WITHDRAWN

VOLUME I

The Papers of John Marshall

A Descriptive Calendar

John Marshall as Chief Justice
from the portrait by John Wesley Jarvis

COURTESY OF RICHARD C. MARSHALL

The Papers of John Marshall

A Descriptive Calendar

IRWIN S. RHODES

I

UNIVERSITY OF OKLAHOMA PRESS

NORMAN

039769

Standard Book Number: 8061–0861–4

Library of Congress Catalog Card Number: 69–10622

Copyright 1969 by the University of Oklahoma Press, publishing division of the University. Composed and printed at Norman, Oklahoma, U.S.A., by the University of Oklahoma Press.
First edition.

INTRODUCTION

"A DESIRE TO KNOW intimately those illustrious personages, who have performed a conspicuous part on the great theater of the world, is, perhaps, implanted in every human bosom."

So wrote John Marshall in the preface to his *Life of George Washington*. In their stark simplicity these words describe appropriately the purposes of the present volumes.

John Marshall was born in 1755 in one of the frontier counties of Virginia, then Prince William and shortly to become Fauquier County. His life of eighty years encompassed soldiering in the Revolution, law practice, authorship, landownership, farming, and legislative, executive, and judicial officeholding in his state and in the nation. As Chief Justice of the United States he is the best-known figure in American legal history, but from the point of view of detailed biography, one of the least known. Albert J. Beveridge, his most eminent biographer to date, has pointed out that "Less is known of Marshall than of any of the great Americans."

This fact remains despite Beveridge's mighty work.[1] The main lines of his life and work have been written about by many students, from his own day to the present. And he himself wrote two fragments of autobiography. But the depth of any future biography must rest in considerable part upon his papers, a descriptive calendar of which is contained in these volumes.

Although fifteen years have gone into the preparation of the *Calendar*, it would be rash to claim for it a completeness which must be eschewed by a bibliographer. But the previous surmises (and I can only describe them as that) about the extent of Marshall's literary remains have amounted, at best, to no more than a small fraction of the thousands of items which are described in these pages. The task of compilation has been greatly complicated by the fact that the Marshall papers are widely scattered in federal,

[1] *The Life of John Marshall*, 4 vols. (Boston and New York, Houghton Mifflin Company, 1916–1919).

state, and local archives and libraries, in court records and reports, and in private hands. In short, and unlike the records, personal and public, of many other eminent figures in American history, there is no single, easily accessible source.

Marshall is, of course, best known for his service as Chief Justice of the United States by appointment of President John Adams in 1801 to his death in 1835. His opinions are readily available in any law library containing reports of the Supreme Court, and their ramifications in legal doctrine are profusely documented. Less obvious is the rich store of historical materials in the case papers on deposit at the National Archives.

Of less accessibility and renown are Marshall's opinions in cases before the United States Circuit Court, Virginia District, sitting at Richmond, in the conduct of which he long had a continuous and preponderant part. These are found in the reports of John W. Brockenbrough. To these have been added herein cases of special interest in connection with Marshall, including reference to autograph documents. The court record books and case papers on deposit at the Virginia State Library have been of importance.

The United States Circuit Court, North Carolina District, sitting at Raleigh, required an arduous journey for Marshall twice a year. Its sessions were brief, its load light, and the remaining records of its proceedings meager.

Because of the importance and extent of Marshall's judicial pronouncements, it was felt necessary to brief, in some detail, their factual, procedural, and legal content. Aside from their importance as legal rulings, they reveal a picture of social and commercial activities of the times. They also point to a concentration of Marshall's judicial efforts on mundane matters, interspersed with constitutional issues, most of which arose in his middle and later years on the bench.

Marshall's record as a practicing lawyer extends from 1781, after which he spent a few years in the local courts of his native Fauquier County, to his ascent to the United States Supreme Court. In 1783 he married and moved to Richmond to devote himself to practice in the superior courts of the state, which had recently opened following the American Revolution. Through a combination of ability, affability, and excellent connections, he quickly established an extensive practice, which dwindled only on his departure in 1797 as one of the ministers plenipotentiary to France in the XYZ Affair and by reason of his political commitments thereafter.

His wide legal practice has been heretofore reported and is apparent in his "Account Book," but we know of no prior attempt to reconstruct it in depth. It has been done in the present volumes from printed reports, as well as more remote original court records and case papers from county to

Supreme Court levels. The case papers, where extant, have been most revealing, and being holographic have disclosed a great mass of Marshall manuscript material, heretofore considered rare. Many of the case papers have been destroyed—for example, those of the Court of Appeals of Virginia and the High Court of Chancery—and county records were found spotty and traceable only in part. Those uncovered represent perhaps one-fifth of Marshall's actual practice, but they are sufficient to indicate its wide character and scope.

Especially rewarding were the previously unexplored case papers of the United States Circuit Court of Virginia mentioned above, which reveal Marshall's great activity in that court. Of some interest is his frequent participation in the British debt cases. He represented Virginia debtors to such an extent as to warrant the printing of forms of defenses bearing his name as counsel (defenses, incidentally, which he persisted in despite frequent overruling). One form interlined with James Innes' name was used in the famous case of *Ware v. Hylton* in which Marshall was defeated in his lone argument before the United States Supreme Court, and in which he pleaded for doctrines contrary to his later judicial pronouncements. Also disclosed is his personal initiation in this court of litigation in *Martin v. Hunter,* a controversy in which he had a continuing active interest and financial stake.

I have considered it important to present the cases of his legal practice step by step in order to indicate the time and effort involved in their prosecution. One gets the impression that litigation then was as tortuous and time-consuming as that of the present day, if not more so.

Second only to Marshall's legal and judicial activities was his interest in land acquisitions, understandable for his times, when land was the prime medium of wealth and speculation, and its development a basic government policy. The ownership and management of landholdings gripped Marshall early in life and persisted as a major interest to his death. Military land warrants for land in Kentucky, his father's position as surveyor of Fayette County, and the migration of much of his family to that area early brought thoughts of moving to the "Western Country."[2] Marriage and early success at politics and the bar probably were factors in diverting such a move, and the acquisition with his brother and others of the vast claims of the Fairfax Estate in the Northern Neck of Virginia shifted his attention from western lands. Thereafter his landholdings in various counties of Virginia, and in and around Richmond, payment for them, sales, leasing, farming, their legal protection, and final transmission to his descendants became consum-

[2] Marshall's interest in Kentucky and Ohio lands is treated in an article by the author, "John Marshall and the Western Country, Early Days," *Historical and Philosophical Society of Ohio Bulletin,* Vol. XVIII (April, 1960), 19–22.

ing interests paralleling his preoccupation with law. In my view, he exceeded the limits of propriety by active promotion and counseling in the litigation which was to end in his court and establish title of his brother and himself to a great part of the Fairfax purchase (*Fairfax v. Hunter*). The same may be said of his actions in *Fitzsimmons v. Ogden,* in which his interest and that of his brother were involved.

The authorship of *The Life of George Washington* was undoubtedly one of the most absorbing activities of Marshall's life.[3] It went far beyond conceit or money-making. He spent from 1803 to near the end of his days on this project, devoting years of intensive effort to its first writing, thereafter to concern about the errors it contained and the corrections required for a second edition, and to the commencement of assembling for publication the Washington letters. The latter project he graciously and wisely relinquished to Jared Sparks.

His *Life of George Washington* was not a great work in either style or content, but it was so close to Marshall's heart as to be a measure of the man. He rated it highly among his personal ambitions, and to him it was a means of self-fulfillment. Such were his credence and effort that he may have hoped to be remembered more for it than for his judicial writings. The collection of manuscripts concerning it at the Historical Society of Pennsylvania tells an absorbing story of the interplay between him, Bushrod Washington, C. P. Wayne, and Parson Weems.

Marshall's political activities prior to his becoming Chief Justice of the United States Supreme Court are a lengthy record in themselves. His role as delegate to the Constitutional Convention of Virginia appears in the several printed reporter accounts of that body; as member of the House of Delegates of Virginia and the Council of State, in the official minutes and journals of these bodies; and as member of Richmond Common Council, recorder, and as a member of the Court of Hustings, at the Virginia State Library and in the court records. Of particular interest are his activities in the Court of Hustings, representing as they do his early judicial experience, here on a local level.

His diplomatic venture as one of the ministers plenipotentiary to France in the XYZ Affair brought national attention. Official documenta-

3 *The Life of George Washington, Commander in Chief of the American Forces, During the War Which Established the Independence of His Country, and First President of the United States. Compiled Under the Inspection of the Honourable Bushrod Washington, from Original Papers Bequeathed to Him by His Deceased Relative, and Now in Possession of the Author, to Which is Prefixed, an Introduction, Containing a Compendious View of the Colonies Planted by the English on the Continent of North America, from Their Settlement to the Commencement of That War Which Terminated in Their Independence.* 5 vols. (Philadelphia, C. P. Wayne, . . . 1804–1807.)

tion appears in the Annals of Congress and other publications; in the manuscript collections of the National Archives, Washington, and Yale University; and in copies at the Library of Congress of holdings of the Bibliothèque Nationale, Paris. His own journal is on deposit at the Massachusetts Historical Society. His correspondence with George Washington during his French sojourn is of particular interest. There is some irony in the fact that his acclaim is based on his adamant refusal to pass monetary rewards, and that thereafter, as Secretary of State, he spent much time and effort in providing gifts and emoluments in appeasement of the Barbary Powers.

His career as Secretary of State under John Adams for the year preceding his chief justiceship is amply documented in the records of the National Archives. They show him busily engaged at the new seat of government in affairs with foreign powers as well as in domestic matters of administration and appointments. He worked closely and respectfully with the absent President, and because of chaotic political conditions was cast into position of resident second to the President. His term of less than a year was too short to admit of sound appraisal other than that of efficiency and circumspection. The treaty with Great Britain settling mutual debts, one of the few major events, was completed by the distant minister, Rufus King, by his own skill and on the basis of instructions of Marshall's predecessor in office, Timothy Pickering.

It is of interest that the record of contact between Marshall and Adams, following the latter's political eclipse, is negligible, whereas that between Adams and Jefferson, and, parenthetically, that between Marshall and Pickering, persisted through the years. This may indicate that Adams's last great act in office, the appointment of Marshall as Chief Justice, was one of political expediency rather than of personal attachment.

Of Marshall's personal and private life, the record shows for the most part merely occasional and fleeting glimpses. The most consecutive body of data in this area consists of the letters to his wife, Mary Willis Ambler, whom he affectionately called "Polly," collected and published in *My Dearest Polly* by Frances Norton Mason,[4] and his account book covering the years 1783 to 1795, privately held, but copies of which are in various depositories.

Marshall married Mary Willis Ambler, a girl of seventeen, member of a large and prominent family of Yorktown and Richmond, on January 3, 1783. This and the marriage of his brother William into the wealthy and

[4] Francis Norton Mason, ed., *My Dearest Polly: Letters of Chief Justice John Marshall to His Wife, with Their Background, Political and Domestic, 1779–1831* (Richmond, Garrett and Massie, 1961).

accredited Adams family of Richmond, and that of his brother James M. to the daughter of the financier-speculator Robert Morris assured Marshall of social acceptability, a matter of no small concern to a rising lawyer. Marshall's correspondence with Polly and his deep mourning at her death four years before his own express a romantic beginning and a deep devotion to her throughout his life. They also show an apparent lack of communication from her during his frequent absences. His great concern was for her health, for Polly suffered an undefined malady for many years of her life, confined herself largely to her room, was disturbed by noise and excitement. It is quite apparent that she was not a companion in his worldly activities.

Ten children were born of the marriage between 1784 and 1805, three of whom died shortly after birth and another at age four. Marshall built and provided an excellent home for his family and himself, surrounded by residences of relatives and friends. His account book for the earlier years attests to a detailed attention on his part to expenditure for it and its stocking and management. Of his five sons, three attended Harvard, one, Yale; the fifth dabbled in but did not practice medicine. Only one of them turned to law, commencing practice, but soon dropping out. All of them gravitated to the various Marshall farm holdings in Fauquier County and devoted themselves to farming. Marshall's only surviving daughter, Mary, married well and lived near him in Richmond.

Marshall had an affable and engaging personality, a characteristic which apparently stood him well throughout his life. He was obviously astute in bending men to his ways. In his earlier days his gains and losses at whist were considerable, and quoits (at which he was expert) took the place for him of present-day golf. Tradition and anecdotes concerning him are numerous, as are the comments and appraisals of his contemporaries. These of necessity have no place in the present volumes.

An autobiographical source of data on Marshall is a letter written by him from Richmond, March 22, 1818, to Joseph Delaplaine of Philadelphia. A more extensive primary source is an autobiographical sketch composed by Marshall, undated, but noted by the recipient, Joseph Story, as of 1827. It was published in 1937 under the editorship of John S. Adams as *An Autobiographical Sketch by John Marshall.*[5] This document is hereinafter referred to as *Autobiography*. It was used extensively by Joseph Story in three articles which are of particular import because of their contemporaneous character and because of Story's intimate association with Marshall.

5 John S. Adams, ed., *An Autobiographical Sketch of John Marshall; Written at the Request of Joseph Story and Now Printed for the First Time from the Original Manuscript Preserved at the William L. Clements Library* (Ann Arbor, University of Michigan Press, 1937), 48 pp.

The three-volume collection of memorial addresses given on the hundredth anniversary of Marshall's ascent to the bench, together with earlier addresses by Story, John F. Dillon, and others (edited by Dillon), is a rich secondary source of biographical information.[6] An authoritative genealogical and biographical account appears in W. M. Paxton, *The Marshall Family*.[7]

The resources for Marshall study are not by any means small. James A. Servies of the College of William and Mary published his bibliography in 1956 containing no fewer than 1,822 items, including books, articles, and pamphlets by and about Marshall.[8] The listings embrace only printed materials, exclusive of newspaper articles. As the compiler aptly points out in his introduction, Marshall, like Washington, Jefferson, and Lee, "has been the unwitting foil for hosts of orators. Almost entirely eulogistic in substance, these addresses constitute the largest single bloc of literature on the Chief Justice—and usually supply the smallest percentage reward. Yet the 'legend' of John Marshall has grown through the years on this material, each contribution built, coral-like, upon the skeleton of the preceding oration."

The present work, which may add another dimension to the foregoing biographical resources, is, in a sense, a compromise with objectives which I had developed many years ago—in short, to publish under my editorship all of the known papers of John Marshall. The co-operation of the American Bar Association was generously extended to me, from the conviction that the embellishment of the greatest name in American constitutional law should be a duty. The reluctance, however, of the National Historical Records Commission in Washington to approve my undertaking and my effort as a nonprofessional (and I might add, nonsubsidized) devotee of historical research in this field constituted a barrier which almost caused me to abandon even the idea of this *Calendar*. Under the encouragement of my esteemed friend Savoie Lottinville and my publishers at the University of Oklahoma Press, I determined upon the course which is represented in these volumes.

[6] John F. Dillon, ed., *John Marshall; Life, Character and Judicial Services as Portrayed in the Centenary and Memorial Addresses and Proceedings Throughout the United States on Marshall Day, 1901, and in the Classic Orations of Binney, Story, Phelps, Waite, and Rawle* (Chicago, Callaghan, 1903). 3 vols.

[7] W. M. Paxton, *The Marshall Family, or a Genealogical Chart of the Descendants of John Marshall and Elizabeth Markham, His Wife, Sketches of Individuals and Notices of Families Connected With Them* (Cincinnati, Clarke, 1885).

[8] James A. Servies, *A Bibliography of John Marshall* (Washington, United States Commission for the Celebration of the Two Hundredth Anniversary of the Birth of John Marshall, 1956).

Aside from my conviction, after much thought, that a descriptive calendar might provide the greatest immediate service to the name of John Marshall, considering the long and signal neglect of his widely dispersed papers, I have felt that such a compilation will be of fairly general usefulness in American legal, cultural, and intellectual history. The method thus chosen reduces Marshall's literary remains in form though not in content, the latter phrase being understood descriptively. In fact, my present work is designed as not merely exploratory and directional in nature, but as a workable tool for research and, hopefully, of sufficient readability to hold interest.

The speed with which the great personal and public documents in American legal history are being made available to scholars everywhere through microfilm is suggestive of at least one further research use for these volumes. Ultimately, wherever or whenever a particular Marshall paper is needed for examination or quotation *in extenso,* as determined from its descriptive content in the *Calendar,* it may be ordered out at minimal cost.

I do not wish this opportunity to pass without extending my thanks to Mrs. Dorothy Hill Gersack of Bethesda, Maryland.

Any discussion of John Marshall must devote itself in substantial part to that phase of his judicial career for which he is most famous; namely, the establishment of the Supreme Court as the final arbiter in the political scheme of questions involving acts of government allegedly in conflict with the Constitution, as well as interpreter of the meaning and scope of that document. This doctrine is generally and euphemistically called "the rule of law" and is traced in part to the dramatic case of *Marbury v. Madison.* More accurately it should be termed "the rule of judicial law."

The essential fact, which is so often unmentioned, is that the Constitution, either designedly or in deference to the delicacy of the question, left a hiatus as to the enforcement of the Constitution itself. It set up a structure characterized by a large measure of separation of functions in the legislative, executive, and judicial arms of government, but with a subordination of the judiciary through its appointment and control by the other two branches. It might very well have been assumed that, in the strictly national area, as well as in that of conflicting state action, enforcement would result from an interplay and accommodation, and by future events. Such was the not untenable position of Jefferson.

Although there was some tendency on the part of the judiciary prior to *Marbury v. Madison* to wield the ultimate power, its exercise was generally limited to negating judicial authority itself, for example, against the judiciary's giving of advice to the executive, or the exercise of administrative duties by the former. There was no conceded governmental axiom or practice, and no established legal maxim that the judiciary should be the repository of ultimate power. In fact, it is remarkable that this power came to be in the hands of the organ of government least democratically controlled, an organ with no means of finally enforcing its mandate other than by concession, and that it came to be exercised over the national authority which initiates government processes and controls the purse, and over that power which appoints, executes the processes, and wields its force, as well as over the semi-independent state structures.

Such, however, was the essence of Marshall's daring pronouncement in *Marbury v. Madison*, a case unimportant for what it decided, but important in that it showed the teeth of the Supreme Court and got away with it. It was ultimately to change the Court from the status of pronouncer and interpreter in individual disputes to that of an active arm in the political process, a weaver of unity, and, aided by the doctrine of implied powers, a vehicle of primary importance in the movement toward nationalism.

That Marshall, from his vantage point, strained to pronounce the doctrine of judicial supremacy at the earliest moment, in a situation which did not require it, in a case in which, because of prior entanglement, he should never have participated, and in a manner which could not be gainsaid, is a measure of his political acumen, his daring, and his ambition for himself and for the judicial institution in which he sat as leading advocate.

It must be remembered, however, that when his position was seriously threatened by the Chase impeachment proceedings, he was willing to retrench and defer to Congress as the final arbiter of the Constitution; and in the Burr trial, he stopped short of asserting the judicial will over the executive. During his entire subsequent career he was never called upon, nor is it certain he would have felt the Court's position strong enough, to assert supremacy over the legislative or executive branch at the national level. Rather, the direction was to uphold exertions of their powers, to limit incursions by the states, and to meet the needs of an expanding and hopefully unified nation.

For Marshall's abiding vision was that of centralized national strength, as opposed to the proven weakness of a confederacy of states, with the Court as a tool of national cohesion. Here he was able to act mightily in bringing to bear compulsions of the Constitution and, through division and counter-interests of opponents, to prevail. Thus by boldness, tenacity, persuasion, and longevity he was able to assert and reiterate the power of the judiciary and generally make it effective.

He never felt secure, however, in this drive to national unity; and to the very end of his days when the Court was gainsaid, or political dissension reached a threatened breaking point, he despaired of the life of the Union.

Marshall's greatness in the field of constitutional law lies not in the novelty of his views but in the fact that he was able to announce them from a high rostrum. For the most part his pronouncements were the common property of great statesmen and able advocates who preceded and surrounded him. Partly by happy chance, partly by inexorable political, economic, and social development, the growth of the nation coincided with his pattern, and the Court's ascendancy, though often questioned, was largely accepted. How far, however, and to what ends his path of judicial supremacy need be or should be followed are constantly recurring problems, at all times open to scrutiny and review.

"The events of my life are too unimportant, and have too little interest for any person not of my immediate family, to render them worth communicating or preserving." So wrote Marshall. Nothing could be further from the fact.

To its refutation I dedicate this book.

IRWIN S. RHODES

Cincinnati, Ohio

August 9, 1969

CONTENTS

TABLES

ARRANGEMENT

ABBREVIATIONS

THE GENERAL ARRANGEMENT of materials herein has been largely chronological. Within a given year, it has been found convenient to block off cohesive groups such as legal practice, court opinions, and land transactions, and to arrange these chronologically where feasible. Law cases have been arranged by citation if published, otherwise alphabetically, with the date of rendering or final order taken as the year of entry. Separate groupings also have been made according to court of final decision. Occasionally an activity or litigation has been carried through beyond its principal year of listing. Citations of depositories have been abbreviated in conformity with the Union List; others have been devised.

Abridgement, Debates of Congress Thomas Hart Benton. *Abridgement of the Debates of Congress; 1789–1856.* 16 vols. New York, Appleton, 1857–1861.

Adams, *J. Adams Works* Charles P. Adams, ed. *John Adams Works.* 10 vols. Boston, Little, Brown, 1850–1856.

Adams, *Memoirs* J. Q. Adams. *Memoirs of John Quincy Adams.* Ed. by Charles Francis Adams. Philadelphia, J. B. Lippincott & Co., 1874–1877.

Adams, *Sparks* Herbert Baxton Adams. *The Life and Writings of Jared Sparks.* Boston, Houghton Mifflin, 1893.

AHR *American Historical Review.* New York, Macmillan, 1896–19——.

Annals U.S. Congress. *Debates and Proceedings in the Congress of the United States.* (*Annals of Congress.*) Washington, Gales and Seaton, 1834–1856.

ASP *American State Papers. State Papers and Publick Documents of the United States.* 2nd ed. Boston, Wait, 1817.

ASP (Claims) U.S. Congress. *American State Papers. Documents Legis-*

lative and Executive of the Congress of the United States. (Class IX. Claims.) Washington, Gales and Seaton, 1832–1861.

ASP (Commerce) ———. *(Class IV. Commerce and Navigation.)*

ASP (Finance) ———. *(Class III. Finance.)*

ASP (For. Rel.) ———. *(Class I. Foreign Relations.)*

ASP (Misc.) ———. *(Class IX. Miscellaneous.)*

ASP (Public Lands) ———. *(Class VIII. Public Lands.)*

Barbary Powers U.S. Office of Naval Records and Library. *Naval Documents Related to the United States War with the Barbary Powers.* 4 vols. Washington, G.P.O., 1939–1942.

Beveridge, *Marshall* Albert J. Beveridge. *The Life of John Marshall.* 4 vols. Boston, Houghton, Mifflin, 1916–1919.

Branch Hist. Papers *John P. Branch Historical Papers of Randolph-Macon College.* Richmond, Jones (various dates).

Brockenbrough John W. Brockenbrough, ed. *Reports of Cases Decided by John Marshall.* Philadelphia, Kay, 1837.

Brunner's Coll. Cases Albert Brunner, ed. *Reports of Cases Argued and Determined in the Circuit Courts of the United States.* San Francisco, Sumner Whitney, 1884.

Call Daniel Call, ed. *Reports of Cases Argued and Determined in the Court of Appeals of Virginia.* Richmond, Cottom, 1824.

———. 3 vols. Richmond, Smith, 1833.

Car. L. Rep. *The Carolina Law Repository.* 2 vols. Raleigh, Gales, 1814.

Colton, *Clay* Calvin Colton. *The Life and Correspondence of Henry Clay.* 5 vols. New York, Barnes, 1855–1857.

Coombs, *Burr* J. J. Coombs. *The Trial of Aaron Burr.* Washington, Morrison, 1864.

Cotton Joseph P. Cotton, ed. *The Constitutional Decisions of John Marshall.* 2 vols. New York, Putnam's, 1905.

Cranch William Cranch, ed. *Reports of Cases Argued and Adjudged in the Supreme Court of the United States, 1801–1803.* 9 vols. Philadelphia, Carey and Lea, 1830–1854.

Crosskey, *Politics and Constitution* William Winslow Crosskey. *Politics and the Constitution in the History of the United States.* 2 vols. Chicago, University of Chicago Press, 1953.

CSmH Henry E. Huntington Library. San Marino, Calif.

C St Stanford University. Palo Alto, Calif.

CtHi Connecticut Historical Society. Hartford, Conn.

CtY Yale University. New Haven, Conn.

CtY-P Yale University, Peabody Museum. New Haven, Conn.

CVSP *Calendar of Virginia State Papers and Other Manuscripts.* 11 vols. Richmond, 1875–1893.

DeHi Historical Society of Delaware. Wilmington, Del.

Dillon, *Decisions* John M. Dillon, ed. *Complete Constitutional Decisions of John Marshall.* Chicago, Callaghan & Co., 1903.

Dillon, *Marshall* John F. Dillon, ed. *John Marshall. Life Character and Judicial Services.* 2 vols. Chicago, Callahan, 1903.

DLC Library of Congress. Washington, D.C.

DNA National Archives. Washington, D.C.

Elliot, *Debates* Jonathan Elliot, ed. *The Debates . . . on the Adoption of the Federal Constitution.* 5 vols. Philadelphia, Lippincott, 1836–1859.

Flanders, *Marshall* Henry Flanders. *The Life of John Marshall.* Philadelphia, Johnson, 1904.

French Spoliation *Messages from the President of the United States Transmitting Copies of the Several Instructions to the Ministers of the United States to the Government of France and of the Correspondence with said Government Having Reference to the Spoliation Committed by that Power on the Commerce of the United States Anterior to Sept. 30, 1800.* In keeping with a resolution of the Senate (19 Cong., 1 sess.), dated May 20, 1826. Washington, D.C., Gales and Seaton, 1826.

G Georgia State Department of Archives and History Library. Atlanta, Ga.

Gibbs, *Memoirs* George Gibbs, ed. *Memoirs of the Administration of Washington and John Adams; edited from the papers of Oliver Wolcott.* 2 vols. New York, W. Van Norden, 1846.

Gwathmey, *Historical Register* John Hastings Gwathmey. *Historical Register of Virginia in the Revolution. Soldiers, Sailors, Marines, 1775–1783.* Richmond, Dietz Press, 1938.

Hamilton, *Monroe* Stanislaus M. Hamilton. *The Writings of James Monroe.* New York, Putnam's, 1898–1903.

Hamilton, *Works* John C. Hamilton, ed. *Alexander Hamilton Works.* 7 vols. New York, Francis, 1851.

Haywood John Haywood, ed. *Reports of Cases Adjudged in the Superior Courts for the State of North Carolina.* 2 vols. Halifax and Raleigh, N.C., 1799–1806.

Heitman, *Historical Register* Francis Bernard Heitman. *Historical Register of Officers of the Continental Army During the War of the Revolution.* Washington, W. H. Lowdermilk & Co., 1893. Revised and enlarged. Washington, Rare Book Shop Publishing Co., 1914.

Hening, Stat. William W. Hening, ed. *The Statutes at Large: Being a collection of all the Laws of Virginia from the First Session of the Legislature in the year 1619.* 13 vols. Richmond, Desilver, 1810–1823.

Herring, *Marshall* "John Marshall, LL.D., Chief Justice of the United States," in James Herring and James B. Longacre, eds., *The National Portrait Gallery of Distinguished Americans.* 2 vols. Vol. I. New York, Monson Bancroft, 1834–1839.

ICHi Chicago Historical Society. Chicago, Illinois.

ICU University of Chicago. Chicago, Illinois.

Iles, *Little Masterpieces* George Iles, ed. *Little Masterpieces of Autobiography.* New York, Doubleday, Page, 1908.

InU Indiana University. Bloomington, Indiana.

Jefferson, *Writings* Andrew A. Lipscomb and Albert Ellery Bergh, eds. *The Writings of Thomas Jefferson.* 20 vols. Washington, The Thomas Jefferson Memorial Assoc., 1905.

Journal, Council of State *Journals of the Council of State of Virginia.* 3 vols. Richmond, Virginia State Library, 1931–1952.

Journal, H. of D. *Journal, House of Delegates of Virginia.*

King, *Life* Charles R. King. *Life and Correspondence of Rufus King.* New York, Putnam's, 1894–1900.

KU University of Kansas. Lawrence, Kansas.

KyHi Kentucky Historical Society. Frankfort, Ky.

KyLF Filson Club. Louisville, Ky.

KyU University of Kentucky. Lexington, Ky.

Littell, *Political Transactions* William Littell. *Political Transactions in and concerning Kentucky from the First Settlement Thereof Until It Became an Independent State.* Frankfort, Hunter, 1806.

Magruder, *Marshall* Allan M. Magruder. *John Marshall.* Boston, Houghton Mifflin, 1885.

Marshall, *Autobiography* John Stokes Adams, ed. *An Autobiographical Sketch by John Marshall.* Ann Arbor, University of Michigan Press, 1937.

Marshall, *Life of Washington* John Marshall. *The Life of George Washington.* For various editions, see herein pp. 510–11. The edition cited herein is that published by The Citizens' Guild of Washington's Boyhood Home, Fredericksburg, Va., 1926.

Marshall, *Writings* *The Writings of John Marshall.* Boston, Munroe, 1839.

Mason, *Polly* Frances Norton Mason. *My Dearest Polly.* Richmond, Garrett and Massie, 1961.

MB Boston Public Library. Boston, Mass.

MdBJ Johns Hopkins University. Baltimore, Md.

MdBP Peabody Institute. Baltimore, Md.
MdHi Maryland Historical Society. Baltimore, Md.
MH Harvard University Libraries. Cambridge, Mass.
MHi Massachusetts Historical Society. Boston, Mass.
MHi Coll. Massachusetts Historical Society, *Collections.*
MHi Proc. Massachusetts Historical Society, *Proceedings.*
MiD Detroit Public Library. Detroit, Mich.
MiD-B Detroit Public Library, Burton Historical Collections. Detroit, Mich.
MiU University of Michigan. Ann Arbor, Mich.
MiU-C University of Michigan, William L. Clements Library of American History. Ann Arbor, Mich.
MoSW Washington University. St. Louis, Mo.
MWA American Antiquarian Society. Worchester, Mass.
N New York State Library. Albany, N.Y.
NbO Omaha Public Library. Omaha, Nebraska.
NcD Duke University. Durham, N.C.
NCR *National Corporation Reporter.*
NcU University of North Carolina. Chapel Hill, N.C.
NhD Dartmouth College. Hanover, N.H.
NhHi New Hampshire Historical Society. Concord, N.H.
NIC Cornell University. Ithaca, N.Y.
Niles *Niles' Weekly Register.*
NjP Princeton University. Princeton, N.J.
NjR Rutgers University. New Brunswick, N.J.
NN New York Public Library. New York, N.Y.
NNC Columbia University. New York, N.Y.
NNMM Metropolitan Museum of Arts. New York, N.Y.
NRU University of Rochester. Rochester, N.Y.
NSDR National Society, Daughters of the American Revolution. Washington, D.C.
OCHP Historical and Philosophical Society of Ohio. Cincinnati, O. (Now Cincinnati Historical Society.)
OHi Ohio State Archaeological & Historical Society. Columbus, Ohio.
OMC Marietta College. Marietta, Ohio.
Oster, *Marshall* John E. Oster. *The Political and Economic Doctrines of John Marshall.* New York, Neale, 1914.
OU Ohio State University. Columbus, Ohio.
Peters Richard Peters, ed. *Reports of Cases Argued in the Supreme Court of the United States.* 16 vols. Philadelphia, Nicklin, 1828–1843.
PHC Haverford College. Haverford, Pa.

PMHB *Pennsylvania Magazine of History and Biography.*

PP Free Library of Philadelphia. Philadelphia, Pa.

PPAP American Philosophical Society. Philadelphia, Pa.

PPHi Historical Society of Pennsylvania. Philadelphia, Pa.

PPL Library Company of Philadelphia. Philadelphia, Pa.

PWbH Wyoming Historical and Genealogical Society. Wilkes Barre, Pa.

Quasi-War–U.S. and France U.S. Office of Naval Records and Library. *Naval Documents Related to the Quasi-War between the United States and France.* 7 vols. Washington, G.P.O., 1935–1938.

Quincy, *Life* Edmund Quincy. *Life of Josiah Quincy.* 2 vols. 6th ed. Boston, Little and Brown, 1874.

R.G. Record Group (National Archives).

Robertson, *Burr* David Robertson. *Reports of the Trial of Aaron Burr for Treason and for a Misdemeanor, Take in Shorthand.* Philadelphia, Hopkins and Earle, 1808.

ScCc Clemson College. Clemson, S.C.

ScU University of South Carolina. Columbia, S.C.

Smith, *St. Clair* William Henry Smith. *The St. Clair Papers. The Life and Services of Arthur St. Clair.* Cincinnati, R. Clarke & Co., 1882.

Sparks, *Washington* Jared Sparks, ed. *Writings of George Washington.* 12 vols. Boston, American Stationers Company, 1834–1837.

Story, *Life and Letters* William W. Story, ed. *Life and Letters of Joseph Story.* 2 vols. Boston, Little and Brown, 1851.

Thayer, *Marshall* James B. Thayer. *John Marshall.* Boston, Houghton Mifflin, 1901.

TKL Lawson-McGee Library. Knoxville, Tenn.

TNV Vanderbilt University. Nashville, Tenn.

TxU University of Texas. Austin, Texas.

Tyler's *Tyler's Quarterly Historical and Genealogical Magazine.*

U.S. U.S. Supreme Court. *United States Reports.* Washington, 1798 ——.

V Virginia State Library. Richmond, Va.

Va. Cas. Judges Brockenbrough and Holmes, eds. *Collection of Cases Decided by the General Court of Virginia.* Vol. I. Philadelphia, Webster, 1815.

William Brockenbrough, ed. *Virginia Cases or Decisions of the General Court of Virginia.* Vol. II. Richmond, Cottom, 1826.

Va. Debates Virginia Constitutional Convention of 1788. *Debates and Other Proceedings.* 2nd ed. Richmond, Enquirer Press, 1805.

Va. Gaz. and G. A. *Virginia Gazette and General Advertiser.*

VHi Virginia Historical Society. Richmond, Va.

VHS Hampden-Sydney College. Hampden-Sydney, Va.

VMH *Virginia Magazine of History.*

VU University of Virginia. Charlottesville, Va.

VW College of William and Mary. Williamsburg, Va.

Warren, *Supreme Court* Charles Warren. *The Supreme Court in United States History.* 2 vols. Rev. ed. Boston, Little Brown, 1937.

Washington Bushrod Washington, ed. *Reports of Cases Argued and Determined in the Court of Appeals of Virginia.* 2 vols. Richmond, Nicolson, 1789–1799.

Washingtoniana *The Washingtoniana: Containing a Biographical Sketch of the Late Gen. George Washington.* Baltimore, Samuel Sower, 1800.

Webster, *Correspondence* Fletcher Webster, ed. *Private Correspondence of Daniel Webster.* 2 vols. Boston, Little, Brown, 1857.

Webster, *Writings* *Writings and Speeches of Daniel Webster.* 18 vols. Boston, Little, Brown, 1903.

Wheaton Henry Wheaton, ed. *Reports of Cases Argued and Adjudged in the Supreme Court of the United States.* 12 vols. Philadelphia, Carey, 1816–1827.

Wheeler Crim. Cases Jacob D. Wheeler, ed. *Reports of Criminal and Law Cases . . . .* 3 vols. Albany, Gould Banks & Gould, 1857.

WHi The State Historical Society of Wisconsin. Madison, Wisconsin.

WMQ *William and Mary Quarterly.*

Wythe George Wythe. *Decisions of Cases in Virginia High Court of Chancery, 1780–1795.* Richmond, Weston, 1795.

———. 2nd ed., B. B. Minor, ed. Richmond, Randolph, 1852.

Calendar

Calendar

1755

RECORD OF BIRTH

Sept. 4 *Bible Record*

J.M. was born in what is now Fauquier, then Prince William County, Virginia, to Thomas and Mary Marshall. Marshall Family Bible Record, VHi, Bible Record, VU; J.M. to Delaplaine (herein Mar. 22, 1818); Marshall, *Autobiography*, 3.

(He was born in a log cabin on Licking Run, near Germantown, Fauquier County, located in an angle made by the intersection of the Southern Railroad and the old stagecoach road from Warrenton to Fredericksburg. In 1902 a memorial tablet was placed at the site of the house, then gone, by the Marshall Chapter of the Phi Delta Phi legal fraternity. Maria Newton Marshall, "The Marshall Memorial Tablet," *Green Bag*, Vol. XIV [Aug., 1902], 372.)

1759–1789

THOMAS MARSHALL—PUBLIC OFFICES

May 24, 1759 Bond, £300, by Thomas Marshall, James Keith, Cuthbert Bullitt; appointment of Thomas Marshall under commission from president and masters of William and Mary College as surveyor of Fauquier County, Va., Fauquier County Deed Book 1, 1.

July 1, 1765 Bond £500, by Thomas Marshall, Thomas Rutherford, James Wood; appointment of Thomas Marshall under commission from president and masters of William and Mary College as surveyor of Frederick County, Va. Recorded July 2, 1765, Fauquier County Deed Book 10, 379.

He served as member of the House of Burgesses of Virginia from 1761 through 1768. He was re-elected in 1769 and served until 1773. In 1775 he was again elected. Journal, House of Burgesses, Va. (1761–1765), 3; (1766–1769), 147, 257; (1773–1776), ———.

Oct. 26, 1767 Bond by Thomas Marshall, Jeremiah Darnall, James Scott, William Pickett, £1,000 Va., and £50 Va., conditioned on commission of Governor, Oct. 20, appointing Thomas Marshall sheriff of Fauquier County. County Court, Fauquier, Minute Book 1764–1767, 32. See Journal, House of Burgesses (1766–1769), 147, 257.

Mar. 28, 1769 Bond of Thomas Marshall and Thomas Keith to the King, 30,000 lbs. tobacco, conditioned on Thomas Marshall's collecting county levies and paying county creditors. Fauquier County Deed Book 3, 359; County Court, Fauquier, Minute Book 1768–1772, 60. See Journal, House of Burgesses (1766–1769), 272, 290, 291.

Apr. 23, 1770 Reappointed, justice of County Court in Chancery and of Oyer and Terminer. Same, 181.

Sept. 1, 1769 Justice of peace and justice of County Court in Chancery, County Court, Fauquier, Minute Book 1768–1773, 137.

May 7, 1771 Appointed to take list of tithes, Leeds Parish. Same, 298. Aug. 26, 1771. Tithes returned. Same, 322.

In 1773 served as clerk of courts of Dunmore (now Shenandoah) County, Va. Journal, House of Burgesses (1773–1776), 9.

In 1782 was one of Virginia commissioners to the Western Country. See Gov. Benjamin Harrison to Thomas Marshall and other commissioners, "Powers and Instructions to Commissioners Appointed to the Western Country," Jan. 29, 1782. V, Exec. Letter Book 1, 41.

He visited Kentucky in 1780 preparatory to moving there; in 1781, was appointed surveyor of Fayette County; and in Sept., 1782, opened surveyor's office. In 1785, he moved permanently to Kentucky, accompanied by his wife, two sons, and five married daughters. Humphrey Marshall,

The History of Kentucky (Frankfort, Robinson, 1824), I, 103–104, 120–21, 149. See Rhodes, "John Marshall and the Western Country, Early Days," *Bulletin Historical and Philosophical Society of Ohio*, Vol. XVII (Apr., 1960), 19–22.

In 1789 appointed receiver for the District of Kentucky. See letter, Governor of Virginia to Thomas Marshall, Richmond, Feb. 13, 1789. V, Exec. Letter Book 1789–1792, 10.

For several years he held the office of collector of revenue for the District of Ohio. (See herein letter of resignation, Apr. 28, 1797.)

1765

DOCUMENT

Oct. 12
FAUQUIER COUNTY, VA. *Lease*

To Thomas Marshall, Fauquier County, by Thomas Ludwell Lee and Molly, his wife, Richard Henry Lee and Anne, his wife; 330 acres north side of Goose Creek, commencing at a white oak at the mouth of a small branch of Goose Creek at spur of Naked Mountain whereon Thomas Marshall resides, during life of Thomas and his wife, Mary, and of his son, John; yearly rent £5 current money, quitrents and land tax. Fauquier County, Va., Records, Deed Book 2, 424–28.

Land located in a valley of the Blue Ridge Mountains known as "The Hollow." See Beveridge, *Marshall*, I, 34ff.; "The Thomas Marshall Cabin," *Fauquier County, Va., Court Records*, compiled by Miss A. M. Seymour and Mrs. W. T. Jewell (and hereinafter cited as Seymour & Jewell), III, 29–30, typescript on deposit at NSDR.

1768

DOCUMENT

Oct. 22
FAUQUIER COUNTY, VA. *Lease*

Thomas Lord Fairfax to J.M. for life and natural lives of wife Mary and son Thomas. Fauquier County, Deed Book 3, 230. (An obvious error in transposition of names.) Recorded, Aug. 22, 1768. County Court, Fauquier, Minute Book 1768–1773, 2.

1769

SCHOOLING

J.M. AT AGE OF fourteen spent one year under the tutorship of Rev. Archibald Campbell, Westmoreland County, Va., and thereafter a year under the tutorship of a Scotsman, James Thompson, pastor of the parish at his home. Marshall, *Autobiography*, 4. See Beveridge, *Marshall*, I, 53.

1773

DOCUMENT

Jan.
FAUQUIER COUNTY, VA. *Deed*

Thomas Turner to Thomas Marshall, 1,700 acres adjacent to North Mountain, Fauquier County; consideration £912:10 current Virginia. Fauquier County, Va., Records, Deed Book 5, 282. (House built known as "Oak Hill," later given by J.M. to his son Thomas. New house built adjacent [*circa* 1815]. Beveridge, *Marshall*, I, 55–56; IV, 74; Seymour & Jewell, *supra*, I, 57–58.)

1775–1779

MILITARY SERVICE

May, 1775 *Virginia Militia*

Eyewitness account and paraphrase of speech by J.M. to his men on assuming command as lieutenant of a company of Virginia Militia. Justice Horace Gray in Dillon, *Marshall*, I, 48; Horace Binney in Dillon, *Marshall*, III, 286–88.

Sept.–Nov., 1775 *Militia Service*

Lieutenant in Virginia Militia "Minute Men." Assembled for service Sept. 1; in a few days marched to lower country to defend against forces commanded by Lord Dunmore; first to Williamsburg; engaged in battle of the Great Bridge in October or November; marched with provincials to Norfolk, present at burning and evacuation of city. Marshall, *Autobiography*, 5. Affidavits of J.M. supporting pension applications of David Jamison, Feb. 6, 1832; William Payne, Apr. 26, 1832; Robert Pollard, June 20, 1832; letter, J.M. to Samuel Templeton, Sept. 16, 1832 (which see herein); Joseph Story in Dillon, *Marshall*, III, 335; Herring, *Marshall*, 3–4. Letter, J.M. to Delaplaine (herein Mar. 22, 1818) states entered service in Sept., 1775, as a subaltern.

Mar., 1776 *Military Discharge*

The Culpeper Battalion Minute Men, of which J.M., a lieutenant, were discharged at Suffolk, Va. Affidavit of J.M. supporting pension application of David Jamison, Feb. 6, 1832; same for William Payne, Apr. 26, 1832; same for Robert Pollard, June 20, 1832 (which see herein).

July 30, 1776 *Continental Line, First Lieutenant*

Enlisted in the 3rd Virginia Regiment, Continental Line; commissioned first lieutenant, under Capt. William Blackwell in regiment commanded by Col. McGraw; his company transferred to the 11th Virginia Regiment, Continental Line, commanded by Col. Daniel Morgan and later by Col. Christian Fabiger. Pension application of J.M., Jan. 26, 1833 (herein); Marshall, *Autobiography*, 5.

Dec., 1776 *Captain-Lieutenant*

Promoted to captain-lieutenant in the Continental Army, dating from July 31, 1776, and transferred to the 15th Virginia Regiment. Gwathmey, *Historical Register*, 501; Heitman, *Historical Register*, 285.

Jan.–Feb., 1777 *Smallpox*

Among officers in Philadelphia "for the purpose of being carried through the small pox." J.M. to William Stark, June 12, 1832 (herein).

Sept. 11, 1777 *Battles*

Engaged in the skirmish at Iron Hill and the subsequent battle of Brandywine of this date, also in the battle at Germantown Oct. 4.

For J.M.'s description of the battle of Brandywine, see his *Life of Washington*, II, 298–306.

For that of the battle of Germantown, see Same, II, 321–28.

Nov. 20, 1777
HEADQUARTERS, WHITE MARSH *Deputy Judge Advocate*

Orders of Gen. George Washington appointing Lieut. J.M. Deputy Judge Advocate in the Army of the United States by the Judge Advocate General. DNA, War Dept. Coll. of Rev. War Records, War of the Rev., Orderly Book, June 11, 1777, to Dec. 10, 1779, p. 89. R.G. 93; John P. G. Muhlenberg, "Orderly Book of Gen. John Peter Gabriel Muhlenberg

Mar. 26–Dec. 20, 1777," PMHB, Vol. XXXV (1911), 156, at 182; George Weedon, *Valley Forge Orderly Book* (New York, Dodd, Mead, 1902), 134; Heitman, *Historical Register*, 285; Gwathmey, *Historical Register*, 501.

1777–1778
VALLEY FORGE

From Dec., 1777, to June, 1778, J. M. was in the encampment at Valley Forge. Affidavits of J.M. for pension application of Humphrey Marshall, June 12, 1832 (herein).

For J.M.'s description of conditions at Valley Forge, see his *Life of Washington*, II, 406–34.

COMPANY MUSTER ROLL

J.M., 1st Lieut.
Capt. Wm. Blackwell's Company of 11th Virginia Regiment of Foot, Commanded by Col. Daniel Morgan.

1777

Month	Roll Dated	Remarks	Other
Mar.–Apr.	May 16	Philadelphia	Commissioned July 31, 1776
May–June	Aug. 5	Philadelphia	
July	Aug. 4		
Aug.	Sept. 2	on command	
Sept.	Oct. 13		
Oct.	Nov. 4		
Nov.	Dec. 22		
Dec.	Jan. 8, 1778		

DNA, Rev. War Records, Military Card Records. R.G. 93.

COMPANY PAY ROLL—1777

Month	Time	Pay per Mo	Whole Pay	Bal. Due	
Mar.–Apr.	1 mo.	£10:2:6	£10:2:6	£14:24:6	J.M. 1st Lieut. Capt. Wm. Black-
June–July	1 mo.	$27	$27		well's Co. 11th
July	1 mo.	$27	$27		Va., commanded by Col. Daniel Morgan
Aug.			$47		Omitted, being drawn for as adjutant in May. Abstract from May 1 to 16, $20

Sept.	1 mo.	$27	$27	
Oct.	Oct. 1–31	$27	£8:2	Capt. Blackwell's Co. 11th Va., commanded by Col. Geo. Nicholas
Nov.	Nov. 1–31	$27	£8:2	
Dec.	Dec. 1–31	$27		
		The U.S. to Lieut. J.M. to additional pay as lieutenant from July 30, 1776, to Oct. 23 following at $9 per mo. $25		Same, commanded by Daniel Morgan.

DNA, Rev. War Records, Military Card Records. R.G. 93.

Feb. 27, 1778, *n.p.* *Assignment of Wages*

Assignment of wages by Robert Colwell (Caldwell) to Lieut. Marshall directed to paymaster of Col. Grayson's regiment. DNA., Rev. War MSS, Military Receipts 16653 and 18868. 9W–4. R.G. 93.

Mar. 24, 1778, *n.p.* *Deputy Judge Advocate General*

David William indebtedness to Daniell Willett, clothing, $6.00 equal £1:16:0. Proved J.M., Deputy Judge Advocate General. DNA, Rev. War MSS, Military Receipts 16791. 9W–4. R.G. 93.

May 8, 1778, *n.p.* *Deputy Judge Advocate General*

Jeremiah Goldsburry debt to Richard Conner, cash lent, £1:7:6. Sworn before J.M., Deputy Judge Advocate General. DNA, Rev. War MSS, Military Receipts 16768. 9W–4. R.G. 93.

May 10, 1778, *n.p.* *Deputy Judge Advocate General*

Sgt. Nollen of Capt. Ricces [*sic*] Co. to John Rooke, $7.00. Proved by J.M., Deputy Judge Advocate General. DNA, Rev. War MSS, Military Receipts 16665. 9W–4. R.G. 93.

May 18, 1778, *n.p.* *Deputy Judge Advocate General*

Duncan Cowen account with Wm. Pope, money lent £1:6:3, dated Apr. 6, 1778. Proved by J.M., Deputy Judge Advocate General. DNA, Rev. War MSS, Military Receipts 16772. 9W–4. R.G. 93.

June 8, 1778, *n.p.* *Deputy Judge Advocate General*

Claim of Andrew Dunn against John Williamson for wages agreed to give to exchange company, $26⅔. Proved by J.M., Deputy Judge Advocate General. DNA, Rev. War MSS, Military Receipts 16580. 9W–4. R.G. 93.

June 16, 1778, *n.p.* *Deputy Judge Advocate General*

Isaac Brown debt to Thos. Thomas, cash lent £1:15:0, dated Apr. 23, 1778. Sworn before J.M., Deputy Judge Advocate General. DNA, Rev. War MSS, Military Receipts 16659. 9W–4. R.G. 93.

Aug. 18, 1778, *n.p.* *Deputy Judge Advocate General*

Dr. Duncan Meade account with Capt. John Chilton's Estate, shirts, breeches, balance £3:7. Autograph oath of Capt. Blackwell, 3rd Virginia Regiment, found account in books of Chilton before J.M., Deputy Judge Advocate General. DNA, Rev. War MSS, Military Receipts 16517. 9W–4. R.G. 93.

Sept., 1778
NEWARK *Captaincy*

Promoted to full captaincy in army, commission dated July 1, 1777 (see pay and muster rolls herein).

Beveridge refers to J.M.'s appointment as July 1, 1778, quoting Heitman, *Historical Register*, 285. J.M. in his *Autobiography*, 6, and in his pension application, Jan. 26, 1833 (herein), refers to the captaincy as of May, 1777, apparently in error.

Sept. 14, 1778 *Transfer of Regiment*

J.M. transferred to the 7th Virginia Regiment, formerly the 11th. Gwathmey, *Historical Register* 501.

Furlough

After the campaign of 1778, visited his family on furlough. Affidavit of J.M. for pension application of Humphrey Marshall, June 12, 1832 (herein). For description of his visit home, see Sallie E. Marshall Hardy, "John Marshall, Third Chief Justice of the United States, As Son, Brother, Husband and Friend," *Green Bag*, Vol. VIII (Dec., 1896), 480.

June 28, 1778 *Battle of Monmouth*

Engaged in Battle of Monmouth. Marshall, *Autobiography*, 6.

For J.M.'s description of battle, see his *Life of Washington*, III, 16–29.

Aug. 10, 1778, *n.p.* *Deputy Judge Advocate General*

Lieut. James Davis account with James Thompson, cash lent; handkerchief, washing by wife, £5:16:3. Proved by J.M., Deputy Judge Advocate General. DNA, Rev. War MSS, Military Receipts 16707. 9W–4. R.G. 93.

Aug. 10, 1778, *n.p.* *Deputy Judge Advocate General*

Lieut. Jesse Davis, 11th Regiment, debt to John Blackwell, cash lent 1777 at Philadelphia, £1:4. Proved by J.M., Deputy Judge Advocate General. DNA, Rev. War MSS, Military Receipts 16657. 9W–4. R.G. 93.

Aug. 10, 1778, *n.p.* *Deputy Judge Advocate General*

Anthony Meadry account with Timothy Shechan, cash lent $12.00. Sworn by J.M., Deputy Judge Advocate General. DNA, Rev. War MSS, Military Receipts 16841. 9W–4. R.G. 93.

Aug. 10, 1778, *n.p.* *Deputy Judge Advocate General*

Geo. Tiggart debt to Capt. Geo. Rich, Mar., 1777, cash lent, $2.00, £0:12:0. Proved by J.M., Deputy Judge Advocate General. DNA, Rev. War MSS, Military Receipts 16653. 9W–4. R.G. 93.

Aug. 12, 1778, *n.p.* *Deputy Judge Advocate General*

Wm. Berry, soldier Capt. Porterfield's Co., indebtedness to Dimit Collett, £2:12:8. Proved by J.M., Deputy Judge Advocate General. DNA, Rev. War MSS, Military Receipts 16634. 9W–4. R.G. 93.

Aug. 16, 1778, *n.p.* *Deputy Judge Advocate General*

Sgt. Aquilla Harvill account with Roger McMahon, cash lent, balance £3:7:6. Proved by J.M., Deputy Judge Advocate General. DNA, Rev. War MSS, Military Receipts 16773. 9W–4. R.G. 93.

Aug. 16, 1778, *n.p.* *Deputy Judge Advocate General*

Geo. Tagart account with Robt. Sharman, cash lent, 1777, £2:18:9. Proved by J.M., Deputy Judge Advocate General. DNA, Rev. War MSS, Military Receipts 16814. 9W–4. R.G. 93.

COMPANY MUSTER ROLL—1778

Month	Roll Dated	Remarks	Other Data
Jan.	Feb. 3	on command	J.M. 1st Lieut., Capt. Wm. Blackwell's Co. in 11th Va. Reg. of Foot, commanded by Capt. Chas. Porterfield.

Feb.	Valley Forge, Mar. 7	Acting as Judge Advocate	Same, commanded by Major Thos. Sneed
Mar.	Valley Forge, Apr. 6	Acting as Judge Advocate	
Apr.	Valley Forge, May 1	Acting as Judge Advocate	Late Capt. Wm. Blackwell's Co. of 11th Va. Reg., commanded by Col. John Cropper.
May	Valley Forge, June 7	Acting as Judge Advocate	Same, commanded by Lt. Col. John Cropper.
June	Paramus, July 13	Acting as Judge Advocate	Lieut. Col. Cropper's Co. 11th–15th Va., selected from Capt. Blackwell's, Capt. Grymes', Capt. Harris' Companies in 2nd Battalion of Gen'l Woodford's Brigade, commanded by Lieut. Col. John Cropper.
July	White Plains, Aug. 4	Judge Advocate in court martial	
Aug.	Same, Sept. 1	Acting Judge Advocate	Col. John Cropper's Co. 11th–15th Va. Reg. of 1st Battalion of Gen'l Woodford's Brigade commanded by Col. Daniel Morgan
Sept.	Camp Newark, Oct. 28		J.M. Captain in Same.
Oct.	Camp Pompton Plains, Nov. 6		J.M. Captain in Same.
Nov.	Same, Dec. 1		J.M. Captain in Same.
Dec.	Camp Middlebrook, Jan. 13, 1779	On furlough in Virginia	

DNA, Rev. War Records, Military Card Record. R.G. 93.

FIELD AND STAFF MUSTER ROLL—1778

Col. M., 11th & 15th Va., Lieut. J.M., 1st Co.
Lt. Col. Cropper, Command of Col. Daniel Morgan

Month	Place	Company	Date	Other Data
July	White Plains	1	Aug. 4	Commissioned July 31, 1776
Aug.	White Plains	1	Sept. 1	

Sept.	Newark	1	Oct. 28	Captain J.M.'s Co. under Col. Morgan (7th Va.)
Oct.	Pompton Plains	1	Nov. 6	Col. Morgan (7th Va.)
Nov.	Pompton Plains	1	Dec. 2	Col. Morgan (7th Va.)
Dec.	Middlebrook	3	Jan. 13, 1779	On furlough in Virginia

DNA, Rev. War Records, Military Card Record. R.G. 93.

COMPANY PAY ROLL—1778

Month	Time	Pay per Month	Whole Pay	Other Data
Jan.	Dec. 31–Jan. 31	$27	£8:2	J.M. 1st Lieut., Capt. Wm. Blackwell's Co. in
Feb.	1 mo.	$27	£8:2	11th Va. Reg. of Foot
Mar.	1 mo.	$27	£8:2	commanded by Capt. Chas. Porterfield
Apr.	1 mo.	$27	£8:2	Same commanded by Col. John Cropper
May	1 mo.	$27	£8:2	
June	1 mo.	$26⅔	Subsistence	About May, 1778, the
July	1 mo.	$26⅔	$10, total £11 Subsistence $10, total £11	11th & 15th Va. Regs. were incorporated to 11th–15th Va., until Sept., 1778; (also elements of 3rd & 7th Va.).
Aug.	1 mo.	$26⅔	Subsistence $10, total £11	Lieut. Col. Cropper's Co. in 11th–15th Reg. commanded by Col. Daniel Morgan.
Sept.	1 mo.	$40	Subsistence $20, total £18	J.M. Captain in Same (commission dated July 1, 1777)
Oct.	1 mo.	$40	Subsistence $20, total £18	Same in 11th–15th Reg. of Gen'l Woodford's Brigade commanded by Col. Daniel Morgan
Nov.	1 mo.	$40	Subsistence $20, total £18	Capt. J.M.'s Co. in 7th Va. Reg. commanded by
Dec.	1 mo.		On furlough	Col. Daniel Morgan

DNA, Rev. War Records, Military Card Records. R.G. 93.

June 15, 1779 *Battle of Stony Point*

Took part in storming. Pension application of J.M., Jan. 26, 1833 (herein).

For description of battle, see Marshall, *Life of Washington*, III, 126–29.

Aug. 18, 1779 *Engagements in New York*

Engaged in cover action after capture of British at Powles Hook; continued in service along Hudson. Pension application of J.M., Jan. 26, 1833 (herein).

Description of engagement, Marshall, *Life of Washington*, III, 135–39.

Dec., 1779 *Ordered Home*

Virginia regiments of the Northern Army under command of Col. Thomas Marshall encamped at Morristown, N.J.; three-year term of men expired; officers including J.M. ordered home. DNA, Pension Bureau. Affidavit of J.M. on pension application of Humphrey Marshall, June 12, 1832 (herein); Marshall, *Autobiography*, 6.

COMPANY MUSTER ROLL—1779

Jan.	Camp Middlebrook, Feb. 3	On furlough in Virginia	Capt. J.M.'s Co in 7th Va. Reg. in Gen'l Woodford's
Feb.	Same, Mar. 4	On furlough in Virginia	Brigade commanded by Col. Morgan.
Mar.	Same, Apr. 3	On furlough in Virginia	
Apr.	Same, May 5	On furlough	
May	Camp Smith's Cove, June 11	in Virginia	Commenced July (1,) 1777
June	Same, July 2		Commenced July (1,) 1777
July	Camp at Rammapough, [*sic*] Aug. 3		Commenced July (1,) 1777
Aug.	Sept. 6		
Sept.	Oct. 1	On command at Morristown	
Oct.	Haverstraw, Nov. 8		
Nov.	Camp Morristown, Dec. 9		

DNA, Rev. War Records, Military Card Records. R.G. 93.

FIELD AND STAFF MUSTER ROLL—1779

Captain J.M.'s Co., 7th Va., Under Col. Morgan.

Month	Place	Company	Date	Other Data
Jan.	Camp Middlebrook	3	Feb. 3	On furlough in Virginia
Feb.	Camp Middlebrook	3	Mar. 4	On furlough in Virginia
Mar.	Camp Middlebrook	3	Apr. 3	On furlough in Virginia
Apr.	Camp Middlebrook	3	May	
May	Camp Smith's Cove	2	June 11	
June	Camp Smith's Cove	2	July 2	
July	Camp Rammapough [*sic*]	2	Aug. 3	
Aug.	Camp Smith's Cove	2	Sept. 6	
Sept.	Camp Ramipaugh [*sic*]	2	Oct. 1	Court martial Morristown
Oct.	Camp Ramipaugh [*sic*]	2	Nov. 8	
Nov.	Camp near Morristown	2	Dec. 9	

DNA, Rev. War Records, Military Card Record. R.G. 93.

COMPANY PAY ROLL—1779

Month	Time	Pay per Month	Whole Pay	
Jan.	1 mo.	\$40–\$20 subsistence	£18	Captain J.M.'s Co. in 7th Va. Reg. commanded by Col. Daniel Morgan.
	Same	Through July		
Aug.	1 mo.	\$40–subsistence \$97	\$137	
Sept.	1 mo.	\$40–subsistence \$200	\$240	
Oct.	1 mo.	\$40–subsistence \$200	\$240	

DNA, Rev. War Records, Military Card Records. R.G. 93.

1780

DOCUMENTS

Jan. 3 *Treasury Warrant*

Treasury Warrant 2036, issued to Thomas Marshall, 5,000 acres, \$2,000, survey dated Jan. 3, 1783, for 1,640 acres assigned to J.M., Jr., lying in

Fayette County, Kentucky. V, Old Treasury Warrants. (Many other entries were made this same day, probably involving J.M. directly or indirectly. Some of these were entered as "John Marshall," some as "John Marshall, Jr." The use of the suffix "Jr.," because of its interchangeable use in related transactions, may have been a trading device employed by Thomas, John's father, or it might have referred to J.M. in order to distinguish him from other persons of the same name, such as John's uncle. Transactions herein listed have included only those in which it is clear or probable because of extrinsic evidence that our J.M. was involved. For exhaustive listings, see William Rouse Jillson, *Old Kentucky Entries and Deeds* [Louisville, Standard Printing Co., 1926], 124, 245, and Jillson, *The Kentucky Land Grants* [Louisville, Standard Printing Co., 1925], 83, 206. See also Finley Table of Entries, WHi, Draper MSS 12 ZZ–130; Survey of 1,560 acres, Aug. 11, 1785, Same, MSS 12 ZZ–117.)

Mar. *College Attendance*

Went to Williamsburg, remaining until July; attended law lectures of Chancellor George Wythe, and lectures of natural philosophy given by Rev. James Madison, president of William and Mary College. DNA, Pension Bureau, affidavit of J.M. supporting pension application of Humphrey Marshall, June 12, 1832 (herein); Marshall, *Autobiography*, 6; Joseph Story in Dillon, *Marshall*, 336.

His name appeared on the college walls, probably in two places. WMQ (ser. 1) Vol. X (Oct., 1901), 132; WMQ (ser. 2) Vol. VIII (Oct., 1928), 288; date given is 1775, which is necessarily in error.

May 18
WILLIAMSBURG, VA. *Phi Beta Kappa*

J.M. was recommended, balloted, voted in as member of Phi Beta Kappa Chapter at William and Mary College, member No. 40. WMQ (ser. 1) Vol. IV (Jan., 1896), 215, 236; "John Marshall," *Green Bag*, Vol. XIII, (Apr., 1901), 164. Meetings: May 21. Named to argue question whether any form of government more favorable than Commonwealth. June 3, argued. WMQ, *supra*, 252.

June 15
JEFFERSON COUNTY, KY. *Land Entry*

J.M., Jun., assignee enters 14,717 acres of land on treasury warrant to begin at a black oak with Indian marks on north side of North Fork of Licking Creek on the east side of the road leading from the head of Lawrence Creek to the Lower Salt Licks adjoining George Dickinson's pre-emption, Richard Wade's settlement, Hugh Shannon's line, George Clark or William Crow's settlement and pre-emption, and Alex McClennan's pre-emption. Jefferson County, Ky., Records, Deed Book A, 133. This tract was surveyed and patented by J.M.'s father, Thomas, on Nov. 28, 1784. Kentucky Land Office, Frankfort, Ky., Va. Grants, Book 8, 154. It was devised by him to his son, Thomas, on Feb. 15, 1803.

June 15
JEFFERSON COUNTY, KY. *Land Entry*

J.M., Jun., assignee, enters 15,000 acres on three treasury warrants to begin at road that leads from the mouth of Cabin Creek to the Upper Salt Lick where the road crosses the dividing ridge between the waters of Cabin Creek and the North Fork of Licking Creek adjoining McDrummitt's settlement and pre-emption. Jefferson County, Ky., Records, Deed Book A, 133.

June 15
JEFFERSON COUNTY, KY. *Land Entry*

J.M., entry June 15, 1780. Surveyed Nov. 18, 1784. (This notation is of entries of 14,717 acres on the North Fork of the Licking and 15,000 acres on Same.) Finley Table of Entries. WHi, Draper MSS 12 ZZ–130.

June 24
JEFFERSON COUNTY, KY. *Land Entry*

J.M. (designated as J.M., Jn'r), assignee of Thomas Marshall, entry for 5,000 acres on North Fork of Elkhorn and crossing branches and drains of the South Fork of the Licking River, less prior entries. Jefferson County, Ky., Records, Deed Book A, 150. See herein July 29, 1799.

Aug. 28
FAUQUIER COUNTY, VA. *Admission to Bar*

Admission of J.M. to bar of Fauquier County. County Court, Fauquier, Minute Book 1773–1780, 473.

1781

DOCUMENTS

Feb. 12 *Resignation from Army*

Before invasion of Virginia by Phillips resigned his commission in the army, there being a redundancy of officers, "desiring to give attention to future prospects in life." Marshall, *Autobiography*, 6; J.M. to Joseph Delaplaine, Mar. 22, 1818 (herein); Gwathmey, *Historical Register*, 501.

Feb. 19
RICHMOND *to William B. Giles*

Autograph memorandum. Listed in E. Lazare, ed., *American Book-Prices Current* (New York, Dodd, Mead & Co., 1931), 757. Present owner unknown.

Mar. 5
WINCHESTER, VA. *Military Document*

Authentication by J.M. of handwriting of the late Gen. (James) Wood; order to Maj. John Roberts concerning management of Hessian prisoners. DNA, Rev. War Pension Files, John Roberts, W2347 Var. (segregated files). R.G. 15–A.

1782

DOCUMENTS

Nov. 30 *Military Land Certificate*

Certification by William Davies, War Office, Virginia, that Capt. J.M. entitled to captain's allowance for three years' service as officer in army. Land Office Certificate No. 30 issued. V, Land Office Military Certificates, John Marshall, Rev. War Records, Folder 11; V, Land Office, Military Certificates No. 1, 1–1805, p. 6; Records Ky. Dept. of State, Frankfort, Military Warrants, Book I, 10; DNA, Rev. War MSS Coll., No. 17449, R.G. 93. Gains M. Brumbaugh, *Revolutionary War Records, Virginia* (Washington, Lancaster, Pa., Press, 1936), I, 104.

Nov. 30
FRANKFORT, KY. *Survey Order*

Survey order on Military Warrant No. 30, issued to J.M., three years' service in army, 4,000 acres land, pursuant to certificate of Commissioner of War. Records Ky. Dept. of State, Frankfort, Military Warrants, Book I, 10.

HOUSE OF DELEGATES OF VIRGINIA
COUNCIL OF STATE (PRIVY COUNCIL)

J.M. WAS ELECTED to the Virginia House of Delegates from Fauquier County in May. Marshall, *Autobiography*, 7; J.M. to Joseph Delaplaine, Mar. 22, 1818 (herein).

He served during the October session until Nov. 30, 1782, having been elected by it to the Virginia Privy Council or Council of State on Nov. 20. He resigned from the Privy Council Apr. 1, 1784.

Nov. 9 Member of Committee for Courts of Justice. Journal, H.D., 1781–1785 (Oct. sess., 1782), 10. (Reprint, Richmond, Thos. W. White, 1828). DLC; V.

Nov. 12 On special committee "to form a plan of national defense against invasion, etc." Same, 14.

Nov. 13 On special committee to frame a bill to amend the ordinance of convention. Same, 15.

Nov. 18 Voted for bill allowing John McLean to return to Virginia. Passed. Same, 22.

On committee to plan for more speedy promulgation of laws and journals of General Assembly. Same, 23.

On committee to bring in bill for reorganization of militia. Same. 23.

On committee concerning bill for appropriating public revenue; redemption of certificates. Same, 25.

Nov. 20 Leave given J.M. to prepare and bring in bill to amend act concerning pensioners. Same, 27.

Elected member of Privy Council or Council of State of Virginia by joint ballot of House of Delegates and Senate. Same, 27.

On committee to examine books and papers of commercial agent and determine payment of debts. Same, 27.

Nov. 25 Added to Committee of Privileged and Elections. Same, 36.

Nov. 26 Voted for bill to discourage extensive credit and repeal act concerning proving of book debts. Same, 37–38.

Nov. 27 Ordered with Tazewell and Arthur Campbell to prepare and bring in bill concerning surveyors. Same, 42.

Nov. 29 Voted against motion to postpone militia bill. Motion carried. Same, 45.

Nov. 30 J.M. presented certificate of membership in Privy Council or Council of State, qualified by oath before J. Ambler, alderman, V, Journal of the Council (of State, Va.), 1782–1783, 13; V, Exec. Papers, Box Nov. 1–30, 1782, Folder Nov. 21–30; Journal, Council of State, III, 184; CVSP, III, 386; Marshall, *Autobiography*, 7; Oster, *Marshall*, 196. He served on this body until Apr. 1, 1784. (See herein that date.)

LEGAL PRACTICE

County Court, Fauquier

Lawrence Washington, Attorney for John Washington v. John Baites and James Wren.

July 23. Action of debt. Special bail, plea payment; continued; discontinued as to Baites. J.M. for Wren.

County Court, Fauquier, Minute Book 1781–1784, 57.

For revival of judgment and execution against James Wren and Minor Wren, his common bail, see Same, Minute Book 1784–1786, 149.

1783

DOCUMENTS

Jan. 1 *Marriage Bond*

J.M. and Mary W. Ambler. NSDR, "Henrico County, Va., Records, Marriage Bonds" (typescript compilation), p. 130.

Jan. 3 *Marriage*

J.M. and Mary Willis Ambler married. VU, Marshall Bible Record; Marshall, *Autobiography*, 7; J.M. to Joseph Delaplaine, Mar. 22, 1818 (herein). His courtship is described by him in J.M. to Polly Marshall, Feb. 23, 1824 (herein). Also by Betsy Ambler Carrington, his sister-in-law, in "An Old Virginia Correspondence," *Atlantic Monthly*, Vol. LXXXIV, (Oct., 1899), 535–49.

Jan. 11
Frankfort, Ky. *Land Entry*

Entry in name of J.M., Jr., of 4,002 acres of land in Kentucky on Lawrence Creek, waters of Licking, on Treasury Warrants 11251 and 13924. Kentucky Land Office, Frankfort, Ky., Fayette Entries, Book 2, 34; Jillson, *Old Kentucky Entries and Deeds*, 124. (See July 26, 1799, herein for patent of 1,239 acres; survey of above, Dec., 1785, in name of J.M.) KyHi.

Jan. 11
FRANKFORT, KY. *Land Entry*

Entry by J.M., Jr., assignee of Thomas Marshall, who was assignee of J.M. 8,304 acres on south side of North Fork of Licking, Kentucky, on part of Treasury Warrant 12971. Surveyed. Kentucky Land Office, Fayette Entries, Book 2, 44.

Jan. 11
FRANKFORT, KY. *Land Entry*

Entry by J.M., Jr., 10,659½ acres in Kentucky on South Fork of Licking Creek (Mason Co., Ky.), on Treasury Warrants 14011 and 12143, assigned to him by Benjamin Netherland, and 12718, assigned to him by Jesse Glover. 5,413 acres assigned for J.M., Jr. Kentucky Land Office, Fayette Entries, Book 2, 39–40. (See herein June 14, 1799; Apr. 3, 1812; Sept. 10, 1805; July 29, 1799 [J.M.'s power of attorney].)

Jan. 11
FRANKFORT, KY. *Land Entry*

Entry by J.M. for 14,150 acres Kentucky land on the Ohio River. Kentucky Land Office, Fayette Entries, Book 2, 47.

Jan. 11
FRANKFORT, KY. *Land Entry*

Entry by J.M., Jr., assignee of Thomas Marshall, who was assignee of J.M., 4,000 acres south side of North Fork of Licking, Kentucky, on part of Treasury Warrant 12971. Surveyed Apr. 7, 1786. Kentucky Land Office, Fayette Entries, Book 2, 45. See *Ward v. Fox's heirs*, Hughes' Reports, at 433 (Supreme Court and Court of Appeals, Kentucky).

Jan. 13 *Treasury Warrant*

For 500 acres, Fayette County, Ky., assigned to Thomas Marshall, assignee of J.M., who was assignee of Samuel Beal. Grant issued to Nathaniel Randolph, assignee, 2,962 acres, plus current money, Apr. 26, 1784. V, Land Office, Old Treasury Warrants, Book M, folio.

Jan. 31 *Land Warrants*

Folio page for Warrant No. 2036 issued in name of Col. Thomas Marshall, 5,000 acres, Fayette County, Ky., dated Jan. 13, 1780; on above date 1,640 acres assigned to J.M., Jr.; grant issued Mar. 11, 1784, recorded in Book K, folio 340. (See herein Mar. 11, 1784.)

Also assignment of 1,700 acres of the 5,000 acres, Nov. 24, 1783, to Thomas Marshall, the younger, by Thomas Marshall, assignee of J.M., assignee of Thomas Marshall. V, Land Office, Old Treasury Warrants, 1–4327, 1779–1780. See also Franklin County District Court Records, 1797–1830, Order Book 1, 1–7, Frankfort, Ky.

Feb. 12
RICHMOND *to William Pierce*

Discusses war and finance, rumors of peace; social activities, Richmond Assembly. NjP.

Mar. 5
RICHMOND *to Col. William Heth*

Acknowledges letter; assures that if any tobacco was drawn by officers on certificates, it was before Heth's was entrusted to him. No tobacco in Treasury; some expected. Banks not in town; will consult Ross. Made application to Treasurer; refused. Col. T. M. Randolph concerning price on horse to Pryor. Discourages Heth on appointment as state naval officer. VU, Selden MSS, Deposit 5071.

Sept. 17
FRANKFORT, KY. *Land Warrants—Entries*

J.M. is listed as owner of three treasury warrants: No. 19450 for 25,000 acres, £40,000 current money; No. 19451, same noted as survey made of 3,956 acres for Thomas Marshall, Sen., Fayette; No. 19452, 6,121 acres, £9,795 current money. V, Old Treasury Warrants, 16416–19999, 1783.

On Dec. 27, 1783, he entered 56,121 acres of land in Kentucky on the North Fork of the Licking on these warrants. Kentucky Land Office, Fayette Entries, Book 3, 110.

On Nov. 8, 1785, he withdrew 5,000 acres from the above and re-entered it on the same river, south side below Crook Mill Creek. Same, Fayette Entries, Book 4, 233.

Oct. 23
RICHMOND *Account Book and Legal Notes*

This is the first date of entry in J.M.'s account book of income and expenses, appearing on p. 3. Prior entries were probably of the prior month or months. The last entries were Sept., 1795. J.M. Account Book, Marshall House, Richmond, Va.; DLC; VW.

The notes of law propositions written in rear of book and running in counter direction are undated. Beveridge says the notes were of Wythe lectures, but he says further that many were probably made after J.M. left college. Beveridge, *Marshall,* I, 174, 176n. Mason indicates doubt, saying that the book might have been "clean as a new sail," or it might have already held a scheme of law notes gathered before J.M.'s army years. She says he turned his law notes upside down and began the accounts in 1783. Mason, *Polly,* 7, 20. The numbering of the pages, however, would indicate otherwise. It is suggested that the notes were started in rear of the book after commencement of the account book in 1783.

Nov. 10, *n.p.* *Bounty Warrant*

Certificate that Richard Marshall enlisted and served in 11th Virginia Regiment; signed by J.M. as captain. V, Rev. War Records, Bounty Warrants.

Nov. 30
FRANKFORT, KY. *Land Entry*

Entry by J.M. of 40,000 acres Kentucky land on Salt Lick Creek near Ohio River adjoining entry by J.M., 14,150 acres, on Treasury Warrant 17721. Kentucky Land Office, Fayette Entries, Book 3, 19.

Dec. 9
RICHMOND *to Col. Leven Powell, of Loudon County, Va.*

Concerning Powell suit against Burwell; will be at Fauquier March court; judgment taken by Commonwealth against Powell. Discusses the General Assembly, the bills concerning commutables, elections, and attendance of members. Branch Hist. Papers, June, 1902, 130–31; Robert C. Powell, *A Biographical Sketch of Col. Leven Powell* (Alexandria, Va., Ramey, 1877), 99–100.

Apr. 8, 1786. The case of *Powell v. Burwell's Executor* finished, J.M. received fee of £10 from Powell. Account Book, 68.

Dec. 12
RICHMOND *to James Monroe*

Delivered letters to Gen. Clarke and Banks; letter to Maj. Crittenden mentioned. Col. R. H. Lee and Col. Harry Lee in the Assembly. Commutable bill and citizenship bill discussed. Jones, Henry, Taylor, Nicholas mentioned. Survey of Cumberland lands; Crittenden and military warrants. Cession (of Kentucky) by Congress discussed. Thomas Marshall departed to Western Country. WHi, Draper MSS, 522–97 (2); DLC, Beveridge Coll.; Oster, *Marshall,* 86–88; Reuben G. Thwaites, "A Letter of Marshall to Jefferson, 1783." AHR, Vol. X (July, 1905), 816–17. (In these last two printings Thomas Jefferson is named as addressee, which is undoubtedly incorrect. See Beveridge, *Marshall*, I, 208.)

Dec. 18, *n.p.* *Military Document*

Certificate by J.M. that Lieut. Benjamin Ashley served in 7th Virginia Regiment in 1777 in continental service. Signed by J.M., as "then Cap't. 7th V.R." V, Rev. War Pension Records.

n.d. *Land Survey*

Survey in name of J.M. of 1790 acres on part of entry of 4,002 acres on Lawrence Creek, Mason County, Ky. (see herein Jan. 11, 1783); 1,239 acres of same entry patented in name of J.M. and designated as adjoining (see herein July 26, 1799). This survey of J.M. is referred to, with plat, in *Ward v. Fox's Heirs*, Hughes' Reports, at 414 (Supreme Court and Court of Appeals, Kentucky).

n.d., FAUQUIER COUNTY, VA. *Tax List*

J.M. listed as owning one Negro and three horses. V, Fauquier County, Tithable Book, 1783–1784.

COUNCIL OF STATE

Mar. 12 At request of Governor, the Council of State appointed two of its members, J.M. and James Monroe, to examine what progress the Solicitor had made in settling accounts of the state against the Continent (the United States). V, Journal, Council of State, III, 230.

Mar. 25 Report by J.M. and James Monroe in Council of State on progress made by Virginia Solicitor in settling accounts of the state against the Continent (the United States), reporting great abuses and misapplication of funds. Same, 234–35.

May 22 J.M. sat as member of Council of State of Virginia at session approving warrant on the contingent fund to reimburse Thomas Marshall (his father) for advances by him to commissioners to settle accounts in the Western Country. Same, 259.

LEGAL PRACTICE

J.M.'s ACCOUNT BOOK records of his fees for legal services commence undated and are obviously incomplete, referring themselves to the carryover of a balance from some other record. The only entries which definitely refer to legal fees are those from Crohan, part fee £3; Ernest, £2:10; Reid, £2.8; Hancock Lee, £2.11; and possibly £1:14:9 received from Keith Thomas.

J.M.'s letter of Dec. 9 to Col. Leven Powell refers to a suit by Powell against Burwell, and a judgment against Powell by the Commonwealth. (See herein Dec. 9, 1783.)

County Court, Fauquier

Charles Carter v. Jesse Williams.

J.M. for defendant.

May 28. Dismissed.

County Court, Fauquier, Minute Book 1781–1784, 128.

Fees: Sept., 1784, £1:16; Apr. 18, 1785, £4:16. Account Book 14, 32.

Col. Thomas Marshall v. Katherine Rector, executrix of John Rector.

Action on security bond, £600, 1771. J.M. for defendant.

Sept. 22, 1783. Defendant by attorney confessed £581:6:1 with interest from January, 1775; j. entered £281:6:1, to be levied on goods of decedent, execution stayed ninety days.

County Court, Fauquier, Minute Book 1781–1784, 176.

(See letter J.M. to Cuthbert Bullett, herein, Mar. 16, 1785.)

1784

DOCUMENTS

Richmond *to James Monroe*

Greatest man on earth dead, superior man, heart overflows with gratitude. Will meet requests on pecuniary and other subjects. Letter to Maj. Crittenden sent in hands of Gen. Clark, in Western County February or March; Crittenden to attend to Monroe's military warrant. Speaker of House of Delegates left Richmond; may not be present for next session. Laments exclusion of delegates in Congress from legislature; fear of Congress chimerical. Regrets troubling Monroe with resolution on cession of Western Territory; resolution to Congress from Col. Mercer, dated September. DLC, Papers of James Monroe.

Feb. 7

Richmond *to James Monroe*

Post setting out, enclosing bill as best method within J.M.'s reach of sending money due a delegate to Congress; $104 drawn expended on land warrant now in hands of surveyor. DLC, Papers of James Monroe.

Feb. 19
RICHMOND *to James Monroe—Addressed to Annapolis*

Opportunity of sending by gentleman waiting duplicates of bills sent by post but possibly detained by hard weather; deliver to those for whom drawn. Requests he receive Maury and introduce to confreres in Congress. Jefferson better acquainted with him. New York Society Library.

Feb. 24
RICHMOND *to James Monroe*

Inability to raise money for Monroe on his warrants; Ege and Mrs. Shera pressing for money. Social gossip concerning Little Stewart, Kitty Hair, Dunn, Tabby Eppes, Carrington, Young Seldon, Wright, Foster Webb. Political comment concerning Lomax, Nelson, Randolph, Short. NN, Papers of James Monroe; DLC, Beveridge Coll.; Beveridge, *Marshall*, I, 181–83 (excerpt).

Feb.
RICHMOND *Tax List*

Return to the Common Hall of the inhabitants and assessments of Ward No. 1 Richmond.

J.M., councilor, abode—1 year, lot 630, age 28, wheels of riding carriages—4 (tax 5 shillings), tax £1:2; Mary Willis Marshall, age 17; no. of white male tithables, 1; no. females, 1, tax 10 shillings; Hannah, age 25; Moses, age 10; Beah, age 10, tax 15 shillings; total tax to J.M. £2:7. V, Common Hall Records 1782–1793, I, 300–301.

Assessment of lots and tenements with their improvements in Wardship 1, Richmond, 1784.

J.M. tenant, lot 680, value £15, bracketed with Wm. Cocke, lot 630, value £15, tax on both 6 shillings; value of improvements £150, tax 15 shillings, total tax £1:1. Same, 361.

Mar. 11
FRANKFORT, KY. *Land Grant*

Kentucky land grant to J.M., assignee of Thomas Marshall, 1,640 acres in Fayette County, head branch of John Constant's and Morgans Fork of Strodes' Fork of the Licking River, on Treasury Warrant 2036, issued Jan. 13, 1783, survey Jan. 31, 1783. Kentucky Land Office, Va. Grants, Book 2,

85; V. (See also Will of Thomas Marshall, June 26, 1798, and Land Warrants, Jan. 31, 1783, herein.)

Mar. 24
FRANKFORT, KY. *Land Entries*

Involved in an entry of 60,000 acres of Kentucky land on the North Fork of the Elkhorn and Eagle Creek jointly with John Crittenden and Zuke Kennon on Treasury Warrant 19453. (See letter of James Monroe, Dec. 12, 1783, herein.) Kentucky Land Office, Fayette Entries, Book 3, 237. On Jan. 5, 1785, 30,000 acres was re-entered on Slate Creek. Same, Book 4, 82. J.M.'s share of the 60,000 acres was 5,000 acres, which he withdrew Mar. 7, 1785. Same, Book 4, 130. This was re-entered on the Main Licking, Apr. 20, 1785. Same, Book 4, 153. Thereafter July 30, 1785, re-entered on Cabin Creek. Same, Book 4, 213.

For entry of J.M. and John Crittenden Treasury Warrants, see V, Old Treasury Warrants, 16416–19999, 1783, folio page Sept. 17.

Apr. 1
RICHMOND *to Gov. Benjamin Harrison*

Resignation from Council of State of Virginia. V, Exec. Comm. Box, Benj. Harrison, Nov. 30, 1781–Nov. 30, 1784, Folder May 3, 1784; Marshall, *Autobiography*, 7; J.M. to Joseph Delaplaine (Mar. 22, 1818, herein).

J.M. had attended sessions and signed the proceedings of two hundred meetings of the Council between Nov. 30, 1782, and Apr. 1, 1784. He missed comparatively few sessions. Journal, Council of State, III, 184–344.

Apr. 17
RICHMOND *to Arthur Lee—Addressed to Annapolis, Md.*

Sale of tobacco for Lee; warehouses of Byrd and Shockoe. Interest in Western Country; intention of J.M. to move to Kentucky. Separation from Virginia approved. Resignation from Executive Council; at Richmond General Court bar. Encloses bill for £100. VHi, Lee Transcripts.

Apr. 17
RICHMOND *to James Monroe*

Acknowledges letter of Mar. 12. Resignation from Executive Council, judges opposed to legal practice. Considering candidacy (to Virginia House of Delegates) from Fauquier County. Various representatives elected. Trying to sell Monroe's warrants; discuss £100 sent (incomplete). NN, Papers of James Monroe; DLC, Beveridge Coll.; Beveridge, *Marshall*, I, 212 (excerpt reproduced).

May 2
RICHMOND *L. Wood to Governor of Virginia*

Mentions appointment of Marshall and Monroe as a committee of the Executive Council concerning Continental accounts. Feb. 7, 1783; both now out of office. V, Exec. Papers, Box Apr.–July, 1784, Folder May 1–10.

May 15
RICHMOND *to James Monroe*

Thanks for enclosures. Col. Grayson has not arrived; Nicholas has. House made on Wednesday; committees being appointed. Henry charged high to delay collection of taxes; speeches. Believes citizenship bill will be taken up. J.M. considers self a moderate. Compliment to Mercer. £100 in Treasury. May and Crittenden re-elected for Fayette County. J.M. anxious to learn of Monroe's land from them. If Dr. Lee not in Annapolis, take J.M.'s letter to him. DLC, Papers of James Monroe.

June 16
RICHMOND *to Charles Simms*

Acknowledges receipt of petition and bond; advises need to advertise petition; may be able to carry it through House. Believes no prospect of amending circuit court system in Virginia so as to put more power in judges rather than magistrates. Approves pending bill to restrict foreign vessels to certain ports; will benefit Norfolk and Alexandria. Also favors bill to hold one session of the House each year. Going to Fauquier when session ends; plans to spend summers there and winters in Richmond; uncertain if plan will hold. DLC, Chas. Simms Papers; Corra Bacon-Foster, *Early Chapters in the Development of the Potomac Route to the West* (Washington, Columbia Hist. Society, 1912), 254–55.

Dec. 2
RICHMOND *to James Monroe*

Acknowledges letter of Nov. 14; congratulates on safe return to Atlantic part of world. Agrees in regretting resolution on British debts; excuse for holding forts; weakens federal bonds resolution pending for payment by installments. Bill passed exclusive privilege to Rumsey to navigate new boats; regrets bill to encourage intermarriage with Indians rejected; general assessment and circuit court bill may fail. Regrets members of Council appointed before knew Col. Mercer desired; mortified not able to elect Carrington. Showed father part of letter concerning Western Country; latter will render service, also Humphrey Marshall, who, being better acquainted with lands, able to choose to advantage. Recommends Monroe sell western lands; will be poor during lifetime unless moves to Western Country. DLC, Papers of James Monroe; Oster, *Marshall*, 55–59; George Bancroft, *History of the Formation of the Constitution* (New York, Appleton, 1883) I, 398–400; W. H. Henry, *Life and Correspondence of Patrick Henry* (New York, Charles Scribner's Sons, 1891), II, 219.

HOUSE OF DELEGATES OF VIRGINIA
(Session of May 3, 1784–Jan. 7, 1785)

J.M. RE-ELECTED to Virginia House of Delegates from Fauquier County, although only a nominal resident; immediately after the election he established self in Richmond to practice law in the superior courts. Marshall, *Autobiography*, 7; Joseph Story in Dillon, *Marshall*, III, 337; Herring, *Marshall*, 5.

May 13 J.M. admitted to his seat in House of Delegates on paying fees for tardy attendance, representing Fauquier County. Journal, H.D. (May sess., 1784), 5. (Reprint, Richmond, Thos. W. White, 1828. DLC; V.)

May 13 J.M. appointed on Standing Committee for Propositions and Grievances, and on Committee on Courts of Justice. Same, 5.

May 19 On committee to bring in bill providing for reapportionment of debts of states to Congress under 8th article of Articles of Confederacy, and bill to allow retaliatory trade laws. Same, 11–12. Latter bill reported and passed. Same 37, 81. Hening, Stat., XI, 388. Presented amendments to bill for the relief of Thomas Paine. Beveridge, *Marshall*, I, 213.

May 20 Voted against bill containing act adjusting claims for property impressed and public service. Bill rejected. Journal, H.D., 12.

May 21 On committee on forgery of military certificates. Journal, H.D., 16.

June 2 J.M. and Spencer Roane were added to committee to bring in bill "to amend the act for establishing county courts and regulating proceedings." Same, 32.

June 7 Voted for act repealing Virginia acts which prevent compliance with treaty with Great Britain. Bill defeated. Same, 41.

June 11 Voted for amendment of bill changing seat of government to provide for opinion of citizens. Passed. Same, 51.

June 17 Voted against bill to restrict foreign vessels to certain ports of Virginia. Bill passed. Same, 61.

June 18 On committee to bring in bill "to compel the delinquent counties within the state to pay up delinquencies for recruiting of troops to serve in U.S. Army." Same, 65. Bill passed. Hening, Stat., XI, 390.

June 19 Resolution for joint balloting with Senate to select two members of Privy Council in place of J.M. and Thomas Lomax, resigned. Journal, H.D., 67.

June 21 Voted for amendment of resolution rejecting petition of Augusta County as beyond powers of General Assembly by striking reference to reform of constitution by majority of people. Amendment rejected. Same, 70–71.

On committee to bring bill extending time to establish settlement and pre-emption rights. Same, 71.

June 22 Joint balloting held with Senate for selection of two Privy Council members, one vacancy created by J.M.'s resignation. J.M. on committee to meet with Senate committee to examine ballots. Same, 72; V, Exec. Papers, Box Apr.–July, 1784, Folder June 21–30, "Appointment and Election to Offices."

June 23 On resolution to Congress for remonstrance against violations by Great Britain of treaty, and withholding co-operation of General Assembly until rectified voted for amendments eliminating latter clause and substituting merely submission of claims of Virginians, or withholding payment to British claimants. Both amendments defeated; resolution passed. Journal, H.D., 74–75.

June 25 Did not vote on bill for sale of public lands in and near Richmond. Same, 78.

June 28 Same as to bill concerning marriages. Same, 81–82.

June 30 J.M. on behalf of committee reported amendments to bill vesting public land in Thomas Payne. Bill rejected. Also similar bill of Madison, rejected. Same, 86.

July 5 J.M. received £34:4 for services in the General Assembly. Account Book, 10.

Nov. 1 Committee on Courts of Justice, of which J.M. member, to meet and adjourn from day to day; also Committee on Propositions and Grievances. Journal, H.D., (Oct. sess., 1784), 7.

Nov. 2 On committee to prepare bills to amend militia acts and to provide against invasion and insurrection. Same, 8.

Nov. 5 On committee to prepare bill to amend acts imposing duties on imports; providing for appointment of controller. Same, 12.

Nov. 11 No vote recorded for J.M. on bill for tax or contribution for support of Christian religion. Same, 19.

Nov. 12 On committee to prepare bill applying receipts of import duties to creditors of state instead of to the United States. Same, 20.

Nov. 13 On committee to bring in bill to explain and amend, entitled "An act for discouraging extensive credit," and repealing the act prescribing methods of proving book debts. Same, 22.

Nov. 15 George Washington visit to Richmond; J.M. not on waiting committee. Same, 24.

Nov. 17 On committee for appointment of attorney general for Kentucky District. Same, 27.

Bill for incorporation of all societies of Christian religion; no vote recorded for J.M. Same, 27.

Nov. 18 Visit of Lafayette to Richmond; J.M. not on waiting committee. Same, 28.

Nov. 22 Bill for incorporation of Cincinnati Society of Virginia to Committee on Courts of Justice, of which J.M. member. Same, 33. Dec. 2, committee relieved of bill; to Committee of Whole House. Same, 51.

Nov. 25 Reported before Committee of the Whole House that his committee had considered bill concerning entries and surveys on the Western waters; offered amendments; read and offered bill. Same, 38. Nov. 30, asked to carry bill to Senate. Same, 46.

Petition of Thomas Marshall for payment as state officer; 1777, major 3rd Virginia Regiment, command of regiment of artillery in state service; to Committee of Propositions and Grievances. Same, 39.

Nov. 26 Voted for amendment to bill punishing offenses against tranquility of Commonwealth, permitting extradition to foreign countries. Amendment passed. Same, 41. Nov. 27, voted for bill. Passed. Same, 42.

Nov. 27 On committee concerning claim of Oliver Pollock. Same, 43. Dec. 4, report on same by Ronald. Same, 55. Dec. 10, Senate amendment thereto agreed to. Same, 64.

Nov. 29 On committee to prepare bill settling title to unpatented land prior to establishment of Land Office. Same, 45. Dec. 2, J.M. presented above bill. Same, 51. Dec. 30, ordered to acquaint Senate of agreement to amendments. Same, 96.

Dec. 18 No vote recorded for J.M. on bill to issue certificates to officers of 1st and 2nd Virginia regiments. Bill passed. Same, 75.

Dec. 22 Voted for bill incorporating Protestant Episcopal Church. Bill passed. Same, 79.

Dec. 24 Voted against postponement of third reading of bill for teachers of Christian religion. Postponement passed; opinion of people requested. Same, 82.

Dec. 30 Voted for bill allowing western counties to pay arrears of taxes in hemp. Bill passed. Same, 95.

Ordered to carry to Senate bill allowing exchange of British land warrants issued under Proclamation of 1763 to those serving in U.S. Army from May 1, 1779, for warrants to land in Virginia military lands on eastern side of Ohio River. Same, 97. Jan. 3, 1785. Same House agreement on amendments to resolution. Same, 103.

LEGAL PRACTICE

Account book record of fees collected in legal practice during this year is not as descriptive and dated as might be desired. It would appear from what is probably an incomplete record that he was engaged in some ninety-eight legal matters which but for few exceptions were litigated matters in civil court. The nature of these may be gained from notations as land cases involving caveats and contracts to convey; appeals, certiorari; debt and detinue; chancery suits; injunctions; and attendant motions. Only one criminal case involving robbery appears, for which he received a fee of £3. He received several fees for advice, in each case less than £2. In a matter involving the will of Eppes, he received £10, a comparatively large fee.

His income from legal practice for the year as recorded by him totaled £498:16. The great majority of his fees were in the £2 bracket. In addition to the above mentioned, one for a chancery suit was for £7, two such suits for £7:10, a supersedeas proceedings £4:16, three suits in General Court £12.

During this year he practiced not only before the courts in Richmond which had now reopened, but also in Fauquier County. His entry of July 31 shows the receipt of £2:14 from Fauquier County business, and his letter Dec. 9, 1783, to Col. Leven Powell (which see herein), refers to his attendance at the Fauquier March court.

Caveats

Sept. 3 *JM., Jr. v. John Craig, assignee of Pemberton Rowlings.*

1,000 acres pre-emption rights (Kentucky land) north of line extending east from northeast corner Craig's Settlement, falls within entry of 200 acres of J.M., Jr., at Surveyor's Office on Treasury Warrant, 1784. V, Virginia Land Office, Caveats, I, 113.

Oct. 19 *George Easterly v. John Benson, Frederick Kaylor, assignee, and Frederick Foland, assignee.*

J.M. for plaintiffs. Land in Rockingham County, formerly Augusta County, adjoining lands of Fairfax's heir and Knight and Bowman, surveyed by Benson, 1774. Easterly claiming part by assignment from Kaylor after purchased from Benson and before Foland. V, Virginia Land Office, Caveats, I, 122. Oct. 23, 1784. Same as to 230 acres. Same, I, 124–25.

Fee: Oct. 14, 1784, £2:10. Account Book, 18.

County Court, Fauquier

Rawley Smith, administrator of Joseph Smith v. William Smith.

Assumpsit. J.M. for defendant.

Aug. 27. V.j. for plaintiff, £8:17.

County Court, Fauquier, Minute Book 1784–1786, 51.

Fees: May 2, 1787, "apl. in cas" £5; Sept., 1794, "old suit," £5. Account Book, 114, 396.

John Ashby v. William Grant.

Aug. 27. Order dissolving injunction against j. at common law. J.M. for plaintiff.

County Court, Fauquier, Minute Book 1784–1786, 47.

Fee: Oct. 3, 1786, "Appeal" £1:8. Account Book, 84.

1785–1788

RECORDER FOR TOWN OF RICHMOND
Richmond City Hustings Court

July 5, 1785 In accordance with act of 1782 incorporating the City of Richmond, as amended, triannual election of body corporate, sixteen freeholders elected from approximately seventy-six contenders. J.M. received 121 votes, exceeded only by Gabriel Galt with 122. V, Common Hall Records 1782–1792, I, 105–106.

(The sixteen so elected for three-year terms constituted the city corporate body, and elected from their number a mayor annually, a recorder, six aldermen, and eight common councilmen. They sat at the Common Hall, at least seven required for a quorum; one being the mayor, recorder, or eldest alderman.)

July 17, 1785 J.M. elected Recorder of City of Richmond by vote of the sixteen corporators. V, Common Hall Records 1782–1792, I, 105–106. As Recorder J.M.'s duties included keeping records and signing orders of the Board of Aldermen. He also recorded deeds conveying property in Richmond, and wills. See V, Common Hall Records 1782–1792, I.

J.M. sat ex officio as member of Richmond City Hustings Court, composed of the mayor, recorder, and a varying number of aldermen, totaling not less than four. The court was one of original jurisdiction having the same civil and criminal jurisdiction as the County Court in cases originating in the city, excepting larger penal cases not involving violation of city ordinances. Its members had powers of justices of the peace.

The court met on the first Monday of each month. It generally completed its calendar in not to exceed two days. Orders of the court were generally signed by J.M. as recorder; if J.M. not present, by the mayor. V, Richmond City Hustings Court, Order Books 1 and 2.

(J.M. resigned office Mar. 10, 1788. His final signature to the records of the court appears Jan. 28, 1788. See herein. He was succeeded in office by William Hay.)

July 18, 1785 The first session of the court attended by J.M. together with John Harvie, mayor, and three aldermen. V, Richmond City Hustings Court, Order Book I (1782–1787), 295.

He attended the following monthly sessions of the court during his term in office:

1785—Aug. 15 (300); Sept. 19 (308); Dec. 19 (346).

1786—Jan. 16 (362); Feb. 20 (377), 21 (389), 22 (396); Apr. 17 (423), absent 18 (435); May 15 (448); June 19 (462); Aug. 21 (517); Sept. 18 (553), 28 (582); Nov. 20 (612).

1787—Jan. 16 (672), absent 17 (675); Feb. 20 (Order Book 2, Feb., 1787–Mar., 1792, 12); Mar. 12 (30), 26 (33), absent 27 (50); May 28 (67), 29 (88), 30 (99); June 25 (109), 26 (120), absent 27 (126); July 24 (156), 25 (164); Aug. 8 (175), 27 (176), 28 (187); Sept. 24 (198), 25 (210).

1788—Jan. 28 (262), absent 29 (264) but signed minutes (265).

Jan. 29, 1788 Final signature of J.M. as recorder appearing on Order Books of Richmond City Hustings Court. V, Richmond City Hustings Court, Order Book II, 265.

Common Hall of Richmond

The Common Hall with some irregularity held its regular meetings monthly and in addition special meetings called by the mayor. Each meeting was completed in a single day. During J.M.'s tenure as recorder, commencing with the meeting of July 11, 1785, and ending with that of Mar. 10, 1788, forty-five meetings were held, thirty-four of which J.M. attended.

Aug. 8, 1785 J.M. as recorder appointed in Common Hall on committee to list all fines and penalties annexed to certain offenses. Richmond City Common Hall Records 1782–1793, I, 111; V.

Sept. 12, 1785 Resolution of Common Hall. J.M. as recorder with mayor and alderman requested to set early day for cases of suspected vagabonds; that landholders and inhabitants be called on to inform as to persons not requiring legal residence and within legal description of vagrants or vagabonds; appointment of constables authorized. Same, 112.

Jan. 2, 1786 J.M. as recorder on committee of five to draw scheme of lottery for £1,500 pursuant to act of legislature to raise money for construction of Masonic Hall. Same, 118.

Jan. 9, 1786 Report of Masonic Hall lottery made, agreed to, and managers named (not including J.M.). Same, 118.

(The lottery was not successful. Same, 130, 136–37, 142–43.)

Feb. 13, 1786 J.M. as recorder ordered to bring suit in General Court against assessors who failed to report, requisite fees to be paid. Same, 121.

Mar. 19, 1786 Fines against J.M. remitted for nonattendance at Oct. and Nov., 1785, meetings; excuse made. Same, 123.

Sept. 26, 1786 J.M. as recorder on committee to draft petition to General Assembly for amendment of act of incorporation of Richmond. Same, 135.

Dec. 11, 1786 J.M. laid before Common Hall letter of mayor resigning office. Same, 137.

Jan. 24, 1787 J.M. on committee to draft ordinance concerning precautions in case of fire. Same, 140.

July 9, 1787 J.M. on committee to draft ordinance concerning gunpowder. Same, 147.

Jan. 17, 1788 J.M. as recorder presented ordinances concerning fires and gunpowder, both of which were adopted. Same, 155.

Mar. 10, 1788 Letter of resignation by J.M. as recorder of Richmond noted as received by Mayor John Beckley. The Hall proceeded to fill the vacancy, appointing William Hay. Same, 160.

1785

DOCUMENTS

Jan. 3
RICHMOND *to Governor of Virginia*

Enclosing petition of inhabitants of Prince William County for clemency to unnamed prisoner; adding that prisoner did not ask for gun and acted under influence of others. C St.

Jan. 7
RICHMOND *to George Muter*

Thanking for account of affairs in Western Country. Time for separation approaching or arrived; solicitous it be done wisely; expects migration of good element; Virginia cannot legislate for Kentucky. Innes chosen attorney general for district; Muter's name withdrawn from nomination of judge because Cyrus Griffin on list; if Griffin withdraws, will back Muter; salary £300. Bills passed legislature of utmost consequence, to open communication between James and Potomac rivers and Western waters; also Ramsey's scheme for navigating boats upstream obviates need for opening Mississippi River. J.M.'s father to set out for Kentucky in early spring. Compliments to acquaintances. Tyler's, Vol. I (July, 1919), 28, from *The Commonwealth*, Frankfort, Ky., May 23, 1838. Also in *H.R. Rep. No. 353*, 29 Cong., 1 sess., 22–25 (1845–1846).

Mar. 15
RICHMOND *Deed*

Jacquelin Ambler, Richmond, to J.M., one-half-acre lot in Richmond on Shockhoe Hill, No. 480 Plan of Richmond, £10 current. Delivered to Fisher Apr. 3, 1801. Richmond City Hustings and Chancery Court, Deed Book 1, 29; V.

Acknowledged by Ambler and ordered recorded. Same, Order Book 1, 250; V.

Mar. 16
FAUQUIER COUNTY, VA. *Deed*

Thomas Marshall, Leeds Manor, Fauquier County, to J.M., of same parish and county, his son, for five shillings and natural affection tract of land purchased of Thomas Turner, sheriff of King George, now Westmoreland County, lying in Fauquier County, 1,824 acres, excepting 1,000 acres sold by Thomas Marshall to Thomas Murray, located on Goose Creek and extending to foot of North Cobler Mountain. Recorded Apr. 26, 1785. Fauquier County, Deed Book 8, 241–42.

Above deed of gift with receipt endorsed proved by oath of Martin Pickett, Thomas Maddox, Thomas Chilton, and recorded County Court, Fauquier, Minute Book 1784–1786, 102.

Mar. 16
FAUQUIER COUNTY, VA. *to Cuthbert Bullett*

Gives permission to Bullett, attorney for plaintiffs, to file declaration in suit by Col. Thomas Marshall and Martin Pickett against Katherine Rector, executrix of John Rector, in County Court of Fauquier County, in which as attorney for defendant confessed judgment. Suit on a security bond, £600, of 1771; confessed j. Sept. 12, 1783. County Court, Fauquier. Original File Papers, 1783.

Mar. 17, *n.p.* *to Unnamed Client*

Concerning ejectment suit. Letter delivered by Brooke. NP.

Mar. 26 *Marriage Bond*

Signer of marriage bond of Elizabeth Jacquelin Ambler (sister-in-law of J.M.) to Col. William Brent. ICU. (After death of William Brent, married Col. Edward Carrington.)

Apr. 29 *Admission to Practice*

J.M. qualified as counselor before Virginia Supreme Court of Appeals; oath of fidelity to Commonwealth and oath of attorney taken. V, Court of Appeals of Virginia, Richmond City (Williamsburg), Order Book I, 47.

He was the sixth lawyer to be admitted to practice before the court. See list. Same, Order Book IV, following p. 332.

Oct. 7
FAYETTE COUNTY, KY. *Land Entry*

Entry of 600 acres in Kentucky for J.M. (or J.M., Jr.), obtained by Thomas Marshall, on waters of Well's Creek and the North Fork of the Licking, surveyed. Kentucky Land Office, Fayette Entries, Book 4, 225. *Ward v. Fox's Heirs*, Hughes' Reports, 432–33. (Sup. Ct. & Ct. App., Ky.)

n.d., RICHMOND *Tax List*

J.M. owned at Richmond two Negroes, two horses, and twelve head of cattle. V, Henrico County Titheable Book; Beveridge, *Marshall*, I, 187–88.

LEGAL PRACTICE

J.M.'s LEGAL PRACTICE during this year was quite active for one so lately commencing. His account book shows fees collected for some 150 legal matters. Fees especially for civil matters were modest, one of £11:8, only five reaching the £7 level, two in the £6 bracket, a scattering in the £5 bracket, and the balance lower and for the most part in the £2 bracket. Criminal causes appeared to pay better; of six such listed, one for horse stealing was £5:13, another undesignated £8, for murder £8, for forgery £12. Fees for advice were generally in the £1 and £2 bracket. J.M.'s total income for the year was £848:7.

His practice was of the normally varied sort. The thirty-six civil matters described by him were appeals, five; supersedeas, three; injunctions, two; mandamus, two; habeas corpus, two; motions, one; ejectments, four; caveats, four; wills, two; chancery, four; advice, four; debt, one; trespass, one; libel, one.

During this year he was admitted to practice in the Supreme Court of Appeals (see herein, Apr. 29, 1785), and immediately thereafter entered into the famous case of *Hite v. Fairfax*, which after many continuances was argued the following year.

J.M. records the receipt of thirteen fees from Fauquier County, which must have represented practice before the March term of the court of that county. Account Book, 26. During April, he went to Oak Hill and Winchester, possibly to practice before the courts in Fauquier and Frederick counties. Account Book, 27.

During this year he received and transmitted a substantial amount of money arising from sale of warrants and interest, and from military funds to the respective owners and parties. Account Book, 60–61.

County Court, Fauquier

William Jones v. Thomas Maddox.

Action on replevin bond. J.M. for plaintiff.
Apr. 26. J. for plaintiff £3:4:10.
County Court, Fauquier, Minute Book 1784–1786, 125.
Fee: Oct. 13, 1785, £2:10. Account Book, 52.

Maddox v. Edmonds.

In case. J.M. for defendant.
Apr. 26. Discontinued.
County Court, Fauquier, Minute Book 1784–1786, 120.
Fee: Nov. 17, 1785, £2. Account Book, 54.

See also *Edmonds v. Maddox*, case, dismissed, agreed defendant paying costs. County Court, Fauquier, Minute Book 1781–1784, 61.

James Winn v. James Grigsby.

In case. J.M. for defendant.
May 26, 1783. Deposition by plaintiff.
County Court, Fauquier, Minute Book 1781–1784, 113.
Aug. 22, 1785. V.j. for plaintiff £25:18:3.
Same, Minute Book 1784–1786, 206.
Aug. 24, 1785. J. set aside, new trial. Same, 218.
Mar. 31, 1786. V.j. £20:10:14. Same, 342.

Also on same day, *Same v. Same*, Case, verdict £4:7, j. being less than £5, nonsuit, j. against plaintiff five shillings and costs. Same, 343–44.

Fee: Feb., 1785, £2:13:4. Account Book, 26.

Caveats

Aug. 1 *Adam Mann v. Hugh Caperton and Paul Lang.*

J.M. for Mann. 200 acres Greenbrier County, on Laurel Creek branch of Indian Creek, adjoining Valentine Cook and James Bradshaw, saltpeter mine in bounds of Singing Cave; claiming failure of Caperton to survey and obtain grant in time limit. V, Virginia Land Office, Caveats, I, 212.

Fee: Aug. 3, 1785, £1:8. Account Book, 46.

Nov. 25 *Thomas Marshall, assignee of J.M., Jr. v. Henry Crutcher and John Tibbs.*

3,000 acres Fayette County (Kentucky), entry Nov. 8, 1783, on Treasury Warrant 17735.

Same v. Same, 10,000 acres, Fayette County, by prior entry Oct. 17, 1783, on treasury warrant, survey Mar. 14, 1784. V, Virginia Land Office, Caveats, I, 247.

Nov. 25 *Thomas Marshall v. Henry Lee.*

4,000 acres Fayette County, (Kentucky) entered May 15, 1780, on treasury warrant or so much as fall within 10,500–acre survey made on subsequent but special location of Thomas Marshall on treasury warrants; claims Lee's entry vague and survey contrary to entry. V, Virginia Land Office, Caveats, I, 248.

Expense Item: Dec. 3, 1785, £15. Account Book, 57.

1786

DOCUMENTS

June 15
Frankfort, Ky. *Land Grant*

To J.M., 1,000 acres in Military District on Lost Creek, a branch of the Ohio (in present Livingston County, Ky.) on Military Warrant No. 30, surveyed May 20, 1783. Kentucky Land Office, Va. Grants, Book 3, 315; V, Virginia Grants, II, 187.

June 15
Frankfort, Ky. *Land Grant*

To J.M., 1,000 acres in Kentucky on Clay Lick Creek (in present Livingston County) on Military Warrant No. 30. Kentucky Land Office, Va. Grants, Book 3, 316; V, Virginia Grants, II, 189.

Oct.
RICHMOND *Commissioner on Claim*

Act of General Assembly appointing J.M. as one of commissioners on claim for tobacco destroyed in Byrd's warehouse fire. V, Virginia Acts, Box Oct., 1786, chap. XXIV, 18–19; Hening, Stat., XII, 280.

Oct.
RICHMOND *Road Commissioner*

J.M., Jr., one of commissioners to receive subscriptions for road from Falls of Great Kanawha to Lexington. V, Virginia Acts, Box Oct., 1786, chap. XXV, 19. (Not known whether this is J.M.)

Nov. 14
RICHMOND *Masonic Lodge*

Deputy Grand Master of Richmond Lodge No. 10, Masonic Order; in 1793–1794 Grand Master. David K. Walthall, *History of Richmond Lodge, No. 10* (Richmond, Ware and Duke, 1909), 22, 34–35.

In 1792 J.M. became Grand Master pro tempore of the Grand Lodge; in 1793 he was named Grand Master of the Masons of Virginia, serving through 1795. On his retirement, he was presented with a Past Master's Jewel. Beveridge, *Marshall,* II, 176–77; John Dove, *Proceedings of the M. W. Grand Lodge of Ancient New Masons of the State of Virginia, from 1778 to 1822* (Richmond, Goode, 1874), I, 121, 139, 144.

Nov. 20
RICHMOND *to Unknown—Kentucky Land*

Urging addressee to call on Bullitt to settle dispute over land purchased of addressee by J.M.; requests assignment from Bullitt to J.M. 4,900-acre survey on Licking (Ky.); patent issuing. Willing to convey one-half of survey to addressee. Requests entries on Sandy and Kentucky rivers be surveyed. Allows to draw on J.M. for expense. MB.

Nov. *Candidacy for Attorney Generalship*

Ran against Col. Innes for attorney generalship of Virginia before the House of Delegates. Lost, but had a "handsome" vote. Letters, James Madison to George Washington, Richmond, Nov. 1, 1786, and Dec. 4, 1786. Gaillard Hunt, *The Writings of James Madison,* 9 vols. (New York, G. P. Putman's Sons, 1900–1910), II, 282, 289 at 294.

Dec. 20
RICHMOND *Report on Sanity*

Report by J.M. and others in inquest as to sanity of James Goss. V, Exec. Papers, Box Dec., 1786, Folder Dec. 21–30.

Dec. 28
RICHMOND *Commissioner on Claim*

Award of J.M. and Cyrus Griffin as commissioners in claim of Simon Nathan against Commonwealth of Virginia on bills of exchange. V, House of Delegates, Va., Exec. Comm., Box Exec. Comm. Sessions Oct. 16, 1786—Jan. 11, 1787; Oct. 15, 1787—Jan. 8, 1788.

Dec. 30
RICHMOND *Edmund Randolph to Speaker of House of Delegates*

Enclosing award of J.M. and Cyrus Griffin in dispute between Simon Nathan and the Commonwealth. V, House of Delegates, Va., Exec. Comm., Box Exec. Comm. Sessions Oct. 16, 1786—Jan. 11, 1787; Oct. 15, 1787—Jan. 8, 1788.

n.d., FRANKFORT, KY. *Kentucky Statehood*

Memorial of members of Kentucky convention of Sept., 1786, giving reasons why act of Virginia Assembly on Kentucky statehood could not be acted on because of absence of members of Clark and Logan expedition. Forwarded to J.M. for presentation to Virginia Assembly as political agent. Hening, Stat., XII, 240; Littell, *Political Transactions*, App. VII, 17; Thomas Marshall Green, *The Spanish Conspiracy* (Cincinnati, Robert Clarke, 1891), 102; Marshall, *History of Kentucky*, I, 251, 254.

n.d., n.p. *Memorandum to Hall*

Perkins request Hall pay Jones balance due from Gen. Clark; inform Jones get money due J.M. in execution against Pope, £40. Transfer credit £2 to Capt. Easton; Perkins settle with Hall; J.M. won at piquet but account owing at store. V, James Innes Papers.

n.d. *Albert Gallatin*

"John Marshall . . . in 1786, offered to take me into his office without a fee, and assured me that I would become a distinguished lawyer."

Excerpt from letter, Albert Gallatin to Wm. Maxwell, corresponding secretary of the Virginia Historical Society. VHi, *Virginia Historical Register and Literary Companion* (Richmond, Virginia, Historical Society, Jan., 1848—Oct., 1853), I, 94–95.

LEGAL PRACTICE

RECORDS SHOW THAT during the year J.M. was paid for approximately 118 legal matters. Total receipts from legal practice was approximately £837:6. (J.M. totals at £808:4:10) Account Book, 93.

Sixteen instances of fees were for advice, five of which for advice as to wills. Fee was ordinarily between £1 and £2, in one instance as much as £3:10. Two fees were for drawing deeds, one for contract to lease a tavern, these fees less than £2.

Except for two criminal matters, one for robbery, fee £3 in part payment, the other concerning indictment, fee £2:16, and two habeas corpus proceedings, the balance of designated fees were for civil litigated matters. Seventeen are listed as chancery suits; thirteen as appeals; four, supersedeas proceedings; seven, ejectment; one, trespass; three caveats; admiralty, debt, and injunction, two each; plus one retainer.

An outstanding fee for the year was £70 from Pringle & Co. for an admiralty case. (July 26) Account Book, 78. J.M. also received a £21 fee for several chancery cases; a £20 fee for a single such case; and £18 fee in an ejectment case; four £14 fees, one of which was for drafting a will; and two £10 fees. Otherwise in civil litigated matters fees were between £2 and £5. Account Book, 64–80.

During this year Edmund Randolph was elected Governor of the Commonwealth, and on Nov. 10 advertised to his clients that J.M. would succeed to his practice. W. Asbury Christian, *Richmond, Her Past and Present* (Richmond, L. H. Jenkins, 1912), 29–30. J.M. offered to take Albert Gallatin into his office. (See herein, Gallatin to Wm. Maxwell, n.d., Documents, 1786.)

In August, J.M. went to Winchester, Berkeley Court House, and Fauquier County attending to legal matters. Account Book, 81.

CAVEATS

Jan. 12 *Richard Graham v. Charles Marshall, Simon Morgan, and William Marshall, Jr.*

4,437½ acres, surveyed on Treasury Warrant 20317, on Cabin Creek (Ky.), beginning at northeast corner John Marshall, Jr. 15,000 acres. V, Virginia Land Office, Caveats, I, 268.

Jan. 17 *Thomas Marshall, George Muter, Charles Dabney, John Montgomery, George Walls, Christopher Roane, John Rogers, Nathaniel Welch, Humphrey Marshall, Nathaniel Rice, Superintendents for the Virginia State Line and Navy v. George Rogers Clark.*

36,932 acres, Lincoln County (Kentucky), south side of Tennessee River on the Ohio, claimed by caveators under grant by act of General Assembly to officers and soldiers of Virginia State Line and Navy; entry and survey vague and upon tract not liable under law to location under treasury warrants. Same, Caveats, I, 270.

Jan. 17 *Same v. William Ronald.*

10,000 acres, Lincoln County on Rivers Mississippi and Ohio; same reason omitting vagueness. Same, Caveats, I, 271.

Jan. 17 *Same v. Jacob Myers.*

10,000 acres on Mississippi opposite point of first island below mouth of Ohio, Lincoln County; same reason. Same, Caveats, I, 272.

Probably filed by J.M., who represented officers in the case. (See herein Sept. 15, 1789.)

Apr. 14 *Isaac Roman v. Arthur Campbell.*

J.M. for caveator. Thirty-five acres Washington County, south side Middle Fork of Holstein River, surveyed under pre-emption warrant. Campbell claimed under prior entry certificate from Commissioner's Court and patent. Same, Caveats, I, 286.

Fee: Oct. 5, 1786, £2:10. Account Book, 84.

General Court

Jan. 10
Hampshire County, Va.
Ephraim Lloyd v. Zare Osborne.

Ejectment, one plantation, one messuage, one garden, 400 acres. J.M. for defendant.

Apr., 1786. Plea not guilty.

Oct., 1786—Sept., 1790. Continuances.

Apr., 1791. Dismissed.

VU, McGregor Libr., Marshall Family Papers.

Jan. 11
Hardy County, Va.
Ephraim Lloyd v. Barnet Lambert.

Ejectment, one plantation, one messuage, one garden, 500 acres. J.M. for defendant.

Apr., 1786. Plea not guilty.

Oct., 1786—Sept., 1790. Continuances.
Apr., 1791. Dismissed.
VU, McGregor Libr., Marshall Family Papers.

Mar. 30
FREDERICK COUNTY, VA.
Hugh Douglass, executor of William Douglass, deceased v. Bryan Bruin.

Action of debt on written obligation dated Oct. 28, 1771, £594:19:5; damage £400. J.M. for plaintiff. Autograph petition.

Apr. 1786—Dec., 1789. Continuances.

Sept., 1790. V.j. for plaintiff £156:19:9, with interest from Oct. 28, 1776, £97:9:9, and one penny damages.

VU, McGregor Libr., Marshall Family Papers.

Apr. 8
RICHMOND
Col. Clark v. Cornelius Free.

J.M. for plaintiff; receipt by J.M. of bond and fee.
KyLF, Clark-Hite Coll.

Apr. 11
HARDY COUNTY, VA.
Ephraim Lloyd v. John Smith.

Ejectment, one plantation, one messuage, one garden, 400 acres.
J.M. for defendant.
Apr., 1786. Plea not guilty.
Oct., 1786—Sept., 1790. Continuances.
Apr., 1791. Dismissed.
V, Ac. 24111.

n.d., FREDERICK COUNTY, VA.
William Bayless v. William Maston.

Petition for supersedeas and reversal of judgment of County Court of Frederick, Oct., 1784, £36, payable by £18, on joint bond of Bayless and Craig for debt of Craig. Grounds: obligee withheld suit until Craig "went away"; no declaration filed in suit. Granted on giving bond. J.M. for petitioner. Autograph petition and certificate signed "John Marshall one of the attornies practising in the General Court."

Apr., 1787—Nov., 1789. Continuances.
Apr., 1789. Discontinued.
VU, McGregor Libr., Marshall Family Papers.

Court of Appeals of Virginia

Hite et al. v. Fairfax et al., 4 Call 42, 69–81.

J.M. represented tenants and citizens of Virginia, holding under Lord Fairfax. This was his first case before the Supreme Court of Appeals. In 1730, by British Order of Council, John and Isaac Vanmeter were allowed 30,000 acres which they assigned to Joist Hite; and Hite and Robert M'Kay were allowed another 100,000 acres in the Shenandoah Valley, largely within the bounds of the Fairfax proprietorship, conditioned on establishing 100 families therein by 1735. Hite established 54 families and made twenty-seven surveys of 37,834 acres. In a controversy between Fairfax and the Crown as to the boundaries of the proprietorship and the right of the Crown to grant or patent the land, a convention was arrived at in 1748 establishing the bounds and providing that Fairfax would confirm patents and grants heretofore issued to settlers. Fairfax refused to make grants to Hite and his associates under their surveys on grounds that they were inadequate, even though some years before he had agreed to do so, and granted parts thereof to others. Hite brought action in 1749 in General Court to enforce his claim, and in 1769 and 1771 the Court ruled in his favor as to Vanmeter's 30,000 acres and 54,000 acres of the 100,000, subject to the rights of others who had received grants therein from Fairfax. In 1780, Hite appealed to the Court of Appeals, where the decree was amended to give Hite title to the surveyed land (37,834 acres), subject to the rights of persons affected—except heirs, devisees, and executors of Fairfax—including those who claimed equity by contract or conduct of Hite, to assert their equity in High Court of Chancery within three months. Others holding the land within the twenty-seven surveys were required to convey to Hite.

J.M. in his argument stressed the validity of the Fairfax title to the Northern Neck of Virginia. Same, 69–72.

The record of the case in the Virginia Court of Appeals is as follows:

Aug. 29, 1780. Order giving Hite and others time until next court to file records and prosecute appeal, it appearing by certificate of clerk of High Court of Chancery that application made by him and Robert Green for transcript of record of General Court in Chancery for appeal to King in Privy Council. Court of Appeals, Va., Order Book I, 8–9.

Aug. 30, 1780. Reprimand to clerk of High Chancery for failure to prepare transcript. Same, 10.

Mar. 9, 1781. Clerk excused for nonattendance. See *Commonwealth v. Beckley*, 4 Call 4.

Mar. 29, 1781. Further time allowed. Court of Appeals, Va., Order Book I, 14.

Apr. 29, 1782. Time allowed. Same, 15–16.

Oct. 29, 1782. Suit revived in name of administrators or executors of Thomas Lord Fairfax, appellee. Same, 17–18.

Apr. 29, 1783. Case now entitled *Representatives of Joist Hite and Robert Green v. Representatives of Thomas Lord Fairfax*. Continued. Same, 23–24.

Oct. 29, 1783. Continued. Same, 29–30.

Apr. 29, 1784. Continued. Same, 35.

Nov. 2, 1784. Continued. Same, 43.

May 1, 1786. Cause partly heard on record and arguments of counsel; continued. Same, 70.

May 2. Cause partly heard on arguments of counsel; continued. Same, 71.

May 3. Cause further heard in argument of counsel; continued. Same, 71–72.

May 4. Title of case now enumerates all heirs, devisees, and representatives of both Hite and Green, both deceased. Further argument of counsel; adjourned to next day. Same, 72–74.

May 5. Case fully heard and taken under advisement. Same, 74–75.

May 6. Judgment of Court, reversing perpetual injunction by General Court against judgment of William Ewing and others against Hite; also decreeing as follows:

Heirs and devisees of Lord Fairfax and those deriving title from him after Dec. 25, 1735, convey to appellants land within twenty-seven surveys stated in memorial of Thomas Marshall and others, excepting those holding under appellants and confirmed by Fairfax, also reserving right of those claiming equity by action of appellants to apply to High Court of Chancery within three months; others in possession to convey title to appellants by Jan., 1787; granting appellants profits of land since Jan. 1, 1749–1750, less improvements, paid out of Fairfax Estate subject to exceptions; issuance of grants to appellants of land ungranted by Fairfax. Same, 77–80.

Nov. 7, 8, 9, 1786. Exceptions by Fairfax Estate to report on profits owing. Same, 97, 98, 100.

Nov. 1 and 6, 1787. Exceptions to same. Same, 108.

Nov. 14. Affirming account of profits and report, subject to exceptions. Same, 117–18.

See *Transcript of Record, Representatives of Joist Hite and Robert Green, appellants v. Right Hon. Thomas Lord Fairfax, appellee, commenced in*

General Court of Virginia, 1749. Filed in Court of Appeals of Virginia, 1782. Clerk of Circuit Court, Frederick County, Va. Deposited at Handley Library, Va.

IN THE FOLLOWING cases before the High Court of Chancery and Court of Appeals, J.M. represented claimants to land who sought to bring themselves within the reservation in the decree of May 8, 1786, as deriving, or equitably entitled to title through conveyances or transactions with Hite or his associates as of 1770. There were approximately forty-one such claims filed against the representatives of Joist Hite, Robert Green, Williams Duff, and Robert McCoy, J.M. acting as attorney in most of these. A few were settled by the parties by remitting underpayment of purchase price, apparently without J.M.'s intervention. It appears that two were handled by George Nicholas, (*William Grubbs, Robert Baylor, and David Kennedy v. Hite's Representatives et al. and Daniel Storer v. Same*). KyLF, Clark-Hite Papers.

The decrees of the High Court of Chancery in these proceedings were dated Aug. 5, 1790, with few exceptions noted.

Joshua Browning, John Ritson Browning, William Keating and Roseman, his wife v. Hite's Representatives et al.

1,200 acres on Potowmac Run, Berkeley County, Va. (now W. Va.) on which Van Swearingin, Peter Williamson, Vachael Medcalf, George Obder, Thomas and Benjamin Boydstone, Peter Palmer, and John Lewis live, sold by Joist Hite to John Browning, who died 1741, devising to sons and daughter, under whom claimants hold. Allowed. KyLF, Clark-Hite Papers.

Fees: "Lewis," Nov., 1791, £6:18 (?). Account Book, 438.

Robert Bull, John Grantham, Nicholas Schull, and Simeon Hyatt v. Hite's Representatives et al.

320 acres on Opeckon, sold by Joist Hite to William Hyett, from whom derived by intermediate conveyances. Allowed on evidence Joseph Hyatt inserted in entry book of surveyor, Joist Hite directed survey in his name, sale Hyatt to Thomas, compromise, subsequent sale by both, grant to present possessors by Fairfax. Allowed, claimants to pay £7:10 with interest from 1736.

Oct. 24, 1793. Appeal to Court of Appeals, Va., affirmed. Court of Appeals, Va., Order Book II, 115, 189, 243, 244. KyLF, Clark-Hite Papers.

Fee: Amount illegible. Account Book, 439; Mar., 1791, £5. Account Book, 276.

Walter Clarke, William Grub, Lancelot Lee, Owen Thomas, and Thornton Washington v. Hite's Representatives et al.

650 acres on Bull Skin, Berkeley County, Va. (now W. Va.) sold by Joist Hite to John Grub, in bill of original case, derived by conveyance from Grubb. No record of disposition available. Allowed. KyLF, Clark-Hite Papers.

Fees: "Lancelot Lee," £2:12; Same, May, 1790, £4:10; Aug., 1790, "Washington," £6. Account Book, 438, 440.

Mary Clevenger, widow and executrix of John Clevenger v. Hite's Representatives et al.

——— acres on South River, Shenandoah County, Va., devised by Robert McKay, original grantee and partner of Hite, by one devise to Shadrach Parlour, 1755, then by conveyances to claimant.

Aug. 5, 1790. Allowed.

Nov. 12, 1791. Reversed; not within reservation; no partition between McCoy and Hite; title derived from one with partial interest; decree amended allowing equitable right on partition; division between various purchasers preferring those from specific devisees to purchasers from residuary devisees. Court of Appeals, Va., Order Book II, 119–21.

Mar. 19, 1792. Mandate entered by High Court of Chancery. KyLF, Clark-Hite Papers.

Fee: £1:8. Account Book, 439.

Representatives of Hite et al. v. Christian Copp, Henry Snarr, Mary and Jacob Sellers, and William Strother.

Land in North Mountain tract. Claim allowed on payment of purchase price.

Nov. 16, 1791. Appeal to Court of Appeals, affirmed. Court of Appeals, Va., Order Book II, 118, 127. KyLF, Clark-Hite Papers.

Fee: Aug., 1789, "on account of motion," £0:18.

Adam Cunninghame v. Hite's Representatives et al.

Part of 7,000 acres on South River, Shenandoah County; sold by Robert McKay, an original grantee to claimant as stated in original bill of Hite.

Aug. 5, 1790. Dismissed, no evidence of identity of land or money paid; evidence before commissioners in 1770 that claimant then claimed purchase from other persons. Disallowed. KyLF, Clark-Hite Papers.

Walter Cunninghame v. Hite's Representatives et al.

Part of 7,000 acres called South River tract, Shenandoah County, in possession of Walter Cunninghame, Adam Cunninghame, and William Baxter, sold by Robert McKay, partner of Joist Hite to Thomas Grubbs, thence to Walter Cunninghame, died intestate, son Edward sold to claimant.

Aug. 5, 1790. Dismissed; sale of some land to Walter Cunninghame admitted in original bill, but no evidence of contract, what land sold, or that claimant derived equity from original Walter Cunninghame.

Appeal to Court of Appeals of Virginia by claimant, and by defendants seeking accounting for rents and profits after original decree. (Record not found.) KyLF, Clark-Hite Papers.

Fees: £1; Sept., 1790, appeal, £5:12. Account Book, 439, 438.

John Denton and Jacob Cockenhour v. Hite's Representatives et al.

——— acres, Denton and Palmer survey on North River, Shenandoah County, Va., sold Joist Hite to Jonah and John Denton and Thomas Palmer, bond Mar., 1735, two-thirds held by John Denton as heir, one-third by Cockenhour, purchaser from Palmer.

Allowed on payment of unpaid part purchase money of Denton share, which was paid. KyLF, Clark-Hite Papers.

Fee: £2:16. Account Book, 439.

Note fee "From Spigle" (part of Dentons tract, 1789 (88), £1:8. Account Book, 438.

John Hoop v. Hite's Representatives et al.

——— acres part of Great Cove survey, Shenandoah County, sold by Joist Hite to William Clarke, under whom claim by intermediate conveyances.

Aug. 5, 1790. Allowed on payment of original purchase price.

Nov. 18, 1791. Appeal by Hite, *et al.*, to Court of Appeals, Va., held purchase price proved by delivery of horse and saddle, affirmed. Court of Appeals, Va., Order Book II, 116, 130–31.

Mar. 19, 1792. Mandate entered in High Court of Chancery. KyLF, Clark-Hite Papers.

Fee: Sept., 1790, £3. Account Book, 438.

Simeon Hyatt, George Cloke, John Daniel, John Bees, Jr., and Adam Livingston v. Hite's Representatives et al.

Tract of ——— acres, Berkeley County, sold by Joist Hite to ——— under whom orators claim.

Aug. 5, 1790. Dismissed, bill not state land or manner claimed. KyLF, Clark-Hite Papers.

Fee: Amount not stated. Account Book, 439.

George Keller and Henry Somervalt v. Hite's Representatives et al.

500 acres, part of 9,860 acres, Powells Fort, Shenandoah County, sold by Joist Hite and Robert McKay to Abraham Delbach, to claimants.

Aug. 5, 1790. Dismissed. Evidence not prove contract.

KyLF, Clark-Hite Papers.

Benjamin Layman, George Bowman, Jacob Pickle, Nicholas Severn, David Funkhouser, Jacob Shamon, John Leman, ——— Coffman, John Correll, Nicholas Wenman, George Federman and George Korn v. Hite's Representatives et al.

1,585 acres of 4,600 acres, North Mountain, purchased by John Bougham of Joist Hite, 1739, to Benjamin Layman, parts to claimants. Evidence three horses to Hite. Allowed. KyLF, Clark-Hite Papers.

Fees: 1789 (88), "Layman," £1:8; May, 1790, "Leman," £2:10. Account Book, 438.

Ebenezer Leith v. Hite's Representatives et al.

Three-hundredth part of 7,000 acres of land called South River tract, Shenandoah County, sold by Joist Hite and partners to Wm. Burk, from whom title derived.

Aug. 5, 1790. Dismissed, paper produced before commissioners in 1770 not proved, no other evidence of title.

Appeal to Court of Appeals of Virginia by claimant, and by defendant seeking accounting for rents and profits since decree.

Nov. 15, 1791. Affirmed. Court of Appeals, Va., Order Book II, 118, 126.

Mar. 1, 1792. Mandate entered, High Court of Chancery.

KyLF, Clark-Hite Papers.

Fees: n.d., £1:8; Aug., 1790, £2:8; Sept., 1790, £2:12. Account Book, 440, 438.

James Leith v. Hite's Representatives et al.

200 acres, part of 7,000 acres on south side of South Branch Shenandoah River; heir of Ephraim Leith, who purchased from father, James Leith, who purchased from original grantee, bond of which signature torn off.

Aug. 5, 1790. Allowed on evidence of execution of bond and payment, admission by one defendant belief in sale.

Nov. 14, 1791. Appeal to Court of Appeals, Va., affirmed. Court of Appeals, Va., Order Book II, 116, 125.

Mar. 1, 1792. Mandate entered, High Court of Chancery.

KyLF, Clark-Hite Papers.

Fees: n.d., £1:8; Aug., 1790, £2:8. Account Book, 440, 438.

William and John Leman, Nicholas and Edward Mercer v. Hite's Representatives et al.

Land on south side of Opekon, 360 acres purchased by John Lilburne from Hites, part of 700 acre tract. Deed Hite to Vanmeter in 1736, 475 acres, part of 700 acres, residue belonging to Lilburne.

Aug. 5, 1790. Denied.

Nov. 21, 1791. Appeal to Court of Appeals, reversed and remanded, claimant permitted to make survey to identify land, on retrial not permitted to examine witnesses. Court of Appeals, Va., Order Book II, 118, 133.

On retrial in High Court of Chancery, Jan. 7, 1793, claim disallowed. Appealed to Court of Appeals.

Nov. 3, 1801. Reversed, payment made to Jonathan Clark, agent of Hite, £400, for relinquishment of title. Court of Appeals, Va., Order Book IV, 7, 43, 67, 116, 376. KyLF, Clark-Hite Papers.

Fees: £5; Nov., 1791, "Leman v. Hite," £6:18. Account Book, 439, 438.

John Lindsay, Jun., Thomas Lindsay, Albion Throckmorton, Isaac Laine, Warner Washington (and Edmund Clair) v. Hite's Representatives et al.

860 acres on Long Marsh, Berkeley County, Va., (now W. Va.), sold Joist Hite to Nathaniel Doherty, power of attorney to John Lindsay. Isaac Hite admitted sale; present possessors to prove title and payment. Allowed. KyLF, Clark-Hite Papers.

Fees: "Lindsay and Throckmorton," £2:16; "Clair," £1:10. Account Book, 439.

Solomon Mathews v. Hite's Representatives et al.

400 acres part of Great Cove survey, Shenandoah County, sold by Joist Hite to William Clarke, by sons and devisees to Burr Harrison, to claimant.

Aug. 5, 1790. Allowed on payment of original purchase price.

Nov. 18, 1791. Appeal by Hite, *et al.*, to Court of Appeals, Va.; held delivery of horse and saddle for purchase money proved, allowed at appellants' costs. Court of Appeals, Va., Order Book II, 116, 130–31.

Mar. 19, 1792. Mandate entered. KyLF, Clark-Hite Papers.

Fee: "Harrison," £3:16; Same, May, 1790, £2:8. Account Book, 439, 438.

Jacob Miller, Robert Lowry, Philip Ingle, Abraham Neill, Gordon Swift, and William Dark, claimants in proceedings entitled *John and Isaac Hite et al. v. Representatives of Thomas Lord Fairfax et al.*

Part of 1,300 acres on Elk Branch claimed under Thomas Hart, purchaser from Joist Hite, also by grant from Fairfax except part granted by Fairfax to George William Fairfax.

Aug. 5, 1793. Allowed as to all but part granted to George William Fairfax, no evidence of disclaimer of title by Hart by delivery of contract by Joist Hite to son, or acceptance by Hart of Fairfax grant. KyLF, Clark-Hite Papers.

Fees: £9:17, £1:8. Account Book, 440.

Peter Miller v. Hite's Representatives et al.

——— acres of land on South River, Shenandoah County, devised by Robert McKay, original grantee and partner of Hite on devisees to Zachary McKay, sold to claimant.

Aug. 5, 1790. Allowed.

Nov. 14, 1791. Appeal to Court of Appeals, decree reversed and amended allowing equitable right to land after survey, no partition of land having been made by original grantee. Court of Appeals, Va., Order Book II, 112, 122–23. (See *Mary Cleavenger v. Hite,* herein.)

Mar. 20, 1792. Mandate entered, High Court of Chancery.

KyLF, Clark-Hite Papers.

John Netherton, Henry Netherton, John Overall, and Abraham Keller v. Hite's Representatives et al.

500 acres on South River, Shenandoah County, Va., sold by Joist Hite to Paul Froman, who sold 200 acres to Henry Speers, title bond from Hite, intermediate conveyances to Nethertons; 300 acres to two daughters, intermarried with Abraham Keller and William Overall; latter sold to John Overall.

Defendants admitted original sale and payments, order to lay off according to contract. KyLF, Clark-Hite Papers.

Fee: £2:16. Account Book, 439.

Jonathan Odell and Samuel Odell v. Hite's Representatives et al.

200 acres of South River tract, Shenandoah County (200th part of 7,000 acres). Robert McCoy sold to Joseph White, consideration to build house, not completed. Hite paid £7:10 Pa. to complete; White sold to Odell, left state, wrote to McCoy for money for work done; Odell left in possession without deed.

Aug. 5, 1790. Dismissed.

Nov. 18, 1791. Reversed on appeal to Court of Appeals; presumed Odell to keep land on paying for finishing house; quieted in title on payment of £6 with interest from 1749. Court of Appeals, Va., Order Book II, 118, 131–32. KyLF, Clark-Hite Papers.

Fees: 1787, £5:2, Sept., 1790, £5; £1:8. Account Book, 438, 440.

James Odell v. Hite's Representative et al.

Land on South River. Claim disallowed. KyLF, Clark-Hite Papers.

Fee: £1:8. Account Book, 439.

Edward Snickers, Joseph and Cornelias Anderson, Jasper Ball, Thomas Shepherd, and Warner Washington, Jr. v. Hite's Representatives et al.

450 acres on Arnold's Marsh, Frederick County, Va., sold by Joist Hite to Thomas Morgan, to Bartholomew Anderson; devised to Joseph and Cornelias Anderson and other children; sold to Snickers, Ball, and Shepherd.

Aug. 5, 1790. Allowed, on payment of £4 with interest from 1740 unpaid purchase price. KyLF, Clark-Hite Papers.

Fee: £3:12. Account Book, 440.

Adam Stephens v. Hite's Representatives et al.

Land on Lick Branch.

Claim denied. Case appealed; probably purchase money paid in settlement. No further record. KyLF, Clark-Hite Papers.

Fee: May, 1795, "Smith in Hite adv. Stevens," £5. Account Book, 416.

Francis Stubling and John Milton v. Hite's Representatives et al.

Shuckster's stone house.

Claim allowed. KyLF, Clark-Hite Papers.

Fee: £1:12 (?). Account Book, 440.

William Taylor, John Milton and William Booth v. Hite's Representatives et al.

147 acres Buck Marsh, sold by Joist Hite to Pennington, patented to Isaac Remington, 1734, by conveyances to claimant.

Defendant Isaac Hite admitted sale, not in twenty-seven surveys, questioned purchase money, held no title.

Claim allowed. KyLF, Clark-Hite Papers.

Fee: Amount illegible. Account Book, 440.

George Washington v. Hite's Representatives et al.

Land on Bull Skin, Berkeley County, Va. (now W. Va.).

Purchase money paid Hite, case settled. KyLF, Clark-Hite Papers.

Fee: £1:4. Account Book, 439.

John Augustine Washington v. Hite's Representatives et al.

——— acres on Bullskin, Berkeley County, Va. (now W. Va.), sold Joist Hite to Patrick Mathews, by intermediate conveyances to claimant; all other land as devisee of father, Laurence Washington.

Defendants admitted sale; no money received; claims land if deserted.

Case agreed. KyLF, Clark-Hite Papers.

Fee: £1:4. Account Book, 439.

Jeremiah Whitson v. Hite's Representatives et al.

——— acres on South River, Shenandoah County, Va., purchased of James and Zachariah McKay, sons of Robert McKay, grantee and partner of Joist Hite, to William Whitson, to Charles Whitson, to claimant, eldest son, in name of mother.

Aug. 5, 1790. Allowed.

Nov. 14, 1791. Appeal to Court of Appeals, reversed; sale to William Whitson recognized; decree to claimants subject to partition of land, as in *Clevenger* case; costs borne by each. Court of Appeals, Va., Order Book II, 112, 122.

Mar. 20, 1792. Mandate entered, High Court of Chancery. KyLF, Clark-Hite Papers.

Fee: £1:8; Nov., 1791, £4:4. Account Book, 440, 438.

John Yates v. Hite's Representatives et al.

Land on South River.

Aug. 5, 1790. Allowed.

Nov. 15, 1791. Appeal to Court of Appeals, affirmed. Court of Appeals, Va., Order Book II, 118, 126. KyLF, Clark-Hite Papers.

Fees: Feb., 1791, £4:16; (1789), £1:16; ——— £1:18. Account Book, 274, 438, 440.

Edwin Young v. Hite's Representatives et al.

Land on South River.

May 8, 1786. Claim based on purchase from heirs of Robert McCoy, denied by High Court of Chancery.

Nov. 14, 1791. Appeal to Court of Appeals, reversed, subject to partition of land. Court of Appeals, Va., Order Book II, 112, 124.

Mar. 19, 1792. Mandate entered by High Court of Chancery. KyLF. Clark-Hite Papers.

Fee: Sept., 1787, £2:10. Account Book, 124.

Edward Rice v. Walter Jones, 4 Call 89.

Case adjourned from General Court for difficulty. J.M. for Rice.

Will probated 1784 in North Carolina; Rice named executor; thereafter probate revoked on grounds incapacity of testator, letters testamentary to Dickinson. In 1785, Rice brought first will to General Court of Virginia for probate opposed. Opinion holding General Court can receive will as affects land in Virginia regardless of North Carolina ruling.

Aug. 29, 1785. Continued. Court of Appeals, Va., Order Book I, 47.

Nov. 2, 1786. Heard. Same, 93.

Nov. 9, 1786. Opinion rendered. Same, 99.

Fee: Oct., 1788, £4:10. Account Book, 168.

1787

DOCUMENTS

Jan. 1
RICHMOND *to James Wilkinson*

Disappointed in request for passport for Wilkinson from government of Virginia. Effect of separation of Kentucky from Virginia; berates political dissension in Massachusetts; fears another revolution. ICU; VHi; AHR, Vol. XII (1907), 347–48 (dated 5th); Oster, *Marshall,* 88–90 (same).

Jan. 7
RICHMOND *to George Muter*

Acknowledges letter of Sept. 23 by Fowler. (Memorial of members of Kentucky, Danville convention of Sept., 1786, giving reasons why act of Virginia Assembly on Kentucky statehood could not be acted on because of absence of members on Clark and Logan expedition. Forwarded to J.M. for presentation to Virginia Assembly. Unknown. Reference in Green, *The Spanish Conspiracy,* 102.) Regrets delay of Kentucky convention on separation; shortness of time by Congress thought sufficient; Congress desires Kentucky to have statehood; Congress avoided extending convention life; up to them. Objection to Article 7 not well founded; owners of both sides of stream reciprocal rights. Discusses treaty with Spain as affects use of Mississippi River by Kentucky; not worth staying out for. Decries melancholy events in Massachusetts; violence possible. Amendment to Constitution to give government greater power suggested. Tyler's, Vol. I (July, 1919), 29–30; J.M. Brown, *Political Beginnings of Kentucky* (Louisville, Morton, Filson Club, 1889), 77–79.

Jan. 17
RICHMOND *to Cadwallader Jones, of Petersburg, Va.*

Requests payment of order for 2,000 wt. of tobacco on William Constable, of Philadelphia, in favor for Gratz. J.M. represented Gratz. PPHi, Etting Jurists Coll.; DLC, Beveridge Coll.

Jan. [after 10th]
RICHMOND *to Thomas Marshall*

Explaining his inability, in appearance before committee of the General Assembly of Virginia, to obtain amendment of existing act for separation of Kentucky from Virginia according to memorial sent him by Danville convention; instead new act passed (Jan. 10) for new convention and extending time. Recommends passage of law extending present convention or calling for new one. Advises of Virginia resolution opposing the ceding of navigation of the Mississippi to Spain. Littell, *Political Transactions,* App. VII, 17; App. VIII, 21; Brown, *Political Beginnings of Kentucky,* 77–79; Marshall, *History of Kentucky,* I, 254; Green, *Spanish Conspiracy,* 102–104 (extract); 108–109n., 112.

Feb. 10
RICHMOND *to John Alexander*

Will speak to Randolph about amendment of Alexander's bill. Injunction to be continued to final hearing. Inquires of conversation with Alexander concerning employment in Belfield matter; offered high fees by latter to represent him. DLC, John Marshall Papers, Ac. 9475.

Fee: Sept., 1787, £11 from Alexander. Account Book, 122.

Feb. 11
RICHMOND *to George Muter, Danville, Kentucky*

Inquires of opinion of measures of last Assembly as affect the Western Country (Kentucky). Expects separation to be decided on. Col. Carrington delegate in Congress; doubts Congress will admit to Union; Virginia will approve. Navigation of Mississippi by treaty for term of years approved by many friends of Western Country; J.M. not favorable to such. Suggests Muter consider marriage. DLC, John Marshall Papers; Tyler's, Vol. I (July, 1919), 28–29.

Mar. 5
RICHMOND *to Arthur Lee—Addressed to New York*

Has not forwarded letter to Imlay; has notes inquired for. Fears unthinking men of Western Country will embroil us in war with Spain unless government acts. Refers to memorial from Kentucky incriminating Gen. Clarke. J.M. has no decided opinion on cession for a time of navigation of Mississippi because of lack of information. (Patrick) Henry is opposed. Congratulates suppression of insurrection in Massachusetts. Elections; debtors seeking Assembly seats. VHi, Lee Transcripts, No. 2; Richard Henry Lee, *Life of Arthur Lee* (Boston, Wells and Lilly, 1829), II, 321–22; Oster, *Marshall*, 40.

May 3 — *to John Breckenridge, Attorney at Law,*
RICHMOND — *Albemarle County, Va.*

Acknowledges letter of Apr. 23. Pleased to communicate on legal and other subjects for what it is worth. Certificate sent to clerk; will issue writ of habeas corpus. Describes procedure as to bail; advises let writ find defendant; describes return to General Court. DLC, Papers of Breckenridge Family, IV.

Sept. 28
RICHMOND — *to John Breckenridge*

Acknowledges letter and appeal in *Hill v. Henley*; mistake made; inquire of clerk; mention to Hill; wrote other day, by Harvie, answering inquiries. DLC, Papers of Breckenridge Family, IV.

Oct. 18
FAUQUIER COUNTY, VA. — *Deed*

Aquilla Dyson and wife, Lucy, to J.M., Richmond, land in Fauquier County adjoining lands of estate of Lord Fairfax, George Ash, Wharton Ransdell, and William Moore, along deep branch, 268 acres with house. Consideration £160 Va. Recorded Feb. 25, 1788. Fauquier County, Deed Book 10, 29.

HOUSE OF DELEGATES OF VIRGINIA

J.M. SERVED IN the House of Delegates of Virginia, representing Henrico County, for the session commencing Oct. 15, 1787, and ending Jan. 8, 1788.

Oct. 16 On Committee of Propositions and Grievances and for Courts of Justice. Journal, H.D. (Oct. sess., 1787), 4. (Reprint, Richmond, Thos. W. White, 1828). DLC; V; NcU.

Oct. 20 On committee to prepare bills concerning militia, authorizing executive to acquire 1,000 stands of arms, relieving militia from providing own arms, annexing corps of cavalry in each county. Same, 10.

Oct. 25 Resolutions for state convention to consider adoption of federal Constitution; proceedings of federal convention to "convention of the people, for their full and free investigation and discussion"; every citizen freeholder eligible to a seat; one delegate to each county with two delegates in legislature, and to each city, town, or corporation eligible; election as for delegates to General Assembly, on March next first day of court; convention at State House, Richmond, May 4 next; 2,000 copies of resolution for distribution. Passed; Mathews to carry to Senate. Same, 15. Oct. 31, Senate agreed. Same, 25.

Dec. 4, Bill presented by P. Henry, convention in June. Same, 81. Dec. 7, amendments proposed by committee. Same, 86. Dec. 8, bill with amendments engrossed, for third reading. Same, 88. Dec. 11, passed unanimously; Dawson ordered to carry to Senate. Same, 90. Dec. 13, Senate approval. Same, 95. Dec. 26, Governor to transmit copies of act to executives and legislatures of other states. Same, 119.

Oct. 27 Voted for resolution absolving M'Aulay, a member of the House, from charge that represented General Assembly in ordering New to leave town. Passed. Same, 19.

Nov. 2 On committee to amend act establishing High Court of Chancery. Journal, H.D., 27. Nov. 26, bill presented by J.M. Same, 70. Dec. 22, amended by committee. Same, 115. Dec. 31, agreed to at second reading. Same, 126. Jan. 1, 1788, passed. J.M. ordered to carry to Senate. Same, 127. Jan. 2, agreed to by Senate. Same, 130.

Nov. 13 Committee to bring in bill for district court on Western waters; probably Thomas Marshall, J.M.'s father, a member of the House. Same, 42.

Nov. 17 Voted for resolution repealing acts of Virginia repugnant to treaty with Great Britain, but suspending until other states pass similar laws. Same, 52. Thomas Marshall voted similarly. Same. Both voted against amendments making resolution subject to Britain complying with treaty, or subject to act limiting payment of debts due British subjects. Both amendments were rejected. Same, 51, 52. J.M. on committee to bring in bill pursuant to resolution. Same, 52 (see herein Dec. 3).

Nov. 19 Thomas Marshall on committee to draft bill for county courts of Kentucky to establish ferries. Same, 55.

Nov. 24 No vote recorded by J.M. on bills to amend charter of Norfolk; to declare tobacco receivable for taxes, 1787. Both passed. Same, 65, 66.

Nov. 26 On committee to bring in bill amending act preventing fraudulent gift of slaves. Same, 70.

Dec. 3 House in Committee of Whole, bill to repeal lawful impediments to collection of debts to and from British under treaty provision. Repeal section passed; also amendment making it provisional on British to withdraw troops from ports and return or compensate for slaves removed. J.M. and Thomas Marshall voted against amendment. Same, 79–80. Dec. 4, passed as amended. Same, 80. Dec. 11, Senate passed bill with amendments. Same, 91. Dec. 12, accepted some Senate amendments, rejected others. Same, 94. Dec. 13, Senate receded from amendments. Same, 95.

Dec. 4 Committee on Propositions and Grievances, of which J.M. a member, returned no resolution on petition of Presbyterian Church against provision of act repealing act incorporating Episcopal Church which reserved to latter churches and glebes. Resolution made in Committee of Whole House allowing disposition of glebe lands derived from contribution of people, where no Episcopalian minister, for public purposes. Rejected. No vote recorded for J.M. or Thomas Marshall. Same, 82.

Dec. 6 On committee to bring in bill establishing district courts, and reforming county courts. Same, 85.

Dec. 10 On committee to bring in bill amending act imposing new taxes. Same, 90.

Dec. 13 Account of Jacquelin Ambler, Treasurer, to committee. Same, 96–97. Dec. 19, committee resolution deficiency of £2,919:6:1 be payable by Ambler in securities of state. Passed. No recorded vote of J.M.; Thomas Marshall voted for. Same, 108–109. Dec. 21, Ambler re-elected Treasurer. Same, 113.

Dec. 15 Voted against bill authorizing debtors and creditors to arrange judgment bonds for debt without court action. Rejected. Same, 101.

Dec. 17 On committee to call on commissioners adjusting expenses incurred by state in ceding Northwest Territory. Same, 105. Jan. 7, 1788, report of committee. Same, 137–39.

Dec. 18 Voted against bill establishing district courts. Bill passed. (Thomas Marshall voted in favor.) Same, 105–106. Jan. 3, 1788, Senate amendments resolved. Same, 130–31.

Dec. 22 On committee to bring in bill regulating rights of cities, etc., and jurisdiction of corporation courts. Same, 115. Jan. 3, 1788, bill passed. Same, 131.

J.M. a manager for free conference with Senate on amendments to bills on roads and tobacco inspection. Same, 115. Dec. 24, met as to latter bill. Same, 117.

Dec. 31 On committee to bring in bill punishing stealing free persons or selling them for slaves. Same, 126. Jan. 8, 1788. Bill passed. Same, 141.

Jan. 1, 1788 Instructed to carry to Senate bills for amending act establishing High Court of Chancery and act directing patents for surveys of Richard Rigg. Same, 127.

Amendment to bill concerning manumission of slaves requiring emancipated slave to leave state within twelve months, authorizing sale of poor into slavery by overseer; J.M. voted against. Amendment defeated. Same, 128. Jan. 2, bill passed. Same, 129.

Jan. 2 Voted for resolution, sale of present building occupied by General Assembly, apply to new building. Passed. Same, 129–30.

Jan. 3 On committee to prepare bill repealing act establishing Courts of Assize. Same, 132. J.M. presented bill. Same. Jan. 4, passed. J.M. ordered to carry to Senate. Same. Jan. 5, J.M. acquaint Senate of House agreement to Senate amendment. Same, 136.

Jan. 5 Bill to enable citizens partners of British subjects recover proportion of debts; motion to postpone to March. J.M. voted against; motion defeated. Voted against bill; bill defeated. Same, 135.

LEGAL PRACTICE

For this year J.M. entered 336 fees received for a total of £1,134:3:5. Account Book, 96–138.

His major activity was in the trial of causes, only thirty-six of the fees being in the category of office work. Of these, fourteen are listed as the giving of advice, with the client's name not listed; eleven are of the same, with the listing of client's name. One is for several office fees, £1:8. Of the remaining ten, five are for advice as to specified wills, four for advising or drawing deeds, and one for drawing an answer. Fees for these services were all in the £1 bracket, predominantly £1:8, except for three fees in the £2 bracket.

Exceptional fees noted were from Dr. Stuart, £16:16; Hunter's administrator, £14; Col. R. Randolph's Executors, £14 (designated "retainer"); Alexander, £11; Harrison, for suit forwarded from Philadelphia,

£10. From T. Randolph for a fee of £2:10 he received three barrels of corn.

The remainder of his practice appears to be in litigated matters. His predominant fee collected was in the £2 bracket, with a goodly number as high as £4 and £5.

It appears that his work was predominantely in the appellate courts, twenty-four cases being marked "Appeals" (probably General Court and Supreme Court of Appeals), twelve "Supersedeas," one "Writ of Error." Twenty-five cases are marked "Chancery," which include appeals to the Superior Court of Chancery as well as original equity matters.

Cases, the nature of which he has designated, are divided between actions of debt, replevin, injunction, trespass, ejectment. There are no criminal matters mentioned. Two habeas corpera (Morris and Young, administrator of Rorrick) possibly arose from civil debt matters. There appears to be a dearth of land cases—one caveat (Wilkinson) and one land matter in Fauquier County.

His practice carried him to Petersburg, from which source he noted receipt of £50, a substantial item. Among other places the record reveals him active in litigation before the district courts at Prince Edward County and Fredericksburg City (see herein).

Beveridge states that J.M.'s practice was growing, "although slowly." Beveridge, *Marshall*, I, 190. This would appear to be an understatement, inasmuch as his income considerably exceeded that of the previous year.

During this year, Mar. 5, J.M.'s brother James was admitted to practice before the Henrico County Court. County Court, Henrico, Order Book II, 613.

Court of Appeals of Virginia

George Pickett v. Robert and William Claiborne, 4 Call 99.

Error to General Court which reversed j. County Court of Henrico for plaintiff in error. Reversed.

J.M. for plaintiff in error.

Pickett brought action for 1,000 pounds crop tobacco; no declaration filed; case continued in County Court by consent; note by Claibornes to several attorneys authorizing to confess judgment for 65,440 pounds of tobacco, which done. General Court reversed and annulled j. on grounds of lack of declaration. Held, agreement to confess judgment waived want of declaration and other matters of form; judges of General Court now retract and agree.

May 2, 1785. Writ of error allowed. Court of Appeals, Va., Order Book I, 49.

Apr. 3, 1787. Continued. Same, 102.

Oct. 30, 1787. Heard. Same, 106.

Nov. 1, 1787. Order reversing General Court and affirming County Court. Same, 107.

High Court of Chancery

William Farrar v. Francis Jackson, Wythe, 88.

Appeal from County Court of Amelia.

J. for appellee, defendant below, reversed. J.M. for defendant. Father of plaintiff, tenant in tail of land to which slaves annexed, sold two slaves for his life to one who resold; bought by defendant from purchaser who thought title in seller. Action by son, heir in tail, for slaves and offspring, unable to locate until five years after death. Plea of defendant, statute of limitations, purchase innocent, learned later. Reply; took warranty at purchase and knew of title; removed slaves; did not notify when learned but planned to conceal. County Court dismissed bill. Reversed by divided Court, two judges holding defendant could not avail of statute of limitations; Wythe dissenting.

Fee: Apr. 23, 1787, £4:16:8. Account Book, 110.

Oct. 29

Richmond

Dr. Walker adv. Col. Syme, chancery.

Receipt for £5 from Walker. Autograph signed. VHi.

The following fees were collected in this matter: Oct. 29, 1787, £5; Oct. 19, 1789, £4:10; Aug., 1792, £5. Account Book, 132, 218, 334. (See herein July 9, 1789; 1792, n.d.)

Mar. 3, 1787. Entry of fee of £2:10 on *Walker v. Syme*, debt case. Account Book, 100.

General Court

Apr.

Berkley County, Va.

James Ware v. Cornelius Conway.

Action for conversion of dark bay mare, lost by plaintiff Jan. 10, 1786, detained by defendant, value £30, damages £50. J.M. for plaintiff. (Autograph complaint.)

Jan. 29, 1788. Plea, not guilty.

Apr., 1788—Apr., 1791. Continuances.

Sept., 1791. V.j. for plaintiff.

VU, McGregor Libr., Marshall Family Papers.

Fee: Apr. 11, 1787, £2:10. Account Book 106.

Aug. 31
Berkley County, Va.
Frederick Havely v. Garrett Hammersly.

Debt. Action on bond, sealed obligation dated May 3, 1784, £45 Maryland money of value of £36 Virginia money. J.M. for plaintiff. (Autograph declaration.)

Feb. 29, 1788. Court order on defendant.

Mar. 29, 1788. Court order against defendant, confessed.

Apr., 1788. Plea, payment. Continued.

Sept., 1789. Continued.

Apr. 1790. V.j. £13:9:4 with interest from May 22, 1790, until paid, damages one penny. VU, McGregor Libr., Marshall Family Papers.

Sept. 7
Hampshire County, Va.
John Dawson v. James M. Lingan.

Ejectment, two messuages, two plantations, 225 acres, ejector claiming under twenty-year lease from Dawson dated June 26, 1787. Damages £1,000.

Endorsed "not guilty, Mar." (Endorsement not definitely identified as handwriting of J.M., acting as attorney for defendant.)

V.j. for plaintiff, one penny damages. VU, McGregor Libr., Fairfax and Lee Family MSS.

District Court, Accomack and Northampton

William and Smith Brickhouse, executors of Hezekiah Brickhouse v. Major, John, Sr., and George Brickhouse, Jr.

Debt (two cases). J.M. for one of parties in appeal proceedings, 1787.

One action in County Court, Northampton, in 1786 on sealed obligation of £100 by Hezekiah against Major and Hezekiah, and agreement to compromise for £50; j. for plaintiff appealed to General Court, Mar. 15, 1787.

Another action in Court of Quarter Sessions, Northampton County, in 1786 by Hezekiah against Major and John on sealed obligation, £110, in which j. against defendants for £79:2:3 was also appealed to General Court.

These cases were long delayed and js. were not finally affirmed (note entry of dismissal of one by consent in 1795) by the District Court until 1799 and 1795, respectively, J.M. not participating. See District Court, Accomack and Northampton, Order Book 1789–1791, 36; Order Book 1794–1797, 243; Order Book 1789–1797, 247, 339, 356, 394, 402, 423, 428.

Fee: Nov. 11, 1786, £2:8, "Appeal." Account Book, 90.

PERSONAL PROPERTY LISTS, RICHMOND CITY, IN NAME OF JOHN MARSHALL—1787–1835

Date	White Male Tithables over 21	White Males over 16 under 21	Blacks above 16	Blacks under 16	Horses, Mules, etc.	Tax	Cattle	Carriages, Wheels
1787	1	1	5	5	2		2	
1788	1		6	1	1	£25 at 5%—£1.5.0		
				over 12 under 16				
1789	2		7	2		£20 at 5% £1.0.0		
1791	2		10	1	2	£40 at 1¼% £0.1.0		6
								Chariots
1792	1		9	1	2	£50 at 1¼% £0.12.6		4
1793	1		9	1	3	£50 at £0.16.8 per £100—£0.8.4		4

Date	Whites above 16	Blacks above 12	Blacks above 16	Horses, Mules, etc.	Ordinary Licenses	Billiard Tables	Tax	Carriages, Coaches
1794	1	1	8	3	1	1	£50 at £0.16.8 per £100 £0.8.4	1 1 4-wheel carriage 1 2-wheel carriage
							Tax—Yearly rent lots	
1795	1	1	9	4	1	1	£5 at £0.16.8 per 100 £0.0.10	1
1796	2—J.M. and John Smith		9	3			pt. of lot— £3 at £0.16.8 per £100 £0.0.6	1
1797	2	1	8	2			£150 at 5%, £7.10.0	4

PERSONAL PROPERTY LISTS (*continued*)

Date	Blacks above 12	Horses & Mules	Carriage Wheels	Tax	Yearly rent	Tax	Name of Persons Owning Houses & lots	Tenant
1798	10	2	2 Chariots	$ 7.68	$ 5.00	$ .23	J.M.	Benj. Taylor
1799	8	3	4 Chariots	8.88	50.00	2.23	J.M.	Benj. Taylor
1800	8	3	4 Coaches	8.88	50.00	2.63	J.M.	
1801	8	3	4 Coaches	8.88	50.00	2.63	J.M.	
1802	8	3	4 Coaches	8.88	75.00	3.93	J.M.	
1803	11	4	4 Coaches	10.32	50.00	2.63	J.M.	
1804	11	4	4 Coaches	10.32	50.00	2.60	J.M.	
1805	9	4	4 Coaches	9.44	50.00	2.63	J.M.	
1806	9	3	4 Coaches	9.32	50.00	2.63	J.M.	
1807	9	3	4 Coaches	9.32	60.00	3.13	J.M.	
1809	11	2	8 Coaches & chariots	15.08	60.00	3.13	J.M.	
1810	10	3	10 Chariots	15.62	60.00	3.12	J.M.	
1811	10	3	10 Chariots	15.62	90.00	4.68	J.M.	
1812	6	3	8 Chariots	13.00	400.00	6.24	J.M.	
1813	7	3	4—$300	12.61	400.00	8.32	J.M.	Carter & Page
			4—$100		450.00	9.36		Carter & Page
			Studs / Valuation				No. lots	Valuation
1814	7	3	1 / $350.00	13.24	500.00	13.85	786–791 / 787–792	$25,000.00

Date	White Males above 16	Blacks above 12	Horses & Mules	Valuation	Tax
1816	1	9	3	$600.00	14.84
1817	1	9	3	600.00	14.84
1818	1	8	3	300.50	11.64
1819	1	9	3	50.50 300.50	12.34

	Blacks above 12	Horses & Mules	Val.	Pers. Prop. Tax	No. lots	Name of Streets	Rate	Total Rents	Tax Rents	Total Tax
1820	9	3	$200.05	$11.84	783	K & 9th	$3.2	$500.	$15.00	$26.84
				11.84	786	J & 9th		500.	15.00	26.84
1821	8	3	200.50	9.64½	783	K & 9th	2¼	775.	17.44	27.08½
			200.50	9.64½	786	J & 9th	2¼	775.	17.44	27.08½
1822	8	3	200.05	9.64½	783	K & 9th	2¼	775.	17.44	27.08½
				9.64½	786	J & 9th	2¼	775.	17.44	27.08½

	Slaves above 12	Horses	Carriages	Carriage Tax	Tax Pers. Prop.	Lot	St.	Rent	Tax	Total Tax
1823	8	3	gig—30.	$50	$6.12	783	K. & 9th	$700.	$14.21	$20.33
			coach—150.	50		786	J. & 9th	700.	14.21	20.33

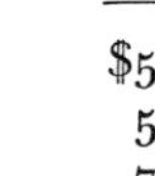

PERSONAL PROPERTY LISTS (*continued*)

Monroe Ward, Richmond

	Slaves over 12	Horses	Gen. Descrip. Carriages	Value Carriages	Tax Carriages	Total Tax
1824	7	3	coach	$150.	$2.00	$6.15
			gig	30.	.50	6.15
1825	6	3	gig	30.	.50	5.68
			coach	150.	2.00	
1826	6	3	gig	30.	.50	5.68
			coach	150.	2.00	
1827	10	3	gig	50.	.50	7.56
			carriage	200.	2.50	
1828	7	3	1 4-wheel	200.	2.50	6.17
			1 chair	20.		
1829	7	3	Same	Same	Same	5.60
1830	7	3	Same	Same	Same	5.19
1831	7	3	1 4-wheel	150.	2.00	4.43
			1 gig	20.	.50	
1832	7	3	Same	Same	Same	4.43
1833	7	3	1 4-wheel	Same	Same	4.43
			1 chair			
1834	7	3	Same	Same	Same	4.43
1835	1					.25

1788

DOCUMENTS

Jan. 9
RICHMOND *Land Grant*

To J.M., Jr., 40,000 acres Fayette County, Kentucky, on waters of Ohio, containing 1,800 acre survey of J.M. Land Office Treasury Warrant 17721, dated July 12, 1783; survey Mar. 15, 1785. Kentucky Land Office, Va. Grants, Book 12, 162; V, Land Grants 15, 1787 (bound), 393–97.

Mar. 8
RICHMOND *Law Suit*

Robert Greenhow, executor of John Greenhow v. John Harvie, J.M., and Samuel McCraw.

Action on bond dated Oct. 1, 1787, J.M. and McCraw sureties. Confessed j. against Harvie £1,000 Va., in gold at £5:6:8 specie, or silver six shillings eight pence specie per ounce. County Court, Henrico, Order Book III, 224; V.

May 5
RICHMOND *Appeal to Privy Council*

Certificate signed by J.M. and others who had been several times at billiard table of Robert Means (Minns) and considered it an orderly house. Filed in papers of appeal to Governor and Privy Council of Virginia against conviction for unlawful retailing of liquor. Fine remitted, Aug. 4. V, Exec. Papers, Box Apr.–June, 1788, Folder May 1–5.

June *Poem*

Doggerel on Convention of 1788 (by J.M.). VU; Mason, *Polly*, 52.

July 23 *to George Chapman*

Concerning land case in Virginia, affidavits, etc. Listed in Lazare, *Book-Prices* (1964), 843; *The Month at Goodspeed's*, Vol. xxxix, Nov. 2–3 (Nov.–Dec., 1967). Present owner unknown.

Sept. 15
RICHMOND *to George Washington*

Excuse for late answer to letter of Aug. 15, absent from Richmond. Explains procedure on caveats; caveat will be continued and new process issued if caveator show court nonservice of process accidental, not due to his negligence, as defendant living out of state or county; otherwise, dismissed; certified to register of Land Office; patent to applicant. Dismission not to impair title; junior patentee must sue in chancery, as must do if caveat against him. CSmH, RB 39003:8 (p. 436).

Dec. 20
RICHMOND *Club Membership*

J.M. was elected to membership in the Amicable Society of Richmond, probably the predecessor of the Buchanan Spring Quoit Club in which he was active during most of his life. Record books of the latter were destroyed by fire in 1865. Edmund Berkeley, Jr. "Quoits, the Sport of Gentlemen," *Virginia Cavalcade*, Summer, 1965, 11–12. Quoting from *American Turf Register and Sporting Magazine*, 1829.

RICHMOND *Tax List*

1 white male above 16, 6 tithable slaves, 1 horse, etc. Tax £2:4:0. V, Common Hall Records 1782–1793, I, 413.

Return of taxable property in the City of Richmond for the year 1788. J.M., taxable value £200, tax 10 shillings. Same, 417.

Lot No. 630 marked unimproved and unclaimed, value £35, tax 19 shillings. (This lot was marked occupied by J.M. in the return of 1784.) Same, 420.

VIRGINIA CONVENTION OF 1788 ON ADOPTION OF FEDERAL CONSTITUTION (Held at Richmond)

Mar. J.M. delegate from Henrico County. V, Journal of Convention of Virginia 1788, ii.

Apr. Return of sheriff certifying election of J.M. as representative to Virginia convention on federal Constitution. V, Folder Election Certificates, Convention of Virginia 1788, Henrico County.

June 2 Entry of fees, £13:0:0 for attendance at convention from June 2. V, Attendance Book of Convention of Virginia 1788, Henrico County.

June 2 Appointed on Committee of Privileges and Elections. V, Journal of Convention of Virginia 1788, 2; Elliot, *Debates*, III, 1. Several contested elections were heard. V, Journal of Convention of Virginia 1788, 7–11; Elliot, *Debates*, III, 5–6.

June 10 Debate. Answer to Patrick Henry objections. (Report of comment by J.M. that the speeches at the convention were poorly reported. VMH, Vol. LXVI [July, 1958], 365–67.) Legislative criminal indictment attacked. Navigation of Mississippi not endangered; opposes amendment prior to adoption; federal convention not to exceed powers; possibility of abuse; no objection to representative government and delegated powers. Answer to Gov. Randolph: delegation of taxing power as against state requisitions necessary; direct taxation supported; payment of state debts furthered; no rejection by Rhode Island; adoption by New Hampshire forecast; extent of country no objection; check on government by American spirit; secrecy in government no objection; answers argument same agency power to declare war should conduct it; urges amendment after ratification if necessary rather than before; Constitution better than British; will not encroach on state governments. Va. Debates, 163–72; Elliot, *Debates,* III, 222–36; Oster, *Marshall,* 253–67; Magruder, *Marshall,* 68–79; Frank Moore, ed., *American Eloquence* (New York, Appleton, 1859), II, 10–16; E. B. Williston, *Eloquence of the United States* (Middletown, Conn., Clark, 1827), I, 226–39.

June 16 Debate. Answering William Grayson; states retain power to control militia; Congressional power to call out and regulate is necessary. Va. Debates, 297–99; Elliot, *Debates,* III, 419–21 (dated June 14); Magruder, *Marshall,* 80–82.

June 20 Debate. Defense of judiciary provisions of proposed Constitution; federal courts will provide fair trial; objection to Congress establishing inferior courts refuted; jurisdiction under Constitution and laws thereunder proper; courts will declare void laws outside Constitution; state courts' jurisdiction not infringed on; provision as to suit between state and citizen of another state enables state to sue but not to be sued; no injustice in citizen of one state suing that of another; jurisdiction where state and foreign state parties prevents disputes; selection of jury within ten miles defended; Fairfax Estate titles determinable in state courts; trial by jury will be properly regulated by Congress; federal courts will not be used oppressively. Va. Debates, 391–99; Elliot, *Debates,* III, 551–62; Oster, *Marshall,* 267–78 (erroneously dated June 28); Magruder, *Marshall,* 82–86; Moore, *American Eloquence,* II, 16–20.

June 23 Debate. J.M. with Patrick Henry on J.M.'s assertion that trial by jury as well secured under new Constitution as in the Virginia bill of rights. Elliot, *Debates,* III, 577–78.

June 25 Vote opposing amendment to resolution of approval to require declaration of rights and amendments to be referred to other states prior to approval of federal Constitution. V, Journal of Convention of Virginia 1788, 27, 30.

June 25 Vote for approval of federal Constitution with amendments recommended to Congress. V, Journal of Convention of Virginia 1788, 23, 31; Elliot, *Debates*, III, 655.

June 25 On committee to prepare form of ratification of federal Constitution and report amendments. V, Journal of Convention of Virginia 1788, 33; Elliot, *Debates*, III, 656.

June 27 Vote opposing amendment to proposed bill of rights by striking article concerning direct taxes and contribution by states. The negative won, provision approved. V, Journal of Convention of Virginia 1788, 63–64; Elliot, *Debates*, III, 662.

LEGAL PRACTICE

During the year 1788, J.M. accounted for the receipt of £1,169:15:16 in fees received for legal services. The number of fees recorded was 326.

They were, for the most part, in the range of from £2 to £7, tending predominantly to the lower end of this range; seven fees were in considerably larger amounts, two for £14 from Hiron for his law business and from Eppes (Account Book, 154, 170); one for £20 from Beal (Same, 148); £24 from Hancock; £28 from Brett Randolph (Same, 152; see herein, 1789 Legal Practice, County Court, Henrico); £29:10:2 as Harrison's balance (Same, 174); £30 from Tyler for sundry suits (Same, 162). Of some interest is a retainer fee from Robert Morris of £4:4 (Same, 156), a client for whom he handled considerable business and who was in Richmond at the time, May 2, during elections for the constitutional convention. (See herein, Legal Practice, 1787. See also Beveridge, *Marshall*, I, 401 n.)

Of the thirty fees designated as for advice, all but five were in the £1 bracket. Of these five, one was for 18 shillings, three were in the £2 bracket, and one was for £5. Three small fees were for drawing deeds or instruments, two for services to corporations, one of which was from an Alexandria corporation (Account Book, 164). A fee of £2.8 came from Ladly concerning the riot at Morgantown. Nov. 4, 1788, £2:8. (Same, 176).

In 105 instances, the nature of the cases involved are designated. Of these, forty-five are appellate in nature, thirty-five marked appeals, including two in chancery, nine supersedeas, and one writ of error. The other large group was in chancery, twenty-four; and injunctions, eleven. Land cases involved six ejectments and two caveats. Miscellaneous litigation were replevins, two; debt, one; fraud, one; attachments, four; motions, four.

During this year, Aug. 4, William Marshall, J.M.'s brother, who was licensed to practice law as an attorney in the inferior courts of the Commonwealth, took oaths of fidelity and of an attorney and was allowed to practice in the Henrico County, Va., Court. County Court, Henrico, Order Book III, 357.

Court of Appeals of Virginia

John Robinson, surviving executor of Philip Grymes, and Presley Thornton, acting executor of Francis Thornton, etc. v. Edmund Pendleton and Peter Lyons, administrators of John Robinson, 4 Call 130.

Error to j. General Court, Nov. 5, 1779, against representatives of two deceased on letter of credit, £2,700 with interest from 1757. Reversed. J.M. for plaintiff in error, apparently with Randolph, who is reported as their attorney.

Held, representatives of two deceased persons cannot be joined in same action even on joint obligation; failure to plea to issue fatal despite jury verdict.

Nov. 8, 1785. Writ of error allowed. Court of Appeals, Va., Order Book I, 76.

Apr. 30, 1787. Continued. Same, 102.

Oct. 29, 1787. Abated by death of plaintiff, revived. Same, 105.

Nov. 8, 1787. Heard. Same, 112.

Nov. 12, 1787. Continued. Same, 117.

May 1, 1788. Reheard. Same, 120.

May 6, 1788. Reversed without prejudice. Same, 123.

Fee: Mar., 1791, £9. Account Book, 276.

Hare v. Gay, 4 Call 151.

Case adjourned from General Court for novelty and difficulty. J.M. for Hare.

Hare, having a j. on replevin bond, sued out writ of *fieri facias* prior to Jan. 4, 1788; only part of debt levied; second writ sued out later; sought to have endorsed that no security be taken contrary to act passed Jan. 4, 1788. Opinion certified, no such endorsement to be made.

May 3, 1788. Heard. Court of Appeals, Va., Order Book I, 122.

May 8, 1788. Opinion. Same, 125.

Fee: May 22, 1788, "Hare, advice," £1:8. Account Book, 158.

Caveats

July 2 *David Hunter v. Joseph Thomson.*

J.M. for Thomson. 403 acres Hampshire County on North River of Great Cacapon, surveyed by Thomson, Feb. 9, 1788, entry Jan. 2, 1786, Hunter claiming by previous warrant. V, Virginia Land Office, Caveats, II, 46.

(For further proceedings, see herein 1790, Legal Practice, District Court, Frederick.)

Fee: Oct., 1788, £5. Account Book, 168.

Oct. 7 *Samuel Duval, Jr. v. William Reynolds.*

J.M. for Reynolds. 127 acres in Henrico County on main run of Chickahominy Swamp, surveyed by Matthews Feb. 18, 1784, on treasury warrant, Duval claiming under entry of Aug. 27, 1773, and claiming Reynolds failed to file plat and certificate at Land Office in time. Same, Caveats, II, 15.

Fee: Oct. 7, 1788, £1:12. Account Book, 170.

Oct. 30 *Denny Fairfax v. Charles M. Thurston and Dorsey Penticoast.*

Filed by J.M. 5,490 acres in Northern Neck, Fauquier County, Virginia, adjoining the Manor of Leeds and Hedgman River, surveyed by Thurston and William Robinson, May 10, 1787, claimed by Fairfax under devise from Thomas Lord Fairfax. Caveats, II, 51.

Dec. 10 *Denny Fairfax v. John Thompson.*

Filed by J.M., 297 acres, Hampshire County on the waters of Little Cacapon, claimed under devise from Thomas Lord Fairfax. Same, Caveats, II, 54.

Dec. 20 *Denny Fairfax v. Robert Stephens, assignee of David Hunter.*

Filed by J.M. 2,144 acres on River Potomack, Berkeley County; surveyed by Hunter, May 30, 1788; assigned June 19, 1788; returned to Land Office, July 1, 1788; claimed by Fairfax under devise from Thomas Lord Fairfax. Same, Caveats II, 55.

Same v. Same.

1,050 acres in Berkeley County, Va., beginning at Warm Springs, surveyed June 10, 1789, returned July 1, 1788. Same, Caveats, II, 55.

Same v. Same.

400 acres in Berkeley County, Va., surveyed June 5, 1788, returned July 1, 1788. Same, Caveats, II, 56.

(For proceedings on above caveats, see herein 1790, Legal Practice, District Court, Frederick County, *Hunter v. Thompson, Fairfax v. Hunter, Fairfax v. Stephens*; also 1791, Legal Practice, General Court, *Fairfax v. Stephens* and *Fairfax v. Hunter.*)

1789

DOCUMENTS

Jan. 10
HENRICO COUNTY, VA. *Trust Deed*

George Webb, Buckingham County, to J.M. and John Beckley, Richmond, nine negro slaves to hire out, in trust for Hannah Webb, wife of George Webb, Sr., during his life; after death of both, to George Webb, Jr. Henrico County, Va., Deed Book 3, 38.

Apr. 7, 1789. Proved and recorded. County Court, Henrico, Order Book III, 570.

Feb. 4
RICHMOND *to Governor of Virginia*

Report on insanity of Catherine Crull, signed by J.M. V, Exec. Papers, Box 1789, Jan.-Feb., Folder Feb. 1–10.

Mar. 7
MOUNT VERNON, VA. *from George Washington*

Enclosing protested bill of exchange of executors of William Armstead for collection; previous action by Col. Fielding Lewis and Lund Washington referred to. Requests J.M. to handle caveat on Washington's land on the Ohio against claims of heirs of Michael Cresap. DLC, Papers of George Washington, Letter Book 9, Box 312, 139–40. (July 29, 1785, caveat filed *George Washington, Esq. v. M. Cresap's Heirs,* 400 acres in Ohio County on Ohio River, bottom called Round-Bottom. Washington grant based on legal survey. V, Virginia Land Office, Caveats, I, 212.)

Mar. 26
RICHMOND *to George Washington*

Asking for proof of protest of bill of exchange, notice to executors of William Armstead (n.f.). Referred to in George Washington to J.M., Apr. 5, 1789 (herein).

Apr. 5
MOUNT VERNON, VA. *from George Washington*

Acknowledges letter of Mar. 26. Advises no proof of notice to Armstead's executors concerning protest of note. Refers to Col. Fielding Lewis, deceased, as his former attorney. Requests information on effect of dismission of caveat against Cresap's heirs. DLC, Papers of George Washington, Letter Book 9, Box 312, 170.

Apr. 8 *to George Washington*

Acknowledged and answered by George Washington, Apr. 11, 1789 (n.f.).

Apr. 11 *from George Washington*

Letter of 8th acknowledged. Advises not to press claim against Mrs. Armstead. Mention made of Col. Pendleton and Montgomerie. DLC, Papers of George Washington, Letter Book 9, Box 312, 184.

Apr. 25
RICHMOND *to John Dandridge, of New Kent Court House, Va.*

Opinion to addressee, an attorney, as to liability of holder of personal property of deceased to claims. V, Ac. 216895; VW.

Apr. 30 *Admission to Practice*

J.M., James Monroe, John Taylor, John and Robert Brooke, Oliver Fowler, John Fellesces, Charles Simms, Bushrod Washington, Richard Brent, John James Moand, William Waller Henning admitted to practice; oath of fidelity to Commonwealth, subject to payment of £15 tax, on which question adjourned to General Court at Richmond. District Court, Fredericksburg Law Orders, A, 1789–1793, 6.

June 22
RICHMOND *to John Breckenridge*

J.M. unable to appear in cases in Albemarle and Prince Edward counties, forwarded cases to Breckenridge. DLC, Papers of Breckenridge Family; V; VMH, Vol. LXXI (Jan., 1963), 30.

June 26
WOODFORD COUNTY, KY. *Thomas Marshall to George Washington*

Suggesting that if necessary to make commands, safe conveyance under cover to son, John Marshall, in Richmond, to whom will write. Jared Sparks,

Correspondence of the American Revolution (Boston, Nettle, Brown & Co., 1853), IV, 261.

July 7
HENRICO COUNTY, VA. *Deed*

Philip Turpin and Caroline, his wife, Powhatan County, to J.M., Richmond, one-half acre lot in Richmond, Town Plan 786; £150. Recorded same date. Henrico County, Deed Book 3, 74–75; The John Marshall House. (This is the J.M. home plot.)

July 9
RICHMOND *to Dr. Thomas Walker, of Albemarle*

Encloses draft of answer to Syme's bill regarding claim for purchase of Negroes. Endorsed by J.M. "not useful." VU, Page and Walker MSS, Deposit No. 3098. (See herein, Legal Practice, Oct. 29, 1787; 1792, n.d.)

July 17
RICHMOND *to John Breckenridge*

Offering to communicate and assist in legal and other subjects. DLC, Papers of the Breckenridge Family; V. (See "John Breckenridge and Kentucky Land," 1789, VMH, Vol. LXXI [Jan., 1963], 29–30.)

Aug. 10
RICHMOND *to Dr. Stuart*

Addressed through George Washington (n.f.). See letter from Washington, Aug. 15, 1789 (herein).

Aug. 15
MOUNT VERNON, VA. *from George Washington*

Acknowledges letter of 10th to Dr. Stuart enclosing summons to L. Washington. Asks advice as to procedure in clearing title to land against claims of heirs of Michael Cresap (for caveat, see herein, Mar. 7, 1789), represented by Luther Martin. Washington acted on advice of Randolph. DLC, Papers of George Washington, Letter Book 6, Box 311, 217–18.

Sept. 15
FAYETTE COUNTY, KY. *Thomas Marshall to Gov. Randolph*

Discusses pending litigation as to relative rights to Kentucky land of officers of the state line and claimants under treasury warrants. Refers to J.M., to be engaged on part of officers. V, Exec. Papers, Box 1788, folder Sept. 11–20. (See herein 1786, Legal Practice, Caveats, Jan. 17.)

Sept. 24
WASHINGTON *U.S. Attorney*

Nomination of J.M. as U.S. Attorney for Virginia sent to U.S. Senate by President Washington. Journal of the Senate of the United States, I, 19. Affirmed by Senate Sept. 26. Same, I, 31. DNA, Legislative Dept., Office of Senate Financial Clerk. R.G. 46.

Sept. 26
NEW YORK *Commission—U.S. Attorney*

Commission as U.S. Attorney, Virginia District. DNA, State Dept., Misc. Commissions, Permanent, 1789–1802, Vol. B, 39.

Oct. 14
RICHMOND *to George Washington*

Declining appointment as U.S. Attorney for the District of Virginia. Listed in Lazare, *Book-Prices* (1959), 585. Present owner unknown. (See herein Washington letter of Nov. 23, 1789.)

Reason by J.M. for declining: federal courts at two distinct places distant from Richmond where superior courts of state sat, would be detriment to legal practice. Marshall, *Autobiography*, 12.

Nov. 23
NEW YORK *from George Washington*

Acknowledges letter of [Oct.] 14 declining appointment as Attorney for the District of Virginia, recommended by Col. Samuel Griffin at request of J.M. (List of persons who have requested Griffin to recommend them: J.M. as U.S. Attorney for Virginia. Bureau of Appointments, Dept. of State, in Gaillard Hunt, *Calendar of Applications and Recommendations for Office During the Presidency of George Washington* [Washington, D.C., Dept. of State, Libr. of Congress, 1800; G.P.O., 1901], 53.) Return of commission requested. DLC, Papers of George Washington, Letter Book 7, Box 318, 199; DNA, General Records Dept. of State, Misc. Letters. R.G. 59.

n.d., n.p. *Legal Opinion*

Legal opinion by J.M. in answer to questions as to rights of various parties where trust deed to secure payment of a debt assigned to third party. Parties involved: Baskerville, Delony, Burton, Jefferson. VHi, Baskerville Family of Mechlenburg County, Va.

Papers pertaining to *Baskerville adv. Hill*, for which entry of fee, £1:10, Apr. 15, 1789. Account Book, 193.

HOUSE OF DELEGATES OF VIRGINIA

J.M. WAS ELECTED member of the Virginia House of Delegates as representative of the City of Richmond, a newly created office. He attended sessions commencing Oct. 19, 1789, and ending Dec. 29, 1790. Marshall, *Autobiography*, 12–13.

Oct. 20 On committees of Privileges and Elections, and on Courts of Justice. Journal, H.D., (Oct. sess., 1789) (Reprint, Richmond, Thos. W. White, 1828), 4. DLC; V; NcU.

Oct. 22 On committee to bring in bill amending Court of Appeals Act as to safekeeping of prisoners of the United States in state jails, reducing reward for apprehending horse thieves, increasing security of jails. Same, 7.

Oct. 23 On committee to bring in bill to amend act establishing District Courts, and regulating General Court. Same, 8.

Resolution to President of the United States to supply powder and lead to Chickasaw Indians for defense against Creeks; no vote of record by J.M. Passed. Same, 9.

Oct. 24 On committee to examine in details enumerated and report on revision of laws of Commonwealth. Same, 10–11; V, Va. Acts (Nov. 18), Box Oct., 1789, Chap. IX, 227; Hening, Stat., XIII, Chap. 9, 8–9. Oct. 31, report submitted by Edward Carrington, with recommendation for further committee; to Committee of Whole House. Same, 25–29. Nov. 2, bill ordered. Same, 29–33.

Oct. 27 On committee to prepare bill amending statute of descent. Same, 16. Dec. 18, bill passed; J.M. ordered to carry to Senate. Same, 136.

Nov. 5 On committee ordered to prepare bill for cession of ten square miles to the United States for permanent seat of government. Same, 41. Nov. 28, bill passed. Same, 87–88.

Nov. 9 No vote of record on amendment to bill fixing salaries of civil officers, concerning Council of State. Amendment passed. Same, 47. Nov. 10, no vote on bill. Same, 57–58.

Nov. 16 On committee to bring in bill to appropriate the public revenue. Same, 63.

On committee to examine and report on letter of Governor concerning lost or destroyed records of Henrico County. Same. Nov. 19, on committee to bring in bill concerning same. Same, 69. Nov. 23, bill passed. Same, 76.

Nov. 23 Added to committee considering divorce petition of Ann Destigue. Same, 78. Committee report. Same, 103. Bill of divorcement passed. Same, 141.

Nov. 25 On committee to prepare and bring in bill to amend acts concerning mode of proceeding under certain executions. Same, 82.

Nov. 28 On committee to meet with committee of Senate to examine and report on joint ballots for choice of Governor of Commonwealth. Same, 88; V, Exec. Papers, Box Nov.–Dec., 1789, Folder Nov. 21–31. Same as to vacancies in Council of State. Journal, H.D., 88.

Nov. 30 On committee to prepare and bring in bill amending act establishing Supreme Court in District of Kentucky. Journal, H.D., 90.

On committee to prepare and bring in bill on method of procedure in impeachments. Same, 90.

On committee to draw bill granting Kentucky statehood. Same, 96. Bill passed. Same, 115, 131, 141. Beveridge states that J.M. probably drew the bill. Beveridge, *Marshall*, II, 55.

Dec. 2 On committee to bring in bill for revival and amendment of act of 1785 concerning statehood of Kentucky. Same, 96.

Dec. 5 On committee to prepare and bring in bill concerning allowances to commissioners in High Court of Chancery. Journal, H.D., 101. Dec. 7, presented bill. Same, 106. Dec. 9, J.M. ordered to carry bill to Senate. Same, 112. Dec. 11, passed by Senate. Same, 118.

Voted against amendment to resolution urging Congress reconsider amendments to Constitution recommended by Virginia but not adopted. Amendment defeated; resolution passed. Same, 101–102.

Dec. 7 On committee to notify Beverly Randolph of re-election as Governor of the Commonwealth. Same, 107.

Dec. 9 Ordered to acquaint Senate of agreement of House to amendment to bill concerning proceedings in certain criminal cases. Same, 112–13.

Affirmative vote on resolution to postpone consideration of memorial of Baptist Association. Postponed. Same, 113.

On committee to consider letter of Governor enclosing letter from President of the United States on proposals of foreigners to establish woolen mill in Commonwealth. Same, 114.

Dec. 11 On committee to bring bill for collection of arrears of taxes, Boutetort County, prior to 1788. Same, 117.

Dec. 12 On committee to confer with Senate committee concerning amendments to the Constitution of the United States. Same, 119.

Dec. 14 Amendments of Senate to resolutions concerning permanent seat of general government agreed to by House; J.M. ordered to acquaint Senate. Same, 129.

LEGAL PRACTICE

DURING 1789, J.M. recorded his income from legal fees at £1,114:2, derived from a total of 302 fees paid and representing approximately 305 matters. Account Book, 184–228. Of these, thirty-seven fees are designated as for advice, and of these three in connection with wills and four with drawing of deeds. For this office work his fees were generally over £1 but less than £2. In one will matter he charged £5, in an estate matter £4:2, and for conveyances, which must have been several, £4:4.

The remaining matters involved litigation, of which he designated the nature of the proceedings in ninety-six instances. These were predominantly chancery cases and appeals, twenty-nine of the former and thirty-one of the latter. Fees ranged generally between £2 and £5. One fee was over £27, three were for £14, one for £12:10, two in the £11 bracket. From Morris, he received glass and nails, probably as compensation, valued at £56:0:5, and from Maj. Jones a hogshead of tobacco. One fee, £4:17:6, was for representing the famous Frenchman, Caron de Beaumarchais, in litigation against one Smith. Account Book, 200. He later represented Beaumarchais through the latter's agent Chevallie in proceedings against Virginia for supplies furnished during the Revolution. (See herein 1801, Court of Appeals of Virginia.) During the XYZ Affair, proposals (which J.M. rebuffed) were made that £50,000 of the claim be assigned and paid to Talleyrand. (See J.M.'s Diary, herein, Dec. 17, 1797.) Beveridge, *Marshall,* II, 173n., 292, 314, 317.

HIGH COURT OF CHANCERY

John Holcomb Overstreet v. Richard Randolph and David Meade Randolph, executors of Richard Randolph, and William Griffin, Wythe 115.

Injunction refused. J.M. for Overstreet.

Obligation of £300 by Overstreet to Richard Randolph, testator, in payment for Negro slaves; transaction an unfair bargain, would have warranted defense in action by obligee. Note assigned for value to purchaser in good faith.

Held, injunction not issued against assignee to prevent enforcement of note or execution on judgment, equity superior to maker; act of 1748 giving assignee right to sue and allowing discounts against assignor as set off does not apply to defense of unfairness.

Fee: Apr. 3, 1786. "In part," £2:16. Account Book, 68.

DISTRICT COURT, ACCOMACK AND NORTHAMPTON

Severn Kellum v. Jeremiah West.

Case, slander, alleging statement that plaintiff "forsworn," i.e., perjured self as witness. J.M. for plaintiff.

Feb. 29, 1788. Defendant defaulting, office j. for plaintiff, writ of inquiry to determine damages at General Court, Richmond.

Apr., Oct., 1788. Continued by plaintiff's attorney. General Court.

Oct. 16, 1789. District Court, Accomack and Northampton, George Parker, attorney for plaintiff; writ of inquiry set aside; plea not guilty. V.j. guilty, damages £10. District Court, Accomack and Northampton, Order Book 1789–1791, 4; Same, Order Book 1789–1797, 21.

Fee: Aug. 25, 1787, £2:10. "Chr." Account Book, 120.

DISTRICT COURT, AUGUSTA

Florence and Joseph Bell, executrix and executor of David Bell v. John and Thomas Patterson.

Oct., 1786. General Court. Action on sealed obligation, April 3, 1780, £2,631 Va., penal sum £5,262. Edmund Randolph, attorney for plaintiff; also J.M.

Apr., 1786–Oct., 1788. Continued.

Sept. 2, 1789. District Court.

No plea; j. £5,262 payable by £43:17 specie, agreeable to scale of depreciation. District Court, Augusta, Order Book 1789–1793, 1; Same, Order Book 1789–1797, 8.

Fee: May 11, 1790, £5. Account Book, 246.

John Brown v. Elizabeth Brown, administrix of Thomas Brown.

Case, money had and received, £62:12:8. Alexander Stuart signed petition as attorney for plaintiff, J.M. probably for same.

Oct., 1786. Petition filed in General Court.

Continued successively through Apr., 1789.

Sept. 5, 1789. Plea *non assumpsit*; office j. set aside. V.j. £52:13:10 against estate of intestate. District Court, Augusta, Order Book 1789–1793, 28; Same, Order Book 1789–1797, 18.

Fee: Jan. 4, 1787, £2:10. Account Book, 96.

Superior (District) Court, Frederick

William Glascock v. James G. Dowdall.

In case. J.M. for defendant.

Sept. 5, 1789. V.j. for defendant.

Superior Court, Frederick, Order Book 1789–1793, 24.

Fee: Aug., 1786, £4:16. Account Book, 80.

District Court, Fredericksburg

Andrew Bourne v. Charles Porter.

In case. J.M. for plaintiff.

Oct. 1, 1789. Abated by death of plaintiff.

District Court, Fredericksburg, Law Orders A, 1789–1793, 16.

Fee: Oct. 22, 1788, £2:16. Account Book, 172.

Richard Corbin v. John Hatley Norton and George F. Norton, s.p. John Norton & Sons.

Debt, money advanced and expended, £1, 893:8, May 31, 1779. Filed in General Court Apr., 1784, by Tazewell for plaintiff, Frederick County. J.M. for defendant.

Apr., 1785—Oct., 1788. Continued.

Oct. 8, 1789. Confessed j. £1,289:18:4½ current; execution extended over three-year period.

Oct. 10, 1793. Writ of *scire facias,* by consent plea and demurrer withdrawn, sent back to rules.

Oct. 9, 1794. *Scire facias,* demurrer to plea of defendant overruled, costs against plaintiff.

District Court, Fredericksburg, Record Book 1789–1792, 119–20; Law Orders A, 1789–1793, 538; Same, B, 1794–1798, 103.

Fee: Aug., 1789, £2:10. Account Book, 206.

Overton Cosby and James Gregory, s.p. James Mills and Co. v. David Hening, executor of Samuel Hening.

Debt, on joint sealed obligation, £1,300 current, Jan. 4, 1794, damages £10. Filed in General Court Apr., 1786. Culpeper County. J.M. for defendant.

Apr., 1787—Oct., 1788. Continued.

Oct. 6, 1789. V.j. £1,300 current, payable £482:13:6 on goods of testator.

District Court, Fredericksburg, Record Book 1789–1792, 86–87; Law Orders A, 1789–1793, 55.

Fee: Apr. 17, 1787, £2:10. Account Book, 108.

Overton Cosby and James Gregory, s.p. James Mills & Co. v. Samuel McCherney and Alexander Stewart.

Debt, £1,580. Filed in General Court. J.M. for McCherney (probable).

Oct. 7, 1789. Confessed j., £1,580, payable by £536:4:6 with interest 5 per cent from June 19, 1775.

District Court, Fredericksburg, Law Orders A, 1789–1793, 63.

Fee: Apr. 26, 1787, £2:10. Account Book, 112.

Langhorne Dade v. Frances Suttle.

Debt, on sealed obligation, 14,000 pounds newly inspected crop tobacco and casks (value £420 Va.), Mar. 21, 1784, damages £50. Filed in General Court Apr., 1785. Culpeper County. J.M. for defendant.

Oct., 1786—Oct. 1788. Continued.

Oct. 5, 1789. (District Court) Confessed by security, j. against defendant and security 14,000 pounds newly inspected crop tobacco and casks, payable by 5,000 same, each cask 1,000 weight net.

District Court, Fredericksburg, Record Book 1789–1792, 69–70; Law Orders A, 1789–1793, 47.

Fee: Apr., 1785, £2:10. Account Book 30.

William Dudley and Henry Fleet, executors of Edwin Fleet v. William and

Joseph Elliott Payne, executors of John Elliott.

Debt, on sealed obligation, £478:12:3, May 4, 1765, damages £10. Filed in General Court Oct., 1784. Petition signed by Edmund Randolph. J.M. for plaintiff.

Mar., 1785—Oct., 1788. Continued.

Oct. 3, 1789. (District Court) V.j. for plaintiff £478:12:3 payable by £95:16:6, with interest 5 per cent from June, 1772.

District Court, Fredericksburg, Record Book 1789–1792, 40–41; Law Orders A, 1789–1793, 37.

Fee: Feb., 1790, £5:2. Account Book, 234.

Elizabeth Eggleston v. Thomas and John Chiles and John Sutton, Jr.

Debt, on penal bill £70, penal sum £140, July 1, 1782; damages £5. Filed in General Court Apr., 1785. Caroline County. J.M. for plaintiff. Petition signed.

Oct. 10, 1785. Security for defendant.

Oct. 1, 1789. (District Court) V.j. for plaintiff £140, one penny damages.

District Court, Fredericksburg, Record Book 1789–1792, 29–30; Law Orders A, 1789–1793, 26.

Fee: Mar., 1788, £1:2. Account Book, 148.

Gabriel Johnston, administrator of John Drake v. Elijah Morton, executor of William Morton.

Debt. J.M. for defendant (probable).

Oct. 5, 1789. Abated by death of defendant.

District Court, Fredericksburg, Law Orders A, 1789–1793, 41.

Fee: Sept., 1787, £1:8. Account Book, 122.

Christopher and Robert Johnston v. William Wiatt.

Action for money had and received, £600, 1779, filed in General Court Oct., 1783. Defense money given for purchase of goods by defendant lost in accidental rearing of horse and loss of saddle bags, probably taken by British forces. Spotsylvania County. J.M. for defendant.

Aug., 1784. General issue; agreement for arbitration in 1783 apparently not completed.

Oct., 1784—Oct., 1787. Continued.

Apr. 16, 1788. Jury trial, juror withdrawn.

Apr. 17, 1788. Deposition witness in Kentucky.

Oct., 1788. Continued.

Oct. 1, 1789 (District Court) V.j. for defendant.

District Court, Fredericksburg, Record Book 1789–1792, 4–8; Law Orders A, 1789–1793, 16.

Fees: Oct., 1787, £2; Oct., 1789, £1:2. Account Book, 130, 216.

William Jones v. Joseph Hoomes and Abram Simons.

Appeal. J.M. for Jones (probable).

Oct. 9, 1789. Dismissed on motion of appellee.

District Court, Fredericksburg, Law Orders A, 1789–1793, 72.

Fee: Oct., 1789, £2:8. Account Book 216.

Thomas Latham v. Richard Gaines, John McBargon, and John Camp.

Assault, "with swords, staves, knives," etc., on plaintiff, in fact by whipping. Damages £5,000. Filed in General Court Apr., 1783, Edmund Randolph for plaintiff. Culpeper County. J.M. for plaintiff.

Oct., 1784—Oct., 1788. Continued.

Oct. 8, 1789. V.j. £100. Testimony of one of group, not doing beating but agreeing to pay share of damages if sued, held inadmissible, excepted to.

District Court, Fredericksburg, Record Book, 1789–1792, 112–16; Law Orders A, 1789–1793, 65, 68.

Fee: Sept. 5, 1785, "finished," £2:10. Account Book, 48.

Benjamin Leitch, assignee of Charles Holloway v. James Thomas.

Debt, on sealed obligation, Mar. 5, 1784, £100, damages £10. Filed General Court Oct., 1785. J.M. for plaintiff. (Petition signed.)

Oct., 1786—Oct., 1788. Continued.

Oct. 5, 1789. V.j. £100, one penny damages, payable by £20:2:4.

District Court, Fredericksburg, Record Book 1789–1792, 47–49; Law Orders A, 1789–1793, 42.

Fee: Oct. 4, 1785, £2:10. Account Book 50.

John McGeehee, assignee of Charles Lynch v. Charles Carter.

Debt, on sealed obligation, £203 Va., Nov. 8, 1783, assigned to plaintiff. Filed in General Court Apr., 1785. J.M. for plaintiff. (Petition signed.)

June, 1785—Oct., 1788. Continued.

Oct. 2, 1789. (District Court) Confessed j. for plaintiff against defendant and security, £203 Va. in gold or silver, payable by £101:10 specie and interest.

District Court, Fredericksburg, Record Book 1789–1792, 33; Law Orders A, 1789–1793, 33.

Fee: Dec., 1784, £2:10. Account Book, 22.

Battaile Muse, assignee of Patrick Cavens v. Thomas Ludwell Lee.

Debt, on sealed obligation, £80, June 1, 1785, damages £10. Filed General Court Apr., 1787. Stafford County. J.M. for plaintiff. (Petition signed.)

Oct., 1787—Oct., 1788. Continued.

Oct. 3, 1789. Confessed by security. J. against defendant and security, £80 Va. payable £40 Va.

District Court, Fredericksburg, Record Book 1789–1792, 45–46; Law Orders A, 1789–1793, 39.

Samuel Parsons and Samuel Smith v. William Almond, Robert Broadus, and Parke Goodall.

Debt, on obligation sealed, Apr. 24, 1782, £120 gold or silver.

Filed in General Court Oct., 1783, Duval for plaintiff. J.M. for defendant Almond (probable).

Apr., 1784. J. against Broadus and security, Emanuel Almond, non-appearance.

Apr., 1785. Confessed j. against Goodall and his security, John Madison.

Oct. 1, 1789. V.j. against defendant Almond and his security, Spilsley Davis, £120 gold or silver, payable by £60 gold or silver at rate of £5 per ounce of gold, six shillings, eight pence per ounce for coined silver.

J.M. probably attorney for one of the parties in last action.

District Court, Fredericksburg, Record Book 1789–1792, 13–16; Law Orders A, 1789–1793, 29.

Fee: Feb., 1789, "Parsons v. Adams," £2:7. Account Book, 186.

William and Joseph Payne, executors of John Elliott Payne v. William Tailor, Elijah Kirtley and Zachariah Tailor.

Debt, on sealed obligation, £172:10, Dec. 22, 1785. Filed in General Court Apr., 1787. Culpeper County. J.M. for defendants.

May, 1787. Court order against Kirtley and James Slaughter, sheriff Culpeper County. Capias against Tailor.

Oct., 1787. Payment by sheriff for Kirtley.

Apr., 1788. Continued as to Kirtley.

June, July, 1788. Court order against Tailors, Slaughter, Ben Winslow, deputy sheriff Orange County.

Oct., 1788. Tailors arrested, not appearing; j. against Tailors, Slaughter, and Winslow £172:10 payable by £86:5.

Oct. 7, 1789. Confessed j. against Kirtley and Slaughter, surety for Kirtley, same as above.

District Court, Fredericksburg, Record Book 1789–1792, 96–98; Law Orders A, 1789–1793, 61.

Fee: Oct., 1787, £2:10. Account Book, 126.

Christopher Perfect v. John Page, executor of Mann Page.

Debt, on bond to convey. Filed in General Court. J.M. for plaintiff.

Oct. 2, 1789. Abated by death of defendant.

District Court, Fredericksburg, Law Orders A, 33.

Fee: Oct., 1784, £3. Account Book, 14.

Robert Pollard v. Richard Gaines.

Debt, on sealed bill penal, 1,286 pounds crop tobacco, penal amount 2,500 pounds, Jan. 1, 1784. Filed in General Court Oct., 1785. Culpeper County. J.M. for plaintiff. (Petition signed.)

Apr., 1786—Oct., 1788. Continued.

Oct. 5, 1789. Confessed by security. J. 2,500 pounds crop tobacco payable by 1,286 pounds.

District Court, Fredericksburg, Record Book 1789–1792, 54–55; Law Orders A, 1789–1793, 44.

Fee: Mar. 14, 1786, £2:10. Account Book, 66.

Thomas Powell v. Thomas Carr.

In case, appeal from j. Court of Spotsylvania County, Mar. 7, 1787, £127:17:4 in favor of Carr (John Minor, his attorney) based on promise to pay debt of John Powell of Georgia. Appeal filed in General Court Apr., 1787. J.M. for appellant.

Apr., 1787—Nov., 1789. Continued.

Oct. 6, 1789. (District Court) J. reversed, lack of consideration.

District Court, Fredericksburg, Record Book 1789–1792, 299–302; Law Orders A, 1789–1793, 164.

Fees: Mar. 28, 1787, £4:16; Apr., 1790, £1:8. Account Book, 104, 242.

Robert Price, administrator of Thomas Price v. William Nelson, executor, and Maria Armistead, executrix of William Armistead.

Debt, £200 St. Filed in General Court. J.M. for plaintiff.

Oct. 7, 1789. Verdict damages £254:9; j. £200 St., value of £266:13:4 Va., and damages assessed.

District Court, Fredericksburg, Law Orders A, 1789–1793, 60.

Fees: Oct., 1789, £5; June, 1791, £5. Account Book, 214, 290.

Thomas Mann Randolph v. Charles Carter.

Debt, on sealed obligation, £532:19, Jan. 6, 1778, damages £10.

Filed in General Court, Apr., 1787. Stafford County. J.M. for plaintiff. (Petition signed.)

Oct., 1787—Oct., 1788. Continued.

Oct. 7, 1789. (District Court) Confessed j. against defendant £532:19 current, payable by £127:15:8.

District Court, Fredericksburg, Record Book 1789–1792, 91–92; Law Orders A, 1789–1793, 59.

Elizabeth Segar, by Richard Segar, guardian v. Joseph Sutton.

Case. Filed in General Court. J.M. for defendant.

Oct. 6, 1789. Dismissed by agreement.

District Court, Fredericksburg, Law Orders A, 1789–1793, 52.

Fee: Apr. 9, 1787, £1:8. Account Book, 106.

Jacob Souther v. William Thompson.

Debt, on sealed obligation, £40:2 current, May 13, 1785. Filed in General Court Oct., 1785. Spotsylvania County. J.M. for plaintiff. (Petition signed.)

Oct., 1786—Oct., 1788. Continued.

Oct. 5, 1789. V.j. £40:2, payable by £26:8 current.

District Court, Fredericksburg, Record Book 1789–1792, 52–53; Law Orders A, 1789–1793, 44.

Fee: Apr. 14, 1786, £2:10. Account Book, 70.

Elliott Vawter v. James Reynolds.

In case. J.M. for defendant.

Oct. 7, 1789. Abated by death of defendant.

District Court, Fredericksburg, Law Orders A, 1789–1793, 58.

Fee: Oct., 1787, £2:10. Account Book, 126.

Vincent Voss v. Rosey Keith.

Detinue, for return of lost slave detained by defendant, value £200. Filed in General Court, Apr., 1786. Spotsylvania County. J.M. for defendant.

Oct., 1786—Oct., 1788. Continued.

Oct. 6, 1789. V.j. for defendant.

District Court, Fredericksburg, Record Book 1789–1792, 82; Law Orders A, 1789–1793, 54.

Fee: Nov. 14, 1786, £2:16. Account Book, 90.

District Court, Northumberland

Joseph Simon v. Richard Lee.

Debt, on note or bill of exchange. J.M. for plaintiff.

Sept. 10, 1789. Former plea relinquished, confessed j. £224:12:10 St., against defendant and Robert Sanford, undersheriff of Westmoreland County, also twelve shillings for costs and charges of protest, interest at 10 per cent from June 7, 1784, to date, thereafter 5 per cent; execution stayed by agreement until Apr. 1 next. District Court, Northumberland, 1789–1792, 30.

Fee: Aug. 5, 1788, £2:8, "old suit." Account book, 164.

District Court, Prince Edward

Walter Brame and James Smith, executors of Melcheredeck Brame v. Humphrey Haley, George Grey, and Joseph Richardson.

Debt, on obligation sealed, Aug. 6, 1772, £40. Halifax County. J.M. for plaintiff. Petition signed.

Feb. 28, 1787. Order on defendant, security confirmed.

Apr., 1787. Payment for security.

1789. V.j. £11:0:7.

District Court, Prince Edward, Records at Large 1789–1792, 42–44.

Philimon Halcombe v. Richard Burks.

Trespass on case for slander, "a rogue . . . stole two negroes of defendant." Damages £500. Filed in General Court, Dec. 30, 1784. Prince Edward County. J.M. for defendant.

1789. V.j. for plaintiff £30.

District Court, Prince Edward, Records at Large 1789–1792, 1.

Fee: Apr., 1785, £2:16. Account Book, 30.

A similar suit for slander was filed by plaintiff against defendant in County Court of Prince Edward in 1783 for calling plaintiff a foreigner, £500 damages. May 17, 1785, v.j. for plaintiff £90; affirmed in District Court on writ of supersedeas, Sept. 9, 1791. It does not appear whether J.M.

was counsel in this cause. District Court, Prince Edward, Records at Large 1789–1792, 421.

William Hall v. Zachariah Robertson.

Debt, on obligation sealed, Apr. 8, 1776, £125 current, payable in one year, penal sum £250. J.M. for defendant.

Dec., 1785. Order against defendant, security made.

1789. Verdict for plaintiff, one penny damages, j. £250, payable by £93:19:8 current, with interest 5 per cent from June 7, 1778.

District Court, Prince Edward, Records at Large 1789–1792, 33.

Fee: Sept., 1789, £1:4. Account Book, 210.

John Dreadnought, lessee of Robert Jones v. John Lewis.

Ejectment. J.M. for defendant.

Sept. 5, 1789. Dismissed by plaintiff. District Court, Prince Edward, Order Book 1789–1792, 37.

Fee: Oct. 7, 1787, £2:6. Account Book, 128.

James McGraw v. John Passnell. (2 cases)

Trespass, assault and battery. J.M. for plaintiff.

Sept. 2, 1789. Dismissed by consent at plaintiff's costs. District Court, Prince Edward, Order Book 1789–1792, 7, 8.

Fee: Dec. 2, 1788, £2:16. Account Book, 180.

County Court, Henrico

Brett Randolph v. David Meade Randolph, administrator of Ryland Randolph, deceased, of the goods and chattels of Ryland unadministrated by Richard Randolph, deceased.

Action in debt. J.M. for plaintiff.

May 8, 1789. J. £150 payable by £81:4:4½.

County Court, Henrico, Order Book III, 630.

Fee: June 16, 1788, £28. Account Book, 152.

1790

DOCUMENTS

Jan. 3
Richmond *to Albert Gallatin*

Acknowledges letter of Dec. 23, 1789; states cannot answer satisfactorily query about Virginia judiciary prior to entering bar; colonial system law and equity one judge; at Revolution separated; reasons, movement to unite; jury trial in early chancery court, elimination; difficulty and advantages of blending common law and chancery. Encloses requested act; condolence for loss by death. NNHi; Henry Adams, *The Life of Albert Gallatin* (Philadelphia, J. B. Lippincott & Co., 1879), 81–82; Oster, *Marshall,* 38–39.

Jan. 18
HENRICO COUNTY, VA. *Trust Deed*

Henry Banks, Richmond, to J.M., 4¼ acres in Richmond, for exoneration and indemnifaction of John Harvie on bond for Banks in suit pending in District Court, Henrico County, against him by Micajah Clark on £250 note. Recorded July 6, 1790. Henrico County, Va., Deed Book 3, 264–66.

Feb. 9
RICHMOND *to William B. Giles*

Acknowledges letter received on 8th with legal papers. Comments on suit against Booker, action of detinue; bills against Call. NN. Misc Papers.

Feb. 29
RICHMOND *to James Mercer*

Listed in Lazare, *Book-Prices* (1926), 819. Present owner unknown.

Mar. 24 *Robert Brooke to Governor of Virginia*

Stating that J.M. refused request of Governor to assist in advising the escheator for the County of Frederick concerning claims of Commonwealth to real estate of late Bryan Martin because engaged for Martin's family. CVSP, IX, 12; Oster, *Marshall,* 33–34.

Mar. 28
RICHMOND *to John Breckenridge*

Recommends Breckenridge as attorney. DLC, Papers of Breckenridge Family, VI.

Apr. 3
RICHMOND *to John Breckenridge*

Vest shown Breckenridge's memorandum in suit against Fore. Blames self for insufficient attention in failing to forward papers; now sent to Charlottesville; hopes for continuance. DLC, Papers of Breckenridge Family, VI.

Apr. 26
RICHMOND *to —— Reid*

Acknowledges receipt of power of attorney; assuming cause will be expeditiously handled. V, Ac. 22528.

Probably *Reid v. Burnsides,* for which fee of £9 received Mar. 10. Account Book, 238.

May 23, *n.p.* *Legal Document*

Agreement between Isaac Hite and Corbin Washington, devisee of John Augustine Washington, settling action over land in Berkeley County, Va., pending in High Court of Chancery. Surveyed by Joist Hite; sold to Patrick Mathews, under whom Washington holds; bond of conveyance from Hite lost. Entry quieting title to be made on payment of £3 per hundred acres with interest from 1738. In handwriting of, and witnessed by, J.M. KyLF, Clark-Hite Coll.

J.M. represented Washington in action against Hite. Fee of £5 received May, 1790. Account Book, 244.

July 14
RICHMOND *to John Conrad Rhuling, Portsmouth*

Concerning trial of libel against the *Pamela* and other legal matters; legal opinion enclosed. Listed in Lazare, *Book-Prices* (1932), 557. Present owner unknown.

Aug. 3
RICHMOND *to Patrick Henry*

Acknowledges letter by Francisco; unable to furnish paper requested, no copy of Randolph will, with Hay. Recollects that no general clause in will subjecting lands to payment of debts; bond creditors can collect as against devises; J.M. opinion general creditors cannot, but doubtful because of contrary view of some of "ablest men and soundest lawyers, includes Mr. Jefferson among these." Sending copy of interlocutory order in Randolph executors and creditors case. VU, Lee Papers; V.

Aug. 3
[RICHMOND] *to Charles Simms, Alexandria*

Received letter from gentleman who does J.M.'s business on eastern shore; judgment against Wilkins and his writ to discharge in money. Inquires for instructions; asks if will take money instead of tobacco, and basis. Bond put into J.M.'s hands by Simms. DLC, Chas. Simms Papers, IV, 34689–90.

Sept. 29
RICHMOND *Recommendation*

Recommendation of Tatham's map of southern divisions of the United States, signed by J.M. Va. Gaz. and G.A., Sept. 29, 1790, 3; also in Same, Oct. 6, 1790, 1.

Nov. 29
RICHMOND *to James Madison*

Letter of introduction of William B. Giles. DLC, James Madison Papers; Oster, *Marshall*, 178.

Dec. 20
RICHMOND *Lottery Trustee*

J.M. trustee in lottery for Nathaniel Twining. V, Virginia Acts, Box Oct., 1790, Chap. XVVI, 31; Hening, Stat., XIII, 174.

n.d., n.p. *to John Breckenridge*

Enclosing papers in case of *Vest v. Fore*, detinue in Prince Edward District Court. J.M.'s fee was dependent on success, a negro or £50; Breckenridge to handle case on same basis. DLC, Papers of Breckenridge Family. Nov. 30, 1790—Dec. 27, 1791. (See herein, Legal Practice, Prince Edward County, Sept. 4, 1790.)

Buckingham County Land

Purchased land in Buckingham County, Va., from Charles Minor Thurston with oral promise of seller to pay off existing mortgage held by Caron de Beaumarchais; failed to do so; litigation ensued. (See herein Jan. 28, 1803.)

The Buckingham County records were largely destroyed in 1868. Evidence of J.M.'s holdings appear in the County Tax Lists, as follows: 1804, 2,792 acres; 1807–1809, 2,255 acres; 1813–1814, 2,255 acres and 390½ acres, both on Randolph's Creek, eighteen miles east of courthouse. V, Buckingham County, Va., Land Book I.

HOUSE OF DELEGATES OF VIRGINIA

Oct. 19 On Committee on Religion; of Privileges and Elections; of Propositions and Grievances; and on Courts of Justice. V, Journal, H.D., 1790, 3–4. (Reprint, Richmond, Thos. W. White, 1828.)

Oct. 21 On committee to bring in bill to amend Act of Descents; carried same to Senate. Same, 7, 136.

Nov. 3 Voted for amendment to resolution disapproving federal Assumption Act as beyond constitutional power of Congress; the amendment approved the act. Amendment defeated. Same, 35, 36. Voted against resolution, which passed. Same, 36. See Beveridge, *Marshall*, II, 65–69. See also Same 38, 44, 141.

Nov. 6 On committee to consider report of committee on revision of laws. Same, 41.

On committee to estimate revenue and needs of state. Same, 43.

Nov. 11 On committee to bring in bill to repeal tax on attorneys, physicians, surgeons, and apothecaries. Same, 51.

Nov. 12 No vote of record on resolution admitting Severn Major as citizen. Same, 52. Nov. 24, same on bill. Same, 85–86.

Nov. 15 On committee to bring in bill repealing tax on clerks of court. Same, 58.

Nov. 19 Voted against resolution for sale of glebe land, excepting privately donated. Resolution defeated. Same, 73–74.

Nov. 22 On committee to draw bill to provide funds for lunatic hospital, Williamsburg. Same, 79–80.

Nov. 24 No vote of record on bill for relief of sheriffs and collectors of revenue. Same, 85.

Nov. 26 On joint committee to examine ballots for election of two members of Privy Council. Same, 90.

Dec. 1 On committee to draw bill concerning sessions of High Court of Chancery. Same, 106. Dec. 2, presented bill. Same, 108.

Dec. 3 Jacquelin Ambler, Treasurer's account. Same, 110–12.

Dec. 6 Revision of acts concerning City of Richmond, etc., ordered to carry to Senate. Same, 116.

Dec. 8 On committee to prepare bill for appointment of persons learned in law to revise Virginia statutes and determine suitable British statutes; former committee on English statutes continued. Same, 121–22.

Dec. 14 No vote of record on bill for relief of Peter Francisco. Same, 131.

Voted for bill limiting tax collection for 1791 to one-third. Passed. Same, 135.

Dec. 15 Voted for amendment to bill for improvement of James River. Passed. Same, 138.

Dec. 18 On committee for bill remitting militia fines since adoption of federal government. Same, 145.

Dec. 20 Voted for agreement with Senate to bill for several lotteries, etc. Passed. Same, 147.

On committee to prepare bill to amend act concerning High Court of Appeals. Same, 148. Dec. 23, presented bill. Same, 153. Dec. 25, passed. Directed to carry bill to Senate. Same, 159.

On committee to prepare bill for reducing revenue tax for 1790. Same, 148. Dec. 24, bill rejected. J.M. on new committee for bill directing proportion of tax for 1790. Same, 156.

Dec. 23 No vote of record on bill to collect arrearages of taxes, Botetourt County. Same, 152.

Dec. 24 On committee to bring in bill for payment of workmen, and for completion of Capitol. Same, 157.

Dec. 27 On committee to bring in bill repealing certain revenue laws. Same, 161.

Dec. 28 On committee to bring in bill for payment to Nicholson for printing and regulating salary of jailer. Journal of Senate. Same, 163. Dec. 29, ordered to carry to Senate. Same, 166.

Dec. 29 On committee to bring in bill for duplicates of certificates and warrants; presented; passed; ordered to carry to Senate. Same, 166.

LEGAL PRACTICE

In the year 1790, J.M. recorded receipt of £1,445:10:6 in legal fees, 329 in number. This represented a substantial increase in income over former years occasioned by a high number of comparatively large fees. Of these eighteen fees over £10; one was for £42, two of £30, and four were in the £20 bracket. Of thirty-one fees for advice, all but four were in the usual £1 bracket.

Of the forty-five fees designated in the category of court appearances and litigated matters, the majority were in Chancery Court proceedings, fifteen, and appeals, eighteen, of which five were appeals in Chancery. The balance was of scattered type. Of particular interest are the nine instances of fees for cases in the Supreme Court of Appeals.

U.S. Circuit Court, Virginia

Nov. 26 J.M., together with Inman Baker, Burwell Starke, and John Wickham, admitted to appear as counsel and attorney in the U.S. Circuit Court, Middle Circuit, held at Williamsburg. U.S. Circuit Court, Va. Order Book I, 4.

Court of Appeals of Virginia

John Pinchback Crump and John Meade, executors of Sarah Crump v. William Dudley and wife, 3 Call 439, 442–45.

Appeal from High Court of Chancery. J. for appellees, reversed. J.M. for appellee.

Will provided for slave to daughter Sarah for life, on her death to son John, with residue clause to four children, including above; John predeceased Sarah. Anne, the surviving daughter of the eldest son William, a day before marriage conveyed her rights in the slave to Sarah, not disclosing the fact to her intended husband. On the death of Sarah, Anne and her husband claimed the slave and increase against Sarah's executor as descending to her father as eldest son, and that deed of sale was invalid as in derogation of marriage. Held, Court inclined to view that slave covered by residue clause, not by intestacy, that sale from Anne was valid.

June 21–22. Heard. Court of Appeals, Va., Order Book II, 1.

June 23. Reversed, bill dismissed. Same, 3.

Samuel Beale v. James Edmundson, 3 Call 446, 446–48.

Adjourned case from General Court. J.M. for plaintiff. Action for goods sold and delivered in 1781; alleged express promise to pay in 1783. Held, although action barred as a book account by act of 1779 to discourage credits and limiting actions based on proof of book account to six months, express promise thereafter with moral obligation as consideration supports action which may be brought within five year statute of limitations.

July 3. Case heard. Court of Appeals Va., Order Book II, 18.

July 7. Ruling that District Court of King and Queen Courthouse enter j. on verdict. Same, 21.

Johnstons v. Meriwether, 3 Call 454, 456–59.

Writ of error denied from judgment to Meriwether on forthcoming bond. J.M. and John Taylor represented Meriwether opposing motion.

Cole obtained j. against Johnston; execution levied by Meriwether, coroner, on slaves; forthcoming bond executed by Johnston for redelivery; condition of bond broken. Meriwether brought action, damages £10, j. rendered for £750. Held, bond to officer instead of judgement creditor valid, not barred by statute, oppressive or uncertain; verdict on collateral bond for more than laid in declaration valid.

June 22. Motion for writ of error to j. District Court, Charlottesville.

Apr. 24, 1790. Continued. Court of Appeals, Va., Order Book II, 2.

June 26, 29, 30, July 1. Continued. Same 7, 11, 13, 15–16.

July 2. Motion overruled. Same, 16.

David Barrett v. Berry Floyd, Archibald Garrison, John Floyd, and John Widgeon, 3 Call 460, 461–63, 463–64.

Appeal from High Court of Chancery. Injunction against j., affirmed. J.M. for appellant.

Barrett and Floyd co-operated in rescue of abandoned vessel under agreement for shares if determined a prize, or what each entitled to for salvage if not. Court of Admiralty determined prize; thereafter Barrett brought action in County Court for greater share based on cargo he saved, recovered. J. enjoined.

May 9, 1788. Decree affirmed, power of equity to enjoin judgments discussed.

July 2, 1790. Heard. Court of Appeals, Va., Order Book II, 17.

July 6. Affirmed. Same, 20.

Fee: Dec., 1785, £5:4 "Barrett adv. Fly, injunction." Account Book, 56.

John Hughes, Sen. v. Henry Clayton and wife Theodosia, administratrix of Anderson Hughes, her late husband, 3 Call 478.

Detinue, appeal from j. District Court of Petersburg, Sept. 22, 1789, against appellant for nine slaves valued £60 to £100 each, and £70 damages. Affirmed. J.M. for appellant.

Contention that appellee should have been nonsuited below for failure to prove administration of the estate, also because gift of slaves to her from her father not by deed.

Held, declaration was on possession of defendant while unmarried and so proved; that in absence of notice, letters of administration need not be proved in detinue case; that alleged gift by father conditioned on marriage to Hughes a proper question for jury.

July 9, 1790. Heard. Court of Appeals, Va., Order Book II, 24.

July 10. Affirmed. Same, 25.

Fee: Nov. 2, 1786, £2:8, Oct., 1789, £4:18. Account Book, 90, 218.

John Syme, Jr. v. Thomas and William Johnston, executors of Richard Johnston, 3 Call 482, 485–87.

Appeal from decree of High Court of Chancery, Nov. 2, 1789, denying injunction against j. General Court for purchase money of land, affirmed.

J.M. and John Taylor for appellant.

Richard Johnston and one Gaines purchased in partnership land leased of College of William and Mary; were refused separate leases; lease to Johnston; agreed division. Johnston's part sold at public sale under will by executor, announcing selling testator's interest only and division; adjoining owner announced claim to part. In General Court action for purchase money buyer agreed to confessed j., thereafter sought injunction claiming hard of hearing, did not know terms and claims, price too high. Thereafter College agreed to separate lease. Held, no fraudulent concealment; purchase confirmed by agreement.

June 30, July 1, 1790. Motion for additional security denied. Court of Appeals, Va., Order Book II, 14–16. *Syme v. Johnston*, 3 Call 453.

Dec. 13. Affirmed. Same, 53.

Fee: Oct., 1789, £5. Account Book, 214.

J.M. mentioned his counselship in this case in *Peyton v. Brooke*, 3 Cranch 92, 94 (1805).

Daniel Ross v. Benjamin Pynes, 3 Call 490, 491–92.

Appeal from High Court of Chancery. Dismissal of injunction and affirmation of verdict, affirmed. J.M. and Inman Baker for appellant.

The High Court of Chancery enjoined a j. against Ross of £500 for slandering title to slaves, at General Court. On retrial the verdict was £1,000; the General Court entered no j. and certified to Chancery that j.

would be against evidence. Chancery dismissed the injunction, entered j. of £500. Affirmed.

Oct. 12, 1789. Opinion in Chancery, 4 Wythe 71.

Dec. 6, 1790. Heard. Court of Appeals, Va., Order Book II, 42.

Dec. 8, 1790. Affirmed. Same, 45.

Fee: Dec., 1790, £7:4. Account Book, 268.

Rev. John Bracken v. The Governors or Visitors of William and Mary College, 3 Call 495, 499–501.

J.M. represented William and Mary College.

Claimed before General Court in mandamus proceeding to reinstate professor, that visitors of College had no power to change course resulting in vacancy.

Case adjourned to Court of Appeals. Held, visitors had such power, and no mandamus lies against eleemosynary institution.

July 8, 1790. Case heard. Court of Appeals, Va., Order Book II, 22.

July 13. Rehearing ordered. Same, 29.

Dec. 7. Case reheard. Same, 43.

Dec. 8. Reversal of order of General Court awarding writ of mandamus to restore Bracken to office of grammar master and professor of humanity. Same, 46.

Apr. 26, 1796. Appeal from judgment of District Court, Williamsburg, denying Bracken relief, May 8, 1794. Continued. Same, Book III, 116.

Nov. 6, 1797. Case submitted. Same, 189.

Nov. 9. J. affirmed. Same, 191.

Fee: Dec., 1790, £20. Account Book, 268.

See *Same v. Same*, 1 Call 139 (1797) refusing arrears of salary. Wickham for Bracken; Randolph for College.

Samuel Beale v. Martin Cockburn, 4 Call 162, 180–195.

Appeal from decree of High Court of Chancery, Mar. 11, 1789.

J.M. and John Wickham for appellant.

Beale, a merchant of Williamsburg, agreed to transmit for collection bills for sterling money owed Cockburn drawn on his brothers in Jamaica. Beale was to pay Cockburn on the basis of £7 in loan office certificates if bills honored. By intermediate transactions, including endorsement of the bills, he managed to collect in part in 1780 after giving extension of time to the payee. The balance was dishonored because stopped by Cockburn. In 1781 he settled with Cockburn for the part collected on an approximate

20 to 1 basis. By that time depreciation scale was 250 to 1. In 1789, Beale sued Cockburn for causing the protest of the bills, and Cockburn brought a suit in chancery in which Beale's action at law was enjoined and judgment had against Beale in what was now specie equivalent of the money collected, based on grounds of delay in collection and breach of agreement by endorsing the bills. Affirmed.

Nov. 25, 1789. Continued. Court of Appeals, Va., Order Book I, 150.

July 5, 1790. Case heard. Same, II, 19.

July 12. Chancery decree of Mar. 11, 1789, against appellant, £1,146:12:3 Va. and enjoining action at law, affirmed. Same, 27.

Fees from "Mr. Beale": Mar. 30, 1788, £20; Mar. 7, 1789, £4:11:8; July 30, 1789, £10; Aug. 5, 1789, £5:12. Account Book, 148, 188, 204, 206.

William Johnston (Johnson), etc. v. William Macon, late sheriff of Hanover, 4 Call 367; 1 Washington 4.

Appeal from j. District Court, Richmond. Sept. 7, 1789.

J.M. represented Macon, who had been sued as sheriff by the creditor in General Court for alleged negligent escape of a debtor; judgment for Macon was affirmed despite some misdirection to the jury.

Dec. 1, 1790. Heard. Court of Appeals, Va., Order Book II, 35.

Dec. 15, 1790. Affirmed. Same, 54.

Daniel and Joseph Dejarnett v. Robert Burton.

Appeal from j. against appellant, District Court, Fredericksburg, Apr. 29, 1790, £556:6:2 Va., payable by £234:16:6. (The proceedings in General and District Courts were as follows:

(Debt, on sealed obligation £556:6:2 Va., Nov. 15, 1787. Filed in General Court, Oct., 1788.

(Oct. 9, 1789. Office j. set aside, case at issue.

(May 2, 1790. [District Court] Confessed j.

(May 8, 1790. Appeal allowed.

(District Court, Fredericksburg, Record Book 1789–1792, 143–45; Law Orders A, 1789–1793, 72, 95.)

J.M. for appellant.

Dec. 14, 1790. Appellant did not appear; case submitted, affirmed. Court of Appeals, Va., Order Book II, 50–51.

Fee: Mar., 1789, £2:10. Account Book, 188.

Francis Eppes v. Saint George Tucker, 4 Call 346.

Adjourned case from High Court of Chancery. J.M. for plaintiff.

Defendant, owner of schooner and tobacco in Virginia in 1779, loaned plaintiff six hogsheads of tobacco of cargo to be transported to Europe to be sold and invested in specified merchandise and returned, one-half of proceeds to defendant for freight and risk. Schooner went to Surinam, South America, because of risk; sold tobacco and bought merchandise. On return voyage fell in with British cruisers, ran aground to avoid capture; fought off British; saved cargo, but lost ship. Plaintiff notified; thereafter deposited notes with defendant for loan, too large in amount; asked for payment or tobacco for surplus; received back entire notes from defendant. Plaintiff claimed agreement not canceled by receiving back notes, that entitled to one-half saved merchandise from proceeds of the six hogsheads; defendant claimed canceled; if not should deduct freight, salvage cost, and contribution for loss of vessel.

Held, not canceled; defendant accountable to plaintiff for share of merchandise saved which was purchased by proceeds of the six hogsheads, full freight and reasonable salvage to be charged, but exempt from average contribution for loss of vessel or other goods.

The case was first heard before the Court of Appeals as originally constituted by the Chancellors, Judges of the General Court, and of Admiralty, who could not agree.

Apr. 29, Nov. 4, 1784, May 6, 1785. Continued. Court of Appeals, Va., Order Book I, 36, 46, 54.

May 3, 1786. Heard. Same, 93.

Apr. 30, Oct. 30, 1787. Continued for rehearing. Same, 102, 106.

May 1, 1788. Continued. Same, 119.

Thereafter it was heard by the Court of Appeals as constituted a separate court under act of Dec. 22, 1788.

June 22, 1790. Heard. Court of Appeals, Va., Order Book II, 2.

June 24, 1790. Opinion. Same, 4.

Fee: Dec., 1787, £7. Account Book, 38.

John Groves v. Francis Graves. 1 Washington 1

Appeal from High Court of Chancery Aug. 13, 1790, j. against appellant on contract to deliver certificates for mortgage on land. J.M. for appellant.

Nov. 27, 1790. Continued. Court of Appeals, Va., Order Book II, 33.

Dec. 8, 9. Heard. Same, 46.

Dec. 18. Reversed. Contract not usurious in calling for repayment by twenty shillings certificates for every twenty-six pence specie advanced, as such was the market; penalty of certificates taken at half value improper; value at date deliverable and not at time of trial. Agreed by parties certificates at Nov. 1, 1787, date of delivery, twenty-eight pence half penny and sum owed £285 specie.

Injunction against j. perpetual if paid, otherwise land sold. Same, 59–60.

Fee: Dec., 1790, £14. Account Book, 268.

John Hord and William Waring, executors of Ambrose Hord v. John Upshaw, Thomas Roane, and James Upshaw.

Adjourned case from High Court of Chancery. J.M. for appellees.

Oct. 30, 1783. Continued. Court of Appeals, Va., Order Book II, 33.

May 1, 1784. Continued. Same, 37.

May 3, 1784. Continued, depositions, wills admitted. Same, 38.

Nov. 2, 1784. Continued. Same, 39, 44, 45.

Nov. 4, 1784. Sent back for proper parties to be added. Same, 45.

(No further record shown in Court of Appeals.)

Fee: June, 1790, £1:8. Account Book, 250.

Peter Jones, executor of Peter Jones, Jun. v. John Verrell, Jun., and Martha, his wife.

Appeal from decree High Court of Chancery, June 2, 1789, £3,-327:17:4. J.M. for appellant.

July 9, 1790. By consent of parties, oath of Burwell Starke, j. reversed to £1,980, costs and lawyers' fees. Court of Appeals, Va., Order Book II, 24.

Fee: June, 1789, £5. Account Book, 202.

High Court of Chancery

Thomas Walker v. Nicholas Cabell, executor and devisee of Thomas Cabell, Edward Carter, Alexander Trent, and John Wilkinson.

Bill in equity, High Court of Chancery, signed by J.M. as attorney for petitioner. VU, Page and Walker MSS, Dep. No. 3898.

Bill alleges partnership agreement, Dec. 28, 1770, to erect and put in repair furnace forge, grist and saw mill, and buildings to make pig iron and castings; one-third Wilkinson, one-sixth others; Wilkinson to pay in £1,000, others £500; Wilkinson manager. When discovered such condition did not operate at profit, agreed to complete on credit of company. Petitioner paid £678:18; works never paid profit, Wilkinson in advance to company; scheme abandoned for many years; prayer that works be sold and accounting made.

Fees: May, 1790, "final chancery," £3: Aug. 3, 1790, £4:4. Account Book, 256.

(See herein Feb. 23, 1793, concerning attachment on Wilkinson; also *Wilkinson adv. Trents,* Nov. 8, 1787, £7:4. Account Book, 134.)

Caveats

June *Fairfax v. Pendleton,* £28. Account Book, 250. (Case records not found.)

District Court, Accomack and Northampton

Griffin Stith, Jr., v. John Stratton, Sr.

Detinue. J.M. for plaintiff.

Oct. 15, 1789. Continued. District Court, Accomack and Northampton, Order Book 1789–1797, 15.

May 15, 1790. Continued; commission for depositions. Same, 40. No further record.

Fee: Nov. 18, 1789, £11:16. Account Book, 222.

District Court, Augusta

Daniel Joseph v. Robert Bratton.

Writ of supersedeas to j. County Court, Augusta, against Joseph and Jasper Solling, his security, May 18, 1785. J.M. for defendant.

Apr. 6, 1790. Abated by death of defendant. District Court, Augusta, Order Book 1789–1797, 39.

Fee: Mar. 3, 1787, £2:16. Account Book, 100.

George Keisel v. Andrew Donnally.

In case. Appeal filed in General Court from j. County Court, Augusta, Aug. 22, 1787, £110:11, granted on motion against appellant on common bail bond. Reversed. J.M. for appellant.

Oct., 1787, through Nov., 1789. Continuances in General Court.

Apr., 1790. Continuance in District Court, Staunton.

Sept. 3, 1790. Reversed; wrong remedy pursued; action by Donnally was based on common bail for Keizel, not as security on note, bond, or obligation. District Court, Augusta, Order Book 1789–1793, 107–108; Same, Order Book 1789–1797, 42, 56.

Fee: Mar. 8, 1788, £2:20. Account Book, 146.

John McElheny v. Thomas Hughes.

Case. J.M. for plaintiff, petition signed by J.M.

Action in General Court, Oct., 1786, on promissory note of Apr. 2, 1782, £50 specie or hemp at 35 shillings per hundred.

Continued in General Court successively through Oct., 1788.

Apr., 1789; Sept. 4, 1790; Apr. 2, 1790. District Court, continuances.

Sept. 1, 1790. V.j. £70:16:8. District Court, Augusta, Order Book 1789–1793, 81; Same, Order Book 1789–1797, 17.

Robert Page v. William Allen.

Case. J.M. for defendant, petition signed by Edmund Randolph.

Oct., 1784. Action filed in General Court on agreement of Apr. 15, 1783, defendant to deliver at Richmond one ton merchantable hemp on Oct. 1 following, penalty two tons same, on failure five tons of same, damages £50; Page to pay Allen all money hemp fetches less £30 and interest.

Jan., 1785. *Non assumpsit* (Marshall). Continued in General Court through Apr., 1788.

Sept., 1789. Continued, in District Court.

Apr. 2, 1790. V.j. £39:15. District Court, Augusta, Order Book 1789–1793, 34; Same, Order Book 1789–1797, 24.

Fee: Oct., 1784, £0:18, "in part." Account Book, 18.

District Court, Franklin

Joseph Poindexter v. James Gatewood.

In case. J.M. for defendant.

Apr. 17, 1790. Commission to plaintiff, deposition of Jerman Baker, John Gatewood, and Micajah Clark of District of Kentucky; of William Meredith about to move to Kentucky. District Court, Franklin, Order Book I, 1789–1793, 53.

Sept. 23, 1790. V.j. for defendant. Same, 125.

Fee: Apr. 14, 1788, £2:8 "in part." Account Book, 152.

Guy Smith v. Bourne Price.

Assault and battery. J.M. for defendant.

Sept. 24, 1790. Discontinued by plaintiff. District Court, Franklin, Order Book I, 1789–1793, 129.

Fee: Sept. 6, 1785. £2:10, "finished." Account Book, 48.

Superior (District) Court, Frederick

William Askew v. Francis Willis.

Appeal from Berkeley County Court, j. Mar., 1787, £96:10. J.M. for appellant.

Apr. 23, 1790. Affirmed.

Superior Court, Frederick, Order Book 1789–1793, 87.
Fee: Jan., 1791, £5. Account Book, 272.

Duncan Campbell v. Thomas Reed.
Debt. (two cases) J.M. for defendant.
Apr. 20, 1790. V.j. for plaintiff £233, payable by £116:10 in each.
Superior Court, Frederick, Order Book 1789–1793, 60, 61.
Fee: May 4, 1785, £2:10. Account Book, 36.

Denny Fairfax v. David Hunter.
Three caveats. J.M. for plaintiff.
Apr. 17, 1790. Continued for hearing. Superior Court, Frederick, Order Book 1789–1793, 48.
Apr. 24, 1790. Adjourned to General Court for novelty. Same, 102.
Sept. 1, 1791. Return of General Court, dismissed. Same, 207–208.
Sept. 6, 1791. Caveats, adjourned to General Court for novelty. Same, 241 (no further record).
(For ruling of General Court, see herein 1791, Legal Practice, General Court.)

Denny Fairfax v. Robert Stephen.
Caveat. J.M. for plaintiff.
Apr. 17, 1790. Continued for hearings. Superior Court, Frederick, Order Book 1789–1793, 47.
Apr. 24, 1790. Adjourned to General Court for novelty. Same, 102.
Sept. 1, 1791. Return of General Court, dismissed. Same, 207–208.
Sept. 6, 1791. Caveats, adjourned to General Court for novelty. Same, 241 (no further record).
(For ruling of General Court, see herein 1791, Legal Practice, General Court.)

John Fitzgerald v. George Noble.
Debt. J.M. for defendant.
Sept. 7, 1789. Confessed j., £532 Va., payable by £237. Superior Court, Frederick, Order Book 1789–1793, 34.
Fee: Aug., 1786, "2 suits habeas corpus," £4:8. Account Book, 80.

Frederick Havely v. Gerret Hammersly.
Debt, for £45 Md. of value of £36 Va., Berkeley County. J.M. for plaintiff.

Aug. 31, 1787. Declaration filed in General Court. (Printed declaration filled in and signed by J.M. VU, McGregor Libr., Marshall Family Papers.)

Feb. 29, 1788. Special bail and common order on defendant.

Apr., 1788. Plea payment.

Oct., 1788, Sept., 1789. Continued.

Apr. 22, 1790. V.j. for plaintiff, £45 Md. of value of £36 Va., payable by £13:9:4 current.

Superior Court, Frederick, Order Book 1789–1793, 76.

John Hawkins' Executors v. Charles Smith's Executors.

Debt. J.M. for plaintiff.

Sept. 7, 1789. Continued. Superior Court, Frederick, Order Book 1789–1793, 30.

Apr. 20, 1790. V.j. for plaintiff, £688, payable by £128:16. Same, 65.

Fees: Feb., 1792 "Hawkins ex'r adv. Smith," £3. Account Book, 314.

Richard Henderson, etc. v. William Brooke; Same v. William Brooke and Magnes Tate.

Case. (Two cases) J.M. for defendant.

Apr. 17, 1790. Dismissed by consent. Superior Court, Frederick, Order Book 1789–1793, 52, 57.

Fee: Oct. 5, 1786, £2:8. Account Book, 84.

David Hunter v. Joseph Thompson.

Caveat. 403 acres, Hampshire County, North River of Great Cacapon. J.M. for Thompson.

Apr. 17, 1790. Continued for hearing. Superior Court, Frederick, Order Book 1789–1793, 46.

Apr. 20, 1790. Heard, adjourned to General Court. Same, 69.

Sept. 1, 1791. Mandate of General Court, caveats dismissed. Same, 207–208.

Fee: Oct. 10, 1788, £5. Account Book, 168.

David Kennedy, Samuel Reid, and George Riley v. Beard's Executor.

Appeal from j. Berkeley County Court Mar., 1787, j. £241:7:6, payable £120:13:9. J.M. for appellants.

Apr. 23, 1790. Reversed, defective replevin bond. Superior Court, Frederick, Order Book 1789–1793, 91.

Fee: Apr. 12, 1787, £2:5. Account Book, 106.

George Lewis v. William Richardson.

In case. J.M. for defendant.

Sept. 7, 1790. V.j. for defendant, 150 pounds tobacco assessed.
Superior Court, Frederick, Order Book 1789–1793, 127.
Fee: Oct., 1787, £2:10. Account Book, 126.

Lessee of James M. Lingan v. John Dawson.

Ejectment, two messuages, two plantations, and 220 acres, Hampshire County. J.M. for defendant.

Sept. 7, 1787. Declaration filed in General Court. (Original of complaint endorsed "not guilty, Mar." VU, Fairfax and Lee Family MSS.)

Sept. 5, 1789. Depositions. Superior Court, Frederick, Order Book 1789–1793, 26.

Apr. 21, 1790. V.j. for plaintiff. Same, 70.

Fee: Apr. 5, 1788, £3:16. Account Book, 150.

Michael McKewn v. William and John McKeen.

Debt. J.M. for defendants.

Apr. 20, 1790. V.j. for plaintiff £400 Pa., value of £320 Va., payable £120 Va. Superior Court, Frederick, Order Book 1789–1793, 66.

Fee: Mar. 30, 1788, £2:10. Account Book, 148.

Robert Throckmorton v. Richard Gray.

Appeal. J.M. for appellant.

Apr. 23, 1790. Abated by death of appellant. Superior Court, Frederick, Order Book 1789–1793, 92.

Fee: Feb. 4, 1789, £2:10. Account Book, 186.

Lewis Walker, executor of Jolliffe v. Tavenor Beale, executor of John Hite.

Debt. J.M. for defendant.
Apr. 20, 1790. V.j. for plaintiff, £1,800 payable by £900.
Superior Court, Frederick, Order Book 1789–1793, 63.
Fee: Apr. 1, 1786, £2:10. Account Book, 68.

Edwin Young v. John Allen.

In case. J.M. for plaintiff.
Apr. 20, 1790. Dismissed by consent.
Superior Court, Frederick, Order Book 1789–1793, 61.
Fee: Oct. 10, 1785, £1:10. Account Book, 52.

Edwin Young v. Mounce Bird.

In case. J.M. for plaintiff.
Sept. 2, 1790. Dismissed by agreement.

Superior Court, Frederick, Order Book 1789–1793, 114.
Fee: Oct. 13, 1788, £2:10. Account Book, 170.

District Court, Fredericksburg

William Peachey et al., executors of Henry Armistead v. John Spotswood and William Fontaine, executors of Bowles Armistead.

Debt, on sealed bill of testator, acknowledging 16,700 pounds net crop tobacco Fredericksburg or Falmouth inspection and obligating heirs, etc., to pay 33,556 pounds, damages £5. Filed in District Court Apr., 1789. John Minor for plaintiff. J.M. for defendants (probable).

May 1, 1790. V.j. 33,556 pounds, payable by 3,394 pounds from property of estate.

District Court, Fredericksburg, Law Orders A, 1789–1793, 87.

Fee: Sept., 1795, £5. Account Book, 420.

Samuel H. Bradford and Jno. W. Willis, appellants v. Machen Boswell.

Appeal from j. Court of Spotsylvania County, Aug. 7, 1787, against appellant £773:6, payable by £386:13. J.M. for appellants.

Oct. 7, 1790. Affirmed. District Court, Fredericksburg, Law Orders A, 1789–1793, 178.

Fee: Apr., 1791, "Bradford and Wills appeals," £2:8. Account Book, 282.

John Conner and Thomas Latham v. Robert Spratt.

Debt, appeal from Court of Culpeper County, Nov. 22, 1787; action by appellee against appellant, j. £146:17:2½ and costs. Filed in General Court Apr., 1788. J.M. for appellee.

Apr., 1788—Nov., 1789. Continued.

Oct. 1, 1790. Affirmed.

District Court, Fredericksburg, Record Book 1789–1792, 223–26; Law Orders A, 1789–1793, 137.

Fee: May, 1788, £2:10. Account Book, 156.

Commonwealth of Virginia at instance of Gavin Lawson & Co. v. James, Robert, and Lawrence Slaughter, and William Ball.

Debt, £10,000. J.M. probably for one or all Slaughters; John Minor for John M. Bell and French Strother, sureties.

May 1, 1790. Bell and Strother against whom writ of enquiry pending for failure of appearance of defendants allowed to plead for defendants, condition performed.

May 2, 1790. Bond for defendants filed, plea against securities set aside.

Oct. 2, 1790. V.j. £10,000, discharged by £214:18:6.

District Court, Fredericksburg, Law Orders A, 1789–1793, 94, 99, 144.

Fee: June, 1790, £2:8. Account Book, 252.

James Craig v. Robert Hart, administrator of John Marshall, Louisa County, Va.

Action to recover £762:10, advanced to Marshall Dec. 12, 1776, to purchase tobacco on designated account, promise to repay in crop tobacco. Filed General Court, 1785. J.M. for defendant.

Oct., 1785. Not assumed; fully administered.

Apr., 1786—Oct., 1788. Continued.

Oct. 7, 1790. (District Court) J. for plaintiff, £1,016:13:4.

District Court, Fredericksburg, Record Book 1789–1792, 377–81; Law Orders A, 1789–1793, 41, 185.

Fee: Apr., 1790, £5. Account Book, 242.

John Crutchfield v. Edward Herndon.

Detinue. J.M. for defendant (probable).

Oct. 8–9, 1789. Jury disagreed.

Oct. 4, 1790. Dismissed, agreed between parties.

District Court, Fredericksburg, Law Orders A, 1789–1793, 71, 73, 153.

Fee: Apr. 19, 1787, £2:8. Account Book, 110.

Culpeper Justices at instance of John Thompson and Jane, his wife v. John Slaughter et al., administrators of Thomas Howison.

Action on obligation sealed, June 16, 1769, £8,000, Va., executed by Slaughter, *et al.*, to sitting members of Court of Culpeper County, for not administering estate according to law. Filed in General Court Oct., 1787. James Monroe for plaintiffs, J.M. for Slaughter (probable).

Oct. 4, 1790. V.j. for plaintiff, £8,000, Va., payable by £1,610:12:2 as assessed by jury.

District Court, Fredericksburg, Record Book 1789–1792, 261–71, Law Orders A, 1789–1793, 154.

Fees: Oct., 1787, £2:10, "Slaughter pd on"; Dec., 1788, £2:10. Account Book, 130, 180.

William Edgar v. Daniel Grinnan.

Appeal. J.M. for appellant.

Apr. 9, 1790. Dismissed, parties agreed.

District Court, Fredericksburg, Law Orders A, 1789–1793, 75.

Fee: Dec. 4, 1786, "Edgar v. Greenhil," £1:4. Account Book, 92.

John Elam v. Burges Ball and Elam Frazer.

Debt. £200 St. and ten shillings, six pence, 1775, probably protested bill of exchange. Filed in General Court. J.M. for Frazer (probable).

Oct. 2, 1789. Continued.

Oct. 8, 1790. V.j. for plaintiff £200 St. and 10 per cent per annum from June 22, 1775, and ten shillings, six pence Gr. Br., payable by £290 St. with interest at 5 per cent from date of j. until paid.

District Court, Fredericksburg, Law Orders A, 1789–1793, 31, 188.

Fee: Oct., 1790, £3. Account Book, 260.

Robert Gilchrist, assignee of Benjamin Tompkins v. John B., William, and Nicholas Fitzhugh, executors of Henry Fitzhugh.

Debt, on note £35, 1773, filed in General Court, 1787, King George County. J.M. for defendants.

Jan., Feb., Apr., Oct., 1788. Court orders on defendants.

May 6, 1790. Heard in District Court. Writ of enquiry set aside, plea *non assumpsit,* v.j. £35 and £17:10 damages, to be levied against goods of testator, if insufficient costs against defendants.

District Court, Fredericksburg, Record Book 1789–1792, 171; Law Orders A, 1789–1793, 109.

Fee: Apr.–May, 1792, £5. Account Book, 322.

George Gray v. Henry Alexander Ashton.

Action for deficiency in land sold to plaintiff, Loudon County, on Horse Pen Run, £200 owing, breach of agreement to convey further land. Filed Apr. 1, 1789, King George County. J.M. for defendant.

Sept., 1789. Answer by J.M., not assume.

May 4, 1790. Confessed j. £110 in full for deficiency.

District Court, Fredericksburg, Record Book 1789–1792, 165–67; Law Orders A, 1789–1793, 66, 102.

Fee: Oct., 1789, £1:16:8. Account Book, 216.

Peter Hansbrough v. William Smallwood.

Ejectment, undivided one-third 500 acres, King George County. Damages, £100. Filed in General Court, Apr., 1786. Answer, not guilty, J. T. Mercer. King George County. J.M. for defendant.

Oct., 1786—Sept., 1789. Continued.

May 8, 1790. (District Court) V.j. for plaintiff; writ stayed pending determination of case in High Court of Chancery, "*Mercer v. Smallwood.*"

District Court, Fredericksburg, Record Book 1789–1792, 213–15; Law Orders A, 1789–1793, 49, 63, 125.

Fee: Mar. 3, 1790, £17. Account Book, 236.

See *Representatives of William Smallwood v. John F. Mercer and Peter Hansborough*, 1 Washington 290 (herein 1794, Legal Practice), wherein Smallwood's claim to land under contract was denied, affirming dismissal of bill by High Court of Chancery, which would result in judgment for plaintiff in this case.

John Hindman & Co. v. Burgess Ball.

Assumpsit, on protested bill of exchange drawn on London, England, Jan. 6, 1776, £100 St., damages £100 with 10 per cent interest from 1776; nine shillings, three pence protest charges. Filed in General Court Apr., 1788. Culpeper County. J.M. for plaintiff. (Petition signed.)

Oct., 1788, J. Monroe receipt of payment indicates was co-counsel.

Sept. 30—Oct. 1, 1790. (District Court) V.j. for plaintiff; £100:9:3 with 10 per cent interest on £100 from Jan., 1776, payable by £177:14:9 St.

District Court, Fredericksburg, Record Book 1789–1792, 220–23; Law Orders A, 1789–1793, 133, 136.

William Howe, merchant, Falmouth, Stafford County v. Daniel Triplett.

Action for malicious attachment alleging absconding, destruction of credit and business. Filed in General Court Oct., 1786. Stafford County. Baker for plaintiff.

May 4, 1790. Writ of enquiry set aside. V.j. for plaintiff; damages £300.

Also Davenport and Triplett v. William Howe.

Appeal from order of Stafford County Court, Aug., 1786, attachment sued out by appellant on grounds appellee absconding, quashed.

Apr., 1787—Nov., 1789. Continued.

May 6, 1790. (District Court) Affirmed, damages £5, or 1,000 pounds tobacco.

J.M. was attorney in this controversy, probably for Triplett.

District Court, Fredericksburg, Record Book 1789–1792, 167–70, 175–76; Law Orders A, 1789–1793, 105, 110.

Fees: May, 1790, £2:16; July, 1790, £4:3:2; Sept., 1790, £3:16. Account Book, 246, 254, 260.

Joseph James v. Benjamin Lillard.

Case, libel. J.M. for defendant.

May 7–8, 1790. V.j. for plaintiff, one penny damages.

District Court, Fredericksburg, Law Orders A, 1789–1793, 117, 119.

Fee: Oct., 1788, £2:10. Account Book, 170.

James Johnston v. William Fauntelroy Gray.

Case. Filed in General Court. J.M. for plaintiff.

Oct. 3, 1789. Referred by consent to arbitrators, award to be binding, arbitrators authorized to proceed ex parte if either party not appear on notice.

Oct. 8, 1790. J. on award for defendant.

District Court, Fredericksburg, Law Orders A, 1789–1793, 34, 196.

Fee: Oct., 1789, £0:18. Account Book, 216.

James Monroe v. Benjamin Johnston.

Case, on account for goods and merchandise, £400, damages £200. Filed in General Court Apr., 1788. J.M. for defendant.

May 8, 1790. Consent j. for plaintiff £381:14:9; agreed that adjustments defendant can make appear to Lovell, gent., within twenty days allowed against j.

District Court, Fredericksburg, Record Book 1789–1792, 210–11; Law Orders A, 1789–1793, 210.

Fee: Apr., 1785, £2:10. Account Book, 34.

Oxley and Hancock v. John Short.

Assumpsit, on two bills of exchange drawn by Short, merchant of Falmouth, Stafford County, on London drawee, Aug. 19, 1785, and Jan. 5, 1786, each £700, refused and protested. Damages £2,000. Filed Apr., 1789, J. Minor for plaintiff. King George County. J.M. for defendant.

May 7, 1790. V.j. for plaintiff £1,040:14:9.

Fredericksburg District Court, Record Book 1789–1792; Law Orders 1789–1793, 115.

Fee: Nov., 1789, £7. Account Book, 222. Also Oct., 1789, "Oxley and Hancock," £14. Account Book, 220.

John Peyton and Thomas Dixon, executors of John Dixon v. John Whitaker Willis.

Debt, (two cases) on sealed obligations, £1,146:10 Va., Aug. 6, 1788, and £487:19:2 Va., July 15, 1787. Filed Apr. term, 1789, John T. Brooke for plaintiff. Spotsylvania County. J.M. for plaintiff. Monroe mentioned.

May 3, 1790. Abated as to Peyton by death. Confessed j. for Dixon, £1,146:10 Va., payable by £573:5, and £487:19:2 Va., payable by £243:7.

District Court, Fredericksburg, Record Book 1789–1792, 147–52; Law Orders A, 1789–1793, 96.

Fees: Nov., 1792, £4:10; May, 1793, £0:10. Account Book, 342, 360.

Alexander Spotswood v. William Walker.

Appeal. J.M. for appellee.

Apr. 29, 1790. Dismissed, appellant not prosecuting.

District Court, Fredericksburg, Law Orders A, 1789–1793, 76.

Fee: Apr., 1790, £5. Account Book, 246.

French Strother v. Layton Yancey.

Appeal from j. Court of Culpeper County, Mar. 22, 1787, allowing *scire facias* against Strother security on j. obtained by Yancey against James Gray, Feb. 1, 1783, in same court, 8,000 pounds crop tobacco of Fredericksburg and costs payable by 4,000 pounds tobacco, also 215 pounds tobacco and fifteen shillings or 150 pounds of tobacco as costs, representing difference in exchange by Yancey of stud horse, the property of the public, for a horse of Gray's. Strother claimed failure of Yancey to account for proceeds of sale of certificates and of horse received. Appeal filed in General Court Apr., 1787. J.M. for Yancey.

Apr., 1787—Nov., 1789. Continued.

Oct. 6, 1790. (District Court) J. affirmed, appellant assessed damages for retarding execution.

Sept. 30, 1791. On motion Yancey obtained j. for 13,722 pounds crop tobacco and £14:1:2, the penalty of bond on *fiere facias*, payable by 6,861 pounds crop tobacco and £7:0:7, negro and horse having been seized on execution.

District Court, Fredericksburg, Record Book 1789–1792, 302–305, 554. Law Orders A, 1789–1793, 164, 275.

Fee: Apr., 1790, £1:8. Account Book, 240.

John Wiley v. Thomas Towles, executor of Nicholas Lewis.

Debt. J.M. for defendant.

Oct. 2, 1789. Continued.

May 4, 1790. Continued by plaintiff; commission to plaintiff to examine witnesses *de bene esse*; motion by defendant to dismiss if plaintiff fails to give security for costs in sixty days. (No further record.)

District Court, Fredericksburg, Law Orders A, 1789–1793, 34, 104.

Fee: Oct., 1789, £3. Account Book, 216.

Nathaniel Williams v. John Frisbie and Original Young, executors of John Rolls, Sr., executor of John Rolls, Jr.

Action in case. J.M. for plaintiff.

Oct. 3, 1789. Continued.

May 3, 1790. Referred by consent to arbitrators, award to be made j.

District Court, Fredericksburg, Law Orders A, 1789–1793, 36, 106.

Fee: Oct., 1789, £1:8. Account Book, 216.

Robert Wilson v. Robert Hart, administrator of John Marshall, deceased, of Louisa County.

Assumpsit. Breach of contract, Dec. 13, 1776, £1,600 advanced on agreement to lay out in tobacco or other staple articles to be delivered by planters, commission to be paid. Damages, £1,000. Filed in General Court Oct., 1787. J.M. for plaintiff. (Petition signed.)

Apr., Oct., 1788. Continued.

May 6, 1790. (District Court) V.j. for plaintiff £611:10½.

District Court, Fredericksburg, Record Book 1789–1792, 185–88; Law Orders A, 1789–1793, 112.

Fee: Dec., 1789, £4:16. Account Book, 226.

District Court, Northumberland

Aminidab Seekright, lessee of Merryman Payne v. Francis George.

Ejectment, two messuages and two gardens and 450 acres, premises Richard Merryman devised to grandson, plaintiff herein. J.M. for defendant.

Apr. 10, 1790. V.j. for plaintiff, damages one penny, possession awarded as of Dec. 25 next. District Court, Northumberland, Order Book 1789–1792, 72.

Fee: Dec., 1785, £8 (?). Account Book, 56.

Thomas Yerby v. Thomas Taff.

Upon an appeal. Nature of case not known. J.M. for plaintiff.

The only record available is of repeated continuances from Apr. 2, 1790, through Apr. 1, 1796. District Court, Northumberland, Order Book 1789–1793, 38, 139, 156, 182; Same, Order Book 1793–1802, 10, 56, 80, 109.

Yerby died sometime before Sept. 1, 1801. Same, 393.

Fee: Feb. 8, 1790, £7; Mar. 1, 1790, £2:5. Account Book, 232, 236.

John Fowler, surviving obligee of John and George Fowler v. Richard Parker, and Henry S. Redman, security for his appearance.

Debt. J.M. for defendant.

Apr. 7, 1790. Plea of Redman withdrawn. Confessed j. against both, £130 current money as in declaration alleged, payable by £65:0:10½ with legal interest from June 8, 1773. District Court, Northumberland, Order Book 1789–1793, 64.

Fee: Apr. 6, 1787, £2:16. Account Book, 104.

Walter Jones and John Shearman Woodcock, executors of William Flood v. Richard Lee.

Debt. (Seven cases) J.M. for plaintiff.

Sept. 3, 1789. Undertaking for defendant; j. at rules against defendant and security set aside; plea, payment. Continued. District Court, Northumberland, Order Book 1789–1793, 12–15.

Sept. 7, 1790. J. for plaintiff in seven cases: £600, Va., payable by £300 with interest from Apr. 1, 1773; £600 payable by £109:13:6 Va., with interest on £300 from Apr. 1, 1776; £600 Va., payable by £300 with interest from Apr. 1, 1774; £600 Va., payable by £100 with interest from Apr. 1, 1775; £120 Va., payable by £60 with interest from Apr. 1, 1774; £600, payable by £30 with interest from Apr. 1, 1776; £30 Va., payable by £15 with interest from Apr. 1, 1777. Same, 92–93.

Sept. 9, 1790. One of js. set aside and amended to £600 Va., payable by £86:16:9 with interest on £300 from Apr. 1, 1776, until Sept. 7, 1790; thereafter on £86:16:9. Same, 102.

Fee: Sept. 23, 1788, £2:10. Account Book, 166.

District Court, Prince Edward

James Edmundson v. Obediah Hunt and Benjamin Morris.

Debt, on penal bill sealed, Jan. 12, 1786, £100 current payable Mar. 10, 1787, by £120, penal sum £240. Buckingham County. J.M. for plaintiff. (Petition signed.)

Feb. 28, 1787. Order against Morris and security; *capias* against Hunt.

Apr., 1787. Continued.

Oct., 1787. Payment by security, defendant arrested.

Apr., 1790. Special bail and payment. V.j. not paid, damages one penny; j. £240, payable by £120.

District Court, Prince Edward, Records at Large 1789–1792, 94–95.

Creid Haskins v. Garrard Ellyson.

Appeal from j. £127:3 in attachment by Ellyson of four slaves of Haskins in County Court of Cumberland, May 2, 1787, reimbursement of payment as security for Haskins and Mann of debt j. against them by John S. Langhorn, Apr. 26, 1785, £26:10, payable by £130:2. J.M. for appellee.

June 1, 1787. J. on attachment affirmed. Appeal bond filed.

Sept. 4, 1790. Affirmed.

V, District Court, Prince Edward, Records at Large 1789–1792, 203–204; Same, Order Book 1789–1792, 119.

Fee: Apr., 1788, £2:16. Account Book, 152.

Edward Robertson v. William Thomas Jr., and John Hobson, Jr., John Clarke, Edward Dillon, Crud Haskin, and Denny Hatcher.

Trespass, assault and battery, beat and bruised, damages £1,500. Cumberland County. J.M. for defendant. (Henry for plaintiff.)

Sept., 1789. Conditional j. arrested; capias.

Oct., 1789. Confirmed.

Apr., 1790. Satisfaction as to Thomas Hobson, others arrested.

Sept., 1790. V.j. against Thomas and John Hobson, and John Clarke £45; other defendants acquitted.

Also *Field Robertson v. Same.*

Trespass, assault and battery.

Sept., 1790. V.j. against John Hobson and John Clarke £18.

District Court, Prince Edward, Records at Large 1789–1792, 282, 284.

Fee: Apr. 9, 1787, £6 (with *Ransom v. Same*). Account Book, 106.

Phenehas Thomas v. Anne Price.

Appeal from j. in detinue County Court of Cumberland, Aug. 20, 1780, against appellant for return of five slaves lost by appellee and detained by appellant, one man valued at £100, two at £50 each, one woman at £100, one at £50, plus £30 damages. Filed in General Court. J.M. for appellee. (Samuel Anderson was attorney for defendant below, and John Nicholas for plaintiff below.)

Sept. 5, 1790. Appellant did not appear. Affirmed on record.

District Court, Prince Edward, Records at Large 1789–1792, 208–209.

Fee: Oct., 1788, £2:10. Account Book, 168.

James Vest v. Joseph Fore.

Detinue, for four slaves, three women, one man, £100 each, delivered to defendant and detained after demand for return, 1786. Prince Edward County. J.M. for plaintiff. (Petition signed.)

Nov., 1788. Order on defendant and security.

Sept. 1789. Special bail, order for appearance.

Apr., 1790. Continued by plaintiff; at issue.

Sept., 1790. V. j. for plaintiff, man £75, women £80, £75, and £70, and damages (no amount stated).

District Court, Prince Edward, Records at Large 1789–1792, 265–66.

County Court, Henrico

Carter Braxton v. Samuel Beale.

Action on case. J.M. for defendant.

May 6, 1788. Submitted to arbitration.

County Court, Henrico, Order Book III, 308.

Mar. 2, 1790. Dismissed by agreement. Same, IV, 171.

Fee: May 4, 1789, £4:4. Account Book, 196.

Other fees of Beale, Mar. 29, 1788, £20; July 30, 1789, £10. Account Book, 148, 204.

1791

DOCUMENTS

Jan. 4
Richmond *Deed*

James Hayes and Ann Dent, his wife, to J.M., lot No. 787 Plan of Richmond, one-half acre in square where J.M. resides, purchased from Philip Turpin; £50. Recorded Jan. 24, 1791. Richmond City Hustings and Chancery Court, Deed Book 1, 454–55.

Jan. 5
Richmond *Executor of Estate*

Advertising sale of household furniture, etc., of Serafina Farmicola, deceased, in front of Eagle's Tavern; signed J.M., executor. Va. Gaz. & G.A., Jan. 5, 1791, 2; also in issue of Jan. 12, 1791.

Jan. 19
Richmond *Lottery*

Notice of lottery for Nathaniel Twining, signed J.M., *et al.*, trustees. Va. Gaz. & G.A., Jan. 19, 1791, 3; repeated intermittently through May 11, 1791, 4.

Feb. 20
Richmond *Executor of Estate*

Notice to creditors and debtors for payment of debts to, and filing claims against, estate of Serafina Farmicola, signed J.M., executor. Va. Gaz. & G.A., Mar. 2, 1791, 1; Same, Mar. 16, 1793, 3.

Feb. *n.d.*
RICHMOND *to John Breckenridge*

Enclosing declarations against John Turner and Co. and Robert Duncan and Co.; damages higher than writ, in current money and including interest; variance attacked only by plea in abatement. Fears statute of limitations; must be put in writing if raised. Note appended: Breckenridge appeared for J.M. in suits in Albemarle (Va.) District Court; brought wrong and dismissal; renewed according to J.M.'s instructions; four bills and two declarations involved. DLC, Papers of Breckenridge Family, VII.

Mar. 31
PHILADELPHIA *from J. S. (Joseph Simon)*

Letter sent by Barnard Gratz, Philadelphia. Reports payment on Richard Lee execution order on Seth Barton of Baltimore; bill of exchange sent by J.M., protested by Reid; endorser on bill, John Ballantine; request suit be brought in General Court on bills in hands of Bushrod Washington; fee of four joes. PPL.
See fee: May 16, 1787. *Gratz v. Lee,* in name of "Simons," £2:3. Account Book, 114.

Apr. 1, *n.p.* *to Thomas Jefferson*

Opinion signed by J.M. and Andrew Ronald as to claim of Farrel and Jones against Randolph and Wayler for indemnity on shipment. DLC, Papers of Thomas Jefferson, LXII, folio 10826; Oster, *Marshall,* 181.

May 25
RICHMOND *Family Marriage*

Marriage of Lucy Marshall (sister of J.M.) to John Ambler of Jamestown. Va. Gaz. & G.A., May 25, 1791, 3; Mason, *Polly,* 59.

June 10
RICHMOND *to John Breckenridge*

Acknowledges letter of May 29 concerning suits against Robert Duncan; chagrined, culpable in conducting; asks if writs issued from County or General Court and if in case or debt. Had hoped to amend faulty writ, agreement of attorneys in General Court to allow; overdesire for 10 per cent. File new bill in case against Robert Duncan and Co., if partners name Duncan and John Turner separately. As to bills not accepted, action on case against drawees; if partnership, Duncan sued as firm of John Turner and Co.; if not, in chancery. Cautions against mentioning statute of limitations; defense of prior action not good. Will draw declarations when hears writ issued. DLC, Papers of Breckenridge Family, VII.

Aug. 5
RICHMOND *Militia*

J.M. confirmed as colonel in battalion of militia for City of Richmond. County Court, Henrico, Order Book IV, 597.

Sept. 14
FREDERICKSBURG, VA. *Lottery*

Notice of lottery for enlarging building of Fredericksburg Academy; J.M. and Benjamin Harrison obliging by disposing of some tickets. Notice dated June, 1791. Va. Gaz. & G.A., Sept. 14, 1791, 4.

Dec. 5, *n.p.* *from Wilson Cary Nicholas*

Advises has given Col. Lindsey an order on J.M. for £12, which will pay in ten days on visit to Richmond or will win of J.M. at whist. Receipt of Lindsey noted in handwriting of J.M. VU, Wilson Cary Nicholas Papers, No. 2343.

Dec. 11
RICHMOND *Court Commissioner*

Sale by decree of High Court of Chancery at Eagle Tavern, Richmond, Feb. 20, Chissels Lead Mines and 1,400 acres subject to lease to Moses Austin and Co., signed by J.M. and William Hay, commissioners. Va. Gaz. & G.A., Dec. 28, 1791, 1. Repeated intermittently in issues to July, 1792.

n.d., RICHMOND *to John Breckenridge*

Johnston informed that defect in declaration in *Luts v. Duncan* prevented judgment, attributes lack of attention to agreement between lawyers of General Court to allow amendments; not certain court will allow to amend writ; if not, dismiss and refile. DLC, Papers of Breckenridge Family, VII.

n.d., *n.p.* *to John Breckenridge*

Advises Harris to bring suit in chancery against Watkins for possession of land, rents, and profits; sees no error in decree, sue out writ of *habere facias possessionem*. DLC, Papers of Breckenridge Family, Nov. 30, 1790–Dec. 27, 1791.

It appears that Harris brought the following suits as advised by J.M.:
May 11, 1792 *Benjamin Harris v. Nathaniel Watkins, Samuel Wood, et al.*, chancery action, 800 acres, County Court, Albemarle, Order Book 1791–1793, 134. Continued from year to year. Order Book 1793–1795, 60, 261, 313, 419; Order Book 1795–1798, 62, 192, 317, 366, 426.

Mar. 6, 1798. Abated by defendant's death. Same, 468.

Mar. 15, 1794 *Benjamin Harris v. Nathaniel Watkins, Thomas Ballew, et al.*, chancery. Same, Order Book 1793–1795, 64, 134, 512.

Dec. 13, 1794 *Benjamin Harris v. Nathaniel Watkins*, action on protested bill. Same, 295. May 4, 1795. Continued. Same, 359. June 3, 1795.

Default j. £2:9:8. Same, 397.

June, 1788. Advice fee, £1:2:6. Account Book, 166.

n.d., n.p. *to John Breckenridge*

Acknowledges letter; certiorari obtained, court rising, will send certiorari next post. Requests money from Harris. In court, apologizes for paper scraps used. DLC, Papers of Breckenridge Family, Nov. 30, 1790—Dec. 27, 1791.

LEGAL PRACTICE

During the year 1791, J.M., according to his records, received £1,247:5:3 from 270 legal fees. Fees designated as for advice numbered thirty and followed the usual pattern of being predominately less than £2. One fee of £1:8 was for drawing a mortgage; £4 was received from Robert Morris as a retainer.

In twenty-seven instances of court matters and litigation described, twelve were appeals, of which three were appeals in chancery; seven were chancery matters. Eight cases were designated as in federal court. A fee of £14 was made for defense in a murder trial, and £3 in a separate maintenance case.

Sizable fees included one for £33; two for £28, one of which was from the executors of Lord Fairfax. A fee of £20 was paid by Robinson's administrators. Account Book, 272–308.

Feb. 14 List of orders by the clerk of the Common Hall, Richmond, for the payment of money: Part of No. 88, J.M., as a fee for defending suit against Corporation by Mrs. Mary Byrd, £10. Paid Sept. 26, 1792. Richmond Common Hall Records 1782–1793, I, no page number.

Order of Common Hall for payment of the above fee, also £10 to James Innes, co-counsel with J.M. Same, 226.

Feb. 18 Appeal in case of *Orandorf v. Welch.* Original in Law Library of University of Virginia. VU, No. 1172.

U.S. CIRCUIT COURT, VIRGINIA

James and Robert Donald and Co. v. Zacharias Taliaferro and John Wyatt. (Two cases)

Debt. J.M. for defendants.

May 24, 1791. Judgment entered by clerk set aside.

Pleas: payment; Britisher not recover.

Motion to send back to rule docket. U.S. Circuit Court, Va., Order Book I, 13, 14. Same, Record Book Index, Nov., 1791. V, U.S. Circuit Court Case Papers.

Robinson, Sanderson, and Rumny, merchants, Great Britain v. Andrew Lewis, Va.

Debt, on obligation under seal, £798:0:9½ Va., 1787.

J.M. for plaintiff.

Nov. 24, 1791. Default j. against defendant and his security, £798:0:9½ Va., payable by £399:0:4½ Va. U.S. Circuit Court, Va., Record Book I, 31. V, U.S. Circuit Court Case Papers, containing petition form filled in by J.M. and signed.

COURT OF APPEALS OF VIRGINIA

Andrew and William Hamilton v. James Maze, 4 Call 196, 204–205, reversing in part Wythe, 36–46.

Action concerning land, Greenbriar County.

J.M. for Maze, defendant in error.

Maze claimed 400 acres settlement in 1764, 1,000 acres pre-emption adjoining, surveyed; Hamilton claimed latter under survey 1774–1775 and grant of Greenbriar Company; order of Council to Company, 1751. Commissioners directed for Hamilton; caveat filed; order reversed by General Court, Oct. 9, 1782, allowing 400 acres and pre-emption to Maze. Appeal to Court of Appeals dismissed, lack of jurisdiction. Injunction granted High Court of Chancery, decree for Maze on payment of £3 per 100 acres to Greenbriar Company. Reversed by Court of Appeals, June 20, 1791, allowing Maze 400-acre settlement with cabin south of an agreed line, Hamilton to convey such part as within his 1,100-acre survey, Maze to find his balance elsewhere.

Earlier proceedings:

Apr. 30, 1783. Writ of error and supersedeas staying proceedings on

j. of General Court, Oct. 19, 1782, against Hamiltons on caveat. Court of Appeals, Va., Order Book I, 26.

Oct. 29, 1783. Writ quashed, dismissed, court no jurisdiction over js. of General Court on caveats reviewing js. of district commissioners. Same, 31.

Oct. 30, 1783. Order of Oct. 29 set aside. Same, 32.

Nov. 1, 1783. Writ quashed, dismissed, same reason as order of Oct. 29. Same, 34.

Present proceedings:

Dec. 14, 1790. Appeal from injunction of High Court of Chancery, continued. Court of Appeals, Va., Order Book II, 51.

June 8, 10, 1791. Heard. Same, 71, 74.

June 20, 1791. Reversed, decree amended. Same, 81.

William Calvert v. Preeson Bowdoin, surviving partner Phripp and Bowdoin, 4 Call, 217, 219.

Appeal from j. District Court at Suffolk affirming j. Court of Hustings, Norfolk, May 25, 1789, against appellant, reversed.

J.M. and William Duval for appellant.

Action for breach of agreement to buy land from money received; plea, statute of limitations. Proof, receipt of 1779 of different amount, and purpose objected to because more than five years elapsed. J. for plaintiff below based on assumption of obligation. Held, statute of limitations applied; variance of proof by receipt from declaration. Nonsuit, new trial refused.

Dec. 14, 1790. Appeal dismissed, failure to appear. Court of Appeals, Va., Order Book II, 50.

June 9, 1791. Set aside. Same, 55.

June 10. Reversed, nonsuit, Same, 74.

Thomas Marshall, George Muter, Charles Dabney, John Montgomery, George Walls, Christopher Roane, Nathaniel Welsh, John Rogers. Humphrey Marshall, and Nathaniel Rice v. George Rogers Clark, 4 Call 268.

Adjourned case from the Supreme Court District of Kentucky, answering seven questions. Opinion given that Cherokee Indian title to land bounded by North Carolina land, and Tennessee, Ohio, and Mississippi rivers could be extinguished by act of Virginia Legislature (insufficient facts to determine if so done and if lands waste and unappropriated), of no consequence in rival claims of citizens. Act of 1779 permitted acquisition on treasury warrants; that act establishing pay and survey of land to officers of military not retroactive and did not invalidate previous entries and locations.

Dec. 1, 1790. Continued. Court of Appeals, Va., Order Book II, 35.

Nov. 16, 1791. Heard. Same, 127.

Nov. 21. Opinion. Same, 133.

J.M. represented officers. See letter Thomas Marshall to Gov. Randolph, Sept. 15, 1788, herein.

Carter Braxton et al. surviving executor of Philip W. Claiborne v. Peter Winslow, Joseph Brock, and John Crane, surviving justices of Spotsylvania County, 4 Call 308, 312–14. I Washington 31.

Error from j. General Court, Oct. 14, 1785, against surety on executor's bond based on waste by executor, reversed.

J.M. and John Taylor for plaintiff in error.

Action against Claiborne, surety on executor's bond, on grounds executor failed to pay protested bill and judgment; plea condition performed, no waste. Evidence that debts of inferior dignity paid, but no proof of lack of assets to pay bill and judgment, and no suit against executor. Held, under Virginia statute creditors may sue on executor's bond, but must first sue executor, prove waste of assets, and prove debt unpaid.

June 23 and Nov. 3, 1790. Three judges disqualified themselves. Court of Appeals Va., Order Book II, 2, 34.

June 1, 2, 1791. Continued. Same, 61, 62

June 3, 1791. Heard. Same, 63.

June 4. Continued. Same, 64.

June 6. Reversed, j. against creditor 150 pounds tobacco for false clamour, also costs and expenses. Same, 64–65.

Note: N.W. Dandridge was drawee and endorsee of bill of exchange involved. J.M. was involved in litigation by Claiborne's executor against him. See fee, *Hanover Justices (Claiborne's Executors) v. Dandridge*, Feb., 1792, £2:16. Account Book, 314.

Charles Hudson v. Thomas Johnson, a minor, 1 Washington 10.

Debt, appeal from j. for appellee, defendant below, District Court of Charlottesville, Sept., 1790, which affirmed j. County Court of Louisa. Affirmed in part. J.M. for appellant. After suit plaintiff referred defendant to his attorney to whom payment made. In trial court demurrer to evidence of payment overruled and j. for defendant with full costs. In District Court affirmed as to payment, reversed as to costs before payment and j. for plaintiff below as to such costs plus damages against defendant for delaying execution. In Court of Appeals, affirmed as to payment and division of costs but reversed as to damages for retarding execution.

July 1, 1791. Heard. Court of Appeals, Va., Order Book II, 110.

July 2, 1791. Affirmed. Same, 111.

Fee: Aug. 2, 1788, £0:14. Account Book, 164.

David Ross v. James Norvell, 1 Washington 14.

Appeal from High Court of Chancery, decrees Oct. 31, 1789, appellant to deliver slaves to appellee; Mar. 12, 1790, dismissing cross bill of appellant. Affirmed. J.M. for appellee. Slaves conveyed by appellee by absolute deed 1765; claimed oral agreement that conveyed as security for debt redeemable on payment of principal and interest. Bill filed in 1779 to redeem; cross bill on notes for hire of slaves by appellee 1765–1767 and dismissal of decree in first suit requiring redelivery of slaves. Evidence that in 1770 and 1772 appellant admitted appellee had right to redeem.

Held, parol proof admissible under the circumstances to vary written document; action not barred by time; no statute of limitations in equitable redemption; twenty years usual period.

June 21–22, 1791. Heard. Court of Appeals, Va., Order Book II, 85, 89.

June 28, 1791. Decree of redemption affirmed; decree of dismissal of cross bill affirmed. Same, 103, 104.

Fee: Dec. 20, 1789, £5. Account Book, 226.

Rawleigh Downman, Jr. v. John Chinn, Joseph B. and Rawleigh W. Downman, executors of Rawleigh Downman, 1 Washington 26.

Debt, appeal from j. for appellee, District Court, Northumberland Courthouse, Apr. 3, 1790, £106 Va. payable by £53 with interest from 1769 to 1789 and costs. Affirmed. J.M. for appellee.

After office judgment had been confirmed, defendant sought to plead tender of principal and interest in 1781 in Virginia currency, which was refused; at all times was and is ready to pay, and bring same into court. On motion plea refused as too late, and that money brought was once paper money but now not money; j. as above.

Held, under circumstances of country and disperse situation of attorneys and clients, courts should not adhere to rigorous requirements of time of pleading, discretion of judge; plea bad in form in not stating sum certain tendered, and that ready to pay only since time of tender, twelve years after due; plea did not say what kind of money tendered, and money brought to court not money current. J. entry wrong in stopping interest after twenty years, rightly might have included penalty of obligation.

Dec. 14, 1790. Hearing. Court of Appeals, Va., Order Book II, 51.

Dec. 18, 1790. Continued, rehearing. Same, 60.

June 8, 1791. Reheard. Same, 69.

June 10, 1791. Affirmed. Same, 72.

Fees: May, 1790, £5; Feb., 1792, £5:10 and £11:10. Account Book 244, 314.

See: *Downman et al., executors of Downman v. Downman et al.*, 2 Call 426 (1800) for later proceedings on judgment.

Vertinda Dade, widow, Baldwin Dade, Buckner Smith, Lawrence Taliaferro, William Bowling, and Richard Ratcliff v. Charles and Robert Alexander, 1 Washington, 30.

Appeal from decree of High Court of Chancery, May 25, 1790. J.M. for appellees.

Held, that where will directs purchase of slaves to be annexed to land devised in same will in tail, bequest considered slaves and pass with land; that where feme sole entitled to slaves in remainder of reversion, marries and dies before determination of the prior estate, the right vests in husband.

June 14, 1791. Heard. Court of Appeals, Va., Order Book II, 78.

June 17, 1791. Affirmed. Same, 79.

Fees: May, 1789, £14; June, 1791, £14. Account Book, 196, 290.

John Wilcox v. James Calloway, 1 Washington 38.

Appeal from High Court of Chancery, Nov. 1, 1790, dismissing bill without prejudice, affirmed. J.M. for ———.

Wilcox and Calloway purchased and received patents two tracts of land 1764. Wilcox agreed to sell to Donaldson in 1768, gave him delinquent quitrents. Cox in 1767 had petitioned for tracts for nonpayment of quitrents; Donaldson bought his rights; j. was had in 1772 and patent in 1774, which he sold to Calloway in 1776. In 1783, Wilcox had filed a caveat against issuance of patent under j. for failure of Cox to pay quitrents and obtain patent within six months, and in 1783 he obtained j. and patents and filed action against Calloway only.

Held, Calloway a purchaser for valuable consideration without notice of fraud, if any; dismissal without prejudice allows Wilcox to proceed against Calloway, if fraud, for purchase money.

June 25, 1791. Continued. Court of Appeals, Va., Order Book II, 101.

Nov. 3, 4, 7, 1791. Heard. Same, 113, 114, 115.

Nov. 25, 1791. Affirmed. Same, 143.

Fees: June 4, 1790, £7; Nov., 1791, £28. Account Book, 250, 304.

Lessee of William Mayo v. Paul and Nathan Carrington et al., 4 Call 472, 1 Washington 45.

Error from General Court.

Ejectment by appellant as heir of testator against residuary legatees, j. for latter, affirmed. J.M. for defendant in error.

Will provided for petition to General Assembly for manumission of slaves and other property to named legatees. Manumission effected; heir claimed Mecklenburg County land on grounds residuary clause contingent on manumission failure, and did not include land. Held, residuary clause absolute; "other property" includes land.

July 13, 1790. Writ of error, two js. allowed. Court of Appeals, Va., Book Order II, 29.

Nov. 29, 1791. Heard. Same, 147.

Dec. 1. Affirmed. Same, 148.

Fees: June 19, 1790, £10; June, 1791, £12; Apr.–May, 1792, £8; Sept., 1794, £5. Account Book, 252, 290, 322, 398.

Thomas and John Roane, James Upshaw and William Latane, executors of William Roane v. Frederick William Hearne and wife, Anne, widow of William Roane, 1 Washington 47, affirming Wythe, 111.

Appeal from decree of High Court of Chancery, action to enforce premarital agreement. Affirmed. J.M. for appellants. Testator entered into premarital agreement with Anne, in lieu of dower, twenty slaves of which he died possessed, but not less than one-third, also carriage with horses belonging to same. During arrangements but prior to execution, conveyed fourteen or fifteen slaves to two sons (Spencer and Thomas). Executors in distribution included, among the twenty, ten slaves belonging to Anne at marriage; two horses with carriage. Anne claimed exclusion of slaves owned by her, inclusion of gift to sons, four horses.

Held, slaves owned by Anne to be excluded, also gift to sons, twenty or one-third from remainder; two horses proper for normal use.

Nov. 17–18, 1791. Heard. Court of Appeals, Va., Order Book II, 128, 132.

Nov. 21, 1791. Affirmed. Same, 136.

Fees: Oct., 1789, £3; Dec., 1790, £2. Account Book, 218, 264.

David, William, and Samuel Shelton, executors of Joseph Shelton v. John Shelton, Jun., 1 Washington 53.

Appeal from decree High Court of Chancery, Aug. 5, 1790, decree reversed and amended in part, dismissed as to other. J.M. for appellee.

Action brought in High Court of Chancery by appellee as heir at law of testator for after-acquired slaves, and proportion of surplus residue of personal estate and crops; also legacy of £200 of deceased brother. Will of testator in 1770 devised to three brothers each a plantation "and appurtenances"; to nephew, John, appellee, a plantation with cattle subject to life estate to testator's sister, the latter including named slaves; and to nephew William, brother of John, a plantation and cattle, providing if either should die without heirs then to the other; also "all negroes young and old at all plantations named equally to three brothers," including those named to sister; no residue clause. Before death, testator purchased additional plantation "Williamson," to which removed part of slaves and purchased others, part put on "Williamson," three of these temporarily absent from "Williamson" at time of death. Chancery Court decreed to appellee £200 legacy with interest; slaves and profits not settled on devised land or named to sister; surplus of personal estate, excluding sheep on devised lands, but including emblements on "Williamson" and crop raised thereon during year of testator's death.

Held, that parol proof of the situation and circumstances of testator at time of will and time of death admissible to prove his intent; that the clause as to slaves to brothers restricted to slaves attached to named plantations at time of death whenever acquired, excluding those on "Williamson," but including any temporarily absent; all others (sixteen in number) to appellee as heir at law; that growing crops did not pass with land devised as "appurtenances," but after harvesting and paying of charges as prescribed by Virginia act, surplus not to heirs but to executors.

Dec. 14, 1790. Continued. Court of Appeals, Va., Order Book II, 50.

June 6, 7, 1791. Heard. Same, 66, 67.

July 1, 1791. Continued for rehearing. Same, 110.

Nov. 2, 1791. Reheard. Same, 113.

Nov. 10, 1791. Decree reversed, bill dismissed, appellee to receive £200 bequest with interest, sixteen slaves, and £272:10 profits. Same, 117.

Fee: Oct. 9, 1787, £5; June, 1791, £14; Apr., 1793, £2:14; Jan., 1794, £5. Account Book, 128, 290, 358, 380.

Note: The case was reheard because "the court not having a library at hand, or leisure to digest the variety of adjudged cases relied on in argument . . . . That has been done this term; and the court has derived much satisfaction from the laborious researches, and able reasoning of the gentlemen at the bar" (p. 55).

William Armistead v. Mathew Jordon.

Appeal from District Court, Prince Edward Courthouse, Sept. 4, 1790, affirmance of j. against appellant in County Court of Charlotte, Aug. 6, 1787, £90:10:6. J.M. for appellee.

June 22, 1791. Affirmed on inspection of record. Court of Appeals, Va., Order Book II, 88.

Fee: Oct., 1787, £2:10. Account Book, 128.

John Birch and William Jaco v. Timothy Goodtitle, lessees of Charles Alexander.

Ejectment and trespass. Appeal from District Court, Dumfries, Oct. 22, 1790, j. for appellee in his action for undivided moiety land patented to Robert Howsom on Potomac River and Great Hunting Creek, also land patented to James Robertson on Long Branch, twelve messuages and 3,300 acres, Fairfax County. Filed General Court, Oct. 26, 1782. J.M. for appellants.

Nov. 17, 1791. Affirmed. Court of Appeals, Va., Order Book II, 128.

May, 1792. Order of Court of Appeals filed in District Court, Prince William, Land Causes 1789–1793, 422.

For record of this case in District Court, Same, 89, 100 ff.

For related cases, *Same v. Charles Little and William Herbert,* Same, 91, 456, 470; *Same v. William Bryan, Charles Curtis, William Reedy, John Lemaster et al.,* Same, 101, 451, 466, 489; *Same v. John West,* Same, 491, 494; *Same v. James Web and William Short,* Same, 492; *Same v. John Ball, Jeremiah Thaft, and Caleb Richards,* Same, 498.

Fee: May, 1792, "Alexander v. his tenants," £7. Account Book, 326.

Mary Bolling v. Lessee of Elizabeth Ramsey.

Ejectment, appeal from j. District Court, Petersburg, Apr. 15, 1790. J.M. for appellee.

June 13, 1791. Dismissed for failure to prosecute. Court of Appeals, Va., Order Book II, 77.

Fee: Nov., 1790, £14. Account Book, 266.

John Daugherty v. William Crow, of Kentucky.

Appeal from decree of Supreme Court District of Kentucky, Sept., 1787, dismissing bill of Daugherty and decreeing Crow might proceed in ejectment. J.M. for appellee.

Dec. 17, 1790. Partly heard; continued. Court of Appeals, Va., Order Book II, 57.

Dec. 18, 1790. Continued. Same, 61.

June 27, 1791. Case heard. Same, 104.

June 30, 1791. Affirmed. Same, 106.

Fee: June, 1791, £4:10. Account Book, 290.

Samuel Dew v. William McIlwaine.

Appeal from decree for appellee, District Court, Winchester, Apr. 15, 1790, for term in 384 acres, house, and garden in Hampshire County.

J.M. for appellant.

June 20, 1791. Reversed and new trial for refusal to allow deed in evidence. Court of Appeals, Va., Order Book II, 83.

Fee: June, 1791, £5. Account Book, 290.

Andrew Donally v. John Hutchinson.

Appeal from District Court, Lewisburg, Greenbrier County, May 20, 1790, £62:8:3 for appellee.

J.M. for appellee.

June 9, 1791. Case submitted, affirmed. Court of Appeals, Va., Order Book II, 71.

Fee: Oct., 1790, £5. Account Book, 264.

William Faris v. William Ladd.

Appeal from j. against appellant. District Court, Richmond, Apr. 5, 1791, two negro slaves, £150 and £75, or said amounts and £75 damages.

J.M. for appellant.

Nov. 26, 1791. Appellee not appear, case submitted, reversed and j. for appellant, 150 pounds tobacco. Court of Appeals, Va., Order Book II, 144.

Fee: Apr. 27, 1786, £2:10. Account Book, 72.

James Hambleton, David Bradford, and John Decker v. Solomon Saveatt, lessee of Alexander Wells.

Appeal from j. of ejectment against appellants, District Court, Monongalia County, Sept. 20, 1790, 200 acres. J.M. for appellants.

Dec. 18, 1790. Order to certify record. Court of Appeals, Va., Order Book II, 60.

June 21, 1791. Heard. Same, 102.

June 29. Reversed for failure to allow proof that knew survey not made when patented. Same, 105.

Fees: Aug., 1787, £4:16; May, 1791, £2:8. Account Book, 120, 286.

William Helm and Walter Clark v. William Armstrong.

Appeal from j. District Court at Winchester, Sept. 4, 1790, £313:11:1, payable by £156:15:6½. J.M. for appellant.

June 21, 1791. Case submitted, affirmed. Order Book II, 84.

Fee: Dec., 1791, £5. Account Book, 308.

Benjamin Harrison v. Christopher McRae.

Appeal from j. District Court, Prince Edward Courthouse, Apr. 6, 1791, affirming j. Court of Cumberland County, Aug. 28, 1788, £67. J.M. for appellee.

Nov. 21, 1791. Appellant not appear, submitted. Order Book II, 138.

Nov. 23, 1791. Affirmed. Same, 141.

Fee: Apr., 1791, £5. Account Book, 282.

Thomas Hudnall v. Joseph Hudnall, Jr.

Appeal from j. for appellee, District Court, Northumberland Courthouse, Apr. 6, 1791, for four slaves if to be had, otherwise from £20 to £50 each and £20 damages. Not known which party J.M. represented.

Nov. 21, 1791. Submitted. Court of Appeals, Va., Order Book II, 139.

Nov. 23, 1791. Affirmed. Same, 141.

Fee: June, 1791, £7. Account Book, 290.

Anne Hungerford v. Margaret Pratt and Thomas Bunbury, executrix and executor of Thomas Pratt.

Appeal from High Court of Chancery Mar. 9, 1789, affirming decree of County Court of King George against appellant. J.M. for appellant.

June 13, 1791. Consent decree reversing decrees and j. for appellant against estate, £50. Court of Appeals, Va., Order Book II, 76.

Fee: May 12, 1789, £2:16. Account Book, 196.

James Lee v. George Gayle.

Appeal from j. against appellant District Court, King and Queen County, Apr. 23, 1791, affirming j. Court of Middlesex County, May 26, 1788, £21:2. J.M. for appellee.

Nov. 22, 1791. Submitted, affirmed. Court of Appeals, Va., Order Book II, 140.

Fee: Jan., 1792, £2:10. Account Book, 312.

Michael Wallace v. Smith and Morton, assignees of Henry and Zachariah Vowles.

Supersedeas to j. for appellee against Wallace, sheriff of King George County, as security, and William Piper, District Court, Fredericksburg, May 8, 1790, for debt £2,084:3:3½, payable by £1,042:1:73. (District Court, Fredericksburg, Law Orders A, 1789–1793, 122; Same, Record Book 1789–1792, 207–208. Oct. 7, 1791, j. by District Court, Fredericksburg, on mandate of Court of Appeals. Same, 322.) J.M. for appellee.

June 20, 21, 1791. Heard. Court of Appeals, Va., Order Book II, 82, 83.

June 23, 1791. Affirmed. Same, 89.
Fee: Apr., 1790, £2:8. Account Book, 242.

General Court of Virginia

Denny Fairfax v. Robert Stephen; Same v. David Hunter. Va. Cas. I, 3–4.

Opinion on causes adjourned from District Court of Winchester, Frederick County, for novelty. (See herein, 1790, Legal Practice, Frederick County.)

June 20. Several caveats entered by clerk of court upon copies from Land Office certified by its clerk instead of its register void, dismissed.

The Commonwealth v. John Crane, the Younger, Va. Cas. I, 10.

Adjourned question to General Court from District Court of Winchester, indictment for murder, Sept., 1791; opinion guilty of murder, not manslaughter. J.M. for Crane.

Challenges to fight, threats, and altercations between accused and his reapers and those of adjoining owner resulting second day in fight in which accused knifed and killed his adversary.

Special verdict, guilty of murder or manslaughter.

Held, murder.

Fee: Nov., 1791, £14. Account Book, 304.

High Court of Chancery

Thomas Cobs v. John Mosby, Wythe, 71.

Bill in equity for relief against verdict dismissed where only showing of cause was denial of new trial. J.M. for defendant.

Fees: May, 1790, £2:10 (probably first case); Nov., 1790, £2:2, Sept., 1794, "App. finished," £1:20. Account Book, 248, 266, 394.

John Dandridge and William Armistead, executors of Bartholomew Dandridge v. Thomas Lyon. Wythe, 30.

Father bequeathed entire estate to wife except future increase of slave to daughter; the latter bequeathed all remainder of her estate to mother (wife above) for life and then "to return" to Poindexter, under whom Dandridge claims. Heir of daughter claimed the increase on grounds father could not bequeath slaves not in being at time of will, belonged to mother for life, and "remainder" in daughter's will not include them; j. County Court of James City in favor of heir of daughter. Injunction allowed against j., bequest of future acquired property approved. J.M. represented Dandridge.

Fee: June 30, 1789, £5. Account Book, 202.

Joseph Woodson v. John Woodson, Wythe, 55–57.

Appeal from Court of Goochland County.

Dismissal of bill, reversed.

J.M. for ———.

Pledgee of slave for 13,000 pounds of tobacco required to account for profits during time used; first to apply to interest, though none mentioned, surplus to principal. Pledgee claimed all profits without deductions.

Fee: Apr., 1788, £10 (2 Chr.); May, 1791, £——; May, 1793, £——. Account Book, 154, 288, 362.

Robert Gaines Beverley v. John Rennolds, executor of Leroy Hipkins, Wythe, 105–106.

Injunction sought against j. £300 obtained against Beverley under agreement to arbitrate damages for disavowal of contract to sell real estate for pittance made during minority. Granted. J.M. for petitioner.

Fees: May, 1789, £5:12; Oct., 1789, £5:20. Account Book, 21, 216.

District Court, Accomack and Northampton

Susanna Linton v. John Cropper.

Detinue. Action filed Oct. 31, 1788. J.M. for defendant.

Oct. 18, 19, 1791. Special verdict. In 1763, Watts sold to plaintiff Negro woman, Comfort, reserving possession during own life and that of wife, Esther, or survivor; he died 1765. Esther sold Comfort to father of defendant for term of Esther's life; Esther died 1784. Comfort and offspring in possession of defendant since 1786. Value of Comfort, £10:18; her offspring, £10:18, £27:1, £23:4:10, £7:1. District Court, Accomack and Northampton, Order Book 1789–1797, 177, 180.

Oct. 21, 1791, through May 15, 1793. Continued. Same, 188, 212, 216, 244.

May 15, 1794. Dismissed, case agreed. Same, 311.

Also *Same v. Same.*

In case, for conversion of Negro women slaves.

Oct. 19–21, 1791. V.j. for plaintiff, £59. Same, 182, 184, 186.

Fee: Dec., 1791, £5:14:6. Account Book, 308.

District Court, Augusta

John McKean, Benjamin Lewis, and Alexander Roberts, administrator of Patrick Couts v. William Bowyer.

Debt. Action in General Court, Apr., 1788, on sealed obligation to pay

£509:7:4, payable by £254:13:8; damages £10. J.M. for plaintiffs. (Petition signed by J.M.)

June, 1788. Plea, payment.

Oct., 1788. General Court. Continuance.

Sept., 1789, Apr. and Sept., 1790. District Court. Continuances. Same, Order Book 1789–1797, 20, 29, 50, 93.

Apr. 6, 1791. V.j. for defendant. Same, Order Book 1789–1793, 233–56.

(Note, extensive mercantile accounts and correspondence between Richmond and Staunton merchants contained in record.)

William Peachy, assignee of Thomas Carneal who was assignee of John Fulton v. Samuel and Alexander Craig.

Debt. Action on sealed obligation (note) to Fulton dated Mar. 12, 1783, £45, penal sum £90, payable in three years; part payment, £33:13:9, May 3, 1788; assigned to Carneal Sept., 1788; thereafter by Carneal to Peachy. J.M. for Peachy (probable); declaration signed by A. Stuart as attorney for plaintiff.

Apr. 2, 1791. Security bond for defendant Alexander.

Apr. 8, 1791. Common order against Alexander; abatement as to Samuel.

May 9, 1791. Common order confirmed.

Sept. 3, 1791. Default j. £90, payable by £11:6:3 and interest. District Court, August, Order Book 1789–1793, 326.

Similar action filed at same time on note dated Aug. 9, 1783, £45, penal sum £90, payable Mar. 12, 1787, same persons and assigns.

Sept. 3, 1791. Default j. £90, payable by £45 and interest. Same, 329.

Also, on note by and to same parties and assigns, same date, payable Mar. 12, 1788.

Sept. 3, 1791. Default j. £90, payable by £45 and interest. Same, 331.

Also, on similar note of same date, payable Mar. 12, 1789.

Sept. 3, 1791. Default j. £45 with interest. Same, 334.

Fee: July 19, 1788, £7:10, "3 suits." Account Book, 162.

John Robinson, administrator of Solomon Carpenter v. Elizabeth and Samuel McDowell, administrators of James McDowell.

Debt. Action on sealed obligation (note) of July 10, 1771, £50, penal sum £100, for land. Damages £50. J.M. for defendants.

Sept., 1789. Filed.

Oct., 1789. Plea, payment.

Apr. 5, 1790. Commission for deposition.

Sept. 2, 1790. Continued.

Apr. 4, 1791. V.j. £100, payable by £50 against estate, costs against defendants if no property in estate. District Court, Augusta, Order Book 1789–1793, 191.

Fee: June, 1791, £5. Account Book, 290.

District Court, Franklin

William Jones v. Richard Brown.

Assault and battery. J.M. for defendant.

Sept. 22, 1791. Continued. District Court, Franklin, Order Book I, 1789–1793, 225.

Apr. 17, 1792. Discontinued, agreed by parties. Same, 242.

Fee: Aug., 1791, £3. Account Book, 294.

Superior (District) Court, Frederick

William Dark v. William Burns.

Case. J.M. for plaintiff.

Sept. 8, 1790. Continued. Superior Court, Frederick, Order Book 1789–1793, 148.

Apr. 18, 1791. J. for plaintiff £100. Same, 172.

Apr. 26, 1791. Appeal. Same, 203.

Fee: May 18, 1790, £5. Account Book, 248.

John Moore v. Reubin Moore, Jr.

Appeal from j. County Court of Shenandoah, June 2, 1787, £15:1:7½. J.M. for ——.

Apr. 25, 1791. Affirmed. Superior Court, Frederick, Order Book 1789–1793, 193.

Fee: Sept., 1787, £2:10. Account Book, 124.

Morgan Morgan, Sheriff of Berkeley County v. Leakin Dorsey.

Appeal from j. Court of Berkeley County, June 19, 1787, £370:14:10 payable by £185:7:5. J.M. for appellee.

Apr. 15, 1791. Reversed, not shown Wilson in custody of sheriff under escape warrant. Superior Court, Frederick, Order Book 1789–1793, 166.

Fee: Feb., 1789, £1:16. Account Book, 186.

John H. Norton v. Beverly Whiting, administrator, d.b.n. of Francis Whiting.

Debt. J.M. for defendant.

Sept. 6, 1791. Confessed j. £150 with 5 per cent interest from Aug. 5,

1768, and 141 pounds tobacco and fifteen shillings, as in declaration, levied against goods of decedent. Superior Court, Frederick, Order Book 1789–1793, 239–40.

Fee: May, 1795, £5:2. Account Book, 412.

James Ware v. Cornelius Conway.

Case, trover, damages for retention of bay mare lost by plaintiff, found by defendant, 1786, value £30, damages £50, Berkeley County. J.M. for defendant.

Dec. 29, 1787. Declaration dated Apr., 1787, filed in General Court. (Autograph signed declaration. VU, McGregor Libr., Marshall Family Papers.)

Jan., 1788. Plea, not guilty.

Apr., 1788—Apr., 1790. Continued. Superior Court, Frederick, Order Book 1789–1793, 35, 74.

Sept. 6, 1791. V.j. for plaintiff £20. Same, 235.

Fee: Apr. 11, 1787, £2:10. Account Book, 106.

District Court, Fredericksburg

William Allen v. William Wilson.

Case, action for breach of agreement that plaintiff give possession of store and dwelling in town of Falmouth to defendant and remove his goods to vacant house and hold plaintiff harmless for rent due and unpaid. Damages, £100. Filed Apr., 1789. Stafford County. J.M. for plaintiff. (Petition signed.)

May 1, 1790. Plea *non assumpsit*; writ of enquiry set aside; continued in District Court, Fredericksburg, Law Orders A, 1789–1793, 93.

Oct. 6, 1790. Continued. Same, 166.

May 2, 1791. Continued. Same, 221.

Oct. 3, 1791. J. for plaintiff £30. Same, 294.

District Court, Fredericksburg, Record Book 1789–1792, 600–601.

John Almond v. John Tribrue, assignee, etc.

Appeal from j. Court of Orange County, Nov. 29, 1787, against appellant £46, payable by £23. J.M. for appellee.

May 2, 1791. Appellees's attorney appeared; appellant did not; record examined, affirmed, damages against appellant according to law for obstructing execution. District Court, Fredericksburg, Law Orders A, 1789–1793, 225.

Fee: Sept., 1790, £2:10. Account Book, 258.

Hardin Burnley v. John Thornley, deputy inspector.

Case, filed in General Court. J.M. for defendant.

Oct. 6, 1789. Continued by consent. District Court, Fredericksburg, Law Orders A, 1789–1793, 55.

May 5, 1791. Continued by plaintiff. Same, 240.

Sept. 30, 1791. D. j. for defendant, failure to prosecute; j. for defendant 150 pounds tobacco, cost of defense. Same, 274.

Fee: Sept., 1789, £2:8. Account Book, 260.

George Cammock v. William Drummond, assignee of James Couts.

Debt. Appeal from consent j. on bill sealed May 6, 1788, £100, County Court of Caroline, Nov., 1789. J.M. for appellant (probable).

May 7, 1791. Affirmed. District Court, Fredericksburg, Law Orders A, 1789–1793, 260; Record Book 1789–1792, 531–33.

Fee: May, 1791, "Commock (finished)," £8. Account Book, 286.

Jesse Carter v. Ann Gaddis.

Ejectment, 140 acres, Parish of Overwharton, Stafford County.

J.M. for plaintiff.

Oct. 1, 1790. General issue, commission for deposition by defendant. District Court, Fredericksburg, Law Orders A, 1789–1793, 140.

Oct. 6, 1791. Dismissed, agreed between parties. Same, 307.

Fee: Jan., 1790, £5. Account Book, 230.

Samuel Coleman, Jr. v. Richard Wyatt, Jr.

Action in case. J.M. for plaintiff. (Signed petition.)

Petition alleged defendant borrowed of plaintiff £100 of military officers specie certificates bearing 6 per cent interest, Nov. 20, 1783; promised to repay, refused on demand, £120 damages. Filed in General Court, Oct., 1785, from Caroline County.

Feb. 8, 1786. Plea, not assume.

Apr., 1786—Oct., 1788. Continued.

Sept., 1789. Continued at plaintiff's costs.

May 3, 1791. V.j. for defendant. District Court, Fredericksburg, Law Orders A, 1789–1793, 23; Same, Record Book 1789–1792, 474–75.

Francis Dade and Lawrence Taliaferro v. Charles Carter.

Appeal from County Court of Orange. J.M. for appellee.

Oct. 6, 1790. Motion by appellee for diminution of record. District Court, Fredericksburg, Law Orders A, 1789–1793, 163.

Apr. 30, 1791. Dismissed, agreed between parties. Same, 200.

Fee: Mar., 1788, £2:10. Account Book, 148.

William Dawson v. James Mercer.

Action for breach of contract of employment alleging, in 1772, defendant hired plaintiff overseer of several plantations and large number of slaves; for three years, compensation £30 and £40, sufficient grain, one-eighth of middle plantation; breach in 1774 by driving off without compensation. Filed in General Court, Oct., 1785. Spotsylvania County. J.M. for defendant.

Apr., 1786. Plea, not assume; statute of limitations.

Apr., 1786—Oct., 1788. Continued.

Oct. 5, 1789. Referred to arbitrators. District Court, Fredericksburg, Law Orders A, 1789–1793, 47.

May 5, 1790. Continued. Same, 107.

Oct. 8, 1790. Commission to defendant for depositions. Same, 186.

May 4, 1791. Plaintiff nonsuited, failure to prosecute. Same, 235; Same, Record Book 1789–1792, 475–77.

Fee: Sept., 1790, £2:16. Account Book, 260.

Francis Eppes, Henry Skipwith, and Thomas Jefferson, executors of John Wayles v. Thomas Lomax.

Debt, on obligation sealed, Nov. 27, 1775, £184:10. Filed Sept., 1789. Caroline County. J.M. for plaintiffs. (Petition signed.)

May 1, 1790. Plea payment; office j. set aside; continued.

District Court, Fredericksburg, Law Orders A, 1789–1793, 89.

Oct. 1, 1791. J. for plaintiffs, £184:10 current, payable by £92:5, interest 5 per cent from Nov. 27, 1773 (obligation in evidence dated Nov. 27, 1774). Same, 282. Same, Record Book 1789–1792, 574–75.

Robert Goodloe v. Joseph Brock, William and John Carter, executors of John Carter.

Detinue. J.M. for defendant.

Oct. 7, 1789. Continued by consent. District Court, Fredericksburg, Law Orders A, 1789–1793, 58.

Oct. 5, 1790. Same. Same, 156.

May 3, 1791. Abated by death of plaintiff. Same, 232.

Fees: Dec. 4, 1786, £3; Oct., 1789, £1:10. Account Book, 92, 216.

John Graham v. William Elliott, John Woolfolk, John Hoomes, and Richard Bowles.

Debt. (two cases) On obligation sealed, May 14, 1787, £384; May 14, 1789, £387:14. J.M. for plaintiff. (Petition signed.)

June, 1790. Abated as to Bowles, bail filed and oyer as to others.

Sept. 29, 1790. Plea payment, office j. set aside. District Court, Fredericksburg, Law Orders A, 1789–1793, 131.

Oct. 6, 1791. Confessed js., £384, payable by £180:19; £387:14:8, payable by £186:16. Same, 311. Same, Record Book 1789–1792, 642–45.

Fee: Feb., 1790, "Graham v. Hoomes et al.," £3:12. Account Book, 234.

John Graham v. William Harrison.

Debt, on bill of exchange drawn June 11, 1785, £100:10:6 on Samuel Gist, London, to Henry Banks, assigned to plaintiff. Filed Apr., 1789, Spotsylvania County. J.M. for plaintiff. (Petition signed.)

Oct. 3, 1791. J. for plaintiff, £100 St. and ten shillings, six pence St. cost of protest, and 10 per cent interest from June 11, 1785, plus damages £40. District Court, Fredericksburg, Law Orders A, 1789–1793, 295; Record Book 1789–1792, 601–603.

Fee: Apr. 7, 1789, £1:15, Account Book, 192.

James Johnston v. William Rennolds.

Debt, on bill sealed, £16,000 current, Aug. 14, 1781, penal sum £32,000. Filed in General Court Oct., 1786. Caroline County.

J.M. for defendant.

Oct., 1787–Oct., 1789. Continued. District Court, Fredericksburg, Law Orders A, 1789–1793, 52.

Apr. 1790. Plea by security, special bail payment. Same, 108.

May 5, 1791. (District Court) V.j. for defendant, debt paid. Same, 241. Same, Record Book 1789–1792, 487–88.

Fee: Oct., 1787, £1:8 (in part). Account Book, 126.

Thomas Lea v. William Foushee.

Action in case. J.M. for defendant.

Sept. 29, 1789. Motion for depositions. District Court, Fredericksburg, Law Orders A, 1789–1793, 12.

May 2, 1790. Jury disagreement. Same, 99.

Oct. 6, 1791. V.j. for defendant, appeal certified to Court of Appeals, no record appeal pursued. Same, 312.

Fee: Sept. 22, 1789, £2:8. Account Book, 212.

(See herein *Foushee v. Lea,* 1795, Legal Practice, Court of Appeals, Va.)

John Lewis v. Richard Dixon, assignee.

Writ of supersedeas to Court of Spotsylvania County, j. for appellee,

May 2, 1787, £267:13:4, payable by £103:6:8. Filed in General Court. J.M. for appellant.

May 5, 1791. Affirmed, damages against appellant for retarding execution. District Court, Fredericksburg, Law Orders A, 1789–1793, 238; Same, Record Book 1789–1792, 480, 483.

Fee: Oct., 1789, "Lewis v. Dicken," £2:10. Account Book, 214.

Francis Madison, assignee of James Madison v. James Pendleton, Sheriff, Culpeper County.

Writ of supersedeas to j. Court of Culpeper County, Aug., 1789, rejecting motion for sheriff to pay over money received on execution. Filed Apr., 1790. J.M. for Pendleton.

Madison levied execution on j. against Richard Thomas and John Piper. Sheriff's return, property of Piper sold £19:6:5½, less tax for 1788, clerk's fee, cost of removing, balance paid to Joseph Strother under order of court for old arrears of taxes instead of to Madison.

Oct. 9, 1789. Writ awarded. District Court, Fredericksburg, Law Orders A, 1789–1793, 72.

May 7, 1791. Reversed, j. £14:10:½, amount made on execution. Same, 260; Same, Record Book, 1789–1792, 534–35.

Fee: Oct., 1789, £1:8. Account Book, 216.

Cornelius McLaney v. Reuben George, executor of John George.

Case. Oct. 1, 1789. Continued. District Court, Fredericksburg, Law Orders A, 1789–1793, 16.

Oct. 6, 1790. Jury disagreed. Same, 169.

May 4–5, 1791. Jury disagreed, submitted to arbitrators, award to be j. Same, 235, 236.

May 6, 1791. Award and j. for plaintiff, £7. Same, 246.

Fee: July, 1792, "Clanahan v. George," £2:8. Account Book, 332.

James Miller v. Philip Johnston.

Trespass and ejectment. Appeal from j. of Court of Caroline County, May, 1789, dismissing appellant's bill. 500 acres Caroline County claimed under indenture of appellee's father, July 18, 1768, to appellant conditioned on payment of £152 (a mortgage).

Deposition of other son, resident of Kentucky, and former executor allowed to prove payment, exceptions. Filed in General Court, Oct., 1788. J.M. for appellant.

May 10, 1791. (District Court) Affirmed. District Court, Fredericksburg, Law Orders A, 1789–1793, 267; Same, Record Book 1789–1792, 544–50.

Fees: Oct., 1785, £7, "finished suits"; Oct., 1789, "Miller, ejectment, chr.," £14. Account Book, 52, 216.

John Mitchell v. John Williams.

Debt, on obligation sealed, June 17, 1774, £238:10:5. Filed in General Court, Oct., 1788. Culpeper County. J.M. for defendant and James Williams, surety.

Oct. 1, 1789. Answer, payment, plaintiff British subject not recover in court under Virginia Act 783 suspending executions on certain judgments; office j. set aside; at issue. District Court, Fredericksburg, Law Orders, 1789–1793, 29.

May 5, 1791. Continued by consent. Same, 241.

Oct. 4, 1791. (District Court) On case agreed that Oct. 25, 1773, plaintiff conveyed all his estate including bond sued on to trustee (for creditors), some due British subjects. Same, 302.

Oct. 8, 1791. J. for plaintiff, £169:5:10, interest 5 per cent from June 17, 1774. Same, 330. Same, Record Book 1789–1792, 622–24.

Fee: Oct. 22, 1788, £2:10. Account Book, 172.

John Mitchell v. John Williams et al., executors of William Williams.

Debt, on obligation sealed, July 18, 1774, £140:6:4. Filed in General Court, Oct., 1788. Caroline County. J.M. for defendants.

Nov. 30, 1788. Appearance by J.M., oyer, special imparlance.

Oct. 8, 1791. On agreed case in lieu of special verdict, Oct. 25, 1773, Mitchell conveyed estate to trustee (for creditors) including bond sued on, some creditors British. J. for plaintiff £140:6:4, payable by £70:3:2, 5 per cent interest from Feb. 18, 1775. District Court, Fredericksburg, Law Orders A, 1789–1793, 330; Same, Record Book 1789–1792, 665–67.

Fee: Oct. 22, 1788, £2:10. Account Book, 172. Also "Williams adv. Mitchell," Same.

John Mitchell v. Robert Yancy, executor of Lewis Davis Yancy.

Debt, action on bond sealed executed by testator May, 1773, £263:8. Filed in General Court, Oct., 1788, Culpeper County. J.M. for defendant.

Oct. 1, 1789. Plea, debt due British citizen not recoverable under Virginia act deferring execution. District Court, Fredericksburg, Law Orders A, 1789–1793, 30.

May 7, 1791. (District Court) Agreed case in lieu of special verdict, on Oct. 25, 1773, testator conveyed all his estate and all debts, including the bond to trustee a citizen of Virginia for benefit of creditors, some of whom were British; testator executed bond on which suit brought. J. for plaintiff,

£236:8, payable by £134:3, interest 5 per cent from May 15, 1775, from estate. Same, 254; Same, Record Book 1789–1792, 511–12.

Also, *John Mitchell v. Robert Yancy.*

Oct. 5, 1793. Writ of inquiry set aside on motion of defendant who pleaded "not guilty;" plaintiff replied to plea. Same, Law Orders A, 1789–1793, 525.

Oct. 3, 1794. Suits dismissed, failure to prosecute. Same, Law Orders B, 1794–1798, 64.

Oct. 12, 1797. V.j. defendant not guilty, plaintiff assessed cost of defendant's defense. Same, 344.

Oct. 14, 1797. Appeal to Court of Appeals allowed. Same, 358. No record of appeal taken.

Fee: Oct., 1788, £2:10. Account Book, 172.

Oxley and Hancock v. Robert Brent.

Debt. J.M. for defendant.

Oct. 3, 1791. Continued by defendant. District Court, Fredericksburg, Law Orders A, 1789–1793, 291.

May 9, 1792. By consent award of J.M. and Bushrod Washington to be made judgment of court. No further entry. Same, 380.

Fee: May, 1791, £2:8. Account Book, 286.

Samuel Smith v. John Stockdale and John Young.

Debt, on obligation sealed, £700, filed Apr., 1790, Caroline County. J.M. for plaintiff. (Petition signed.)

Oct. 1, 1791. Confessed j. for plaintiff, £700, payable by £328. District Court, Fredericksburg, Law Orders A, 1789–1793, 93, 279; Same, Record Book 1789–1792, 562–64.

Fee: Oct., 1789, £2:16. Account Book, 216.

James Quarles, executor of Henry Washington v. Thacker Washington.

Case, on bill of exchange made by George Weedon, Dec. 22, 1786, on defendant in favor of testator, accepted by defendant, £150 specie. J.M. for defendant.

Oct. 3, 1791. J. for plaintiff, £185:16:8. District Court, Fredericksburg, Law Orders A, 1789–1793, 292; Same, Record Book 1789–1792, 594–96.

Fee: May, 1790, £5. Account Book, 244.

William Staunton v. Humphrey Richards.

Appeal from j. against appellant, Court of Culpeper County, Aug. 19, 1788, on replevin bond £748:3:7, payable by £374:1:9.

Filed in General Court Oct., 1788. J.M. for appellant.

Apr. 30, 1791. (District Court) J. affirmed. District Court, Fredericksburg, Law Orders A, 1789–1793, 214; Same, Record Book 1789–1792, 448–50.

Fee: Oct., 1788, £2:10. Account Book, 168.

John Stiles, lessee of William Fitzhugh v. William G. Stewart.

Ejectment, 100 acres land King George County. Filed District Court, Sept., 1789. J.M. for defendant.

May 6, 1791. V.j. for plaintiff. District Court, Fredericksburg, Law Orders A, 1789–1793, 247; Same, Record Book 1789–1792, 501–502.

Fee: Apr., 1790, £2:16. Account Book, 242.

Eppaphodilas Thornley v. Jeremiah Pickett.

Trespass, assault and battery. V.j. in Court of Quarterly Sessions, King George County, for Thornley, Mar. 5, 1787, £56:5 damages, reversed in General Court, Apr. 18, 1787. J.M. for Thornley.

Oct. 7, 1789. Continued. District Court, Fredericksburg, Law Orders A, 1789–1793, 56.

May 5, 1791. (District Court) On new trial, v.j. for Thornley, £50. Same, 242; Same, Record Book 1789–1792, 490–92.

Fee: Apr. 13, 1787, £2:10. Account Book, 106.

See also *Pickett v. Thornley.*

Case. Oct. 7, 1789. Continued. Same, Law Orders A, 1789–1793, 56.

May 5, 1791. Dismissed, failure to prosecute. Same, 230.

George Turner, assignee of Nathaniel Sanders v. Robert Scott.

Debt, on written obligation, defendant to deliver goods and merchandise, Mar. 15, 1789; defense, refusal of plaintiff to accept. J.M. for plaintiff (probable).

Sept. 30, 1789. Office j. against defendant and surety, John Mitchell, set aside; at issue. District Court, Fredericksburg, Law Orders A, 1789–1793, 15.

May 8, 1790. Answer, denial. Same, 125.

Oct. 5, 6, 1790. Jury disagreed. Same, 162, 166.

May 3, 1791. Same. Same, 230.

Sept. 30, 1791. Dismissed, agreed between parties. Same, 273.

Fee: May, 1791, £2:8. Account Book, 286.

George Weir v. William Elliott, John G. Woolfolk, Richard Bowles, d.b.a. William Elliott & Co.

Case. Debt on obligation sealed, £364:13:10½. J.M. for plaintiff.

(Signed petition.)

Sept., 1789. Filed.

Oct., 1789. Common order. Security.

Nov., 1789. Continued.

Jan., 1790. Common order confirmed.

Apr., 1790. Bail; plea payment. District Court, Fredericksburg, Law Orders A, 1789–1793, 76.

Oct. 3, 1791. Confessed j. £364:13:10½, payable by £182:6:11¼. Same, 291; Same, Record Book 1789–1792, 591.

Fee: June, 1789, £2:8. Account Book, 200.

John W. Willis and Samuel K. Bradford v. Mary Sullivan.

Appeal from j. Court of Spotsylvania County, Nov. 6, 1787, by appellee against appellants on replevin bond taken on writ of *fieri facias* against Willis, £302:19:9. Filed in General Court, Apr., 1788. J.M. for appellants.

Apr., 1788—Nov., 1789. Continued.

Apr. 30, 1791. Appellants not appear. Affirmed on record.

District Court, Fredericksburg, Law Orders A, 1789–1793, 296; Record Book 1789–1792, 413–14.

Fee: Apr., 1791 (District Court), "Bradford and Willis, App.," £2:8. Account Book, 282.

Samuel Yager v. Thomas Sampson.

Trespass, assault and battery. J.M. for defendant.

May 3, 1791. Dismissed, agreed between parties. District Court, Fredericksburg, Law Orders A, 1789–1793, 232.

Fee: Apr., 1788, £2:10. Account Book, 154.

Isaac Zane v. Mason Pitcher and Edward Dickerson.

Case. J.M. for plaintiff.

Oct. 7, 1789. Abated as to Dickerson, death; writ of enquiry of damages as to other. District Court, Fredericksburg, Law Orders A, 1789–1793, 60.

May 3, 1791. Abated, death of defendant. Same, 231.

Fee: Dec., 1789, "retainer," £2:8. Account Book, 228.

District Court, Prince Edward

James Burnett v. Robert Easley.

Appeal from j. against appellant County Court, Buckingham, May, 1788, £39:11:3. J.M. for appellee.

Apr. 4, 1791. Submitted. District Court, Prince Edward, Order Book 1789–1792, 165.

Apr. 5, 1791. Reversed, declaration insufficient. Same, 168–69.

For further proceedings between parties probably in same cause for abusive use of stud horse, resulting in v.j. for Easley Apr. 11, 1792, of £37:3:6, Breckenridge, his attorney of record, see Prince Edward, Records at Large 1792–1795, 32.

Fee: Oct. 4, 1788, £2:16 "Easly adv. Burnet (John Allen) appeal." Account Book, 166.

Charles Cotteral v. Benjamin Jordan.

Detinue. J.M. for plaintiff.

Sept. 7, 1789. Continued. District Court, Prince Edward, Order Book 1789–1792, 40.

Apr. 6, 1790. Continued. Same, 78.

Sept. 7, 1790. Continued, commission for deposition. Same, 131.

Apr. 2, 1791. Dismissed by consent. Same, 163.

Fees: July 20, 1786, £2:10, "Buckingham"; Oct. 2, 1786, £2:8 "detinue." Account Book, 78, 84.

Philimon Halcombe (Overstreet) v. John Bibb, assignee of William Walker.

Writ of supersedeas to j. County Court, Prince Edward, for defendant, Aug. 18, 1790, £204 current. J.M. for defendant.

Apr. 9, 1791. Abated by death of defendant. District Court, Prince Edward, Order Book 1789–1792, 187.

Fee: July, 1793, £5. Account Book, 368.

Richard James and William Spears v. John Cobbs.

Appeal from County Court, Cumberland, j. for appellee, Mar. 28, 1787, £226:0:3½. J.M. for appellant.

Sept. 2, 1790. Dismissed by consent. District Court, Prince Edward, Order Book 1789–1792, 112.

Sept. 3, 1790. Reinstated by appellant. Same, 115.

Sept. 8, 1790. Continued. Same, 134.

Apr. 4, 1791. Dismissed by consent. Same, 165.

Fee: Sept. 24, 1787, £2:10 "appear." Account Book, 122.

John Overton and Richard Morris v. John George, William Carr, and John Ramey.

Case. J.M. for defendants.

Apr. 9, 1790. Continued. District Court, Prince Edward, Order Book 1789–1792, 94.

Apr. 7, 1791. Continued. Same, 178.

Sept. 8, 1791. V.j. £89:4:5 against George and securities; George released from custody. Same, 210.

Fee: Oct. 2, 1788, £1:4. Account Book, 168.

Richard Taylor v. George Miller, late Deputy Sheriff and Collector of Revenue Buckingham County.

Case, for extorting and exacting under colour of office public taxes and county and parish levies for year 1788 in amount of £3 Va., damages £200. J.M. for defendant.

Apr. 7, 1791. V.j. for plaintiff, £50.

Apr. 8, 1791. Motion for new trial denied. (Exhibits contain interesting land tax, court costs, sheriff's fees, etc.) District Court, Prince Edward, Records at Large 1789–1792, 364–71.

Fee: Aug., 1791, £5. Account Book, 294.

Joseph Vest v. Edmund King.

Case, money had and received, £100, Halifax County. J.M. for plaintiff. (Signed petition.)

Controversy involved sale of land in Pittsylvania County, 850 acres, of which 565 acres conveyed; j. by Vest in General Court Apr., 1784, for £50 payment; injunction in High Court of Chancery, Nov. 17, 1784, against execution on j. dissolved if tender of balance of land less remit of £10 as determined by arbitrators.

Sept. 1, 1789. Special bail, common order.

Apr., 1790, 1791. Continued, *non assumpsit.*

Sept. 8, 1791. V.j. for defendant. District Court, Prince Edward, Records at Large 1789–1792, 426.

Fee: Dec. 15, 1787, £2:10. Account Book, 138.

Benjamin Wilson, trustee for Christopher McCrae, executor of John Harris v. George Keeling.

Detinue, for fourteen slaves, valued £50 each, lost and found and detained by defendant. Cumberland County. J.M. for defendant.

Sept. 2, 1791. Confessed j. for plaintiff, one shilling damages.

District Court, Prince Edward, Records at Large 1789–1792, 381–82.

Also *Same v. Same.*

Ejectment, for 750-acre farm.

Sept. 2, 1791. Confessed j. for plaintiff. Same, 383–85.

Fee: May, 1792, £1:16. Account Book, 322.

District Court, Prince William

David Ross and Thomas Pleasants, for selves and for partners, David Ross & Co. v. William Hunter, Jun., for self and John Allison.

Debt. Record of case incomplete. J.M. for defendants.

Oct. 13, 1794. Alias *scire facias* against Hunter. District Court, Prince William, Order Book 1794–1798, 8.

May 13, 1795. Not returned. Same, 95.

Oct. 13, 1795. Same. Same, 151.

May 13, 1796. Another writ issued. Same, 209.

May 20, 1797. Continued. Same, 351.

Oct. 20, 1797. Continued. Same, 432.

Fee: Oct., 1791, £4:10. Account Book, 302.

1792

DOCUMENTS

Jan. 4
Richmond *State Bank*

Call for meeting of merchants and others in Richmond at Eagle Tavern, Dec. 3, 1791, to consider proposition of merchants of Petersburg to apply to legislature for state bank; further meeting of citizens called for May 1, 1792; J.M. named as present at original meeting. Va. Gaz. & G.A., Jan. 4, 1792, 4, through Jan. 25, 1792, 3.

Jan. 31
Richmond *Potomac Company*

Legal opinion by J.M. concerning act for opening and extending navigation of Potomac River; advising, under section 11 of act, condemnation of land on side of canal not permissible after canal cut; powers under section 12 may be exercised after canal completed. *Opinion of Judge Marshall, in Relation to the Potomac Company; and Agreement by the Potomac Company with General Henry Lee* (Georgetown, D.C. Rind, 1817).

Mar. 17
Richmond *Bond-Sinking Fund*

J.M. bondsman with others for Harry Heth as agent to the Sinking Fund of Virginia. V, Exec. Papers, Box 1792, Jan.-Mar., Folder Mar. 11–20.

June 18
RICHMOND *Bridge Lottery*

J.M. appointed by Common Hall of Richmond on committee of managers of lottery to raise not to exceed £1,200 for building bridge over Shockoe Creek. Plan adopted for £1,125; 6,250 tickets. V, Richmond Common Hall Records 1782–1793, I, 259–60.

Aug. 1. Plan for lottery revised to £450 and 2,500 tickets; J.M. on committee of managers. Same, 263.

Aug. 9. Notice of lottery published (see herein, Aug. 9).

Nov. 10. Drawing of lottery authorized when 600 tickets sold. Same, 271.

Nov. 15. Managers authorized to dispose of unsold tickets of lottery on terms deemed beneficial to city. Same, 272.

July 13
RICHMOND *State Treasurer Accounts*

Warrant of payment by state of £11:15:0 under heading "Public Warehouse." (Identity of J.M. named uncertain.) V, Warrants Issued July 2–Sept. 31, 1792, Exec. Papers, Box July–Sept., 1792, Folder Sept. 21–30.

Aug. 9
RICHMOND *Bridge Lottery*

Notice of lottery to build stone bridge over Shockoe Creek, signed J.M. and others, managers. Va. Gaz. & G.A., Sept. 5, 1792, 4; through Oct. 24, 1792, 2.

Aug.
RICHMOND *to Polly Marshall*

Letter in verse deploring loss of two children, attempting to reconcile wife and urging her to return home from her mother's (Ambler). (n.f.) Described by J.M. in letter to Joseph Story, June 26, 1831 (herein). MHi. Proc. (ser. 2), Vol. XIV (Nov., 1900), 344–46; Oster, *Marshall*, 133–36; Mason, *Polly*, 60–62.

Sept. 14 *to John A. Chevallie*

Concerning an Assembly meeting. Listed in Lazare, (1960), 606. Present owner unknown.

Sept. 24
FAUQUIER COUNTY, VA. *Law Suit*

J.M., Esq. v. John T. Waller and Thomas Simpson. Debt on replevin bond taken on distress for rent. Default j. £35:14 Va. payable £17:17. County Court, Fauquier, Minute Book 1791–1793, 212.

Nov. 7
RICHMOND *to James Webb*

Acknowledges letter of 5th; legal matter will be attended to. NcD, John Rutherford Papers.

Dec. 23
RICHMOND *Bank of Richmond*

Charter for Bank of Richmond granted to J.M. and others. V, Va. Acts, Box Oct., 1792, Chap. LXXVII, 105–107; Hening, Stat., XIII, 599.

n.d., RICHMOND *to (Thomas) Walker*

Concerning affidavits in case against Syme. DLC, Rives Papers. (See herein, 1787, Legal Practice; July 9, 1789.)

Militia—Brigadier General

J.M. named brigadier general of Second Brigade, Virginia Militia under act of General Assembly at sessions of 1792 and 1793. V, War 10 (Militia-Commissions, General Orders, 1782–1809), 5.

Charter, Insurance Company

J.M. on committee to examine plan for fire insurance company and petition legislature for charter; charter granted "Mutual Assurance Society of Virginia." V, Memorial of Wm. F. Ast and others; Christian, *Richmond, Her Past and Present,* 46.

LEGAL PRACTICE

DURING THE YEAR 1792, income from legal fees declined to £973:14:1, and the number of fees collected to 205.

Of these, approximately twenty-four are designated as for advice, and fees were in the £1 bracket with the exception of advice on the Fairfax will, which was £2:8.

In litigated matters (in thirty-three of which the nature is noted) the shift appeared to be toward federal court cases, fees for nine of which are entered. Appeals total eight, and chancery matters nine, two of which are appeals in chancery. The "defense of Branch" may have been the only criminal case.

There is a slight tendency toward higher individual fees for litigated cases, with sixty-four such fees in the £5 bracket and fourteen in the £7, together accounting for over one-third of this total number. There were, however, only fourteen fees over £10; two in the £11 bracket, one in the £12, four in the £14, one of £28, one of £30, one of £35, and £50 from Norton.

Mar., *n.p.* *Adams Will*

Legal opinion on will of Thomas Adams, deceased, in answer to queries as to subjection of bequeathed land to exoneration of slaves and payment of debts and distribution by executor where debts. VHi.

Fee: Mar., 1792, £1:8. Account Book, 316.

U.S. Circuit Court, Virginia

John McCall v. Peter McDougall and Co.

Petition for injunction against default j. in U.S. Circuit Court, May, 1792, on sealed obligation, £900 Va., payable by £450 (see Record Book 1, 97); grounds surprise, refusal to give credit of £300:3:9. J.M. for petitioner.

Dec. 5, 1792. Allowed as to part paid. U.S. Circuit Court, Va., Order Book I, 138.

V, U.S. Circuit Court Case Papers, containing autograph petition.

McCall and Shedden v. William Banks.

Petition to enjoin default j. in U.S. Circuit Court on penal bond of 1774, £180 Va. payable by £90, Nov. 24, 1791 (see Record Book 1, 40–42; Order Book 1, 81, 113, 133); grounds plaintiffs British, attorney failed to defend; interest not due during War. May 23, 1792. J.M. for petitioner.

Dec. 5, 1792. Granted as to £25:5:2. U.S. Circuit Court, Va., Order Book I, 138.

V, U.S. Circuit Court Case Papers, containing autograph petition.

James and Bruce Wilson, London merchants v. James Wilson.

Debt, for goods sold and delivered, £1,500. J.M. for plaintiff.

Filed 1791 and continued until May 25, 1792, when dismissed. U.S. Circuit Court, Va., Order Book I, 99. Record Book Index, Civil, May T 1792.

V, U.S. Circuit Court Case Papers. (Autograph petition.)

Fees: See *Wilson v. Wills*, Mar., 1790, £5, Account Book, 236. Also *Wilsons v. Wilson*, Chancery, £4:16. Account Book, 146.

Court of Appeals of Virginia

Tabb v. Gregory, 4 Call 225, 226–27.

Error from j. May 3, 1791, District Court, Brunswick Courthouse. J. for defendant in error, affirmed. J.M. for plaintiff in error.

Gregory, candidate for House of Delegates, brought action of slander alleging words spoken in 1789, amended to 1788 before trial, during trial leave granted to amend to 1789. Held, transitory action, date immaterial; practice as to amendments discussed.

Apr. 13, 1792. Heard. Court of Appeals, Va., Order Book II, 153.

Apr. 14. Affirmed. Same, 155–56.

Further proceedings—Apr. 16, 1794. Order for record of District Court, action on order. Same, 264.

Nov. 6, 1794. Same. Same, III, 24.

Apr. 17, 1795. Appeal dismissed. Same, 49.

Fee: Nov., 1791, £10. Account Book, 304.

Elisha White v. Wood Jones' Heirs, 4 Call 253, 256–57, 1 Washington 116, affirming Wythe, 100–101.

Appeal from decree of High Court of Chancery, June 1, 1791, reversing decree of County Court of Charlotte, May 4, 1789, affirmed.

J.M. for appellee.

White brought action for 426 acres land purchased from Hatcher in 1762, who had surveyed land in 1740 without order of Council, and failed to apply for patent, pay quitrents, or cultivate. In 1744, Jones received order of Council and surveyed 2,000 acres. White petitioned for land as lapsed and received patent in 1764 relating Hatcher's survey; but prior thereto Jones received patent for the 2,000 acres. The lower court entered j. against Jones for the 426 acres, apparently on grounds of fraud or relating back of White's patent. The Court of Chancery declared issue of fraud for court of law, but reversed on grounds of delay in asserting rights by White. Held, issue of fraud cognizable in equity or law, but affirmed because no proof of fraud or that prior rights of Hatcher preserved.

Oct. 11–12. Heard. Court of Appeals, Va., Order Book II, 182–83.

Oct. 13. Affirmed. Same, 184.

Fee: May 11, 1790, £5. Account Book 246.

Note: J.M. cited two unpublished cases "known only to few of the profession" (p. 257).

John Hoomes v. Jacob Kuhn, 4 Call 274, affirming Wythe, 70.

Assault and battery. Appeal from decree High Court of Chancery, Oct. 28, 1791, refusing injunction against j. District Court, Fredericksburg, against appellant, £100. Affirmed. J.M. for appellant.

Altercation over whipping of slave of Hoomes by Kuhn for supposed theft. In action by Kuhn against Hoomes for assault and battery, witnesses of latter sick and several late; motions for new trial denied.

Held, no relief in equity; delinquency and negligence of petitioner noted; discretion of trial judge as to new trial noted.

Oct. 18, 1792. Heard. Court of Appeals, Va., Order Book II, 187.

Oct. 20, 1792. Affirmed. Same, 188.

Fees: Apr. 23, 1787, £3; Oct., 1791, £5:12; Sept., 1792, £10. Account Book, 110, 300, 338.

Trespass, assault and battery, damages, £2,000, filed in General Court Oct., 1786, Caroline County; J.M. was one of counsel for Hoomes.

Oct., 1787—Sept., 1789. Continued.

May 6, 1791. (General Court) V.j. for plaintiff £100. District Court, Fredericksburg, Record Book 1789–1792, 498–99; Same, Law Orders A, 1789–1793, 62, 245.

Josiah Wood v. Isaac Davis, 1 Washington 69.

Appeal from j. District Court of Charlottesville, Apr. 25, 1791, for appellee on forthcoming bond, affirmed. J.M. for appellee. J. on bond for 32,325 pounds tobacco and £9:10, payable 16,164 pounds tobacco; objection that bond did not state that delivery date was day of sale.

Held, not required.

Apr. 11, 1792. Submitted. Court of Appeals, Va., Order Book II, 150.

Apr. 12, 1792. Affirmed. Same, 152.

Fee: June, 1791, £2:16. Account Book, 290.

James and Thomas Evans and Tom Beale v. William Smith, 1 Washington 72.

Debt, appeal from j. against appellant, District Court of King and Queen Courthouse. Apr. 23, 1791, £535:19, payable by £267:19:6, affirmed. J.M. for appellee.

Objection to evidence, variance of bond sued on and declaration; bond stating defendants "of the County of Essex" and not so stated in declaration; objection overruled.

Apr. 13, 1792. Dismissed, failure to prosecute. Court of Appeals, Va., Order Book II, 154.

Apr. 17, 1792. Order set aside; appellant not appearing, j. affirmed. Same, 160.

Fees: Apr., 1792, £8; Apr., 1793, £5. Account Book, 320, 358.

George Asberry, John Chastain, and Jeremiah Hatcher v. James Callaway and William Leftwich, administrators of Gross Scruggs, 1 Washington 72.

Writ of supersedeas to District Court of New London, Apr. 22, 1791, affirming in part j. for defendant in error by County Court of Bedford, Jan. 5, 1791, penalty of bond, payable by £651:8:3 with damages at 20 per cent per annum, reversed. J.M. for plaintiff in error. Administrators of sheriff on motion under statutory proceedings obtained above judgment against Trent and Asberry, his deputy sheriffs and sureties on their bonds for revenue tax due 1783 and damages recovered by Commonwealth against him. Trent denied executing joint sheriff's bond sued on by acknowledgment or delivery; j. had against him, Asberry and securities affirmed by District Court except as to Trent remanded for jury trial. Held, error to give j. on bond not proved executed by Trent; act of 1780 under which action brought calling for 20 per cent altered by act of 1783 which reduced damages assessable against sheriff to 15 per cent; j. should be for sum under sheriff chargeable and not penalty of bond, payable by such sum.

Apr. 16, 1792. Submitted on record, defendant in error not appearing. Court of Appeals, Va., Order Book II, 158.

Apr. 18, 1792. Reversed and remanded. Same, 158.

Fee: May, 1791, £4:4. Account Book, 288.

John Butler v. Mary Parks, executrix of John Parks, 1 Washington 76.

Appeal from District Court, King and Queen Courthouse, Apr. 25, 1791, reversing j. of County Court of King William, May, 1784, reversed.

J.M. for appellee.

Detinue by Butler for five slaves; j. rendered for four; issue as to fifth not determined. Held, j. properly reversed but error in failing to order new trial.

June 21, 1791. Supersedeas. Court of Appeals, Va., Order Book II, 83.

Apr. 20, 1792. Reversed. Same, 164.

Fee: Apr., 1789, £0:12. Account Book, 192.

John Scott v. Alexander and Peterfield Trent, merchants, 1 Washington 77.

Appeal from j. against appellant, District Court of Charlottesville, Sept., 1791, £251:18:8. J.M. for appellant.

Action by partnership for goods sold and delivered and money lent.

Appellant offered receipts of payments signed by one Trent partner with whom had individual account and not stating if for partnership account; also receipts signed by same Trent for payment of debts which he agreed to pay and apply balance to debts due Trent and due partnership; balance not shown. Court refused to admit as evidence.

Held, not admissible; receipts not show payment for company account; balance unsettled amount. Court suggested if balance due partnership in partners hands, injunction would lie against partnership.

Apr. 16, 1792. Submitted. Court of Appeals, Va., Order Book II, 158.

Apr. 21, 1792. Affirmed. Same, 165.

Fee: Mar., 1792, £2:8. Account Book, 316.

Cochran v. Street, 1 Washington 79, 80, reversing Wythe, 69.

Appeal from High Court of Chancery, May 16, 1792, reversing Hanover County Court, reversed. J.M. for appellant.

Street brought action of slander; j. £150; motion in arrest of judgment refused; reversed by injunction on chancery side of same court, and new trial ordered on basis of surprise and mistake of jury in arriving at verdict believing majority ruled. Held, no evidence of surprise; verdict based on mistake of jury.

Apr. 24, 1792. Order of reversal. Court of Appeals, Va., Order Book II, 166.

Fee: Apr., 1789, £4:16, "Cochran 2 appeals." Account Book, 192.

Jesse Thornton v. William Smith, 1 Washington 81.

Slander, writ of error to j. District Court, Richmond, Sept. 5, 1791, reversing j. Court of Hustings, Richmond, Sept. 25, 1787, £55, affirmed. J.M. for appellant.

Declaration commencing "City of Richmond" and laying words spoken "in the city aforesaid," failed to state "within jurisdiction of the court."

Held, fatal defect, even where not raised at trial. The president of the court dissented, stating English precedents not applicable in America; Statute of Jeofails cures; words required "cabalistical."

Argument of J.M. on a point declared not sound (p. 86).

Nov. 29, 1791. Writ issued. Court of Appeals, Va., Order Book II, 146.

Apr. 17, 1792. Heard. Same, 159.

Apr. 28, 1792. Affirmed. Same, 169.

Fee: Mar. 10, 1788, £2:10. "Appeal" to District Court. Account Book, 146.

David Ross v. Erasmus Gill and Sarah, his wife, 1 Washington 87.

Error from District Court of Petersburg, Sept. 24, 1790, reversing j. Court of Hustings for Richmond, Sept. 5, 1787, and dismissing.

Action of debt, j. for appellees, plaintiff below, affirmed.

J.M. for appellees.

Action for rent by ward after reaching majority on parol lease, supported by written memorandum by guardian, for seven years occupancy at £70. Term of lease until ward of age or marries; privilege to give up at expiration of any year. Declaration made in two counts; proof of one only. Held, unproved count surplusage; refusal of nonsuit not ground for exception; lease interpreted as year to year; ward has privity and may sue where rent reserved to her.

June 29, 1791. Heard. Court of Appeals, Va., Order Book II, 105.

July 1. Continued for rehearing. Same, 110.

Apr. 14, 1792. Heard. Same, 156.

Apr. 28. Affirmed. Same, 169.

Fee: Sept. 18, 1790, £4:4. Account Book, 260.

(See related case, herein 1794, Legal Practice, Court of Appeals, Va., *Ross v. Gill,* 4 Call 250.)

Richard Bibb and John Watson v. Commonwealth for benefit of Catherine Cauthorne, 1 Washington 91.

Appeal from j. District Court, Apr. 8, 1791, for defendant in error, reversed and amended. J.M. for appellants.

Action of debt in name of Commonwealth for benefit of Cauthorne on bond of William Bibb, former sheriff, against sureties for execution and sale of property of Cauthorne despite writs of supersedeas against judgments on which execution levied.

V.j. for Commonwealth for benefit of Cauthorne in amount of bond, £1,000, dischargable by damages of £260 "and such other damages, as may be hereafter assessed, upon suing out a *fieri facias* and assigning new breaches."

Held, action sustainable by Commonwealth on bond made to it under act of 1748, which considered by legislature still in force by its act of 1782, repealing it in part only, that the bond need not be made out to the justices as provided in act of 1776.

Further, however, error in judgment in providing recovery for future injuries by Cauthorne only, excluding all others. J. ordered amended.

Nov. 21, 1791. Continued. Court of Appeals, Va., Order Book II, 138.

Apr. 25, 1792. Heard. Same, 167.

Apr. 30, 1792. Reversed and amended.

Fees: Nov., 1791, £2:8; Apr., 1792, £2:10. Account Book, 306, 320.

Jesse Taylor v. John Dundass, 1 Washington 92.

Appeal from District Court, Dumfries, Apr. 18, 1791, reversing County Court of Fairfax, June 26, 1790, which quashed execution against appellee; reversed and County Court affirmed. J.M. for appellee.

Appellee with judgment against Hendricks and Taylor, his security, levied execution on effects of former and replevin bond taken. The security being insufficient, appellee sued out second execution directed to property of Taylor.

Held, second execution properly quashed; replevin bond with execution not quashed is bar to second execution.

Apr. 30, 1792. Heard. Court of Appeals, Va., Order Book II, 170.

May 3, 1792. Reversed. Same, 179.

Fee: Oct., 1791, £7. Account Book, 302.

Richard Kennon v. Archibald McRoberts and Elizabeth, 1 Washington 96.

Ejectment, appeal from j. District Court, Brunswick Courthouse, Oct. 4, 1790, to appellee 1,000 acres, reversed. J.M. for appellant.

Testator in his will stated in preamble disposition of his "temporal estate"; among devises willed and bequeathed to his eldest son Robert "all my lands at the Ochaneachy island," without further description of interest, and to his wife and daughter "all the rest of my estate real and personal."

Held, the devise was in fee; the residuary clause did not pass the reversion, the heir of the devisee, not the reversioner, taking. English cases were extensively reviewed, the result of efforts of counsel for appellee.

Nov. 18, 1791. Heard. Court of Appeals, Va., Order Book II, 132.

Dec. 1, 1791. Continued. Same, 148.

Apr. 21, 1792. Reheard. Same, 165.

Apr. 23, 1792. Continued one day. Same, 166.

Apr. 24, 1792. Heard further. Same, 166.

Apr. 30, 1792. Law on agreed case for appellant, bill dismissed. Same, 170.

Fee: Nov., 1791, £7:10. Account Book, 304.

Mary Sloman Scott, executrix of Thomas Scott v. William Call, surviving partner of Field and Call, 1 Washington 115.

Debt, appeal from j. for appellee District Court of Petersburg, Sept. 3, 1790, £509:3:6 St., rate of exchange settled at 33⅓ per cent, reversed. J.M. for appellant.

Action on protested bill of exchange, £187:15 St. "of the value of £250:6:8 current," protest fees, interest at 10 per cent from due date. Error based on failure to prove protested bill presented to drawer under act allowing 10 per cent.

Held, not decided, declaration faulty in claiming current money on bill payable in sterling only.

June 30, 1791. Heard. Circuit Court of Appeals, Va., Order Book II, 109.

Apr. 28, 1792. Rehearing. Same, 169.

May 5, 1792. Continued. Same, 180.

Oct. 13, 1792. Reheard. Same, 184.

Oct. 29, 1792. Reversed. Same, 202.

Fee: Mar. 31, 1788, £2:12. Account Book, 148.

Ross v. Poythress, I Washington 120, 122.

Appeal from District Court, Petersburg.

J. dismissing action, affirmed. J.M. for appellee.

Action of debt by Ross against sheriff for breach of prison bounds bond; prisoner released because j. on which detained enjoined by High Court of Chancery. Held, prisoner properly discharged.

Oct. 16, 1792. Heard. Court of Appeals, Va., Order Book II, 185.

Oct. 17. Affirmed. Same, 186.

William Thompson v. David and James Davenport, 1 Washington 125.

Appeal from decree High Court of Chancery, Oct. 24, 1791, allowing injunction of judgment of law, reversed and amended. J.M. for defendants in error. J. had in County Court of Hanover for appellant on bond by appellees, £113:16:4, purchase price at foreclosure sale of land under defaulted mortgage of £40:18:7 to secure debt of 1756. Bill claimed title defective because of prior auction sale of land to father of one appellee, concealment of mortgage claim at time, and payment of mortgage foreclosed. There was a running account between appellant and mortgagee subsequent to mortgage, which appellees claimed paid off the mortgage and left merely an account due. Chancery Court applying one specific payment to reduction of mortgage, balance to running account, enjoined proceeding on judgment at law on bond above amount due on mortgage, £29:1:3 with interest, less costs in action at law and in chancery proceedings.

Held, payments on mortgage properly determined and separated from running account; decree erroneous in assessing appellant costs of action at law and failing to order sale under mortgage and application of funds.

Oct. 15, 1792. Heard. Court of Appeals, Va., Order Book II, 185.
Oct. 20, 1792. Reversed, amended order. Same, 188.
Fee: Feb., 1791, £4:10. Account Book, 274.

James Hill and Carter Braxton v. Roger Gregory, executor of Fendall Southerland, 1 Washington 128, amending Wythe, 13.

Appeal from decree, High Court of Chancery, Oct. 27, 1790, enjoining enforcement of j. by appellee against appellant, except amount determined, reversed and amended. J.M. for appellee.

Hill endorser of protested bill of exchange, 1776, drawn by Braxton to Southerland, suit pending thereon in county court; parties agree to confessed j. £778:7:4 and interest; Braxton failed to enter same and in 1784 without notice obtained j. on account for £361:6:10; on supersedeas by Braxton, reversed. In 1787, Southerland in new suit against Hill, j. £1,400:5:9. Injunction sought against this j., claiming credits against bill of exchange and involving running mercantile account between Braxton and Southerland.

Held, Chancery Court reversed on principles for settling account; amount agreed by parties in 1776 adopted; two bonds given to Southerland by Braxton in 1783 applied to protested bill account, rather than other accounts between them, reducing Hill's obligation to £34:17:9½; in adjusting running account between Braxton and Southerland 1777–1780, goods delivered by Braxton set off against a bond of Braxton and general account at nominal sum (not using scale of depreciation), but residue of Braxton account set off against Southerland debt at legal scale of depreciation, 80 to 1, balance due from Braxton to Southerland on account £70:0:4.

Oct. 10, 1792. Heard, Hill not appearing. Court of Appeals, Va., Order Book II, 186.

Oct. 29, 1792. Reversed, amended decree. Same, 197–98.

Fees: Aug., 1787, £2:10; Sept. 4, 1788, £3:16; Oct. 24, 1788, £1:8; Oct., 1792, £7. Account Book, 120, 166, 172, 340.

Daniel Smith v. Thomas Walker and Nicholas Lewis, executors of John Mickie, 1 Washington 135.

Case, appeal from District Court of Charlottesville, Apr., 1791, reversing j. for appellant in County Court of Albemarle, Aug. 12, 1788, £240:14. Reversed and dismissed. J.M. for appellee.

Declaration claimed marriage of appellant to granddaughter of testator on promise to receive as much of estate as any of own children, not give as much as some. Pleas, not assume, not assume within five years, concluding to country. Jury found did assume, but not within five years; j. for appellant.

District Court reversed on general rejection of evidence by defendant of suit in chancery between parties in which specific performance of contract denied.

Held, declaration defective in failing to state amount of claim, what given to others, and time; plea of five years defective failing to state before institution of suit, and by concluding to country rather than court; verdict inconsistent; District Court order defective in reversing without dismissing, granting new trial, or repleader; verdict not cure defects in declaration.

Apr. 13, 1792. Certiorari to certify record. Court of Appeals, Va., Order Book II, 155.

Oct. 21, 1792. Heard. Same, 189.

Oct. 24, 1792. Reversed and dismissed. Same, 192.

Fee: Oct., 1791, £5. Account Book, 300.

William Nelson v. Thomas and John Nelson, 1 Washington 136.

Appeal from High Court of Chancery, Nov. 7, 1791, dismissing appellant's bill, affirmed. J.M. for appellee.

Elder son claimed oral agreement in 1787 with brother to divide estate of father equally, regardless of will; latter lived with father who was infirm and always declared intention to give equally; thereafter, will gave larger estate to younger son.

Held, such agreement generally irreverence to parent and not enforced; might be under circumstances, but agreement not proved.

Oct. 24, 1792. Heard. Court of Appeals, Va., Order Book II, 192.

Oct. 25, 1792. Affirmed. Same, 193.

Fees: Mar. 25, 1789, "Chr.," £2:15; Oct., 1790, £25; Feb., 1795, £5. Account Book, 188, 264, 404.

Keel and Roberts v. Thomas Herbert's Executors, 1 Washington 138.

Writ of supersedeas against j. District Court, Suffolk, May 8, 1790, affirming j. Borough Court of Norfolk, Sept. 5, 1787, for Herbert £220 damages and costs. Reversed. J.M. for defendant in error.

June 25, 1791. Writ formerly issued not returned; new writ of certiorari for record. Court of Appeals, Va., Order Book II, 103.

Apr. 13, 1792. New writ issued. Same, 154.

Apr. 27, 1792. Defendant dead, writ of Apr. 13 set aside, new writ against executrix. Same, 168.

Oct. 23, 1792. Writ quashed, *scire facias* annulled, executrix cannot use on bond for previous writ, a new proceedings. Same, 190.

Apr. 12, 1793. Continued. Same, 260.

Oct. 19, 1793. Defendant in error not appearing, writ annulled; lower court ruled on sufficiency of evidence, a question for jury.

Fees: May, 1789, "adv. Herbert's," £5:8; May, 1791, "Herbert, Ch.," £5. Account Book, 286.

Francis Thornton, William Thornton, and Fielding Lewis, executors of Rev. John Thompson, clerk; George Gray and Mildren, his wife v. Alexander Spotswood. 1 Washington 142.

Appeal from High Court of Chancery, Oct. 14, 1789, reversing decree of County Court of Spotsylvania against appellants, Aug. 7, 1788. J.M. for appellants.

Grandfather of appellee settled annuity of £500 on wife chargeable on mine tract, devised land to son in tail. Wife remarried; husband and his legatee brought suit in equity on bonds and bills given for arrears of annuity by son before death. County Court decreed to appellants amount of bills of exchange plus 10 per cent damages, amount of bonds, annuity payment due; ordered mine land sold to satisfy.

Held, relief not in equity but law; also, in equity annuity extinguished by payment of bonds and bills.

Dec. 2, 1790. Three judges disqualify selves. Court of Appeals, Va., Order Book II, 36.

June 24, 1791. Same. Same, 101.

Nov. 19. General Court judges not appear though requested. Same, 146.

Oct. 10, 1792. Special Court of Appeals not appear. Same, 182.

Nov. 21, 22. Heard. Same, 204, 205.

Nov. 24. Reversed. Same, 206.

Fee: Oct., 1789, £30. Account Book, 220.

Adam Hunter and Abner Vernon, executors of James Hunter, and Edward Herndon and James Lewis, executors of John Herndon v. Alexander Spotswood, 1 Washington 145.

Appeal from High Court of Chancery, Nov. 24, 1790.

J. for appellee, affirmed. J.M. with co-counsel Warden and Stark for appellants.

Executors of John Spotswood obtained j. against Campbell, a nonresident, for breach of trust in receiving monies under agreement with appellants for sale of interest in iron works, and against appellants for attached assets of Campbell in their hands. Reversed for failure of record to show published service on Campbell except by certificate of clerk; later affirmed on correction of record.

Jan. 30, 1791. Three judges disqualify for interest. Court of Appeals, Va., Order Book II, 106.

Nov. 29. Judges of General Court did not appear. Same, 146.

Oct. 10, 1792. Continued, three judges disqualified for interest or otherwise. Same, II, 182.

Nov. 21–23. Heard. Same, 204–205.

Nov. 26. Reversed. Same, 205.

Apr. 30, 1793. Three judges disqualified selves. Same, 229.

June 21. Heard. Same, 231.

June 23. Publication of service noted, affirmed. Same, 232.

Fees: Apr. 22, 1789, £2:8; May, 1791, £6; Nov., 1792, £14. Account Book, 194, 233, 286, 342.

Commonwealth v. Churchill Gibbs, late Lieutenant in First Virginia State Regiment.

Appeal from District Court, Richmond, Sept. 10, 1791, ordering certificate for five years' full pay in commutation of half pay for life with interest. J.M. for appellee.

May 1, 1792. Affirmed. Court of Appeals, Va., Order Book II, 172.

(See herein, affidavit of J.M.)

Commonwealth v. William Graves late a coronet and quartermaster of cavalry of Col. Dabney's legion.

Appeal from judgments of District Court, Richmond, Sept. 9, 1791, ordering certificate for five years' full pay in commutation of half pay for life with interest. J.M. for defendant.

Apr. 25, 1792. Heard. Court of Appeals, Va., Order Book II, 167.

May 2, 1792. Reversed on grounds defendant discharged on Feb. 9, 1783, prior to signing of preliminary Articles of Peace. Same, 172.

Fee: Oct., 1788, £4:20. Account Book, 170.

Related case involving commutation for half pay: *Commonwealth v. James Mercer, administrator of Alexander Dick, late Major to Dabney's legion,* Order Book II, 171; *Same v. Ludowick Brodie, late Surgeon in Second Virginia State Regiment and Dabney's legion.* Same, 172; *Same v. James McClung, late Physician and Director General of the State Hospitals.* Same, 173; *Same v. John Nelson, late surgeon in the Cavalry, raised for defence of State.* Same, 174; *Same v. William Thompson, late Captain in State regiment of artillery.* Same, 176; *Same v. James Quarles, late Major in Virginia State Line.* Same, 177; *Same v. Joseph Hay, late Surgeon in State Hospitals.* Same, 178.

Commonwealth v. James M. Marshall, late lieutenant in state regiment of artillery; Thomas Marshall, Jr., late captain and paymaster of same; Humphrey Marshall, late captain lieutenant in same; and others.

Appeal from order District Court, Richmond, Sept., 1791, Auditor of Public Accounts to issue certificate for five years' full pay for life, and interest from Apr. 22, 1783, to Apr. 26, 1783, day of discharge.

Oct. 26, 1792. Reversed by consent of parties, appeal from Auditor dismissed, lack of sufficient proof. Court of Appeals, Va., Order Book II, 201–202.

J.M. undoubtedly took part in these proceedings involving his brothers and brother-in-law and cousin, Humphrey.

Francis Willis, Jun. v. William Dandridge Claiborne, assignee of Fendall Southerland.

Appeal from District Court, Williamsburg. J.M. for appellee.

Apr. 14, 1792. Discontinued, appellant not prosecuting. Court of Appeals, Va., Order Book II, 156.

Fee: Feb., 1792, £5. Account Book, 314.

Benjamin Smith v. Mary Ewing.

Writ of supersedeas to j. District Court at Staunton. J.M. for appellant.

Oct. 10, 1792. Dismissed, appellant not prosecuting. Court of Appeals, Va., Order Book II, 182.

Fee: Aug., 1791, £4:10. Account Book, 294.

Edmund Winder v. Thomas Eddy, administrator of John McKean.

Appeal from j. District Court, Fredericksburg, reversing and nonsuiting j. for appellant by Court of Hustings for Corporation of Fredericksburg, Mar. 28, 1789, £207:8:3 and three pence damages for goods sold and delivered, affirmed. J.M. for appellant.

May 7, 1791. J. of District Court reversing and nonsuiting on grounds declaration not state cause within jurisdiction of Corporation Court, District Court, Fredericksburg, Record Book 1789–1792, 518–20; Law Orders A, 1789–1792, 256.

May 10, 1791. Appeal to Court of Appeals granted. Same, Law Orders A, 1789–1793, 268.

Oct. 25, 1792. Submitted and affirmed. Court of Appeals, Va., Order Book II, 194.

May 9, 1793. Mandate of Court of Appeals entered. District Court, Fredericksburg, Law Orders A, 1789–1793, 491.

Fee: May, 1791, £4:4. Account Book, 286.

John Smith v. Ralph Wormeley, Jun., Mann Page, Francis Lightfoot Lee, George Plater, John Taylor Corbin, Warner Lewis, Jun., Edward Loyd, Thomas Lawson, surviving executors of John Taylor.

Appeal from j. debt against appellant. District Court, Northumberland Courthouse, Sept. 10, 1791, £2,645:15:10, one penny damage, payable by £1,322:7:11. J.M. for appellant.

Oct. 15, 1792. Abatement as to Plater and Lewis by death. Affirmed. Court of Appeals, Va., Order Book II, 184.

Fee: Oct., 1787, £2:3. Account Book, 128.

District Court, Accomack and Northampton

John Stringer v. Thomas Dolby and John Guy, executors of John Burton.

Detinue. J.M. probably for defendants.

1786. Complaint filed in General Court.

Oct. 15, 1789. Continued. District Court, Accomack and Northampton, Order Book 1789–1797, 17.

May 21, 1790. Special verdict, Thomas Dolby orally gave slave Judah to son, John, and delivered possession; John held possession until his death in 1778, meantime having married Susanna, to whom he bequeathed the slave. Susanna married Stringer, the plaintiff, the same year, and he held possession of slave until 1780. In 1779, Thomas made deed of gift to daughter, Bridget Burton, wife of John Burton, of same slave and four offspring born while in possession of John and Stringer Dolby; deed recorded; possession taken from Stringer by Burton. Stringer brought replevin action in County Court, Northampton; j. for him reversed in General Court, and brought present action. Same, 85.

Oct. 23, 1790. Issue adjourned to General Court for novelty if act of Dec., 1787, for preventing fraudulent gift of slaves controls operation of act of 1758 for preventing fraudulent gift of slaves and applies to verbal gift prior to passage of act of 1787. Same, 118.

Oct. 19, 1791. Continued. Same, 180.

May 15, 1792. Transcript of opinion General Court, for plaintiff; jury to assess values and damages. Same, 201.

Oct. 15, 1792. Jury determined value of four of offspring: £58:9, £50, £40, £20; j. accordingly if not delivered; also damages £65. Same, 217.

District Court, Accomack, Complete Record Book 1791–1794, 259–264.

Fees: May 29, 1787, £2:11, "Replevin"; Dec., 1790, £——, "General Court." Account Book, 114, 268.

John Eyre, executor of Littleton Eyre v. John Savage.

Debt. J.M. for plaintiff.

Oct. 18, 1791. Continued. District Court, Accomack and Northampton, Order Book 1789–1797, 177.

May 15, 1792. Dismissed by consent. Same, 199.

Fee: May 30, 1789, £2:11 "Appeal." Account Book, 114.

Nathaniel Wilkins, executor of John Wilkins v. William Jarvis.

Appeal from j. in action of debt, County Court, Northampton, Mar. 16, 1792, £180. Affirmed. J.M. for appellee.

May 18, 1792. Continued. District Court, Accomack and Northampton, Order Book 1789–1797, 212.

Oct. 18, 1792. Affirmed. Same, 232. Same, Record Book 1791–1794, 302–305.

Fee: May, 1794, £5. Account Book, 386.

District Court, Augusta

Isabella Burns, executrix of Robert Burns v. Richard Mathews and William Chambers.

Debt. J.M. for plaintiff (?); Alexander Stuart signed petition as attorney for plaintiff.

Sept., 1791. Action on sealed obligation, Jan. 18, 1790, £170 conditioned on paying j. described below and costs if injunction proceedings dissolved; also against Mathews on unpaid j. against him, £65:13:4 debt and £24:18 damages and 360 pounds tobacco, and costs of injunction proceedings against the j. which resulted in dismissal of the injunction.

Apr. 6, 1792. Office j. against Chambers set aside. V.j. against Chambers on written obligation, £170, payable by £95:9:5. Discussed as to Mathews. District Court, Augusta, Order Book 1789–1793, 427; Same, Order Book 1789–1797, 169.

Fee: Mar., 1794, £5. Account Book 384.

John Smith v. John Lowry and John McPheeters.

Debt. J.M. for plaintiff, petition signed by J.M.

Action filed in General Court on sealed obligation dated Feb. 13, 1783, £500, conditioned on fulfillment of agreement of Lowry to deliver two male Negroes, 16 and 25 years old, in return for wagon and team of four horses delivered by Smith to Lowry.

May, 1786. Common order against McPheeters.

Jan., 1787. Same against Lowry.

Continued through Apr., 1789.

Sept. 3, 1789. District Court, Staunton. Default of appearance by defendants; writ of inquiry as to damages awarded.

May 2, 1792. V.j. £500, payable by £159. District Court, Augusta, Order Book 1789–1793, 36; Same, Order Book 1789–1797, 11, 26.

Fee: May 19, 1785, £2:10. Account Book, 36.

County Court, Fauquier

J.M. v. John T. Waller and Thomas Simpson.

Action of debt on replevin bond for property seized in distress for rent and returned. Sept. 24, 1792, j. £35:14 payable by £17:17. County Court, Fauquier, Minute Book 1791–1793, 212.

Superior (District) Court, Frederick

James M. Lingan v. John Dawson.

Trespass. J.M. for defendant.

Apr. 25, 1792. J. for plaintiff, one penny. Superior Court, Frederick, Order Book 1789–1793, 327.

(See *Same v. Same,* herein 1790, Legal Practice, Superior Court, Frederick County.)

Fee: Apr. 5, 1788, £3:16. Account Book, 150.

Michael Rorrock v. Edwin Young.

Debt. J.M. for defendant.

Apr. 17, 1792. Dismissed, lack of prosecution. Superior Court, Frederick, Order Book 1789–1793, 286.

Fees: Apr. 20, 1785, £2:10 "supersedeas." Account Book, 34. See also May 9, 1787, £2:10 "Young adv. Rorrock, habeas corpus." Account Book, 114.

Francis Willis, Jr. v. Robert White; Same v. Thomas Violett; Same v. Joseph Holmes.

Detinue. J.M. for defendants.

Apr. 17, 1790—Apr. 11, 1792. Continued.

Sept. 3, 1792. Discontinued. Superior Court, Frederick, Order Book 1789–1793, 50, 212, 282, 354.

Fees: White. Apr. 14, 1786, £2:16; Violett, May, 1785, £2:10; Holmes, Mar. 30, 1786, £2:10. Account Book, 70, 36, 66.

DISTRICT COURT, FREDERICKSBURG

James Brown, executor of Hugh Patton v. Charles P. Howard and John Ware.

Debt, £1,595:12:1½. J.M. for plaintiff.

Oct. 6, 1792. Confessed j. £1,595:12:1½, payable by £290:14:3.

District Court, Fredericksburg, Law Orders A, 1789–1793, 420.

Also *Same v. Charles P. Howard.*

May 7, 1793. Plea payment, office j. set aside. Same, 475.

May 3, 1794. Dismissed, agreed between parties. District Court, Fredericksburg, Law Orders B, 1794–1798, 42.

Fees: Feb. 12, 1790. Advice concerning Patton's will to Howard, same to Brown. £2:8; £2:16. Account Book, 232.

William and Benjamin Chapman v. Erasmus Chapman and James Allen.

Debt, on sealed obligation, filed Apr., 1791, Culpeper County.

J.M. for defendant.

Oct. 8, 1792. Confessed j. £68, payable by £34. District Court, Fredericksburg, Record Book 1790–1793, 51.

Fee: Sept., 1790, £13:16. Account Book, 260.

The Commonwealth v. William Adams.

Indictment for felony, passing counterfeit certificates. J.M. for defendant.

Oct. 3, 1792. Special verdict, possessed of counterfeit certificates; when called before magistrate, tore up certificates; circumstantial evidence knew counterfeit, not positive proof thereof. District Court, Fredericksburg, Law Orders A, 1789–1793.

Oct. 10, 1792. Acquitted. Same, 436.

Fee: Oct. 4, 1785, £2:10. Account Book, 50. (Query if same case, lapse of time.)

Henderson, Ferguson, and Gibson, merchants v. Benjamin Johnston.

Debt, on bond sealed, Mar. 4, 1790, £198.10 specie. Filed Sept., 1790, King George County. J.M. for defendant.

Oct., 1790. Bail. District Court, Fredericksburg, Law Orders A, 1789–1793, 170.

May 4, 1791. Plea, payment, by James Monroe. Same, 233.

May 7, 1792. J. for plaintiff, £198:10 specie, payable by £99:5 specie, interest on £3:7:11, May, 1786, on £95:17:1, June, 1787. Same, 368. Record Book 1789–1792, 705–707.

Fee: Feb., 1786, £2:8. Account Book, 66.

George Malone and Lucy, his wife v. William Edwards, administrator of John Carter.

Trespass on the case, breach of agreement for use of three tracts of land, Stafford County, by defendant, 1,000 pounds tobacco for seven years, 7,000 pounds and 70 pounds tobacco. Filed Apr., 1790, Stafford County. J.M. for plaintiff. (Petition signed.)

May 4, 1792. V.j. £100. District Court, Fredericksburg, Law Orders A, 1789–1793, 358; Record Book 1789–1792, 692–94.

Fee: Jan., 1789, £1:8. Account Book, 184.

James Ritchie & Co. v. Hezekiah Brown.

Appeal from j. Court of Culpeper County, May 19, 1789, denying appellant's motion for execution on replevin bond, costs against appellant. J.M. for appellant.

May 10, 1791. Reversed; continued for substitute j. District Court, Fredericksburg, Law Orders A, 1789–1793, 265.

May 5, 1792. Sent back to County Court to render judgment shall seem right. Same, 363.

Fee: Oct., 1789, £2:16. Account Book, 214.

District Court, Northumberland

Samuel L. Staughan v. Lewis abb [sic] *Lewis Lamkin.*

Error to j. County Court, Northumberland, in favor of Lamkin, May 12, 1786, 1,000 pounds tobacco. J.M. for defendant in error. Action for breach of contract.

Apr. 5, 1792. Reversed on grounds suit brought for uncertain damages. District Court, Northumberland, Order Book 1789–1792, 193.

Fee: Dec. 5, 1787, £2:10 "writ of error." Account Book, 138.

District Court, Prince Edward

Richard Burks v. Martha, Peter, Andrew, and Charles Johnston, executors, etc., of Peter Johnston.

Detinue. J.M. for plaintiff (probable).

Sept. 4, 1792. Dismissed at rules for want of prosecution. District Court, Prince Edward, Order Book 1789–1792, 285.

Apr. 3, 1793. Nonsuit for want of declaration set aside. Same, Order Book 1793–1799, 17, 57.

Fee: Apr. 16, 1785, £4:4, "Burks adv. Johnston." Account Book, 32.

William Hubbard v. Seraphino Farmicola.

Appeal from j. for appellee, County Court, Charlotte, Aug. 4, 1790, £230, dischargable by £65 specie or 6,000 pounds Petersburg inspected tobacco. J.M. for appellee.

Apr. 7, 1791. Appeal abated by appellee's death. District Court, Prince Edward, Order Book 1789–1792, 177.

Nathaniel Williams v. John Ragland and John Pettus, executors of John Pettus.

Debt, on obligation sealed, July 8, 1774, £200. J.M. for defendants.

Apr. 5, 1792. V.j. £200 from estate, if insufficient, costs against defendants. District Court, Prince Edward, Records at Large 1789–1792, 484–85.

Fee: Apr.–May, 1792, £5. Account Book, 322.

Same v. Same.

Covenant. J.M. for defendants.

Apr. 3, 7, and Sept. 7, 1793. Commissions for depositions of witnesses in Georgia, commissioners appointed. District Court, Prince Edward, Order Book 1793–1799, 24, 31, 79.

Apr. 4, 1794. Dismissed by consent. Same, 106.

Fee: May, 1795, £5. Account Book, 414.

1793

DOCUMENTS

Jan. 18 *to Richard Henry Lee*
RICHMOND *—Addressed to Chantilly, Westmoreland, Virginia*

Acknowledges letter of 14th. J.M. has contract with brother, James, now in London, to make valuable purchase; James has power to bind him and another to make payments. J.M. purchased stock for William Lee and bound self to pay; if complete purchase, will make transfer of stock and accept loss himself. Will hear definitely from London in March or April. VU, Lee Papers, No. 436.

Jan. 24
RICHMOND *Bank Subscription*

Notice of opening of books of subscription for Bank of Richmond, signed J.M. and others. Va. Gaz. & G.A., Jan. 30, 1793, 3, and intermittently through Same (Extraordinary), Mar. 20, 1793, 4.

[Jan.]
[RICHMOND] *to James Henderson*

Enclosing dispensation (for Masonic Lodge); affix seal of lodge and attest. CSmH, BR Box 22.

Feb. 8
[RICHMOND] [*to Charles Yauncey*]

Dispensation to Free Masons of Buckingham County, Virginia, to form Buckingham Union Lodge No. 38; Yauncey, Master. Signed by J.M., Deputy Grand Master of Virginia.

Note of J.M. (no addressee) enclosing dispensation requesting affix seal of lodge and attestation. CSmH, BR Box 22.

Feb. 23
RICHMOND *to Francis Walker—Addressed to Albamarle*

Advising taking testimony of Meriwether as to value of land and situation of tracts involved in agreement; recommending attachment on Wilkinson in suit against Cabell. VU, Page and Walker Mss, Deposit No. 3098.

(See herein 1790, Legal Practice, High Court of Chancery, *Walker v. Cabell et al.*, involving partnership in iron works, etc.)

Apr. 6
RICHMOND *Dispensation for Masonic Lodge*

Dispensation to applicants Nimrod Long, Charles Vowls, and George Lathan to form Stevensburg Lodge No. 40, Stevensburg, Culpeper County, Va. Signed by J.M., Deputy Grand Master of Masons of Virginia. CSmH, BR Box 22.

April
RICHMOND *to John Cabell*

Acknowledges letter by Cabell's son. Advises against defending suit brought by Campbell; J.M. represents Campbell.* In Cabell's injunction against Cooper nothing done; depositions necessary before final hearing in spring. DLC, Breckenridge Long Papers, Autograph Coll. (231).

* Fee received in *Campbell v. Cabell*, Apr. 1793, £5. Account Book, 358.

May 13
RICHMOND *Militia*

At the request of the Governor the Court recommended officers of the city militia; J.M. as lieutenant colonel commandant. Richmond City Hustings and Chancery Court, Order Book 3, 1792–1797, 110.

June 10
RICHMOND *Militia*

Presented commission to Court and took oath as lieutenant colonel commandant of the 19th (City of Richmond) Regiment of militia.* Richmond City Hustings and Chancery Court, Order Book 3, 1792–1797, 123; V.

* Jan. 13, 1794. Court recommended David Lambert to this command. Richmond City Hustings and Chancery Court, Minute Book 1, 1793–1797, 20.

June
RICHMOND *Resolution—Genet*

Drew up resolution passed at public meeting in Richmond condemning activities of M. Genet, the French minister to the United States. *Daily National Intelligence* (Washington), July 9, 1835. See Marshall, *Autobiography*, 13–15.

July 2
RICHMOND *Legal Opinion—City Appropriation*

Resolution of Common Hall of Richmond; legal opinion of J.M. and Andrew Ronald if thirty acres belonging to Dr. Philip Turpin appropriated for public buildings was within Richmond and could be used for public market; fee £10. V, Richmond Common Hall Records 1793–1795, II, 20.

July 15. Opinion not within city limits, no jurisdiction over markets. Ronald relinquished his part of "liberal fee to poor." Same, 21–27. Committee appointed to petition legislature for relief. Same, 27.

Aug. 6
RICHMOND *to Benjamin Rush, of Philadelphia*

Advises that Trumbull refuses to have Rush and another as commissioners in Trumbull case. PPL.

Aug. 22
RICHMOND *Militia*

Circular by Lieut. Gov. James Wood to commanding officers of militia of counties in Virginia where ports of navigation prohibiting asylum to any cruiser or privateer of either party at war. V, Exec. Letter Books 1792–1794, 236.

Aug. 23
RICHMOND *from Lieut. Gov. James Wood*

Order to J.M. as lieutenant colonel commandant of the city militia to organize guard over public arms in Richmond. V, Exec. Letter Books, 1792–1794, 235–36.

Sept. 12
RICHMOND *to Governor and Executive Council of Virginia*

Petition for mercy in behalf of Angelica Barnet, convicted of murder, by J.M., alleging her good character. Pardoned. V, Exec. Papers, Box 1793, July-Sept., Folder Sept. 11–20.

Sept. 23
RICHMOND *from Robert Mitchell*

Concerning suspicion of Negro uprising and protection by city militia of which J.M. colonel. V, Exec. Papers, Box 1793, July-Sept., Folder Sept. 20–30.

Sept. 23
RICHMOND *to Gov. Henry Lee*

Acknowledges letter of 21st; has written officers of the guard. States need for rations and sentry box for (Richmond) guards. V, Exec. Papers, Box 1793, July-Sept., Folder Sept. 20–30. CVSP, VI, 546; Oster, *Marshall*, 31.

Sept. 24
RICHMOND *to Gov. [Henry] Lee*

Enclosing Mitchell letter, and suggesting guards receive cartridges. V, Exec. Papers, Box 1793, July-Sept., Folder Sept. 20–30; CVSP, VI, 547; Oster, *Marshall*, 31–32.

Sept. 29
NEW BRUNSWICK, N. J. *from Anthony W. White*

Introducing brother-in-law, Judge Paterson, requests civilities in his official visits to Virginia. Complains of long time since previous letter of J.M. (n.f.) concerning demands against "Tobacco Gentlemen"; proof and vouchers in J.M.'s hands; suit should have been filed and collection made. Requests obtain deposition from Shingleton that received $27,000 from White during war for recruiting. Advised by J.M. that Virginia Senate rejected White petition; must settle public accounts with the United States; requests return of paper money left with J.M., receipts and papers. Inquires if obtained Howell certificates from Scott, received to discharge Howell's obligation on tobacco contract; should be delivered to White. Asks concerning claim against Erskin and Boyer; if latter not collectible in Virginia, return tobacco account for suit in Philadelphia. Inquires about Peyton notes; requests suit against David Leitch; if in Kentucky, will sue there. Inquires if J.M. has sent writer's land warrants to Col. Anderson and if patent issued. Decries action of Virginia toward him, an officer, advanced money; creditor of another state not able to recover in Virginia. Will pay for legal services. NjR.

Oct. 5
RICHMOND *to Gov. [Henry] Lee*

Suggests officer of guard contract with butcher for rations. V, Exec. Papers, Box 1793, Oct.-Dec., Folder Oct. 1–10; CVSP, VI, 581; Oster, *Marshall,* 32.

Oct. 12
RICHMOND *to James Breckenridge, of Botetourt, Virginia*

Requesting affidavits of his client for deposition of witness residing in Kentucky; possible arbitration, suit against McGraw. J.M. farming in neighborhood and in need of plow horse; asks that offer be made to Nowd to take horse for J.M.'s claim against him. NhD.

Oct. 15
RICHMOND *to Gov. [Henry] Lee*

Report of examination of the captain and passengers of the vessel *Phoenix* as to possible contagion from Philadelphia; recommends impose quarantine. V, Exec. Papers, Box 1793, Oct.–Dec., Folder Oct. 11–20; CVSP, IV, 600–601; Oster, *Marshall,* 32–33.

Oct. 15
RICHMOND *Militia*

Order of Gov. Henry Lee to J.M., lieutenant colonel commandant of the militia of Richmond, to provide escort of sloop *Phoenix* to quarantine. V, Exec. Letter Books, 1792–1794, 278.

Oct.
RICHMOND *to Gov. [Henry] Lee*

Transmitting payroll of Richmond Guards; officer ration not estimated.

V, Exec. Papers, Box 1793, Oct.-Dec., Folder Oct. 1–10; CVSP, VI, 581; Oster, *Marshall*, 32.

Dec. 2
RICHMOND *Militia*

Order establishing militia of Virginia under acts of General Assembly, 1792, 93. J.M. named brigadier general of the Second Brigade. V, War 10, Militia Commissions, Gen'l. Orders, 1782–1809, 1, 5.

Dec. 28
RICHMOND *to Charles Lee*

Acknowledges letter of 22nd. Presence of Mrs. Tumbull at trial not material but may attend, trial in March. Asks Lee to get testimony in Alexandria, suit for separate maintenance of consequences, fortune of Tumbull, injury to that of Mrs. Tumbull, expenses. Lee to be serviceable at trial. The John Marshall House, Richmond, Va.

n.d. [circa *1793*], *n.p.* *to Charles Lee*

J.M. relying on Lee's word to attend to his legal business in Fredericksburg, little remaining as policy for some time not to engage in anything new. Two suits with difficulties; trespass case opposed by Warden; noted issues for demurrer and for taking issue; Lee to use his judgment. Small suit, Chew interested, a poor client; consult with Washington and Brooke. Other suits plain business; one about lost tobacco hogshead, will lose unless plaintiff drops case. The John Marshall House, Richmond, Va.

n.d. [circa *1793*], *n.p.* *to Charles Lee*

Has transmitted to clerk of Dumfries traverse to Fauquier inquest drawn in name of purchaser; suggests demurrer. Federal court open to J.M., although closed to Fairfax; reason must not be disclosed. Requested Patton of Fredericksburg pay Potowmac [*sic*] Company treasurer J.M.'s account; asks that be checked. Legislature growing worse and worse; hopes session soon determined. The John Marshall House, Richmond, Va.

n.d. [circa *1793*], *n.p.* *to William Mumford*

Will receive Kennon's negroes in deduction of $4.00 per month each. Would like to know if coming before J.M. leaves town Wednesday or Thursday. Alonzo not accustomed to field work, will not suit. The John Marshall House, Richmond, Va.

n.d., n.p. *to Gabriel Jones*

J.M. wrote Gabriel Jones, lawyer, concerning Genet, the French minister (n.f.). Referred to in James Monroe to Thomas Jefferson, Sept. 8, 1798, Hamilton, *Monroe*, I, 274–75.

n.d., n.p. *from John Wise*

Attesting to general character of John Eyre and Thomas Newton, applicants for admission to Society of Masons. CSmH, BR Box 22.

LEGAL PRACTICE

DURING THE YEAR 1793, J.M. recorded the receipt of 247 legal fees totaling £1,030:19:8. Thirty-nine fees are designated as for advice, all in the £1 bracket, except two in the £2 and one in the £3 bracket.

Appeals to upper state courts predominated in litigated matters. Federal Circuit Court cases remained active, nine fees being recorded for such in matters principally involving defense against collection of pre-war debts by Britishers.

Amounts of fees ranged generally from £2 to £7, with £5 predominating. Nine fees were of £10 or more; £14 was collected in connection with Wilcox's will; the largest, of £21, was in the case of *Maeze v. Hamilton*. Account Book, 346–78.

U.S. CIRCUIT COURT, VIRGINIA

Joseph Ball, executor of John Ball, Pa. v. Edward Hill, Va.

Covenant on penal bond under seal, 24,450 lbs. tobacco and £36:17:5, May 24, 1793. U.S. Circuit Court, Va., Order Book, 1, 1421. J.M. for plaintiff.

Dec. 3, 1793. V.j. $1,290.50. Same, 237.

Same, Record Book I, 393–95. V, U.S. Circuit Court Case Papers. (Autograph petition.)

Fee: Oct., 1792, £5. Account Book, 340.

John Bowman, s.p. Alexander Spiers, John Bowman and Co., Glasgow, Great Britain v. William Bowyer, Augusta County, Va.

Debt, on obligation under seal, £212:17:4 Va., 1772. J.M. for defendant.

May 29, 1792. Pleas: payment; Britisher disabled from recovery; violation of Treaty of Paris; Declaration of Independence. Demurrer to last four pleas by plaintiff. U.S. Circuit Court, Va., Order Book I, 114.

Security for Bowyer. Same, 120.

Nov. 28, 1793. Demurrer for plaintiff. V.j. £212:17:4 Va., payable by $354.77. Same, 203.

Same, Record Book I, 395–403.

V, U.S. Circuit Court Case Papers.

Fee: May, 1792, £4:4. Account Book, 326.

Hugh Colquehoun et al., of Alexander Donald and Co., merchants, Glasgow, Great Britain v. Robert Crawley, Mecklenburg County, Va.

Debt, on obligation under seal, 1773, £577:17 Va. J.M. for defendant.

May 24, 1791. Henry Heth security for defendant. Existing judgment set aside. Answer: payment; British subject disabled by Virginia law. U.S. Circuit Court, Va., Order Book I, 9, 10.

Nov. 28, 1791. Second plea withdrawn. Answer: Virginia laws disabling Britisher; violation of Treaty of Paris; Declaration of Independence. Demurrer by plaintiff. Same, 62.

Dec. 5, 1791. Bail released. Same, 85.

Nov. 23, 1793. Demurrer for plaintiff. V.j. £577:17 Va., payable $577.20. Same, 169–70.

Same, Record Book I, 468–77.

V, U.S. Circuit Court Case Papers.

Fee: Oct., 1790, £7:10 (part). Account Book, 266.

John Dobson et al., s.p. Dobson, Daltera, and Walker, Great Britain v. Garland Anderson, Hanover County, Va.

Case, goods sold, £623:12:8 St., 1770. J.M. for defendant.

Dec. 3, 1791. Answer: not assume; British enemy disabled by Virginia law; violation of Treaty of Paris; Declaration of Independence. Demurrer by plaintiff. U.S. Circuit Court, Va., Order Book I, 84.

Nov. 22, 1793 (O.B. says June 8). Demurrer for plaintiff. V.j. $2,462.88. Same, 166.

Same, Record Book 1, 341–56.

V, U.S. Circuit Court Case Papers.

Fees: Apr.–May, 1792, £2:10, Nov., 1793, £2:16. Account Book, 322, 374. Also Jan., 1791, "Anderson adv.," £2:10. Account Book, 272.

Dobson and Daltera, s.p. Dobson, Daltera, and Walker, Great Britain v. Joseph Eggleston, Sr., Amelia County, Va.

Case, £250. J.M. for defendant.

Dec. 3, 1791. Prior pleas 2 and 3 withdrawn.

Pleas: not assume; payment to Loan Office; violation of Treaty of Paris;

Declaration of Independence. Demurrer by plaintiff. U.S. Circuit Court, Va., Order Book I, 79.

May 25, 1792. Depositions in England. Same, 96.

Dec. 2, 1793. Abated by death of defendant. Same, 224.

Same, Record Book Index. Dismissed, Nov. R [Rules], 1793.

V, U.S. Circuit Court Case Papers, containing answer on J.M.'s printed forms, filled in by him.

Fee: Jan., 1791, £2:10. Account Book, 272.

Robert Donald et al., s.p. James and Robert Donald and Co., merchants, Glasgow, Great Britain v. Jesse and Robert Burton, executors of Robert Burton, Albemarle County, Va.

Debt, on obligation under seal, 1775, £1,829:6:4 Va. J.M. for defendants.

Nov. 30, 1791. Answer: payment; Britisher disability under Virginia laws; violation of Treaty of Paris. Demurrer by plaintiff. U.S. Circuit Court, Va., Order Book I, 68.

Nov. 26, 1793. For plaintiff on demurrer. V.j. £1,829:6:4 Va. payable by $2,647.82. Same, 185–86.

Same, Record Book II, 122–28.

V, U.S. Circuit Court Case Papers.

Fee: Feb., 1791, £5. Account Book, 274.

Robert Donald et al., s.p. James and Robert Donald and Co., Glasgow, Great Britain v. James and William Clarke, administrators of Charles Clarke, Powhatan County, Va.

Debt, on obligation under seal, £559:7:1 Va., 1776. J.M. for defendants.

Nov. 29, 1792. Answer: payment; Britisher disability under Virginia law; breach of Treaty of Paris; Declaration of Independence. Demurrer by plaintiff. U.S. Circuit Court, Va., Order Book I, 124.

Nov. 30, 1793. For plaintiff on demurrer. V.j. £579.7:1 payable by $932.25. Same, 220–21.

Same, Record Book II, 81.

V, U.S. Circuit Court Case Papers, containing answer of James Clarke naming J.M. as attorney; autograph answer of Charles Clarke.

Fee: Nov., 1791. £2:16. Account Book, 306.

Robert Donald et al., s.p. James and Robert Donald and Co., merchants, Glasgow, Great Britain v. Ischarner Degraffenredt, Lunenburg County, Va. (Two suits)

Debt, on obligation under seal, £200 Va., 1774. J.M. for defendant.

May 28, 1792. Pleas: payment; not recoverable by Britisher; violation of Treaty of Paris; Declaration of Independence. Demurrer by plaintiff. U.S. Circuit Court, Va., Order Book I, 111.

Nov. 29, 1793. Demurrer for plaintiff. V.j. £200 Va. payable by $333.33. Same, 211.

Same v.j. in second suit. Same, 212.

Same, Record Book II, 68–72 and 72–76.

V, U.S. Circuit Court Case Papers.

Robert Donald et al., s.p. James and Robert Donald and Co., merchants, Glasgow, Great Britain v. John Harris, Powhatan County, Va.

Debt, on obligation under seal, £218:10:10 Va., 1774. J.M. for defendant.

May 24, 1792. Security for defendant. U.S. Circuit Court, Va., Order Book I, 93.

May 28, 1792. Pleas: payment; no recovery by Britisher; violation of Treaty of Paris; Declaration of Independence. Demurrer. Same, 111.

Nov. 29, 1793. Demurrer for plaintiff. V.j. £218:10:10 Va., payable by $134.48. Same, 209.

Same, Record Book I, 100–105.

V, U.S. Circuit Court Case Papers.

Fee: Oct., 1791, £2:8. Account Book, 300.

Robert Donald et al., s.p. James and Robert Donald and Co., merchants, Glasgow, Great Britain v. Charles Lynch, Va. (Two cases)

Debt, on obligation under seal, £200 and £192, Va., 1772. J.M. for defendant.

May 28, 1792. Security for defendant. Pleas: payment; no recovery by Britisher; violation of Treaty of Paris; Declaration of Independence. Demurrer by plaintiff. U.S. Circuit Court, Va., Order Book I, 109.

Nov. 28, 1793. V.js. £200, payable by $333.33 and £192:2 payable by $118.62. Same, 205.

Same, Record Book I, 59–63, 63–67.

V, U.S. Circuit Court Case Papers.

Robert Donald et al., s.p. James and Robert Donald and Co., Glasgow, Great Britain v. Thomas Owen, Henrico County, Va.

Debt, on written obligation under seal, 1772, £395:8:3 Va. J.M. for defendant. (Two suits)

May 24, 1790. Existing judgment set aside. Answer: Payment; Britisher disabled by Virginia law. Demurrer by plaintiff. U.S. Circuit Court, Va., Order Book I, 12.

Nov. 28, 1791. Second plea withdrawn. New pleas: Britisher disabled by Virginia law; breach of Treaty of Paris; Declaration of Independence. Demurrer by plaintiff. Same, 62.

May 26, 1792. Robert Donald death noted. Same, 104.

Nov. 22, 1793. Demurrer for plaintiff. V.j. £395:8:3 Va. payable $251.68. Same, 170.

Same, Record Book II, 90–95.

Same v. Same.

Debt, on obligation under seal, £400 Va., 1772. J.M. for defendant.

Pleadings same as other action. Order Book 1, 13, 62, 104.

Nov. 23, 1793. V.j. £400 Va. payable by $666.66⅔. Same, 170.

Same, Record Book I, 95–100.

U.S. Circuit Court Case Papers.

Fee: May, 1791, £5. Account Book, 288.

Robert Donald et al., s.p. James and Robert Donald and Co., merchants, Glasgow, Great Britain v. John Ware, Fluvanna County, Va.

Debt, on obligation under seal, £1,041:10:5 Va., 1772. J.M. for defendant.

Nov. 25, 1790. J. entered by Clerk set aside. Pleas: payment; no recovery by Britisher. U.S. Circuit Court, Va., Order Book I, 15.

Nov. 28, 1791. Second plea withdrawn. New pleas: Britisher disabled by Virginia law; violation of Treaty of Paris; Declaration of Independence. Demurrer by plaintiff. Same, 62.

Nov. 23, 1793. Demurrer for plaintiff. V.j. £1,041:10:5 Va., payable by $1,603.57. Same, 173.

Same, Record Book 1, 110–16.

V, U.S. Circuit Court Case Papers.

Robert Donald et al., s.p. James and Robert Donald and Co., merchants, Glasgow, Great Britain v. Allen Williamson, Henrico County, Va.

Debt, obligation under seal, £189:17:8 Va., 1774. J.M. for defendant.

Nov. 25, 1790. J. entered by Clerk set aside. Pleas: payment; no recovery by Britisher. U.S. Circuit Court, Va., Order Book I, 15.

Nov. 28, 1791. Second plea withdrawn. New pleas: Britisher disabled by Virginia law; breach of Treaty of Paris; Declaration of Independence.

Demurrer by plaintiff. Same, 62.

Nov. 23, 1793. Demurrer for plaintiff. V.j. £189:17:8, payable $502.41. Same, 171.

Same, Record Book I, 105–110.

V, U.S. Circuit Court Case Papers.

Robert Donald et al., s.p. James and Robert Donald and Co., merchants, Glasgow, Great Britain v. Daniel Winn, Lunenburg County, Va.

Debt, on obligation under seal, £200 Va., 1774. J.M. for defendant.

May 28, 1792. Pleas: payment; not recoverable by Britisher; violation of Treaty of Paris; Declaration of Independence. Demurrer. U.S. Circuit Court, Va., Order Book I, 111.

Nov. 30, 1793. Demurrer for plaintiff. V.j. £200 Va., payable by $333.33. Same, 219.

Same, Record Book II, 77–81.

V, U.S. Circuit Court Case Papers.

Gizzel Gills et al., executrix and executor of William Donald, Glasgow, Great Britain v. Anne and Simon Miller, executrix and executor of Simon Miller.

Debt, on promissory note, £152:3:3½ Va., 1776. J.M. for defendant.

May 27, 1793. Answer: payment; Britisher disability under laws of Virginia; violation of Treaty of Paris; Declaration of Independence.

Reply; rejoinder; demurrer to last three pleas. U.S. Circuit Court, Va., Order Book I, 144.

Dec. 2, 1793. Demurrer for plaintiff. V.j. £512:3:3½ Va., payable by $220.20. Same, 227–28.

Same, Record Book IV, 4.

V, U.S. Circuit Court Case Papers.

Fee: May, 1793, £5. Account Book, 362.

Richard Hanson, Great Britain v. Roger Atkinson, Dunwiddie County, Va.

Debt, on protested bill of exchange, by Atkinson on Gale, Fearvin and Co. to Hanson, £4,000 St., 1774. J.M. for defendant.

Nov. 28, 1794. Pleas: payment to Loan Office; Britisher not recover; Declaration of Independence; violation of Treaty of Paris; nil debit. Demurrer by plaintiff. U.S. Circuit Court, Va., Order Book I, 63.

Dec. 6, 1793. Demurrer for plaintiff. V.j., £4,000 St., value of $16.760. Same, 251.

Record Book II, 289–300.

V, U.S. Circuit Court Case Papers, containing pleas on J.M. forms, filled in by him; also autograph bond for defendant.

Richard Hanson, Great Britain, assignee of Robert Kennon v. George Markham, Chesterfield County, Va.

Debt on bond, £500 Va., 1774. J.M. for defendant.

Nov. 28, 1791. Pleas: payment; Britisher not recover; violation of Treaty of Paris. Demurrer by plaintiff. U.S. Circuit Court, Va., Order Book I, 63.

Nov. 25, 1793. Dismissed for lack of prosecution. Same, 179. Same, Record Book Index. Dismissed, Nov. R, 1793.

V, U.S. Circuit Court Case Papers, containing pleas on printed forms filled in by J.M.

Richard Hanson, Great Britain v. Richard Taylor, Prince George County, Va.

Debt, on obligation under seal £500 Va., 1770. J.M. for defendant.

Nov. 25, 1790. Existing j. set aside. Answer: payment; British subject disability. U.S. Circuit Court, Va., Order Book I, 5.

Nov. 29, 1791. Second plea withdrawn. Answer: Disability of plaintiff under Virginia law; breach of Treaty of Paris; Declaration of Independence; payment. Demurrer by plaintiff. Same, 67.

Nov. 30, 1793. Demurrer for plaintiff to first three. V.j. £500 Va., payable $833.33. Same, 216.

Same, Record Book 2, 263–74.

V, U.S. Circuit Court Case Papers. (Pleas on J.M. forms.)

Robert Hastie et al., s.p. of Buchanan, Hastie and Co., merchants, Great Britain v. Rice Newman, executor of Richard Newman, Va.

Case, assumpsit for goods sold, commissions, and advances, 1776, £497:1:2. J.M. for defendant.

Answer: not assume; five-year limitation; defendant British. Reply, rejoinder, surrejoinder.

Nov. 26, 1793. Second plea withdrawn. Demurrer to third plea, for plaintiff. V.j. $1,655.27. U.S. Circuit Court, Va., Order Book I, 184–85.

Same, Record Book 1, 356–93.

V, U.S. Circuit Court Case Papers, containing autograph pleadings.

Robert Hastie et al., s.p. John Lindsay and Co., merchants, Great Britain v. John Pettus, executor of John Pettus, Charlotta County, Va.

Debt, on obligation under seal, £385:2:½ Va., 1774. The record shows Richard Duval as attorney for the defendant, but inasmuch as J.M. received a fee from defendant of £5 on Dec., 1792, he either consulted or acted as co-counsel (see Account Book, 344).

May 29, 1792. Pleas: payment; Britisher not recover; breach of Treaty of Paris; Declaration of Independence. Demurrer. U.S. Circuit Court, Va., Order Book I, 118.

Dec. 2, 1793. Demurrer for plaintiff. V.j., not paid; £385:2:½ Va., payable by $641.84. Same, 224.

Same, Record Book I, 457–68.

V, U.S. Circuit Court Case Papers.

Fee: Dec., 1792, £5. Account Book 344.

Henderson, McCaul and Co., merchants, Great Britain v. Edward Walls, Samuel Burke, and William Watts, Va.

Debt, on obligation under seal, £1,943:9 Va., value of $6,378.16⁶⁄₁₀, 1777. J.M. for defendants.

May 30, 1793. Pleas: payment; Britisher not recover under Virginia law; violation of Treaty of Paris; Declaration of Independence. Demurrer to last three by plaintiff. U.S. Circuit Court, Va., Order Book I, 146.

Dec. 3, 1792. Demurrer for plaintiff. V.j. £1,943:9 Va., payable by $809.76. Same, 238.

Same, Record Book II, 301–309, Nov., 1793.

V, U.S. Circuit Court Case Papers.

Fee: May, 1793, £7. Account Book, 360.

William R. Lidderdale, executor of John Lidderdale, Great Britain v. Carter Braxton, Henrico County, Va.

Case, for goods sold and commissions, £784:8:1 St. value of £1,045:17:6 Va., 1767. J.M. for defendant.

Answer: not assume; five-year statute of limitation; Britisher disability.

Dec. 8, 1791. Depositions to be taken in London. U.S. Circuit Court, Va., Order Book I, 92.

Nov. 25, 1793. Demurrer to second and third pleas for plaintiff. V.j. for defendant on *no assumpsit*. Same, 179.

Same, Record Book I, 319–32.

V, U.S. Circuit Court Case Papers, containing autograph pleadings.

McCall and Sheddin v. Richard Jeffries.

Debt, on obligation under seal, £250:8:11 Va., on land contract, 1772. J.M. for defendant.

Dec. 3, 1791. Pleas: payment; Britisher disabled under Virginia laws; violation of Treaty of Paris; Declaration of Independence. Demurrer by plaintiff. U.S. Circuit Court, Va., Order Book I, 77.

Nov. 27, 1793. Demurrer for plaintiff. V.j. £250:8:11 Va., payable by $240.47. Same, 192.

Same, Record Book II, 271–80.

V, U.S. Circuit Court Case Papers, containing printed pleadings filled in by J.M.

William Snodgrass, Great Britain v. Sarah Covington, executrix of Luke Covington.

Debt, on bill penal, £307:12:3¼, penalty £615:4:6, 1770. J.M. for defendant.

Pleas: payment; Britisher disabled by Virginia laws; violation of Treaty of Paris; Declaration of Independence. Demurrer by plaintiff. U.S. Circuit Court, Va., Order Book I, 66–67.

Nov. 25, 1793. Demurrer for plaintiff. V.j. £615:4:6 payable by $1,591.11. Same, 180.

Same, Record Book II, 336–43. Nov., 1793.

V, U.S. Circuit Court Case Papers.

Fee: May, 1791, £2:10. Account Book, 288.

William Snodgrass, Great Britain v. Thomas Miller.

Debt, on penal bond, £289.8, penalty £578:17:8½ Va., 1770. J.M. for defendant.

Dec. 3, 1791. Pleas: Britisher not recover under Virginia laws; violation of Treaty of Paris; Declaration of Independence; payment.

Demurrer by plaintiff. U.S. Circuit Court, Va., Order Book 1, 77.

Nov. 26, 1793. Demurrer for plaintiff. V.j. £578:17:6½ Va., payable by $188.17. Same, 189.

Same, Record Book II, 343–51. Nov., 1793.

V, U.S. Circuit Court Case papers.

Fee: May, 1791, £2:10. Account Book, 258.

Andrew Van Bibber, Md. v. George Green, Va.

Debt, on obligation under seal, £400 Md., 1791. J.M. for plaintiff.

June 3, 1793. Plea payment. U.S. Circuit Court, Va., Order Book 1, 148.

Dec. 3, 1793. V.j. £400 Md. value $1,066.66⅔ payable $533.33. Same, 235.

Same, Record Book II, 352–55.

V, U.S. Circuit Court Case Papers, containing autograph petition signed.

Fees: Aug., 1791, £2:8; Jan., 1792, £7:10. Account Book, 294, 312.

(See herein, Apr. 18, 1796.)

Wallis and Bartlett, merchants, London, Great Britain v. Ralph Wormsley, Francis Lightfoot Lee, Mann Page, George Plator, John Taylor Corbin, Warner Lewis, Jr., Edward Loyd, and Thomas Lawson, executors of John Taylor, Richmond.

Debt, on protested bill of exchange by William Black on William Lea to Taylor, endorsed to James Gibson and Co., then to plaintiff, £150 St. J.M. for defendants.

Nov. 29, 1791. Pleas: Britisher not recover; violation of Treaty of Paris; Declaration of Independence; payment. Demurrer by plaintiff. U.S. Circuit Court, Va., Order Book 1, 66.

Nov. 26, 1793. Demurrer for plaintiff. V.j. £150 St., payable by $614.71. Same, 183.

Same, Record Book II, 355.

V, U.S. Circuit Court Case Papers.

U.S. District Court, Virginia

Samuel Swann v. Sloop Polly.

Libel of sloop, tackle, and apparel for value of 1,100 bushels of coal shipped to Philadelphia for delivery to one Lowndes, delivered instead to Wood, owner of sloop. J.M. for respondents Basil Wood, owner, and Ebenezer Prentis, captain of sloop.

Dec. 20, 1792. Answer in handwriting of J.M. alleging delivery as ordered.

Mar., 1793. Dismissed by agreement.

V, U.S. District Court, Va., District End Cases, 1793, Box 3.

Court of Appeals of Virginia

John Verell v. John Scott Coleman, 4 Call 230.

Writ of supersedeas to District Court of Petersburg.

Debt, default j. for defendant in error, affirmed.

J.M. for defendant in error.

Coleman brought action in County Court. Plea, payment; issue joined.

Verell removed cause by habeas corpus to District Court where Coleman plead over, took default j. Apr. 17, 1790. Verell claimed error in pleading over and not proceeding on old pleadings. Held, no error.

Apr. 11, 1793. Heard. Court of Appeals, Va., Order Book II, 150.

Apr. 12. J. 21,600 pounds crop tobacco of Petersburg, payable by 10,830 pounds, also £170 payable by £85 specie, affirmed. Same, 151, 152.

Fee: Nov. 1791, £4:18. Account Book, 306.

Edward Stevens v. John Taliaferro, administrator of John Thornton, 1 Washington 155, 155–56.

Writ of supersedeas to j. District Court of Fredericksburg, May 10, 1792 (District Court of Fredericksburg, Law Orders A, 1789–1793, 385), reversing j. Court of King George County, Nov. 6, 1789. J.M. for appellant.

Stevens brought action on bond; plea, another jointly bound; reply, not joint, but if so under act of 1786, surviving obligor may be sued separately. J. for £60, payable by £30 with 5 per cent interest from Apr. 15, 1776; reversed by District Court.

Held, plea sufficient; replication faulty, not stating date of death.

Apr. 13, 1793. Heard. Court of Appeals, Va., Order Book II, 212.

Apr. 16. Affirmed. Same, 214–15.

William White v. Thomas Johnson, 1 Washington 158.

Supersedeas to j. of General Court, Oct. 1, 1783, £50, against John Watson and appellant, reversed. J.M. for White.

White, deputy sheriff of Louisa County, returned writ in action brought by Johnson on the case in General Court; endorsed executed without name of his principal on it. Defendant failed to appear and no appearance bail taken; common order and writ of enquiry had against defendant and White; v.j. against White.

Held, despite practice to contrary, j. must be against the sheriff and not deputy sheriff for failure to take bail.

Apr. 16, 1793. Heard. Court of Appeals, Va., Order Book II, 213.

Apr. 17, 1793. Reversed. Same, 217.

Fee: Jan. 23, 1790, £2:10. Account Book, 230.

Kennedy v. Baylor, 1 Washington 162, 163.

Appeal from High Court of Chancery, June 2, 1792, affirming decree Court of Berkeley County, Nov. 20, 1790, affirmed.

J. for foreclosure of equity of redemption in land bought by Baylor. J.M. for appellant.

Objection on appeal, did not allow credits claimed in answer and not replied to; decree for more than commissioner's report; other objections not considered by court. Held, all credits allowed but are not proved; allowance of interest on interest adjusted by agreement of parties on account of miscalculations.

Apr. 18, 1793. Appellee did not appear. Court of Appeals, Va., Order Book II, 217.

Apr. 24, Same, J.M. argued. Affirmed. Same, 222.

William Reynolds v. John Waller, heir and administrator of Edward Waller, 1 Washington 164.

Appeal from decree High Court of Chancery, May 30, 1792, restitution of land and military warrants fraudulently obtained, affirmed and amended. J.M. for appellee.

Warrants for over 5,000 acres of land purchased by Valentine for self and Reynolds for £20 while testator drunk; acquired by Reynolds, part of land warrants assigned to Waller. Decree annulling sale as fraudulent; Reynolds a partner though not party to fraud; damages for land warrants not received; return of military certificates for Waller pay and depreciation pay of £283:16:7, or if not available, other certificates of equal value.

Held, decree amended to payment of present value of certificates not available for return.

Apr. 19, 1793. Heard. Court of Appeals, Va., Order Book II, 218.

Apr. 24, 1793. Affirmed and amended. Same, 222.

Fees: Mar., 1792, £7; June, 1792, £5:12; Apr., 1793, £3. Account Book, 316, 330, 358.

John Baird and Gray Briggs, surviving partners John Baird and Co. v. Henry Blaigrove, executor of Henry Blaigrove, 1 Washington 170, 171.

Appeal from District Court of New London, Sept. 19, 1791.

Order arresting jury verdict £413:6:1½ reversed, j. for appellants same amount. J.M. for appellee.

Action in case brought by appellants, written agreement by appellee to pay judgment debt from proceeds of property sale, subsequent oral agreement to pay balance. Order arresting verdict based on grounds instrument sealed, case not lie. Held, doubtful if scrolls indicate sealed; action lies on subsequent oral agreement.

Apr. 11, 1793. Case presented on record. Court of Appeals, Va., Order Book II, 210.

Apr. 13. Reversed, j. for appellants. Same, 212.

Fees: Oct., 1788, £2:10; Nov., 1791, £5. Account Book, 168, 306.

Neil Buchanan and Duncan Rose, executors of John Bannister v Thomas Shore, administrator of Martha Shore, 1 Washington 173, 175–76.

Appeal from High Court of Chancery, June 1, 1792.

J. for defendant in error reversed. J.M. and Andrew Ronald for appellee. Action by Bannister for £1,000 alleged promised by father of deceased wife as marriage portion. Proof that father stated intended to give money, and later advised by letter that intended to give land instead; land thereafter deeded to son.

Held, no jurisdiction in equity; mere intention; no binding promise. Query, if tenant by courtesy so as to bring action for land.

Apr. 19, 1793. Heard. Court of Appeals, Va., Order Book II, 218.

Apr. 24. Reversed. Same, 222.

Fees: Apr., 1790, £5:12; Feb. 1, 1793, £5. Account Book, 242, 348.

John Clayborn, executor of A. Clayborn v. Hill, 1 Washington 177, 180–83.

Appeal from High Court of Chancery, June 5, 1792.

Decree in favor of appellee, affirmed. J.M. and John Warden for appellee. Action by creditor to set aside as fraudulant conveyance of slaves from father to son by way of mortgage, on which levied execution. Mortgage recorded, slaves in possession of son who was given release and bill of sale not recorded until after execution. Held, fraudulent.

Apr. 24, 1793. Heard. Court of Appeals, Va., Order Book II, 221.

Apr. 29. Affirmed. Same, 226.

Fees: Mar., 1790, £5; Sept., 1792, £2:8. Account Book, 236, 338.

Thomas Anderson v. William R. Bernard, 1 Washington 186, 187.

Error to District Court of Prince Edward, Sept. 5, 1792.

Trespass, j. for defendant below, affirmed by divided court. J.M. for appellee.

Action against deputy sheriff for seizing saddle in levying distress for fees due deputy clerk of General Court. Plea of general issue. Allowed to put in evidence an account showing fees due deputy clerk, no exceptions taken to admission, but in bill of exceptions.

Apr. 18. Heard. Court of Appeals, Va., Order Book II, 217.

Apr. 19. Affirmed. Same, 218.

Fee: Apr., 1793, £5. Account Book, 356.

Johnson v. Bourn, 1 Washington 187, 188.

Error to District Court of Charlottesville, Sept. 21, 1791, £90 damages. Action by plaintiff in error assault and battery, j. for defendant in error, reversed. J.M. for defendant in error.

Testimony of witness being sued in separate action for assault at same time rejected.

Held, error. J.M. admitted counsel of opponent stated law correctly, but that General Court determined otherwise.

Apr. 13, 1792. Writ of supersedeas. Court of Appeals, Va., Order Book II, 154.

Apr. 12, 1793. Submitted. Same, 210.

Apr. 13. Reversed. Same, 211.

Fee: Mar. 22, 1793, £3. Account Book, 354.

Tomlin, Mitchell & How v. Kelly, 1 Washington 190.

Writ of supersedeas j. District Court, Northumberland Courthouse, Apr. 9, 1791, on special verdict dismissing action, reversed with j. for plaintiff in error. J.M. for plaintiff in error in earlier proceedings, Campbell for same herein. Action for goods sold and delivered brought in General Court, sent to District Court, special verdict for plaintiff £100:9:6½ if plaintiff can maintain action where kept no retail store, sold at public auction at wharf, suit brought after twelve months. Va. act of 1779 recited injury to Commonwealth of act of 1748 allowing retail merchants to prove accounts by own oath, and required "actions on accounts for goods sold and delivered, or for any article charged in any store account" be brought within six months.

Held, following earlier case, act applied only to retail store accounts.

Oct. 24, 1792. Continued. Court of Appeals, Va., Order Book II, 193.

Apr. 13, 1793. Reversed, j. for plaintiff in error. £110:9:6½. Same, 211.

Fee: Apr. 23, 1787, £2:8. Account Book, 110.

For proceedings below, see District Court, Northumberland, Order Book 1789–1792, 38, 106, 142; Same, Order Book 1793–1802, 1.

James McAlister v. John McAlister, 1 Washington 193.

Action case on account, j. District Court, Winchester, Sept., 1791 (District Court, Frederick County, Order Book 1789–1793, 270), reversing j. County Court of Berkeley, Aug., 1790, dismissing defendants writ for admission as evidence the oath of one of the parties, ordering umpire finding set aside, and remanding.

J.M. for ———.

Arbitrators not agreeing, umpire gave opinion of dismissal having over objection allowed in evidence depositions of defendant and wife. County Court refused plaintiff's evidence of admission of depositions, dismissed; District Court reversed and remanded for new trial.

Held, depositions not admissible; reversed and sent back to County Court to receive proof of their admission.

Apr. 22, 1793. Continued. Court of Appeals, Va., Order Book II, 220.

Oct. 11, 1793. Heard. Same, 233.

Oct. 12, 1793. Reversed, remanded. Same, 234.

Fee: Apr., 1793, £5. Account Book, 356.

Apr. 22, 1794. Order of District Court conforming to mandate of Court of Appeals. District Court, Frederick County, Order Book 1794–1797, 36–37.

William Eustace v. Thomas Gaskins, executor of John Eustace, 1 Washington 188, 189–90.

Appeal from decree High Court of Chancery, May 4, 1792, reversing County Court of Lancaster which granted relief to appellant; both reversed. J.M. for appellant.

Bill in equity for compensation for land. Testator gave son William land, provided in will that if recovered from him for defect son John, principal legatee, should purchase other. Recovery of land had in 1744; testator died 1785; suit filed 1788; reason for delay, promise of testator to provide for in will. Wife of John, newly appointed executrix, disallowed as party.

Held, sufficient evidence to combat presumption of satisfaction by lapse of time; insufficient evidence of recovery of land; wife of John proper party.

Apr. 18, 1793. Heard. Court of Appeals, Va., Order Book II, 217.

Apr. 20. Both decrees reversed, new trial. Same, 219.

Fees: Mar., 1795, £5; July, 1795, £2:16; Sept., 1795, £3:12. Account Book, 396, 406, 418.

Wilson and M'Rae v. Keeling, 1 Washington 194, 196.

Appeal from High Court of Chancery, May 23, 1792, affirmed. J.M. for appellee.

Appellee in Apr., 1788, borrowed £422:18 paper money, gave mortgage to secure. After due, tendered payment in paper money; refused. Action for injunction and liberty to redeem equity of redemption on payment according to scale of depreciation at time of loan. Allowed, on payment of £84:11:8 with remission of interest from time of tender until demand.

Oct. 17, 1793. Order affirming. Court of Appeals, Va., Order Book II, 236.

Fee: Apr.–May, 1792, £1:16 designated "old suit." Account Book, 322.

William Payne, executor of John Payne v. William Dudley et al., executors of Fleet, 1 Washington 196, 198.

Appeal from decree High Court of Chancery, May 12, 1792.

Injunction against judgment denied; affirmed. J.M. for appellee. Creditor received j. in 1766, acceded to conveyance in trust by debtor for creditors. In 1789 creditors' representative obtained j. on same debt. Injunction refused on grounds agreement to trust not bar action; delay justified.

Oct. 16, 1793. Heard. Court of Appeals, Va., Order Book II, 236.

Oct. 18. Affirmed. Same, 238.

John Hawkins' Executors v. Nelson Berkley, 1 Washington 204, 205–206.

Error to District Court of Richmond, Sept. 12, 1792, affirming County Court of Hanover, Nov. 6, 1790, £914:15, affirmed. J.M. for appellant.

J. against agent for failure to bring suits on accounts under collection undertaking and to account. J.M. argued a variance, no express duty to file suits.

Held, variance not material, power to bring suit implied, objection too late after verdict.

Oct. 17, 1793. Order of affirmance. Court of Appeals, Order Book II, 237.

Fees: Aug., 1791, £4:10; July, 1793, £4:2. Account Book, 294, 366.

See also May, 1790, "Hawkins' ex. v. sundries," £4; Sept., 1790, "Hawkins' Ex'r," £1:4; Sept., 1792, "Mr. Thomas from Mrs. Hawkins," £2:16. Account Book, 248, 258, 336.

For later proceedings in same matter holding giving bonds to lawyer to collect a sufficient compliance, and ruling on remitting of proceeds, see *Hawkins' Executors v. Minor, executor of Berkeley*, 5 Call 118 (1804).

Hooe and Harrison and others v. George Mason, 1 Washington 207, 209–11.

Error to District Court of Dumfries, May 21, 1791.

J. for defendant in error, action against him for freight, reversed.

J.M. for defendant in error.

Shipment from Amsterdam for Alexandria, Virginia, on armed merchantman carrying letter of marque, cruising prohibited; changed course several points; gave chase to enemy vessel prospective prize; disabled in encounter; put in at Dartmouth, New England; goods transshipped by shipper's agent to Virginia.

Held, shipper liable for freight pro rata.

Apr. 26, 1793. Mason dead; revived name of executor. Court of Appeals, Va., Order Book II, 225.

Oct. 24. Reversed, j. for £20. Same, 246.

Thweat and Hinton v. Adam Finch, 1 Washington 217, 219.

Error to District Court of Petersburg, Sept. 19, 1789.

J. for defendant in error, £96:15:2, affirmed. J.M. for defendant in error.

Action against warehouseman for failure to deliver note for inspected tobacco on order of owner, declaring delivered to another on a forged order.

Held, nonsuit properly refused, question for jury if counterfeit; declaration implies a public warehouse, not multifarious.

June 7, 1791. Appellant dead, *scire facias*. Court of Appeals, Va., Order Book II, 67.

Apr. 12, 1792. Alias against George Thwait, executor. Same, 151.

Oct. 10. *Pluries scire facias*. Same, 183.

Apr. 12, 1793. Continued. Same, 209.

Oct. 22. Heard. Same, 242.

Oct. 23. Affirmed. Same, 242–43.

Fee: Oct., 1793, £5:8, Apr., 1795, £4:16. Account Book, 372, 410. Also Finch adv. Thweat, chancery, May, 1795, £5. Account Book, 412.

Judith Brown, administratrix of William Burnett Brown v. John Garland, Parke Goodall, and Geddis Winston, 1 Washington, 221, 222, 223.

Appeal from District Court of Richmond, Apr. 7, 1792.

J. for appellees, reversed. J.M., John Warden, and William Duval for appellees.

Action of debt by administratrix on bond; offset of bonds due from intestate acquired by assignment since trial allowed.

Held, error; also advertisement of discount to creditors who purchased at public auction not applicable.

Oct. 17, 1793. Order reversing. Court of Appeals, Va., Order Book II, 237.

Abraham Sallee, Bernard Markham, and Edward Moseley, executors of Benjamin Harris, and Benjamin and William W. Harris v. William and Sarah Yates, 1 Washington 226.

Appeal from decree High Court of Chancery, Sept. 6, 1792, reported in Wythe, 2nd edition, 163, reversed. J.M. for appellants.

Testator devised £300 to daughter, 1776, £100 payable after eighteen years old, balance as soon as obtainable. First payment made by executor to Sallee, guardian, 1778; balance, 1779. Latter lent out £200, repaid in 1780, £100 retained; funded entirety when paper money called in at one for a thousand. Chancery Court decreed payment by executors of £300, less payments made at then true value.

Held, executors discharged by payments to guardian in paper; guardian not accountable for further depreciation; act of 1781 concerning repayment of paper money claims cited.

Dismissed as to executors and legatees; remanded for accounting by guardian.

Oct. 24, 1793. Heard. Court of Appeals, Va., Order Book II, 244.

Nov. 2, 1793. Reversed. Same, 248.

Fees: Feb., 1790, £5; Sept., 1792, £2:2. Account Book, 234, 336.

Jacob Westfall v. John Singleton, 1 Washington 227.

Appeal from High Court of Chancery, May 18, 1792, dismissing bill for injunction of ejectment judgment in County Court of Hampshire and conveyance of land, reversed. J.M. for appellee.

Abel Westfall purchased land in Northern Neck from earlier settler and held to death, 1775, no deed from Fairfax; Cornelius, the elder son took possession in 1773, was refused lease by Lord Fairfax. Singleton claimed through purchase from younger son who claimed to hold under deathbed donation; Fairfax issued lease to Singleton.

Held, Singleton convey Fairfax lease to Cornelius, the rightful heir; eviction action enjoined.

Apr. 29, 1793. Heard. Court of Appeals, Va., Order Book II, 227.

May 1, 1793. Continued for rehearing. Same, 230.

Oct. 12, 1793. Rehearing. Same, 234.

Nov. 1, 1793. Second rehearing. Same, 247.

Nov. 4, 1793. Reversed, injunction perpetual. Same, 250.

Fees: July 30, 1790, £5:3; Nov., 1792, £7:5. Account Book, 254, 342.

Jones v. Williams and Tomlinson, 1 Washington 230, 230–31, reversing Wythe, 46.

Appeal from High Court of Chancery, May 28, 1792.

J. for appellees, plaintiffs below, reversed. J.M. for appellant.

Bill for land claimed under right of settlement prior to 1775 affirmed by commissioners in 1780 against patentee under military warrant located 1775, surveyed 1776, patent 1784. Court heard case as though on caveat which had been dismissed by accident.

Held, no right of settlement of former Crown lands prior to act of May, 1779; applies only to waste and unappropriated land, not land held under warrant.

Apr. 30, 1793. Heard. Court of Appeals, Va., Order Book II, 228.

May 1. Continued for rehearing. Same, 230.

Nov. 2. Reheard. Same, 249.

Nov. 4. Reversed, dismissed. Same, 251.

Fees: Nov. 29, 1789, £5; Oct., 1791, £2:8; May, 1792, £5; Mar., 1794, £3. Account Book, 224, 302, 326, 382.

Coleman v. Dick and Pat, 1 Washington 233, 236–37, 238.

Error to District Court of Petersburg.

Action assault and battery, false imprisonment, j. for appellees, one shilling, affirmed by equally divided court. J.M. with Alexander Campbell for appellees.

Issue if appellees, plaintiffs below, free or slaves. Special verdict, descended by maternal line from Indian brought into state after 1705.

Held, several plaintiffs may join in tort action which in substance action for freedom; under act of 1705, American Indian cannot be slave, foreign Indian can. Court divided on presumption under verdict.

Nov. 7–8, 1793. Heard. Court of Appeals, Va., Order Book II, 253, 255.

Nov. 9. Affirmed. Same, 255.

Josias Granberry, executor of Josiah Granberry v. Josiah and James Granberry, etc., 1 Washington 246.

Appeal from decree High Court of Chancery on bill of appellee against appellant for accounting, exceptions to Auditor's report as confirmed by court, reversed. J.M. apparently involved in case; counsel of record, Ronald, for appellant; Campbell for appellee.

Held, improper to scale paper money received by executor on day received, but appellant, having adopted the method, is bound by it; interest should not be charged executor except on yearly balance; 5 per cent commission due executor as compensation, even though beneficiary and bequest not in lieu of compensation; accounting with executor in payments made estate for loan taken as paper and reduced by scale of depreciation as any creditor.

Oct. 23–24, Nov. 5, 1793. Heard. Court of Appeals, Va., Order Book II, 243, 244, 251.

Nov. 8, 1793. Order of reversal and instructions. Same, 254.

Fees: Aug., 1790, £7; Sept., 1794, £9. Account Book, 256, 398.

Robert Draffin v. John Thomas.

Appeal from j. against appellant, District Court, Charlottesville, Sept. 20, 1792. J.M. for appellant.

Oct. 24, 1793. Dismissed, agreement of parties. Court of Appeals, Va., Order Book II, 246.

Fee: Oct., 1791, £5. Account Book, 300.

Joseph Jones v. Henry Anderson.
Same v. Henry Anderson, Smith Tandy, and David Ross and Co.

Appeal from High Court of Chancery, Sept. 1, 1792. J.M. for appellant.

Oct. 19, 1793. Heard. Court of Appeals, Va., Order Book II, 240.

Oct. 22. Affirmed. Same, 243.

Fee: Jan. 10, 1787, £2:10 (High Court of Chancery). Account Book, 96.

Orlando Jones and John Hudson v. Nicholas Davis.

Appeal from j. against appellant District Court, Sept. 19, 1791, £218, payable by £113.:12:11½. J.M. for appellee.

Apr. 18, 1793. Affirmed, appellants not appearing. Court of Appeals, Va., Order Book II, 161.

Fee: July 13, 1789, £2:10. Account Book, 204.

Archer Payne v. Thomas Oliver.

Appeal from j. against appellant District Court, Richmond, Apr. 4, 1793. J.M. for appellant.

Oct. 10, 1793. Dismissed, neither party appearing. Court of Appeals, Va., Order Book II, 240.

Fee: Sept., 1789, £2:8; Sept., 1790, £2:12. Account Book, 210, 258.

Edward Washington, executor of Edward Washington v. Samuel Tillett.

Appeal from High Court of Chancery, June 4, 1792. J.M. for appellant.

Apr. 27, 1793. Dismissed, failure to prosecute. Court of Appeals, Va., Order Book II, 225.

Fee: May, 1791, £4:4. Account Book, 286.

High Court of Chancery

Thomas Bailey and Anne, his wife v. Levin Teackle, executor of Ralph Justice et al., Wythe 8.

J.M. represented petitioner (Anne).

Testator devised plantation to wife during widowhood then to daughter Alice; also other land and Negro to daughter Anne, adding if both children die without heirs, plantation to wife; on death, to brother. Testator died 1750; wife remarried 1756; Alice died an infant and her personal property distributed to mother, Anne, and two half-sisters. In action by Anne, held, wife entitled to remainder on event regardless of remarriage, also to dower;

Anne entitled to two-thirds of profits of plantation after mother's remarriage, also to one-half personal property of Alice, which can recover from half sisters; statute of limitations docked because infant at time; also testator can sign will at top instead of bottom.

Fees: Oct., 1792, £2:14; Apr., 1793, £5. Account Book, 340, 356.

Miles Cary and Grizzel, his wife, and Josiah Buxton v. Nathaniel Buxton, Wythe 26.

J.M. represented defendant herein (heir of eldest son).

Testator, having both land in fee and other land in tail, devised former to eldest son without words of inheritance, latter to two younger sons. Eldest son took all, claiming will invalid as to entailed. In action in General Court against heir of eldest son by claimant under one younger son, former obtained j. in his favor. Injunction against j. allowed; testator intended to provide for younger sons; oldest son having elected to take entailed, his heir must relinquish fee land, account for rents and profits and slaves belonging to younger under will.

Fees: May, 1789, £2:8 (lower court); Mar., 1792, £4:10 (Chancery). Account Book, 198, 316.

Daniel Lawrence Hylton v. Adam Hunter and Abner Vernon, executors of James Hunter, Wythe 78.

Controversy involved sale of bonds by executors of Hunter to Hylton based on correspondence of 1788; J.M. not attorney in case; testimony that correction of correspondence referred to various lawyers, first Henry Banks and William Hay, then to Jerman Baker and J.M., lastly to George Weir (p. 810).

Sarah Hooe, survivor of husband Gerrard Hooe, and John Alexander and Elizabeth, his wife v. Mary Kelsick, survivor of husband Younger Kelsick, and Johnathan Beckwith, survivor of wife Rebecca.
Also *Beckwith et al. v. Hooe et al.,* Wythe 102.

J.M. for Hooe and Alexander.

Unequal distribution of estate by codicil of testator among three daughters set aside despite court verdict of 1761 approving codicil; equity based on assertions of intentions by testator to suitors of daughters.

Fees: Apr. 3, 1786, £8:8; Apr., 1792, £12:10; May, 1792, £3. Account Book, 68, 322, 326.

County Court, Cumberland

Republica v. Richard Randolph.

J.M.'s notes of evidence in examination of Randolph, committed and charged with felonious murder of child said to be born to Nancy Randolph. Copied from original by John Randolph of Roanoke in Williamsburg, June 28, 1793. VHi, MSS 2 M 3567. J.M. co-counsel with Patrick Henry and Alexander Campbell for defendant. Found not guilty and discharged. V, County Court of Cumberland, Order Book, 1792–1797, 88; see also W. C. Bruce, *John Randolph of Roanoke* (New York, Putnam, 1922), 112–19; Henry, *Patrick Henry*, II, 491.

District Court, Franklin

John Letcher, assignee of William Noll v. Rawleigh White.

Debt. J.M. for plaintiff.

Apr. 20, 1793. Abated by death of plaintiff. District Court, Franklin, Order Book I, 1789–1793, 329.

Fee: Mar., 1789, £1:8, "old appeal." Account Book, 190.

District Court, Northumberland

John Lunsford, assignee of John Hunton v. George Glascock, Jr.

Motion for j. upon bond for forthcoming of property taken on execution. J.M. for plaintiff.

Sept. 9, 1791. Submitted by agreement to arbitrators John James Mound, Francis F. Brooke, John Monroe, and William Brown. District Court, Northumberland, Order Book 1789–1792, 167.

Apr. 7, 1792. Order of reference set aside, continued. Same, 196.

Sept. 2, 1793. Default j., £120 Va., payable by £45 with interest from Aug. 1, 1789, also 500 pounds gross tobacco and fifteen shillings, $5.64 and nine shillings with interest from May 17, 1793. Same, Order Book 1793–1802, 2.

Fee: May, 1794, £5. Account Book, 386.

Superior (District) Court, Frederick

Lewis Stephens v. Isaac Hite.

Writ of supersedeas to County Court, Frederick; j. against plaintiff in error, Oct., 1790, £142:8:7½, payable by £71:4:3½, which included four js. against Jacob Widner and Stephens, his special bail.

J.M. for Stephens.

Apr. 20, 1792. Continued. Superior Court, Frederick, Order Book 1789–1793, 302.

Sept. 10. Continued. Same, 383.

Apr. 22, 1793. Reversed, except as to £15. Same, 505.

Fee: Jan., 1794, £5. Account Book, 380.

Edwin Young v. Abraham Byrd.

Trespass, assault and battery. J.M. for plaintiff.

Apr. 22, 1793. Abated by death of plaintiff.

Superior Court, Frederick, Order Book 1789–1793, 502.

Fee: Oct. 13, 1788, £2:10. Account Book, 170.

See *Same v. Maurice Bird.* Case, Sept. 2, 1790. Dismissed by agreement. Same, Order Book 1789–1793, 114.

District Court, Fredericksburg

William and Mary Almond, administrator and administratrix of James Yarbrough v. David Davenport.

Writ of supersedeas from j. County Court of Caroline against plaintiff's testator for three slaves or £100, £5 damages.

J.M. for Davenport.

Apr. 29, 1790. Diminution of record, writ of certiorari granted. District Court, Fredericksburg, Law Orders A, 1789–1793, 79.

Oct. 4, 1793. Held, j. upon replevin bond was against Benjamin Tompkins only; execution against defendant and Tompkins erroneous. Proceedings in County Court after j. set aside; plaintiffs allowed appeal to Court of Appeals. (No record in latter court.) Same, 303.

Fee: Apr., 1790, £2:8. Account Book, 242.

John Brown and John Cook v. William Hewitt.

Trespass on case; plaintiffs hired boat, rigging, etc., to defendant, three shillings per day, to be returned in good condition; failure to return; damages £200. Filed in General Court, 1784. J.M. for plaintiff.

Apr., 1786—Oct., 1789. Continued. District Court, Fredericksburg, Law Orders 1789–1793, 40.

May 5, 1790. Referred to arbitrators. Same, 106.

May 6, 1793. J. on award for Brown, £20. Same, 474.

Same, Law Orders 1790–1793, 105–106.

Fee: Oct., 1788, £1:8. Account Book, 168.

Bennett Brown & Co. v. Thomas Short et al.

Debt. J.M. for plaintiff.

Oct. 3, 1791. Abated as to Bennett Brown by death, continued. District Court, Fredericksburg, Law Orders A, 1789–1793, 292.

May 7, 1792. Continued by plaintiff. Same, 364.

May 7, 1793. Abated by death of plaintiff. Same, 484.

Fee: Mar., 1789, £4:16. Account Book, 190.

The Commonwealth v. George T. Tod.

Indictment for murder. J.M. for defendant.

Apr. 30, 1793. Verdict, acquittal. District Court, Fredericksburg, Law Orders A, 1789–1793, 444.

Fees: June, 1792, £2:10. Account Book, 330. Also Sept., 1795, "*Tod v. Commonwealth,*" £5. Account Book, 420.

James Ewell v. Burgess Ball.

Debt, on obligation sealed, £1,000 current, Dec. 24, 1773. Filed Apr., 1790, Stafford County. J.M. for defendant.

Oct. 7, 1791. Special verdict, if payment in paper currency subsequent to 1777 in nominal sum constitutes payment of debt due in money current, verdict for defendant; if subject to scale of depreciation, for plaintiff £447:9:19 with interest on £397:19 from 1778. District Court, Fredericksburg, Law Orders A, 1789–1793, 324.

Oct. 10, 1791. Exceptions to admission of evidence by third person, in absence of defendant, that agent of defendant in selling defendant's land to him stated doing so to pay plaintiff on bond sued upon. Same, 334.

May 9, 1793. J. on special verdict for defendant. Same, 490.

Law Orders 1790–1793, 129.

Fee: Sept., 1790, £2:10. Account Book, 260.

Mansanna Hunter, assignee of John Russell Spence v. Alexander Spotswood.

Debt. J.M. for plaintiff.

May 2, 1793. Office j. set aside. District Court, Fredericksburg, Law Orders A, 1789–1793, 454.

Oct. 10, 1793. Consent j., £449:18, payable by £224:19. Same, 539.

Fee: May, 1793, £4:16. Account Book, 360.

Thomas Porter v. and adv. Henry Ayler. (Two suits by Porter, one by Ayler)

Debt and covenant. J.M. for Porter.

May 9, 1791. By consent, to arbitrators for final award. District Court, Fredericksburg, Law Orders A, 1789–1793, 263.

Oct. 8, 1791. Orders of references set aside, put on calendar. Same, 331.

Oct. 3, 1792. On motion of Porter in his suits, surveyor of Culpeper County to survey land; justice of court to meet him, take depositions of witnesses, sheriff attend. Same, 405.

May 6, 1793. Dismissed, parties agreed, costs split. Same, 472.

Fee: Jan., 1790, £6:14. Account Book, 230.

Thomas Terry and George Booker v. John Scott.

Ejectment, 1,000 acres called "Arnolds," Parish of St. Margaret, County of Caroline; wills, estate in tail, residuary estates, survival. Filed in General Court, Oct., 1786. J.M. for defendant.

Oct. 3, 1789. By consent to arbitration, award to be final.

District Court, Fredericksburg, Law Orders A, 1789–1793, 37.

May 7, 1793. Report of arbitrators. John Brumskill died in Europe, 1761; will devised land to daughter Isabella Scott in fee, attested by one witness and not proved in handwriting of testator. Son William held heir; will of 1770 left to sister Isabella and heirs of body; if no heir, right of appointment to poor children of her sister; residue of estate to children of three sisters—Isabella, Martha Booker, Hannah Scott—excluding children of other sisters—Mary Clarke and Elizabeth Terry—and George Booker. Elizabeth survived William, and was survived by sisters Martha, Hannah, and Elizabeth, and daughters of Mary Clarke. Surviving claimants when suit filed were George Booker (son and heir of Martha) and Thomas Terry (only son and heir of Elizabeth Thomas), who died pending suit.

Held, John Brumskill will void. Thomas Brumskill will gave Isabella a fee in tail; provision for appointment void for uncertainty and unexercised. Three sisters—Martha, Elizabeth, and Hannah—took as coparceners under residuary clause; children of Mary Clarke excluded. The three sisters died intestate, leaving plaintiffs Thomas and George sole heirs; and former having died pending suit, George entitled to entire premises. Same, 478; Law Orders 1790–1793, 111.

Fees: Oct., 1789, £5; Mar., 1793, £2:8. Account Book, 214, 350.

District Court, Prince Edward

William Hubbard v. John Marshall, executor of Seraphine Farmicola.

On a delivery bond, appeal from j. of County Court, Charlotte. J.M., executor of appellee.

July 2, 1792. J.M. as executor brought action, County Court, Charlotte, on delivery bond, Paul Carrington, Jr., his attorney; bond executed Mar. 22, 1792, by Hubbard and others for £172:11:16½ current money or 15,100 pounds inspected Petersburg tobacco, on condition that if Hubbard and others deliver to sheriff a Negro fellow named Ben, levied on in execution for £86:5:9 current money or 7,550 pounds tobacco, bond to be void. J. for latter amount on failure to deliver. Appeal to District Court. Apr. 1, 1793. Affirmed. District Court, Prince Edward, Order Book 1792–1795, 149; Same, Order Book 1793–1799, 2–3.

James Lyle, administrator of Joseph Calland v. Nicholas Calland, executor of William Cabell.

Sept. 8, 1792. Motion to show cause why writ of error not issue to j. for defendant, plaintiff below, against intestate in County Court, Cumberland, June 27, 1785, £889:17:7½, payable by £444:18:9[3] with interest at 5 per cent from July 8, 1771. District Court, Prince Edward, Order Book 1789–1792, 319.

Apr. 1, 1793. Continued. Same, Order Book 1793–1799, 4.

Apr. 5. Writ awarded. Same, 24.

No further record.

See also:

Apr. 11, 1793. *Same v. Same.* Writ of error awarded to j. County Court, Cumberland, *Cabell v. Calland,* Nov. 26, 1788. Same, 45.

Sept. 3, 1793. Reversed, defendant in error admitting erroneous. Same, Order Book 1793–1799, 75.

Fee: Oct. 10, 1788, £2:10, "Writ of error." Account Book, 108.

District Court, Prince William

Townshend Dade; William G. Stuart; and John, George, William, Thomas, Nicholas, and Richard, Mordecai, Balail, and Giles, infants, and Sarah Fitzhugh v. Lewis Saunders.

Ejectment, plantation of six messuages, one garden, 500 acres, Fairfax County, damages £500. Filed in General Court, Richmond, Oct., 1785. J.M. for plaintiffs. (Signed declaration.)

Oct., 1785. Answer, not guilty.

Apr., 1786. Survey order.

Oct., 1787, through Oct., 1789. Continued.

May, 1790. Leave to amend declaration.

May 13, 1791. Objections to amendments as changing materially the demise, overruled, exceptions.

Oct. 14, 15, 1791. Trial. Depositions for plaintiff referring to contents of deposition of another witness, which latter was held by plaintiff and presented at trial; objection by defendant to use of former depositions. Ruling, can be used, but portion referring to latter deposition excluded. Exception by plaintiff.

Oct. 17, 1791. Special verdict for plaintiff if proper parties to bring action under will of testator, prior owner; continued.

May 12, 1792. By consent verdict set aside, j. for plaintiffs. District Court, Prince William, Land Causes 1789–1793, 361–421.

Fee: July 22, 1784, £8:8. Account Book, 12.

William Hunter, Andrew Wailes, Robert Lyle, and Thomas Hewet, executors of Robert Lyle v. Elisha C. Dick.

Debt, £76, damages £90 on sealed obligation, Fairfax County.

J.M. for defendant.

Nov., 1790. Bond, delivery, special bail, common order.

Dec., 1790. Order confirmed.

May, 1791. Order set aside; defense, payment.

Oct. 17, 1793. V.j. £76, payable by £38; damages one penny.

District Court, Prince William, Records at Large 1793, 285.

Fee: Apr. 7, 1787, two suits, £5:12. Account Book, 104.

Richards v. Fallis.

J.M. for defendant.

District Court, Prince William, Records at Large, 504 (so listed in Record Book but existing record does not include to that page).

Fees: Nov., 1791, £2:8; Mar., 1792, £1:8. Account Book, 304–316.

William Wilson v. Robert Powell.

Case, on acceptance of bill of exchange assigned to plaintiff, $112, damages $50, Fairfax County. J.M. for plaintiff.

Mar. 5, 1790. Summons.

June, 1790. Common order.

Aug., 1790. Order confirmed.

Oct. 14, 1793. V.j. £43:19:8. District Court, Prince William, Records at Large 1793, 37.

Fee: Nov. 3, 1786, "from Allen in supersedeas *Wilson v. Powell,*" £2:10. Account Book, 90.

District Court, City of Richmond

Rawleigh Colston, administrator of Thomas Webb, surviving partner

Thomas Webb and Isaac Beale, deceased, d.b.a. Thomas Webb & Co. v. Robert Morris and Carter Braxton, d.b.a. Morris & Braxton.

Case. J.M. for plaintiff.

Action on account arising from purchaser of arms in Curaçao by Morris & Braxton sold in the United States on credit of Thomas Webb & Co. and not repaid by Morris.

Apr., 1793. V.j. £9,812:10:19. In evidence *Francis Webb et al. v. Rawleigh Colston,* Superior Court of Chancery, Winchester, Frederick County, Va., Record Book 1784–1820, 1, 37; see also Same, V, 39, 84–85.

Dec. 8, 1796. Colston wrote to J.M. to make personal application to legatees of Thomas Webb and Warden and Smith concerning proffered means of settlement and collection of judgment against Robert Morris (n.f.). Letters Colston to Robert Morris and to James Webb, Dec. 9, 1796. Same, Record Book 1784–1820, I, 180, 183. In Oct., 1796, he had enclosed several letters to "Mr. Marshall" concerning this matter for forwarding. Letter Colston to Henry Hill, Oct. 18, 1796; Hill to Colston, Oct. 5, 1796. Same, Record Book 1784–1820, 1, 44, 177.

J.M. conferred with William Smith, advising him of Colston's desire to settle the claim of legatees of Webb against Colston. Letter William Smith to Colston, n.d. (1796). Same, Record Book 1784–1820, 1, 62.

Fees of £15, and £10, June, 1790, to J.M. for the above matter entered in account current Rawleigh Colston with Thomas Webb & Co. Same, 22, 115.

LAND TRANSACTIONS

Fauquier County, Virginia

July 25 *Lease*

J.M., Richmond, to Thomas Smith, Fauquier County, five shillings, part of Oak Hill bounded by Burr Harrison, Phil Mallory, Maj. Massie, John Rust, Benjamin Rector, John Lawson, during lives of grantee, wife, and son. £50 yearly rental, Jan. 1; obligation to plant 100 apple trees, ten acres in timothy or clover, build dwelling 16 x 24 ft. and barn 34 x 16 ft.; fifty acres to remain unclaimed, no right to sell without consent. Fauquier County, Va., Records, Deed Book 11, 538. Recorded Apr. 28, 1794. County Court, Fauquier, Minute Book 1793–1795, 96. xxx

July 25 *Lease*

J.M., Richmond, to Thomas Simpson, Fauquier County, five shillings, land purchased by J.M. of Acquilla Dyson, for life of grantee, wife, and son; yearly rental £10, Jan. 1, quitrents and taxes; obligation to plant 200 apple trees, ten acres in timothy or clover, build dwelling 16 x 24 ft., barn 34 x 16 ft. Fauquier County, Va., Records, Deed Book 12, 29–30. Recorded July 28, 1794. County Court, Fauquier, Minute Book 1793–1795, 168. Proved and certified Sept. 23, 1793. Same, 1791–1793, 455.

July 25 *Lease*

J.M., Richmond, to Edward S. Shacklett, Fauquier County, five shillings, land part of Oak Hill bounded by outer lot on main road and lot of John Clarke, for life of grantee, wife, and son; yearly rental £6, Jan. 1, obligation to plant 150 apple trees, 7½ acres in timothy or clover, build house 16 x 24 ft., barn 34 x 16 ft. Fauquier County, Va., Records, Deed Book 12, 30–32. Recorded Sept. 23, 1793. County Court, Fauquier, Minute Book 1793–1795, 168. Proved and certified, Sept. 23, 1793. Same, 1791–1793, 455.

July 25 *Lease*

J.M., Richmond, to Benjamin Rector, Fauquier County, five shillings, land part of Oak Hill bounded by two out lines of Oak Hill tract, for life of grantee, wife, and son; yearly rental £15, Jan. 1; obligation to plant 150 apple trees, 7½ acres in timothy or clover, build dwelling 16 x 24 ft., barn 34 x 16 ft. Fauquier County, Va., Records, Deed Book 12, 32–33. Recorded July 28, 1794. County Court, Fauquier, Minute Book 1793–1795, 168. Proved and certified, Sept. 23, 1793. Same, 1791–1793, 465.

July 25 *Lease*

J.M., Richmond, to William Hume, Fauquier County, five shillings, land part of Oak Hill bounded by out line land of John Rust, and road; yearly rental £8, Jan. 1; obligation to plant 100 apple trees, five acres in timothy or clover, building dwelling 16 x 24 ft., barn 34 x 16 ft. Fauquier County, Va., Records, Deed Book 15, 584–86. Recorded Apr. 28, 1804. County Court, Fauquier, Minute Book 1791–1793, 479. Proved and certified Oct. 28, 1793. Same, 1791–1793, 478.

1794

DOCUMENTS

Jan. 17, *n.p.* *Bill of Exchange*

Order by J.M. on Rev. David Jones, Eastown, Chester County, Va., to pay Garrett Cottinger one hundred dollars. PP, Rare Book Dept.

Jan. 21
NEW YORK

James M. Marshall to Secretary of State Edmund Randolph

Received by post four packets and one letter to Thomas Pinkney, one for Mrs. Randolph, one for Gennings; no letter of advice for Anderson and Co. necessary. Sailing American bottom for Falmouth; no instructions to destroy dispatches if driven into French port. DNA, General Records Dept. of State, Misc. Letters. R.G. 59.

(James M. Marshall went to Europe as special agent for President Washington to obtain release of Lafayette. See letters of Thomas Pinckney to J.M. Marshall, Mar. 28, 1794; Apr. 3, 1794; June 14, 1794; and July 18, 1794. ScHi. Also Marshall, *Life of Washington.* V, 262. At same time he contracted for purchase of Fairfax Estate lands in Virginia. See herein Jan. 18, 1793, Feb. 1, 1794; Beveridge, *Marshall,* II, 203–204.)

Feb. 1
LONDON

South Branch Manor Purchase

Deed of Denny Martin Fairfax to J.M. of Manor of South Branch, Hampshire and Hardy counties, Va., first executed on this day. Resealed and delivered Feb. 1, 1797. (See herein, that date, 1797. Documents.)

Mar. 27
RICHMOND

to Archibald Stuart, Attorney at Law, Staunton, Va.

Encloses letter to Bell; comments on record in Mills case; not employed by Mathews, Duval is; Burns case appearance; represents Rankin, cannot represent Donaghoe. Congratulates on marriage; reminds of winter trip to Philadelphia to see Congress open. Fears war, outrages beyond human bearing. VHi; WMQ (ser. 2) Vol. V (Oct., 1925), 286–87 (incomplete); *Green Bag,* Vol. X (Jan., 1898), 24 (incomplete); Magruder, *Marshall,* 92–93; Iles, *Little Masterpieces,* I, 115–16 (dated as 1793).

Apr. 8
RICHMOND

Legal Practice

Release by J.M. as attorney for plaintiff of portion of judgment if appeal be not prosecuted by the state in case of Samuel Bacon Cunningham against Virginia. V, Exec. Papers, Box 1794, Feb.-Apr., Folder Apr. 1–10; CVSP, VII, 101–102; Oster, *Marshall,* 20. (See herein 1794, Legal Practice, Court of Appeals, *Commonwealth v. Cunningham and Co.*)

Apr. 25
RICHMOND *to Lieut. Gov. James Wood*

Applies for arms for militia of Richmond. V, Exec. Papers, Box 1794, Feb.-Apr., Folder Apr. 21–30; CVSP, VII, 120; Oster, *Marshall*, 20–21.

May 20
RICHMOND *to Gov. Henry Lee*

Request for house for field pieces of Richmond militia. Endorsed, rejected. V, Exec. Papers, Box 1794, May-June, Folder May 11–20, CVSP, VII, 148; Oster, *Marshall*, 21.

May 28
RICHMOND *to Archibald Stuart*

Giving adverse opinion on merits from record of slander suit brought by Clay. Inconsistent pleas of not guilty and jurisdiction permissible; whether truth a defense unsettled. Received letters from Philadelphia of military action from Canada; hopes democratic society of Philadelphia or "upper brethren" will demolish; if true must prepare for serious war. VHi; WMQ (ser. 2), Vol. V (Oct., 1925), 287–88 (dated 1790).

June 17
RICHMOND *Militia*

Orders of Henry Lee, Governor and commander-in-chief of militia, Virginia, calling up detachment of militia on requisition of President of the United States (for service in "Whisky Rebellion"); Maj. Gen. Hopkins in command; Brigs. J.M., Meade, Williams, and Zane under him. V, Exec. Papers, Box 1794, May-June, Folder June 21–30; Va. Gaz and G.A., July 9, 1794, 3.

June 30
RICHMOND *Militia*

Rough general orders of Governor to militia, called up to suppress "Whisky Rebellion"; J.M. brigadier general. CVSP, VII, 202. See also Edward Carrington to Lieut. Gov. Wood, Sept. 1, 1794, CVSP, VII, 287–88.

For J.M.'s description of the Whisky Rebellion and its suppression, see his *Life of Washington*, IV, 452–58, V, 170–85.

July 4 *Power of Attorney*

Power of attorney J.M. to Charles Marshall to execute bond or instrument as security for Denny Fairfax that will account to Commonwealth of

Virginia for rent of Manor of Leeds if same should be escheated, and will prosecute suits of Fairfax into effect. Fauquier County, Va., Records, Deed Book 2, 375. Recorded Oct. 27, 1795. County Court of Fauquier, Minute Book 1795–1797, 16.

July 7
RICHMOND *to [Gov. Henry Lee]*

Contest in 19th Regiment of militia between light infantry and grenadier companies as to rank, former claiming rank under senior commissions, latter claiming military usage gives grenadiers right as privilege of company regardless of rank of captain; other regiments have same differences. Request general rule. CSmH, RB 39006.

July 19
RICHMOND *Militia*

Offer to J.M., brigadier general, of officers of artillery to make first tour of duty required from the President, signed by A. Quarrier. V, Exec. Papers, Box 1794, July-Aug., Folder 11–20.

July 21
RICHMOND *Militia*

Particular orders of Gov. Henry Lee to J.M. as brigadier general of militia to proceed to Smithfield; cavalry and artillery of Second Brigade to move with him; Second Battalion of Nineteenth Brigade follow by water; light infantry from Petersburg under Marshall's command; information to be obtained from Maj. Taylor. Knows dignity and rights of Comonwealth safe in J.M.'s hands; instructed to report on misconduct of lieutenant colonel commandant of Isle of Wight. V, War 10, Militia Commissions, General Orders 1782–1809, 20–21.

July 23
SMITHFIELD, VA. *to Governor of Virginia, Henry Lee*

Report of arrival of troops at Smithfield and action taken to halt arming of privateer *Unicorn*, seizure of cannon, etc.; returning with troops to Richmond. V, Exec. Papers, Box 1794, July-Aug., Folder July 21–31; CVSP, VII, 228–29; Oster, *Marshall*, 21–23.

July 28
RICHMOND *to Gov. Henry Lee*

Further report of Virginia militia Smithfield expedition. V, Exec.

Papers, Box 1794, July-Aug., Folder July 21–31; CVSP, VII, 234–35; Oster, *Marshall*, 23–25.

July 30
RICHMOND *from Gov. Henry Lee*

Commending J.M. on conduct of Richmond and Petersburg militia under his command in interposition of militia to support civil authority. V, Exec. Letter Books, 1792–1794, 474.

Aug. 6
PETERSBURG *Maj. G. K. Taylor to Gov. Henry Lee*

Detailed report of Smithfield incident; arrival of Gen. Marshall on Tuesday; opposition vanished; Marshall command and orders praised; departed on Friday. V, Exec. Papers, Box 1794, July-Aug., Folder Aug. 1–10.

Aug. 15
RICHMOND *Militia*

Order of Gov. Henry Lee as commander-in-chief of Virginia militia; J.M. as brigadier on Board of General Officers to complete settlement of rank of second detachment of militia called for by President of the United States to protect frontiers from Indians and seaboard in case of war. Va. Gaz. and G.A., Aug. 20, 1794, 3.

Aug. 19
PETERSBURG *Maj. G. K. Taylor to Gov. Henry Lee*

Enclosing report of Smithfield incident dated Aug. 4, held to submit to J.M., but latter sick. Also account of expenditures, includes one or two charges against J.M. not presented to him for payment in Smithfield. V, Exec. Papers, Box 1794, July-Aug., Folder Aug. 11–20; CVSP, VII, 264–65.

Sept. 4
RICHMOND *Militia*

Order of James Wood, Lieutenant Governor of Virginia, to J.M. authorizing expenditures for subsistence and transportation of baggage of militia to Winchester, the place of rendezvous; J.M. addressed as "Brigadier." V, Exec. Letter Books, 1792–1794, 506–507.

Sept. 13
RICHMOND *to Gov. Henry Lee*

Enclosing statement by captain of Richmond artillery as to needs for equipping for action. V, Exec. Papers, Box 1794, Sept.-Nov., Folder Sept. 11–20; CVSP, VII, 309; Oster, *Marshall*, 27.

Sept. 30 *Autograph*

J.M.'s name is inscribed twice on front page of George Washington's diary preceding entry of above date. DLC, Diary of George Washington.

Oct. 4

RICHMOND *Opinion as State Attorney—Militia Fines*

Lieut. Gov. James Wood to Brig. Gen. Martin, order to institute legal proceedings on delinquencies under requisitions of President of the United States; enclosed opinion of J.M., acting as Virginia State Attorney in absence of Attorney General. (n.f.) WHi, Draper MSS. 2 XX—45.

(James Innes, Attorney General of Virginia, departed for Kentucky bearing communications between the President of the United States and the executive of Kentucky. He claimed not to be in violation of Virginia statutes forbidding the holding of federal and state offices coterminously. See letter Innes to James Wood, Lieutenant Governor, Lancaster, Nov. 20, 1794. V, Exec. Papers, Box 1794, Sept.-Nov., Folder Nov. 11–20.)

Oct. 16

RICHMOND *Opinion as State Attorney—Tax Arrearages*

Opinion by J.M. as acting Attorney of Commonwealth of Virginia concerning disposition of gain from proceeds of sale by state agent collecting arrears of taxes; profits from resale to state; on subject of agent Davies' letter. V, Exec. Papers, Box 1794, Sept.-Nov., Folder Oct. 11–20; CVSP, VII, 347; Oster, *Marshall*, 25–26.

Oct. 16

RICHMOND *Opinion as State Attorney—Militia Fines*

Opinion of J.M. as acting Attorney of Commonwealth of Virginia as to fines under the militia laws; failure to obey requisition punishable under federal law, one year's pay; state act of fine $10.00 not apply; neither fine applies to foreign citizens. V, Exec. Papers, Box 1794, Sept.-Nov., Folder Oct. 11–20; CVSP, VII, 347–48; Oster, *Marshall*, 26–27.

Oct. 27

RICHMOND *to Edmund Randolph*

Answering inquiry as to law of Virginia on proof of book debts, English statute giving right ex parte proof by British suing in Virginia terminated;

same proof for British debt as American. DNA, Dept. of State, Misc. Letters, Oct.–Dec., 1794.* NNHi.

* Randolph advised John Jay received opinion from "professional friend." Randolph to Jay, Oct. 11 and 19, 1794. DNA, General Records, Dept. of State, Domestic Letters, VII, 352–53, R.G. 59; ASP (For. Rel.), I, 498–99. Later he corroborated statement by J.M., sending copy of J.M.'s letter by Bayard to England. Randolph to Jay, Nov. 3 and 7, 1794 ASP (For. Rel.), I, 501.

Nov. 28
RICHMOND *Opinion as State Attorney—Sheriff Bond*

Opinion of J.M. as acting Attorney of Commonwealth of Virginia concerning filing of bond and security by Elisha White under commission as sheriff of Hanover County. V, Exec. Papers, Box 1794, Sept.-Nov., Folder Nov. 21–30; CVSP, VII, 383–84; Oster, *Marshall*, 27–28.

Dec. 12
RICHMOND *to Charles Simms*

Acknowledges letter of Nov. 28; glad tobacco in Simms' hands; feared miscarriage. Little versed in marine law; never practiced in court of admiralty; answer to inquiry not to be much relied on. Question if finder of wreck at sea entitled to vessel or salvage; J.M. believes latter; but in any case, charterer of vessel no claim. DLC, Chas. Simms Papers, III, 34809.

Dec. 18
RICHMOND *Opinion as State Attorney—Sale by Sheriff*

Opinion by J.M. as acting Attorney of Commonwealth of Virginia concerning sale of Robert Craig's land by sheriff of Washington County as fraudulent and irregular; property passes to representative of sheriff to sell. (In original document, J.M.'s report referred to on cover, but no opinion included.) See Auditor's Report re Sale of Land, dated Dec. 18, 1794. V, Exec. Papers, 1794, Dec., Folder Dec. 11–20; CVSP, II, 403–404; Oster, *Marshall*, 28–29.

n.d., n.p. *to Archibald Stuart*

Inquires if bonds and papers sent him last summer were given by Clendinnan, Donnelly, or Judge Bullitt, and if received. If concerned about case of *Gaston adv. Devier*, speak to friend Nicholas concerning half fee due Marshall. Sent letter from McClain concerning Bains business; executors may be necessary. VHi.

n.d., RICHMOND *Opinion as State Attorney—Rose's Executor*

Opinion of J.M. as acting Attorney General of Virginia that commencement of action against executor gives no priority; creditor purchasing at sale of estate property cannot enjoin judgment against him for price so as to gain preference over claims of superior or equal dignity; if suit on simple contract at issue against executor and fear of deficiency of assets, latter should change plea to want of assets unless plaintiff willing to take judgment if and when assets. NIC.

COMMON COUNCIL OF RICHMOND

July 1 J.M. elected at triannual election as one of sixteen corporate directors of the City of Richmond; eighth on list with 106 votes, William Richardson having highest vote of 120; J.M.'s brother William and Bushrod Washington also elected. Common Hall Records 1793–1795, II, 58.

July 2 Elected mayor of City of Richmond; meeting attended by eleven of the sixteen directors, not including J.M. Same, 58–59.

July 12 Refused office of mayor; qualified and took oath as common councilman. Same, 59.

Appointed on committees to amend police ordinances and ordinance for appointment of chamberlain. Same, 60.

Absent from meetings of Common Hall July 26 and Aug. 6. Same, 61, 63.

Aug. 18 Presented ordinance concerning appointment of chamberlain, passed. Same, 64.
Absent from meeting of Nov. 12. Same, 66. Present at meeting of Dec. 9. Same, 67. Absent from meeting of Jan. 19, 1795. Same, 67–70. Absent from meeting of Jan. 29. Same, 71.

Feb. 16, 1795 Present at meeting; appointed on committee to confer with James River Co. to supply water to city reservoir in return for passing canal through streets. Same, 72.

Mar. 26 Present at meeting. Same, 74. Absent at meeting of May 18. Same, 76.

No further records extant. (See herein Oct. 22, 1795, committee conveyance of land for tanyard.)

LEGAL PRACTICE

THE NUMBER OF FEES noted by J.M. for this year diminished to 164, totaling a return of £975:4:2. The decreases in number of fees was in part made up by a number of larger fees. Eight of these were in the £20 to £30 bracket; one was for £50 (*Pendleton Pannell et al. v. Spotswood*). A fee of £15 was received from Caron de Beaumarchais in his proceedings against the Commonwealth for supplies and moneys advanced during the Revolution.

No fees are entered for February, April, October, and December, probably because of J.M.'s activities in the militia and as acting Attorney for the Commonwealth.

Of the fees listed, fifteen were for advice, ranging from £1 to £3 each. One hundred thirty-four cases were listed by their titles. In twenty-five instances the courts were named, eight in federal, seven in chancery, seven in appeals, and two in district courts, reflecting the emphasis of J.M.'s practice on federal and appellate court matters.

U.S. Circuit Court, Virginia

Nathaniel Allen v. Isaac Smith, Littleton Savage, Peter Bowdoin, Griffin Stith, and William Stith.

Debt. Chancery. J.M. for defendant Smith.

Dec. 6, 1792. To rules for proceedings. U.S. Circuit Court, Va., Order Book I, 140.

May 27, 1794. Continued. Cost bond. Same, 373.

Nov. 27, 1794. Dismissed by plaintiff. Same, 411.

Same, Record Book Index, Nov. Rules, 1794.

V, U.S. Circuit Court Case Papers.

Fees: Apr.–May, 1792, £5:2; Nov., 1793, £3. Account Book, 322, 376.

William Anderson, Askew Burkel, and William Fowke, merchants, London, d.b.a. William Anderson and Co. v. Moses and Stephen Austin, merchants, Virginia, d.b.a. Moses Austin and Co.

Case, assumpsit on bills of exchange dated 1790. J.M. for plaintiff.

June 2, 1794. V.j. for plaintiff £1,105. U.S. Circuit Court, Va., Order Book I, 388.

Same, Record Book 2, 237–40.

V, U.S. Circuit Court Case Papers.

William and Mary Asselby, executor and executrix of Mary Asselby, who was executrix of Thomas Asselby, Great Britain v. Robert and Thomas Pleasants, Henrico County.

Case, assumpsit on bill of exchange by Thomas Mann Randolph to Asselby on and accepted by Pleasants, dated 1775. J.M. for defendant.

Answer: not assume; five-year limitation; defendant British.

Dec. 2, 1794. Default on defendant's bond, J.M. a signer, $1,552.54 payable by $378.45. U.S. Circuit Court, Va., Order Book I, 428.

Same, Record Book I, 444–56.

V, U.S. Circuit Court Case Papers. (Answer above on printed form bearing J.M.'s printed name and filled out by him.)

James Blanchard v. Thomas and Mary Wishart.

Ejectment, plantation and messuage, 258 acres, Princess Ann County. J.M. for defendants.

Nov. 24, 1792. Order to make party defendants. U.S. Circuit Court, Va., Order Book I, 123.

May 22, 1793. Admitted as defendants, plea of general issue. Same, 143.

Dec. 3, 1793. Continued. Order for security by plaintiff. Depositions. Same, 237.

May 27, 1794. Security for plaintiff. Same, 373.

Dec. 1, 1794. Plaintiff ordered to pay costs assessed or suit dismissed. Same, 423.

Same, Record Book Index, May Term, 1795.

V, U.S. Circuit Court Case Papers.

Fees: Aug., 1792, £5; May, 1795, £9. Account Book 334, 414.

Hugh Colquhoun et al., s.p. Alexander Donald Co., merchants, Glasgow, Great Britain v. Samuel Hopkins, Mecklenburg County, Va.

Debt, on obligation under seal, £1,137:13:9 Va., 1772. J.M. for defendant.

Nov. 28, 1791. Second plea withdrawn. Pleas: payment; Britisher disability under Virginia laws; treaty violation; Declaration of Independence. Demurrer by plaintiff. U.S. Circuit Court, Va., Order Book I, 62.

Nov. 22, 1793. V.j. for plaintiff. Same, 165–66.

Nov. 30, 1793. Judgment set aside by consent. Same, 216.

Dec. 4, 1794. Consent judgment, £1,137:13:9 payable by $1,896.06½. Same, 456–57.

Same, Record Book II, 513–23.

V, U.S. Circuit Court Case Papers.

Fee: Oct., 1790, £7:10 (part). Account Book, 266.

James Craxall, Philip Rogers, and Samuel Owings, one of American assignees of Clermont Richards of France, assignee of Bagness and Combor of Great Britain, assignee of Mathew Dobson of Great Britain v. Thomas Bates, Va.

Debt, written obligation £600 St., 1785. J.M. for defendant.

Answer, payment.

Dec. 3, 1793. V.j. £600 St., value of $2,406, payable $1,332. Stayed for equity hearing. U.S. Circuit Court, Va., Order Book I, 234.

May 26, 1794. *Bates v. Dobson,* chancery. Injunction dissolved. Continued. Same, 369.

Dec. 4, 1794. Decree of dismissal of equity suit. Same, 444.

Same, Record Book I, 422–25.

V, U.S. Circuit Court Case Papers.

Fee: Mar., 1791, £2:9. Account Book, 280.

John Dobson and James Daltera, d.b.a. Dobson, Daltera, and Walker, Great Britain v. Alexander and Porterfield Trent and James Callaway, d.b.a. Trents and Callaway.

Action on two bills of exchange, 1772, £5,360 St. and £500. J.M. for defendant.

Nov. 29, 1791. Pleas of British subject and sequestration withdrawn. Plea: payment to loan office; British subjects; violation of Treaty of 1783; effect of Declaration of Independence. Demurrer by plaintiff.

U.S. Circuit Court, Va., Order Book I, 65.

May 25, 1792. Depositions in England. Same, 96.

Disposition of case uncertain. Case papers indicate dismissed, May, 1794.

U.S. Circuit Court Case Papers. (Answer on J.M.'s forms, filled in by him.)

Dobson and Daltera, s.p. Dobson, Daltera, and Walker, merchants, Great Britain v. Trents, Crump, and Bates.

Debt on bill of exchange, £3,250, 1772, and case. J.M. for defendant.

Nov. 29, 1791. Third and fourth pleas withdrawn.

Pleas: payment to Loan Office; Britisher not recover; violation of Treaty of Paris; Declaration of Independence. Demurrer by plaintiff.

U.S. Circuit Court, Va., Order Book 1, 65.

Dec. 3, 1791. Same. Pleas: not assume, otherwise same. Same, 79.

May 25, 1792. Depositions in England. Same, 96.

Nov. 27, 1793. Depositions. Same, 194.

Nov. 26, 1794. Debt case dismissed, grounds bill of exchange dated in Virginia but executed in Great Britain. Same, 405.

V, U.S. Circuit Court Case Papers. (Pleas on J.M.'s printed form.)

Fees: Apr., 1790, advice and retainer, £5:12; Mar., 1791, £9:12. Account Book, 243, 278.

Samuel Donaldson, s.p. Gibson, Donaldson, and Hamilton v. John Winston, Hanover County, Va.

Case, for money advanced, £398:19:½ Va., 1774. J.M. for defendant.

Nov. 29, 1793. V.j. one cent. U.S. Circuit Court, Va., Order Book I, 214.

Dec. 5, 1793. Motion for new trial. Same, 247.

May 24, 1794. Denied. Same, 362.

Same, Record Book IV, 1–4.

V, U.S. Circuit Court Case Papers.

Fee: July, 1790, £11:4. Account Book, 254.

Richard Hanson, Great Britain v. Wills Cowper, Nansemond County, Va.

Debt, on promissory note, £500 St., 1775. J.M. for defendant.

Nov. 24, 1791. Security for defendant. U.S. Circuit Court, Va., Order Book 1, 55.

Nov. 29, 1791. Pleas: payment; Britisher disabled under Virginia laws; violation of Treaty of Paris; Declaration of Independence. Same, 66.

Nov. 25, 1793. Demurrer to last three pleas. Juror withdrawn. Same, 274.

May 24, 1794. Continued. Same, 361.

Nov. 26, 27, 1794. Jury called. J. confessed, £500 St. payable by $470. Same, 407, 408.

Same, Record Book III, 90–104.

V, U.S. Circuit Court Case Papers. (Printed pleas filled in by J.M.)

Thomas and Benjamin Harwood, assignees of William Whitecroft, Md. v. John Lewis, Va.

Same v. Robert Throckmorton and John Lewis, Va.

Debt, on obligation under seal, £6,000 Va., or £3,000 money plus £3,000 in officer's certificates, 1784. J.M. for plaintiff.

May 29, 1793. Security for defendant by Robert Brooke and John Minor. U.S. Circuit Court, Va., Order Book I, 146.

Dec. 2, 1793. Continued. Same, 226.

May 24, 1794. Answer by Bushrod Washington for defendant. Plea: payment to Whitecroft and performance. Same, 363.

Reply by J.M.

May 28, 1794. V. $7,680.45, j. $11,279.16, £6,000 Va. valued $20,000, payable by verdict amount. Same, 376–77.

May 31, 1794. Motion to set aside judgment. Same, 387.

Dec. 6, 1794. Denied. Same, 451.

Confessed judgment by Throckmorton, £6,000 valued at $20,000 payable by $11,279.16. Same, 453.

Same, Record Book III, 52–65.

V, U.S. Circuit Court Case Papers. (Autograph petition and reply.)

Robert Hastic et al., s.p. Buchanan, Hastic and Co., merchants, Glasgow, Great Britain v. Charles Sullivant, Jr., and Dudley Brooke, Va.

In chancery, action to foreclose mortgage deed to 240 acres land Charlotte County, Va., 1774, to secure debt executed by Sullivant; land thereafter to Brooke; £133:14:6½ Va.

May 10, 1792. J.M. for defendant Brooke. Answer: tender and refusal.

Nov. 30, Dec. 2, 1793. Plaintiff Buchanan dead; defendant ordered to answer, not a native of the country. U.S. Circuit Court, Va., Order Book 1, 231.

May 31, 1794. Sullivant ordered to appear. Same, 385.

Dec. 6, 1794. Default as to Sullivant. Sale ordered, £130:15:10½ with 5 per cent interest, eight years interest to abate. Same, 448.

Same, Record Book II, 389–400.

V, U.S. Circuit Court Case Papers. (Answer of Brooke in J.M.'s handwriting; autograph notice for deposition.)

Harman Leroy and William Bayard, d.b.a. Leroy and Bayard, merchants, New York v. David Ross and Co., merchants, Va.

Debt, on protested bill of exchange by Ross on Ezekiel Edwards, London, to James Murdock and endorsed to plaintiff, £2,000 St., 1783. J.M. for plaintiff.

Dec. 3, 1793. Plea: general issue. U.S. Circuit Court, Va., Order Book 1, 239.

May 30, 1794. Confessed j., £4,089:18:2 St. value of $18,159.20. Same, 381.

Same, Record Book II, 132–34.

V, U.S. Circuit Court Case Papers. (Autograph petition signed.)

William Robinson Lidderdale, executor of John Lidderdale, Great Britain v. George Butler and Thomas Reade.

Chancery, on bond for purchase price of two tracts of land Charlotte County, Va. 400 acres and 264 acres, to Butler, £166 Va., 1772. J.M. for defendant Reade.

Answer: purchase of 400-acre tract by Reade, 1778, from Butler for £200; defended against escheat.

Dec. 2, 1793. Butler, a foreigner, ordered to answer, advertised. U.S. Circuit Court, Va., Order Book 1, 230.

May 31, 1794. Same. Same, 385.

Dec. 5, 1794. Decree sale of lots successively to plaintiff £273:2:11. Same, 446.

Same, Record Book III, 105–17.

V, U.S. Circuit Court Case Papers.

Fee: Nov., 1791. £5. Account Book, 304.

William R. Lidderdale, executor of John Lidderdale, London v. Munford Dejarnett.

Chancery, action on sale to defendant tract of land, No. 23 of plat, Charlotte County, supposed to contain 512 acres at £25 per 100 acres, total £128. Purchaser in possession; because of war, no payments made. Inquest of office found land escheated to Commonwealth; finding enjoined by High Court of Chancery, Oct. 27, 1789, and land decreed to Dejarnett on paying plaintiff the contract price of £128 plus £56:15 for 227 acres excess over 512 acres in plot. On resurvey the plot was found to contain 812 acres; additional £24:10 sought. J.M. for defendant.

June 5, 1793. Default by defendant. Sale ordered, £206:5 for plaintiff. U.S. Circuit Court, Va., Order Book I, 155.

Nov. 26, 1793. Decree set aside; answer filed claiming £128 price for entire tract. Same, 184.

Dec. 5, 1794. Decree of sale, £216 for plaintiff; interest held by court. Same, 445.

Same, Record Book III, 133–39.

V, U.S. Circuit Court Case Papers. (Autograph answer.)

John Lloyd, executor of Osgood Hanbury, merchant, Great Britain v. Mary Byrd, executrix of Hon. William Byrd.

Debt, on bill of exchange on Capel and Osgood Hanbury to Capt. John Hylton, £191:4:4½ St. J.M. for defendant.

Plea, testator did not assume.

May 27, 1794. V.j. $1,798.28. U.S. Circuit Court, Va., Order Book I, 372.

Same, Record Book II, 129–32.

V, U.S. Circuit Court Case Papers.

Fee: Jan., 1793, £7. Account Book, 346.

John Lynch v. Robert Donald et al., surviving partner Robert Donald & Co.; Charles Lynch v. Same.

Injunctions against js. obtained by default against plaintiffs.

J.M. for plaintiffs in early proceedings.

John Lynch case:

Dec. 4, 1794. Petition alleged bond given Mar. 30, 1773, £570:15:10 payable by £285:7:11, paid by attached list of credits; j. obtained against him in the U.S. Circuit Court, May, 1792, by default, no lawyer, £570:15:10 payable by £170:8:7[6] and interest. Proceedings on j. stayed for hearing, bond filed. U.S. Circuit Court, Va., Order Book I, 441.

Dec. 4, 1794. Defendants not appearing, order to appear advertised. Same, III, 143.

June 4, 1805. Hearing on objections of defendants to report of commission, allowing in part injunction dissolved as to £62:13:8 of j. Same, V, 130. J.M. and Cyrus Griffin sitting.

June 7, 1806. Objection by defendants to report as to £30 disallowed; injunction perpetual as to this amount. Same, 323.

Charles Lynch case:

Dec. 4, 1796. Petition stating Charles and John gave bond Sept., 1764, for all debts due at two stores, at Warwick operated by Robert, at Rockridge by brother Alexander, deed of trust as security, agreed paid and bond returned. J. by default in Circuit Court, Nov., 1793, not learned of until later.

Also j. taken by default on bond of Sept., 1772, on account of Bedford store, not properly adjusted. Prayer for accounting, injunction.

Dec. 8, 1802. Motion by plaintiff for commissioners. Same, III, 259.

May 29, 1805. Executrix Anselm Lynch substituted on death of plaintiff. Order on defendant to appear, advertised. Same, V, 102.

June 12, 1806. Commissioners on motion of plaintiff. Same, 349.

Dec. 10, 1806. Injunction dissolved as to $329.79 part of one j., perpetual as to other j. of $118.22. Same, VI, 79.

V, U.S. Circuit Court Case Papers.

(J.M. sat at hearing from Dec., 1802, on. Autograph petitions for plaintiffs by J.M. Advertisements in *Lynchburg Weekly Gazette*, Feb. 16, Mar. 2 and 16, 1799.)

Alexander McComb, executor of John Rucker, Pa. v. John F. Mercer, Va.

Debt, on protested bills of exchange drawn on Joshua Johnston, London, to Benjamin Harrison, Jr., endorsed to plaintiff, 1786, £400 St. with 10 per cent interest. J.M. for plaintiff.

June 2, 1794. Consent verdict, £685:8:8½ value $3,043.40. U.S. Circuit Court, Va., Order Book I, 388.

Same, Record Book II, 146–50.

V, U.S. Circuit Court Case Papers, containing autograph petition.

James Robb and Co. v. Musco Garnett, administrator of William Hunter.

Debt, on obligation under seal, £2,477 Va., 1773. J.M. for defendant.

Dec. 3, 1793. Answer: payment. U.S. Circuit Court, Va., Order Book I, 236.

Dec. 1, 1794. Verdict for plaintiff. Judgment arrested for failure of declaration to show jurisdiction. Same, 424.

Same, Record Book III, 164–65.

V, U.S. Circuit Court Case Papers, containing autograph reply and motion.

Philip Slater, s.p. Willings and Slater, druggists, London, Great Britain v. John Minson Galt, apothecary, Williamsburg, York County, Va.

Debt, on note, £1,181:11:7 St., 1775. J.M. for defendant.

Nov. 21, 1791. Pleas: Britisher not recover under Virginia laws; violation of Treaty of Paris; Declaration of Independence; payment. Demurrer by plaintiff as to first three. U.S. Circuit Court, Va., Order Book I, 66.

May 26, 1794. Demurrer for plaintiff. V, $2,625.50, j. £1,181:11:7 St. value of £1,575:8:9 Va., payable by verdict amount. Same, 364.

Same, Record Book II, 193. May T, 1794.

V, U.S. Circuit Court Case Papers.

Fee: Sept., 1795, £4:16. Account Book, 422.

Miller Southgate, Great Britain v. William Winslow, Beverly Winslow, and William Mills, Va. (Two cases)

Case, on obligation under seal, £600 Va. value of $2,000, 1792, in each case. J.M. for plaintiff.

May 28, 1794. Plea, payment. U.S. Circuit Court, Va., Order Book I, 375.

Dec. 3, 1794. V.j. in each case, £600 Va., payable $1,000. Same, 433, 434. Same, Record Book III, 168–69; 170–71, Nov. T, 1794.

V, U.S. Circuit Court Case Papers.

Fee: Dec., 1793, £5:12. Account Book, 378.

For further proceedings on bond, j. against Winslow, 1795, Order Book II, 7, 8; case against Mills dismissed, 1795–1796. Same, II, 135.

Court of Appeals of Virginia

David Ross v. Erasmus Gill and wife, 4 Call 250, 251.

Error to District Court of Petersburg, Sept. 6, 1791.

Action waste under lease, j. for appellee £777, reversed. J.M. for appellees.

Lease by wife's guardian for one year beyond majority or marriage unless canceled.

Held, void as beyond term of guardianship despite power to terminate; no recovery for waste.

Oct. 26–27, Nov. 2, 4, 5, 1793. Heard. Court of Appeals, Va., Order Book II, 194–95, 202, 249, 251, 252.

Nov. 1. Reversed, dismissed. Same, 257.

Nov. 13. Reversal set aside. Same, 260.

Apr. 15, 1794. Continued. Same, 263.

Oct. 29. Reheard. Same, III, 20.

Nov. 22. Reversed, dismissed. Same, 42.

(For related case, see herein 1792, Legal Practice, Court of Appeals, Ross v. Gill, 1 Washington 87.)

Fees: Apr., 1791, £4:4; Sept., 1793, £5. Account Book, 284, 370.

Commonwealth v. Cunningham and Co., 4 Call 331, 335.

Appeal from District Court of Richmond, reversed; on appeal from second j., affirmed in part. J.M. for appellee.

Cunningham owner of vessel impressed by Governor under resolution of General Assembly, 1781; invasion by British; sunk by enemy.

Auditor of Accounts refused claim; delay in submitting; authority terminated; claim against the United States. On petition to District Court, on Sept. 12, 1792, court adopted valuation in certificate issues by County Court of Nansemond, June 14, 1784, £2,959:8:3½ for vessel, £1,288:17:9 tobacco cargo (145,000 pounds), and ordered Auditor to issue warrants.

Held, impressment authorized; State liable; valuation by original appraisement, or if none, by verdict.

On issue in District Court, verdict and j. £4,264:8:3½ for vessel, cargo, £2,771:17:4½ interest.

On second appeal to Court of Appeals, principal affirmed, interest denied.

Apr. 26, 1793. Heard in part. Court of Appeals, Va., Order Book II, 225.

May 1. Continued. Same, 230.

Nov. 5, 7. Heard. Same, 252, 253.

Nov. 11. Reversed, new trial. Same, 258–59.

Apr. 15, 1794. J. of District Court of Apr. 5 affirmed. Same, 263.

Copy of j. V, Exec. Papers, Box 1794, Feb.-Apr., Folder Apr. 1–10.

Fee: May, 1794, £15. Account Book, 386.

(See herein Apr. 8, 1794, remission of part of j. in agreement not to prosecute appeal.)

Taylor's Administratrix v. Peyton's Administratrix, 1 Washington 252, 253.

Appeal from District Court of Northumberland.

J. for appellee, plaintiff below, Apr. 11, 1793, £3,000:0:1, affirmed. J.M. for appellee.

Action debt on bond in common form; plea payment; bond proved by copy; original burnt. Held, production of original waived by accepting oyer of copy and pleading.

Apr. 10, 1794. Case submitted. Court of Appeals, Va., Order Book II, 264.

Apr. 18. Affirmed. Same, 266.

Smith and Moreton v. Michael Wallace, 1 Washington 254, 256.

Appeal from High Court of Chancery, Mar. 12, 1793.

Injunction against j. against appellee and William Piper in District Court of Fredericksburg, affirmed. J.M. and Alexander Campbell for appellee.

Suit in General Court, sheriff released two defendants from arrest on promise to give bail. Bond submitted named one defendant; objected to by sheriff; plaintiff's counsel approved; clerk by error thinking bail bond bad, entered as plea of payment for sheriff against whom j. taken.

Held, bail piece sufficient; surprise and accident grounds for relief.

Apr. 15, 1794. Heard. Court of Appeals, Va., Order Book II, 263.

Apr. 18. Affirmed. Same, 266.

Fees: Mar., 1793, £3:10; Oct., 1793, £7:4. Account Book, 352, 372.

Carr v. Gooch, 1 Washington 260, 261.

Appeal from District Court of Charlottesville. J. for appellee, plaintiff below, Sept. 18, 1793, £156:7:4½, affirmed. J.M. for appellee.

Action in case. Auctioneer sold land at public sale; one executor objected to sale, other agreed to hold auctioneer harmless if confirmed sale and not cry over. Recovery had by promisee and other executors against auctioneer.

Held, agreement to indemnify valid, consideration not immoral or illegal.

Apr. 22, 1794. Case submitted. Court of Appeals, Va., Order Book II, 270.

Apr. 24. Affirmed. Same, 272.

Fee: Nov., 1793, £3. Account Book, 376.

William Cole v. William Clayborn, 1 Washington 262, 264.

Appeal from District Court of Charlottesville.

J. for appellee, Sept. 19, 1793, three slaves and £45, affirmed. J.M. for appellant.

Action of detinue, contest between heirs over ownership of slave and offspring allotted to widow in dower; residuary clause in will for equal division among children held to cover these rather than passing to testator's son as undisposed of interest.

Apr. 23, 1794. Case submitted. Court of Appeals, Va., Order Book II, 271.

Apr. 24. Affirmed. Same, 272.

William Shermer, executor v. Dudley Richardson, John Shermer's executor, 1 Washington 266–68.

Appeal from High Court of Chancery, Sept. 27, 1792, affirmed. J.M. for appellee.

Testator left estate to wife for life; thereafter, one-half to her appointees, one-half to his brother. Wife, on her death, failed to appoint; executors sold and distributed one-half to her relatives. In action by brother for entirety, held, intention one-half to go to wife's family, allowing to go to her legal representatives equivalent to appointment.

Apr. 14, 1794. Continued. Court of Appeals, Va., Order Book II, 262.

Oct. 13. Heard. Same, III, 2.

Oct. 18. Affirmed. Same, 6.

Fee: Oct., 1787, "Shermer's Ex'tr" £28. Account Book, 130.

Ward v. Webber and wife, 1 Washington 274, 275, 277–78.

Appeal from High Court of Chancery, May 14, 1792.

Bill of review of former j. for appellees refused, affirmed. J.M. for appellants.

Father deeded land to daughter pursuant to promise if she married to please him; thereafter, canceled it. J. obtained in General Court against father and his executors. Bill of review by appellant alleging deed conditional, made because of pending prosecution threatening father's life, to be reconveyed. Held, no proof of condition or implied trust.

Apr. 10, 1794. Continued. Court of Appeals, Va., Order Book II, 261.

Oct. 13. Heard. Same, III, 2.

Oct. 17. Affirmed. Same, 4–5.

Fees: Mar., 1795, £4:2:6; Oct., 1795, £3. Account Book, 406, 420.

Elizabeth and Jane Applebury et al. v. James Anthony's Executors, 1 Washington 287, 288.

Appeal from High Court of Chancery May 24, 1793, reversing County Court, j. for appellants, affirmed. J.M. for appellees.

In compromise of action by son-in-law against father on marriage agreement, latter deeded slave to grandchildren; next day by agreement paid £60 and slave retained, deed returned unrecorded. Action by grandchildren against executors of grandfather for slave. Held, no legal or equitable claim.

Oct. 10, 1794. Heard. Court of Appeals, Va., Order Book III, 5.

Oct. 20. Affirmed. Same, 7.

Fees: Apr.–May, 1792, £5; Oct., 1793, £5; Oct., 1794, £4:16; May, 1795, £2:8. Account Book, 322, 372, 398, 408.

Representative of William Smallwood v. John F. Mercer and Peter Hansborough, 1 Washington 290, 292–93.

Appeal from High Court of Chancery, Mar. 11, 1793, dismissing bill of appellant, affirmed. J.M. for appellant.

Appellant purchased land knowing third person claimed interest therein relying on arbitration agreement between seller and claimant who agreed to convey in accordance with finding; arbitration not completed because arbitrators refused to act. Appellant brought specific performance action against claimant. Held, agreement never perfected, not enforcible.

Oct. 16–17, 1794. Heard. Court of Appeals, Va., Order Book III, 4, 5.

Oct. 20. Affirmed. Same, 7.

(See herein 1790, Legal Practice, Fredericksburg District Court, *Hansbrough v. Smallwood.*)

Callohill Minnis, executor of William Aylett, et al. v. Philip Aylett, 1 Washington, 300, 301.

Appeal from High Court of Chancery, May 21, 1793, reported in Wythe, 2nd ed., 219.

J. for appellee, petitioner below, reversed. J.M. for appellee, probably also for petitioner below, although Wythe states case argued by Calthorp for petitioner, Gerwin for defendant.

Will devising to son "all his lands in the county of King William," held to pass freehold lands but not leaseholds, the latter going to the residue.

Oct. 20. Heard. Court of Appeals, Va., Order Book III, 8.

Oct. 21. Reversed.

Fees: Mar. 10, 1789, £5; Apr. 1794, £3. Account Book, 188, 384.

John Pierce and William Browne, executors of John Browne, s.p. Eaton and Brown v. Benjamin Putney, 1 Washington 302.

Appeal from District Court of Williamsburg.

Assumpsit, j. for appellee, May 9, 1793, £514:5:7, reversed. J.M. for appellee.

Action brought Aug., 1791, on claim dated Mar., 1786. Plea, statute of limitations. Defense, writ in case filed Oct., 1786, same cause, Court of Hustings, Williamsburg, abated as to one partner not inhabitant, as to other by death.

Held, statute of limitations applies, failed to recommence suit within one year after abatement as provided in act.

Apr., 1794. Death of John Browne, *scire facias* against executors. Court of Appeals, Va., Order Book II, 271.

Oct. 21. Submitted. Same, III, 9.

Oct. 22. Reversed. Same, 10–11.

Fee: Apr. 2, 1787, £2:10. Account Book, 106.

Augustine Leftwich and wife v. Bartholomew Stovall et al., 1 Washington 303, 304.

Error to District Court of New London, Sept. 24, 1790, affirming County Court of Bedford, Aug. 28, 1786, 13,812 pounds tobacco and damages for retarding execution, affirmed. J.M. for plaintiffs in error.

Action upon case for damages. Writ sued out, no declaration. Held, agreement for arbitration agreement dispensed with need of declaration.

Oct. 21, 1794. Heard. Court of Appeals, Va., Order Book III, 9.

Oct. 23. Affirmed. Same, 11.

Fee: Aug., 1793, £1:16. Account Book, 368.

J.M. represented the same parties in proceedings in District Court.

Sept. 24, 1790. Affirmed. District Court, Franklin, Order Book I, 1789–1793, 128.

Sept. 18, 1793. Allowance to sheriff for execution against Henry Jeter, one Negro and eleven head of cattle taken. Same, 360.

Apr. 23, 1794. Record certified to Court of Appeals, certiorari of Aug. 22, 1793. Same, II, 1794–1796, 42.

Apr. 17, 1795. Motion to quash execution, continued. Same, 107.

Apr. 23, 1795. Motion overruled. Motion to quash replevin bond of Jeter, Dec. 3, 1790, on writ of fieri facias, granted. Same, 136.

Fee: Aug. 25, 1787, £2:10, "Stoval et al. (Jeter) v. Stoval's exrs." Account Book, 120.

Charles Lee, executor of Robert Daniel v. Thomas Cooke, 1 Washington 306, 307, 308.

Appeal from District Court of King and Queen.

J. for appellee, plaintiff below, Apr. 19, 1793, £94:10:5, affirmed. J.M. for appellee.

Action of covenant on warranty of deed conveying Negro by testator; action against executor. Breach, recovery from buyer by third person in action of detinue, not stated notice thereof to executor. Held, sale of personalty, executor bound; notice not necessary, evidence excluded by appellant.

Oct. 21, 1794. Heard. Court of Appeals, Va., Order Book III, 9.

Oct. 24. Affirmed. Same, 12.

Fee: Oct., 1793, £5. Account Book, 372.

Zachariah Burnley v. Charles Lambert, 1 Washington 308, 311.

Appeal from District Court of Fredericksburg. (For record, District Court, Fredericksburg, Law Orders 1790–1793, 89.)

J. for apellee, plaintiff below, May 3, 1793, four slaves and £47:10, affirmed. J.M. and John Warden for appellant.

Detinue, by devisee of slaves who had received distribution from executors against purchaser of same, seized on execution by creditor and sold at coroner's sale. Held, need prove merely possession by defendant anterior to writ; creditor cannot proceed against individual legatee; against executor or join all legatees in equity.

Oct. 21, 1794. Heard. Court of Appeals, Va., Order Book III, 9.

Oct. 22. Affirmed. Same, 10.

Fees: Jan. 1793, £7; July, 1793, £3. Account Book, 346, 366.

John Cook, special bail for Francis Willis, Jr. v. Samuel Beale's executors, 1 Washington 313, 314–15.

Appeal from District Court of Winchester, Apr. 25, 1792, affirming County Court of Frederick, May 3, 1787.

J. against appellant reversed. J.M. for appellant.

Action by judgment creditor against special bail of defendant; defense delivery of body of defendant to sheriff, not alleging filed receipt with clerk.

Held, bail released by delivery, filing of receipt merely directory; error in refusing to allow amendment of declaration that filed receipt.

Oct. 22, 1794. Heard. Court of Appeals, Va., Order Book III, 10.

Oct. 24. Reversed, new trial. Same, 13.

William Dandridge v. Samuel Harris, 1 Washington 326.

Appeal from High Court of Chancery, June 5, 1793, dismissing bill for specific performance, and injunction against j. District Court of Richmond reversing County Court, reversed. J.M. and William Duval for plaintiff in error.

Harris agreed to repair mill for Dandridge, payment in money or property to be appraised; alternative payment not in written contract. In county court action Dandridge allowed to show failure to insert alternative payment clause as agreed by Harris; reversed on ground parol evidence varying written agreement.

Held, failure to insert fraudulent; evidence admissible; by consent of Dandridge ordered to pay j. of £45 heretofore found by jury, but without costs.

Oct. 25, 1794. Heard. Court of Appeals, Va., Order Book III, 14.

Oct. 27. Reversed. Same, 17.

Fees: Apr., 1790, £7; Aug., 1792, £2:10; Mar., 1793, £0:18; May, 1793, £?:10; Sept., 1794, £5. Account Book, 240, 336, 352, 360, 398.

John Nicholas v. Nathan Fletcher, 1 Washington 330.

Appeal from District Court of Petersburg, Apr. 20, 1793, affirming j. County Court of Amelia against appellant, Mar. 24, 1791, 60,740 pounds tobacco and £4:9:4, payable by half, affirmed. J.M. for appellee.

Action on forthcoming bond for nondelivery. Held, burden of proof on obligee of bond to show performance.

Oct. 25, 1794. Order affirming. Court of Appeals, Va., Order Book III, 15.

Fee: Aug., 1793, £2:4. Account Book, 368.

Jacob Watson and William Hartsborne v. William Thornton Alexander, 1 Washington 340, 347–49.

Appeal from District Court of Dumfries, j. for appellee, May 21, 1792, £626 specie, reversed. J.M. and Bushrod Washington for appellee.

Action for nine years' rent on leasehold lots in Alexandria executed in 1779. Jury verdict for appellee; court for no reasons given ruled rent expected paid in money current at time due, entered j. in specie without scaling under act of Nov., 1781.

Held, error; court no power to depart from statutory scale except under valid procedures appearing on record.

Oct. 20, 1793. Heard. Court of Appeals, Va., Order Book II, 246.

Nov. 2; Apr. 11, 1794. Continued. Same, 248, 261.

Nov. 5, 1794. Heard. Same, III, 23.
Nov. 12. Reversed. Same, 32.

William Wroe v. William Washington, Beckwith Butler, and James Nevison, 1 Washington 357, 358, 361–62.

Appeal from District Court of Northumberland Courthouse, Apr. 10, 1793, reversing Court of Westmoreland County, Mar., 1791, j. £59:19:1 for appellee, nonsuit awarded, reversed. J.M. for appellant. Action for rent and board furnished at house in Leeds Town; some variance between declaration and proof as to rentals. District Court nonsuited appellant. Held, no power to compel a nonsuit; evidence relates to all material parts of contract.

Apr. 16, 1794. Heard. Court of Appeals, Va., Order Book II, 204.
Apr. 26. Continued. Same, 273.
Nov. 5. Heard. Same, III, 24.
Nov. 14. Reversed, j. of County Court reinstated. Same, 34.

Overton Cosby, executor of David Loudon v. Isaac Hite, 1 Washington 365, 366.

Appeal from District Court of Winchester, Apr. 5, 1793, reversing County Court of Frederick, Mar., 1792, affirmed. J.M. for appellee. Appellant, plaintiff below, action in assumpsit; plea, general issue. Appellant filled in blanks in declaration in material points when issue joined which court refused to strike and refused to allow appellee to plead over, intending to plead statute of limitations. Refusal held error.

Nov. 10, 1794. Heard. Court of Appeals, Va., Order Book III, 30.
Nov. 11. Affirmed. Same, 31.

James Hewlett, executor of Austin Hewlett v. Byrd Chamberlayne, 1 Washington 367, 368.

Appeal from District Court of Williamsburg, Sept. 11, 1793, £103:18:11½.

Action of debt by appellee on forthcoming bond, j. for appellee, affirmed. J.M. for appellee.

Bond taken by sheriff on execution issued at suit of appellee; property not delivered up or money paid. Bond failed to state amount of execution; action sustained.

Nov. 10, 1794. Affirmed. Court of Appeals, Va., Order Book III, 30.

Carter Braxton v. Thomas Willing and Robert Morris, 1 Washington 380.

Appeal from decree High Court of Chancery requiring £20 bond and security for appeal from county court, affirmed. J.M. for Morris. On rule to show cause Braxton sought to require bond to cover entire decree involved.

Held, that required by Chancellor was only bond authorized under statute.

Apr. 15, 1794. Motion dismissed. Court of Appeals, Va., Order Book I, 275.

Fee: Feb., 1787, £8:10. Account Book, 98.

(See later proceedings herein 1795, Legal Practice, Court of Appeals, Va.; also letters from Morris Feb. 29 and Dec. 29, 1795, herein.)

Philip Pendleton et al. v. Jacob Vandevier, 1 Washington 381, 387–88.

Appeal from District Court of Winchester.

Ejectment, brought by appellee against appellant, j. for appellee reversed and amended. J.M. and Bartlet Williams for appellant. Testator devised part of tract of land to "heirs lawfully begotten" on body of daughter, and parts to other children; all described accurately except one at issue.

J. given holder under granddaughter but to smaller of two possible parts as described. Held, will construed to devise to heir apparent of daughter at testator's decease; error in description from omission of line which supplied to form larger tract.

Nov. 3, 1794. Caces submitted. Court of Appeals, Va., Order Book III, 22.

Nov. 7. Reversed, j. entered for appellee to larger tract. Same, 27.

Fee: Oct., 1793, £7. Account Book, 372.

John Walden, executor of Charles Walden v. David Payne, 2 Washington 1, 2–5, 6–7.

Appeal from District Court of Fredericksburg.

Action of debt on bond brought by appellee against appellant, j. £150 payable with £75, affirmed. J.M. for appellant.

Executor sold personal assets except slaves, offered to pay creditor in 1778 a specie debt with paper money depreciated one for one thousand. In court action by legatees required to distribute slaves. J. against him for full amount of principal and interest. Held, slaves personal property in executor's hands; court order required distribution only after debts paid; specie debts not scaled.

Nov. 17, 1794. Case revived and heard. Court of Appeals, Va., Order Book III, 36.

Nov. 20. Affirmed. Same, 38–39.

Fee: Nov., 1794, £10. Account Book, 400.

James Roy, guardian of James and Mary Roy, infants v. Muscoe Garnett, 2 Washington 9, 23–30.

Appeal from District Court of King and Queen Courthouse.

Ejectment by appellant against appellee, j. dismissing bill, Sept. 25, 1792, affirmed. J.M. and Alexander Campbell for appellants.

Testator devised land to son James for life, remainder to son Muscoe in trust to sons of James in tail male, if no male issue to Muscoe for life, etc. James died without male issue and devised land to daughter under whom appellant claims. Held, estate of James not converted by construction or act of Virginia into fee; estate passed to Muscoe as next remainderman.

Nov. 31, 1793. Continued. Court of Appeals, Va., Order Book II, 248.

Apr. 11, 1794. Continued. Same, 261.

Oct. 29, 31; Nov. 1, 1794. Heard. Order Book III, 20–22.

Nov. 20. Dismissal of bill affirmed. Same, 38.

Fees: Apr., 1793, £7; Oct., 1793, £7. Account Book, 356, 372.

James Burnsides v. Andrew Reid, Samuel Culbertson, and Thomas Walker. Andrew Reid, attorney in fact and assignee of Samuel Culbertson v. James Burnsides. 2 Washington 43.

Appeal from High Court of Chancery, May 15, 1792 (reported in Wythe, 49) enjoining and reversing General Court, reversed. J.M. for Reid (Culbertson).

Culbertson claimed land, 400 acres and 600 adjoining under settlement in 1753, Burnsides under purchase from Loyal Company (Greenbrier) in 1775. Court of Commissioners in 1782 decided in favor of Burnsides; caveat filed, reversed by General Court in 1784, gave to Culbertson. On appeal High Court of Chancery decreed 400 acres to Culbertson on paying $3.00 per acre, 600 acres elsewhere. Reversed by Court of Appeals, Culbertson given right to 400 acres and 600 adjoining under settlement.

Nov. 13, 1793. Continued for rehearing. Court of Appeals, Va., Order Book II, 259.

Apr. 11, 1794. Continued. Same, 261.

Nov. 4. Heard. Same, III, 23.

Nov. 19. Reversed, decree amended. Same, 37.

Fees: Mar. 10, 1790, £9; Oct., 1793, £3:13. Account Book, 238, 372.

Hannah Fitzhugh v. Philip Ludwell Grymes, son and heir of Philip Grymes.

Appeal from decree of High Court of Chancery, Sept. 18, 1792. J.M. for appellant.

Apr. 14, 1794. Heard. Court of Appeals, Va., Order Book II, 262.

Apr. 25. Continued for rehearing. Same, 273.

Nov. 18. Rehearing. Order Book III, 36.
Nov. 19. Affirmed. Same, 37.
Fee: May, 1793, £5:12. Account Book, 362.

Daniel Kidd v. Hugh Donagho and Joseph Bell.

Appeal from High Court of Chancery, Sept. 20, 1792, affirming j. against appellants County Court of Augusta, Aug. 20, 1789. J.M. for appellants.

Apr. 15, 1794. Heard, appellee not appear. Court of Appeals, Va., Order Book II, 263.

Apr. 19. Affirmed. Same, 269.

Fee: Jan., 1792, £2:12, Account Book, 312.

High Court of Chancery

Carter Bassett Harrison and Mary Howell, his wife, et. al. v. William Allen, Wythe 33.

Testator's father by will of 1783 devised to him all his estate and thereafter purchased land in James City County. Testator devised this land and others to son John, other land to son William, and residue to both; John predeceased testator, who died July, 1793. William claimed all the land as against his three sisters. Held, Virginia act of 1785 providing for descent of intestate real estate to children and permitting devise of after acquired land was in effect, the repealer act of 1792, which repeated its provisions, being suspended during the same session of legislature; that the residue clause of the will did not include the lapsed devise to John, which descended to all the heirs of testator.

Affirmed by Court of Appeals, Oct. 22, 1802, 3 Call 251.

J.M. represented petitioners in Chancery Court.

Fees: Mar., 1794, £6; Nov., 1794, £24. Account Book, 382, 402.

Archibald Hamilton v. William Urquhart, executor of Nathaniel Fleming, Wythe 113.

Ruling against petitioner, holding depreciation statute of Nov., 1781, not apply to debt secured by bond in 1777 due for dealing between parties in years before depreciation began; sec. 5 of 1781 act applied.

J.M. represented defendant.

Fees: Nov. 2, 1788, £5; Aug. 3, 1790, £3. Account Book, 176, 256.

District Court, Accomack and Northampton

Michael Dunton and Sarah, his wife, administrator and administratrix of Mary Scott v. Major and John Brickhouse, and John Kendall, Sr.

Debt. J.M. for plaintiffs.

Oct. 18, 1793. Office j. set aside; plea, covenant performed. District Court, Accomack and Northampton, Order Book 1789–1797, 285.

May 19, 1794. Confessed j., £180 payable by £60:19:8½. Same, 336.

Fee: Feb. 18, 1786, £2:10, "Appeal." Account Book, 64.

DISTRICT COURT, FRANKLIN

Jacob Faris, administrator of John Faris v. Richard Faris.

Writ of supersedeas to j. County Court, Campbell, recovered by defendant Mar. 2, 1792, £10. J.M. for defendant.

Sept. 18, 1794. Reversed, j. entered that defendant take nothing by his bill. District Court, Franklin, Order Book II, 1794–1796, 64.

Fee: Mar., 1792, £5. Account Book, 316.

SUPERIOR (DISTRICT) COURT, FREDERICK

Robert Coan, surviving executor of Thomas Whiting v. Warner Washington's Executor.

Debt. J.M. for plaintiff.

Sept. 12, 1794. V.j., £174:15:½, payable £87:7:6. Superior Court, Frederick, Order Book 1794–1797, 109.

Fee: See *Whiting v. Washington,* May 2, 1787, £2:4 "Trespass." Account Book, 114.

Apr. 24 *Fairfax Escheat*

Commonwealth v. Denny Fairfax.

Motion to quash inquisition of escheat against Fairfax by Charles Mynn Thruston, escheator for County of Frederick.

Held, inquisition defective and insufficient; set aside and quashed. Charles Marshall, attorney for Fairfax. Superior Court, Frederick, Order Book 1794–1797, 45.

Note: Ruling on same day as in *David Hunter v. Denny Fairfax.*

(For related proceedings in Fauquier County, see herein July 10, 1795; also herein 1798, Legal Practice, Court of Appeals, *Commonwealth v. Fairfax.*)

DISTRICT COURT, FREDERICKSBURG

Commonwealth v. Benjamin Grymes.

Indictment for murder. J.M. for Grymes.

Oct. 9, 1794. Acquittal. District Court Fredericksburg, Law Orders B, 1794–1798, 106.

Fee: Oct.–Nov., 1793, £5. Account Book, 374.

Thomas Hungerford v. William Thornton Alexander.

Case. J.M. for plaintiff.

May 4, 1793. Commission to plaintiff for deposition. District Court, Fredericksburg, Law Orders A, 1789–1793, 464.

Oct. 4, 1793. Leave to defendant to file pleas, writ of enquiry to be set aside and case sent back to rules. Same, 522.

Oct. 6, 1794. Demurrer to second plea of defendant sustained; v.j. for plaintiff £100 damages. Law Orders B, 1794–1798, 82.

Fee: Sept., 1790, £1:10. Account Book, 260.

Adam Hunter, surviving obligee of Adam Hunter, and Abner Vernon, executors of James Hunter v. Basil Nooe.

Debt, £237 Va. J.M. for defendant.

Oct. 8, 1794. V.j. £237 Va. and damages one penny, payable by £168:10. District Court, Fredericksburg, Law Orders B, 1794–1798, 99.

Fee: Oct., 1788, £2:8. Account Book, 168.

John Fitzpatrick v. Thomas Wood.

Case. J.M. for defendant.

Oct. 6, 1790. Case reinstated by plaintiff, had been dismissed for want of declaration. District Court, Fredericksburg, Law Orders A, 1789–1793, 174.

Oct. 9, 1792. Continued by consent. Same, 431.

May 2, 1793. Continued by plaintiff. Same, 449.

May 4, 1793. Submitted to arbitrators, award to be j., ex parte hearings. Same, 463.

May 1, 1794. Award at Orange County Courthouse, May 4, 1793, for defendant. Same, Law Orders B, 1794–1798, 13.

Fee: Oct., 1788, £2:10. Account Book, 168.

1795

DOCUMENTS

Jan. 11

RICHMOND *to Henry Tazewell*

Comments on bad postal service. Wheat in Virginia three shillings less than Philadelphia and New York; aristocrats blame on moneyed men, perverse on refusal to allow British Bank to discount at 6 per cent; Democrats blame on Hamilton, Jay, and devil. Listed in Lazare *Book-Prices* (1932), 557. Present owner unknown.

Feb. 2 *Admission to Practice*

J.M. admitted to practice as counselor before the U.S. Supreme Court. U.S. Sup. Ct., Minute Book A, 41.

Feb. 29
PHILADELPHIA *from Robert Morris*

Acknowledges J.M. letter of Nov. 23, 1794 (n.f.); promised $1,500 not available; comments on decree in favor of Braxton. DLC, Robert Morris Letter Book, Vol. 1, Pt. 2, folio 646.

Mar. 2
RICHMOND *to Governor of Virginia* [*Robert Brooke*]

Writes as attorney for Fairfax in case with Commonwealth in Court of Appeals; wishes approval of bill in equity requiring purchaser to assert title without awaiting service so as to expedite. V, Exec. Papers, Box 1795, Jan.-Mar., Folder Mar. 1–10; CVSP, VII, 446; Oster, *Marshall*, 29. (See herein, 1798, Legal Practice, Court of Appeals, Va., *Commonwealth v. Fairfax*.)

Mar. 21
RICHMOND *from Robert Brooke, Governor of Virginia*

Replying to letter of J.M. concerning case in Court of Appeals between Commonwealth and Fairfax; refuses to dispense with usual procedures. V, Exec. Letter Books, 1794–1800, 45; CVSP, VII, 446; Oster, *Marshall*, 29.

Mar. 21
RICHMOND *from Robert Brooke, Governor of Virginia*

Requesting opinion of enclosed legal papers for the information of the escheator of Fairfax; inquisition in hands of Attorney General and not returned; asks if second jury be impaneled. (J.M. law officer of the state in absence of Attorney General.) V, Exec. Letter Books, 1794–1800, 56.

Mar. 23 *Robert Brooke, Governor of Virginia,*
RICHMOND *to Roger West, Escheator of Fairfax*

Enclosing copy of letter of J.M. giving opinion as law officer of state (n.f.); orders to convene another jury to make findings. V, Exec. Letter Books, 1794–1800, 56.

Apr. 15
RICHMOND *Election*

Notice of election of J.M. to represent City of Richmond in General Assembly. Va. Gaz. & G.A., Apr. 15, 1795, Postscript, 2.

Apr. 30
RICHMOND *from Robert Brooke, Governor of Virginia*

To J.M. and other brigadier generals of the militia, list of arms and accoutrements; request for report. V, Exec. Letter Books, 1794–1800, 69.

May 13 *Receipt for Fee*

Receipt for payment of fee by client, Orandorf, witnessed by J.M. VU, No. 1172, original in law library.

A fee of £30 is noted in the account book from Orandorf, May, 1795. Account Book, 412. A further entry appears: *Littlejohn v. Cookus* (in *Orandorf v. Cookus*) £3, Mar., 1795. Account Book, 408.

June 21
RICHMOND *Witness*

J.M. witness to signature of Henry Lee on deed by Lee and wife Anne to Bushrod Washington of tract of land, Henrico County, Va., known as Belvidere. Proved by J.M. in General Court, Nov. 13, 1795, VHi.

July 10
FAUQUIER CO., VA. *Bond—Fairfax Escheat*

Bond, J.M. by Charles Marshall, his attorney in fact, Charles Marshall, Martin Pickett, and Septmus Norris to Robert Brooke, Governor of Virginia, £1,000 current; bond to indemnify and hold harmless John Blackwell, escheator, for rents and profits collected by J.M. from lands of Denny Fairfax devise, jury having determined Fairfax an alien. Fauquier County, Va., Records, Deed Book 12, 376–78. Recorded Oct. 26, 1795. County Court of Fauquier, Minute Book 1795–1797, 6.

July 12
RICHMOND *[to Attorney at Law]*

Note to an attorney concerning action in Supreme Court. Listed in Lazare, *Book-Prices* (1929), 741. Present owner unknown.

Aug. 26
PHILADELPHIA *from George Washington*

Offering appointment to attorney generalship of the United States.

DLC, Papers of George Washington, Vol. 275, 10. DLC, George Washington Letter Book XII, 126; Sparks, *Washington,* XI, 62; *Green Bag,* Vol. X (Jan., 1898), 24–25; Oster, *Marshall,* 193.

Aug. 31
RICHMOND *to George Washington*

Acknowledges letter of 26th. Refuses appointment as Attorney General of United States. DNA, General Records, Dept. of State, Misc. Letters, Aug.–Dec., 1795, 14, R.G. 59. Beveridge, *Marshall,* II, 123. J.M. stated he was too deeply engaged in practice to accept. Marshall, *Autobiography,* 20.

Sept.
RICHMOND *to Col. Thomas Marshall*

Telling of death of sister, Lucy Marshall Ambler (n.f.). Referred to in letter Col. Thomas Marshall to J.M., herein Nov. 6, 1795.

Oct. 9
MOUNT VERNON *George Washington to Edward Carrington*

Asking assistance of Carrington and J.M. in offering appointment of Attorney General of the United States to Col. James Innes, or of Secretary of State to Patrick Henry; enclosing letter to latter. DLC; Sparks, *Washington,* XI, 78.

For letter of Washington to Henry, see DLC, Washington Letter Book 5; Sparks, *Washington,* XI, 81; Marshall, *Life of Washington,* V, 396.

Oct. 13
RICHMOND *Edward Carrington to George Washington*

Giving reasons for J.M. and Carrington reversing order of approach by submitting offer of appointment to Patrick Henry as Secretary of State without first approaching Innes as to attorney generalship. DLC, Washington Letter Book 5; Sparks, *Washington,* XI, 79–82n. See also letters from Same to Same, Oct. 8 and Oct. 20, 1795. DLC, Washington Letter Book 5.

Oct. 22
RICHMOND *Lease*

J.M., Edward Carrington, William Duval, committee appointed by mayor, recorder and commonalty of Richmond in Common Hall to Samuel Parsons, Goochland County; for tanyard purposes, property of city, twenty-one years from Feb. 1, 1796; $30.00 per year rent and taxes; erect and deliver up improvements for tanning business at end of term. Assigned by Parsons to

Benjamin Tate, tanner and currier, Oct. 23, 1795. Recorded July 11, 1796. Richmond City Hustings and Chancery Court, Deed Book 2, 264–67. Entry to record. Same, Order Book 3, 489.

Nov. 2
PHILADELPHIA *from Robert Morris*

Advises that James M. Marshall and wife (Morris' daughter) left by sea two weeks ago; encloses Lytle note for $2,000 and promises $1,500 in few days, according to promise to James. DLC, Robert Morris Letter Book, Vol. 1, Pt. 2, folio 577–78.

Nov. 6
BUCKPOND, KY. *from Thomas Marshall*

Lamenting death of his daughter, Lucy Ambler; Molly (Mrs. Humphrey Marshall) ill. Intends to leave Lucy's share of his estate to her husband. Is informed that J.M. has been appointed and has accepted attorney generalship of the United States. Complains lack of U.S. Attorney in Kentucky impedes his duties as federal Collector of Revenue. Paxton, *Marshall Family*, 22–23; Mason, *Polly*, 72.

Nov. 9, *n.p.* *to Heth*

Advises Heth that no way of securing payment of gambling debt by representative of debtor except by bond of third person unacquainted with nature of debt. VU, Heth Papers, Dep. No. 38, 114.

Nov. 16 *to Hudson Martin, of Albemarle, Va.*

Acknowledges letter of Oct. 19 concerning suits between Banks, Clendinnen, and Martin; refers to Anderson. DLC, Marshall Papers, Ac. DR, D 3072.

Dec. 29
PHILADELPHIA *from Robert Morris*

Postponed answering J.M.'s of Nov. 23 (n.f.) hoping to send $1,000 as directed by James M. Marshall; will not rest until business is accomplished. Criticizes legal principles and motives of Judge Edward Pendleton in case of *Carter Braxton v. Thomas Willing and Robert Morris*. (See herein 1795, Legal Practice, Court of Appeals, *Va., Braxton v. Willing, Morris and Co.*) Will advise of arrival of *Pennsylvania* with James M. and wife aboard. DLC, Robert Morris Letter Book, I, 646.

to N.W. Price, Grand Secretary,
n.d., RICHMOND *Virginia Grand Lodge of Freemasons*

Warrant signed by J.M., Most Worshipful Grand Master, order to Grand Tyler to summon committee of masters and past masters of Virginia lodges to meet at Masons Hall Sunday morning to consider difference between Jacob Abrahams and I. K. Read. CSmH, BR Box 22.

COMMON COUNCIL OF RICHMOND

FOR J.M.'S SERVICE as councilman of Common Council of Richmond during this year, see herein 1794, Common Council of Richmond.

HOUSE OF DELEGATES OF VIRGINIA
(November Session, 1795)

J.M. SERVED AS representative of the City of Richmond in the Virginia House of Delegates for the session commencing Nov. 10, 1795, and ending Dec. 29, 1795. See V, Journal, H.D., (Nov. sess., 1795), 1–138. (Reprint, Richmond, Augustine Davis, MDCC, XCV.)

Nov. 11 Appointed on the Committees of Privileges and Elections, Same, 3–4; on Committee of Propositions and Grievances, Same, 4; on Committee of Courts of Justice, Same, 5.

Nov. 13 On committee to prepare and bring in a bill on proceedings in equity against debtors and defendants, and attachment against absconding debtors. Same, 12.

Nov. 16 On committee on revision of penal code. Same, 14.

Nov. 17 Bill to subject lands to be sold under execution for debts; seconded motion for record vote; voted for bill; bill defeated. Same, 20.

Nov. 20 Voted for amendment to resolution approving vote of Virginia senators in Congress against Jay Treaty, amendment that House no mature opinion. Amendment defeated. Same, 26–27. Voted against resolution; passed. Same, 27–28. Nov. 21, resolution approving the motives of the President in ratifying treaty amended to approve vote of Virginia senators and disavowing censure of President. J.M. voted against amendment. Passed. Same, 28–29. Nov. 24, 25. Senate agreement and amendment. Same,

38, 41. Dec. 4, House agreed to amended resolution, J.M. voting for it. Same, 71–72. Argument in debate was published and favorably received by Federalists in Congress. Marshall, *Autobiography*, 17–19. See letter Joseph Jones to James Madison, Fredericksburg, Va., Nov. 22, 1795. MHi Proc. (ser. 2), Vol. XV (June, 1901), 151–52.

Nov. 23 No vote of record on amendment to salaries bill, amendment to reduce allowance to members of General Assembly from $2.00 per day to $1.66⅔. Amendment defeated. Same, 32–33.

Nov. 26 Voted for bill supplementing act for appointments to civil offices. Defeated, 16 to 99. Same, 46.

Nov. 27 No vote recorded on resolution to repeal acts vesting glebe lands in Protestant Episcopal Church. Defeated. Same, 47.

On committee to examine treasury and state of James River Canal. Same, 49.

Nov. 28 On committee to bring in bill allowing branches of Bank of the United States. Same, 50. Presented bill. Same, 53. Dec. 8, voted for bill. Passed. Same, 79.

On committee to bring in bill authorizing payment in species of arrears of tax certificates in certain counties. Same, 50.

Dec. 1 Ordered to carry bill to establish fire insurance company to Senate. Same, 63.

Dec. 2 No vote of record on bill for relief for arrears of certificate taxes in certain counties. Same, 64–65.

Dec. 3 Ordered to carry bill for appointing agents for certain lands to Senate. Same, 68.

Submitted report on state and treasury of James River Canal; committed to whole House. Same, 69.

Dec. 5 One of managers at free conference with Senate on amendments to bill fixing allowance to members of General Assembly. Same, 73. Dec. 7, ordered to attend conference; reported. Same, 78. Dec. 15, voted against acceding to Senate. Passed. Same, 97–98. Dec. 10, no vote of record on extension of act concerning executions, and relief of insolvent debtors. Passed. Same, 86–87. Dec. 15, ordered to advise Senate of disagreement to amendments. Same, 97.

Dec. 12 Resolutions that senators and representatives of Virginia in Congress seek amendment of federal Constitution requiring approval of House of Representatives for treaties; a separate tribunal for impeachments; staggering tenure of senators one-third annually; forbidding judges to hold other offices. Amendment to postpone. J.M. voting for, defeated. Same, 91–92. Resolutions passed, J.M. voting against. Same, 92. See Beveridge, *Marshall,* II, 141–43.

Dec. 15 On committee to consider letter concerning prisoners in jail, district of Washington. Same, 97.

Dec. 16 No vote of record on postponement of petition for sale of certain glebe lands. Postponed. Same, 101.

Dec. 18 Jacquelin Ambler. Treasurer accounts. Same, 105–109.

On committee to bring in bill for appointment of Public Printer. Same, 111.

No vote on resolution relieving Davis, public printer, of disability because also acting as postmaster. Defeated. Same, 111.

Dec. 19 On committee to draft bill authorizing Executive to supply clothes and necessities to prisoners in certain counties, and advances to jailors, Same, 113; on committee to meet with Senate committee to examine ballots in election of brigadier general, Same, 113; on committee to draft amendments to act consolidating acts concerning slaves, free Negroes, and mulattos, Same, 114.

Dec. 21 On committee to bring in bill authorizing state subscription to stock of James River Company, and Potomac Company. Same, 119.

Dec. 22 Voted for bill fixing date of meeting of General Assembly. Passed. Same, 120.

Bill concerning slaves, etc., recommitted to committee of which J.M. a member. Same, 120.

On committee to bring in bill to amend act concerning suits for stealing money, rates of exchange, and damages. Same, 121. On second reading recommitted to committee. Same, 123.

Dec. 24 No vote of record on bill to complete navigation of Potomac River. Passed. Same, 124.

Ordered to carry to Senate bill to complete navigation of James River. Same, 125.

Voted against bill allowing embargo of Indian corn and meal. Bill defeated. Same, 125–26.

Added to committee to consider letter of Attorney General, causes for delay in suits against public debtors. Same, 126. Dec. 29, report of committee; J.M. voted for postponement to next session. Passed. Same, 135–36.

Dec. 25 Resolution denying right of federal court to decide cases concerning title to land granted by state, and empowering Governor to employ counsel to prosecute writ of error to the U.S. Supreme Court in *Hunter v. Fairfax*; ordered to lie on table. Same, 129. Dec. 29, postponed. Same, 126.

Dec. 26 On committee to bring bill increasing salaries of judges of High Court of Chancery to $1,666.67. Same, 131.

Dec. 28 Voted for bill to extend navigation of Appomatox River. Passed. Same, 133.

Ordered to carry to Senate agreement to amendments of bill for completion of James River navigation project. Same, 134.

LEGAL PRACTICE

J.M. RECORDED THE RECEIPT of 199 fees for legal services during the year, totaling £1,025:18:7.

The largest fees were one of £30 from one Orandorf (see herein, 1795, Documents, May 13) and same amount in the federal Circuit Court case of *Douglas and Prentis v. Lord* [*sic*]. (*Joseph Larelle v. William Douglas* and *Same v. William Prentis*. Case, both dismissed for failure of plaintiff to give security for costs, May 30, 1796. U.S. Circuit Court, Va., Order Book II, 66, 134.) Advice fees numbered twenty-four. Sixteen of these were in the £1 and £2 brackets, the largest £8. Only one fee for drawing a deed appears (£1:2:6), and only one caveat.

One hundred forty-five litigations are named by title; in only fourteen of these is the court or nature designated; and for the most part, these are divided between federal and state appellate courts. Account Book, 404–422.

J.M. was admitted to practice as counselor before the U.S. Supreme Court (see herein, 1795, Documents, Feb. 2).

U.S. CIRCUIT COURT, VIRGINIA

Thomas Belfield, surviving executor of William Smith v. McColl and Elliott and John McColl and Co.

Dec. 4, 1792. Injunction against j. against Hancock Lee, executor of Smith on penal bond of 1774, £235:10 of j. for £250, Nov. 24, 1791. J.M. for petitioner. U.S. Circuit Court, Va., Order Book I, 136.

June 8, 1793. Dissolved, except to £85:10 Va. Same, 162.

June 6, 1795. Dissolved. Same, 539.

Same, Record Book I, 42–46.

Fee: May, 1792, £5. Account Book, 320.

Thomas Blaine, Great Britain v. Thomas Archer, Va.

Case, for goods sold and delivered, 1790, $500. Answer: not assume.

J.M. for plaintiff.

Nov. 28 (30), 1795. V.j. $3,472.89. U.S. Circuit Court, Va., Order Book II, 35.

Same, Record Book III, 436–39.

V, U.S. Circuit Court Case Papers, containing autograph petition signed.

Fee: Jan., 1794, £7 (with *Blaine v. Hobson*). Account Book, 380.

Thomas Blaine, Great Britain v. Richard Hobday, Va.

Case, for goods sold and delivered, $4,000. J.M. for plaintiff.

Dec., 1794. Capias.

June, 1795. Continued.

July, 1795. Alias.

Dec., 1795. Dismissed.

U.S. Circuit Court, Va., Record Book Index, Civil, Dec. T, 1795.

V, U.S. Circuit Court Case Papers, containing autograph petition signed and notation of dismissal in J.M.'s handwriting signed.

John Bowman et al., s.p. Alexander Spiers, John Bowman and Co., merchants, Great Britain v. Vivion Brooking, executor of Robert Munford, Amelia County, Va.

Debt, on penal bond, £207:14:6½ Va., payable by £103:17:3, 1775. Plea, payment. J.M. for defendant.

Dec. 4, 1794. Plea payment. U.S. Circuit Court, Va., Order Book I, 442.

May 30, 1795. V.j. £207:14:6½ Va. payable by $346.20. Same, 512.

Same, Record Book III, 263, May T, 1795.

V, U.S. Circuit Court Case Papers.
Fee: July, 1794, £5. Account Book, 392.

William Brown v. Thomas Jett.
Record Book Index, Civil, Jan. R, 1795.
V, U.S. Circuit Court Case Papers.
Fee: Oct.–Nov., 1793, £4:10. Account Book, 374.

John Buchanan, Jr., executor of William Buchanan, Glasgow, Great Britain v. William Call and Richard Taylor, surviving obligees of said Call and Taylor, and John King, Prince George County, Va.

Debt, on obligation under seal, £5,587:14:4 Va., 1777. J.M. for defendant.

May 28, 1792. Answer: payment; Britisher disability under Virginia laws; violation of Treaty of Paris; Declaration of Independence. Reply and demurrer to last three pleas. U.S. Circuit Court, Va., Order Book I, 112.

May 25, 1795. V.j. on issue of payment, £5,587:14:4, payable by $3,725.17. Same, 471.

Dec. 8, 1795. By agreement j. to be discharged agreeable to scale of depreciation. (Paid 2½ to 1 June 26, 1796.) Same, Order Book II, 69.

Same, Record Book III, 202–10.
V, U.S. Circuit Court Case Papers.
Fee: Feb., 1792, £6:14. Account Book, 314.

Buchanan Hastic and Co., Great Britain v. Boswell Goodwin (Goodwyn).
Debt. J.M. for securities of defendant.

May 26, 1792. Pleas: payment; not recoverable by Britisher; breach of Treaty of Paris; Declaration of Independence. Demurrer by plaintiff. U.S. Circuit Court, Va., Order Book I, 109.

May 25, 1795. Demurrer for plaintiff. V.j. £3,013:5:7 Va., payable by $2,903.62. Scaled 2½ to 1. Same, 470.

Not indexed in Record Book.
V, U.S. Circuit Court, Case Papers.
Fee: Nov., 1791, £4:4. Account Book, 306.

James Dennistoun et al., d.b.a. Donald Scot and Co., Glasgow, Great Britain v. Gabriel Penn and Daniel Gaines, executors of Henry Gilbert, Amherst County, Va.

Debt, on obligation under seal, £731:4:3 Va., 1774. J.M. for defendant.

May 24, 1791. Judgment clerk's office set aside. Pleas: payment; Britisher no standing. U.S. Circuit Court, Va., Order Book I, 16.

Nov. 25, 1794. Plea: assets administered. Same, 400.

May 22, 1795. Plea no assets withdrawn for plaintiff on question of standing. V.j. £731:4:3 Va., payable by $951.71. Same, 461.

Same, Record Book III, 198–202.

V, U.S. Circuit Court Case Papers.

Fee: Jan., 1791, £5:12. Account Book, 272.

James Halton, New York v. Thomas Ker, Va.

Debt, on promissory note, £256:15:8 N.Y., 1793. J.M. for plaintiff.

Nov. 27, 1795. Security for defendant. U.S. Circuit Court, Va., Order Book II, 22.

Same, Record Book Index, Office Judgment, 1795.

V, U.S. Circuit Court Case Papers, containing autograph petition.

Fee: Apr., 1795, £10. Account Book, 410. (Refers only to Ker.)

Henderson, McCaul and Co., merchants, Great Britain v. William Farrar, Goochland County, Va.

Debt, on obligation £274:14:10 Va., 1776. J.M. for defendant.

June 6, 1795. Bond undertaking by J.M. for defendant. Plea: payment. U.S. Circuit Court, Va., Order Book I, 537.

Dec. 1, 1795. Confessed judgment, £274:14:10 Va. value of $915.00 payable by $457.91. Order Book II, 38.

Same, Record Book III, 451–53.

V, U.S. Circuit Court Case Papers.

Fee: May, 1794, £2:16. Account Book, 386.

Thomas and Rowland Hunt, merchants, London v. William Nelson, Caroline County, Va.

Debt, on obligation under seal, £267:3:8, 1773. J.M. for plaintiff.

June 5, 1795. Security for defendant. Plea: payment. U.S. Circuit Court, Va., Order Book I, 532.

Dec. 8, 1795. V.j. £267:3:8 valued at $892, payable by $415.15. Same II, 67.

Same, Record Book IV, 110–12.

V, U.S. Circuit Court Case Papers, containing autograph petition.

John Tyndale Ware, executor of Wm. Jones, s.p. Farrell and Jones v. John Quarles, Jr.

Debt. J.M. for defendant.

Nov. 28, 1791. Second plea in bar; sent back to Rules. U.S. Circuit Court, Va., Order Book I, 63.

Dec. 4, 1793. *Scire facias,* plaintiff Jones dead, Ware substituted. Same, 243.

Dec. 5. Commission, depositions in Great Britain. Same, 249.

Nov. 28, 1794, and Nov. 27, 1795. Continued. Same, 412; Same, II, 23.

May 30, 1796. Demurrer to plea of payment into Treasury sustained, continued on plea of *non assumpsit.* Same, 143.

May 26, 1797. Plaintiff nonsuited, failure to prosecute. Same, 217.

V, U.S. Circuit Court Case Papers.

Fee: July, 1791, £5:2. Account Book, 292. (For this case and *Ware, executor of Jones v. Richeson,* herein.)

The related case of *Ware, executor of Jones v. John Ruffin* was bracketed throughout with the Quarles case, dismissed Nov. 28, 1798. Order Book III, 125. J.M. was undoubtedly counsel in the case.

John T. Ware, executor of William Jones, surviving obligee Farrell and Jones, merchants, Great Britain v. Holt Richeson, King William County, Va.

Debt, on obligation under seal, £200 St., 1772. J.M. for defendant.

Nov. 28, 1791. Answer: payment; Britisher disability under Virginia laws; violation of Treaty of Paris; Declaration of Independence. Demurrer by plaintiff. U.S. Circuit Court, Va., Order Book I, 63–64.

Dec. 4, 1793. Jones death, executor substituted. Same, 242.

Nov. 25, 1794. Demurrer to last three pleas for plaintiff. V.j. £200 Great Britain, payable by $454.57. Same, 401.

Nov. 29, 1794. Judgment set aside. Same, 419.

Dec. 6, 1794. Continued. Same, 457.

Nov. 25, 1795. Demurrer for plaintiff, v.j. £200 Great Britain, payable by $240.95. Same, III, 14.

Same, Record Book III, 429–36.

V, U.S. Circuit Court Case Papers.

Fee: July, 1791, £5:2. Account Book, 292. (For this case and that of *Ware, executor of Jones v. Quarles,* herein above.)

Sir Lyonel Lyde and Samuel Lyde, d.b.a. Lyonel Lyde and Co., merchants, London, Great Britain v. Roger Atkinson.

Chancery, failure to remit on consigned merchandise, 1764; accounting asked. J.M. for defendant.

Answer: goods stolen, other sold for depreciated currency, escheat, breach of treaty, remedy at law.

Dec. 3, 1794. Death of plaintiff, Lyonel. Demurrer to pleas for plaintiff.

Court commissioners ordered to settle accounts. U.S. Circuit Court, Va., Order Book I, 438.

May 29, 1795. Report, consent verdict £1,004:8 Va. value of $3,348.21. Same, 501.

Record Book III, 366–77. May T, 1795.

V, U.S. Circuit Court Case Papers, containing autograph pleadings.

Trustees of John McCall, s.p. McCall and Elliott, Glasgow, Great Britain v. William and Thomas Richards, executors of William Richards, King and Queen County, Va.

Debt, on sealed obligation £646:11:1½, value $2,188.75, 1774. J.M. for defendant.

Nov. 29, 1791. Pleas: payment to Loan Office; British debt not recoverable; Treaty of Paris violation; Declaration of Independence.

Demurrer. U.S. Circuit Court, Va., Order Book I, 65.

Jan. 4, 1794. Plea, payment. Same, 398.

May 29, 1795. V.j., not paid, £656:11:1½ Va. payable by $691.87. Same, 494.

May 30, 1795. Set aside by consent j. £656:11:1½ Va. payable by $628.03. Same, 515.

Same, Record Book III, 393–96.

Autograph, entry of consent to commission to take deposition. VHi.

James Maury, Great Britain v. Moses and Stephen Austin, d.b.a. Moses Austin and Co., Va.

Case, for goods sold and delivered, £324:8:10 St., 1792. J.M. for plaintiff.

June 5, 1795. V.j. $1,790.88. U.S. Circuit Court, Va., Order Book I, 530.

Same, Record Book III, 259–60.

V, U.S. Circuit Court Case Papers.

Fee: Oct., 1793, £5. Account Book, 372.

John Scott v. J. W. Ware, executor of William Jones, s.p. Farrell and Jones, assignee of Thomas Randolph.

Injunction against enforcement of j. held by Ware against Scott as to part of judgment for which Scott claimed a credit, by mistake not presented in defense by J.M., his attorney at trial. Prayer that Richard Hanson, agent of Jones, and executors of Randolph be made party.

The original j. was on a bond of 177— given by Peterfield Trent to William Randolph for account owed, signed by Trent and Alexander Trent, Scott, John Harris and William Gay as security, £600, assigned by

Randolph, 1789, to Jones. Action against Trents abated by death; j. taken against others, Nov. 25, 1794, in U.S. Circuit Court, Va., for £1,200 Va., equal to $4,000, payable by $2,000. U.S. Circuit Court, Va., Order Book I, 402.

Scott, originally represented by Duvall in this case, employed J.M. as attorney and gave him written acknowledgment by Randolph of indebtedness to Scott of £150:12:10. J.M. by mistake or error failed to present it in defense as a credit. In September or October of the following year J.M. found the acknowledgment of Randolph; injunction proceedings commenced Nov. 23, 1795.

Dec. 9, 1795. Subpoena of injunction allowed as to $187.50 of the j. until further hearing. U.S. Circuit Court, Va., Order Book II, 70.

Meantime, Scott had given a forthcoming bond for execution levied against him on the judgment, and on default Ware took judgment against him on the bond for £2,001:10 current money payable by $3,385.84, May 30, 1795. Same, I, 502.

Also Scott on motion directed against Harris and Gay sought to subject them to payment of their proportion of the joint debt; this proceeding was dismissed at plaintiff's cost. May 23, 24, 1796. Same, II, 99, 101. It may be assumed that J.M. represented Scott in these proceedings.

Scott's executors thereafter continued to press action against Harris' executors for contribution. May 8, 1801. Same, IV, 68. On Nov. 23, 1804, with J.M. on the bench, this proceeding was dismissed for failure to prosecute. Same, V, 7.

Meantime, in the original injunction filed by J.M., Richard Hanson filed answer Dec. 3, 1795, denying the discount and refusing to set it off in accounts with the Randolph estate and thereby increase its debts to James estate, his principal, extensive litigation then pending between the two. The cause was continued from Dec., 1799, to July, 1805.

July, 1805, a bill of revivor (*scire facias*) brought in name of Edward and Charles Scott, executors of John Scott, incorporating the original pleadings and evidence, including an account of Randolph acknowledged in 1791 and showing £360:9:2 due Scott; also stating the death of Hanson which deprives of relief against him as agent of James, asking that Ware be made party defendant in revivor action; stating John Wickham of Richmond had effects of Ware, and asking that he be made party defendant. This was allowed Nov. 26, 1805. Same, V, 176.

Nov., 1807. Ware, a nonresident, was summoned to appear; summons advertised in newspaper, but Ware did not enter appearance. John Wickham failed to respond to summons June 10, 1808; attachment was rendered against him and bill taken as confessed.

June 10, 1809. Wickham filed answer asking dismissal, admitting £185:12:4 of Ware assets in his hands. June 21, 1809. On motion, decree against him was set aside. Same, VII, 330.

May 29, 1811. Attachment against Wickham of effects of Ware in his hands was dissolved except as to $187.50 with interest from 1788. Leave given plaintiffs to amend bill to make Thomas M. and William Randolph executors of Thomas Mann Randolph, defendants. Same, VIII, 320.

Nov. 25, 1812. Cause was dismissed at plaintiff's costs. Same, IX, 150.

Same, Record Book Index, Chancery, Nov. T, 1812.

J.M. sat on the bench in this case from 1802 to 1812.

V, U.S. Circuit Court Case Papers, 1812, contain autograph bill for injunction and autograph deposition detailing facts of case, failure to produce paper left with him and finding thereof. These were part of record of case throughout.

William Snodgrass v. James Edmondson.

Debt, on note, £1,072:10:10½, 1770. J.M. for defendant.

Nov. 29, 1791. Pleas: payment; Britisher not recover under Virginia laws; violation of Treaty of Paris; Declaration of Independence. Demurrer as to last three.

Nov. 25, 1793. *Scire facias,* defendant dead. U.S. Circuit Court, Va., Order Book I, 181.

May 25, 1795. Confessed j., John Brockenbrough, administrator, £1,072:10:10½ payable by $902.27. Same, 468.

Same, Record Book III, 216, May T, 1795.

V, U.S. Circuit Court Case Papers, 1793, 1795.

William Snodgrass v. Elliott Sterman and Leroy Dangerfield, executors of William Young, Sr.

Debt, on penal bond £473:13:9¾, penalty £947:7:7½, 1770. J.M. for defendants.

Nov. 29, 1791. Pleas, payment; Britisher not recover under Virginia laws; violation of Treaty of Paris; Declaration of Independence. U.S. Circuit Court, Va., Order Book I, 66.

Nov. 25, 1793. *Scire facias,* Dangerfield substitute for Sterman, who died. Same, 181.

May 24, 1794. Allowed. Same, 361.

May 23, 1795. V.j. £947:7:7½, payable by $1,285.27. Same, 464.

Same, Record Book III, 190–97. May T, 1795.

V, U.S. Circuit Court Case Papers.

Andrew Van Bibber, Md. v. William Robins and William Robins, Jr., Va.

Action on obligation of Oct., 1792, signed in Baltimore, £485:4:10 Md. J.M. for plaintiff.

Dec., 1794. Continued.

Jan., 1795. Court order for defendant's bail.

Feb., 1795. Confessed j.

Same, Record Book Index, office j. 1795.

V, U.S. Circuit Court Case Papers, containing autograph petition. (See herein Apr. 18, 1796, Documents.)

John Vaughan, merchant, Pa. v. Elias Parker and Samuel Paine, Va.

Case, on bill of exchange by Parker on Daniel Parker to Paine, endorsed to plaintiff, $570, 1792. Damage $800. J.M. for plaintiff.

Dec. 9, 1795. Plea: not assume. V.j. $692.97 against Parker. U.S. Circuit Court, Va. Order Book II, 75.

Dec. 12, 1795. Same against Paine. Same, 84.

Same, Record Book IV, 113–16.

V, U.S. Circuit Court Case Papers, containing autograph petition.

Archibald Walker et al., executors of John Stoney v. Mills and John Cowper, s.p. of Scott, Irvine, and Copers.

Case. J.M. for plaintiff.

Dec. 2, 1794. Plea: *non assumpsit.* U.S. Circuit Court, Va., Order Book I, 429.

Nov. 30, 1795. Continued. Same, II, 32.

Dec. 1, 1795. Dismissed by plaintiff. Same, 39.

Same, Record Book Index, Civil, June R, 1794.

V, U.S. Circuit Court Case Papers.

Fee: Nov., 1795, £6. Account Book, 434.

Court of Appeals of Virginia

William Foushee v. Thomas Lea, 4 Call 279, 283–84.

Appeal from High Court of Chancery.

Injunction against j. for appellant in County Court of Henrico and approval of subsequent j. District Court of Fredericksburg for appellee, affirmed. J.M. and Alexander Campbell for appellant.

Action in case by Foushee against Lea for not accepting lease for one year of house in Richmond. Lea's entries subpoenaed, absent; continuance refused; j. for Foushee; motion for new trial next day failed, no quorum. Injunction issued. New trial set by chancellor at Fredericksburg instead of

Henrico as originally ordered; j. for Lea. Held, injunction lies where j. obtained by surprise or inadvertence; ought to have allowed continuance; motion for new trial timely; chancellor had power to set place of trial.

Apr. 25–27, 1793. Heard. Court of Appeals, Va., Order Book II, 223, 225.

May 1. Continued for rehearing. Same, 230.

Apr. 11, 1794. Defendant dead, *scire facias*. Same, 261.

Apr. 13, 1795. Revived; heard. Same, III, 45, 46.

Apr. 16. Affirmed. Same, 47.

Carter Braxton v. Willing, Morris and Co., 4 Call 288.

Appeal from High Court of Chancery, Oct. 5, 1793, reversing decree of Henrico County Court, Nov. 11, 1791, affirmed and reversed as to parts. J.M. for appellee.

Action by Braxton for settlement of commercial accounts, including sale of land to Morris. The accounting in County Court resulted in a balance to Braxton, in Chancery Court a balance to Morris, and in Court of Appeals to further adjustments. Entries in the case in County Court are as follows:

Mar. 10, 1787. Willing and Morris dismissed as individuals, nonresidents of county. County Court of Henrico, Order Book II, 660.

Aug. 6, 1787. Undertaking, release of partnership effects. Same, III, 70.

Aug. 8. Depositions. Same, 101.

Aug. 8, 1789. Exceptions to auditor's report, trial of issue of Morris assumed Braxton's debt to McCall. Same, IV, 69.

Nov. 5, 1789. New auditors. Same, 115.

Mar. 3, 1790. Jury verdict Morris not assume, trial of issue ordered. Same, 175.

Mar. 4. Auditors refuse, new appointed. Same, 200.

Mar. 11, 1791. New auditors refuse. Same, 481.

Nov. 11, 1791. J. against Willing and Morris affirming amounts interlocutory decree and auditor report. Appeal allowed to High Court of Chancery. Same, V, 41.

High Court of Chancery reversed, decree against Braxton £9,627.

On appeal to Supreme Court of Appeals entries were as follows:

Apr. 13, 1794. Motion of appellee for increased appeal bond. Court of Appeals, Order Book II, 275.

Nov. 21. Discharged. Same, III, 40.

Oct. 19, 20, 21, 1795. Case heard. Same, 73.

Oct. 22, 23, 24, 26, 27, 28. Continued. Same, 74–78, 80.

Oct. 29, 31; Nov. 2, 3, 4, 5, 6. Continued. Same, 81, 83, 86–89.

Nov. 7–13. Further rehearing. Same, 90–96.

Nov. 23. Finding on nineteen heads as to state of accounts between parties. Affirming in part and reversing in part. Same, 102–107.

(See letters from Morris, Feb. 29, Dec. 29, 1795, herein; also herein 1794, Legal Practice, Court of Appeals, Same parties.)

Fee: Feb. 2, 1787. "By Alexander," £8:10. Account Book, 98.

John Tuberville v. Stephen Self, 4 Call 580, 585–87, also 2 Washington 71.

On writ of supersedeas, j. District Court of Northumberland Courthouse, Apr. 9, 1794, affirming County Court of Westmoreland, May, 1791, £24:16:8, affirmed. J.M. for appellee.

Tuberville seized slaves of Self in distress for rent in arrears under lease. Replevin by Self showing award of arbitrators made after suit covering accounts to 1775, balance in his favor; set off by Tuberville for tobacco delivered to third person for Self disallowed.

Held, award proper basis for replevin; defendant in replevin cannot set up discounts under Virginia law.

Apr. 24, 1795. Submitted. Court of Appeals, Va., Order Book III, 55.

Apr. 27. Affirmed. Same, 58.

James, Walter, and Dougal Ferguson v. Daniel Moore, 2 Washington 54, 55, 57.

Writ of supersedeas j. District Court of Petersburg, Apr. 20, 1793, affirming j. County Court of Dinwiddie, July 18, 1791, £748:11:2, j. on bond for appellee, reversed. J.M. for appellant.

Moore, owner, directed distress to Sergeant, Court of Hustings of Petersburg, against M'Rae, without owner's consent executed replevin bond returned into County Court of Dinwiddie, on which Moore took judgment. Held, Ferguson tenant in possession; bond returnable and j. obtainable only in court where distress made.

Apr. 15, 1795. Case submitted. Court of Appeals, Va., Order Book III, 46.

Apr. 17. Reversed. Same, 49.

Fee: Apr., 1794, £4. Account Book, 384.

James Currie v. Alexander Donald, 2 Washington 58, 61.

Appeal from order District Court of Richmond, Apr. 10, 1794, denying supersedeas to j. for appellee, Court of Hustings of Richmond, May 15, 1793, affirmed. J.M. and Andrew Ronald for appellee.

Ejectment suit against Donald, allowed to prove Currie not owner by unrecorded deed conveying away property; deed commenced "This indenture" but not indented; delivery proved by parol and signature of witnesses. Held, admissible.

Apr. 22. Case submitted. Court of Appeals, Va., Order Book III, 53.

Apr. 25. Affirmed. Same, 56.

William Shelton v. Sherod Barbour, 2 Washington 64, 64–65.

Appeal from District Court of Charlottesville, Sept. 17, 1794. Action to try right to freedom, j. for appellee, plaintiff below, reversed. J.M. and Bushrod Washington for appellant.

Appellee held as slave by appellant; in action for freedom appellant submitted j. of General Court between person under whom received ownership and mother, finding mother a slave. Submitted to jury as circumstantial but not conclusive evidence. Held, finding as to mother conclusive evidence as to child.

Apr. 11. Case submitted. Court of Appeals, Va., Order Book III, 43.

Apr. 13. Reversed. Same, 45.

Fee: Oct., 1794, £5. Account Book, 398.

Joseph Brook, executor of John Lewis, et al. v. William and Ann Philips and Augustine and Betsy Lewis, infants, 2 Washington 68, 69.

Appeal from High Court of Chancery, Sept. 21, 1793.

Order setting aside conveyance of reversion of land and for distribution according to will, affirmed. J.M. for appellee.

Executor under will giving life estate to half of testator's land to wife, reversion and residue to children, sold reversion to pay debts without court order after delivering moiety to wife. Held, no authority.

Apr. 15, 1795. Heard. Court of Appeals, Va., Order Book III, 46.

Apr. 16. Affirmed. Same, 47.

Fee: Feb., 1792, £5. Account Book, 314.

Hezekiah Turner v. John Moffett, 2 Washington 70, 71.

Appeal from District Court of Dumfries, Oct. 3, 1793.

J. for appellee, reversed. J.M. for appellant.

Assumpsit, declaration against Chilton, capias against Turner and Chilton served on Turner alone. Turner and Moffett agreed to arbitration, j. on award. Counsel argued on several points; court reversed on other ground, that award made on order of reference, the date of which was misrecited.

Oct. 25, 1794. Supersedeas awarded. Court of Appeals, Va., Order Book III, 15.

Apr. 16. Writ of certiorari for record. Same, 48.

Oct. 23. Reversed, new trial. Same, 76.

Alexander Brydie, assignee v. Charles Langham, 2 Washington 72, 74.

Appeal from District Court of Charlottesville, Apr. 19, 1794, affirming County Court of Fluvanna, Sept. 5, 1793.

Order quashing execution against appellee, affirmed. J.M. for appellee.

Appellant having four js. against appellee sued out writs of *capias ad satisfaciendum* directed to sheriff of Henrico County, jailed; never given up permanent residence in Fluvanna County. Held, execution against person in court of residence only.

Apr. 24, 1795. Case submitted. Court of Appeals, Va., Order Book III, 55.

Apr. 27. Record amended. Same, 57.

May 5. Affirmed. Same, 62, 63.

William Bernard v. Richard Brewer, 2 Washington 76, 76–77.

Appeal from District Court of Northumberland Courthouse, Apr. 9, 1794, affirming Court of Richmond, June 3, 1793.

Order granting privilege to build mill, reversed J.M. for appellant.

On application to County Court to build mill, failure to give ten days' notice to appellant whose land to be condemned. Held, error.

Oct. 14, 1795. Case submitted. Court of Appeals, Va., Order Book III, 70.

Oct. 15. Reversed. Same, 71.

Fee: Mar., 1795, £3:18 "Mr. Bernard." Account Book, 406.

Philip M'Rae v. Richard Woods, 2 Washington 80, 81–85.

Appeal from High Court of Chancery, Mar. 8, 1794, reported in Wythe 78. Order injunction and new trial because of uncertainty of verdict, affirmed. J.M. for appellant.

In 1769 three men formed pool of lottery tickets, Roderick McCrae with two tickets to have half share in pool, Woods and Mullens with one ticket each, one-fourth shares. Before drawing, the latter two sold their interest to Roderick, who in turn sold a share to Philip McCrae, who claimed one-half; and by subsequent arbitration between McCraes was held to be entitled to one-half and not one-quarter. Ticket of Roderick won highest prize, a tract of land and lots; although ticket was claimed to have been forcibly taken from Roderick by Philip, Roderick obtained title to the prize land and Woods conveyed his interest in the land to him or his assignee, refusing to convey to Philip. Fifteen years later Philip, unable to recover from Roderick, sued Woods at law for the value of the prize of the whole ticket and obtained j. for £451:18:4. Injunction proceedings before High Court of Chancery decree issued for a new trial.

Held, decree affirmed, the three judges giving various grounds: that evidence of confusion by the jury admissible; variously that Philip entitled to no part, to one-fourth, or to one-half interest, all agreeing that verdict erroneous and issue to be retried.

Apr. 24, 1794. Death of appellant, revived. Court of Appeals, Va., Order Book III, 56.

Oct. 14, 1794. Heard. Same, 69.

Oct. 22, 1794. Affirmed. Same, 74.

Fee: Oct., 1795, £5:4. Account Book, 422. Also Oct., 1791, "McCrae," £7:10. Account Book, 300.

Newell v. The Commonwealth, 2 Washington 88, 91–92.

Appeal from j. District Court of Washington, Oct. 4, 1793, £50 forfeiture, reversed. J.M. for appellee.

J. of guilty on information against justice of peace for accepting bribe in election of county clerk, reversed for insufficiency of information in failing to state election held.

Apr. 21, 1795. Heard. Court of Appeals, Va., Order Book III, 52.

May 9, 1795. Continued. Same, 66.

Oct. 15–16, 1795. Reheard. Same, 71, 72.

Nov. 2, 1795. Reversed. Same, 85.

Fee: Sept., 1794, £12. Account Book, 398.

Rawleigh White v. Roger Atkinson and Stephen Coleman, 2 Washington 94, 96.

Appeal from High Court of Chancery, decree affirmed. J.M. for appellee.

White brought action for specific performance of contract to purchase land from Atkinson under contract 1779 at £6 current money per acre payable June, 1780; tender of price made in specie according to scale of depreciation. Because of great depreciation in paper money, decree was for conveyance on payment of value of land in 1780 determined by jury. Affirmed on condition parties may request redetermination of value as of 1779.

Oct. 16, 1795. Heard. Court of Appeals, Va., Order Book III, 72.

Nov. 10, 1795. Affirmed. Same, 91.

Fees: Mar. 7, 1787, £5, "Chr"; Apr., 1795, £5. Account Book, 100, 410. (For amendment of this decree, see 2 Call 316 [1800].)

Martin and William Picket v. James Dowdall, 2 Washington 106, 107–108, 111–12.

Appeal from High Court of Chancery, Mar. 11, 1794.

Suit for conveyance of land, j. for appellee, reversed. J.M. for appellants.

Predecessor of appellee in 1741 obtained warrant and survey for land in Northern Neck but no grant from Fairfax office within six months as required by rules; grant from Commonwealth in 1788. Appellant's warrant and survey of same land 1762 and 1779, grant from Fairfax office 1780. Held, grant of 1788 not relate back to 1741, abandoned, equity not superior to grant of 1780.

Oct. 23, 24, 1795. Heard. Court of Appeals, Va., Order Book III, 76.

Oct. 26, 1795. Reversed. Same, 77.

Buller Claiborne v. John Parrish, 2 Washington 146, 146–47.

Appeal from District Court of Williamsburg, May 8, 1794, affirming County Court of Kent, Aug. 12, 1793.

Ejectment, j. for appellee, 150 acres, reversed. J.M. for appellee.

At trial testimony introduced as to what witness heard chain bearer say as to his misconduct in surveying. Held, error.

Oct. 30, 1795. Case submitted. Court of Appeals, Va., Order Book III, 86.

Nov. 7, 1795. Reversed, new trial. Same, 89.

Fee: Apr., 1795, £7. Account Book, 410.

John Brown, Jr., et al. v. Anne Brown, administratrix of Thomas Brown, 2 Washington 151, 152.

Decree of High Court of Chancery, Oct. 5, 1793, affirming County Court, reversed. J.M. for appellee.

Case involved item of £386:10:1 not credited in a deceased guardian's account; guardian's estate charged with the amount.

Oct. 29, 1795. Heard. Court of Appeals, Va., Order Book III, 81.

Nov. 12, 1795. Order of reversal. Same, 93–94.

Fee: Jan. 4, 1787, £2:10. Account Book, 96.

William Harrison, executor of Josias Payne v. Stephen Sampson, 2 Washington 155, 155–56.

Appeal from District Court of New London, Sept. 20, 1793.

Covenant, by appellee against appellant, j. for appellee £317:10 affirmed. J.M. for appellee.

Action by grantee of land against grantor's executor for breach of warrant of quiet enjoyment, grantee having been evicted. Question raised if executor could be sued on covenant. Affirmed without opinion.

Oct. 27, 1795. Case submitted. Court of Appeals, Va., Order Book III, 78.

Nov. 6, 1795. Affirmed. Same, 88–89.

J.M. also represented Sampson in action against him by Agatha Payne which resulted in his eviction, Apr. 16, 1786. See fee Mar. 20, 1786, amount illegible, "eject." Account Book, 66; also record of present case below. District Court, Franklin, Order Book 1789–1793, 253, 308; Same, 1794–1796, 192.

Harvey and Wife v. Borden, 2 Washington 156, 158–60.

Appeal from High Court of Chancery, Mar. 11, 1794.

Bill for allotment of land under will, j. for appellee, affirmed. J.M. for appellant.

Will gave each of five daughters 1,000 acres of "all good" land; testator left large tract on James River and smaller one of 2,218 acres on Catawba, the latter being the best. Executor took assignments from four daughters, selecting for self smaller tract and good land out of large tract. Held, in action by assignee of fifth daughter that her share must be taken from Catawba tract; also deed containing privy examination of a wife need not state the commission of the examining officer as justice of peace, will be presumed such.

Apr. 23, 1795. Continued. Court of Appeals, Va., Order Book III, 54.

Oct. 28, 1795. Heard. Same, 79.

Oct. 21, 1795. Affirmed. Same, 83.

Fees: Mar., 1791, £5; June, 1793, £7:12. Account Book, 276, 364.

Mary and Lettice Lee by Richard Bland, guardian v. John Tuberville, 2 Washington 162.

Appeal from District Court of Northumberland Courthouse, Apr. 8, 1794, reversing County Court of Westmoreland, Feb. 25, 1794. J.M. and Charles Lee for appellant.

Richard Lee granted right to build grist mill by County Court; appellee refused to appeal as not a party, obtained supersedeas to District Court, order reversed, J.M. contending could not examine evidence on supersedeas. On appeal District Court reversed and County Court affirmed "on the evidence."

Nov. 20, 1794. Death of Lee, case revived. Court of Appeals, Va., Order Book III, 39.

Oct. 13, 1795. Case set. Same, 69.

Nov. 3, 1795. Heard. Same, 86.

Nov. 4, 1795. Order reversing, affirming County Court. Same, 87.

Benjamin Jordan v. James Neilson, 2 Washington 164.

Supersedeas, j. District Court of Charlottesville, Apr., 1792.

Action of debt by defendant in error, payee, on note for 7,125 pounds crop tobacco, j. for him affirmed by divided court. J.M. for plaintiff in error.

Note sued on executed with amount of tobacco blank, instructions for payee to fill. J.M. contended note not evidence of amount because not made by defendant.

Nov. 9, 1793. Writ of supersedeas. Court of Appeals, Va., Order Book II, 256.

Oct. 13, 1794. Second writ. Same, III, 2.

Apr. 10, 1795. Third writ. Same, 43.

Oct. 12, 1795. Fourth writ. Same, 67.

Nov. 14, 1795. Last writ set aside, case submitted. Same, 98.

Nov. 18, 1795. J. affirmed. Arguments of counsel noted. Same, 100.

Joseph Curd v. George Hooper and Henry Bell.

Appeal from j. District Court, Prince Edward, affirming j. for Hooper, high sheriff of Buckingham County, against Curd, his deputy on official bond, for default in office whereby Hooper subjected to liability, Apr. 2, 1793, £67:11:5[3]. (See District Court, Prince Edward, Order Book 1792–1795, 154; Same, 1793–1799, 42, 98, 118). J.M. for Hooper.

Oct. 29, 1795. Dismissed, failure to prosecute. Court of Appeals, Va., Order Book III, 81.

Fee: Sept., 1794, £5, "Appeal." Account Book, 396.

James Dabney, Sheriff of Louisa County v. Sarah Jerdone, executrix of Francis Jerdone.

Appeal from j. against appellant High Court of Chancery, Oct. 4, 1794, £594:17:10. J.M. for appellee.

Oct. 31, 1795. Appellant not appear, argument of counsel for appellee. Affirmed. Court of Appeals, Va., Order Book III, 83.

Fee: Nov., 1794, £20. Account Book, 400.

Robert Dabney v. Anderson Thompson, William Duval, Martin and James Hawkins, Nelson and Waddy Thompson.

Appeal decree of High Court of Chancery, Mar. 18, 1795. J.M. for appellant.

Nov. 10, 1795. Dismissed, agreement of parties. Court of Appeals, Va., Order Book III, 92.

Fee: Mar., 1795, £5. Account Book, 408.

Baldwin Dade v. Peter Casenove.

J.M. for defendant in error.

Apr. 20, 1795. J. District Court, Dumfries, May 14, 1794, £375:7, affirmed. Court of Appeals, Va., Order Book III, 50.

Oct. 12, 1795. Order of affirmance entered. Prince William County Superior Court (District Court, Dumfries), Order Book 1789–1798, 147.

Fee: Sept., 1794, £6. Account Book, 398.

William Dudley, executor of Edwin Fleet, executor of William Fleet v. James Gregory, executor of David Ker.

Appeal from j. against appellant District Court, King and Queen Courthouse, Sept. 25, 1792. J.M. represented appellee.

Nov. 20, 1795. Dismissed for failure of appellant to appear. Court of Appeals, Va., Order Book III, 101.

Fee: June 2, 1786, £2:8. Account Book, 76.

Charles and Elizabeth Hudson v. Robert Moore, Jr.

Appeal from j. for appellee District Court, Richmond, Sept. 6, 1794, £59:12:7, payable by £29:16:3½. J.M. for appellee.

Oct. 30, 1795. Heard, affirmed. Court of Appeals, Va., Order Book III, 82.

Fee: Mar., 1793, £1:10. Account Book, 354.

Thomas Johnson v. Peter Shelton by Peter Shelton, his trustee.

Appeal from High Court of Chancery, May 13, 1794, dismissing bill of appellant. J.M. for appellee.

Apr. 18, 1795. Security required of appellant. Court of Appeals, Va., Order Book III, 50.

Oct. 13, 14, 1795. Heard. Same, 69, 70.

Oct. 23, 1795. Affirmed. Same, 74.

Fees: Feb., 1793, £5; Sept., 1794, £4:5:6; Oct., 1794, £2:14; Nov., 1795, £2:8. Account Book, 348, 396, 398, 422.

Benjamin and Nathan Morris, and John Land v. James Wood.

Appeal from j. for appellee on delivery bond, District Court, Prince Edward, Apr. 3, 1794, £380:10:7 payable by £190:5:3½ (District Court,

Prince Edward, Order Book 1793–1799, 94, 117); dismissed. J.M. for appellants Morris.

Aug. 23, 1795. Appeal dismissed, appellant not prosecuting. Court of Appeals, Va., Order Book III, 503.

See also related action in case between same parties. District Court, Prince Edward, Order Book 1789–1792, 216, 222, 249; Same, 1792–1795, 14.

Fees: Jan., 1793, £10. Account Book, 346. Also May, 1794, £10, "Morris." Account Book, 386.

Mary Rust Yerby and William Yerby, infants, by Griffin Garland, guardian v. George Yerby, administrator, et al.

Appeal from High Court of Chancery, May 17, 1800, dismissing bill, affirmed. J.M. for ———.

Apr. 15, 1803. Heard. Court of Appeals, Va., Order Book IV, 243.

Apr. 20. Affirmed. Same, 249.

Fee: Mar., 1795, £5:12:6. Account Book, 406 (early stages of proceedings).

District Court, Augusta

Robert Porterfield v. William and James Kinnerly, and James Kinnerly, Jr.

Motion on bond for delivery of property taken into possession of sheriff of Augusta County by virtue of execution. J.M. for Porterfield.

Apr. 2, 1795. Default by defendant, j. £300:16:8. District Court, Augusta, Order Book 1789–1798, 376.

Fee: May, 1795, £5. Account Book, 416.

Superior (District) Court, Frederick

John Lewis v. William Bell and Richard Morgan.

Debt. J.M. for Bell.

Apr. 20, 1795. Consent j. £83:1 and 300 pounds tobacco.

Superior Court, Frederick, Order Book 1794–1797, 147.

Fee: Aug., 1794, £3. Account Book, 394.

District Court, Northumberland

Gilbert Edwards v. Thomas Robinson.

Ejectment, one messuage, one tenement, and 250 acres. J.M. for plaintiff.

Sept. 3, 1794. Notice to appear. District Court, Northumberland, Order Book 1793–1802, 59.

Apr. 1, 1795. Default, writ issued. Same, 81.

Fee: May, 1795, £5, "Edwards adv. Robinson." Account Book, 414.

District Court, Prince Edward

Henry H. Dohrman v. George Anderson.

In case, and account rendered. (2 cases) J.M. for plaintiff.

Sept. 7, 1790. Continued. District Court, Prince Edward, Order Book 1789–1792, 131.

Sept. 3, 1792. Continued for report of referees. Same, 276.

Sept. 3, 1793, and Sept. 5, 1794. Same order. Same, Order Book 1793–1799, 52, 140.

Apr. 2, 1795. On motion of defendant order of reference set aside. Same, 168.

Sept. 7, 1795. Dismissed for failure to prosecute. Same, 213.

Fee: Aug. 9, 1787, £4:4, "2 suits." Account Book, 120.

Anne Woodson, executrix of Charles Woodson, Jr. v. John and Samuel Pankey.

Debt. J.M. for defendant.

Apr. 10, 1794. J. at rules against Samuel and William Pankey, sheriff of Buckingham County, set aside for want of bail. District Court, Prince Edward, Order Book 1793–1799, 113.

Apr. 11 and Sept. 8, 1794. Continued. Same, 128, 152.

Apr. 3, 1795. J. £61:14:6, payable by £30:17:3. Same, 174. Same, Record Book 1792–1795, 560.

Fee: Mar., 1790, £2:8, "app. old." Account Book, 238.

David Ross, assignee of George Holland v. Dick Holland and Joel Maxey.

Recovery allowed on delivery bond, £265:4, penalty of bond.

J.M. for Dick Holland. District Court, Prince Edward, Records at Large 1795–1798, 11.

Fee: Mar. 5, 1790, £2:8. Account Book, 236.

1796

DOCUMENTS

Jan. 8 *Money Transactions with Robert Morris*

Entry in current account book, Dr. Rawleigh Colston with Robert Morris, "to J. Marshall for £8,880 of 6 Jn. Ct. stock for which you desire not to account with 17%, £2,331 Va.; £2,913:15 Pa." "To diff. between the above am't and the rate at which I now settle with Mr. Marshall for sd. £666 V, £832:10 Pa." "To my bill 31st Dec. last on R. Morris Junr. at 60 ds. fav. J. Marshall £6,000 St. le 70, £8160 Va.; £10,200 Pa."

It is not clear if these transactions involve James M. Marshall or J.M. The last possibly represents a loan for purchase of South Branch Manor (see herein Feb. 1, 1797). In evidence *Francis Webb et al. v. Rawleigh Colston*, Superior Court of Chancery, Winchester, Frederick County, Va., Record Book 1784–1820, 1, 139.

Jan. 26
NEW YORK *Charles Lee to President George Washington*

J.M. was sought as commissioner on debts under British treaty, but was considered not available. Sparks, *Correspondence of the American Revolution* (Boston, Little Brown, 1853), IV, 479, 480. See also Lee to Washington, Mar. 20, 1796. Same, 481–82; Beveridge, *Marshall*, II, 200–202.

Jan., *n.p.* *to Major Thomas Massie—Addressed to Frederick*

Acknowledges letter by Page; will attend to suit for title to land. VHi.

Feb. 3
RICHMOND *Unclaimed Letter*

J.M.'s name among list of letters unclaimed at Richmond Post Office. Va. Gaz. & G.A., Feb. 3, 1796, 2.

Feb. 3
PHILADELPHIA *to Polly Marshall*

Journey to Philadelphia on British debt case, *Ware v. Hylton*, absence of Campbell; attended theatre; no information on arrival of vessel of brother and wife; illness of Jacqueline. VW; Mason, *Polly* 76.

Feb. 20
PHILADELPHIA *Land Grant*

Grant President George Washington to J.M. of 1,000 acres on Caesar's Creek, lands northwest of the Ohio, under his Military Warrant 30 pursuant to act of Congress Aug. 10, 1790. Surveyed as Military Survey 1429. DNA, U.S. Dept. of Interior, Bureau of Land Management. R.G. 49.

Feb. 20
PHILADELPHIA *Land Grant*

Grant President George Washington to J.M. of 1,000 acres on Caesar's

Creek, lands northwest of the Ohio, under his Military Warrant 30, pursuant to act of Congress, Aug. 10, 1790. Adjoins above grant. Surveyed as Military Survey 1430. DNA, U.S. Dept. of Interior, Bureau of Land Management. R.G. 49.

Feb. 24
RICHMOND *Insurance Policy*

Application for insurance on J.M. home in Richmond. Reprint by Mutual Assurance Society, Richmond, Va.

Mar. 4
PHILADELPHIA *Robert Morris to James M. Marshall*

Advising J.M. in Philadelphia, letter from him forwarded (n.f.). Could not get case before Supreme Court (*Hunter v. Fairfax, Devisee,* error from U.S. Circuit Court, Virginia); J.M. much concerned, fears disadvantage. DLC, Robert Morris Private Letter Book.

Mar. 8
PHILADELPHIA *from Robert Morris*

Advising of arrival of James M. Marshall in England; news in letter of Dec. 4. DLC, Robert Morris Private Letter Book, Vol. 1, Pt. 2, p. 743.

Mar. 14
RICHMOND *to Unknown*

Conversed with Washington concerning contents of letter; agreement carelessly drawn but interpretation correct; additional proof will aid; declarations held against addressee. PPHi, Am. Statesman Coll.

Apr. 11
PHILADELPHIA *from Robert Morris*

Tells of birth of son to James M. Marshall; acknowledges letter of (Mar.) 15th, agreeable communication (n.f.). DLC, Robert Morris Private Letter Book, Vol. 1, pt. 2, p. 783.

Apr. 18
RICHMOND *to Andrew Van Bibber*

Suit against Robins abated; can renew; will take time. Suit against Green awaits answer. Kingston Galleries, Inc., Somerville, Mass. Catalogue No. 6 (1963), item 114. (Present owner unknown.)

(See herein 1793, Legal Practice, U.S. Circuit Court, *Van Bibber v. Green*; 1795, Same, *Van Bibber v. Robins.*)

Apr. 19
RICHMOND *to Alexander Hamilton*

Acknowledges letter in last mail; decided not to write to H. (Patrick Henry) with whom had not corresponded; asked Gen. Lee to contact him; no answer; will talk to him in Richmond concerning proposition (to be candidate for presidency); expects refusal. DLC, Papers of Alexander Hamilton, Vol. 28; Beveridge, *Marshall*, II, 156–57.

Apr. 25
RICHMOND *to Rufus King*

Encloses letter for forwarding to (Alexander) Hamilton. Irritation of ruling party in Virginia expected by vote of today (approval in Richmond of petition favoring Jay Treaty); counter-resolutions being obtained; charge of improper names used in favorable resolution false. NNHi; King, *Life*, II, 45–46; Oster, *Marshall*, 83.

Apr. 25
RICHMOND *Public Address*

Speech of J.M. at public meeting in Richmond; resolution passed supporting the Jay Treaty. Va. Gaz. & G.A., Apr. 27, 1796, 3; Marshall, *Autobiography*, 16–17; Beveridge, *Marshall*, II, 150–54; Oster, *Marshall*, 15. For above resolution said to be drafted by J.M., see Va. Gaz. & G.A., Apr. 27, 1796, 3. See also "Petition of Inhabitants of Richmond to U.S. House of Representatives opposing Jay Treaty," *The Richmond and Manchester Adv.*, June 10, 1796, 1.

Apr. 25
RICHMOND *to Alexander Hamilton*

Acknowledges letter of the 14th; legislature opposed to Jay Treaty; advises of meeting (in Richmond) approving Jay Treaty with England; will be forwarded to Congress; majority of counties in Virginia will oppose. Treaty valid approved by Senate, Hillhouse; difficulty in engaging H (Henry) in approval. DLC, Papers of Alexander Hamilton, Vol. 28; Hamilton, *Works*, VI, 108–109; Oster, *Marshall*, 93–94.

May 3
PHILADELPHIA *from Robert Morris*

Acknowledges letter of (Apr.) 18th (n.f.); negotiating for bank stock for J.M.; letter of James M. Marshall forwarded (probably announcing birth of son). DLC, Robert Morris Private Letter Book, Vol. 1, Pt. 2, p. 810.

May 6
RICHMOND *Kentucky-Virginia Boundary*

Wrapper on papers respecting boundary line between Virginia and Kentucky. (J.M. one of commissioners.) Contents missing. V, Exec. Papers, 1796, Mar.-Sept., Folder May.

May 6 *Kentucky-Virginia Boundary*

Opinion of J.M. concerning lands involved in question of boundary between Virginia and Kentucky (n.f.). Referred to in Alexander Smyth to the Governor, May 6, 1796. CVSP, VIII, 367.

May 24
RICHMOND *to Rufus King*

J.M. and Gen. Lee conversed with Henry (concerning presidential candidacy); source of inquiry not revealed; Henry unwilling, fearful of difficulty of office. Note appended by King, answered June 1, regrets, need for another person without delay. NNHi; King, *Life*, II, 48; Oster, *Marshall*, 84; Beveridge, *Marshall*, II, 158.

June 16
PHILADELPHIA *from Robert Morris*

Enclosing answer in suit of John Alexander against Morris in Richmond Court of Chancery; bank stock not purchased; can draw money or have stock; complains of tight finances. DLC, Robert Morris Private Letter Book, Vol. 2, Pt. 1, p. 31.

June 23
RICHMOND *Legal Opinion*

Certificate of public debt, opinion of J.M. that judgment obtained by Henry Banks against Commonwealth of Virginia will be affirmed in Court of Appeals; Banks wishes to transfer part of demand. VHi.

July 8
MOUNT VERNON *from George Washington*

Offers appointment as minister to France; asks to forward enclosure (to C. C. Pinckney) if refuses. DLC, Papers of George Washington, Letter Book 12, Box 315, 193–94; Sparks, *Washington*, XI, 143. Oster, *Marshall*, 170.

July 11
RICHMOND *to George Washington*

Acknowledges letter of the 8th; declines appointment as minister to

France; forwarding to C. C. Pinckney. DLC, Papers of George Washington, Vol. 289, 310; Sparks, *Washington,* XI, 143; Oster, *Marshall,* 169–70. J.M. stated that his practice at the bar was more independent and no less honorable than the appointment offered. *Autobiography,* 21.

July 15
MOUNT VERNON *from President George Washington*

Regrets J.M.'s declining offer of ministry to France; asks advice as to qualifications of four possible appointees as Surveyor General. DLC, Papers of George Washington; Sparks, *Washington,* XI, 148–49.

July 18
RICHMOND *to Gen. Henry Lee*

Acknowledging letter of 15th. Purchase of lot on which Alexander Campbell resided; known no title to adjoining; sale to Hylton; negroes subject to Brown's debt. Sale delayed; suicide of Campbell, laudanum; J.M. saw interment. Death "effects us particularly"; delay of "our case" (*Hunter v. Fairfax's Devisees,* herein 1797, Legal Practice, U.S. Supreme Court). Pendleton employed Campbell; too late for another counsel from Virginia; probably not try case; Wickham contacted by J.M.; refused unless applied to. Enclosing letter to Pendleton (n.f.) under cover to Charles Lee; forward by express.

J.M. in Alexandria Monday; visiting Mount Vernon Tuesday; hopes answer by Wednesday. Journey to Philadelphia by J.M. without arguing case a "calamity." NjR, Philip D. Sang Coll.

July 26, *n.p.* *Robert Morris Accounts*

Entry in account book of Robert Morris; account with James M. Marshall; cash, £200 paid to J.M. and credited to James M. Marshall account. DLC, Beveridge Coll.; Beveridge, *Marshall,* II, 210 (facsimile).

[*Circa* July] *to Thomas Marshall, Buckpond, Woodford County, Ky.*

Advising his father that unable to make intended visit to him; writes of the part he is taking in the present "storm" (foreign affairs of the country) (n.f.). Referred to in letter from Thomas Marshall to J.M. Sept. 9, 1796. VW; Mason, *Polly,* 83–84.

Aug. 10
MOUNT VERNON *from President George Washington*

Inquires of letter to Pinckney with bank bills for Charleston fire victims under cover to J.M., not delivered; Pinckney accepts appointment to France. DLC, Papers of George Washington, Letter Book 14, Box 320, 216–17.

Aug. 12
RICHMOND *to President Washington*

Letter of Washington to Gen. Pinckney delivered to postmaster same night; gratified Pinckney will represent United States in France. DLC, Papers of George Washington, Vol. 280, 389.

Aug. 22 *to James McDowell*

Legal opinion on claim to land in Martha's Vineyard. Listed in Lazare, *Book-Prices* (1938), 507. Present owner unknown.

Aug. 24
PHILADELPHIA *from Robert Morris*

Refers to letter of J.M. to Morris (n.f.). Disappointed at not seeing J.M. in Philadelphia. Enclosing certificates for four shares of stock Bank of the United States to return to the gentleman of whom borrowed. Two other shares in name of Geo. Pickett enclosed; will continue remitting before time limited. Dividends to be remitted speedily. DLC, Robert Morris Private Letter Book, II, Pt. 1, p. 83.

Sept. 9
BUCKPOND, KENTUCKY *from Thomas Marshall*

Acknowledges letter of J.M. (n.f.) by Col. Fleming and by Dunlap, pleased family well; death of Colston caused postponement of J.M.'s visit; kept alive by hope of seeing J.M.; will wait one year longer; hears J. Ambler to accompany him. Pleased with part J.M. takes in present "storm"; J.M. never disobliged him in his life. Would like J.M.'s sons Tom and Jaqueline to accompany him except for tender age; if James and Lewis returned from Europe, would like them to come; Charles and Billy do not write.

Means to make division of property near equal between children; part of reason wishes to see J.M.; bond given Susan offered £3,000; to Lewis land £3,000 or £4,000 after death of self and wife; Mrs. Colston and daughter Ambler given nothing. Paid taxes on J.M.'s military lands, not those of grandson Thomas in Fayette. Col. Fleming will give news of country; thinks political horizon clearing. Tell Col. Carrington of Short's account and papers sent to Walcot. VW, John Marshal Papers, Folder 4; Mason, *Polly*, 83–84.

Sept. 12, *n.p.* *Receipt of Legal Fee*

Memorandum in J.M. handwriting; receipt of $20.00 fee in *Means v. Reynolds,* in Chancery, signed by J.M. Valentine Museum, Richmond, Va.

Sept. 22
RICHMOND *Emancipation of Slave*

Deed of emancipation of J.M. of Peter, a black man, purchased by him from Nathaniel Anthony. Henrico County Court, Deed Book 5, 129.

Dec. 5, 1796. Deed proved by oaths of David Lambert and William Marshall and ordered recorded. Same, Order Book 7, 214.

Oct. 10
RICHMOND *Lottery*

J.M. one of managers of Richmond Bridge Lottery. Va. Gaz. & G.A., Nov. 9, 1796, 2, through Same, Dec. 7, 1796, extra, 2.

Oct. 24
RICHMOND *to Joseph Jones, of Fredericksburg, Va.*

Note enclosing three subpoenas in Jones and Smith ejectment case in General Court. NN, James Monroe Papers.

Nov. 11
WASHINGTON *Robert Morris to Rawleigh Colston*

Urging that suit be not brought against him; relying for payment of debt on raising loan by James M. Marshall in Europe; frustrated by tight money; received letter James going to Amsterdam where capitalists propose to supply on hard terms more than sufficient to pay Fairfax; James will accept; first money receives on Morris account will apply to debt. In evidence *Francis Webb et al. v. Rawleigh Colston,* Superior Court of Chancery, Frederick County, Va., Record Book 1784–1820, 1, 45–46; 178–79.

Nov. 24
RICHMOND *to Speaker of House of Delegates of Virginia*

J.M., as one of the purchasers of the Fairfax land and as agent for others, agreeing to relinquish claim to waste and unappropriate land in Northern Neck, Virginia, on condition, according to resolution of the General Assembly, that their title to land appropriated by Fairfax be confirmed in them; petition of citizens of Hampshire, Hardy, and Shenandoah counties to settle numerous suits pending. V, Journal, H.D. (Nov. sess., 1796), 41;

Virginia Acts Nov., 1796, Chap. XIV, passed Dec. 10, 1796; Bull. Va. St. Libr., 7843; *Revised Code of the Laws of Virginia,* (Richmond, Ritchie, 1819), I, 352; *Statutes at Large of Virginia* (n.s.) (Richmond, Shepherd, 1835–36), II, 23; *Marshall's Lessee v. E. Foley,* Circuit Superior Court of Law and Chancery, Fauquier County, Land Causes III, 1833–1850, 8, 35; also filed in cases *Same v. M. Jett,* Same, 52ff; *Same v. Hannah Priest,* Same, 94ff; *Same v. N. Dearing,* Same, 145ff.

Dec. 10
RICHMOND *Agreement—Fairfax Purchase*

Act of Virginia affirming agreement of J.M., in letter of Nov. 24, 1796, to convey waste and unappropriated lands in Fairfax Estate in return for confirmation of title of remainder. V, Virginia Acts, Nov., 1796, Chap. XIV.

Dec. 12
RICHMOND *Virginia-Kentucky Boundary*

Report of commissioners appointed to adjust boundary line between Virginia and Kentucky; J.M. one of commissioners. V, Exec. Papers, Box 1796, Oct.-Dec., File Dec.

Dec. 13
RICHMOND *Militia*

Appointment by Sam Coleman for Simon Morgan, adjutant general, Virginia Militia, of J.M. on board of general officers concerning rank of Maj. Edmund Willis. V, War 10, Militia-Commissions, General Orders, 1782–1809, 67.

Dec. 13
RICHMOND *Militia*

Report of board of general officers of Virginia Militia concerning rank of Maj. Edmund Willis; J.M. a member of board. V, War 10, Militia-Commissions, General Orders, 1782–1809, 67–68.

Dec. 15
RICHMOND *to James Iredell*

Acknowledges letter of 3rd; discusses vote for presidency in North Carolina and Virginia; Marshall's argument in British debt case furnished Dallas. NcD, James Iredell Papers; VU; DLC, Beveridge Papers; Griffith J. McCree, *James Iredell, Life and Correspondence* (New York, Appleton, 1857–58), II, 482–83; Oster, *Marshall,* 44.

Dec. 30
PHILADELPHIA *from Robert Morris*

Acknowledges letter of 10th (n.f.); advises of failure of James M. Marshall to negotiate loan in Amsterdam; Hottenguer trying again; distress in providing funds for Fairfax purchase; approves of compromise with state; sending bank shares; Colston has given authority to J.M. to settle judgment of Braxton against Morris. DLC, Robert Morris Private Letter Book, Vol. 2, Pt. 1, p. 211. (Hottenguer was one of the French agents involved in the XYZ Affair.)

HOUSE OF DELEGATES OF VIRGINIA
(November Session, 1796)

Apr. 13 Election of J.M. to serve in next General Assembly of Virginia, representing City of Richmond. Va. Gaz. & G.A., Apr. 13, 1796, 3. (Richmond, A. Davis, 1796.)

Nov. 8 J.M. attended the House of Delegates as representative of the City of Richmond in the session Nov. 8 to Dec. 27. V, Journal, H.D. (Nov. sess., 1796).

Nov. 9 Appointed on the following committees of the House of Delegates: Religion, Privileges and Election, Court of Justice, Claims, and Propositions and Grievances. Same, 3–4.

Nov. 10 On committee to consider letters and papers concerning boundary line Virginia and Maryland. Same, 7.

Nov. 11 Petition of David and Moses Hunter and Philip Pendleton for public funds to employ counsel to prosecute appeal in U.S. Supreme Court of Denny Fairfax ejectment action, or that purchase price of warrants and expenses be repaid. Referred to Committee for Courts of Justice. Same, 15. Nov. 18, rejected. Same, 24.

Nov. 14 On committee to bring in bill to amend several bills governing descent. Same, 13.

Nov. 16 On committee to meet Committee of Senate to examine ballots in election of Attorney General and to report. Same, 18.

On committee to bring in bill concerning the special Court of Appeals. Same, 20. Nov. 17. Bill presented and passed, and J.M. ordered to carry to Senate. Same, 22.

Nov. 17 On committee to prepare address to President Washington declaring veneration for character and gratitude for services. Same, 22. Nov. 18, resolution presented by Lee; ordered carried to Senate. Same, 26.

Nov. 18 No vote of record on amendment to bill concerning Appomatox River providing for subscription to company by state. Amendment defeated. Same, 23–24.

Nov. 19 On committee to prepare address in accordance with resolution of both houses. Same, 28. Dec. 8, presented by Lee. Tabled. Same, 63–64. Dec. 9, substitute proposed, more lengthy and flattering, referring to his "wisdom." J.M. voted for same. Defeated, 70 to 76. Address tabled. Same, 65. Dec. 10, second substitute submitted. J.M. voted for; defeated 71 to 74. Amendment for strengthening wording; J.M. voted for; defeated 67 to 75. Address agreed to unanimously. Same, 70–71. See Beveridge, *Marshall*, II, 159–64. J.M. erroneously states the word "wisdom" was retained. Marshall, *Autobiography*, 20–21.

Nov. 26 On committee to bring in bill authorizing divorce for adultery. Same, 44.

Nov. (*n.d.*) Report of House of Delegates of Virginia Committee on Laws on edition of acts concerning land, suggesting enlargement of work based on list of laws in possession of Jefferson, signed by J.M. as committee member. Letter of Thomas Jefferson to George Wythe, Jan. 16, 1796, attached. V, Journal of Senate, Virginia, 1800–1802, (Dec. sess., 1800), 36–39; Bull. Va. St. Libr. 7989.

Nov. 28 No vote of record on resolution for convention to revise state constitution. Passed. Same, 47.

Dec. 5 No vote of record on act concerning repayment of paper money, scale of depreciation, made to Loan Office under British debts act. Passed. Same, 58.

Dec. 6 On committee to wait on James Wood to notify election chief magistracy of Commonwealth. Journal, H.D. (Nov. sess., 1796), 59.

Ordered to carry resolution to Senate concerning election of member of Council of State to replace Governor Wood. Same, 60.

On joint committee for election of members of Council of State. Same.

Dec. 7 Voted for bill to amend penal laws. Passed. Same, 61.

On committee to bring in bill concerning methods of proceedings against free person accused of crime. Same. Dec. 12, presented bill. Same, 75.

Dec. 8 On committee to bring in bill concerning collection and publication of land laws. Same, 63.

Dec. 9 Added to committee to prepare bill on county levies, poor rates, clerk's fees. Same, 65.

Dec. 13 On committee to bring in bill to lengthen terms of Fredericksburg, Dumfries, and Winchester District Courts. Same, 75.

On committee to bring in bill concerning keepers of public jails. Same, 75. Dec. 16, passed; J.M. ordered to carry to Senate. Same, 81.

Dec. 15 Voted for bill, salaries of civil officers. Passed. Same, 79–80.

Voted for bill to establish bank in Norfolk. Defeated. Same, 80.

Dec. 17 Ordered to carry bill to Senate as passed by House of Delegates giving the City of Richmond privilege of establishing vendue offices and appointing vendue masters. Same, 83.

Dec. 19 No vote of record on amendment to exempt Quakers and Mennonites from militia duty. Defeated. Same, 87.

Dec. 20 Voted against motion for bill to suspend act to amend penal laws. Passed. Same, 89. Dec. 26, voted against bill. Passed. Same, 92–93.

Dec. 22 Ordered to carry to Senate act passed concerning laws governing slaves, free Negroes, and mulattoes. Same, 92.

Dec. 24 Voted for bill to alter time of annual meeting of General Assembly. Passed. Same, 96.

Voted against rescinding standing order of House for divine service each day. Resolution defeated. Same, 97.

Dec. 26 Resolution passed naming J.M., Thomas Jefferson, Ludwell Lee, Bushrod Washington, and others on committee, any four of members authorized to correspond with committee of Maryland respecting boundary line. Same, 99; Shepherd, Stat. at Large, Virginia (a continuation of Hening, Stat.), II, 1796–1802, 69; Hening, Stat., XV, 69.

LEGAL PRACTICE

July 10 *Receipt for fee*

Receipt of £10 received from Brooking, executor of Isaac Holmes, for prosecuting appeal in District Court. Minneapolis Public Library.

Dec. 9 *Rawleigh Colston to Robert Morris*

Advising that he has written to J.M. requesting him to make personal application to representatives of Webb to authorize proceedings against Morris on debt owed estate. In evidence *Francis Webb et al. v. Rawleigh Colston,* Superior Court of Chancery, Frederick County, Va., Record Book 1784–1820, 1, 154–55.

U.S. Supreme Court

John Tyndale Ware, administrator of William Jones, s.p. Farrell and Jones, Great Britain v. Daniel Lawrence Hylton and Co., Henrico County, and Francis Eppes, Charles City County, Va., 3 Dallas 199.

Error to U.S. Circuit Court, Va.

Action of debt on sealed obligation, ruling of June 7, 1793, overruling demurrer to plea of payment to state loan office, under Virginia sequestration act of Oct. 17, 1777, of part of amount due. V.j. May 31, 1794, for plaintiff in error, plaintiff below, of damages only, $596; reversed. J.M. and Alexander Campbell for defendant in error.

Argument of J.M. before Supreme Court (3 Dallas 210–15):

Virginia at time of confiscation law an independent nation at war; burden on those who would impair sovereignty; confiscation incident to war, applies to civil war; judiciary cannot question law "unless such a jurisdiction is expressly given by the constitution." Property offspring of social state and not state of nature; debt may be restrained by civil authority. Provision for payment to Loan Office is confiscation of debt; no debt in existence at time of treaty; latter applies only to bona fide debts. If covered by treaty, recovery intended against Virginia; revival of debt against debtor who has paid a violation of public faith.

Justice Chase, in his opinion, states J.M. doubted Congress had power to annul Virginia act so as to destroy rights of individual.

Opinions of U.S. Supreme Court:

Justice Chase: Virginia had power after July 4, 1776, to confiscate debts, despite being former part of British Empire, as a right of war; law of nations no objection; Congress prior to 1781 Confederacy had no such power; Virginia act confiscated or discharged paying debtor. Congress under Confederacy had power by treaty to remove "lawful impediments"; Virginia act such; applies to both retrospective and prospective impediments; had power to override state act. Defendant should be reimbursed by state.

Justice Iredell was permitted to file his opinion delivered in court below that treaty did not revive debt, merely announced duty of state to comply.

Proceedings before U.S. Circuit Court, Va.:

Nov. 27, 1790. Petition. Action in debt by William Jones, s.p. Farrell and Jones, Great Britain, merchants, against Hylton and Co. and Eppes on sealed obligation executed July 7, 1774, at Henrico County, on demand £2,976:11:6 St. Damages $500. U.S. Circuit Court, Va., Record Book II, 201 (herein referred to as Record Book).

Dec. 27, 1790. Defendants arrested, not appearing, ordered to appear on j. against them and Edward Carrington, marshal. V, U.S. Circuit Court Case Papers (herein referred to as Case Papers).

May 24, 1791. Recognizance of special bail signed by Thomas Prosser for Hyton and Co. and Eppes.

Motion of James Innes, attorney for defendants, set aside j. in clerk's office against them and Carrington.

Pleas filed by leave:

(1) Payment.

(2) Throughout 1777, plaintiff British subject, defendants citizens of Virginia; on Apr. 27, 1780, latter paid into Virginia Loan Office on account of debt $3,111 1/9, certificate from Commissioner, filed with Governor and Council, receipt pursuant to Virginia act sequestrating British property.

(3) Plaintiff British subjects not recover under laws. Case sent back to rule docket for further proceedings.

Case Papers; U.S. Circuit Court Order Book I, 7 (herein referred to as Order Book).

June 27, 1791. Motion to plaintiff, time given to reply. Same.

July 26, 1791. Reply:

(1) Not paid.

(2) Insufficient at law, but replication that Sept. 3, 1783, Art. IV, Definitive Treaty of Peace, U.S. and Great Britain creditors on either side not to meet with legal impediment recovery in Sterling bona fide debts; under U.S. Constitution Sept. 17, 1787, treaties supreme law of land.

(3) Insufficient at law. Same.

Aug. 26, 1791. Defendants ordered to rejoin to plaintiff's replication to second plea and join in demurrer to third of j. against them third day next court. Same.

Sept. 26, 1791. Motion for same on third day next Court. Same.

Nov. 29, 1791. Consent of parties, second and third pleas, replication and demurrers withdrawn.

New pleas:

(2) Plaintiff not recover as to $3,111⅑ equal to £933:14 St. because July 4, 1776, defendants became citizens of Virginia; plaintiff at all times British; until Sept. 3, 1783, enemies at war; under Va. act of Oct. 20, 1777, British property sequestration act payment made to Virginia Loan Office; certificate signed by T. Jefferson.

(3) Defendants British subjects not recover by reason of Virginia escheat and sequestration acts of May 3, 1779, and May 1, 1782.

(4) No recovery because breach of Definitive Treaty of Peace of 1783 by not withdrawing garrisons, carrying off Negroes, maintaining forts, and aiding Indians.

(5) Declaration of Independence annulled contract.

Case Papers; Record Book, 202–206, 209–211; Order Book I, 65.

(This document in the original case papers is on the printed defense forms of J.M., filled in by him, with his name stricken and that of James Innes inserted in the line originally printed with J.M.'s name as attorney for defendant.)

Reply:

(1) Traverse.

(2) Demurrer; recovery protected by provisions of the Definitive Treaty of Peace of 1783 and U.S. Constitution making treaty law of the land.

(3), (4), and (5) Demurrers.

Case Papers; Record Book II, 206–209, 212–13.

Rejoinder: As to second plea and answer, breach of treaty by British, as above. Traverse as to third, fourth, and fifth. Case Papers; Record Book II, 207, 213–15.

May 30, 1792. Continued to November, Court not yet advised. Case Papers.

Dec. 6, 1792. Continued. Case Papers.

May 23, 1793. Death of Jones, revived in name of Ware, administrator. Case Papers; Order Book I, 141.

June 7, 1793. Court ruling, on demurrer to rejoinder of defendant to reply to second plea for defendant, on demurrers to third, fourth, and fifth for plaintiff. Case Papers; Order Book I, 161.

June 8, 1793. Jury not agree on first issue; juror withdrawn. Case Papers; Order Book I, 162.

May 30, 1794. Jury sent out of court to consult. Case Papers; Order Book I, 381; Record Book II, 215.

May 31, 1794. Verdict, not paid, damages $596 with interest 5 per cent from July 7, 1782; judgment £2,966:11 St. and costs, judgment payable by above damages and interest. Case Papers; Record Book II, 216; Order Book I, 386.

Note, accounts, and letter attached in Record Book.

All items and entries listed above appear also in Case Papers of the Supreme Court, United States, this case. DNA, Records of the Supreme Court, Case No. 4. R.G. 267.

Proceedings before U.S. Supreme Court:

June 6, 1794. Writ of error to U.S. Circuit Court, Va., issued.

U.S. Supreme Court and U.S. Circuit Court Case Papers.

Aug. 1794. Court not advised, continued to Feb. DNA, U.S. Supreme Court, Docket Book A, 7. R.G. 267.

Feb. 18, 1794. Continued. Same.

Aug., 1794. Continued. Same.

Feb. 2, 1795. Continued on request of Tilghman, attorney for Ware. U.S. Supreme Court, Minute Book A, 31.

Feb. 5, 1795. Motion of Campbell, attorney for defendant, Tilghman for plaintiff, general error to be assigned. Same, 43.

Aug. 5, 1795. Continued by consent. Same, 52.

Feb. 11–13, 23–25, 1796. Case heard. Same, 61–63, 67–68.

Mar. 7, 1796. J. for defendant on demurrer to rejoinder of defendant to plaintiff replication to second plea holding payment to Virginia Loan Office a valid defense, reversed; j. for plaintiff £2,976:11:6 St. and costs, payable by $596 and interest and such damages as shall be awarded on writ of enquiry to Circuit Court to ascertain amount really due above $596; remanded. Same, 68–69.

Final proceedings before U.S. Circuit Court, Va., on remand:

May 23, 1796. Decree of U.S. Supreme Court filed by plaintiffs; trial ordered for Nov. 22 next. U.S. Circuit Court, Order Book II, 97–98.

May 26, 1797. V. damages $5,418; j. for plaintiff £2,976:11:6 St., discharged by $596 with interest and $5,418. Same, 214–15.

John Tyndale Ware, executor, etc. v. Daniel L. Hylton, William Foushee, Francis Eppes, and Thos. Prosser.

Motion on forthcoming bond by defendants in execution against estate of Daniel Hylton. Default j. $13,382.12, payable by $6,691.05. U.S. Circuit Court, Order Book III, 69.

J.M. received a retainer fee from Hylton, probably for this case. Apr., 1793, £7. Account Book, 358.

U.S. Circuit Court, Virginia

John Bowman, s.p. Speirs, John Bowman and Co., merchants, Great Britain v. James Gatewood, administrator of Dudley Gatewood, Lynchburg, Va.

Debt, on obligation under seal, £261:2:2 Va., 1775. J.M. for defendant.

June 3, 1795. Pleas: payment. U.S. Circuit Court, Va., Order Book I, 528.

Dec. 8, 1795. Continued, deposition in Kentucky. Same, II, 62.

June 3, 1796. V.j. £261:2:2 Va., value of $870.36, payable $435.18. Same, 168.

Same, Record Book V, 67–74.

V, U.S. Circuit Court Case Papers.

Fee: Apr., 1795, £5. Account Book, 410.

John Bowman, s.p. Alexander Speirs and John Bowman Co. v. William Williams, administrator of Samuel Jordan.

Action on bond dated Feb. 15, 1773, £640:11:11. J.M. for defendant in early proceedings.

May 24, 1796. Plea payment, oyer. U.S. Circuit Court, Va., Order Book II, 100.

May 27, 1797. Plea *non est factum*, continued, agreement cause not abate by death of party. Same, 229.

May 29, 1799. Juror withdrawn, continued. Same, III, 216.

May 23, 1800. Alias *scire facias,* prior one not completed by counsel. Same, 355.

May 23, 1804. V.j. for plaintiff, £640:11:11 Va., value of $2,135.32 as in declaration. Same, IV, 423.

June 5, 1804. Set aside, rehearing, abated to all plaintiffs but Hopkirk by death. Same, 477.

Nov. 24, 1806. V.j., damages one penny; j. £640:11:11 Va., value of $2,135.32 from goods of estate, payable by £320:5:11½ Va., value of $1,067.66 with interest 5 per cent from 1772. Plaintiff agrees to credit of £44:4:4. Same, VI, 5.

V, U.S. Circuit Court Case Papers, 1806, containing autograph answer of J.M. for defendant dated Nov. 22, 1796.

Andrew Cockran, William Cunningham and Co., Great Britain v. Benjamin Rawlings, executor of James Rawlings.

Debt, on obligation under seal, £695:3:2 Va., 1773. J.M. for defendant.

Dec. 8, 1795. Plea: payment. U.S. Circuit Court, Va., Order Book II, 64.

June 4, 1796. V.j. £695:3:2, value of $2,317.19, payable by $889.38. Same, 173.

Same, Record Book V, 76–78.

V, U.S. Circuit Court Case Papers.

Fee: May, 1795, £5:4. Account Book, 414.

William Cunningham and Peter Murdock, s.p. of Cunningham and Co. v. Margaret Booker, administratrix of Richard Booker.

Debt. J.M. for defendant.

Dec. 8, 1795. Plea: payment. U.S. Circuit Court, Va., Order Book II, 64.

June 4, 1796. V.j. £1,086:19:11½ Va., valued at $3,623.90, payable by $1,811.58. Same, 176–77.

Same, Record Book Index, Civil, May T, 1796.

V, U.S. Circuit Court Case Papers.

Fee: Sept., 1795, £7. Account Book, 422.

James Dennistoun, Sr., et al., d.b.a. Donald Scot and Co., merchants, Glasgow, Great Britain v. George Guy, Caroline County, Va.

Debt, on obligation under seal, £194 Va., 1776. J.M. for defendant.

Nov. 28, 1791. Answer, payment; payment into Loan Office; Britisher disability under Virginia laws; violation of Treaty of Paris; Declaration of Independence. U.S. Circuit Court, Va., Order Book I, 61.

May 23, 1796. Confessed judgment, £194 Va., payable by $373.68. Same, Record Book IV, 127–29.

V, U.S. Circuit Court Case Papers, containing defense pleadings on J.M.'s printed forms.

Fee: Jan., 1791, "Guy, federal ct., Caroline," £2:10. Account Book, 272.

Donald Scot and Co. v. John Brown and Charles Thompson, executors of Benjamin Brown.

This initial suit wherein J.M. was not counsel was against Brown's executors.

Debt, on obligation under seal, £229:9:2 Va., 1772.

May 25, 1792. Consent j. £229:9:2 Va. payable by £92:17:7 Va. U.S. Circuit Court, Va., Order Book II, 98.

Same, Record Book I, 78–80.

Thereafter J.M. as counsel for Brown's executors sought to enjoin the judgment.

Dec. 5, 1792. Chancery. Injunction sought on grounds previous counsel had failed to present proper defense as British debt. Same, Order Book I, 138. May 24, 1796. Discontinued by agreement. Same, II, 107.

Same, Record Book Index, Chancery, May T, 1796.

V, U.S. Circuit Court Case Papers, containing autograph petition for injunction.

Joseph Larelle v. William Prentis.
Same v. William Douglass.

Case. J.M. for defendants.

Dec. 8, 1795. Security ordered for plaintiff. U.S. Circuit Court, Va., Order Book II, 66.

May 30, 1796. Dismissed for failure to give security. Same, 134.

Same, Record Book Index, Civil, May T, 1796.

V, U.S. Circuit Court Case Papers.

Fee: Jan., 1795, £30. Account Book, 404.

Elizabeth Randolph, executrix of William Randolph, Bristol, Great Britain v. Henry and Brett Randolph.

Debt, on obligation under seal, £416 St. J.M. for defendants.

Nov. 24, 1795. Undertaking for defendants. Plea: payment. U.S. Circuit Court, Va., Order Book II, 9.

June 4, 1796. V.j. £416 St., value of $1,834.78, payable by $774. 178. Same, Record Book V, 94–97.

V, U.S. Circuit Court Case Papers.

Fees: Apr. 16, 1788, £28; June, 1792, £5. Account Book, 152, 330.

Court of Appeals of Virginia

Sterling Ruffin v. Benjamin Pendleton and William Courtney, executors of Harwood, 2 Washington 184, 185, 186.

Appeal from District Court of King and Queen, Apr. 23, 1795.

Action of debt by appellant, j. for appellee affirmed. J.M. for appellant.

Action on a j. obtained on motion, against appellees as executors claiming assets received after j. and wasted; plea, estate fully administered at time of j., assets received thereafter bound by prior claims. Held, evidence admissible under plea.

Apr. 30, 1796. Heard, affirmed. Court of Appeals, Va., Order Book III, 122.

Edmund Winston, executor of Anthony Winston v. Peter Francisco, 2 Washington 187.

Appeal from District Court, Prince Edward Courthouse, Apr. 7, 1795, affirming j. County Court of Buckingham, Nov. 12, 1793, which arrested j. for appellant, affirmed. J.M. for appellee.

Action of case by appellant; £50 for riding chair and clock sold; bond given by third persons to appellee left with appellant to collect and apply; bond for gaming debt and payment refused; notice to appellee, "promising to pay"; damages £300. V.j. for appellant arrested by County Court because no assignment of bond from third persons to appellee or appellee to appellant, no evidence suit brought or that attempt to collect, declaration uncertain.

Held, no direct averment of assumpsit; "promising to pay" insufficient; gist of action not cured by verdict.

Apr. 19, 1796. Submitted. Court of Appeals, Va., Order Book III, 119.

May 3, 1796. Affirmed. Same, 123.

Sept. 6, 1796. Decree of Court of Appeals entered. District Court, Prince Edward, Records at Large 1795–1798, 177.

Fee: June, 1795, £2:8. Account Book, 416.

John Pearpoint v. Michael Henry, 2 Washington 192.

Appeal from District Court, Monongalia Courthouse, May 5, 1794; trover and conversion; j. for appellee £45, affirmed. J.M. for appellee.

Action of trover and conversion for Negro woman brought by appellee; after verdict for appellee motion in arrest of j. on grounds price or value of Negro not set forth in declaration denied.

Held, in this action need not state price or value of thing converted, action for damages; is necessary in action of detinue.

Nov. 14, 1795. Continued by appellee. Court of Appeals, Va., Order Book III, 98.

May 5, 1796. Submitted. Same, 125.

May 6, 1796. Affirmed, damages against appellant for retarding execution. Same, 126.

Sarah and Thomas Walker, executrix and executor of Thomas R. Walker v. Thomas Walker, 2 Washington 195, 196–97, 198–99.

Appeal from High Court of Chancery, affirming County Court of Princess Anne.

Decree for appellee on exceptions to guardianship account, reversed in part. J.M. for appellant.

Appellant initial guardian of appellee owed balance on guardianship account in 1776; in 1780 he paid £300 on account to successor guardian. In 1786 agreed with successor guardian that payment be scaled for depreciation to £7:10 specie and gave note for £244. Ward, on coming of age in 1787, sued for balance of £468:8:8½. Held, error to apply scale of depreciation of act of 1780 to payment; agreement voided by suit.

Apr. 26, 1796. Heard. Court of Appeals, Va., Order Book III, 116.

May 11. Reversed in part. Same, 130.

Fees: June, 1792, £5; Oct., 1795, £2:12. Account Book, 330, 346.

William Davenport v. William Mason, 2 Washington 200.

Appeal from High Court of Chancery decree granting injunction to j. County Court against appellee, reversing decree of County Court which dissolved temporary injunction and assessed costs against appellee, affirmed.

Counsel for appellant claimed decree of County Court interlocutory until final dismission; J.M. claimed that it was a final because costs were assessed; if not, there was reversible error in assessing costs.

Held, decree of High Court of Chancery affirmed, no reason given.

Apr. 27, 1795. Heard. Court of Appeals, Va., Order Book III, 118.

Apr. 28, 1795. Affirmed. Same.

Fee: Jan., 1793, £5. Account Book, 346.

Edward R. Ragsdale, executor of Edward Ragsdale v. William and John Balte, executors of William Balte, 3 Washington 201.

Writ of supersedeas to j. for defendant in error, District Court, Brunswick Courthouse, Sept. 29, 1794, £32:4:2 Va. with 5 per cent interest from June 16, 1770, one penny damages, 460 pounds gross tobacco costs, reversed and dismissed. J.M. for plaintiff in error.

Action was founded on prior j. for defendant in error in General Court, 1784, £64:8:4 for debt, one penny damages, 460 pounds gross tobacco costs, dischargeable by £32:4:2 with interest from June 16, 1770, damages and costs as above. On plea of payment j. was rendered for latter amount which with interest exceeded the sum for which j. sought in original suit.

Held, error, j. was for penalty of bond and not amount dischargeable; action dismissed at defendant in errors' costs.

Apr. 29, 1786. Heard. Court of Appeals, Va., Order Book III, 120.

Apr. 30, 1796. Reversed and dismissed at defendant in errors' costs. Same, 121.

Fee: May 18, 1790, £5. Account Book, 248.

Lewis Stephens v. Alexander White, 2 Washington 203, 207–208.

Appeal from District Court of Winchester.

Action on case by appellant, j. for appellee affirmed. J.M., Bushrod Washington, and Andrew Ronald for appellee.

Appellee, attorney at law, was sued for neglect in conducting suit on note £62 by failing to file declaration. Verdict against him, £146:18:7; motion for arrest of j. allowed on grounds no consideration or damages alleged. Held, grounds for motion erroneous, but j. affirmed evidence showing appellee not employed until 1784; suit filed in 1779; not liable for error of prior counsel.

Nov. 17, 1795. Appeal docketed. Court of Appeals, Va., Order Book III, 100.

Apr. 27, 1796. Continued. Same, 117.

Oct. 15. Submitted. Same, 135.

Oct. 19. J. affirmed. Same, 136.

Neil Quesnel v. Thomas Woodlief, Edmund Ruffin, Jr., and Edward Harrison, 6 Call 218.

Appeal from decree High Court of Chancery, Oct. 7, 1794, dismissing bill of appellant; reversed and decree for appellant. J.M. for appellees in early proceedings; Call for same herein.

Action for injunction and general relief of contract and purchase money obligations whereby appellant agreed to purchase at fixed price tract of land he and seller, appellee, believed to contain 800 acres, but which contained

608 acres, alleging fraud and collusion. Deed of trust stated 800 acres; deed drawn by seller stated "800 acres, more or less."

Held, error to dismiss; no fraud or collusion but mutual mistake; "more or less" limited to small variance; purchase price proportionately reduced and indemnity provided against suit pending by third party; j. accordingly.

Nov. 7–8, 1796. Heard. Court of Appeals, Va., Order Book II, 146, 147.

Nov. 19, 1796. Reversed, j. as noted. Same, 152–53.

Fee: Apr., 1790, £3:10. Account Book, 240.

George Pickett v. Richard Morris, 2 Washington 255, 257–59, 264–66, 270–71.

Appeal from High Court of Chancery, Mar. 17, 1795.

Injunction of j. against appellee, affirmed. J.M. for appellant. Appellant, assignee of bond, obtained j. against appellee in County Court of Henrico, Court refusing to allow discount of bond of equal amount held by appellee against appellant's assignee; no appeal. Injunction, allowing discount.

Oct. 31–Nov. 1, 1796. Heard. Court of Appeals, Va., Order Book III, 143, 144.

Nov. 11. Affirmed. Same, 149.

Samuel Young v. Sir Peyton Skipwith, 2 Washington 300.

Appeal from decree High Court of Chancery; appellee plaintiff seeking specific execution of contract defendant to purchase land on joint account; relief sought partition as agreed and conveyance. Decree for appellee, surveyor of county to run division line and report quantity. J.M. for appellant.

Held, "after a very lengthy argument," appeal dismissed as premature before final decree, remanded.

Oct. 26, 27, 1796. Heard. Court of Appeals, Va., Order Book III, 140–41.

Nov. 5, 1796. Remanded. Same, 146.

Fees: Dec., 1791, £7; June, 1794, £5. Account Book, 308, 390.

Note: Companion case of *Samuel Young v. Sir Peyton Skipwith, Sherwood, Daniel, and John Hicks, executors of Amos Hicks,* continued through 1799. Court of Appeals, Va., Order Book III, 146, 246, 279, 334.)

Mordecai Booth, executor of William Booth v. William Armstrong, 2 Washington 301.

Appeal from j. of District Court, Winchester, Apr. 23, 1795, £219:3 Va., payable by £109:2:7½ from estate, reversed. J.M. for appellee.

Action debt on a bond given by testator; plea fully administered except

£133:3:3 insufficient to satisfy outstanding judgments. Verdict for plaintiff failed to find assets not administered sufficient to satisfy plaintiff's demand, or value of assets.

Held, verdict insufficient, j. reversed, remanded.

Apr. 27, 1796. Submitted. Court of Appeals, Va., Order Book III, 118.

May 6, 1796. Continued. Same, 129.

Oct. 26, 1796. Resubmitted. Same, 140.

Oct. 31, 1796. J. reversed. Same, 143.

John Dalby v. Thomas Price.

Appeal from decree of High Court of Chancery, June 2, 1795, dismissing bill. J.M. for appellant.

Apr. 30, 1796. Cause heard. Court of Appeals, Va., Order Book III, 121.

May 4, 1796. Reversed on grounds six months not allowed before trial after order for taking depositions and before taken. Same, 125.

Fee: Nov., 1795, £2:14. Account Book, 424.

Richard Harrison v. William Andrews.

Appeal from High Court of Chancery, May 28, 1795. J.M. for defendant.

May 4, 1796. Heard, affirmed. Court of Appeals, Va., Order Book III, 125.

Fee: Mar., 1793, £5. Account Book, 350.

Thomas and Wiley Roy v. William Allason.

Appeal from j. against appellants, District Court, Dumfries, May 16, 1795, £513:18:5½ Va., payable by £256:19:23. J.M. for appellee.

Oct. 29, 1796. Affirmed. Court of Appeals, Va., Order Book III, 142.

Fee: Feb., 1790, £5. Account Book, 232.

Simon Triplett v. Cumberland Wilson and Alexander Campbell.

Appeal from High Court of Chancery, Sept. 3, 1793. J.M. for appellant.

Apr. 25 and Oct. 13, 1795. Continued. Court of Appeals, Va., Order Book III, 56, 59.

Oct. 13, 1796. Three judges disqualify selves. Same, 134.

Nov. 19. Affirmed, in conformity with a decision of the U.S. Supreme Court. (*Ware v. Hylton*, herein 1796, U.S. Supreme Court.) Same, 154.

Fee: Apr., 1795, £6. Account Book, 410. Also May, 1790, "Triplett," £5:12. Account Book, 244.

(This was a bill to foreclose mortgage on land and mill in Loudon County executed by Triplett to secure a debt due Dunlop & Son & Co.,

British merchants; Wilson agent for latter. Triplett set up defense payment into Virginia Treasury under British debts act. Accounts were referred to commissioners, interlocutory decree for sale from which above appeal taken. A bill of review was sought later on grounds Triplett's counsel (J.M.) by mistake failed to claim discount of interest during the war. Denied on grounds not new matter, known to party at the time. *Triplett v. Wilson, et al.*, 6 Call 47 [1806].)

Thomas Woodridge v. Joseph Woodridge.

Appeal from High Court of Chancery, Sept. 29, 1794.

Apr. 29, 1796. Heard. Court of Appeals, Va., Order Book III, 120.

Apr. 30. Affirmed. Same, 121.

Fee: Oct., 1794, £15. Account Book, 398.

High Court of Chancery

William Call v. John Marshall, Elizabeth Moody, widow and relict of Henry Moody, et al.

Action in High Court of Chancery.

Default decree against Francis and Henry Moody, report of master of payments made under deed of trust by Henry Moody; publication required. Va. Gaz. and G.A., Jan. 20, Mar. 16, Apr. 15, Apr. 20, 1796.

Note: J.M. probably acting as attorney in matter.

District Court, Accomack and Northampton

James Henry v. John Gootie.

Debt. J.M. for defendant.

Oct. 19, 1796. V.j. £381:3:6. District Court, Accomack and Northampton, Order Book 1789–1797, 471.

Fees: Sept., 1794, £6. Account Book, 398. Also Nov., 1789, £—— "Chr.," Same, 222.

District (Superior) Court, Franklin

John Markham v. Stephen Coleman, in case; and *Same v. Stephen and Daniel Coleman*, in trespass.

J.M. for Colemans.

Sept. 18, 1794. Continued. District Court, Franklin, Order Book II, 1794–1796, 65.

Apr. 18, 1795. Trespass, continued. Same, 109.

Case, attachment against witness for non-appearance. Same, 110.

Sept. 16, 1795. Trespass, continued. Same, 144.

Case. Continued. Fine of $16.00 against Joseph Akin; attachment. Same, 146, 148.

Apr. 16, 1796. (Superior Court) Case. Nonsuit for failure to prosecute. Same, 193.

Apr. 19, 1796. Trespass, continued. Same, 203.

Apr. 20, 1796. V.j. for defendant. Same, 214.

Fee: May, 1793, £6:2:6. Account Book, 360.

District Court, Fredericksburg

Richard Cave et al. v. Belfield Cave et al.

Upon an issue from High Court of Chancery. J.M. for ———.

May 5, 1796. Dismissed, agreed between parties. District Court, Fredericksburg, Law Orders B, 1794–1798, 186.

Fee: Feb., 1793, £5. Account Book, 348.

William Cunningham, assignee v. William Walker.

Debt, £250. J.M. for defendant.

Apr. 29, 1796. Confessed j. £250, payable by £17:4:8 with interest 5 per cent from Mar. 8, 1775; execution stayed to Oct., 1797, eight years interest deducted. District Court, Fredericksburg, Law Orders B, 1794–1798, 148.

Fee: July, 1790, £15. Account Book, 254.

James Dowdall and Thomas Follis v. James Crap, Jr.

Caveat. J.M. for plaintiff.

Oct. 5, 1796. Dismissed, agreed between parties. District Court, Fredericksburg, Law Orders B, 1794–1798, 245.

An earlier trespass case of *Dowdall v. Crap* resulted in v.j. for defendant. Same. 63. Two actions against James Crap, Sr., abated by death of defendant, May 7, 1794, an action of case. Same, 42; Oct. 8, 1794, action of trespass. Same, 96.

Fee: Mar., 1795, £3:16. Account Book, 406.

District Court, Prince Edward

William Chamberlayne, assignee v. Joel W. Jones and John Jones, Jr.

Debt, on obligation sealed, Feb. 14, 1791, £100, on demand, in successive assignments to plaintiff, notice. Buckingham County. J.M. for defendants.

Apr., 1795. Alias capias and abatement.

Sept., 1795. Final cost price and imparlance.

Oct., 1795. Payment.

Sept. 18, 1796. V.j. for plaintiff, £100, payable by £50. District Court, Prince Edward, Records at Large 1795–1798, 240.

Fee: Sept., 1793, £5. Account Book, 370.

1797

DOCUMENTS

Jan. 14
RICHMOND *Virginia-Maryland Boundary*

Letter from James Wood, Governor of Virginia, enclosing resolutions of General Assembly of Virginia and legislature of Maryland respecting boundary line. Same sent to J.M., Thomas Jefferson, Edmund Randolph, Robert Brooke, Ludwell Lee, Bushrod Washington, John Taylor. V, Exec. Letter Books 1794–1800, 190.

Jan. 23
PHILADELPHIA *from Robert Morris*

Reply to letter of J.M. of Jan. 10 (n.f.). Unable to send bank shares as agreed in last letter; purchasing agreement broken, and lacks funds to purchase. J.M.'s brother unsuccessful in obtaining loan in Holland; at London for loan. Morris unsuccessfully seeking loan from Alexander Baring of the House of Hope and Co.; will introduce Baring to J.M. DLC, Robert Morris Letter Book, Vol. II, Pt. 1, p. 234.

Jan. 24
RICHMOND *to James Wood, Governor of Virginia*

Acknowledging letter of 14th with enclosures of resolutions of General Assembly of Virginia and of the State of Maryland respecting boundary line. PPHi; *Pa. Mag. of Hist. and Biog.*, Vol. LIV (July, 1930), following 196.

Feb. 1
LONDON, GREAT BRITAIN *South Branch Manor—Deed*

Denny Martin Fairfax, Leeds Castle, Great Britain, to J.M., the Manor of South Branch, Northern Neck, Hampshire and Hardy counties, Virginia, premises under will of Thomas Lord Fairfax; 54,596 acres, survey of John Genn, Mar. 31, 1747; and 1,550 acres, survey of Apr. 7, 1748.

£6,000 British; subject to three annuities £100 each per year; excepting grants and leases prior to May 17, 1793. Executed in London by James M. Marshall, attorney in fact for J.M., Feb. 1, 1794. Resealed and delivered by Fairfax and James M. Marshall, attorney for J.M., Feb. 1, 1797. Receipt of payment of £6,000 Feb. 1, 1797. Recorded in Superior Court for District of Hardy, Hampshire and Pendleton counties, Va., Sept. 5, 1797. Hardy County (W. Va.) Records, Deed Book A, 12–17; Tyler's, V, 240–42.

Feb. 1
RICHMOND *Attorney for Virginia*

Duplicate letters from James Wood, Governor of Virginia, to J.M. and Charles Lee, addressed to Philadelphia, appointing them defense attorneys in suit of Indiana Company against the Commonwealth of Virginia. V, Exec. Letter Books 1794–1800, 194.

Feb. 10 *to John Alexander*

Randolph not in Richmond; will speak about amendment to "your" bill. Judges inclined to continue injunction to final hearing. Recalls conversation concerning Belfield suit; latter offering high fee; wishes to know if promised Alexander to act as his attorney. DLC, John Marshall Papers, Ac. 9475.

Feb. 10 *Robert Morris to James M. Marshall—*
PHILADELPHIA *Addressed to London*

J.M. in city, principal business to provide means of paying Lord Fairfax for land purchase; James' letter Nov. 15 blasting hope of loan. Authorizes to sell Gennessee land. DLC, Robert Morris Private Letter Book, II, 265.

Note: James M. Marshall went to Europe to raise money on behalf of Morris, was authorized to make payment from loan to Fairfax on purchase of Virginia land by himself, J.M., and Rawleigh Colston. DLC, Robert Morris to James M. Marshall, Philadelphia, Dec. 3, 1796. Same, 169. James Marshall's account book entry Jan. 25, 1797, shows payment to Denny Fairfax of £7,700, credited to Morris account with him, raised by loan. Beveridge, *Marshall*, II, at 210 (facsimile). Morris expressed pleasure; amount small but first step in securing bargain; hopes he obtains more to complete business. Robert Morris to James M. Marshall, Philadelphia, Apr. 27, 1797. DLC, Robert Morris Private Letter Book, III, 307.

(See also herein, Jan. 8, 1796; Robert Morris to Rawleigh Colston, Nov. 11, 1796, July 10, 1797, Oct. 14, 1797.)

Apr. 20
RICHMOND *to Charles Lee*

Enclosing and criticizing clipping from Pleasant's paper on partisan speech of Pendleton. Virginia strongly pro-French, and public believes government partial to Britain. Elections to legislature going entirely against Federalists; discusses various election races. Brother urges payment on second contract with Fairfax to obtain title; requests remittance by Lee. Authorized to offer to take Lee's interest for $4,000, but prefers he remain partner. MHi, Adams Papers, John Adams Letter Rec'd., L, 208.

Apr. 28, n.p. *Thomas Marshall to President John Adams*

Resignation of Thomas Marshall of commission as supervisor of revenue for the District of Ohio. DNA, General Records, Dept. of State, Misc. Letters 1789–1795. R.G. 59.

May 31
PHILADELPHIA *President John Adams to the Senate*

Message nominating J.M., C. C. Pinckney, and Francis Dana envoys to France. James D. Richardson, *A Compilation of the Messages and Papers of the Presidents, 1789–1897* (Washington, D.C., by Authority of Congress, 1896–1899), I, 245; MHi, Adams Papers, John Adams, Letters Rec'd., VIII, 546, 547–48; Journal, U.S. Senate, I, 241–42, DNA, Legislative Dept., R.G. 46; ASP, (For. Rel.), II, 19.

J.M. states that he accepted the appointment because acquainted with affairs with France, was confident of himself, éclat would come from success, and above all that the mission was temporary and would not injure his practice; that continuance in practice was necessary because of his pending purchase with others of the Fairfax properties. Marshall, *Autobiography*, 21–22.

June 5
PHILADELPHIA *Nomination Envoy to France*

Nomination of envoys to France affirmed. DNA, Records of U.S. Senate. Journal, U.S. Senate, I, 244. R.G. 46.

June 5
PHILADELPHIA *Commission Envoy to France*

Commission to J.M., C. C. Pinckney, and Francis Dana as joint envoys extraordinary and ministers plenipotentiary to France. July 22, Elbridge Gerry in place of Dana, who refused. DNA, General Records Dept. of State, Credences, I, 81. R.G. 59.

June 6
PHILADELPHIA *from Timothy Pickering, Secretary of State*

To J.M. and Francis Dana notifying of appointment as joint envoys to France. DNA, General Records Dept. of State, Domestic Letters, X, 54. R.G. 59; MHi, Pickering MSS, VI, 330.

June 20
PHILADELPHIA *Nomination of Gerry*

Message of President Adams to Senate nominating Elbridge Gerry in place of Francis Dana, who refused, because of health, to become envoy to France with J.M. and C. C. Pinckney. DNA, Legislative Dept., Office of Senate Financial Clerk. R.G. 46.

June 22
PHILADELPHIA *by President John Adams*

Authorization of full power to J.M., Charles Cotesworth Pinckney, and Elbridge Gerry to act as envoys extraordinary and ministers plenipotentiary to French Republic, negotiate on all matters and differences including general commerce and claims, conclude and sign a treaty or convention and transmit to President. ASP (For. Rel.), II, 153. French Spoliation, 465–66.

June 24
ALEXANDRIA *to Polly Marshall*

On way to Philadelphia, spent day at Mount Vernon. Concerned about Polly's ease of mind; sending away Dick; stopping at Uncle Keith's; instructs sending letters left behind. VW; Mason, *Polly*, 90–91.

June 24 *to Gen. Young*

Referred to in letter J.M. to Polly Marshall, June 24, 1797 (n.f.).

June 24 *to James M. Marshall*

Referred to in letter J.M. to Polly Marshall, June 24, 1797 (n.f.)

June 31
PHILADELPHIA *to C. Rodney, Wilmington, Del.*

Acknowledges letter of 28th; thanks for advising him that letters which slipped from J.M.'s pocket in possession of McCullough of New Castle. PP. Rare Book Dept.

July 2
PHILADELPHIA *to Polly Marshall*

Arrival at Philadelphia; dined with President, a plain, sensible man; also with Morris—lives elegantly, gloom hangs over him, hopes to retrieve his affairs; spent evening at Vauxhall; rode out to visit Mrs. Hayward; amusement to prevent brooding absence from beloved wife; urges her to write. VW; DLC, Marshall Papers, Ac. 2535; MHi; WMQ (ser. 2), Vol. III (Apr., 1923), 73–74; Mason, *Polly*, 92.

July 5
PHILADELPHIA *to Polly Marshall*

Complains of not receiving letter; departure plans for next week; celebration of July 4 at dinner of Congressmen; pleased with attention received. VW; DLC, Marshall Papers, Ac. 2535; MHi; WMQ (sec. 2), Vol. III (Apr., 1923), 74–75; Mason, *Polly*, 95–96.

July 6
PHILADELPHIA *from Timothy Pickering*

Advises J.M. and Francis Dana of appointment and confirmation as envoys to France. MHi, Pickering MSS, VI, 330; DNA, General Records Dept. of State, Domestic Letters, X, 54. R.G. 59.

July 7
PHILADELPHIA *to George Washington*

Acknowledges letter with enclosure for delivery in France (J.M. delivered letters dated June 24 to Charles Cotesworth Pinckney and Gen. Dumas. Sparks, *Washington,* XI, 206–209) ; expects to sail next week for Amsterdam and proceed to Paris. Blount matter discussed. DLC, Papers of George Washington, Vol. 285, p. 34; Oster, *Marshall,* 176–77.

July 10
PHILADELPHIA *to Secretary of State* [*Timothy Pickering*]

Requests $3,500 paid to him at Philadelphia; residue of expenses at his command in Amsterdam or Paris. MHi, Pickering MSS, XXI, 177; MHi Proc., XXI, 177.

July 10
PHILADELPHIA *to Polly Marshall*

Acknowledges letter of June 30; thankful health better; hopes to hear her mind tranquil; suspected melancholy; Mrs. Gamble wishes to help. Delay in departure; return depends on events; missing by absence. VW; Mason, *Polly*, 96–97.

July 10
PHILADELPHIA *Robert Morris to Rawleigh Colston*

Concerning payment of judgment against Morris by Colston as administrator of Thomas Webb no harm in delaying answer to Colston; J.M. in Philadelphia; will embark during week for Amsterdam; supposes will be joined by brother James, who is probably in Germany where invited by prospect of loan hoped for. In evidence *Francis Webb et al. v. Rawleigh Colston.* Superior Court of Chancery, Frederick County, Va., Record Book 1784–1820, 1, 53.

July 11
PHILADELPHIA *to Polly Marshall*

Describes attendance at theatre; visited Mrs. Hayward; impatient to depart; longing for home. VW; DLC, John Marshall Papers, Ac. 2535; WMQ (ser. 2), Vol. III (Apr., 1923), 75–76; Mason, *Polly*, 98.

July 12
PHILADELPHIA *to Polly Marshall*

Instructing to file parcel of deeds in desk; surfeited with Philadelphia; anxious to leave. VW; Mason, *Polly*, 99.

July 13
PHILADELPHIA *by President John Adams*

Letters of credence to the executive directory of the French Republic, reciting nomination and appointment of J.M., Charles Cotesworth Pinckney, and Elbridge Gerry as envoys extraordinary and ministers plenipotentiary to terminate differences and restore harmony, good understanding, and commercial and friendly intercourse. ASP (For. Rel.,) II, 153; ASP, III, 473–75.

July 14
PHILADELPHIA *to Polly Marshall*

The *Grace* sailing for Amsterdam next day; J.M. boarding at New Castle; hopes to return by Christmas. Dined at Bingham's home; pleased with Morris family. VW; Mason, *Polly*, 100–101.

July 15
PHILADELPHIA *by Timothy Pickering, Secretary of State*

Instructions to J.M. and other envoys to France; settle claims, alter treaty as to enemy goods and seizure of American goods, arming of privateers, bringing in prizes to American ports; five principles outlined. ASP (For. Rel.), II, 153–57; ASP, III, 457–73.

J.M. is credited with the writing of these instructions in Graham H. Stuart, *The Department of State, a History of Its Origin, Procedure, and Personnel* (New York, Macmillan, 1949), 32, citing Henry J. Ford as source of opinion.

J.M. says that he was instructed to come to Philadelphia to receive the communications of the government prior to departure. Marshall, *Autobiography*, 21.

For J.M.'s description of the mission to France and the XYZ Affair, see his *Life of Washington*, V, 337–44.

July 15
PHILADELPHIA *Passport*

Issued by Timothy Pickering, Secretary of State, for passage to France. DNA, General Records Dept of State, Domestic Letters, 1784–1906, X, 79, R.G. 59.

July 15
PHILADELPHIA *from Timothy Pickering, Secretary of State*

Directed jointly to J.M., Pinckney, and Gerry as envoys extraordinary, etc., to the French Republic, concerning claims of Messrs. Ketland's [*sic*] of Philadelphia for property confiscated by French at Leghorn, June, 1796; with enclosures of list of claims of American citizens; also letters of Fellichi. (Enclosures not found.) Morristown Nat'l. Hist. Park.

July 20
BAY OF DELAWARE *to Polly Marshall*

Describes departure, accommodations on shipboard; urges to write. DLC, Marshall Papers, Ac. 2535; MHi; WMQ (ser. 2), Vol. III (Apr., 1923), 76–77; Mason, *Polly*, 102–103.

July
PHILADELPHIA *to Thomas Marshall, Son of J.M.*

Mentioned in letter to J.M. to Polly Marshall, July 20, 1797 (n.f.).

Aug. 3 and 29
HOLLAND *to Polly Marshall*

Written in part on arrival at mouth of Texel River and part on arrival at Holland; long but comfortable voyage; expresses longing for home. VW; Mason, *Polly*, 107–108.

Aug. 30
LONDON, ENGLAND *Fairfax Purchase—Deed*

Deed by Denny Martin Fairfax, Leeds Castle, Great Britain, to James M. Marshall, Richmond, conveying grantor's lands in the Northern Neck, excepting the Manor of Leeds, quitrents reserved in grants in Northern Neck due or to be due, and excluding 100 acres known as Barry's Ferry; £2,625 Sterling. Recorded at General Court, Richmond, June 11, 1798. *Marshall v. Conrad,* 5 Call 364, 370 (Court of Appeals of Va.); VMH, Vol. XXXIV (1926), 19, at 53. Original deed offered in evidence in *United States v. M. F. Morris et al.* (see herein, 1899). Also entered in evidence in *Philip Martin v. Moffat et al.*, U.S. Circuit Court, Va. V, U.S. Circuit Court Case Papers, 1824.

Note: The following documents were filed as evidence of title to land of the Fairfax Purchase by James M. Marshall in a series of land cases filed in Circuit Superior Court, Fauquier County, Va., in 1833. They are in large part the same documents on which J.M.'s title rested.

1. Act of General Assembly of Virginia of 1736, entitled "An act for confirming and better securing the titles and lands in the Northern Neck held under the Right Honorable Thomas Lord Fairfax, Baron of Camaron in that part of Great Britain called Scotland."

2. Act of General Assembly of Virginia of 1748, entitled "An act for confirming the grants made by His Majesty within the bounds of the Northern Neck as they are now established."

3. Deed from Thomas Lord Fairfax to Thomas Bryan Martin of Frederick County, Aug. 21, 1767, land known as Manor of Leeds, counties of Fauquier, Loudon, and Frederick, Virginia, 122,852 acres, reserving 2,952 acres on Goose Creek.

4. Deeds from Thomas Bryan Martin to Thomas Lord Fairfax, Sept. 4 and 5, 1768, of the same. Recorded in Frederick County, Va., Apr. 4, 1769.

5. Will of Thomas Lord Fairfax devising his one-sixth of lands in Virginia of Culpeper Estate known as the Northern Neck of Virginia to his nephew Denny Martin, if alive; otherwise to Denny's brother, Thomas Bryan Martin, if alive; otherwise to another brother, Philip Martin, subject to annuities to nieces, Nov. 8, 1777. Codicil of Nov. 27, 1779. Recorded in Frederick County, Va., Mar. 5, 1782.

6. Act of General Assembly of Virginia of 1796, entitled "An act concerning certain land lying in the Northern Neck."

7. Deed of Denny Martin Fairfax to James M. Marshall, land in Northern Neck excepting Manor of Leeds, Aug. 30, 1797 (see above).

8. Deed James M. Marshall to Commonwealth of Virginia, Oct. 10, 1798 (see herein).

9. Treaty of Amity and Commerce between the United States and Great Britain, 1794.

10. Will of Denny Martin Fairfax, May 9, 1798, devising all lands in Virginia to youngest brother, Philip Martin. Attested by one of two subscribing witnesses. Recorded, General Court, Richmond, June 12, 1802.

11. Deed from Gen. Philip Martin to J.M., James M. Marshall, and Rawleigh Colston, Oct. 18, 1806 (see herein).

12. Deed. Rawleigh Colston to J.M. and James M. Marshall, (reciprocal deed partitioning land) Oct. 5, 1808.

13. Deed. J.M. to James M. Marshall, division of Leeds Manor, dated Aug. 22, 1816 (see herein).

Marshall's Lessee v. E. Foley, Circuit Superior Court, Fauquier County, Va., Land Causes 1833–1850, III, 8; *Same v. M. Jett*, Same, 52; *Same v. S. Priest*, Same, 94; *Same v. N. Dearing*, Same, 145; *Same v. Brown*, Same, 269; *Same v. Weaver*, Same, II, 700.

Aug. *Law Suit*

J.M. v. Enoch Ashby and Charles C. Chunn, action on debt on replevin bond given for property seized in distress for rent and restored; j. £24 Va., payable by £12. County Court, Fauquier, Minute Book 1795–1797, 143. Case papers in office of Clerk of Courts, Fauquier County, Warrenton, Va.

Sept. 1

THE HAGUE *W. Vans Murray to John Luzac, Leydon*

Advising of Marshall and Pinckney arrival; invites to dinner with them. Morristown Nat'l. Hist. Park.

Sept 2

AMSTERDAM *to Col. Carrington*

Describes voyage and arrival. Discusses British and Dutch naval situation, attitude of Dutch to French, government disorders in France, Talleyrand; hopes for negotiation. Morristown Nat'l. Hist. Park.

Sept. 2
AMSTERDAM *to Timothy Pickering, Secretary of State*

Arrived Aug. 29 at mouth of Texel; British fleet blockade; vessel *Grace* boarded but discharged when learned of U.S. Minister; Dutch fleet. Aug. 30 at Amsterdam, Pinckney at Hague. Discusses French political situation, Directorate for war and Council of 500 approves; peace between Emperor and France. Negotiations for peace between France and Britain. Orders of France for immediate passports to American envoys. DNA, General Records Dept. of State, Diplomatic Despatches, France, 1789–1906, VI, R.G. 59. WMQ (ser. 3) Vol. XII (Oct., 1955), 632–34.

Sept. 9
THE HAGUE *to Timothy Pickering, Secretary of State*

Arrived on 3rd; saw Pinckney; pleased with his information on France; saw despatches of Pinckney and Murray. Directory's arrest of two members of Directory and many of Council of 500; army controlled by Directory; justice on American affairs hoped for from ousted majority; possible military dictatorship. Letter from Gerry; awaiting his arrival. DNA, General Records Dept. of State, Diplomatic Despatches, France, VI, R.G. 59. WMQ, (ser. 3), Vol. 12 (Oct., 1955), 634–37.

See Marshall, *Autobiography*, 22–23. J.M. says the revolution in France blasted hope of accommodation between the United States and France.

Sept. 9
THE HAGUE *to Polly Marshall*

Writes of arrival; met with Pinckney; waiting for Gerry; describes The Hague, Pinckney's daughter; arrests made by Directory in France; discusses return. DLC, John Marshall Papers, Ac. 2535; MHi; WMQ, (ser. 2), Vol. III (Apr., 1923), 78–79; Mason, *Polly*, 108–10.

Sept. 13 *Cover to Pickering by Capt. Izzard*

Note: Pinckney and J.M. left Rotterdam for Paris, Sept. 19; Gerry arrived same day, proceeded to France several days later. DNA, General Records Department of State, Diplomatic Despatches, France, VI. R.G. 59. VW.

Sept. 15
THE HAGUE *to Gen. [George] Washington*

Flattering evidence of Washington's approval and conviction of his interest reason for communication from Europe. British control of seas discussed; arrival in Holland; domination of country by France; new constitution rejected, political conditions; French *coup d'état* 18 Fructidor analyzed. Marshall and Pinckney awaiting Gerry. DLC, Papers of George Washington, Vol. 285, 115; AHR 2 (Jan., 1897), 294–300; Oster, *Marshall*, 154–62; DLC, Beveridge Coll.; Same, Ac. 4314A; MH, Sparks MSS, LXVI.

Sept. 15, 17
THE HAGUE *to Timothy Pickering, Secretary of State*

Describes revolution in France; blow to constitution and freedom; doubts restoration of royalty. Power in hands of those hostile to America. Gerry not arrived, leaving for Paris. Addendum of Sept. 17 concerning French political developments. DNA, General Records Diplomatic Despatches, France, VI, R.G. 59; VW; MH, Sparks MSS, XLVI, 320–33; WMQ (ser. 3), Vol. XII (Oct., 1955), 637–39.

Sept. 19
ROTTERDAM *Charles C. Pinckney to James McHenry*

Traveling with J.M. to Paris; awaiting Gerry. Doubt of successful negotiations because French rely on internal division in America and attachment of large party to them. Morristown Nat'l Hist. Park; B. C. Steiner, *Life and Correspondence of James McHenry* (Cleveland, Burrows, 1907), 274–75.

Sept. 22
ANTWERP *to Charles Lee*

Proceeding to Paris; arrival of Gerry. Discusses *coup d'état* in France and erroneous intelligence concerning it; Moreau, Pickegru and the deportees; recision of motion of Pastoret. Little hope that negotiations with France will terminate as they ought to. Political conditions in France; celebration of anniversary of Republic of Antwerp; French negotiations with Emperor and Britain; prospects of war, Napoleon; departure of Lord Malmsbury, demands on Great Britain. NN, Emmett Coll., No. 2137.

Sept. 25 *Law Suit*

J.M. v. John Rust, debt on replevin bond for goods taken in distress for rent. Default j. £40, payable by £20 and interest from 1795. County Court, Fauquier, Minute Book 1797–1798, 154–55.

Sept. 27, 1797 to Apr. 11, 1798
PARIS *Gen. Marshall's Journal in Paris*

This Journal contains a detailed day-by-day account by J.M. of negotiations carried on by the mission to France. V; DLC; MHi.

Sept. 30
TRENTON *from Timothy Pickering*

Discusses question of seizure by French of American goods in British bottoms; Jefferson; Genet; yellow fever; removal of capital. MHi, Pickering MSS, VII, 7, 244.

Oct. 2
PARIS *to Timothy Pickering*

Advises of arrival Sept. 27; notified minister of foreign affairs unofficially; awaiting arrival of Gerry. Signed by J.M. and Pinckney. DNA, General Records Dept. of State, Diplomatic Despatches, France, 6, R.G. 59; Marshall, *Autobiography*, 23.

Oct. 6
PARIS *to Citizen Minister Talleyrand*

By J.M., Pinckney, and Gerry requesting appointment. ASP (For. Rel.) II, 157–58.

Oct. 12
PARIS *to Charles Lee, U.S. Attorney General, Philadelphia*

Arrival of Gerry; meeting with Talleyrand, negotiations delayed; continued capture and condemnation of American vessels. Letter from Paine enclosed; plan to enforce principle of free bottoms make free goods; letter from envoys acknowledging (n.f.). Privateering from French ports; Americans involved. Italian and Rhine campaigns and French finances discussed. Secret demands for money payment to Talleyrand and Directorate. Expects envoys will receive "marching papers." Includes addendum of Oct. 25 and 27. Unsigned; written by J.M. DNA, General Records Dept. of State, Diplomatic Despatches, France, VI. R.G. 59; French Spoliation, 466 (excerpt).

Oct. 14 *Robert Morris to Rawleigh Colston*

Received letter from James M. Marshall, in Amsterdam; no loan; prospects bad, better if peace. Morris hopes when J.M. joins James able to obtain loan. In evidence *Francis Webb et al. v. Rawleigh Colston*,

Superior Court of Chancery, Frederick County, Va., Record Book 1784–1820, 54–55.

Oct. 22
PARIS *to Timothy Pickering, Secretary of State*

Dispatch No. 1 of J.M., Pinckney, and Gerry; lack of progress of negotiations; visits of X and Y; criticism of President's speech. Postcript of Oct. 27 and enclosures. ASP (For. Rel.) II, 157–61; ASP, III, 475–90; CtY; DNA, General Records Dept. of State, Diplomatic Despatches, France, VI. R.G. 59; French Spoliation, 466–67 (excerpt).

Oct. 24
PARIS *to George Washington*

Discusses agriculture and manufacturing in France, *coup d'état* 18 Fructidor, nationalization of land in France, expropriation of property of emigrants. Hostility of France to United States; doubts reception; captures of American vessels. Discusses French negotiations with Emperor. Addendum of Oct. 27 announces French treaty with Emperor. DLC, Papers of George Washington, Vol. 286, 3–4; MH, Sparks MSS, LXVI 344–49; DLC, Beveridge Coll.; DLC, Ac. 4314A; AHR, 2 (Jan., 1897), 301–303; Oster, *Marshall*, 163–66.

Nov. 3
PARIS *to Charles Lee*

Discusses unsatisfactory status of mission; delay because of French negotiation with Britain; demand for bribe and loan; delay in returning; arrest of American creditor of French government. (Document largely in code, translated.) DLC, Var. Ac. 1752; Beveridge, *Marshall*, II, 283 (excerpt).

Nov. 8
PARIS *to Timothy Pickering, Secretary of State*

Dispatch No. 2 of J.M., Pinckney, and Gerry; thirty-six pages of cipher and eight pages of ciphered exhibits outlining details of negotiations, visits of Hottinguer and Bellami, demand for money payment and loan; refusal of same. Parts dated Oct. 27, 29, 30, and Nov. 1 and 3 with two exhibits dated Nov. 8. DNA, General Records Dept. of State, Diplomatic Despatches, France, VI, R.G. 59; ASP (For. Rel.), II, 161–65. ASP, III, 490–99, IV, 1–14; CtY; French Spoliation, 407–68 (Exhibits A & B only).

Nov. 11
PARIS
to Minister of Foreign Affairs of French Republic [Talleyrand]

Letter by J.M., Pinckney, and Gerry urging negotiations. Enclosed in Dispatch No. 3. DNA, General Records Dept. of State, Diplomatic Despatches, France VI, R.G. 59; ASP (For. Rel.), II, 166; ASP, IV, 16–17; CtY.

Nov. 27
PARIS
to Timothy Pickering, Secretary of State

Dispatch No. 3, signed by J.M., Pinckney, and Gerry; continued condemnation of American vessels; attempt to obtain money; very little prospect of success. Enclosure of letter to Talleyrand of Nov. 11. ASP (For. Rel.), II, 166; ASP, IV, 14–17; CtY.

Nov. 27
PARIS
to Timothy Pickering

Enclosing press reports; seizures of American citizens, Putnam, Murray, forced gifts to government. France's war plans against Britain, Holland, Hamburg, Portugal. Believes France does not wish rupture with America but will not render justice. (No signature.) DNA, General Records Dept. of State, Diplomatic Despatches, France, VI, R.G. 59; WMQ (ser. 3) Vol. XII (Oct., 1955), 639–42; *Green Bag*, Vol. XI (Dec., 1899), 566.

Nov. 27
PARIS
to Polly Marshall

Received no mail from America; return delayed through winter. Describes Paris and his lodging. VW; MHi; DLC, Marshall Papers, Ac. 2535; WMQ (ser. 2), Vol. III (Apr., 1923), 80–81; Mason, *Polly*, 112–13.

Dec. 4
MOUNT VERNON
from George Washington

Reply to letter of Sept. 15 from The Hague. Comments on French mission; conditions in Holland and France; Lafayette's release and son's departure for France. DLC, Papers of George Washington, Vol. 286, 61–66; also Same, Letter Book 16, Box 317, 8–12; Sparks, *Washington*, XI, 223–26.

Dec. 12
RICHMOND
Virginia-Kentucky Boundary

Report to Governor of Virginia of committee composed of J.M., Robert Anderson, John Taylor, and others to review proceedings and statements of commissioners appointed by Governor to adjust contested boundary line with Kentucky, recommending against appointment of new commissioners. CVSP, VIII, 454–55.

Dec. 17 *XYZ—Beaumarchais Claim*

J.M.'s entry of Dec. 17, 1797, tells of meeting Bellami in Gerry's apartment; Bellami regretted could not attend dinner at Beaumarchais'; learned lately J.M. represented latter in cause against State of Virginia; J.M. said cause of great magnitude and uncertain issue (see herein, 1801, Legal Practice, Court of Appeals of Virginia, *Innes (Commonwealth) v. Beaumarchais,* 4 Call 107); Bellami suggested that Beaumarchais would sacrifice £50,000 St. as private "gratification"; J.M. replied not authorized, and would have to be recognition of claims of American citizens and mission; Pinckney opposed. J.M. would require admission of claims for capture by French for want of *rôle d'equipage.* MHi, Journal in Paris (see herein Sept. 27, 1797).

Dec. 20 *to Fulmar Skipwith,*
PARIS *Consul General of the United States to France*

Joint letter J.M., C. C. Pinckney, and E. Gerry answering request for opinion concerning problems of consuls. Advises refund of money advanced and payment for return of American sailors from France, adherence to new American law concerning condemnations, giving of certificate of crew and passengers on French demand. DNA, General Records Dept. of State, Diplomatic Despatches, France, VI. R.G. 59; MHi, Norcross MSS; MHi Proc. (ser. 2), Vol. XV (May, 1901), 89–90; French Spoliation, 469–70 (excerpt).

Dec. 24 *to Rufus King,*
PARIS *Minister of the United States to Great Britain*

Discusses mission to France, futility of negotiations. Cipher and deciphered copy. DLC, Papers of Rufus King–J. D. Shelf; DLC, Ac. 2706.

King wrote to J.M., Pinckney, and Gerry from London, Nov. 24, 1797, urging peace with France, economic and moral reasons; warns against prejudice. Portugal gave money preliminary to treaty with France; Spain alarmed Portugal will fall; war with Austria; England to continue war. King, *Life,* II, 245.

Also King to Same, London, Dec. 9, 1797, information from Hammond American ships delayed by France; intent to sequester. King, *Life,* II, 247–48.

Dec. 24
PARIS *to Timothy Pickering, Secretary of State*

Dispatch No. 4, signed by J.M., Pinckney, and Gerry; no reply from Talleyrand; will write another letter with views of the United States; will not effectuate object of mission unless pay money. Enclosing exhibits Dec. 21, Pinckney's notes on negotiation; Dec. 17, extract from J.M.'s Journal; Dec. 13, undesignated report of events. DNA, General Records Dept. of State, Diplomatic Despatches, France, VI, R.G. 59; ASP (For. Rel.) II, 166–68; ASP, IV, 17–25; CtY; French Spoliation, 470–71 (excerpt).

Dec. 25
FAUQUIER COUNTY, VA. *Law Suits*

J.M. v. Chas. C. Chunn and Robert Jones. Debt on replevin bond given distress for rent. Default j. £18 Va., payable £9, interest from 1796. County Court, Fauquier, Minute Book 1797–1798, 373.

J.M. v. Thos. Simpson and Chas. Chunn. Same. Default j. £29:8:6 Va., payable £14:14, interest from 1795. Same, 374.

J.M. v. Chas. Chunn and Thos. Simpson. Same. Default j. £61 Va., payable £30:15, interest from 1795. Same, 374.

Dec. *Resignation from House of Delegates*

Resignation by J.M. of seat in House of Delegates to accept office under general government. Succeeded by William Foushee. E. G. Swem and John W. Williams, *A Register of General Assembly by Virginia: 1776–1918* (Richmond, Bottom, 1918), 49.

n.d., n.p. *to Zachariah Johnstone*

Acknowledging letter to self and Randolph; concerning withdrawing survey in Phillipsburg and acting as attorney in appeal. (Probably a reply to letter Oct. 17 mentioned in letter of Randolph to Johnstone, Nov. 7, 1797). V, Ac. Item 22031.

Sunday evening—*n.d.,* [1797 or 1798]
[PARIS] *to Maj. Gen. C. C. Pinckney*

Chagrined to find Pinckney's card on return from play in evening. Obliged to go out: Mme de Villette had box at Odeon (Voltaire's *Mahomet*); gave J.M. notice "at night" to accompany her. "What could I do?" Gerry not here; ought to have sent to stop Pinckney. So. Carolina Hist. Society.

LEGAL PRACTICE
U.S. Supreme Court

David Hunter v. Denny Fairfax, 3 Dallas 305.

Error to U.S. Circuit Court, Virginia.

Ejectment, j. for defendant in error, plaintiff below, possession decreed; writ of error dismissed for lack of prosecution. J.M. for defendant in error.

Proceedings before U.S. Circuit Court:

Ejectment brought May 30, 1795 (date given in U.S. Supreme Court Record Book, U.S. Circuit Court Case Papers, undoubtedly in error; no other date available), by "George Goodtitle," by J.M., his attorney, lessee of Denny Fairfax, demised to "Goodtitle" May 10, 1784, thirty years, executed by "Peter Plunderer," May 10, 1794, damages £500.

J.M. for plaintiff. DNA, U.S. Supreme Court Case Papers, No. 29, 1; V, U.S. Circuit Court, Va., Record Book III, 346; V, U.S. Circuit Court Case Papers, 1795.

There is considerable confusion in the record as to the land involved. The petition in transcript of record above and in record below stating one messuage and 788 acres, Shenandoah County, Va.; the agreed case in these same records stating 400 acres, Hampshire County on South Branch of the Potomac, lot No. 53 occupied by Jacob Long and George Triger, patented to Hunter by Commonwealth, James Wood, Lieutenant Governor, Nov. 29, 1794, by virtue of Treasury Warrants 56 and 57, issued Jan. 23, 1788, surveyed Apr. 5, 1794. A copy of this patent is among the U.S. Circuit Court Case Papers. The cover of original Case Papers U.S. Circuit Court similarly says 400 acres, Hampshire County. Title of cause in U.S. Circuit Court Order Book I, 536, says 788 acres in ——— County. [*sic*] Note: Case between same parties pending in state court involved 788 acres in "Shenando" County. (See herein, 1813, U.S. Supreme Court.)

Apr. 4, 1795. Notice to Robert Bodkins, tenant in possession, became defendant. DNA, U.S. Supreme Court Case Papers, No. 29, 2; V, U.S. Circuit Court, Va., Record Book III, 347; V, U.S. Circuit Court Case Papers.

Apr. 17, 1795. Copy of declaration served on Hunter claimant of title. U.S. Supreme Court Case Papers, No. 29, 2–3; U.S. Circuit Court, Va., Record Book III, 347; U.S. Circuit Court Case Papers.

May 30, 1795. Motion by Hunter by his attorney, William C. Williams, admitted as defendant. Plea, general issue, agrees to insist on title only at trial. Case agreed by parties in lieu of special verdict, in J.M.'s handwriting signed by him for plaintiff, by Williams for defendant. So appears in U.S. Circuit Court Case Papers; record of same in full, U.S. Supreme Court Case Papers, No. 29, 3–82; in abbreviated form U.S. Circuit Court, Va., Record Book III, 348–57.

Case agreed (J.M. autograph):

(1) That title to land in Northern Neck in Thomas Lord Fairfax in accordance with recitals and declarations of act of General Assembly, reciting original patent of King Charles II, to Ralph Lord Hopton, Henry Earl of St. Albans and others, confirmation of assignment to the patent to Thomas Lord Culpeper, proprietorship thereof by Thomas Lord Fairfax as heir of Culpeper, to allay uncertainty as to power of Fairfax to grant land because held in tail, all such grants confirmed.

(2) Such grants and charters made part of evidence in case.

(3) That act of General Assembly, 1748, sets boundary of Northern Neck, and with consent of Fairfax confirms Crown grants to others within the limits, to hold under Fairfax.

(4) That Lord Fairfax in 1748 opened and kept office until his death, Dec., 1784, granting waste and ungranted land in fee, with one shilling sterling annual rent, entered in book, also leased for lives and years; was citizen and inhabitant of Virginia capable of holding land and demising.

(5) That neither Lord Fairfax nor Denny Fairfax charged taxes on land.

(6) That land granted, as well as that conveyed to Thomas B. Martin and reconveyed to Lord Fairfax, did pay taxes.

(7) Will of Lord Fairfax, set out in full, devised entire holdings to Rev. Denny Martin, subject to annuities and change of name, and other bequests. States that plaintiff same as Rev. Denny Martin.

(8) That lands are in Northern Neck and same granted to Hunter by James Wood, Lieutenant Governor, patent under Treasury Warrants 56 and 57, Jan. 23, 1788, 400 acres, by survey Apr. 27, 1794, in County of Hampshire, on the South Branch of Potomac River, known by lot No. 53, issued Nov. 29, 1794. That value over $2,000; is in Northern Neck, is waste and ungranted land of Lord Fairfax.

(9) That Lord Fairfax died seized of 300,000 acres, which had been granted in fee to Thomas Bryan Fairfax and reconveyed to him in fee.

(10) That Denny Fairfax born in England in 1750, a British citizen.

(11) Treaty of Peace 1783, pursuant to Provisional Treaty set out in full—note particularly Article IV against impediments.

(12) Several acts of Virginia General Assembly set out a) terms and manner of granting waste and unappropriated land and setting up Land Office; b) land bounty to officers and soldiers; and c) sale of waste and unappropriated £40 per C, surveyor, settlement rights; excepting Indian

land, northwest side of Ohio, Kentucky-Green River, entries, surveys, caveats, grants; abolishing tenure and royal manorial rights:

Act abolishing title in tail.

Act of 1784, prohibiting future confiscations, according to Treaty of 1783.

Act of 1785, records in register of Land Office.

Act confirming entries made before death of Fairfax.

Act abolishing quitrents.

Act of 1779, declaring who were citizens.

Act of 1783, admission of immigrants, and citizenship—right to change.

Act of 1779, repealed.

Act of 1782, concerning surveyors.

Act confirming surveys in office of Fairfax at his death.

Act of 1785, concerning escheators and extending to Northern Neck.

(13) Agreed land not escheated and no inquest of office taken.

(14) Act of 1782, Sec. 20—quitrents to be paid into public treasury.

(15) That defendant citizen of Virginia and possesses by grant.

(16) Acknowledges lease, ouster and entry; that j. be entered according to finding, one penny damages.

June 5, 1795. Case came on by consent of parties, partly argued, continued to next day. U.S. Circuit Court Record Book III, 357. Record in Supreme Court says case coming on by consent, partly argued, continued from day to day, until June 6. U.S. Supreme Court Case Papers, No. 29, 82.

June 6, 1795. Court on mature consideration of case agreed, law for plaintiff, plaintiff recover messuage and land for remaining term, one penny damages, costs; writ to marshal for possession. U.S. Circuit Court, Va., Record Book III, 357; U.S. Circuit Court Order Book I, 536–37; U.S. Supreme Court, Case Papers, No. 29, 82–83.

Proceedings before U.S. Supreme Court:

Jan. 24, 1796. Order of Supreme Court to Circuit Court for record by first Monday February next, in error proceedings. Allowed by Justice James Iredell, U.S. Supreme Court Case Papers, No. 29, A.

A. Petition for writ of error, assigned by Alexander Campbell; allowed by Justice Iredell, noting J.M., counsel for defendants in error personally appeared and waived security for costs. Same, C, D.

Autograph notation service of citation acknowledged by J.M. Same, 88.

Jan. 22, 1796 (filed Feb. 2, 1796). Petition of Hunter to Supreme Court, suit in Circuit Court to try title to unappropriated land of Northern Neck; legislature opened Land Office 1785; grant to Hunter. Was entered as defendant; counsel employed by Executive of State to argue cause for State; petitioner informed argued and judgment for Fairfax. Appeal entered by direction of the Executive; petitioner informed counsel to be sent and no concern in the business. Informed Governor requested General Assembly send counsel; refused on ground title to unapproperiated land and laws concerning not cognizable in U.S. court. Petitioner unprepared to prosecute appeal if advised to do so by Governor and Council of Commonwealth; asks continuance to next term. U.S. Supreme Court Case Papers, No. 29, 87–88.

Mar. 14, 1796. Continued. DNA, U.S. Supreme Court, Docket Book A, 26.

July 29, 1796. Petition of Hunter to Supreme Court. Posted from Martinsburg to clerk for presentation to Court. Petitioner engaged Alexander Campbell to argue cause; informed on 25th that Campbell died July 18; no time to hire counsel for ensuing term; asks continuance to next term. U.S. Supreme Court Case Papers, No. 29, 89–91.

Aug. 6, 1796. Continuance granted on ground that although counsel might be had, case of magnitude requires investigation and study. Reported in 3 Dallas 305. Also noted on above petition; DNA, U.S. Supreme Court, Docket Book A, 26; DNA, U.S. Supreme Court Minute Book A, 78.

Feb. 8, 1797. Lee, U.S. Attorney General, on behalf of defendant, joins in error. U.S. Supreme Court, Docket Book A, 26; Same, Minute Book A, 80.

Feb. 11, 1797. Rule obtained by defendant for argument on 18th or writ of error non-prossed. Same, Docket Book A, 26; Same, Minute Book A, 81.

Feb. 13, 1797. Rule for non pros, with costs. Same, Docket Book A, 26; Same, Minute Book A, 82–83.

U.S. Circuit Court, Virginia

Stephen Bagg, Bristol, Great Britain v. John M. Galt, acting executor of Alexander Craig, Va.

Debt, on obligation under seal, £187:6 St., 1770. J.M. for defendant.

Nov. 29, 1791. Pleas: Payment; Britisher not recover under Virginia law; violation of Treaty of Paris; Declaration of Independence. Demurrer by plaintiff to three last pleas.

May 25, 1796. Demurrer for plaintiff.

May 23, 1797. Plea, full administration, U.S. Circuit Court, Va., Order Book II, 205.

May 26, 1797. V, not paid, fully administered, for defendant. Same, 213. Same, Record Book V, 218–21.

V, U.S. Circuit Court Case Papers containing autograph notations on printed answer forms of J.M. (Note: J.M.'s printed name with line through it; also printed forms used by Baker, plaintiff's counsel, for demurrers.)

Fee: June, 1791, £5 (for two cases). Account Book, 290.

Jesse and Robert Burton, executors of William Burton v. James and Robert Donald and Co.

Chancery, injunction sought against j. of this Court on bond for account by testator £914:13:2, 1775; failed to get credit for land sold by Jesse and purchase money to Donald, also payment to agent of Donald for tobacco sold; balance paid into Loan Office; Patrick Henry representing Burton lost certificate, not put in evidence, plea made by gentleman not employed; statute of limitations not pleaded.

J.M. for petitioner.

Dec. 10, 1793. Petition filed.

Dec. 27. Injunction issued.

Feb. 11, 1794. Answer, credits given, desires legal effect of payment to Loan Office, statute of limitations not pleaded.

May 29, 1794. Motion to deny injunction disallowed. U.S. Circuit Court, Va., Order Book I, 379.

June 7, 1797. Injunction dissolved and dismissed. Same, II, 363–64. Same, Record Book IV, 430–39.

V, U.S. Circuit Court Case Papers containing autograph petition, signed by Burton. Letter, Apr. 11, 1794, from Jesse Burton to J.M. as attorney enclosing certificate of Loan Office, evidence of payment. Autograph endorsements to file in case, see if answer filed, instructions to Ball to deliver to court and obtain receipt from William Marshall.

James Dennistoun et. al., d.b.a. Donald, Scot and Co. v. John Anderson.

Action for £360 Va. on sealed obligation, 1775. J.M. for defendant.

Nov. 28, 1791. Second plea withdrawn. Answer: payment, payment to Loan Office; British subjects; violation of Treaty of 1783; effect of Declaration of Independence. Demurrer by plaintiff. U.S. Circuit Court, Va., Order Book I, 61.

Nov. 22, 1793. Certificate of payment to Loan Office; demurrer. Same, 167.

May 24, 1797. Demurrer for plaintiff. V.j. £364 Va., payable by $606.67. Same, II, 203–204.

Same, Record Book V, 213–17.

V, U.S. Circuit Court Case Papers, containing autograph answer; answer on J.M.'s printed forms naming him; autograph notation on replication forms; autograph appearance bond of Feb. 28, 1791, for defendant.

James Dennistoun et al., d.b.a. Donald Scot and Co., merchants, Glasgow, Great Britain v. Wilson Trevillian, executor of Thomas Trevillian, Hanover County, Va.

Debt, on obligation under seal, £324:18:9½ Va., 1775. J.M. for defendant.

June, 1791. Declaration filed.

Feb. 5, 1792. Answer, payment, British subject, payment of £180 to Loan Office, breach of Treaty of 1783, effect of Declaration of Independence.

May 30, 1796. J. for plaintiff on demurrer to treaty plea. U.S. Circuit Court, Va., Order Book II, 140.

May 30, 1797. For plaintiff on demurrers to other pleas than payment. V.j. £324:18:9½ Va., payable by $514.56. Same, 210.

Same, Record Book V, 257–68.

V, U.S. Circuit Court Case Papers, containing answer on J.M.'s printed form naming him, autograph insertions.

William Fountaine, Va. v. William Henry, North Carolina. (Two cases)

Covenant, on agreement to patent 6,700 acres swamp land in North Carolina, and give 2,000 acres for stud horse, failure to obtain patent, 1788. J.M. for plaintiff.

May 30, 1797. Security for defendant on both. U.S. Circuit Court, Va., Order Book II, 248.

June 7, 1797. Plea: performance. V.j. $4,000. Same, 344.

Same, Record Book IV, 319–22.

Same for 2,000 acres swamp land in North Carolina. J.M. for plaintiff.

June 7, 1797. Plea: performance. V.j. $2,000. Same, Record Book IV, 322–24.

V, U.S. Circuit Court Case Papers containing autograph declarations capias; autograph notations on copy of patent.

Samuel Gist, London v. William Ruffin, s.p. Ritchie, Campbell and Ruffin.

Action on obligation. J.M. for plaintiff.

Dec. 6, 1794. Appearance of defendant. U.S. Circuit Court, Va., Order Book I, 467.

May 25, 1796. Answer, not his deed, not partner. Same, II, 116.

June 2, 1797. Continued. Same, 275.

Nov. 25, 1797. Plaintiff nonsuited, not appear. Same, III, 13.

V, U.S. Circuit Court Case Papers, containing two autograph aliases, two pluries capias.

Thomas and Rowland Hunt, merchants, London v. John Baylor, executor of John Baylor, Va.

Debt, on protested bill of exchange on John Backhouse to Hunts, £169:12:3 St. plus interest from 1773. J.M. for plaintiff.

Dec. 11, 1795. Answer, not owe. U.S. Circuit Court, Va., Order Book I, 79.

May 30, 1796. Continued. Same, 137.

June 2, 1797. V.j. £169:12:3 St. payable by $755.17. 10 per cent interest, less interest during war. Same, 271.

Same, Record Book V, 568–71.

V, U.S. Circuit Court Case Papers, containing autograph declaration.

William Jones, s.p. Farrell and Jones, merchants, Great Britain v. Richard, David M., Brett and Ryland Randolph, executors of Richard Randolph, Henrico County, Va.

Case, for money advanced and goods sold, £446:7:2½ Va. and £342:5:5 St., 1776. J.M. for defendant.

Pleas: not assume; Britisher not recover; fully administered. Demurrer.

Dec. 5, 1793. Depositions in Great Britain. U.S. Circuit Court, Va., Order Book I, 249.

May 24, 1796. Further plea of distribution of assets. Same, II, 102.

May 30, 1797. Demurrer for plaintiff. V.j. no assets on hand; $1,450.15. Same, 251.

Same, Record Book V, 360–74.

V, U.S. Circuit Court Case Papers.

William Jones, s.p. Farrell and Jones, merchants, Great Britain v. Richard Randolph, David Meade Randolph, Brett Randolph, and Ryland Randolph, executors of Richard Randolph, Henrico County, Va.

Case, for reimbursement of payment as broker of £6,664:9:10 of slave ship *Prince of Wales,* consigned to Randolph and John Wales; 280 slaves sold at £7,748 St., 1772. J.M. for defendants.

Pleas: *non assumpsit*; five-year statute of limitations; debt due Britisher not recoverable; full administration of assets. Demurrer as to second and third pleas by plaintiff.

Dec. 1, 3, 1791. Depositions in Great Britain. U.S. Circuit Court, Va., Order Book I, 72, 82.

Dec. 4, 1793. Plaintiff dead, J. T. Ware, executor, substituted. Same, 241.

Nov. 30, 1797. Demurrer for plaintiff. V.j. $52,881.54. Same III, 35. Same, Record Book VIII, 37–52.

V, U.S. Circuit Court Case Papers.

William Jones, s.p. Farrell and Jones v. John Quarles, Jr.

Case, on obligation £153:14:7 St., equal to £204:19:5 Va. J.M. for defendant.

Petition filed in 1791.

Answer: British subject, violation of Treaty of 1783; effect of Declaration of Independence.

Dec. 4, 1793. *Scire facias* to revive in name of J. T. Ware, executor. U.S. Circuit Court, Va., Order Book I, 243.

Dec. 5, 6, 1793. Depositions in Great Britain. Same, 249, 252.

Nov. 27, 1795. Continued. Same II, 23.

May 26, 1797. Plaintiff nonsuited for failure to appear. Same, 217. Same, Record Book Index, Civil May T, 1797.

V, U.S. Circuit Court Case Papers, containing autograph notation on printed answer.

Fee: July, 1791, £5:2. Account Book, 292.

William Jones, s.p. Joseph Farrell and William Jones, merchants, Great Britain v. Thomas Walker, Albemarle County, Va.

Debt, on obligation under seal, £2,903:15:8 St., 1772. J.M. for defendant.

Nov. 23, 1791. Pleas amended: payment to Loan Office of £215:18. Britisher disabled under Virginia law; violation of Treaty of Paris; Declaration of Independence. Demurrer by plaintiff. U.S. Circuit Court, Va., Order Book I, 54.

Dec. 4, 1793. Plaintiff dead; John T. Ware, executor, substituted. Same, 242.

Nov. 25, 1794, and May 24, 1796. Defendant dead. *Scire facias* to revive. Same, I, 401; Same, II, 105.

May 27, 1797. Demurrer of plaintiff allowed. V.j. £2,903:15:8 St., payable by $5,308.08. Same, II, 221.

Same, Record Book V, 287–302.

V, U.S. Circuit Court Case Papers, containing form with J.M.'s name printed thereon as standard answer in British debt cases, autograph notations. Patrick Henry name stricken out; also answer on J.M.'s form, filled in by J.M., noted withdrawn; autograph please of new answer, and rejoinder.

William Robinson Lidderdale, executor of John Lidderdale, merchant, Great Britain v. Thomas Mann Randolph and William Randolph, executors of Thomas Mann Randolph, Henrico and Goochland County, Va. (Three suits)

Debt, on protested bills of exchange on Cappel and Osgood Hanberry, London to Lidderdale, £364:5 St., 1768; same by Archibald Cary on John Lidderdale to Randolph £1,579:5:11 St., endorsed to Lidderdale, 1768; for goods sold and delivered, £2,946:18:3 St., 1768. J.M. for defendants.

Dec. 1, 1791. Pleas as to two actions: payment part to Loan Office; breach of Treaty of Paris; Declaration of Independence. As to third, nil debit. U.S. Circuit Court, Va., Order Book I, 70.

Nov. 30, 1792. Depositions in Great Britain. Same, 130.

Dec. 4, 1793. Defendant dead, *scire facias* to revive. Same, 243.

May 24, 1794. Allowed. Same, 361.

May 24, 1796. Plea: Fully administered assets. Same, II, 106.

June 2, 1797. Demurrer to three pleas above for plaintiff. V.js. £364:15 St., value of £585:13:4 Va., payable by $1,617.36; £579:5:11 St. value of £2,105:14:9 Va., payable by $7,011.75; $19,626.36. Same, 294, 295, 298.

Same, Record Book VI, 126–44; 144–55, 155–62.

V, U.S. Circuit Court Case Papers, containing autograph answer on J.M.'s printed form, payment to Loan Office; also blanks of J.M.'s printed form, five defenses.

Samuel Lyde, s.p. Lyonel and Samuel Lyde v. John Monroe, administrator of Andrew Monroe.

Chancery, foreclosure of mortgage. J.M. for defendant.

Nov. 23, 1797. Order of foreclosure and sale of lands in Fairfax and Westmoreland counties. J. $3,453.74, value of £777:17:4^3 St. U.S. Circuit Court, Va., Order Book III, 6.

Same, Record Book Index, Civil, Nov. T, 1797.

V, U.S. Circuit Court Case Papers.

McCall and Elliott, merchants, Great Britain v. Daniel Triplett and William Richards, executors of John Richards.

Nov. 29, 1791. Debt. J.M. for defendant.

Pleas: payment; payment to Loan Office; Britisher not recover; violation of Treaty of Paris; Declaration of Independence. Demurrer by plaintiff to last four. U.S. Circuit Court, Va., Order Book I, 65.

May 22, 1797. Abated by death of plaintiffs. Same, II, 208.

Same, Record Book Index, May T, 1797.

Consent that commission issue to take deposition of Ballard. Autograph. VHi.

V, U.S. Circuit Court Case Papers, containing answer on J.M.'s printed forms, filled in by him.

Fee: May, 1791, £5 "Richard's ex'rs Federal." Account Book, 286.

Peter McDougall & Co. v. Thomas Banks, surviving executor of Jacob Rubsamon.

Scire facias on j. May 13, 1792, against John McCall and defendant, his security, £900 Va., 160 pounds tobacco. Filed Oct. 2, 1795.

May 25, 1796. Plea, payment. U.S. Circuit Court, Va., Order Book II, 119.

June 6, 1797. Plea, general issue. V. defendant's testator died prior to rendition of j.; j. for defendant. Same, 330.

Same, Record Book IV, 283–89.

V, U.S. Circuit Court Case Papers, containing autograph answer; reply denying death also in J.M.'s handwriting.

John T. Ware, executor of William Jones, s.p. Farrell and Jones, merchants, Great Britain v. Thomas Mann Randolph and William Randolph, executors of Thomas Mann Randolph, Goochland County, Va.

Debt, on obligation under seal by Randolph, Archibald Cary, and Richard Randolph, both deceased, £9,400, 1772. J.M. for defendant.

Dec. 1, 1791. Pleas: general issue; part payment to Loan Office; breach of Treaty of Paris; Declaration of Independence; nil debit. Demurrer by plaintiff. U.S. Circuit Court, Va., Order Book I, 70.

Dec. 4, 1793. Death of defendant; *scire facias*. Same, 243.

June 3, 1797. Pleas: fully administered; payment to Loan Office. Demurrers for plaintiff. V.j., fully administered; £9,400 St. value of £12,533:6:8 Va., payable by $20,484. Same, 296.

Same, Record Book VI, 162–72.

V, U.S. Circuit Court Case Papers.

COURT OF APPEALS OF VIRGINIA

Joseph Cutchin v. William Wilkinson, 1 Call 1, 3–4.

Appeal from District Court of Suffolk, Oct. 2, 1794, reversing County Court Isle of Wight, Nov. 4, 1793, reversed. J.M. and John Wickham for appellant.

County Court appointed brother of deceased widow administrator of estate of husband; District Court reversed in favor of brother of deceased husband. Held, error, widow entitled to estate, her line prevails.

Apr. 14, 1796. Case submitted. Court of Appeals, Va. Order Book III, 111.

Nov. 22, 23. Resubmitted, continued. Same, 154–55.

Apr. 22, 1797. Reversed, County Court affirmed. Same, 167.

Lessee of James Guthrie v. Richard and Elizabeth Guthrie, 1 Call 5, 7, 8–9. (Title reversed.)

Appeal from District Court of King and Queen, Apr. 15, 1794. Ejectment, j. for James, reversed. J.M. for appellants, Richard and Elizabeth.

Testator gave land to James, eldest son; if sells, half of proceeds to second son, Richard; if other land descends to James (from uncle, William), Richard to have it or land devised. Land descended from William; James held both until evicted by Richard in General Court action. Present action by heir of James to dispossess devisee or Richard. Held, James took fee subject to executory devise to Richard which came into effect.

Nov. 9, 1796. Continued. Court of Appeals, Va., Order Book III, 147.

Apr. 20. Reversed, dismissed. Same, 162.

Henry Bell v. Richard Marr, 1 Call 40.

Supersedeas from j. District Court of Prince Edward, Apr. 5, 1796, on forthcoming bond against Bell and Cary Harrison, £2,077:13:6, payable by £1,038:16:9, affirmed. J.M. for appellant.

J. rendered for amount of forthcoming bond which exceeded the amount of execution; thereafter excess released and j's. amended accordingly.

Held, defect cured, j. valid.

Apr. 20, 1797. Record presented. Court of Appeals, Va., Order Book III, 117.

Oct. 27, 1797. Affirmed. Same, 183.

Apr. 3, 1798. Mandate of Court of Appeals entered. District Court, Prince Edward, Records at Large 1795–1798, 444.

Fees: May, 1793, £5:12. Account Book, 360.

See also for earlier proceedings, Sept. 22, 1786, "Marr v. Bell, advance fee," £1:16. Account Book, 82.

William Worsham v. Clough Eggleston, 1 Call 41.

Appeal from j. District Court, Prince Edward Courthouse, Apr. 9, 1796, on forthcoming bond (for record, see District Court, Prince Edward, Records at Large, 1795–1798, 129), reversed and amended. J.M. for appellee. Appellee issued *fieri facias* against appellant, 1794, 6,940 pounds of tobacco and £2:16:6, property taken, forthcoming bond by appellant for 7,342 pounds of tobacco and £2:16:6 including interest, costs, and sheriff's commissions; j. given in this amount.

Held, error to include sheriff's commission in j.; new j. entered for penalty of bond, 14,684 pounds of tobacco and costs, payable by 6,940 pounds of tobacco and £2:16:6 and interest.

Nov. 15, 1797. Submitted. Court of Appeals, Va., Order Book III, 196.

Nov. 16, 1797. Reversed, j. amended. Same, 198.

Fees: May, 1793, £3; Sept., 1793, £2. Account Book, 360, 370.

Note: In proceedings between same parties High Court of Chancery, Mar. 7, 1795, certified issue to District Court, Prince Edward Courthouse to inquire damages to plaintiff by defendant's nonpayment of taxes whereby sixty-nine acres of land sold.

Apr. 8, 1797. V.j. in District Court certified no damage by sale of land in decretal order. District Court, Prince Edward Courthouse, Records at Large 1795–1798, 348.

Philip Ludwell Grymes, son and heir of Philip Grymes, William Thornton, executor of Francis Thornton, who was surviving executor of Presley Thornton, Daniel McCarty, executor of Peter Presley Thornton, both latter decedents, sons, and devisees of Presley Thornton, the elder v. Edmund Pendleton and Peter Lyons, executors of John Robinson, 1 Call 47.

Appeal from decree of High Court of Chancery, Sept. 26, 1793. J.M. for appellants.

Question raised whether appeal lies from interlocutory decree, before final decree, although it may decide title and settle principles. Held, it did not; court no jurisdiction until final decree.

Apr. 16, 18, 1795. Heard. Court of Appeals, Va., Order Book III, 48, 50.

Nov. 19, 1795. Continued for rehearing. Same, 100.

Apr. 26, 1796. Continued for further record. Same, 115.

Oct. 20, 1797. Remanded, decree appealed from not final. Same, 181.

Fees: May 8, 1789, £5; July, 1790, "Grymes," £5:12. Account Book, 196, 254.

For earlier proceedings, see *Grymes v. Pendleton,* 4 Call 130, action on a bond, J.M. not involved.

James Maxwell v. Peter Light, 1 Call 100.

Appeal from two js. against appellant District Court, Winchester, Sept. 11, 1795, replevin, reversed. J.M. for appellee in earlier proceedings; Williams for same herein.

Replevin by appellant for goods taken, alleged by appellee distraint for rent in arrears. Lease recorded on proof of one witness; copy admitted in evidence certified by clerk and without other proof a true copy. J. entered for double rent found by jury due, without allowing appellant to show distraint was for more than due.

Held, reversed, lease improperly recorded, clerk's certificate insufficient, outside proof necessary that true copy; appellant may show distress for rental for more than due to avoid penalty.

Nov. 4, 1796. Certiorari to certify record. Court of Appeals, Va., Order Book III, 145.

Oct. 30, 1797. Submitted. Same, 185.

Nov. 4, 1797. Reversed and remanded. Same, 187.

Fee: Nov., 1794, £7 (including *Light v. Wilson* fee). Account Book, 400.

See also *Light v. Maxwell,* appeal from j. against appellant, District Court, Winchester, Sept. 4, 1794.

Apr. 12, 1796. Docketed. Court of Appeals, Va., Order Book III, 109.

Nov. 4, 1796. Dismissed and remanded, no final j. before appeal granted. Same, 145.

Nov. 7, 1798. Appeal from District Court, Winchester, Apr. 22, 1797, j. for £5, docketed. Court of Appeals, Va., Order Book III, 274.

Nov. 4, 1800. Dismissed as insufficient for jurisdiction. Same, IV, 40.

Elizabeth Towler, widow of James Towler, and six children, devisees of Japeth Towler v. James Jameson and Richard Cameron, s.p. Buchanan Hastie & Co., et al., 1 Call 162.

Appeals from High Court of Chancery, May 12, 1895, reversed. J.M. for appellants in earlier proceedings; Ronald for same herein.

Appellees had mortgage on land, agreed to its conveyance, purchaser to pay mortgage debt; thereafter accepted from purchaser mortgage of eight slaves to secure this and another debt; land sold to appellant. Action to deliver up mortgage; cross bill for sale of land to pay mortgage.

Held, original mortgage extinguished by new security.

Nov. 13, 1797. Heard. Court of Appeals, Va., Order Book III, 193.

Nov. 14, 1797. Continued for rehearing. Same, 194.

Oct. 12–13, 1797. Rehearing. Same, 246, 248.

Oct. 15, 1798. Reversed. Mortgage released, cross bill dismissed. Same, 249–50.

Fee: Jan., 1793, £5. Account Book, 346.

Superior (District) Court, Frederick

The Commonwealth v. Denny Fairfax.

On an inquisition traverse and *monstrans de droit.* J.M. for defendant.

Oct. 7, 1797. Dismissed. Superior Court, Frederick, Order Book 1797–1800, 66.

(See herein, 1797, Legal Practice, District Court, Prince William County, *Thomas B. Martin v. Commonwealth*; 1798, Legal Practice, Court of Appeals, *Denny Fairfax v. Commonwealth.*)

District Court, Fredericksburg

Michael Wallace v. Isaac Smith. (Companion suits against Thomas Kirtley, Job Breeding.)

Writ of right. J.M. for defendant.

Oct. 8, 1792. Order on motion of plaintiff that surveyor of County of Culpeper go on land, make plats and return to court; justice of county meet him, take depositions; sheriff of county attend. District Court, Fredericksburg, Law Orders A, 1789–1793, 429.

May 6, 1795. Continued by defendant; will of Michael Wallace, deceased, subpoened. Same, Law Orders B, 1794–1798, 131.

Oct. 4, 1796. Order as above. Same, 237.

May 4, 1797. Continued; depositions by defendant. Same, 288.

Oct. 3, 1797. Dismissed, demandant not prosecuting, to pay tenants their costs. Same, 353.

Fee: Mar., 1793, £3:10. Account Book, 352.

District Court, Prince Edward

Elijah Clarke, administrator of Mary Richards v. Francis Jackson, administrator of Lewis Jackson.

Case. J.M. for plaintiff.

Apr. 8, 1797. V.j. for plaintiff £51:6. District Court, Prince Edward, Order Book 1793–1799, 362.

Fee: Sept., 1792, £2:8. Account Book, 336.

District Court, Prince William

Elizabeth Graham v. Robert Graham.

Ejectment by stepmother against stepson, 300 acres and other lands of deceased husband. J.M. for ———.

Oct. 23, 1794. Continued. District Court, Prince William, 1794–1798, 69.

May 21, 1795. Death of lessor of plaintiff, continued. Same, 133.

Oct. 15, 1795; May 19, Oct. 21, 1796. Continued. Same, 162, 251, 334.

May 27–29, 1795. Special verdict, numerous conveyances, mortgages, and wills; for defendant as to all but 300 acres. Same, 401, 403.

Oct. 28, 1797. J. for defendant as to all lands. Same, 492.

Fee: Apr. 1791, £7. Account Book, 282.

Henry Lee, Rawleigh Colston, J.M., and James M. Marshall v. The Commonwealth, upon a *monstrans de droit* to an inquisition of office, and *Thomas B. Martin v. Same,* upon a traverse to an inquisition of office.

May 20, 1796. Agreement between Charles Martin, attorney for plaintiffs, and Thomas Swann, attorney for Commonwealth, that cause argued next term, pleadings drawn up during vacation considered now filed, appeal to Court of Appeals by either party, if permitted, heard at next term with pending appeal same subject by Denny Fairfax. Dated May 20, 1795. District Court, Prince William, Order Book 1794–1798, 263–64.

Oct. 13, 1796. Continued. Same, 289.

May 19, 1798. Suit compromised by act of Assembly last session. Same, 344.

(See herein, 1798, Legal Practice, Court of Appeals, *Denny Fairfax v. Commonwealth.*)

Simon Luttrell and Thomas Chapman, executors of William Carr v. Charles Lee, executor of Henry Lee.

Debt. J.M. for defendant.

Oct. 15, 1794. Suits reinstated on motion of plaintiff. District Court, Prince William, Order Book 1794–1798, 10.

Oct. 21, 1795. Submitted to arbitrators. Same, 187.

May 16, Oct. 24, 1796; May 20, 1797. Continued. Same, 236, 294, 350.

Oct. 19, 1797. Award for plaintiff £1,279:7:1 current and 26,082 pounds crop tobacco; j. for plaintiff against estate £2,000 gold at five shillings four pence per pennyweight, or in silver dollars at six shillings, as in declaration, payable by amount of award. Same, 422.

Fee: Apr., 1788, £2:10. Account Book, 152.

LAND TRANSACTIONS
Hardy County, Virginia
(Now West Virginia)

Jan. 12 *Deed*

J.M. to John McNeill, reversionary interest, 216 acres South Branch Manor, leased Thomas Lord Fairfax to Thomas Davies. Consideration £55. Proved and recorded Jan. 15, 1797. Hardy County, Va., Deed Book 4, 160.

Jan. 12 *Deed*

J.M. to John McNeill, reversionary interest, tract South Branch Manor, no acreage mentioned, leased Thomas Lord Fairfax, lease recorded in Hampshire County. Consideration £109:5. Recorded Feb. 15, 1797. Hardy County, Va., Deed Book 4, 161.

Jan. 12 *Deed*

J.M. to Moses Hutton, reversionary interest, 300 acres, South Branch Manor, west side South Branch of Potomac, lease Thomas Lord Fairfax to Hutton, recorded in Hampshire County. Consideration £25. Notation by J.M. that H. M. Hutton has lease for other lands of which reversions to be released. Recorded July 12, 1797. Hardy County, Va., Deed Book 4, 245.

Jan. 12 *Deed*

J.M. to Jonathan Hutton, reversionary interest, eighty-two acres, South Branch Manor, leased Thomas Lord Fairfax to Cornelius Cutright. Consideration £20:10. Recorded July 12, 1797. Hardy County, Va., Deed Book 4, 247.

Jan. 12 *Deed*

J.M. to Moses and Jacob Hutton, reversionary interest, 280 acres, South Branch Manor, east side of South Branch of Potomac, leased Thomas Lord Fairfax to Moses Hutton. Notation by J.M. that reversion of other lands leased by Hutton to be released. Consideration £20. Recorded July 12, 1797. Hardy County, Va., Deed Book 4, 248.

Jan. 12 *Deed*

J.M. to Phebe Couchman, reversionary interest, eighty-one acres, No. 22, South Branch Manor, leased Thomas Lord Fairfax to Adam Couchman, recorded in Hampshire County. Consideration £20:5. Recorded Feb. 14, 1799. Hardy County, Va., Deed Book 4, 412.

Jan. 12 *Deed*

J.M. to Robert Porter, reversionary interest, eighty-six acres, No. 46, South Branch Manor, leased Thomas Lord Fairfax to Robert Porter and Samuel Brink, recorded in Hampshire County. Consideration £31:15. Recorded Feb. 13, 1797; Feb. 14, 1799. Hardy County, Va., Deed Book 4, 417.

Jan. 12 *Deed*

J.M. to Henry Waldeck, reversionary interest, twenty-six acres, No. 21, South Branch Manor, leased Thomas Lord Fairfax to Henry Monk, recorded in Hampshire County. Consideration £19:10. Recorded Mar. 12, 1797; Apr. 15, 1799. Hardy County, Va., Deed Book 4, 430.

Jan. 12 *Deed*

J.M. to Henry Waldeck, 115 acres, South Branch Manor, surveyed by John Foley, June 7, 1791. Consideration £29. Notation by J.M. that grantee claims lease renewable forever under rules of Manor, made entry and survey, and rents and forfeitures of lease extinguished under contract with James M. Marshall. Recorded Mar. 12, 1797; Apr. 14, 1799. Hardy County, Va., Deed Book 4, 431.

Jan. 14 *Deed*

J.M. to John Lawrence, residuary interest, 124 acres, No. 15, South Branch Manor, leased Thomas Lord Fairfax to Lawrence, recorded in Hampshire County, extinguishing rights of Denny Fairfax pursuant to agreement James M. Marshall and Lawrence. Consideration £31. Recorded Apr. 12, 1797. Hardy County, Va., Deed Book 4, 201.

Printed form of above, filled in by hand, signed, listed in Argosy Book Store, Catalogue 450, 19. Present owner unknown.

Jan. 14 *Deed*

J.M. to Abraham Inskeep, reversionary interest, 250 acres, No. 40, and 260 acres, No. 41, South Branch Manor, lease Thomas Lord Fairfax to Inskeep recorded in Hampshire County; conveyance pursuant to agreement of James M. Marshall and Inskeep. Consideration £127. Recorded Apr. 12, 1797. Hardy County, Va., Deed Book 4, 203.

n.d. *Deed*

J.M. to Teakman Our, reversionary interest, two tracts, South Branch Manor, in possession under father's will, leased Thomas Lord Fairfax to John Our, Aug. 3, 1773, recorded Hampshire County, no acreage mentioned. Consideration £14:15. Recorded Sept. 13, 1797. Hardy County, Va., Deed Book 4, 256.

Jan. 16 *Deed*

J.M. to Robert Porter, ten acres, South Branch Manor, surveyed by John Foley. Consideration £2:10. Recorded Feb. 15, 1797. Hardy County, Va., Deed Book 4, 165.

Jan. 16 *Deed*

J.M. to Conrad Moore, reversionary interest, tract South Branch Manor, no acreage mentioned, lease Thomas Lord Fairfax to Moore recorded in Hampshire County, conveyance pursuant to agreement between Moore and James M. Marshall. Consideration £15:10. Recorded Feb. 15, 1797. Hardy County, Va., Deed Book 4, 166.

Jan. 16 *Deed*

J.M. to Daniel Teavehaugh, reversionary interest, 171 acres, South Branch Manor, leased Thomas Lord Fairfax to ———, recorded in Hampshire County, conveyance made pursuant to agreement James M. Marshall and Teavehaugh. Consideration £42:15. Recorded Feb. 15, 1797. Hardy County, Va., Deed Book 4, 168.

Jan. 16 *Deed*

J.M. to Strother McNeill, 279 acres South Branch Manor, purchaser entitled to under contract with James M. Marshall. Consideration £63. Recorded May 9, 1797. Hardy County, Va., Deed Book A, 27.

Jan. 16 *Deed*

J.M. to Daniel McNeill, conveyance of remainder interest in several leases from Thomas Lord Fairfax to tracts in South Branch Manor, Hampshire County, all in possession of grantee, 116 acres leased to Andrew Pancake, 164 acres leased to Abraham Hite, 668 acres and 70 acres and 320 acres to grantee. Consideration £359. Recorded May 9, 1797. Hardy County, Va., Deed Book A, 28.

May 6 *Deed*

J.M., by Rawleigh Colston, attorney in fact, to John Hogbin, conveyance of remainder interest, 60 acres of 175-acre tract, South Branch Manor, Hardy County, No. 49, leased Thomas Lord Fairfax to Alexander Ligget. Consideration twenty years annual rent reserved in lease. Recorded same day. Hardy County, Va., Deed Book A, 1.

May 6 *Deed*

J.M., by Rawleigh Colston, attorney in fact, to John Hogbin, conveyance of remainder interest, eighty-two acres, South Branch Manor, Hardy County, leased by grantee from Thomas Bryan Martin Jan. 4, 1790. Consideration twenty years annual rent reserved in lease. Recorded same day. Hardy County, Va., Deed Book A, 2.

May 6 *Deed*

J.M., by Rawleigh Colston, attorney in fact, to Jesse Welton, conveyance of remainder interest, eighty-eight acres, South Branch Manor, Hardy County, leased Thomas Lord Fairfax to Welton, Aug. 3, 1773, surveyed by Thomas Marshall; also nineteen acres, same, leased Fairfax to Welton, Mar. 9, 1779. Consideration £165:18:37. Recorded May 8, 1797. Hardy County, Va., Deed Book A, 4.

May 11 *Deed*

J.M., by Rawleigh Colston, attorney in fact, to Michael Carr, conveyance of remainder interest, fifty-three and fifty-four acres, South Branch Manor, Hampshire County, leased Thomas Lord Fairfax to Jacob Peterson, Aug. 3, 1773. Consideration £20:5. Recorded Sept. 7, 1797. Hardy County, Va., Deed Book A, 70.

May 11 *Deed*

J.M., by Rawleigh Colston, his attorney, to Jacob Peterson, reversion of lease Aug. 3, 1773, Thomas Lord Fairfax to Peterson, eighty-one acres, Nos. 53 and 54 South Branch Manor. Consideration £20:5. Recorded Sept. 7, 1797. Hardy County, Va., Deed Book A, 71.

May 11 *Deed*

J.M., by Rawleigh Colston, attorney in fact, to Christopher Strader, conveyance of remainder interest in two leases, tracts in South Branch Manor from Thomas Lord Fairfax, Aug. 3, 1773, part in possession of Strader under deed from Godfrey Our, June 7, 1790. Consideration £14:15. Recorded Aug. 6, 1797. Hardy County, Va., Deed Book A, 73.

May 11 *Deed*

J.M., by Rawleigh Colston, attorney in fact, to Christopher Strader, conveyance of remainder interest, fifty-one acres, South Branch Manor, Hardy County, leased Thomas Lord Fairfax to John William Geneitz, Aug. 3, 1773. Consideration £50. Recorded May 7, 1798. Hardy County, Va., Deed Book A, 74.

May 11 *Deed*

J.M., by Rawleigh Colston, attorney in fact, to Teakman Ower (Our), reversionary interest, twenty-one acres, South Branch Manor, leased Denny Martin Fairfax to Ower, Oct. 4, 1790, recorded in Hardy County. Consideration £5:8:4. Recorded Sept. 13, 1797. Hardy County, Va., Deed Book 4, 257.

May 12 *Deed*

J.M., by Rawleigh Colston, attorney in fact, and Commonwealth of Virginia to Jacob Peterson, conveyance of remainder interest, seventy acres, South Branch Manor, Hardy County, leased Denny Martin Fairfax to grantee, May 21, 1790. Consideration £17:10. Recorded Sept. 9, 1797. Hardy County, Va., Deed Book A, 33.

1798

DOCUMENTS

Jan. 8
Paris *to Timothy Pickering, Secretary of State*

Dispatch No. 5 signed by J.M., Pinckney, and Gerry reporting French decree against English merchandise and ports, neutral shipping no hope of being officially received. DNA, General Records Dept. of State, Diplomatic Despatches, France VI. R.G. 59; ASP (For. Rel.) II, 150–51; ASP, III, 451; CtY.

Jan. 17
Paris *to Fulmar Skipwith, Consul General at Paris*

Instructions by J.M., C. C. Pinckney, E. Gerry concerning advances as payment for release of American seamen captured by French on British vessels. NN, Emmett Coll.; CtY.

Jan. 17
PARIS

to French Minister of Foreign Affairs [Talleyrand]

Letter prepared by J.M., signed by him, Pinckney, and Gerry, outlining in detail the American position in the controversy with French. Enclosed in dispatch of envoys No. 6, Feb. 7. DNA, General Records Dept. of State, Diplomatic Despatches, France VI. R.G. 59; *Archives du Ministére,* Vol. 49, folio 10–63 (French translation, folios 65–138); photostats of Same, DLC; ASP (For. Rel.) II, 169–82; ASP, IV, 27–80; CtY. French Spoliation, 471–87 (excerpt dated Jan. 17).

J.M. states that the motive of this memorial, even if French were not impressed, was to show sincerity of envoys, to bring controversy before American people, and to convince them government sought reconciliation. Gerry was opposed and with difficulty was persuaded to sign. Marshall, *Autobiography,* 23–24.

For J.M.'s statement of authorship of this letter and Gerry's delay in signing, see MHi, Journal in Paris, 38–40. Beveridge, *Marshall,* II, 296–97.

Feb. 7
PARIS

to Timothy Pickering, Secretary of State

Dispatch No. 6 signed by J.M., Pinckney, and Gerry, enclosing letter addressed to French minister of foreign affairs, dated Jan. 17; also certain French decrees on navigation. Notation of Mar. 1 by Rufus King that dispatch sent to him unsealed and forwarded; forwarded from The Hague, Feb. 17, by W. V. Murray. DNA, General Records Dept. of State, Diplomatic Despatches, France, VI. R.G. 59; ASP (For. Rel.) II, 169; ASP, IV, 26; CtY.

Feb. 27
PARIS

to French Minister of Foreign Affairs [Talleyrand]

Letter by J.M., Pinckney, and Gerry requesting a personal interview. (Referred to in Same to Timothy Pickering, Mar. 9, 1798, herein.) ASP (For. Rel.) II, 186; CtY; *Archives du Ministére,* Vol. 49, folio 226; photostats of Same DLC.

Feb.
PARIS

to French Minister of Foreign Affairs [Talleyrand]

Letter drafted between Feb. 7 and 19, signed by J.M. and Pinckney; Gerry refusing to sign, not delivered; remonstrating against decree of

Council of French Republic for seizure of neutral vessels bearing English goods, recognizing breakdown of negotiations and mission and demanding passports. DNA, General Records Dept. of State, Diplomatic Despatches, France, VI. R.G. 59. (Referred to in letter envoys to Pickering, Mar. 9, herein; also J.M. to President Adams, Mar. 4, herein.)

Mar. 4 *to French Minister of Foreign Affairs*
PARIS *[Talleyrand]*

Requesting a second interview on 6th. (Answered would receive at eleven o'clock.) (Referred to in letter envoys to Pickering, Mar. 9, herein.) No copy made. See Note to Mar. 9 letter; CtY, copy of Same.

Mar. 4, Mar. 10 [addendum]
PARIS *to President John Adams*

Uncertain as to plans; intend remonstrance against French decree as to effect of carriage of English goods. Disagreement with Gerry as to requested loan to France; need for unanimity and secrecy of agreement; possible plan to return for consultation.

(10th) Loan demanded intended for use by France in war against England. Several meetings with Talleyrand. Regrets undertaking mission. Enclosure for Gen. Washington. Autograph postcript that bearer Lee wishes consulate in France. PP, Jay Treaty Papers, Wm. M. Elkins Coll., Rare Book Dept. (Letter in code and translation, unsigned.); DLC, Ac. 4779.

Mar. 8, Mar. 10 [postscript]
PARIS *to George Washington*

Failure of negotiations with France; possibility of war depending on invasion of England. Secret peace negotiations between France and England; French plans to revolutionize Switzerland, Sardinia, and Naples; the peace treaty at Rastadt. French plans to invade Portugal through Spain; financial strain in France; English invasion loan. French and Swiss encounters reported. MH, Sparks MSS, XLVI, 351–55; DLC, Papers of George Washington, Vol. 287, 113–14; DLC, Beveridge Coll.; DLC, J.M. Var. Access, 4314A; AHR, Vol. II (Jan., 1897), 303–306.

Mar. 9
PARIS *to Timothy Pickering, Secretary of State*

Dispatch No. 7 signed by J.M., Pinckney, and Gerry, recounting progress of mission, interview with Talleyrand. Enclosure dated Mar. 2 forwarded from London, Apr. 6, by Rufus King. DNA, General Records Dept. of State, Diplomatic Despatches, France, VI. R.G. 59; ASP (For. Rel.) II, 186–88; ASP, IV, 82–92; CtY; French Spoliation, 487–88 (excerpt).

Mar. 13
PARIS *to Fulmar Skipwith*

Joint letter with C. C. Pinckney and E. Gerry regretting advances by citizens of the United States cannot be immediately reimbursed; envoys cannot assume it or pay accounts of consuls; must await action of Congress. CtY.

Apr. 3
PARIS *to Timothy Pickering, Secretary of State*

Dispatch No. 8; enclosing letter from Talleyrand to envoys of Mar. 18 in answer to theirs to him of Jan. 17 (herein), and envoys' reply of Apr. 3, signed by J.M., Pinckney and Gerry. DNA, General Records Dept. of State, Diplomatic Despatches, France, VI. R.G. 59; ASP (For. Rel.) II, 188; ASP IV, 93–103; CtY.

Apr. 3
PARIS *to French Minister of Foreign Affairs [Talleyrand]*

Reply of envoys to letter of Mar. 18 concerning prizes in U.S. courts; the treaty of Great Britain; protest against French decree; stating no one of envoys can continue negotiations, and no two will withdraw as long as possibility of treaty; if no such possibility, request passports for all or any number of them wishing to leave. Enclosed in dispatch of envoys No. 8. DNA, General Records Dept. of State, Diplomatic Despatches, Paris, VI. R.G. 59; ASP (For. Rel.) II, 191–99; ASP, IV, 103–57; CtY; *Archives du Ministére*, Vol. 49, folios 259–91; photostats of Same, DLC; French Spoliation, 496–522.

Apr. 3
PHILADELPHIA *President John Adams to the Senate and House of Representatives*

Submitting in confidence the instructions to and dispatches from the envoys extraordinary of the United States to the French Republic. MHi, Adams Papers, XCVII, 54.

Apr. 3
THE HAGUE *William Vans Murray to President John Adams*

Referring to letter received from J.M. and Pinckney at Paris (n.f.); will be off to Bordeaux where arrange credit. MHi, Adams Papers, XCVI, 28.

Apr. 4 *Passport*

Envoi de passeport par Talleyrand et accuses de reception autographes, de Marshall. *Archives du Ministére,* Vol. 49, folios 323, 324; photostats of Same, DLC.

Apr. 9 *to James H. Hooe* (Au Citoyen James H. Hooe,
PARIS au soins du citoyen Dobrie, consul, Nantes [*France*])

Unable to take passage on Dobrus' vessel; uncertain when can leave; will have letter of safe conduct; requests list of vessels departing later date. DLC, Ac. 10754.

Apr. 18
PARIS *to Minister of External Relations*

Acknowledges letter enclosing passport (item 317, dated 23 Geminal) and letter of safe conduct; expected more protection; hopes will prevent turning of vessel out of course; embarking from port of France. *Archives du Ministére,* Vol. 49, V, No. 323; photostats of Same, DLC.

Apr. 21
BORDEAUX *to Fulmar Skipwith*

Enclosing papers neglected to deliver for three months. Taking passage for New York on *The Alexander Hamilton*; awaiting baggage. Greetings to Mme. de Villette; sentiments of friendship. PPHi, Dreer Am. Lawyer's Coll.

Apr. 21
BORDEAUX *to Charles Cotesworth Pinckney*

Describes journey to Bordeaux; sailing on *The Alexander Hamilton.* Pleased to leave Europe. Mentions loveliness of women. DLC, Marshall Papers–Pinckney.

June 6
PHILADELPHIA *Thomas Jefferson to John Page*

J.M. to Amsterdam, returning "for orders"; Gerry remaining, successful, will give facts on both sides. VU, typescript of original owned by Lloyd W. Smith.

June 18
NEW YORK *to Timothy Pickering*

Arrived previous day; leaving for Philadelphia. Refers to copy of letter received from French minister of exterior relations and forwarded J.M.'s passport, sailed from Bordeaux. Gen. Pinckney to South of France because of ill health of daughter. Gerry remaining in Paris; J.M. bearing letter from him to President. NNHi, Vail, 2:66.

June 18
PHILADELPHIA *Reception at Philadelphia*

J.M.'s arrival in Philadelphia from New York; met at Frankfort by Secretary of State and other dignitaries; escorted into town by city cavalry. *Claypoole's Daily Advertiser,* June 20, 1798; PPHi; *Gazette of the United States,* June 20, 1798; Beveridge, *Marshall,* II, 342–43.

June 22
PHILADELPHIA *to George Washington*

Letter to Gen. Duane (Dumas) delivered in Paris; enclosing answer; received flattering attention from him. Acknowledges answer to Hague letter. Going to Winchester where wife is. DLC, Papers of George Washington, Vol. 289, 86; Oster, *Marshall,* 177.

June 23
PHILADELPHIA *from Thomas Jefferson*

Note of compliments and regrets following personal calls on J.M. John Marshall house, Richmond, Va., Assoc. for Preserv. of Va. Antiquities; DLC, Papers of Thomas Jefferson; DLC, Ac. D.R. E1007, Pt. 6; Oster, *Marshall,* 195; Mason, *Polly,* 118–19; Beveridge, *Marshall,* II, 346–47; *Green Bag,* Vol. VIII (Dec., 1896), 483.

Original owned by John Marshall Ribble, Petersburg, Va.

June 23
PHILADELPHIA *Dinner*

Dinner honoring J.M. given by both houses of Congress at Oeller's Hotel; 120 persons, government officials and distinguished public characters; sixteen toasts, notably "Millions for defense, but not a cent for tribute." *Claypoole's Daily Advertiser,* June 25, 1798; PHi.

June 23
PHILADELPHIA *Answer to Glouchester County Grand Jury*

Address of Gloucester County, New Jersey, grand jury praising services, answered. *Claypoole's Daily Advertiser,* June 25, 1798; PPHi; *Gazette of the United States,* June 23, 1798.

June 23
PHILADELPHIA *Payment on French Mission*

J.M. drew $2,000 from Secretary of State Pickering on account of the mission to France. (See account Sept. 3, 1798, herein.)

June 24
PHILADELPHIA *to Thomas Jefferson*

Compliments and regrets, reply to Jefferson note; leaving for Winchester. DLC, Papers of Thomas Jefferson; Mason, *Polly,* 119; Beveridge, *Marshall,* II, 347; Oster, *Marshall,* 182; The John Marshall House.

June 25
PHILADELPHIA *President John Adams to Gen. Belknap*

Discusses envoys to France; critical of Gerry, approving of Marshall and Pinckney. MHi, Belknap MSS, 161, c 37.

June 26
WOODFARD COUNTY, KY. *Will of Thomas Marshall*

Confirmation in will of Thomas Marshall of gift to J.M. of "The Oaks," Fauquier County, Virginia; also two tracts on Strouds' Fork of the Licking, Kentucky, to J.M. Compensation of executors and settlement of disputes by J.M. Mason County, Ky., Records (Maysville, Ky.), Will Book B, 212: Paxton, *Marshall Family,* 23.

Note: The above date is that of execution of the will. Thomas Marshall, father of J.M., died in Mason County, Ky., June 20, 1802, and is buried at the family plot and residence, Washington, Ky. His will was probated Feb. 15, 1803.

July 24
PHILADELPHIA *from Timothy Pickering*

Concerning copies of papers of envoys to France; distribution in Virginia. MHi, Pickering Coll., IX, 88; DNA, General Records Dept. of State, Domestic Letters, XI, 22; DLC, Beveridge Coll.

Memorandum of copies of Ross' edition of papers sent to J.M. DNA, General Records Dept. of State, Misc. Letters 1799–1800.

Aug. 8, *n.p.* *List of Gerry-Talleyrand Letters*

List of letters passing between Elbridge Gerry and Talleyrand Apr.–July, two to Pickering. Autograph note of J.M. explaining copies to government; added two later received from Gerry while he lay at Spithead. CSmH, RK 524.

Aug. 9
PHILADELPHIA *Robert Morris to James M. Marshall*

Opinions of Call and others on Genesee land controversy sent to J.M. for his opinion. VHi.

Aug. 11
RICHMOND *to Timothy Pickering*

Acknowledges letter of July 15, with copy of one to Gerry; also July 24, with copies of dispatches of envoys to France. Anxious as to French propositions made Gerry. Comments on opinion as favorable to administration; criticism analyzed; Alien and Sedition Acts as basis of attack. Anxious about Pinckney departure. J.M. pressed for money because of absence and dispersion of family; need for payment from Treasury; requests order from Secretary of Treasury or by Pickering on Col. Carrington for advance by him. Requests return of Journal. MHi, Pickering MSS, XXIII, 33; DLC, Elbridge Gerry Papers, Ac. 6138; DLC, Beveridge Coll.

Aug. 18
RICHMOND *to Polly Marshall—Addressed to Winchester, Va.*

Comments on children, advises cold baths, etc., to regain health. VW; DLC, Marshall Papers, Ac. 2535; MHi; WMQ (ser. 2), Vol. III (Apr., 1923), 81–82 (misdated Aug. 17); Mason, *Polly*, 121–22; Beveridge, *Marshall*, II, 370–71.

Aug. 24
PHILADELPHIA *from Robert Morris*

Regrets not seeing J.M. and delay in purchase of Fairfax land. Encloses shares of Bank of United States stock, also Pickett bank shares. Brother James M. Marshall in Amsterdam and expects loan. DLC, Robert Morris Letter Book, Vol. 2, Pt. 1, folio 83.

Aug. 27
MOUNT VERNON *George Washington to Bushrod Washington*

Expresses pleasure at the intended visit with him of J.M. and Bushrod Washington. Sparks, *Washington*, 292–93; Ford *Washington*, XIV, 75.

J.M. states that the invitation to spend a few days at Mount Vernon was pressing; Bushrod Washington consented to run for Congress; J.M. objected to doing so because of need for attending his pecuniary affairs, was persuaded to do so because of national crisis. Discussed with George Washington his return to public service as head of army. Marshall, *Autobiography*, 25–26; J.M. to Joseph Delaplaine, Mar. 22, 1818 (herein); J.M. to Paulding, Apr. 4, 1835 (herein).

Aug.
RICHMOND *to Citizens of Richmond, Va.*

Address acknowledging reception by citizens of Richmond on return from French mission; justifying actions of American commissioners in XYZ Affair; possibility of war with France to protect our freedom. *The Columbian Centinel* (Boston, Mass.), Sept. 22, 1798; *Norfolk* (Va.) *Herald*, Aug. 30, 1798; Beveridge, *Marshall*, II, 571–73.

Sept. 3
RICHMOND *Account—Envoy to France*

July, 1797	Outfit as envoy	$ 9,000.00
June 23, 1798	Salary June 20, 1797—July 14, 1798; three months after received passport in Paris and return, one year, twenty-four days at $9,000 per annum	9,591.78
	Salary of secretary, John Brown, July 8, 1797—July 14, 1798, one year six days at $1,350 per annum	1,372.19
		$19,963.97

Received.

July 15, 1797	Cash from T. Pickering in part outfit	$ 3,500.00
	Drafts on Willink, Van Straphorst and Hubbard, bankers for Dept. of State, 1797–1798, 20,000 Guilders at 40¢	8,000.00
	Same for 50 Louis d'or	222.00
June 23 (1798)	Cash from T. Pickering	2,000.00
Oct.	Draft on same this day in favor of Edward Carrington	6,241.97
		$19,963.97

DNA, Treas. Dept., Miscellaneous Accounts Pertaining to Foreign Relations, France, VII, No. 92. R.G. 53.

Sept. 4
TRENTON *from Timothy Pickering, Department of State*

Reply to J.M. letter of Aug. 11. Authorizing advance to J.M. by Col. Carrington for French mission and requesting account; returning J.M.'s Paris Journal; critical of Gerry's correspondence with Talleyrand. MHi, Pickering MSS, IX; DNA, General Records Dept. of State, Domestic Letters, XI, 77. R.G. 59; DLC, Beveridge Coll.

Sept. 12
RICHMOND *from "A Freeholder"*

Letter propounding five questions: (1) Americanism, (2) foreign alliances, (3) alliance with Great Britain, (4) policy and actions of administration toward France, (5) position on repeal of Alien and Sedition Acts. Beveridge, *Marshall*, II, 574; *Columbian Centinel*, Oct. 20, 1798. Beveridge suspected J.M. wrote or suggested these questions. Beveridge, *Marshall*, II, 387n.

Sept. 15
RICHMOND *to Timothy Pickering*

Mentions letter of Griffith concerning impressions at Paris of future intercourse with France. Comment on Talleyrand letter to Gerry demanding names. Asserts Messrs. X, Y, and Z at private Talleyrand dinner with Gerry. Settlement of expense account by Col. Carrington at Richmond. MHi, Pickering MMS, XXIII, 138. (Acknowledged. DNA, General Records Dept. of State, Domestic Letters, XI, 100–101. Sept. 21, 1798.)

Sept. 20
TRENTON *from Timothy Pickering*

Apprehensive J.M. will refuse appointment as Justice of the U.S. Supreme Court tendered by President Adams; inquires if Bushrod Washington would accept. MHi, Pickering MSS, IX, 351; DNA, General Records Dept. of State, Domestic Letters, XI, 98. R.G. 59; DLC, Beveridge Coll.

Sept. 20
RICHMOND *to "A Freeholder"*

Answers by J.M. to five questions in letter of Sept. 12: (1) attached to American principles, (2) opposed to foreign alliances, (3) opposed to alliance with Great Britain, except temporarily against France, (4) policy toward France to preserve neutrality and independence, (5) not an advocate of Alien and Sedition Acts, favors nonrevival. *Columbian Centinel*

(Boston, Mass.), Oct. 20, 1798; *Times and Virginia Advertiser* (Alexandria, Va.), Oct. 11, 1798; Beveridge, *Marshall,* II, 574–77.

Above replied to by "A Freeholder" in letter dated Oct. 11 with further questions, and by a letter signed and undated by "Another Freeholder," addressed "To the Freeholders of the Congressional District of Henrico, etc." *The Virginia Argus* (Richmond, Va.), Oct. 12, 1798, 3; VHi; VMH, Vol. LXIV (Jan., 1956), 104.

Sept. 28
RICHMOND *to Timothy Pickering*

Declining offer of appointment by President Adams to associate justiceship on the U.S. Supreme Court, suggesting Bushrod Washington will accept. (J.M. based refusal on preference for practice at the bar. Bushrod Washington was appointed, "intercepted in his way to Congress." Marshall, *Autobiography,* 26.) Accounts transmitted. Astonished at delay of Gerry arrival. Logan; Pinckney arrival; Hauteval well disposed, devoted to Talleyrand. MHi, Adams Papers, LI, 133; Adams, *J. Adams Works,* VIII, 598n.

Oct. 1 *to Secretary of State*
RICHMOND *[Timothy Pickering]—Addressed to Trenton*

Concerning accounts, has drawn funds authorized of Col. Carrington. Conflict of parties in Virginia; apprehensive of affairs with Franch and Gerry delay. MHi, Pickering MSS, XXIII, 171; DLC, Beveridge Coll.

Oct. 4
TRENTON *from Timothy Pickering*

Arrival of H. M. Rutledge; letter to Gerry, anecdote concerning Gerry's alarm on sailing. Suggests J.M. write "proper animadversions" concerning mission to France; news of coalition against France; Pinckney having difficulties in returning from France. MHi, Pickering MSS, IX, 424; DLC, Beveridge Coll.

Oct. 10
RICHMOND *Receipt—Collection on Bond*

Receipt to William P. Byrd of $1,070 given by Mrs. Mary Byrd to William Shirtliff for £2,000. Jan. 31, 1778; also order on Thomas Willing to William Rawle for $1,333 ⅓ to be credited on bond. Autograph signed. VHi, MSS 2M3567b4.

Oct. 10
RICHMOND *Deed of Release—Fairfax Purchase*

James M. Marshall and wife, Hester, Richmond, on behalf selves and all others claiming title under Denny Fairfax to the Commonwealth of Virginia, pursuant to act of Nov. 8, 1796, to settle claim of State of lands, cases pending in Court of Appeals of Virginia and U.S. Supreme Court, pursuant to letter of J.M. Nov. 24, 1796, accepting settlement resolution of General Assembly, release of all claim or title in Northern Neck waste or unappropriated land at death of Lord Fairfax. Recorded, General Court, Richmond, Nov. 13, 1798, and June 9, 1809. Reproduced in *Marshall's Lessee v. E. Foley*, Fauquier County, Va., Land Causes 1833–1850, III, 8, at 31–36; also entered in evidence in *Philip Martin v. Moffett et al.*, U.S. Circuit Court, Va., Record Book, Chancery, R 1824. V, U.S. Circuit Court Case Papers, 1824.

Oct. 11, n.p. *to Col. Henry Smith, Surveyor of Russell County, Ky.*
(See herein Aug. 30, 1797, note.)

Complaining that two land entries made by him in then Washington County, now Russell County, Ky., improperly attributed to John Marshall of Richmond. Writer was father of Humphrey Marshall and uncle of J.M. VHi.

Oct. 13
TRENTON *from Timothy Pickering*

Letter of Msgr. Hovy advising Pinckney departure from France. Gerry's budget; his opinion of effect of publication of envoy's dispatches on French. Talleyrand's knowledge of XYZ at time of demand for names; comments on French decree lifting embargo on American vassels. MHi, Pickering MSS, IX, 466.

Oct. 15
RICHMOND *to Timothy Pickering*

Acknowledges letter of Oct. 4. Expects support of Gerry by opposition; restrained from publishing comments on French mission by candidacy for Congress and by legal practice. Gerry should be answered if claims negotiations could have been successful. MHi, Pickering MSS, XIII, 231; DLC, Beveridge Coll.

Oct. 16
RICHMOND *Sale—Romney Lots*

Opinion of Virginia Council of State, granting application of James

M. Marshall to pay him proceeds of sale of lots in Romney on filing bond. V, Journal, Council of State, 1797–1798, 318, 320–21.

Oct. 17
RICHMOND *Bond—Romney Lots*

Bond executed by J.M. and James M. Marshall to James Wood, Governor of Virginia, £1,000 in connection with receipt of proceeds of sale of Romney lots; under act of Assembly, Auditor authorized to issue warrant on money in Treasury, James to refund if anyone thereafter produces better title. Witnesses: W. J. Ratcliffe, Benjamin Harrison, Jr., Geo. Pickett. V, Exec. Papers, Box 1798, June-Oct., File Oct.; CVSP VIII, 520–21.

Oct. 19, Oct. 20 [postscript]
TRENTON *from Timothy Pickering*

Returning Journal; copy made. Accuses Gerry of treachery in French negotiations (XYZ Affair); lauds Marshall; suggests J.M. write history of French mission; refers to President Adams criticism of envoys in address from Machias. Journal to be shown to President. In postscript, refers to letter from King quoting Col. Trumbull concerning Hauteval and *douceur* and loan demand. Pinckney commissioned major general. MHi, Pickering MSS, IX, 486; DLC, Beveridge Coll.

Oct. 20
RICHMOND *Bond—Romney Lots*

Approval of bond of J.M. and James M. Marshall by Virginia Council of State covering proceeds of sale of Romney lots. V, Journal, Council of State, 1797–1798, 322–23.

Oct. 22
RICHMOND *to Timothy Pickering*

Acknowledges letter of Oct. 18 (19). Rejoiced at Pinckney's arrival. Denies Gerry contention publication of envoy dispatches prevented French treaty. Influence of "French party" in Virginia; resolution of government censure projected. Pickering letter to people of Prince Edward County; charges against J.M. will recommence. Enclosure of notes to Gen. Pinckney and Maj. Rutlege (n.f.), MHi, Pickering MSS, XXIII, 251; DLC, Elbridge Gerry Papers, Ac. 6138; DLC, Beveridge Coll.

Oct. 26
RICHMOND *Newspaper Item*

Letter to J.M. from "A Republican" questioning him as to position on supremacy of House of Representatives, the treaty with France, a navy and standing army, the public debt, appointments and patronage. *The Virginia Argus*, Oct. 26, 1798, 4.

Nov. 5
TRENTON *from Timothy Pickering*

Concerning controversy with Gerry as to proposals made at Talleyrand dinner; Pickering letter to P. Johnston of Prince Edward County mentioned. Gerry betrayed mission; ought to be impeached. MHi, Pickering MSS, IX, 566.

Nov. 6
TRENTON *Timothy Pickering to George Cabot*

Concerning President's address to people of Machias; Pickering's suggestion J.M. write history of French mission, his refusal because of candidacy and law practice. President's tender of Justice of Supreme Court to J.M., praise of his conduct on mission. President's letter requesting publication of Gerry explanation of Talleyrand dinner; J.M. source of information; Pickering letter to P. Johnston; Gerry guilty of "betraying" colleagues. MHi, Pickering MSS, IX, 574.

Nov. 6
TRENTON *Timothy Pickering to Theodore Sedgwick*

Justification and explanation of J.M.'s answer to the "Freeholder" on Alien and Sedition Acts. Vindication of J.M. in *Columbian Centinel* procured by Cabot. Pinckney's opinion of J.M. as a "sterling fellow." MHi, Pickering MSS, IX, 570; also Same, Theo. Sedgwick, C. 222.

Nov. 6, *n.p.* *Receipt*

Receipt of J.M. to Mrs. Byrd of $150 on bond to William Shirtliff on Jan. 1, 1778, received by Parker. VHi, MSS 2, M3567b3.

Nov. 12
RICHMOND *to Elbridge Gerry*

Refers to Gerry letter to President concerning Pickering letter to Johnston of Prince Edward; justifies statements about Talleyrand dinner. MHi, Pickering MSS, XXIII, 308, and IX, 630; MHi, Adams Papers, LI, 158; DLC, Beveridge Coll.; VW.

Nov. 12
RICHMOND *to Timothy Pickering*

Acknowledges letters of Oct. 19, Nov. 5. Journal received; discounts

President's criticism in address to people of Machias; happy of Presidential approval; unwilling to have Journal shown President. Encloses letter of Nov. 12 to Gerry and certificate of facts; Pinckney to be added. Now of opinion French negotiations might have been successful under certain circumstances. MHi, Pickering MSS, XXIII, 306; DLC, Beveridge Coll.

Nov. 12
RICHMOND *to Timothy Pickering*

Certificate as to facts surrounding money request made on Gerry at Talleyrand dinner; facts published in Pickering letter to Peter Johnston. MHi, Pickering MSS, XXIII, 320.

Nov. 30
RICHMOND *Newspaper Item*

Letter of "Curtius" (John Thompson of Petersburg, Va.; see Beveridge, *Marshall,* II, 398) to J.M., attacking him; characterizing him as "important . . . in this country" and "leader of Federalists in Virginia." *The Virginia Argus,* Nov. 30, 1798, 1; June 18, 1799, 1.

Dec. 1
RICHMOND *to Robert Morris*

Opinion on Morris land litigation; effect of "thinking of the Judges." Condolence for loss of son. NhHi, Morris and Stack Papers, 67.

Dec. 18
RICHMOND *to William Vans Murray*

Enclosing two letters to Sykes, Palais Royal, Paris, on private business (n.f.). States never saw such intemperance as in Virginia General Assembly; fears resolution declaring Alien and Sedition Laws evils will carry; "American party" gains ground in election for national legislature except in New Jersey and Maryland (n.f.). Referred to and quoted in letter Murray to John Quincy Adams, Apr. 1, 1799. MHi, Adams Papers, XCVI, 124.

Dec. 10
RICHMOND *to Henry Banks*

Acknowledges letter of Nov. 20. Refuses to serve in connection with a "trust" involving Banks's affairs. VHi.

Dec. 30
MOUNT VERNON *from George Washington*

Request forwarding packet to Gen. Pinckney. Enclosing charge of

Judge Addison in Alien and Sedition case; comments on opponents; asks to convey charge to Bushrod Washington. Wishes J.M. success in candidacy for Congress; feels responsible for urging him. MH, Sparks MSS, 95; Washington Letters (5), 1786–1789, 385–86; DLC, Papers of George Washington, Letter Book 16, Box 317, 232–33.

Dec.
RICHMOND *Alien and Sedition Acts—Minority Address*

Address from the minority in the Virginia House of Delegates upon the resolution of the majority opposing the Alien and Sedition Laws; authorship attributed to J.M., who affirmed the constitutionality of the acts but opposed them as politically unwise. Journal, H.D. (Dec., 1798), 88–90. *The Address of the Minority in the Virginia Legislature to the People of That State, Containing a Vindication of the Constitutionality of the Alien and Sedition Laws* (Richmond, 1799). See J. Q. Adams to Wm. Vans Murray, Apr. 9, 1799, W. C. Ford (ed.), *The Writings of J. Q. Adams* (New York, Macmillan, 1913), II, 403; Beveridge, *Marshall,* II, 401–405.

n.d., n.p. *Poem, Alien and Sedition Acts*

Poem on the Alien and Sedition Acts, attributed by Thomas Jefferson to J.M.; publication suppressed after the sale of a few copies. (n.f.) See letter Thomas Jefferson to James Madison, May 31, 1798, Jefferson, *Writings,* X, 40 at 43.

n.d., n.p. *to Hopkins*

Enclosing introductory letter to Lee (n.f.); J.M. has written to Lee regularly; no response from him or his government. Wishes pleasant voyage. Long Island Hist. Soc.

LEGAL PRACTICE
U.S. CIRCUIT COURT, VIRGINIA

Dec. 7
RICHMOND *Deposition*

Autograph deposition as to mislaying paper in his hands as attorney. (See herein, 1795, Legal Practice, U.S. Circuit Court, *Scott v. Ware.*)

William and Mary Alexander, New York v. John and Thomas Brockenbrough, executors of Fauntelroy.

Office judgment, on execution for £101:12:8 Spanish milled dollars equal to $254, interest from 1793. J.M. for plaintiff.

Jan. 23, 1799. Execution, no property drawn by executor. J. for plaintiff. U.S. Circuit Court, Va., Record Book Index, O. J., 1798.

V, U.S. Circuit Court Case Papers, containing autograph petition.

Rebecca Backhouse, administratrix of John Backhouse, Great Britain v. John Mickie et al., executors of Robert Donald, Va.

Debt. on note of 1175. J.M. for plaintiff.

Sept. 30, 1796. Petition filed.

Dec. 4, 1797. Pleas: payment; full administration. U.S. Circuit Court, Va. Order Book III, 90.

Dec. 12, 1798. V, damages $5,591; j. £3,231:18:11 St. value of $14,-251.83, payable by verdict damages $5,591. Same, 78.

Same, Record Book Index, Civil, Nov. T, 1798.

V, U.S. Circuit Court Case papers, containing autograph petition.

Fee: Dec., 1789, £2:8. Account Book, 228.

Bank of North America v. Ezekiel Levy, s.p. Abraham Levy & Son.

Case. J.M. for defendant.

Dec. 5, 1792. Deposition. U.S. Circuit Court, Va. Order Book I, 139.

Dec. 4, 1793. Plea, general issue. Same, 245.

Dec. 4, 1794. Security for defendant. Same, 442.

May 26, 1795. Continued for deposition. Same, 479.

May 26, Nov. 22, 1797; Nov. 24, 1798, continued. Same, II, 214; III, 2, 108.

May 28, 1798. V.j. for defendant. Same, III, 209.

Same, Record Book Index, May T, 1798.

See also dismissal of earlier case, Record Book Index, May R, 1791.

Fee: May, 1794, £5:5. Account Book, 388.

John Dobson and Joseph Daltera, s.p. Dobson, Daltera and Walker, Great Britain v. Alexander and Peterfield Trent, Richard Crump, Daniel Bates, d.b.a. Stiles, Trents, Crump, & Bates.

Debt on note £4,100 St., equal £5,466:13:4 Va., 1776, goods sold, filed Nov., 1790. J.M. for defendants.

Nov. 22, 1797. Revival, death of plaintiff. U.S. Circuit Court, Va., Order Book III, 1.

Nov. 26, 1798. V.j. $5,409.33. Same, 112.

V, U.S. Circuit Court Case Papers, containing autograph pleadings on J.M.'s forms.

Dobson and Daltera, s.p. of Dobson, Daltera and Walker, merchants, Great Britain v. John Fowler.

Case, on obligation £6,530:7:4 St., 1775. J.M. for defendant.

Answer, payment to Loan Office, $33,333⅓.

May 25, 1792. Depositions in Great Britain. U.S. Circuit Court, Va., Order Book I, 96.

Nov. 22, 1797. Revival, death of plaintiff. Same III, 1.

Nov. 27, 1798. V.j. $43,260.93. Same, 123.

Same, Record Book Index. Dismissed, Jan. R, 1791; Nov., 1798.

V, U.S. Circuit Court Case Papers, containing answer on J.M.'s printed form filled in by him.

Fee: May, 1793, £4:10. Account Book, 362.

Samuel Donaldson, s.p. Gibson, Donaldson and Hamilton v. Joseph Friend, one of executors of Daniel McCallum.

Action in case, assumpsit for goods sold and delivered, indebted on July 16, 1794, £217:18:9. J.M. for plaintiff.

June 4, 1796. Plea, not assumed; continued. U.S. Circuit Court, Va., Order Book II, 171.

June 7, 1797. Continued. Same, 359.

Endorsed on document below, June, 1797, Common Order; July, Writ of Inquiry.

Nov. 24, 1797. Continued. Same, IV, 9.

Nov. 24, 1798. Dismissed, plaintiff not further prosecuting. Same, 108.

Autograph petition by J.M. NN, Berg Coll.

Related case in chancery, *Samuel Donaldson, s.p. of Gibson, Donaldson and Hamilton v. Joseph Friend, surviving executor of Daniel McCallum, deceased, s.p. Thomas and Donald Alexander & Co., et al.*, resulted in judgment by default, Dec. 10, 1804, £700 with interest from 1776.

U.S. Circuit Court, Va., Order Book V, 60. (J.M. sat on case).

John Tyndale Ware, executor of William Jones, s.p. Farrell and Jones v. Thomas Jefferson, Francis Eppes, Henry Skipwith and Anne, his wife, formerly Anne Wayles, Thomas and Francis Wayles, executors, and Anne, executrix of John Wayles.

Case. J.M. for defendants.

Nov. 26, 1791. Notice of depositions. U.S. Circuit Court, Va., Order Book I, 59.

Dec. 3, 1791. Order for depositions in Great Britain. Order Book I, 81.

Dec. 1, 1792. Pleas: *non assumpsit*; statute of limitations; Britisher not recover; violation of Treaty of Paris; Declaration of Independence. Demurrer by plaintiff to last three. Same, 132.

Dec. 4, 1793. Plaintiff dead; J. T. Ware, executor, substituted. Same, 241, 243.

Dec. 5, 1793. Depositions in Great Britain. Same, 250.

May 29, 1795. Declaration and pleas amended. Same, 501.

May 30, 1796. Continued. Same, II, 138.

May 25, 1797. Hearing. Jury sent out to deliberate. Same, 211.

May 29, 1797. Continued by plaintiff; deposition. Juror withdrawn. Same, 237, 240.

Nov. 26, 1797. Jury impaneled. Juror withdrawn. Same, III, 7.

Nov. 26, 1798. Same. Same, 116.

Nov. 28, 1798. Verdict for defendant, finding that did not assume. Same, 125.

Same, Record Book Index. Civil, Nov. T, 1797; Nov. T, 1798.

V, U.S. Circuit Court Case Papers.

Fee: Mar., 1791, £7. Account Book, 276.

William Jones, s.p. Farrell and Jones v. Francis Ruffin, executor of John Ruffin.

Case, goods sold and delivered, 1769, £196:9:12 St. J.M. for defendant.

May 24, 1791. J. entered by clerk set aside. Pleas: not assume; five-year statute of limitations; Britisher not recover. U.S. Circuit Court, Va., Order Book I, 44.

Nov. 28, 1791. New pleas, payment to Loan Office. Same, 63.

Dec. 3, 1791. Depositions in Great Britain. Same, 82.

Dec. 4, 1793. Plaintiff dead, *scire facias* by J. T. Ware. Same, 243.

Dec. 5, 1793. Depositions. Same, 249.

May 24, 1794. New *scire facias*. Same, 361.

May 30, 1796. Plea of payment to loan office denied. Same, II, 143.

Nov. 24, 1797. Continued. Same, III, 8.

Nov. 28, 1798. Dismissed for failure to prosecute. Same, 125.

V, U.S. Circuit Court Case Papers, containing pleas on J.M.'s printed forms.

Fee: Sept., 1787, £4:12:10. Account Book, 122.

John Lloyd, executor Osgood Hanbury, s.p. Capel and Osgood Hanbury v. Robert Cowne, executor Thomas Whiting.

Case. J.M. for defendant.

May 26, 1796. Continued. U.S. Circuit Court, Va., Order Book II, 122.

May 29, 1797. Continued. Same, 239.

Nov. 23, 1797. Depositions in Great Britain. Same, III, 3.

Nov. 29, 1798. V.j. for defendant. Same, 129.

Same, Record Book Index, Civil, Nov. T, 1798.

Fee: Mar., 1794, £6:4. Account Book, 382.

William Robinson Lidderdale, executor of John Lidderdale v. Benjamin and Carter B. Harrison, administrators of Benjamin Harrison; Carter Page, acting executor of Archibald Cary, s.p. William Prentis & Co.; Beverly and Robert Randolph, sons, and Peter Skipwith Randolph, grandson of Peter Randolph.

In chancery, claim on estate of Peter Randolph on bill of exchange, £150, 1762. J.M. for Randolphs.

Dec. 6, 1793. Depositions by plaintiff. U.S. Circuit Court, Va., Order Book I, 252.

Mar. 14, 1794. Autograph answer by J.M. for Beverly Randolph, alleging large j. taken by Lidderdale against Peter Randolph two years after his death, which occurred in 1767, must have included bill of exchange sued on. V, U.S. Circuit Court Case Papers, 1798.

Dec. 12, 1798. Abated as to Beverly Randolph by his death. J.j. against Harrisons and Page, £159 value of $666 with interest from 1762 and costs, from goods and chattels of estate, if insufficient costs against said defendants. U.S. Circuit Court, Va., Order Book III, 176.

Murdock & Co., Great Britain v. Walter Chisholm.

Office Judgment. Debt, on bond £150 equal to $400. J.M. for plaintiff.

Mar. 26, 1796. Defendant not found.

Jan., 1797. Alias.

U.S. Circuit Court, Va., Record Book Index, O. J., 1798.

V, U.S. Circuit Case Papers.

William Rawle, Philadelphia, attorney, assignee of William and Isaac Wharton, executors of Carpenter Wharton, Philadelphia, assignee of William Shurtliff, Pa. v. Mary Byrd, Va.

Debt, on obligation under seal, £4,000 Va., payable by £2,000, Jan. 31, 1778, J.M. for plaintiff.

Dec. 1, 1798. Plea, payment. Verdict, not paid, damages $31.70. J. £4,000 Va., value of $13,333.33, dischargeable by payment of $31.70 damages. U.S. Circuit Court, Va., Order Book III, 139.

Evidence in case: Oct. 10, 1798, receipt by J.M. from William P. Boyd of $1,070 in part payment of £2,000 bond and order on Thomas Willing to Rawle for $1,333.33.

Nov. 6, 1798, receipt for $150 received by Parker on same, signed by J.M. "Clk."

Same, Record Book VII, 129–38; above receipts at 138.

V, U.S. Circuit Court Case Papers, containing autograph petition.

Court of Appeals of Virginia

David Hunter et al, v.. Adam Hall, 1 Call 178.

Appeal from High Court of Chancery, Sept. 29, 1794, granting appellee right to land, reversed and dismissed. J.M. for appellee.

Bill alleging survey on entry of 400 acres adjoining land of A.K., deceased. Also, 400 acres on the South Branch, adjoining Lord Fairfax's land, at the mouth of Mill Creek. Hall claimed right to survey from the former tract on the east side of the river, crossing the river to the Fairfax tract on the west side. Hunter claimed under survey made on same land as vacant on west side, had brought caveat against Hall, dismissed proceedings because caveat not properly entered, and thereafter received patent. High Court of Chancery ruled for Hall on grounds unfair practice to obtain grant pending caveat.

Held, rights of parties not determined by dismissal of caveat, not on its merits; entry of Hall insufficient to carry survey on east side of river.

Apr. 26, 1796. Continued. Court of Appeals, Va., Order Book III, 116.

Apr. 16, 1798. Heard. Same, 216.

Apr. 19, 1798. Reversed, bill dismissed. Same, 218.

Fee: Mar., 1795, "Hall. an old suit in Court of Appeals finished," £18:2. Account Book, 406.

Charles Fulgham v. Samuel Lightfoot, 1 Call 219.

Writ of supersedeas, j. for defendant in error, trespass on case. District Court, Suffolk, May 17, 1797, affirming County Court Isle of Wight, Aug. 5, 1795, £150, affirmed. J.M. for Fulgham, in early proceedings, Wickham for him herein.

Inspector of lumber of Smithfield, whose certificate required by law for export alleged shipments by plaintiff in error on forged certificates whereby had to resign office, claiming £1,000 damages, stating salary was £50 per year paid by merchants, whereas law provides for individual fees.

Held, declaration sufficient after verdict as to damages, though inartistically drawn.

May 5, 1798. Submitted. Court of Appeals, Va., Order Book III, 232.

May 7, 1798. Affirmed. Same.
Fee: July, 1795, £13. Account Book, 418.

Amos Jolliffe, Isaac and Thomas Brown, Abel and Mordecai Walker, Joseph and Isaac Steer, David and Samuel Lupton, Lewis Neil, Isaac Parkins, Joseph Hackney, David Ridgeway v. Isaac Hite, Jun., and Archibald McDonald, executors of Mary McDonald and Isaac Hite, 1 Call 262.

Appeal from High Court of Chancery Sept. 6, 1796, dismissing bill of appellants, affirmed. J.M. for appellants at earlier date; cause in Court of Appeals, Wickham for appellants, Williams for appellees.

Executors advertised premises for public sale "containing 578 acres"; before sale announced, had deed for such acreage but did not warrant. Survey after purchase showed 512 acres and excluded plot with meeting house purchaser intended to buy. Purchaser refusing to pay full price refused deed, brought action for remission of price.

Held, sale was of tract containing more or less than named acreage, no grounds for remission.

Apr. 18, 1798. Heard. Court of Appeals, Va., Order Book III, 216.
May 11, 1798. Affirmed. Same, 234.
Fee: Nov., 1793, £7. Account Book, 376.

Thomas Dunn and Jeany, his wife v. Charles Bray, personally and administrator of Winter Bray, 1 Call 294.

Appeal from decree High Court of Chancery, Sept. 6, 1795, affirming County Court of Essex, j. for appellee, Aug. 20, 1793. J.M. for appellee in earlier proceedings, Call for same herein.

Will devised land in tail to Winter, by separate item certain slaves to same, if dies without issue to son Charles.

Held, a valid executory devise, Charles taking after death of Winter, as against heirs of latter, following English rule.

Oct. 17, 1798. Heard. Court of Appeals, Va., Order Book III, 253.
Oct. 19, 1798. Affirmed. Same, 254.
Fee: Aug., 1793, £5. Account Book, 368.

William Cabell, Jr., and others v. John Hardwick, 1 Call 301, 302, 304–305.

Appeal from j. District Court, New London, Sept. 18, 1795, for appellee, affirmed. J.M. for appellant.

Debt, action by appellant on an administration bond made out to justices of the court without stating in what capacity bringing action. In District Court the bond was refused in evidence, judgment for defendant.

Oct. 18, 1798. Case submitted. Court of Appeals, Va., Order Book III, 254.

Oct. 23, 1798. Affirmed. Same, 257.

Fee: Oct., 1795, £2:14. Account Book, 422.

John Hopkins v. Thomas Blane et al. 1 Call 315, 319–20.

Appeal from High Court of Chancery, Sept. 2, 1795.

J. dismissing bill of appellant, affirmed. J.M. for appellant. Blane, a London merchant, authorized Hunter, of Alexandria, to purchase grain and ship quickly in vessels sent for purpose, shortage in Europe, draw bills on Blane. Instead Hunter bought tobacco of Hopkins, gave bills on Blane who refused payment, waited three years after protest to sue Blane.

Held, bills taken on Hopkins' credit not in keeping with agency.

Oct. 25, 1798. Heard. Court of Appeals, Va., Order Book II, 259.

Nov. 3. Affirmed. Same, 266.

Pryor v. Adams, 1 Call 332, 334–35, 336.

Appeal from High Court of Chancery, Oct. 2, 1795.

J. for appellee, plaintiff below, reversed. J.M. for appellant.

Bill on indebtedness on bond, 1774, £66:7:10, alleging receipt of £83:1 paper money in 1780, when reduced by scale £1:17 specie, claiming promise to pay by general scale when fixed; bond given up. Decree of May, 1792, dismissing bill set aside. Issue as to promise directed to District Court of Richmond; finding for plaintiff and j. for balance in specie.

Held, Court of Chancery jurisdiction, nature of bill for discovery; proof as to promise clearly for defendant, not to be submitted; act of 1780 setting depreciation scale not apply to debts before 1777 paid before 1781.

Apr. 27, 1797. Heard. Court of Appeals, Va., Order Book III, 169.

Oct. 22, 1798. Reheard. Same, 257.

Oct. 25, 1798. Reversed, original decree for appellee affirmed. Same, 259.

Fee: Sept., 1795, "Col. Pryor," £5. Account Book, 422.

Robert Shaw v. Abraham Clements, 1 Call 373, 374–75.

Appeal from District Court of Staunton, Sept. 6, 1794.

Writ of right, j. for appellee, plaintiff below, affirmed. J.M. for appellee.

Action by purchaser from patentee of 400 acres, Rockbridge County, patented 1740, against purchaser of patentee of 1765 who had received j. in General Court in 1753 that lands forfeited for nonpayment of quitrents, and held possession. Decree for holder under first patent based on special verdict of jury with damages. Held, under Virginia statutes jury may render special verdict and assess damages in action writ of right; common law of England discussed.

Apr. 13, 1796. Case submitted. Court of Appeals, Va., Order Book III, 109.

May 13. Continued for rehearing. Same, 132.

Oct. 19, 1798. Resubmitted. Same, 255.

Nov. 1. Affirmed. Same, 263.

Fee: Apr., 1795, £5. Account Book, 412.

Francis Graves v. Foster Webb, 1 Call 385, 386, 387–88.

Appeal from District Court of Richmond, Sept. 12, 1794, reversing and amending j. Hustings Court of Richmond, Dec. 28, 1789. J.M. for appellee, plaintiff below, affirmed.

J. upon motion by surety on bond against principal for payment of j. against latter of military certificates. J. in Hustings Court was in specie amount £7,950:17:6, specie payable in military certificates of £1,721:12:1. Richmond City, Va., Hustings Court, Order Book II, 469.

Reversed by District Court, j. for military certificates alone.

Held, under Virginia act authorizing recovery by security on motion, j. for things is authorized, contrary to suit at common law.

Oct. 11, 1798. Webb dead, administrator substituted. Court of Appeals, Va., Order Book III, 245.

Nov. 1, 1798. Affirmed. Same, 264.

Fees: Oct., 1784, "Webb for fees," £14; Oct., 1787, "Webb on replevin bond," £2:5. Account Book, 18, 130.

William Jones v. John Jones, 1 Call 396, 397–98.

Appeal from District Court of Prince Edward Courthouse, Apr. 8, 1796.

Writ of right, j. for appellee, demandant below, reversed. J.M. and Edmund Randolph for appellant.

Father, Thomas, and sons John and William obtained patents, 1740, 400 acres each adjoining; Thomas patented 400 acres more in 1746. In 1755 inclusive patent obtained by all three for 2,762 acres including above all adjoining. William in possesssion after father's death of his original patent and that of 1746 to father. Action by John as eldest son and heir for latter tract, claiming father held his 800 acres separately in fee.

Held, joint patent created joint tenancy, existing division on that basis.

Oct. 25, 26, 29, 31. Case heard. Court of Appeals, Va., Order Book III, 259, 260, 263.

Nov. 3. Reversed. Same, 266.

The Auditor of Public Accounts v. Graham, 1 Call 411, 411–12.

Supersedeas to j. General Court, June 20, 1793.

Motion by Commonwealth for penalty under act of 1786, £500, against Clerk of Court of Prince William County for failure to account for fees and services in 1788; overruled under limitation of actions statute, affirmed. J.M. for appellee.

Held, statute of limitations applies to motions under phrase "suits and actions."

Oct. 18, 1798. Record presented. Court of Appeals, Va., Order Book III, 254.

Oct. 22. Affirmed. Same, 256.

Hooe v. Marquess, 4 Call 416, 419–21.

Appeal from High Court of Chancery, May 12, 1795, reversed, new trial, jury issues. J.M. and Bushrod Washington for appellee.

Plaintiff, appellee, purchased land of son who had received deed from father, recorded but destroyed, alleging another substituted with forfeiture clause for noncompliance with terms not in original deed. Father afterwards conveyed to purchaser with notice who sold to appellant with notice. Held, error of court in not determining by decree deed substituted and terms; issue of fraud involving conflicting evidence an issue for the jury.

May 7–8, 1798. Heard. Court of Appeals, Va., Order Book III, 232–33.

May 17. Continued for rehearing. Same, 241.

Oct. 20. Reheard. Same, 256.

Oct. 23. Reversed and remanded. Same, 258.

Samuel Woodson v. Thomas Payne, 1 Call 495.

Appeal from decree High Court of Chancery, Oct. 3, 1796, dismissing bill for injunction of j. of County Court, affirmed. J.M. for Woodson in earlier proceedings; Duval and Randolph for him in this appeal.

Appellant received final settlement or commutation certificates from appellee of £628 agreeing to keep for him and apply as directed. Certain amounts were so applied; other transactions in specie were involved which appellee claimed were to be repaid from interest on the certificates only. The certificates when converted into money by appellee left less than £10 specie due appellant if all credits claimed were allowed. The jury rendered verdict for appellee of £215 specie; new trial denied, j. entered.

Held, although verdict unjust, not a case for interference by equity; appellant had failed in proof to show proper time for conversion into money and values at that time.

Oct. 20, 1798. Heard. Court of Appeals, Va., Order Book III, 263.

Nov. 6, 1798. Affirmed. Same, 271.

Fee: Sept., 1794, "Chr," £1:14. Account Book, 396.

Denny Fairfax, formerly Denny Martin v. The Commonwealth.

Appeal from j. District Court, Prince William County, at Dumfries, Oct. 24, 1794 (District Court, Prince William, Order Book 1794–1798, 82, 84), overruling demurrer to plea of traverse to *monstrans de droit* to the inquisition of office and right to land adjudged in Commonwealth, reversed and inquisition quashed. J.M. for appellant.

May 5–8, 1795. Case heard. Court of Appeals, Va., Order Book III, 63, 65, 66.

Nov. 14. Continued for rehearing. Same, 98.

Nov. 14–18, 1796. Reheard. Same, 150–52.

Oct. 10, 1798. Agreement appellant by attorney and Commonwealth by Attorney General that James M. Marshall claiming under appellant, in accordance with act of Assembly, 1796, act concerning lands in Northern Neck, extinguished his rights to certain lands and Commonwealth its right to lands in inquisition. Reversed, annulled, and quashed. Same, 244–45. (See herein July 10, 1795).

May 10, 1799. Order of Court of Appeals returned at (District) Court at Dumfries and order accordingly. District Court, Prince William, Order Book 1799, 6, 7.

For order of District Court and appeal, District Court, Prince William, Order Book 1794–1798, 82, 84.

(See also herein 1797, Legal Practice, Prince William.)

John Land v. Joseph Curd.

Appeal from High Court of Chancery, May 20, 1795, reversing Court of Buckingham County, Mar. 13, 1793, and dismissing appellant's bill.

J.M. for appellant.

Apr. 21, 1797. Heard. Court of Appeals, Va., Order Book III, 163.

Oct. 12, 1798. Reheard. Same, 247.

Oct. 15, 1798. Reversed, County Court affirmed.

Commissioner erred in using different scales of value of payments and debits, according to statute payments in paper currency credited at nominal value; also failed to credit payment against bond specified. Same, 249.

Fees: Oct., 1794, £5; July, 1795, £5. Account Book, 396, 418.

District Court, Fredericksburg

William Coleman v. James May, et al.

Trespass. J.M. for defendant.

May 14, 1798. Dismissed, agreed between parties. District Court, Fredericksburg, Law Orders B, 1794–1798, 439.

Fee: Aug., 1794, £2:10. Account Book, 394.

Gabriel Johnston v. John Johnston.

Ejectment, messuage, tenement, 226 acres Parish of Hanover, County of King George. J.M. for plaintiff.

May 6, 1790. Continued by defendant; commission to plaintiff for depositions. District Court, Fredericksburg, Law Order A, 1789–1793, 113.

Oct. 2, 1790. On motion of defendant, county surveyor survey land, leave to take depositions. Same, 146.

Oct. 4, 1790. Continued by defendant. Same, 152.

May 4, 1791. Jury disagreement, juror withdrawn. Same, 232.

May 7, 1791. Agreement of parties, if Commonwealth right to grant land in Northern Neck under act of 1785 entitled "An Act for Safe Keeping the Land Papers of the Northern Neck in Registers' Office," j. for plaintiff; otherwise for defendant. Same, 249.

May 8, 1794. Abated by death of defendant. Same, B, 1794–1798, 47.

Oct. 10, 1796. Same agreement by parties. Same, 266.

May 8, 1798. Abated by death of defendant Elizabeth Johnston in whose name had been revived. Same, 405.

Fees: Mar., 1791, £5:12; Sept., 1794, £5. Account Book, 278, 396.

William A. Washington v. John Thornton.

Case. J.M. for plaintiff.

May 6, 1797. Commission for depositions in Pennsylvania, commissioners appointed.

May 2, 1798. Dismissed, agreed between parties. District Court, Fredricksburg, Law Orders B, 1794–1798, 293, 381.

Fee: Oct., 1790, £4:4. Account Book, 262.

County Court, Henrico

James and Stephen Southall, executors of Turner Southall v. J.M., executor of Serefino Farmicola.

Mar. 6, 1798. Case, default j. set aside. Plea, *non assumpsit.* V. j. £43:8. Henrico County Quarterly Court, Order Book III, 598.

LAND TRANSACTIONS
Hardy County, Virginia
(Now West Virginia)

Feb. 7 *Deed*

J.M. by Rawleigh Colston, attorney in fact, to John Rennicks, conveyance of remainder interest 215 acres, leased Thomas Lord Fairfax to John Ulrick Spore, Aug. 3, 1773. Consideration £88:11:4. Recorded May 8, 1798. Hardy County, Va., Deed Book A, 65.

Feb. 7 *Deed*

J.M. by Rawleigh Colston, attorney in fact, to Isaac Pancake, conveyance of remainder interest, ninety acres, leased Thomas Lord Fairfax to John Pancake, Aug. 3, 1773. Consideration £40:17. Recorded May 7, 1798. Hardy County, Va., Deed Book A, 75.

Feb. 7 *Deed*

J.M. by Rawleigh Colston, attorney in fact, to David Welton, 18½ and 26½ acres. Consideration £12 Virginia. Recorded May 7, 1798. Hardy County, Va., Deed Book A, 78.

Feb. 7 *Deed*

J.M. by Rawleigh Colston, attorney in fact, to David Welton, remainder interest, 129 acres, No. 31, east side South Branch of the Potomac, leased Thomas Lord Fairfax to Felix Seymour, Aug. 3, 1773. Consideration £40. Recorded May 7, 1798. Hardy County, Va., Deed Book A, 80.

Feb. 7 *Deed*

J.M. to Rawleigh Colston, attorney in fact, to Job Welton, remainder interest in four leases executed by Denny Martin Fairfax Dec. 4, 1790, 135 acres, 12 acres, 57 acres, and 50 acres. Consideration £100. Recorded May 7, 1798. Hardy County, Va., Deed Book A, 82.

Feb. 7 *Deed*

J.M. by Rawleigh Colston, attorney in fact, to David Welton, conveyance of remainder interest, forty-eight acres, No. 43, west side South Branch of the Potomac, leased by Thomas Lord Fairfax to Michael Ault, Aug. 3, 1773; also seventy-eight acres, leased by Denny Martin Fairfax to

Welton, May 21, 1791. Consideration £40. Recorded May 7, 1798. Hardy County, Va., Deed Book A, 101.

Deed

Feb. 7

J.M. by Rawleigh Colston, attorney in fact, to Anthony Baker, remainder interest, three tracts, 29 acres, No. 30, leased by Thomas Lord Fairfax to Philip Martin; 82 acres, No. 32, leased Same to Same; 113 acres, No. 25, leased Thomas Lord Fairfax to Anthony Baker; all on Aug. 3, 1773. Consideration £78:19:9. Recorded May 8, 1798. Hardy County, Va., Deed Book A, 103.

Deed

Feb. 7

J.M. by Rawleigh Colston, attorney in fact, to Christopher Strader, forty-five acres leased by Denny Martin Fairfax, Dec. 4, 1790. Consideration £64:10:1. Recorded May 8, 1798. Hardy County, Va., Deed Book A, 104.

Deed

Feb. 7

J.M. by Rawleigh Colston, attorney in fact, to Job Welton, remainder interest, five tracts South Branch Manor, Hardy County, 55 acres, No. 70, leased Thomas Lord Fairfax to John Cochran, Aug. 3, 1773; 234 acres, No. 69, to Welton, same date; 55 acres, No. 64, to Welton, same date; 172 acres to Welton, Mar. 9, 1779; ——— acres, No. 73, leased Thomas Lord Fairfax to Sylvester Ward, May 11, 1779. Consideration £200. Recorded May 8, 1798. Hardy County, Va., Deed Book A, 108.

Deed

Feb. 7

J.M. by Rawleigh Colston, attorney in fact, to David Welton, reversion interest, two tracts, eighty-two acres, No. 33, west side South Branch of the Potomac, leased by Thomas Lord Fairfax to Melchior Baker, Aug. 3, 1773; twenty-one acres, No. 29, leased Fairfax to Henry Morsh, same date. Consideration £40. Recorded May 10, 1798. Hardy County, Va., Deed Book A, 119.

Deed

Feb. 7

J.M. by Rawleigh Colston, attorney in fact, to Teakman Our. Thirteen acres on South Mill Creek, surveyed by John Foley, Sept. 7, 1798. Consideration £10 Virginia. Recorded Sept. 7, 1798. Hardy County, Va., Deed Book A, 131.

Feb. 7 *Deed*

J.M. by Rawleigh Colston, attorney in fact, to Robert Darling, reversion interest, 145 acres, No. 18, leased Thomas Lord Fairfax to William Darling, Aug. 3, 1773; 96 acres, No. 17, leased Fairfax to Mansah Hampton, Aug. 3, 1773. Consideration £58:9. Recorded May 6, 1799. Hardy County, Va., Deed Book A, 131.

Feb. 7 *Deed*

J.M. by Rawleigh Colston, attorney in fact, to Isaac Vanmeter, conveyance of reversionary interest in four tracts, 652 acres, No. 2, leased Thomas Lord Fairfax to Garrett Vanmeter; 68 acres, No. 4, Same to Same, Mar. 6, 1780; 187 acres, No. 3, Fairfax to John Sibley, Aug. 3, 1773. Consideration £366:14:1. Recorded May 6, 1799. Hardy County, Va., Deed Book A, 150.

Feb. 7 *Deed*

J.M. by Rawleigh Colston, attorney in fact, to David Welton, remainder interest, 200 acres of 400½-acre tract, No. 29, east side South Branch of the Potomac; 24 acres, No. 31, west side of South Branch of Potomac, leased Thomas Lord Fairfax to Michael Ault, Aug. 3, 1773. Consideration £40. Recorded May 7, 1798. Hardy County, Va., Deed Book A, 157.

Mar. 5 *Deed*

J.M. by Rawleigh Colston, attorney in fact, to Anthony Baker, twenty-eight acres, surveyed by John Foley, Dec. 2, 1797. Consideration £7 Va. Recorded Sept. 7, 1798. Hardy County, Va., Deed Book A, 127.

Apr. 5 *Deed*

J.M. by Rawleigh Colston, attorney in fact, to Anthony Baker, twenty-nine acres, surveyed by John Foley, Sept. 7, 1798. Consideration £7:5 Virginia. Recorded Sept. 7, 1798. Hardy County, Va., Deed Book A, 129.

Apr. 25 *Deed*

J.M. by Rawleigh Colston, attorney in fact, to Jesse Welton, thirty-five acres. Consideration £8:15 Virginia. Recorded May 8, 1798. Hardy County, Va., Deed Book A, 63.

Apr. 25 *Deed*

J.M. by Rawleigh Colston, attorney in fact, to David Welton, 14½ acres, surveyed by John Foley, Feb. 3, 1798. Consideration £4 Virginia. Recorded May 7, 1798. Hardy County, Va., Deed Book A, 77.

Apr. 25 *Deed*

J.M. by Rawleigh Colston, attorney in fact, to Job Welton, fifty-six acres, surveyed by John Foley, Nov. 3, 1791. Consideration £35:0:5. Recorded May 8, 1798. Hardy County, Va., Deed Book A, 105.

May 4 *Deed*

J.M. by Rawleigh Colston, attorney in fact, to Jonathan Hutton, twenty acres, adjoining Hutton's. Consideration £5 Virginia. Recorded May 9, 1798. Hardy County, Va., Deed Book A, 110.

May 4 *Deed*

J.M. by Rawleigh Colston, attorney in fact, to Jonathan Hutton, fifty-three acres. Consideration £13:5 Virginia. Recorded May 9, 1798. Hardy County, Va., Deed Book A, 112.

Aug. 6 *Deed*

J.M. by Rawleigh Colston, attorney in fact, to Jonathan Hutton, twenty-four acres, surveyed by John Foley, Dec. 2, 1797. Consideration £6. Recorded Sept. 9, 1798. Hardy County, Va., Deed Book A, 121.

Nov. 8 *Deed*

J.M. by Rawleigh Colston, attorney in fact, to John Hay, 100 acres, leased Denny Martin Fairfax to Alexander White, Dec. 4, 1790. Consideration £25. Recorded May 6, 1799. Hardy County, Va., Deed Book A, 152.

Dec. 13 *Deed*

J.M. by Rawleigh Colston, attorney in fact, to David Welton, 5¼ acres, and 7 acres 28 poles adjoining own lot, South Branch Manor. Consideration £3:1:3 Virginia. Recorded May 6, 1799. Hardy County, Va., Deed Book A, 159.

1799

DOCUMENTS

PHILADELPHIA *French Mission Papers*

List of persons to whom total of 233 copies of Ross's edition of papers relative to mission to France sent. Six copies to Gen. Marshall July 24, 1798. DNA, General Records Dept. of State, Misc. Letters, Jan.–June, 1799, 1.

Jan. 4
RICHMOND *Pinckney—Visit to Richmond*

Gen. Pinckney invited to home of J.M. during stop at Richmond. Va. Gaz. & G. A., Jan. 4, 1799, 3.

Jan. 8
RICHMOND *to George Washington*

Acknowledges letter of Dec. 30; delivered packet to Gen. Pinckney; latter left on 4th. Thanks for charge of Judge Addison, well written, should be generally read; no arguments moderate opposition, but possible to impress mass of the people; forwarding to (Bushrod) Washington. Despite regret at one of the acts complained of (Alien and Sedition Acts), did not raise tempest; causes deeper. Opposition to any act operating on press captivates public. Serious and alarming debates in Congress on Col. Taylor resolution charging administration seeks monarchy; George K. Taylor resolution on controversy with France and amendment by Col. Nicholas showing Virginia opposition. Comments on men desiring to hold power by any means, even to dissolution of the Union. Next election important; divided legislature in interest of moderation. Uncertain of own election; opposition malignant; if fails, because of temper hostile to government. MH, Sparks MSS, XXIV, MSS Hamilton, etc., 189–91; DLC, John Marshall Papers, Var. Ac. 4314A; Beveridge, *Marshall*, II, 407–408 (excerpt).

Jan. 8 *Patrick Henry to Archibald Blair*

Attacks France; J.M. and colleagues upheld American character. Gratified by J.M.'s public ministry, and esteems as private citizen. Supports J.M.'s candidacy for Congress; prefers to anyone but Washington. Henry, *Patrick Henry*, II, 591–95; Beveridge, *Marshall*, II, 411–12.

Feb. 9
RICHMOND *Trust Sale*

Sale under deed of trust to J.M. to secure debt to William Bentley, guardian of children of William Ronald, deceased, of interest in Black Heath coal pits, Chesterfield County; at Eagle Tavern, Richmond, May 15. Signed J.M. Va. Gaz. & G. A., Feb. 12, 1799, 3. Intermittently in Same to May 3, 1799, 1.

Feb. 19
RICHMOND *to Secretary of State [Timothy Pickering]*

Absence from Richmond delayed acknowledgment of Pickering analysis and commentary on late French negotiations, approves as correct and able; criticizes Gerry letter on the subject. MHi, Pickering MSS, XXIV, 95; Charles W. Upham (Octavius Pickering), *The Life of Timothy Pickering* (Boston, Little, Brown, 1873), III, 389 (excerpt).

Mar. 3
RICHMOND *to Charles Lee*

Letter approving appointment of Murray as commissioner in second French negotiations (n.f.). Referred to in Charles Lee to John Adams, Mar. 14, 1799, and enclosed therein. MHi, Adams Papers, John Adams Letters Rec'd., L, 242; also in Adams, *J. Adams Works,* VIII, 628 and note, and in letter Adams to Lee returning it. Mar. 29. MHi, Adams Papers, John Adams Letter Book, Mar. 29–July 8, 1799, 1.

Mar. 24, *n.p.* *Robert Brooke to the Governor*

J.M. refused to act on the request of the Governor of Virginia together with Robert Brooke and Randolph to advise with respect to claims of Commonwealth to real estate of the late Bryan Martin, supposed to be escheatable because devised to an alien. Inquest to be held by Thruston, escheater for Frederick County on Apr. 16. CVSP, IX, 12.

Apr. 3
RICHMOND *to James M. Marshall*

Acknowledges letters. Approves James bringing ejectment of Winchester land; would have suggested distress, but tenants do not agree that one case will settle; no formal court decision Fairfax held Northern Neck in fee; no objection to such finding; suggests using agreed case between Hunter and Fairfax in which title agreed as model; will send papers in federal court case by Smith; otherwise, use those in Peyton's office; finding as to old town not essential; show particular lot sold. Will bring chancery suit against Pendleton and others; Davies the public printer, subscription to paper. Will advise amounts collected for James at Treasury; not to mention money loaned to Marshall. Dr. Conrad's misquoting J.M. concerning Gerry. J.M.'s election uncertain. Allows discretion in bringing ejectments to collect rent on property. Maj. (George Keith) Taylor and sister Jane relations and marriage intent. Received additional letter with certificate. DLC, Beveridge Coll.; Beveridge, *Marshall,* II, 174–75, 410 (excerpt).

Apr. 28
RICHMOND *from James Innes—to Particular Care of Gov. Lee*

Convey apologies to Court of Appeals for nonattendance. After deducting one year rent due Farmicola's estate (J.M. administrator), and moiety of Norton's bond as security for Jones, balance due Innes £20. Directs to pay Governor for hogshead of wine. VW.

May 1
RICHMOND *to George Washington*

Regrets publication of false statement that office of Secretary of State offered to him by Washington; attributes to political opponents in campaign. DLC, Papers of George Washington, Vol. 295; Oster, *Marshall*, 172–73; Iles, *Little Masterpieces*, I, 96–97 (incomplete); Sparks, *Washington*, XI, 424n.

May 5
MOUNT VERNON *from George Washington*

Congratulates on election to House of Representatives; assures that publication referred to in J.M.'s letter of May 1 not seriously regarded. Asks for further information on elections to Congress and legislature. DLC, Papers of George Washington, Vol. 295; DLC, Beveridge Coll.; *Green Bag*, Vol. VIII (Dec., 1896), 483; Sparks, *Washington*, XI, 424; Iles, *Little Masterpieces*, I, 97 (dated 15th in error).

May 12
MOUNT VERNON *from George Washington*

Asks assistance of J.M. in selection of officers in army; encloses letter from Secretary of War, and data concerning Virginia. DLC, Papers of George Washington, Vol. 295.

May 16
RICHMOND *to George Washington*

Letter of 12th will be referred to Cols. Harrington and Heth. Elections in Virginia to Anti-Federalists; legislature hostile to Union. French war on Austria commented on. DLC, Papers of George Washington, Vol. 296; Oster, *Marshall*, 173–74.

May 16
PHILADELPHIA *from Timothy Pickering*

Answering letter of J.M. of 9th concerning appointment of consul to Glasgow (n.f.). Election in Virginia and New York gives joy. MHi, Pickering MSS, XI, 91.

June 6
MOUNT VERNON *from George Washington*

Acknowledges letter of May 16; asks further advice of J.M., Col. Carrington, and Col. Heth on selection of army officers from Virginia; encloses letter of appointment of Cols. Cropper and Merrill if approved by them. DLC, Papers of George Washington, Vol. 296.

June 12
RICHMOND *to George Washington*

Acknowledges letter of 6th; communicated with Col. Carrington. Held Col. Cropper letter; would be ranked by officers in regular army formerly under his command. Recommends him, Gen. Clarke and Gen. Posey as brigadier general; Minnis, Breckenridge, Porterfield, Blackwell, Swearingen for command of regiment. Report of death of Patrick Henry, his services, loss. DLC, Papers of George Washington, Vol. 296; Oster, *Marshall*, 174–75.

June 14
FRANKFORT, KY. *Land Patent*

Patent to J.M. 847¾ acres Mason County, Ky. Surveyed Oct. 28, 1797. Adjoining a survey of J.M. of 1,239 acres on the south, in consideration of Treasury Warrants 11251, 13924. Land Grant No. 603. Kentucky Land Office, Old Kentucky Grants, Book II, 307–308.

June 14
FRANKFORT, KY. *Land Patent*

Patent to J.M., Jr., 1,934 acres, Mason County, Ky., on waters of the Ohio, adjoining 5,413 acres surveyed for J.M., Jr., on same entry in consideration of Treasury Warrants 14011, 12718, 12143. Delivered to Thomas Marshall, Jr., July 26, 1799. Surveyed Nov. 27, 1797. Patent No. 606. Kentucky Land Office, Old Kentucky Grants, Book II, 311–13.

June 14
FRANKFORT, KY. *Land Patent*

Patent to J.M., Jr., 50¼ acres, Mason County, Ky., north side North Fork of Licking adjoining 5,413 acres of Thomas Marshall, assignee to J.M. on same entry of 10,659½ acres made Jan. 11, 1783, in consideration of Treasury Warrants 14011, 12718, 12143. Delivered to Thomas Marshall,

Jr., July 26, 1799. Surveyed Nov. 27, 1797. Patent No. 607. Kentucky Land Office, Old Kentucky Grants, Book II, 312–13. (See J.M.'s power of attorney of July 29, 1799; deed of Apr. 3, 1812, herein.)

June 16
MOUNT VERNON *from George Washington*

Acknowledges letter of 12th. Withholding of Cropper letter approved; realizes question of rank; will forward revised letter to Cropper to get tender of his service and advice. DLC, Papers of George Washington, Vol. 296.

June 17
MOUNT VERNON *from George Washington*

Enclosing second letter to Col. Cropper, officership in Provisional Army; for inspection by J.M., Carrington, and Heth and forwarding. DLC, Papers of George Washington, Vol. 296; CSmH, HM 5402.

June 21
RICHMOND *to George Washington*

Returning letter to Col. Cropper; happy withholding transmission no offense; second letter forwarded (concerning appointment of Col. Cropper as officer in Provisional Army). DLC, Papers of George Washington, Vol. 296; Oster, *Marshall*, 176.

July 1
MOUNT VERNON *from George Washington*

Acknowledges letter of (June) 21st; thanks for assistance in Col. Cropper appointment. DLC, Papers of George Washington, Vol. 297.

July 25
RICHMOND *Sale by Trustees*

Sale of Negroes at Cross Roads near Four Mile Creek, Henrico County, under deed of trust to pay debt late Richard Randolph, Williamsburg, to Col. William Heth; signed as trustees by J.M., Harry Heth, Edward Carrington. Va.Gaz. & G.A., Aug. 6, 1799, 4, through Sept. 20, 1799. Sale postponed to Oct. 7. Same, Oct. 1, 1799, 4; Oct. 4, 1799, 4.

n.d. *Robbins Case*

Article appearing in the *Virginia Federalist* a few days after Judge Bee's decision in the District Court of South Carolina in the Jonathan Robbins case, July 25, 1799, attributed to J.M., in defense of the conduct of the President of the United States. *Journal of Jurisprudence: A New Series of the Law Journal* (Philadelphia, 1821), 28–32.

Aug. 8
PHILADELPHIA *Timothy Pickering to C. C. Pinckney*

Concerning contents of J.M.'s Journal in Paris; letter to J.M., who was going to Kentucky. MHi, Pickering MSS, XI, 582.

Aug. 23
NEW LONDON *from Inhabitants of Town of New London*

Address approving actions of J.M. as ambassador to France; war better than dishonorable peace. Address handed to J.M. when he passed through town. Va. Gaz. & G.A., Sept. 10, 1799, 3.

Aug. 25
RICHMOND *to Timothy Pickering*

Acknowledges letter of 5th; just returned from visiting father in Kentucky. Gives reasons why controversy over question of *rôle d'equipage* demand should not be left unsettled in negotiations with France, or left to determination by commissioners. Attached copy of three points which President Adams assented as ultimates on Mar. 11, 1799, for negotiations with France: indemnity to U.S. citizens, no condemnation for lack of *rôle d'equipage,* no guaranty of French territory. MHi, Pickering MSS, XXV, 113; Adams Papers, John Adams Letters Rec'd., XLIX, 64 (copy); DLC, Beveridge Coll. (typescript).

Sept. 10
NEW LONDON *to Citizens of New London*

Written address by J.M. thanking for address handed to him while passing through town approving of conduct as envoy to France; sought peace and independence, but peace unattainable; disdain to purchase by surrender of independence. Va. Gaz. & G.A., Sept. 10, 1799, 3.

Sept.
SUPERIOR COURT, HARDY COUNTY, VA. *Law Suit*

J.M. by Charles Magill v. Jonathan Hutton and William Bullett.

Action on bond for £36:10, payable May 9, 1799. Oct., 1799, default judgment, £18:5. May 8, 1800, set aside. Sept. 9, 1800, confessed judgment for £18:5. Superior Court, Hardy County, Va. (now W. Va.), Record Book, 1800–1803, 150; Superior Court, Hardy County, Va. (now W. Va.), Common Law Book, 1797–1803, 235, 283.

Oct. 11
RICHMOND *Power of Attorney*

Power of attorney by John Cox appointing J.M. to receive dividends from U.S. Treasury on stock in name of Cox on books of Commissioner of Loans of Virginia. PHC.

Dec. 16
PHILADELPHIA *to James M. Marshall*

Acknowledges letter of 7th. Pleasant remitted draft, $2,013.75, and certificates fourteen shares bank stock; enclosing power of attorney to transfer and draw dividends to be executed. Eight per cent stock transferred to books in Richmond; probably sold there; writing Hopkins. If remits bills on account of stock, must have money to replace in event of unfortunate decision in Court of Appeals. Approves sale to Vanmetre; change of lease for Swan Ponds; plans respecting Manor of Leeds; suggests writing to Fairfax for conveyance on mortgage, or power of attorney to collect rents.

Renomination of Adams doubtful; displeasure mission to France. Finances of government serious, import not productive, loan to maintain armaments; political dissension as to policy toward France and England. MoSW, Olin Libr., Bixby Coll.; DLC, John Marshall Papers; Beveridge, *Marshall*, II, 438–40 (excerpt).

Dec. 24
RICHMOND *Family Marriage*

Marriage of Jane Marshall (J.M.'s sister) to George Keith Taylor. Va. Gaz. & G.A., Dec. 24, 1799, 3; *The Virginia Argus*, Dec. 27, 1799, 2.

Dec. 29
PHILADELPHIA *to John Ambler*

Congratulations on marriage. Public mourning for death of Washington; temperate session expected in Congress, contrasting with prior year; party politics in Pennsylvania; dismissal of clerks by Governor. DLC, Ac. 422; Oster, *Marshall*, 183–84.

HOUSE OF REPRESENTATIVES

REFERENCES HEREIN to Annals of Congress are to *The Debates and Proceedings in the Congress of the United States . . .* (6 Cong., Dec. 2, 1799—Mar. 3, 1801) Washington, Gales and Seaton, 1834–1856 (1851). The original documentation on which this is based and bearing the same page numbering is the original Journal of the House of Representatives, 6 Cong.; DNA, Legislative Branch. R.G. 46.

Apr. *Election*

Description of election to federal House of Representatives (J.M. against John Clopton, Republican), at which J.M. was elected by a narrow margin. Beveridge, *Marshall,* II, 413–16, from George Wythe Munford, *The Two Parsons; Cupid's Sports; The Dream and the Jewels of Virginia* (Richmond, J. D. K. Sleight, 1884), 208–10.

The race was said to have cost J.M. $6,000. VMH, Vol. XXIX (Apr., 1921), 176–77.

Dec. 2 *Credentials*

Appeared with his credentials and took his seat in the U.S. House of Representatives, Philadelphia. Annals, 6 Cong., 1 sess., 185; Abridgement, Debates of Congress, II, 429; *Marshall Autobiography,* 26–27.

Dec. 2 *Presidential Meeting*

On committee of House of Representatives to wait on President; reported back President's attendance next day at joint session. Annals, 6 Cong., 1 sess., 187, 188. Abridgement, Debates of Congress, II, 430; Va. Gaz. & G. A., Dec. 13, 1799, 2.

Dec. 4, 6, 9, 10 *Answer to President*

Moved resolution for answers to speech of President to House of Congress; appointed on committee to draft answer. J.M. reported address Dec. 6 (DNA, Legislative Branch, Reports of Select Committees H. of R., II, 351; R.G. 46); reported by Committee of the Whole and approved by the House Dec. 9. J.M. on committee to wait on President, reported to be received next day at President's house. Annals, 6 Cong., 1 sess., 191–98. For reference of authorship of address by J.M. see Adams *J. Adams, Works,* IX, 141n; J. B. McMaster, *A History of the People of the United States* (New York, Appleton, 1885), II, 451–52; Beveridge, *Marshall,* II, 433–36.

Dec. 5 *Bankruptcy Act*

Appointed on committee of House of Representatives to bring in a bill for the establishment of a uniform system of bankruptcy. Annals, 6 Cong., 1 sess., 191. Bill, Same, 1452–71. Passed House Feb. 21, Senate Mar., 1800. For J.M.'s authorship of bill, see Beveridge, *Marshall,* II, 481–84.

Dec. 18 *Death of Washington*

Report by J.M. to House of Representatives on death of George

Washington; resolution to adjourn. Annals, 6 Cong., 1 sess., 203; Abridgement, Debates of Congress, II, 433; *Washingtoniana,* 106; Beveridge, *Marshall,* II, 440; Oster, *Marshall,* 278–79.

Dec. 19 Address by J.M. on death of Washington. Annals, 6 Cong., 1 sess., 203–204; Abridgement, Debates of Congress, II, 433–34; NCR, Vol. XIX (Dec. 14, 1899), 544; Oster, *Marshall,* 278–79; *Washingtoniana,* 108–10; Beveridge, *Marshall,* II, 440–43.

For J.M.'s description of receipt of news from stage passenger and announcement to the House, see his *Life of Washington,* V, 364–66.

Dec. 19 Resolutions in House of Representatives on death of George Washington, prepared by Henry Lee and presented by J.M. at conclusion of his speech; to wait on President in condolence; to drape Speaker's chair in black, and members to wear black; Committee with Senate to determine honors; to adjourn to March. J.M. was appointed with Sen. Smith to wait on the President, to arrange for him to receive the House. Annals, 6 Cong., 1 sess., 204–206. Abridgement, Debates of Congress, II, 444; *Washingtoniana,* 110–11; Va. Gaz. & G. A., Dec. 27, 1799, 3.

(See herein J.M. to Charles W. Hanson, Mar. 29, 1832, also *Marshall, Life of Washington,* V, 366.

Dec. 23 Resolutions of joint committee on Washington's death presented to House of Representatives by J.M., calling for a marble monument in Washington, funeral procession and memorial proceeding in the House; recommends wearing of crepe on arm for thirty days; providing a copy to Mrs. Washington. DNA, Legislative Branch, Reports of Select Committees, H. of R., II, 357; Annals, 6 Cong., 1 sess., 207–208; *Washingtoniana,* 115–17; Beveridge, *Marshall,* II, 443.

For J.M.'s account, see his *Life of Washington,* V, 364–72.

Dec. 30 *Census Bill*

Voted against amendment to Census Bill to put marshals under instructions of Secretary of State. Annals, 6 Cong., 1 sess., 222.

Dec. 30 *Washington's Birthday*

Presented resolution of joint committee for public meetings honoring Washington next Feb. 22. Same, 223.

Dec. 31 *Census Bill*

Remarks for sending Census Bill back for reconsideration; not fear executive power; prior vote against wishes. Same, 226.

(For balance of session, see herein 1800, House of Representatives.)

LEGAL PRACTICE

Jan. 1 *Receipt*

Receipt for account against estate of Benjamin Harrison signed by J.M. VU, Dep. No. 2825.

U.S. Circuit Court, Virginia

John Jackson, Great Britain v. William Bowyer.

Case, for goods sold and delivered, 1772–73, £251:16:7 St., value of $1,118.12. J.M. for defendant.

May 30, 1796. Continued. U.S. Circuit Court, Va., Order Book II, 144.

May 30, 1797. Juror withdrawn and continued. Same, 248.

Nov. 29, 1798. V. j. $2,070.50. Same, III, 129.

Dec. 13, 1798. Judgment set aside. Declaration amended. Same, 187.

May 30, 1799. V. j. $2,123.80. Same, 224.

Same, Record Book VI, 193–97.

Fee: May, 1795, £4. Account Book, 414.

Thomas Littleton Savage and Nathaniel Littleton Savage, executors of Nathaniel Littleton Savage v. James Govan, attorney in fact for Archibald Govan.

Injunction of j. against testator on surety in same court in 1794, £1700; part paid in 1777, balance paid into Loan Office, 1780. Obtained by mistake; attorney failed to defend by pleading payment. J.M. for plaintiff.

Case continued from 1795 to 1799.

June 6, 1799. Denied. U.S. Circuit Court, Va., Order Book III, 260.

V, U.S. Circuit Court Case Papers, containing autograph petition.

Joseph Swift v. David Ross.

Trespass on case. $10,000, goods sold and delivered, advances of 1785. J.M. for plaintiff.

Dec. 5, 1799. J. and account agreed by Daniel Call for J.M. acting for Swift. V. j. £921:12:3 St., value of $4,091, less credits approved by William Marshall. U.S. Circuit Court, Va., Order Book III, 328.

V, U.S. Circuit Court Case Papers, containing autograph petition and autograph memorandum.

David Webster, late Widderburne, Great Britain v. Catherine Brown, executrix of William Brown, Va.

Case, for medicines and merchandise. J.M. for plaintiff.

Continued from 1790 through 1798.

May 30, 1799. V. j. $819.74. U.S. Circuit Court, Va., Order Book III, 225.

U.S. Circuit Court, Va., Record Book VI, 175–84.

V, U.S. Circuit Court Case Papers, containing autograph petition.

COURT OF APPEALS OF VIRGINIA

John Proudfit v. Fontaine Murray, 1 Call 343, 346–49.

Appeal from District Court of Fredericksburg, Oct., 1796.

Action of debt, j. for appellee, plaintiff below, reversed. J.M. and John Warden for appellant.

Action Feb., 1793, on bill, £300 St. "for value in current money there received." Act of 1748 allowed 10 per cent damages for eighteen months after protest; repealed by act of Nov., 1792, which in same session, Dec., 1792, was suspended until Oct., 1793. J. given below for £300 St., 10 per cent to j., 5 per cent thereafter.

Held, act of 1748 not repealed when action brought; under act of 1755 j. for current money, not sterling.

Note, discussion of change from English law as to repeal of repealing law reviving original act.

Nov. 3, 1798. Case submitted. Court of Appeals, Va., Order Book III, 267.

Nov. 5. Reversed, j. amended. Same, 269.

Collier and Braxton Harrison v. Henry Harrison, eldest son of Henry Harrison, deceased. 1 Call 364, 369–70.

Appeal from High Court of Chancery, Sept. 28, 1796.

J. for appellee, plaintiff below, reversed. J.M. for appellee.

Action by heir of deceased holder of mortgage on slaves against creditor of mortgagor who held them under execution.

Held, action must be by executor or administrator, or in absence, all heirs must be joined.

Oct. 15, 1799. Partly heard. Court of Appeals, Va., Order Book III, 335.

Oct. 16, 1799. Continued. Same, 337.

Oct. 17, 1799. Hearing. Same, 339.

Oct. 18, 1799. Reversed. Same, 341.

Fees: July, 1790, £3:6; Oct., 1794, £2:8. Account Book, 256, 398.

Robert Beverly v. John Fogg, 1 Call 421, 422.

Appeal from District Court of King and Queen, Sept. 18, 1795.

Writ of right, j. for appellee, plaintiff below, reversed. J.M. for appellee.

Writ for 208 acres land in Essex County, no boundaries of land in count or verdict. Held, j. thereon error.

Nov. 4, 1795. Writ of supersedeas. Court of Appeals, Va., Order Book III, 87.

Apr. 27, 1799. Case submitted. Same, 303.

May 7, 1799. Reversed, dismissed. Same, 316.

Rachel Rowe, widow, and John Rowe, son of Richard Rowe v. John Smith, 1 Call 423, 424.

Appeal from District Court of King and Queen Courthouse, Sept. 20, 1796.

Writ of right, j. for appellee, plaintiff below, reversed. J.M. for appellee.

Action for tenement and sixty-three acres King and Queen County; demandant allowed to introduce depositions taken in trespass case involving defendant and third party. Held, error.

May 2, 1799. Case submitted. Court of Appeals, Va., Order Book III, 309.

May 7. Reversed, new trial. Same, 316.

James Ritchie & Co. v. William Lyne, 1 Call 425, 426–27.

Appeal from District Court of King and Queen Courthouse, Sept. 19, 1796.

Assumpsit for goods sold and delivered for appellee, defendant below, affirmed. J.M. for appellee.

Error alleged in admitting in evidence deposition of factor of appellant made in suit by factor against appellee involving same transaction, which suit had been dismissed because of death of factor.

Held, in nature of cross-suit, admissible.

May 10, 1799. Case submitted. Court of Appeals, Va., Order Book III, 321.

May 11, 1799. Affirmed. Same. 322.

James Eckhols, deputy sheriff Beford County v. Michael Graham and William Trigg, 1 Call 428, 429–30.

Appeal from District Court of New London, Apr. 22, 1796.

Trover, j. for appellee, plaintiff below, affirmed. J.M. for appellee.

Slaves executed on by judgment creditor released by sheriff on informal forthcoming bond; owner sold to appellee; thereafter second execution issued. Held, issuance of second execution waived lien of first, purchaser entitled to slaves.

Apr. 29, 1799. Case submitted. Court of Appeals, Va., Order Book III, 306.

Apr. 30, 1799. Affirmed. Same, 306.

Taylor Noel v. John Sale, 1 Call 431.

Writ of supersedeas to District Court of King and Queen Courthouse, Sept. 21, 1795, affirming j. of County Court of Essex, July 21, 1794, affirmed. J.M. for appellant.

Appellant petitioned County Court for leave to build mill, writ of *ad quod damnum* granted, and inquisition taken. On motion of appellee, the inquisition was quashed, costs against appellant. No grounds given, the record stating merely motion granted "for reasons appearing to the Court." On appeal to District Court, affirmed.

Held, appellant should either move for second inquisition or file bill of exceptions so that may appear on what ground Court acted; in absence of record to contrary, must be assumed Court acted on matter dehors the record, such as misconduct of sheriff, party, or jurors.

Apr. 24, 1796. Writ of supersedeas awarded. Court of Appeals, Va., Order Book III, 113.

Apr. 26, 1799. Case submitted. Same, 299.

Apr. 27. Affirmed. Same, 303.

Charles Lee v. John Love & Co., 1 Call 432, 434.

Appeal from District Court, Prince William.

Case, j. on note and for money had and received, for defendant-appellee, affirmed. J.M. for appellant.

Assignee of note brought action against assignor, payee of note, before suing maker; recovery disallowed.

May 11, 1799. Case submitted. Court of Appeals, Va., Order Book III, 323.

May 13, 1799. Affirmed. Same, 324.

William Wilson v. Angus Rucker, 1 Call 435, 438.

Appeals from both j. District Court of Dumfries (Prince William), Oct. 24, 1794, and j. High Court of Chancery, Sept., 1794, in same cause. Reported in Wythe, 113.

J. of High Court of Chancery for appellee, plaintiff below, affirmed; that of District Court for same, reversed. J.M. for appellee.

Owner of lost military certificate brought trover in District Court against purchaser without notice from finder; j. for owner enjoined by Chancery Court because jury found generally instead of specially on agreed facts; ordered new trial that verdict be certified to it for j. New trial; verdict again for owner; District Court entered final money j.; also certified to Chancery Court, which ordered restitution or money; appeal taken from both js.

Held, unlike owner of money, owner of military certificate may recover from innocent purchaser from finder; Chancery Court, having jurisdiction, had power to certify issue and enter final decree. Judge Covington dissenting on latter point.

Oct. 31, 1795. Case submitted. Court of Appeals, Va., Order Book III, 84.

Apr. 10, 1799. Resubmitted. Same, 284.

May 4, 1799. Order reversing District Court, affirming Chancery Court. Same, 312.

William Garlington v. Jesse Clutton, 1 Call 452, 453, 454, 455.

Appeal from District Court of Northumberland Courthouse, Sept. 6, 1796, affirming County Court of Northumberland, affirmed.

Assumpsit, goods sold and services, j. for appellee, defendant below, £33:11:8, affirmed. J.M. for appellant.

First trial, j. for appellee; agreement made by parties to suit not abated by death of either; on appeal, reversed by District Court for improper evidence; appellee thereafter in 1790 died; at second trial, j. again for plaintiff. Held, agreement against abatement binding and like a release of error, applied to second trial.

Apr. 20, 1799. Case submitted. Court of Appeals, Va., Order Book III, 299.

Apr. 27. Affirmed. Same, 303.

Fee: Oct., 1787, £2:10. Account Book, 128.

John Taliaferro, administrator of John Thornton v. William Minor and Mildred, his wife, and Lawrence Washington, Griffin Stith, and Frances Townshend, his wife, representatives of Thornton Washington. 1 Call 456, 460–61.

Appeal from High Court of Chancery, Sept. 15, 1795. Action for annulment of sale or payment of actual value, decree for appellees, petitioners below, reversed. J.M. for appellees.

Private act of Assembly, 1778, authorizing sale of land by trustees for four devisees, two of whom minors, to reinvest in land. In 1779 two adult devisees purchased, guardians of minors refusing to buy; purchase made for ready money then depreciated; payment deferred by consent of parties and when offered in paper money in 1781 and 1790, further depreciated.

Held, purchasers not accountable for depreciation or application of money; sale affirmed.

Apr. 12, 1799. Continued. Court of Appeals, Va., Order Book III, 280.

May 9, 1799. Reversed. Same, 318.

Sept. 15, 1799. Heard on account of administration. Same, 335.

Oct. 18, 1799. Decree of Sept. 15 reversed with instructions to administrators. Same, 340–41.

Fee: Apr., 1791, £6. Account Book, 282. (See herein, *Same v. Same*, 2 Call 156.)

Martin Hackett v. Thomas Alcock, 1 Call 463, 465.

Appeal from High Court of Chancery, May 15, 1795, affirming County Court of Caroline, Mar. 14, 1794.

Dismissal of bill by appellant for injunction against j. on bond, reversed. J.M. for appellant.

Appellant executed penal bond to secure agreement to convey remainder interest in 400 acres land, not expressing consideration, which originally was to get appellant released from legion and afterwards changed to 16,000 lbs. of tobacco received. Delay occasioned by improper deed prepared by purchaser; latter took j. on penal bond. Held, j. enjoined, to relieve of penalty, on making conveyance; court followed "Courts of that country [England] from which we draw our principles of jurisprudence." (P. 466).

May 2, 1796. Heard. Court of Appeals, Va., Order Book III, 122.

May 4, 1796. Affirmed. Same, 125.

May 6, 1796. Decree set aside. Same, 128.

Oct. 19, 20, 1798. Reheard. Same, 255, 256.

Apr. 16, 1799. Reversed, on condition deed proffered plus 800 lbs. tobacco per year for withholding. Same, 283.

Fee: Apr., 1794 (11,000 cwt. tobacco), £7. Account Book, 384.

William Rose, jailor District of Henrico v. John Shore, 1 Call 469, 471.

Appeal from District Court of Richmond, Sept. 6, 1796, £35:6:3. J. for appellee, plaintiff below, affirmed. J.M., William Duval, and Edmund Randolph for appellant.

Action for money paid by judgment creditor under bond to jailor for maintenance of debtor; debtor out of prison on bond for prison rules, not indigent and not maintained, money turned over to him by jailor.

Held, liable.

May 8, 1799. Case submitted. Court of Appeals, Va., Order Book III, 318.

May 14. Affirmed. Same, 327.

Abraham Smith v. Zebulon Dyer, 1 Call 488, 492.

Appeal from mandamus, District Court of Hardy Courthouse, Sept. 10, 1798, to County Court of Pendleton to restore appellee to office of clerk, affirmed. J.M. and John Wickham for appellee.

May, 1797, Hamilton, then clerk, wrote resignation effective next court; June, Court entered resignation and appointed Dyer; July, Court with some new members entered resignation again, appointed Smith, claimed prior appointment not attested and sent to Governor.

Held, Dyer entitled to office.

Apr. 22, 23, 1799. Heard. Court of Appeals, Va., Order Book III, 287, 288.

Apr. 27, 1799. Affirmed. Same, 304.

William H. Macon v. Benedict Crump, 1 Call 503–504.

Appeal from District Court of Williamsburg, Oct. 3, 1796, affirming County Court of New Kent, May 19, 1795.

Covenant on an award; j. on demurrer to declaration for appellee, plaintiff below, affirmed. J.M. for appellee.

Agreement to refer accounts between Macon and Crump, individually and as executor; award included claim to Crump for building house, and claim to Crump and his co-executor for sale of Negro. Declaration omitted co-executor; it made no profert of the award but submitted it on oyer.

Held, award including co-executor valid; no variance by failure to declare as to latter; inclusion of costs of suit without amount approved. Discussion of right to demurrer where oyer but no profert of instrument.

Nov. 22, 1796. Writ of supersedeas. Court of Appeals, Va., Order Book III, 154.

May 3, 1799. Case submitted. Same, 312.

May 15, 1799. Affirmed. Same, 328.

Caroline, Jane, Lucy, and Mary Fleming, infants by guardian v. Lewis Willis and Anne, his wife, and John Taliaferro, 2 Call 5, 9–10, 11–12.

Appeal from High Court of Chancery.

Bill for specific performance of marriage agreement; j. for appellees, plaintiff below, affirmed. J.M. for appellant.

Marriage agreement called for conveyance by father to son John of "all the lands . . . above Poplar Swamp, and which he had purchased of B"; indenture of same day for tract of land on which lived above "Lamb's Creek, and the land bought of B thereto adjoining." The B purchase was three small tracts, two adjoining the home tract, one of which was below the swamp, the other above the swamp, but separated. The father's will previously made devised all above swamp to John, all below to son William. Decree of three B tracts to John. Held, parol evidence admissible to explain ambiguous marriage agreement.

Oct. 30–31, 1799. Heard; death of Jane, husbands made parties. Court of Appeals, Va., Order Book III, 352, 353.

Nov. 4, 1799. Affirmed. Same, 354.

Peter Eppes, son and heir of Peter Eppes v. Samuel Demoville, administrator of Temple Eppes, 2 Call 19, 20.

Appeal from District Court of Williamsburg; order arresting j. for appellant, plaintiff below, reversed. J.M. and Edmund Randolph for appellant.

Action of debt brought by heir of Peter Eppes on bond for quiet enjoyment of plantation executed by Temple Eppes to his ancestor; violation since death of ancestor by eviction recovery by appellee, granddaughter and heir of Temple; verdict for appellant £679:0:1, set aside on motion to arrest j. Reversed by majority, Judges Roane and Lyon dissenting.

Oct. 23, 1799. Case submitted. Court of Appeals, Va., Order Book III, 344.

Nov. 9. Reversed. Same, 360.

Note: Fee received of Eppes in ejectment, probably that involved in this case, Apr., 1791, £7. Account Book, 282.

Stephen Cooke v. Jesse Simms, 2 Call 33, 35–37.

Appeal from District Court of Dumfries, Oct. 19, 1795, affirming Hustings Court of Alexandria, Mar. 26, 1794. J.M. for appellant. Action in case on promissory note, j. for appellee, plaintiff below, reversed.

First count of declaration stated promissory note in full but failed to allege separately promise to pay. Held, subject to demurrer.

Oct. 19, 20, 21, 1796. Heard. Court of Appeals, Va., Order Book III, 136–37.

Oct. 27, 1798. Order affirming overruling of demurrer but reversing for error in final j., appellee not having entered nolle prosequi. Same, 141.

Nov. 2, 1798. Set aside. Same, 144.
Oct. 21, 1799. Case submitted. Same, 342.
Oct. 28, 1799. Reversed. Same, 350.

James Lawrason, administrator of Windsor Brown v. James and Mary, Daniel, Patrick, and Charity Davenport, 2 Call 79, 81–82.

Appeal from High Court of Chancery, Sept. 6, 1796.

J. for appellees, plaintiffs below, reversed. J.M. for appellee.

Decedent, a native of Ireland residing in Alexandria, left a wife—who remarried to Davenport—and next of kin, all residing in Ireland, except Robert Daugherty, a resident of the United States. The estate included military certificates £1,260, warrants £581:1:4, and other certificates all for services of Brown as officer during war; debts £29:14:5 on note. Robert, claiming entire estate, in Aug., 1791, arranged for sale of certificates and warrants at the same price a dealer had bargained to sell them, and entire proceeds less debt of estate were paid to him by administrator, then ignorant of other claimants.

In action by wife and next of kin against administrator, the High Court of Chancery held sale unjustified, not perishable goods, not necessary for payment of debts, not sold at auction; administrator held liable for present value of certificates and warrants which had greatly increased.

Held by Court of Appeals, sale justified; administrator if acting fairly is judge at time of sale, sale necessary to pay debt and Robert's share; no evidence sale price not market value at Alexandria; proof of market value in Richmond of a "foreign market"; administrator accountable for shares of others turned over to Robert.

Oct. 22, 1799. Heard. Court of Appeals, Va., Order Book III, 342.

Oct. 31, 1799. Reversed and remanded. Same, 352.

Robert Price, executor of George Brooke, William F. Gaines, and Mathew Page, executors of Robert Page v. John Campbell, assignee, 2 Call 92, 97.

Appeal from High Court of Chancery, Mar. 14, 1797.

J. for appellee, plaintiff below, affirmed. J.M. and John Warden for appellants.

Carter Braxton, about to return to Great Britain, sold several bills of exchange to Campbell, drawn on persons in Britain, one an obscure clergyman; gave mortgage of Virginia land to secure in case of protest; later personal sureties added, to whom gave trust deeds as security. J. given against maker and sureties and sale of security. Held, insufficient evidence of usury by debt legally drawing 10 per cent on protest there being no agreement between parties for unlawful interest; the mortgage security not alter debt from bill of exchange so as to draw 5 per cent; statute of limitations docked by payments and transactions to 1792.

Nov. 11, 12, 1799. Heard. Court of Appeals, Va., Order Book III, 361–62.

Nov. 15. Affirmed. Same, 363.

Fee: May, 1794, £4:9:6. Account Book, 388.

Note: Decree of Court of Chancery erroneously was for £2,498:1:2 "currency" instead of sterling, and so affirmed. Held, a bill of review would not lie to correct. *Campbell v. Price, et al.*, 3 Munford's 227. Held also Court of Chancery no power to correct decree as affirmed. *Same v. Same*, 5 Call 115 (1804).

Francis Eppes and Thomas Jefferson, executors of John Wayles v. David Meade Randolph, Richard Ryland, and Brett Randolph, sons and devisees of Richard Randolph, 2 Call 103, 132–41.

Appeal from High Court of Chancery.

Decree dismissing bill of appellants in part and allowing in part, reversed and amended. J.M., Edmund Randolph, and John Warden for appellees.

Action by surety of deceased who paid indebtedness on bond, against sons of deceased to subject lands conveyed to them allegedly in fraud of creditors. Both conveyances in consideration of marriage contracts, one not so stating, the other recorded more than eight months after execution but within four months of re-acknowledgment. Held, both conveyances valid, not subject to claim. Period of j. lien on lands, and rights of surety discussed.

Apr. 30, 1798. Three judges disqualify for interest. Court of Appeals, Va., Order Book III, 226.

Nov. 7, 1798. Same. Same, 274.

May 13, 1799. Same, also revived in name of representative of Richard Randolph. Same, 327.

Nov. 4–7, 1799. Heard. Same, 355–57.

Nov. 9, 1799. Affirmed and amended. Same, 358.

John Taliaferro, administrator of John Thornton v. William and Mildred Minor, and Lawrence Washington, executor, and Frances Townshend, executrix of Thornton Washington, 2 Call 156, 160.

Appeal from High Court of Chancery.

J. on commissioner's report on administrator's account, reversed and amended. J.M. for appellees.

Administrator collected debts of estate in 1778 and 1779 and paid beneficiaries in 1779. Held, error to charge administrator by scale of depreciation between collection and settlement; act of 1781 provides to contrary; commission of 5 instead of 2½ per cent allowed for collecting assets; liability for receipt of counterfeit paper recognized.

Apr. 12, 1799. Continued. Court of Appeals, Va., Order Book III, 280.

May 5–7, 1799. Heard. Same, 312, 313, 317.

May 9, 1799. Decree setting aside sale for paper money, reversed, no fraud. Same, 318.

Oct. 15, 1799. Further hearing. Same, 335.

Oct. 18, 1799. Order reversing and amending, further hearing as to counterfeit paper. Same, 340.

(See *supra* herein, *Same v. Same.* 1 Call 456.)

Jane Anderson, by next friend v. George Anderson, Mary Talley, Nathaniel Anderson, representatives of John Anderson, et al., 2 Call 163, 167.

Appeal from High Court of Chancery.

Decree dismissing bill of appellant, affirmed. J.M. and John Wickham for appellees.

Action by wife to enjoin creditors of husband from proceeding against her remainder interest in slaves, claiming marriage settlement fraudulently drawn, executed Mar., 1787, recorded Sept., 1788. Held, void under act requiring recording in eight months; also lower court loses control over appeal bond first day of term after decree.

Nov. 2, 1799. Heard. Court of Appeals, Va., Order Book III, 354.

Nov. 11, 1799. Affirmed. Same, 360.

Fee: June, 1791, £5; Mar., 1795, £5. Account Book, 290, 408.

Cary Pleasants and Mary, his wife, devisees of John Pleasants, et al. *v. Robert Pleasants, heir and executor of John Pleasants,* 2 Call 270, 279–80.

Appeal from High Court of Chancery, Sept. 12, 1798.

Decree freeing slaves in hands of devisees under provision of will, reversed and amended. J.M. and John Warden for appellee.

Testator devised slaves providing manumission if law permitted at age thirty; action by executor to enforce against devisees. Held, action properly brought by executor; court of equity has jurisdiction; rule against limitation of remainder of chattel upon contingent event not applied to freedom of slaves; error in decreeing unqualified emancipation, contrary to act of 1782 and interest of testator; decree altered so as to provide support bond for slaves over forty-five years, and those under thirty born of mother under thirty. Manumission statutes discussed.

Nov. 5, 6, 1798. Heard, together with *Elizabeth Pleasants v. Ned, a pauper*. Court of Appeals, Va., Order Book III, 270–71.

May 6, 1799. Reversed in part and amended. Same, 313.

George Chapman v. George Chapman, infant, by Susanna Chapman, 4 Call 430, 436–37.

Appeal from High Court of Chancery.

Decree dismissing bill for conveyance of land, affirmed. J.M., Benjamin Botts, and Edmund Randolph for appellant.

Elder brother inheriting land of father orally agreed with mother to convey part to younger brother if mother devises half her estate to him; two parcels conveyed deed to third executed but withheld by will of elder brother. Mother conveyed her lands and devised entire estate to younger son. Held, action by latter against elder brother's devisee for parcel withheld, denied.

Nov. 1, 1797. Continued. Court of Appeals, Va., Order Book III, 186.

Apr. 12, 13, 1799. Heard. Same, 281–82.

Apr. 19, 1799. Affirmed. Same, 286.

Fee: Sept., 1790, £13:16. Account Book, 260.

Chapman Austin v. William O. Winston and Bartlett Anderson, Justices of County Court, Hanover, Benjamin Tyree, et al.

Appeal from decree of High Court of Chancery, May 20, 1797, order of May 24, 1797, affirmed. J.M. for appellant.

Nov. 14, 1799. Case heard. Court of Appeals, Va., Order Book III, 363.

Nov. 16, 1799. Affirmed. Same, 365.

Fee: Oct., 1788, "(2 suits)" £5. Account Book, 172.

Thomas T. Bolling and Hector McNeill v. James Watkins, executor of William Watkins.

Appeal from j. by appellee against appellant, District Court, Petersburg, Sept. 24, 1798. J.M. for appellee.

Oct. 20, 1799. Dismissed, neither party appearing. Court of Appeals, Va., Order Book III, 346.

Fee: Apr., 1792, £4:12:5. Account Book, 320.

Theophilus Field, administrator of Theophilus Field, Sr. v. Richard Taylor, Edmunds B. Holloway, and wives.

Appeal from decree of High Court of Chancery, May 12, 1798. J.M. for appellant.

May 11, 1799. Appellant not appear, dismissed. Court of Appeals, Va., Order Book III, 323.

Fees: Jan., 1791, £5; Sept., 1794, £5. Account Book, 272, 396.

Sarah Hooe, widow of Gerrard Hooe, and John Alexander and Elizabeth, his wife v. Mary Kelsick, widow of Younger Kelsick, and Jonathan Beckwith, widower of Rebecca.

Appeal from High Court of Chancery, *Same v. and adv. Same*. Wythe, 102, reversed. J.M. for appellants.

Codicil to will of testator distributed estate among three daughters unequally, approved by court ruling in 1761. Chancery Court set aside codicil on claim of assertions of testator to Kelsick and Beckwith, then suitors of daughter, of intention to make equal distribution.

Held, evidence conflicting, did not support alleged promise to devise.

Apr. 22, 1794. Continued. Court of Appeals, Va., Order Book II, 271.

Nov. 7, 8, 10, 11, 13, 14, 15, 1794. Abatement as to Mary Kelsick, revival. Hearing, continued. Same, III, 28–35.

Nov. 22, 1794. Continued for rehearing. Same, 42.

Apr. 30, May 1, 2, 1799. Rehearing. Same, 307, 308, 309.

May 7, 1799. Abatement by death of Jonathan Beckwith, revived. Reversed. Same, 315.

Fees: Apr. 3, 1786, £8:8; Apr., 1792, £12:10; May, 1792, £3; Nov., 1794, £20. Account Book, 68, 322, 326, 400.

County Court, Henrico

James Currie v. J.M., executor of Serafino Farmicola, deceased.

Mar. 11, 1799. Order of court setting aside arbitration and continuing the case. Richmond City Hustings and Chancery Court, Order Book IV, 255.

May 14, 1799. V.j. for plaintiff, £10:8 from goods of estate, if insufficient costs against J.M. Same, 279.

LAND TRANSACTIONS

Fairfax Purchase—Various Counties

June 24 *Partition Deed*

James M. Marshall to and by J.M., Rawleigh Colston, and Charles and William Marshall. Pursuant to agreed division of land in Northern Neck conveyed to James by Denny Martin Fairfax, Aug. 30, 1797 (see herein); to J.M. 900 acres called Swan Ponds, 700 acres called Anderson

Bottom, 400 acres on New Creek leased to John Rousscan, 328 acres on Patterson's Creek leased to Corneilus Hogland and occupied by Beale, 430 acres in Allegheny Mts. patented to Charles Lee, 317 acres in same not patented, 872 acres on Capacon of which 672 acres occupied by and patented to Thompson, one-third of two tracts of land in and about the town of Bath, one-half of tract in Berkeley County called Mounds land.

To Rawleigh Colston, tract 2,875 acres in Berkeley County called the Original Manor, 400 acres called Watkin's Ferry, 510 acres on Potomac above Warm Springs, one-third of two tracts in and about the town of Bath.

To Charles and William Marshall, 931 acres in Fauquier County called Moffett's Tract, 367 acres in Blue Ridge at head of Robinson, 250 acres in Fauquier County on Rappahannock Marsh, 300 acres adjoining Goony Run Manor part of Chistuss Tract, 400 acres Shenandoah County called Morgan's Land.

Signed by all parties. Sept. 30, 1800, acknowledged by James at Superior Court, District of Frederick, Berkeley and Shenandoah, at Winchester, Sept. 30, 1800. Superior Court, Frederick County, Order Book 1800–1802, 51. Autograph original entered in evidence in *Philip Martin v. Moffat*, et al. (see U.S. Circuit Court herein 1824).

Hardy County, Virginia (Now West Virginia)

Mar. 13 *Deed*

J.M., by Rawleigh Colston, attorney in fact, to Jesse Welton, thirty-five acres, among three lots of Welton. Consideration £8:15 Virginia. Recorded May 7, 1799. Hardy County, Va., Deed Book A, 175.

Mar. 13 *Deed*

J.M. by Rawleigh Colston, attorney in fact, to Job Welton, fifty-six acres, on drains of Lynches Creek. Consideration £35:0:5. Recorded May 7, 1799. Hardy County, Va., Deed Book A, 177.

Mar. 14 *Deed*

J.M., by Rawleigh Colston, attorney in fact, to David Welton, 1½ acres, also 14 acres, 3 roods, 16 poles. Consideration £3:18 Virginia. Recorded May 6, 1799. Hardy County, Va., Deed Book A, 173.

Mar. 15 *Deed*

J.M., by Rawleigh Colston, attorney in fact, to David Welton, remainder interest, fifty-seven acres, leased Denny Martin Fairfax to Adam Kimble, May 21, 1791. Consideration £14:5. Recorded May 5, 1799. Hardy County, Va., Deed Book A, 166.

May 4 *Deed*

J.M., by Rawleigh Colston, attorney in fact, to William Bullitt, 20 acres. Consideration £5 Virginia. Recorded May 7, 1799. Hardy County, Va., Deed Book A, 185.

May 4 *Deed*

J.M., by Rawleigh Colston, attorney in fact, to Jonathan Hutton, 100 acres, ½ acre, and 93 acres, all on west side South Branch of Potomac. Consideration £36 Virginia. Recorded Sept. 6, 1799. Hardy County, Va., Deed Book A, 203.

May 4 *Deed*

J.M., by Rawleigh Colston, attorney in fact, to Jonathan Hutton, five acres, west side South Branch of the Potomac. Consideration £13:12:6 Virginia. Recorded Sept. 6, 1799. Hardy County, Va., Deed Book A, 206.

May 4 *Deed*

J.M., by Rawleigh Colston, attorney in fact, to James Snodgrass, forty-eight acres and twenty-six acres. Consideration £19:4:9. Recorded May 7, 1799. Hardy County, Va., Deed Book A, 247.

May 4 *Deed*

J.M., by Rawleigh Colston, attorney in fact, to Robert Darling, thirty-three acres. Consideration £8:5. Recorded May 7, 1799. Hardy County, Va., Deed Book A, 249.

Aug. 2 *Deed*

J.M., by Rawleigh Colston, attorney in fact, to David Welton, conveyance of remainder interest, ninety-two acres, No. 42, west side of South Branch of Potomac, leased Thomas Lord Fairfax to John Brygard, Aug. 3, 1773; also ninteen acres, leased Denny Martin Fairfax to same, Nov. 20, 1790. Consideration $85.00. Recorded May 5, 1800. Hardy County, Va., Deed Book A, 253.

Sept. 9 *Deed*

J.M., by Rawleigh Colston, attorney in fact, to Andrew Byrns, *et al.*, remainder interest, four tracts. Forty-eight acres leased Thomas Lord

Fairfax to John Robeson, Mar. 9, 1779; 139 acres, No. 71, leased Same to Same, Aug. 3, 1773; 50 acres, No. 72, leased Fairfax to Sylvester Ward, May 11, 1779; 55 acres, leased Fairfax to George Whitman, Mar. 9, 1779. Consideration £73. Recorded May 5, 1800. Hardy County, Va., Deed Book A, 244.

Sept. 9 *Deed*

J.M., by Rawleigh Colston, attorney in fact, to Rudolph Shobe, remainder interest, three tracts: 165 acres, No. 60, leased Thomas Lord Fairfax to Rudolph Hire, Aug. 3, 1773; 132 acres and 5 acres leased Denny Martin Fairfax to grantee, May 21, 1790. Consideration £75:10. Recorded May 5, 1800. Hardy County, Va., Deed Book A, 251.

Sept. 9 *Deed*

J.M., by Rawleigh Colston, attorney in fact, to John Parsons, remainder interest, 251 acres, No. 6, leased Thomas Lord Fairfax to Parsons, Aug. 3, 1773; also 145 acres, leased Same to Same, Mar. 6, 1780. Consideration £99. Recorded May 6, 1800. Hardy County, Va., Deed Book A, 271.

Sept. 9 *Deed*

J.M., by Rawleigh Colston, attorney in fact, to Abraham Shobe, remainder interest, fifty acres, No. 71, leased Thomas Lord Fairfax to John Cutright, Aug. 3, 1773; also seventy-six acres, leased Fairfax to Same, No. 51. Consideration £31:10. Recorded May 5, 1800. Hardy County, Va., Deed Book A, 243.

Sept. 9 *Deed*

J.M., by Rawleigh Colston, attorney in fact, to Conrad Carr, remainder interest, two tracts: twenty-eight acres and sixteen acres leased Denny Martin Fairfax to Carr, May 28, 1791. Consideration £11. Recorded May 7, 1800. Hardy County, Va., Deed Book A, 285.

Sept. 10 *Deed*

J.M., by Rawleigh Colston, attorney in fact, to John Harness, Sr., three tracts: 260 acres, No. 48, leased Thomas Lord Fairfax to John Harness, Aug. 3, 1773; 11 acres, No. 50, Same to Same, same date; 12 acres, Same. Consideration £70:17:6. Recorded May 5, 1800. Hardy County, Va., Deed Book A, 235.

Sept. 10 *Deed*

J.M., by Rawleigh Colston, attorney in fact, to George Harness, Jr., remainder interest in five tracts: 122 acres, No. 13, leased Thomas Lord Fairfax to Abel Randall, Aug. 3, 1773; 135 acres, leased Fairfax to John Reed, same date; 122 acres, leased Fairfax to John Rennick, same date; 10 acres, Fairfax to George Reed, Mar. 6, 1800; 153 acres, leased Denny Martin Fairfax to Alexander Randal, May 21, 1791. Consideration £146. Recorded May 5, 1800. Hardy County, Va., Deed Book A, 237.

Hampshire County, Virginia
(Now West Virginia)

Feb. 4 *Deed*

John Ashby and Mary, his wife, Fauquier County, Virginia, to J.M., Richmond, sixty-one acres, north bank of Potomac in Hampshire County, Virginia, corner of tract called Swan Ponds, patented to grantor Apr. 19, 1787. Consideration £120. Recorded May 6, 1799. Hardy County, Va., Deed Book A, 147.

Henrico County Land Books—Upper District Land of J.M.

Date	Quantity (acres)	Price per acre (shillings & pence)	Amount	Tax
1799	1035½	9/5	£488:6:1	£7:8:1
1800	Same			
1801	Same			
1802	1053½	9/5	488:16:1	7:8:6
1804	1050	9/5	494:7:6	7:8:6
1805	Same			
1806	1050			
1807	Same			
1809	Same			
1810	1050	9/5	494:7:6	7:9:2
	20	5/8	5:13:4	
1811	Same			
1812	Same			
1813	Same		"on Chickahomy Swamp"	
1814	1070			
	25			
1815	1070		adj. R. Curd's land	
	14½		adj. Daniel Call's land	
1816	Same			
1817	1090		adj. Richard Curd	
	14		adj. Daniel Call	

1818	Same	
1819	Same and	
	41	——— "L" Marshall
1820	1090	adj. R. Curd
	14	adj. D. Call
	41	adj. Curds
	4¾	adj. Curds
1821	Same	
1822	1090	adj. R. Curd
	14	adj. D. Call
	41	adj. Wm. Jarvis
	4¾	adj. Wm. Jarvis
1823	1135	adj. Wm. Jarvis
	14	adj. D. Call
1824	Same	
1825	Same	
1826	Same	
1827	Same	
1828	Same	
1829	1135	adj. Wm. Jarvis
1830	Same	
1831	Same	
1832	Same	
1833	Same	
1834	Same	
1835	Same	(taxes now $20.89)

V, Henrico County Land Books.

Mason County, Kentucky

July 26
Frankfort, Ky. *Land Patent*

Patent to J.M., 1,239 acres Mason County, Ky., on Lawrence Creek and North Fork of Licking in consideration of Treasury Warrants 11251 and 13924, surveyed Oct. 28, 1797, on entry of 4,002 acres by J.M., Jr., adjoining J.M. survey of 1,790 acres made on same entry. Land Grant No. 602. Kentucky Land Office, Frankfort, Ky. Old Kentucky Grants, Book 11, 306. See also *Ward v. Fox' Heirs,* Hughes Reports, at 414. (Supreme Court and Court of Appeals, District of Kentucky) for 1790-acre entry.

July 29 *Power of Attorney*

J.M. appointing Thomas Marshall, Jr., Mason County, Ky., his attorney to sell and convey four tracts of Kentucky land. 1,239 acres on Lawrence Creek and North Fork of Licking, 1,934 acres on waters of the Ohio River, 50¼ acres north side North Fork of Licking, 847¾ acres adjoining his survey of 1,239 acres, upwards of 200 acres being part of his 5,000-acre entry of June 15, 1780. Proved and recorded by William Clark and Humphrey Marshall, May 26, 1807. Mason County, Ky., Deed Book F, 411.

1800

DOCUMENTS

Jan. 2
WASHINGTON *No Addressee*

Concerning J.M.'s efforts to liberate impressed American seamen. Listed in Lazare *Book-Prices* (1935). 634. Present owner unknown.

Jan. 8 *John Hopkins to George Simpson,*
U.S. LOAN OFFICE, VA. *Cashier Bank of the United States*

Bill of exchange on sight on Bank of the United States to pay to J.M. or order drawer's quarterly salary, $375; also $572 transmitted to Treasury for settlement. Autograph of J.M. on reverse. NN, Stauffer Coll.

Jan. 16
PHILADELPHIA *to Samuel Bayard*

Acknowledges oration on death (of Washington). DLC, Marshall Papers, Var. Ac. 3840; Western Reserve Historical Society; Oster, *Marshall* 170; *Homes of American Statesmen, etc.* (New York, Upham. 1861), following 274 (facsimile); Rufus W. Griswold, *The Prose Writers of America* (Philadelphia, Carey & Hart, 1847), (facsimile).

Jan. 20
PHILADELPHIA *to Charles Dabney, of Hanover, Va.*

U.S. financial difficulties; justification of loan for defense purposes; effect of defense efforts reason for French willingness to negotiate. French battleships in West Indies. DLC, Charles Dabney Papers, J.D. Shelf, Dab. 2; NcU, Southern Hist. Coll., Charles W. Dabney Papers, No. 1412; NCR, Vol. XXII (Feb. 28, 1901), 7–8; Beveridge, *Marshall,* II, 479–80 (excerpt).

Feb. 13
WASHINGTON *to James M. Marshall*

Acknowledges letter of 1st enclosing Tucker's letter. Discusses legal relief for rents of Winchester landholders. Ambler debt payment. Fairfax Purchase, J.M. borrowing money, mortgage on property; power of attorney. DLC, Marshall Papers.

Feb. 19
PHILADELPHIA *to James McDowell*

Describing method of collecting internal revenue in Virginia; non-intercourse with France. Listed in Lazare, *Book-Prices* (1938), 507. Present owner unknown.

Feb. 28
PHILADELPHIA *to James M. Marshall*

Settlement of Bell bill; interest on bank stock, power of attorney. Discusses Thomas Nash (Jonathan Robbins) debate. DLC, Beveridge Coll., Beveridge, *Marshall,* II, 463 (in part).

Mar. 16
PHILADELPHIA *to Reuben George, of Richmond, Va.*

Acknowledges letter of Feb. 28; took deposition of Dr. Rush and enclosed to Wickham. Sends parts of newspaper to friends. Discusses Thomas Nash (Jonathan Robbins) case debate; purpose to defeat Adams. Pennsylvania without voting law for Presidential election; predicts Adams election. No news from envoys to France. V, Ac. Item No. 24119.

Apr. 4
PHILADELPHIA *to James M. Marshall*

Pleased with contract made with Vanmetre and Seymour; will execute it this summer. Envoys to Paris arrival; discusses violation of privilege of Senate by publisher Duane; supports power of Congress to provide for counting of votes in elections of President and Vice-President; favors counting by committee in presence of both houses. Democrats abuse J.M. regardless of what he does, so satisfies himself. Four bank shares purchased with money received on bill. CSmH, HM 4684; VHi, (reprint in *Virginia Free Press* (Charlestown, W.Va.), Oct. 31, 1874).

Apr. 11
WALNUT FARM *Bushrod Washington to C.P. Wayne*

Discusses J.M. undertaking writing *Life of Washington*; publication agreement discussed and defined. PPHi, Dreer MSS.

Apr. 23
PHILADELPHIA *to William F(rederick) Ast—Addressed to Richmond*

Acknowledges letter of 23rd. Stamp office law misrepresented; not send to seat of government for stamps; existing offices kept up for sale. Will present petition if directors send, will not succeed, too late for present Congress. CSmH, BR Box 67.

May 7
PHILADELPHIA *Nomination—Secretary of War*

Message of President Adams to the Senate nominating J.M. Secretary of War. Senate, Exec. Journal, I, 352, DNA, Legislative Dept., Office of Senate Financial Clerk. R.G. 46.

May 8
PHILADELPHIA *to President John Adams*

Declining appointment as Secretary of War; private affairs claim his attention. MHi, Adams Papers, John Adams Letters Rec'd. L, 156.

J.M. states that he first learned of appointment in May, 1800, on visits to the War Office to inquire concerning land patents for his military friends; was surprised. Wrote letter to President Adams requesting name be withdrawn from Senate; President did not do so. Left Philadelphia immediately to attend court at Richmond. Marshall, *Autobiography*, 27–28.

May 9
PHILADELPHIA *Confirmation of Appointment*

Senate resolution approving appointment of J.M. as Secretary of War. MHi, Adams Papers. John Adams Letters Rec'd.

May 12
PHILADELPHIA *Nomination—Secretary of State*

Nomination by Presient Adams of J.M. as Secretary of State. Senate, Exec. Journal, I, 353, DNA, Legislative Dept. Office of Senate Financial Clerk. R.G. 46.

See letter Timothy Pickering to President Adams, May 12, 1800, refusing to submit requested resignation. MHi, Adams Papers, Letters Rec'd., XLIX, 102; also Charles Lee to President Adams, May 13, 1800, accepting duties as Secretary of State until new appointment made. Same, L, 253.

May 13
PHILADELPHIA *Confirmation of Appointment*

Confirmation by Senate of President Adams' nomination of J.M. as

Secretary of State. Senate, Exec. Journal, I, 354, DNA, Legislative Dept., Office of Senate Financial Clerk. R.G. 46.

May 13 — *from Charles Lee,*
PHILADELPHIA — *Executing Office of Secretary of State.*

Advising J.M. of appointment as Secretary of State with advise and consent of Senate; enclosing commission; asks for early acceptance. MHi, Pickering MSS, XIII, 58; DLC, Beveridge Coll.

May 13
PHILADELPHIA — *Commission—Secretary of State*

Commission J.M. to serve as Secretary of State during pleasure of President; signed for President by Charles Lee, executing office of Secretary of State. DNA, General Records Dept. of State, Misc. Commissions, Permanent, 1789–1802, Vol. B, 365. R.G. 59.

May 22
RICHMOND — *to Thomas Hungerford of Westmoreland, Va.*

Acknowledges letter of 6th; land warrant forwarded of no value, needs further proof and barred by statute of limitations. VHi.

May 28
PHILADELPHIA — *Charles Lee to President John Adams*

Informing that J.M. has by letter accepted office of Secretary of State (the letter of J.M. is not found). MHi, Adams Papers, John Adams Letters Rec'd, L, 255.

May 28 — *Ben Stoddart, Secretary of War, to*
PHILADELPHIA — *President John Adams*

Advising of arrival of letter of acceptance of office of Secretary of State from J.M. MHi, Adams Papers, John Adams Letters Rec'd, LXIX, 349, 350.

J.M. stated had grave doubts in accepting; still preferred bar, but practice lost by going to Congress. Attacks on him so abusive would have to continue candidacy at Congress. Precisely position wished; felt fitted for it. If Federalists lost power, would return to bar. Marshall, *Autobiography*, 28–29.

May 29
BALTIMORE — *Charles Lee to President John Adams*

Second letter of Lee advising a receipt at Department of State the previous day of letter from J.M. accepting office of Secretary of State; writing to tell J.M. to come to Washington immediately. MHi, Adams Papers, John Adams Letters Rec'd., L 256.

J.M. stated that he was on cordial terms with members of Cabinet, except Wolcott; overcame his doubts as to friendliness. Marshall, *Autobiography*, 29.

May
SUPERIOR COURT, HARDY COUNTY, VA. *Law Suit*

J.M. v. Joseph Inskeep. Action on bond, £450, Jan. 14, 1797, back rent for 136 acres leased land. June, 1800, default judgment against defendant and Isaac Vanmetre. Sept., 1800, set aside. May 8, 1801, confessed judgment £152:17:1 and interest. Hardy County, Va. (now W.Va.), Superior Court, Record Book, 1800–1803, 234; Hardy County, Va. (now W.Va.), Common Law Book, 1797–1803, 289, 331.

n.d. [*circa* May], *n.p.* *to President John Adams*

Unsigned note by J.M. transmitting letters of Gen. Pinckney, dated 1797 and 1798. MHi, Adams Papers, John Adams Letters Rec'd, XLIX, 103.

June 7 *to Governor of Virginia*
ALEXANDRIA [VA.] [*James Monroe*]

Notifying of his appointment as Secretary of State, vacancy of his Congressional seat. V, Exec. Papers, Box 1800, (May-Aug.), File July; CVSP, IX, 115–16; Oster, *Marshall*, 34.

June 7 *J. Wagner to Evans Jones, Consul for the United*
WASHINGTON *States at New Orleans, or Wm. E. Ruling, Vice Consul*

At request of Secretary of State, enclosing for forwarding to Natchez instructions for census of Mississippi Territory. DNA, General Records Dept. of State, Dipl. and Cons. Instrs., V, 342. R.G. 59.

June 9 *to Arthur St. Clair, Governor of Territory*
WASHINGTON *Northwest of Ohio River*

Relating to the Connecticut or Western Reserve (n.f.). Referred to in letter Gov. St. Clair to J.M., Aug. 5, 1800. Smith, *St. Clair*, II, 497; Oster, *Marshall*, 35–36.

June 9 *to Jonathan Trumbell, Jr.,*
WASHINGTON, DEPT. OF STATE *Governor of Connecticut*

Acknowledging letter of May 30 accompanying act of renunciation and deed of cession by state of Connecticut of territory Western Reserve of Connecticut to the United States; laid before President; sufficient; filed in Office of State. CtHi, U.S. Gov't. Letters, No. 73. (Letter Trumbell to J.M., Secretary of State, May 30, 1800, enclosing documents and asking for certificate of acceptance for transmittal by Henry W. Edwards to Governor of the Northwest Territory. CtHi, U.S. Gov't. Letters, No. 71.)

June 10
WASHINGTON *Pardon*

John Burnett, fine $400 for landing product of foreign state without permit, Aug., 1798, U.S. District Court, Pa., remitted. Signed by J.M., Secretary of State, No. 28. DNA, General Records Dept. of State, Pardon Records, I, 34. R.G. 59.

June 12
WASHINGTON *to Arthur St. Clair*

Concerning the act to divide the Northwest Territory (n.f.). Referred to in letter Arthur St. Clair to J.M., Aug. 5, 1800. Smith, *St. Clair, supra,* 497; Oster, *Marshall,* 35–36.

June 13

Notice of removal of offices of Secretary of State to Washington. Quasi-War–U.S. and France, VI, 45, from *The Daily Advertiser* (New York), June 13, 1800; DLC.

June 14 *to William Smith,*
WASHINGTON *Minister of the United States, Portugal*

Described by Smith as a private letter enclosing a copy of the inscription on the Chev. de Ternay's Tomb (n.f.). Acknowledged in letter from Smith, Oct. 15, 1800. DNA, General Records Dept. of State, Dipl. Despatches, Portugal, V, 252. R.G. 59.

June 16 *to Williams Vans Murray,*
WASHINGTON *Minister of the United States, Netherlands*

Requesting official aid to relief sought in Holland by Jeremiah Yellott of Baltimore from decree of Council at Curaçao condemning ship *Mary* as French prize, contrary to proclamation of Batavian Republic. DNA, General Records Dept. of State, Dipl. and Cons. Instrs., V, 342–43. R.G. 59; Quasi-War–U.S. and France, V, 189.

June 18
WASHINGTON *to Don Carlos, King of Spain*

Acknowledging letter of Dec. 22, 1799; congratulating on birth of grandchildren. Signed by J.M., Secretary of State, for the President. DNA, General Records Dept. of State, Credences, I, 107–108; also Same 109–10. R.G. 59.

June 20
PHILADELPHIA *from President John Adams*

Instructions to issue commission to William S. Smith to succeed John Lasher as surveyor and inspector of customs for the port of New York. DNA, General Records Dept. of State, Misc. Letters, June–Dec., 1800, 66. R.G. 59; MHi, Adams Papers.

June 21
CURAÇAO *from Benjamin Hammell Phillips, U.S. Consul at Curaçao*

Acknowledges J.M. letter of Apr. 8 (n.f.) concerning reimbursement for supplies furnished navy. Quasi-War–U.S. and France, VI, 63.

June 23
PHILADELPHIA *from Israel Whelen, Purveyor of Public Supplies*

Requesting directions for purchase of cargo for Algiers; outstanding claim for insurance premium on prior shipment. Enclosure. DNA, General Records Dept. of State, Misc. Letters, June–Dec., 1800, 67. R.G. 59.

A number of letters were received from Whelen on the subject of the Algiers and Tunis shipments, June 25, July 3, July 24, Aug. 6, Aug. 15, 1800. Same, 69, 72, 83, 97, 114. Also from Ebenezer Stevens, June 7, July 12, Aug. 14, 1800. Same, 65, 76, 115.

June 24
WASHINGTON *to President John Adams*

Acknowledges letter of 20th; transmitted commission for Smith (as Collector of New York). King letter of Apr. 7 (No. 66; NNHi); recommends pressing for amicable explanation of sixth article of treaty with Great Britain; Secretaries of War and Navy concur. Suggestions for instructions to minister in Madrid concerning Spanish depredations in American commerce. Plans on making advances to Portuguese sailors stranded at Norfolk. MHi, Adams Papers, John Adams Letters Rec'd., XLIX, 104.

Referred to in John Adams to J.M., July 5, 1800. MHi, Adams Papers,

John Adams Letter Book, 1799–1801, 181; DNA, General Records Dept. of State, Misc. Letters, June–Dec., 1800, 73. R.G. 59.

June 26
WASHINGTON *to President John Adams*

Enclosing letter from King dated Apr. 26 (No. 69; NNHi) concerning conference with Lord Granville in British treaty negotiations. King's dispatch No. 67 not received; further instructions must wait. MHi, Adams Papers, John Adams Letters Rec'd, XLIX, 105.

Referred to in John Adams to J.M., July 5, 1800. MHi, Adams Papers, John Adams Letter Book, 1799–1801, 181; DNA, General Records Dept. of State, Misc. Letters, June–Dec., 1800, 73. R.G. 59.

June 26 *to David Lenox, Agent of the United*
WASHINGTON *States for Seamen in London*

Instructing to renew claim for discharge of John Grayson, impressed by British; enclosing proof of U.S. citizenship. DNA, General Records Dept. of State, Dipl. and Cons. Instrs., V, 343. R.G. 59.

June 28
WASHINGTON *to James A. Bayard, of Wilmington, Del.*

Acknowledges letter of 25th. Passports for missionaries Bishop Asbury and Watcoat will be issued by the government; Department of State not granted power by President; clerkship vacancies in Department of State. Criticizes newspaper *Aurora*. MB.

June 28
WASHINGTON *to Israel Whelen*

Concerning purchase of cargo for Algiers on credit. Answered and referred to in letter Whelen to J.M., Philadelphia, July 3, 1800. DNA, General Records Dept. of State, Misc. Letters, June–Dec., 1800, 72. R.G. 59; Also listed in Lazare, *Book-Prices* (1944), 632. Present owner unknown.

June 29 *to R. G. Van Polanen,*
WASHINGTON *Minister Resident from Netherlands*

Concerning claim of owners of ship *Mary* against the Batavian government (n.f.). Referred to in R. G. Van Polanen to J.M. Dept. of State, Notes from the Netherlands Legation, I, note of July 9, 1800. R.G. 59.

June 30
WASHINGTON *to President John Adams*

Enclosing letter from Swedish government concerning joint action against Barbary Powers. Letter from J. Q. Adams in Berlin concerning French-Austrian negotiations. Wolcott arrived. MHi, Adams Papers, John Adams Letters Rec'd, XLIX, 108. Referred to in John Adams to J.M. July 11, 1800. DNA, General Records Dept. of State, Misc. Letters, June–Dec., 1800, 75. R.G. 59; Adams, *J. Adams Works*, X, 63.

July 3
WASHINGTON *Benjamin Stoddard to Israel Whelen*

"The Secretary of State having his hands full of important business, has obtained my promise to correspond with you, on the subject of the George Washington's cargo . . .," concerning shipments to Algiers. Quasi-War–U.S. and France, VI, 110.

July 3 *to Richard Law*

Concerning 4th volume *Laws of the U.S.* Listed in Lazare, *Book-Prices* (1930), 672. Present owner unknown.

July 12
WASHINGTON *Jacob Wagner to John Adams*

In absence of J.M., in Virginia, enclosing letters from judges of Maryland District; death of marshal; suspending court proceedings and census. MHi, Adams Papers, John Adams Letters Rec'd, XLIX, 110.

July 15
WASHINGTON *Jacob Wagner to John Adams*

J.M. expected to return in day or two. Same, 111.

July 17
WASHINGTON *Jacob Wagner to John Adams*

Received letter from J.M., returning on 19th (n.f.). Same, 113.

July 21
WASHINGTON *to John Adams*

Enclosing King's letter No. 67 (dated Apr. 22, 1800; NNHi); questions whether money settlement with Britain will offend France. Sending dispatches from envoys at Paris; expects negotiations to be protracted. Instructions in letter of July 10 concerning Mediterranean envoys obeyed. MHi, Adams Papers, John Adams Letters Rec'd, XLIX, 114.

Answered by John Adams, July 31, 1800; agrees France protracting negotiations, awaiting pending election in the United States; considers further instructions to envoys rejecting revival of old treaty, rejecting unguarding of shipping until treaty concluded. DNA. General Records Dept. of State, Misc. Letters Jan.–Dec., 1800, 92. Also in letter Aug. 1, 1800. Same, 94, favoring lump sum settlement or appointment of new board in British treaty negotiations.

July 21
WASHINGTON *to John Adams*

Enclosing letters of recommendation for appointee as marshal of Maryland (n.f.). Referred to in John Adams to J.M., July 30, 1800. DNA, General Records Dept. of State, Misc. Letters, June–Dec., 1800, 90; MHi, Adams Papers, John Adams Letter Book July 10, 1799—Mar. 1, 1801, 200; Adams, *J. Adams Works*, IX, 66; also in letters John Adams to John Marshall, July 31, Aug. 1, 1800. Misc. Letters, Same, 92, 94; Adams Papers, Same, 203; Adams, *J. Adams Works*, IX, 67–68, 68–69.

See also letter of John Adams to J.M., July 25, 1800, returning applications for the same and giving J.M. the authority to select the candidate of his choice by filling blank in commission. Misc. Letters, Same, 87. Adams Papers, Same, 195.

July 23 *to John Jay,*
WASHINGTON, DEPT. OF STATE *Governor of New York*

Acknowledging letter of June 28; a short absence. Application made by Gray, inquired into; affair of Dover Cutter settled by Carmichael with Spanish government, Mar. 1784, £300 St.; estate of Carmichael insolvent. Advises only remedy is petition to Congress for sum received by Carmichael. NNC.

July 23
WASHINGTON *to Timothy Pickering*

Enclosing letter from Pickering's son among public letters received from Europe; sorry opened. No data as to success of envoys in France. MHi, Pickering MSS, XXVI, 177; DLC, Beveridge Coll.

July 24 *to John Quincy Adams,*
WASHINGTON *Minister of the United States to Prussia*

Acknowledges dispatches Nos. 160, 161, 162. Refuses to join Sweden and Denmark against Barbary Powers; stationing frigate in Mediterranean hazardous because of hostilities with France. MHi, J. Q. Adams, 1794–1816; MHi, Adams Papers, John Adams Letters Rec'd, XCVII, 78; DNA, General Records Dept. of State, Dipl. and Cons. Instrs., V, 344–45; Quasi-War–U.S. and France, VI, 176; Barbary Powers, I, 364–65.

July 24
WASHINGTON *to President John Adams*

Transmitting originals of dispatches Nos. 71 (May 22, 1800; NNHi) and 72 (May 25, 1800; NNHi) from King. Asks instructions concerning demand for jewels by Tunis. Enclosing letter to John Quincy Adams concerning Swedish and Danish proposal against Barbary Powers; wishes approval and transmittal direct. MHi, Adams Papers, John Adams Letters Recd., XLIX, 18. Referred to in letter John Adams to J.M., Aug. 2, 1800. DNA, General Records Dept. of State, Misc. Letters June–Dec., 1800, 95½. R.G. 59; MHi, Adams Papers, John Adams Letter Book July 10, 1799–Mar. 1, 1801, 205; Adams, *J. Adams Works,* IX, 69–70, approving letter and jewels to Tunis.

July 25 *to Carlos M. de Yrugo, Minister Plenipotentiary*
WASHINGTON *of His Catholic Majesty* [*Spain*] *to the United States*

Advising of decision to return to owners the French vessel *Sandwich,* captured by frigate *Constitution* (n.f.). Acknowledged in letter De Yrugo to J.M. DNA, Dept. of State, Notes from the Spanish Legation, II, notes of July 7, July 31, Oct. 15, 1800. R.G. 59.

July 26
WASHINGTON *to President John Adams*

Acknowledges letter of 19th; directions followed; enclosing German letter, request of schoolmasters to enter country. Directed return of the *Sandwich,* captured by Capt. Talbot, on demand of Spanish minister; consulted heads of departments; did not await instructions. Enclosing letter from Spanish minister objecting to activities of Gen. Bowles. Advises favorably on lump-sum settlement with British for claims under Article 6 of treaty; five million dollars or one million sterling; heads of department concur. MHi, Adams Papers, John Adams Letters Rec'd, XLIX, 119. Answered in letter John Adams to J.M., Aug. 11, 1800. Adams Papers Letter Book, 121; DNA, General Records Dept. of State, Misc. Letters June–Dec., 1800, 104; Report Book I, 159, 63. R.G. 59 (letterpress copy); Adams, *J. Adams Works,* IX, 73.

July 29
WASHINGTON *to President John Adams*

Acknowledges letter of 21st enclosing letters from Gen. Forrest and Wilmer. Consulted with Stoddard on applicants for appointment as marshal for the District of Maryland; discusses qualifications; recommends

Maj. David Hopkins. MHi, Adams Papers, John Adams Letters Rec'd, XLIX, 121. Referred to in letter John Adams to J.M., agreeing to Hopkins, Aug. 7, 1800. MHi, Adams Papers Letter Book, 215; DNA, General Records Dept. of State, Misc. Letters, June-Dec., 103. R.G. 59. Adams, *J. Adams Works*, IX, 71–72.

(See letters of Jacob Wagner, Chief Clerk, Department of State, to President John Adams, enclosing applications and correspondence concerning appointment; J.M. in Virginia. Letters dated July 12, 15, 16, 17, 1800. MHi, Adams Papers, John Adams Letters Rec'd, XLIX, 110, 111, 112, 113.)

July 29 — *to Richard O'Brien,*
WASHINGTON — *Consul General of the United States, Algeria*

The *George Washington* sailing for Algiers with cargo; another vessel to follow. The *Sophia* [*sic*] arrived with letters from O'Brien and Eaton, Papers in Department did not show precise account with Barbary Powers; asks for same and their demands. Desires fixed sum as annuities instead of specific articles; $30,000 to Algiers desirable. Burdensome caprice of Barbary sovereigns cannot always be complied with, despite desire for peace. PPHi; DNA, General Records Dept. of State, Dipl. and Cons. Instrs., V, 345–46; Quasi-War–U.S. and France, VI, 194; Barbary Powers, I, 365. Above referred to and forwarded to Ben Stoddard, Secretary of Navy, July 31, 1800.

July 30 — *to Israel Whelen*

Concerning the brigantine *Sophie*, its sale, etc. Listed in Lazare, *Book-Prices* (1962), 745. Present owner unknown.

July 31 — *President John Adams to*
WASHINGTON — *Don John, Prince Regent, Portugal*

Acknowledging letter of Apr. 22, 1800, congratulations on birth of daughter. Signed by J.M. as Secretary of State. DNA, General Records Dept. of State, Credences, I, 111. R.G. 59.

Aug. 1
WASHINGTON — *Pardon*

Slocum Fowler, Newport, fine 1799, U.S. District Court, Rhode Island, $400 unloading sugar without permit. Fit subject of clemency. Signed by J.M., Secretary of State. No. 30. DNA, General Records Dept. of State, Pardon Records, I, 36. R.G. 59.

Aug. 1 — *to David M. Clarkson, Consul of*
WASHINGTON — *the United States at St. Christopher*

Concerning two American seamen held prisoner at Point Peter, Guadaloupe, under charge of murder; criminal proceedings unlawful; killing of master in rescue of vessel within laws of war; exchange demanded; if refused, United States will retaliate. DNA, General Records Dept. of State, Dipl. and Cons. Instrs., V, 346. R.G. 59; Quasi-War–U.S. and France, VI, 215.

Aug. 1
WASHINGTON — *to President John Adams*

Acknowledges letter of 23rd; uncertain as to President's decision on marshal of Maryland. Transmitting letter from Prince Regent of Portugal with proposed answer. (Returned signed. John Adams to J.M., Aug. 12, 1800. DNA, General Records Dept. of State, Misc. Letters, June–Dec., 1800, 108.) Received letter from King recommending settlement with British for gross sum for claims. MHi, Adams Papers, John Adams Letters Rec'd, XLIX, 125. Referred to in letter John Adams to J.M., Aug. 11, 1800. DNA, General Records Dept. of State, Misc. Letters, June–Dec., 1800, 106. R.G. 59; MHi, Adams Papers, John Adams Letter Book, July 10, 1799—Mar. 1, 1801, 217.

Aug. 2
WASHINGTON — *to President John Adams*

Enclosing letter of Sitgreaves on British negotiations. MHi, Adams Papers, John Adams Letters Rec'd, XLIX, 127.

Aug. 2
WASHINGTON — *to President John Adams*

Acknowledges letter of July 25, authorizing J.M. to select appointee for marshal of Maryland; J.M. awaiting further advice as to President's preference for Chase. Recommends remonstrance, and awaiting instructions concerning prosecution of Daniel Tripe at Guadaloupe. Refusal of Spain to pay Gregorie and Pickard award was violation of treaty, which should be complained of. MHi, Adams Papers, John Adams Letters Rec'd, XLIX, 126. Referred to in letter John Adams to J.M., Aug. 13, 1800. DNA, General Records Dept. of State, Misc. Letters June–Dec., 1800, 109. R.G. 59; MHi, Adams Papers, John Adams Letter Book, July 10, 1799—Mar. 1, 1801, 223. Adams, *J. Adams Works*, IX, 76–77.

Aug. 2 *to David Humphreys,*
WASHINGTON *Minister of the United States to Spain*

Enclosing letter by Charles Lee to Humphreys, dated May 14, 1800 (No. 20); acknowledging letter of Mar. 14, which advised of recall of Don Carlos Martines de Yrugo from Spanish Legation in the United States and appointment of Don Nicholas Blasso de Orosco. DNA, General Records Dept. of State, Dipl. and Cons. Instrs., V, 334. R.G. 59.

Also enclosing copy of letter President to King of Spain congratulating on birth of grandson. DNA, General Records Dept. of State, Dipl. and Cons. Instrs., V, 347. R.G. 59.

Aug. 2 and 7
WASHINGTON *from Timothy Pickering*

Memoranda: Aug. 2, to J.M. acknowledging his of 23rd; Aug. 2, to J.M. enclosing letter to Pinckney; Aug. 7, to J.M. enclosing letter of Capt. Richard O'Brien. MHi, Pickering MSS.

Aug. 4
WASHINGTON *to Job Wall, Consul of the United States, St. Bartholomew*

Bill in favor of Capt. Joseph Dacosta protested; request account of expenditures, relief of sailors costly; bond rejected, securities not citizens. DNA, General Records Dept. of State, Dipl. and Cons. Instrs., V, 347–48. R.G. 59.

For reply, see Job Wall to J.M., St. Bartholomew, Oct. 6, 1800. DNA, Dept. of State, Cons. Despatches, St. Bartholomew, I. R.G. 59.

Aug. 4 *to John Elmslie, Jr.,*
WASHINGTON *Consul of the United States, Cape of Good Hope*

Copy of instructions, amendment. DNA, General Records Dept. of State, Dipl. and Cons. Instrs., V, 347. R.G. 59.

For reply, see John Elmslie, Jr., to J.M., July 10, 1801; DNA, Dept. of State, Cons. Despatches, Cape Town, I. R.G. 59.

Aug. 4
WASHINGTON *to President John Adams*

Transmitting two letters concerning consul at Madeira and oration sent by author. MHi, Adams Papers, John Adams Letters Rec'd, XLIX, 128. Referred to in letter John Adams to J.M., Aug. 15, 1800. DNA, General Records Dept. of State, Misc. Letters June–Dec., 1800, 113. R.G. 59; MHi, Adams Papers, John Adams Letter Book July 10, 1799—Mar. 1, 1801, 228; Adams, *J. Adams Works,* IX, 77.

Aug. 4
WASHINGTON *to Ebenezer Stevens*

Concerning shipment to Tunis (n.f.). Referred to in letter Ebenezer Stevens to J.M., Nov. 18, 1800. DNA, General Records Dept. of State, Misc. Letters Jan.–Dec., 1800, 283. R.G. 59.

(Letter contained commission for John Elmslie as consul for Cape of Good Hope. See reply of E. Stevens to J.M., London, Nov. 29, 1800. DNA, Dept. of State, Cons. Despatches, London, I. R.G. 59.)

Aug. 4 *to Israel Whelen*

Concerning cargoes. Listed in Lazare, *Book-Prices* (1958), 477. Present owner unknown.

Aug. 5
CINCINNATI, O. *from Arthur St. Clair*

Acknowledges letters of July 9 and 12 (n.f.) concerning Connecticut Western Reserve; new county formed. Encloses copy of letter from Col. Hambrum concerning killing; Indian disturbances and war; establishment of court in Trumbull County. OU.

Aug. 5
WASHINGTON *to Harrison Gray Otis*

J.M. paid $40.00 to Dexter for Otis; draft enclosed. Ill news from Virginia, decided Democrat elected to succeed J.M. by enormous majority. New Jersey going badly; Maryland would be right except for current against Federalists of uncalculable force. Tide in affairs of nation, parties, and individuals; fears Americanism is on ebb. MHi, Otis MSS; DLC, Beveridge Coll.

Aug. 7 *from President John Adams*

Requesting opinions of heads of departments as to pardon for Isaac Williams, in prison at Hartford for privateering under French colors. MHi, Adams Papers, John Adams Letter Book, July 10, 1799—Mar. 1, 1801, 212; Quasi-War–U.S. and France, VII, 228; Adams, *J. Adams Works*, IX, 72.

Aug. 7
QUINCY, MASS. *from President John Adams*

Instructing concerning missing papers of patent to clergyman of Braintree for washing machine. DNA, General Records Dept. of State,

Misc. Letters June–Dec., 1800, 102. R.G. 59; MHi, Adams Papers, John Adams Letter Book July 10, 1799—Mar. 1, 1801, 213.

Aug. 8
WASHINGTON *to President John Adams*

Transmitting letter from King, enclosing Swedish complaint for injury to vessel; wrote to Charleston, S.C., collector for inquiry (n.f.). Awaiting instructions from President. MHi, Adams Papers, John Adams Letters Rec'd, XLIX, 129. Answered by John Adams, Aug. 18, 1800, approving action. DNA, General Records Dept. of State, Misc. Letters Jan.–Dec., 1800, 117. R.G. 59; MHi, Adams Papers, John Adams Letter Book, July 10, 1799—Mar. 1, 1801, 229.

Aug. 8
WASHINGTON *to Polly Marshall*

Acknowledges letter of Aug. 5; delighted with account of daughter Mary's dinner and son John's good breeding; approves sending boys to country. Received sermon from Tom, which he had written for (letter n.f.); disappointed not hearing of Polly's health. VW; Mason, *Polly*, 142.

Aug. 11
WASHINGTON *to Timothy Pickering*

Acknowledges letter; Pinckney letter forwarded; Maj. Montflorence and Mitchell mentioned; enclosing letters addressed to Secretary of State. MHi, Pickering MSS, XXVI, 187.

Aug. 11
QUINCY, MASS. *from President John Adams*

Instructing issuance patent for tin cook stove to Frederick Butler. MHi, Adams Papers, John Adams Letter Book July 10, 1799—Mar. 1, 1801, 216.

Aug. 12
WASHINGTON *to President John Adams*

Enclosing letter of Chev. de Yrugo. Acknowledges letter of July 31 with enclosure of letter to Adams from Spanish King. Consulted with Secretary of War, who will write to Col. Hawkins to detach Indians from Bowles; some success already; American troops not desired; British not supporting Bowles· will write De Yrugo as instructed.

Acknowledges letter of July 31 returning dispatches from Paris, and of Aug. 1 with dispatch from King (MHi, Adams Papers, John Adams

Letter Book July 10, 1799—Mar. 1, 1801, 203, 204). Discusses difficulty but desirability of lump-sum settlement of British claims. MHi, Adams Papers, John Adams Letters Rec'd, XLIX, 130.

Referred to in letter John Adams to J.M., Aug. 22, 1800. DNA, General Records Dept. of State, Misc. Letters June–Dec., 1800, 118; DNA, Dept. of State, Report Book I, 165–71 (letterpress copy). R.G. 59; MHi, Adams Papers, John Adams Letter Book July 10, 1799—Mar. 1, 1801, 230 (dated 12th); Adams, *J. Adams Works*, IX, 78.

Aug. 12
WASHINGTON *to Robert Liston*

Requesting minister to communicate with commander of British fleet at Jamaica for release of impressed U.S. seamen (n.f.). Referred to in letter R. Liston to J.M., Aug. 18, 1800. DNA, Dept. of State, Notes from the British Legation, II. R.G. 59.

Aug. 15
WASHINGTON *to Carlos de Yrugo*

Answering letter to President of July 22, effective measures taken against Bowles' activities, to restrain Indians. MHi, Adams Papers, XLIX, John Adams Letters Rec'd., 133.

Aug. 15
WASHINGTON *Appointment—Marshal*

Commission to David Hopkins, office of marshal, Maryland District, signed by J.M., Secretary of State, for President. DNA, General Records Dept. of State, Misc. Temporary Commissions, 1789–1818, Vol. B, 82. R.G. 59. See letters of President Adams to J.M., Aug. 7, 11, 1800, instructing appointment. DNA, General Records Dept. of State, Misc. Letters June–Dec., 1800, 103, 106. R.G. 59; MHi, Adams Papers, John Adams Letter Book July 10, 1799—Mar. 1, 1801, 215.

Aug. 16
WASHINGTON *Pardon*

Isaac Williams, New London, Conn., misdemeanor Oct. 21, Treaty of Amity, Great Britain, U.S. Circuit Court, Conn.; sentenced four months following other indictment; fine $400; poverty; discharged on paying cost of prosecution. No. 29. Signed by J.M., Secretary of State. DNA, General Records Dept. of State, Pardon Records, I, 35. R.G. 59.

Aug. 16
WASHINGTON *to Rufus King, Minister Plenipotentiary of the United States, Great Britain*

Dispatches to No. 74 (dispatch No. 73, June 2, 1800; dispatch No. 74, June 6, 1800; NNHi) received; instructs to congratulate King of Great Britain on escape from assassin; to execute commission of Eaton to purchase jewels for Bay of Tunis. King to be apprised of affairs of Barbary Powers. Hopes for instructions concerning Article 6 of treaty with Great Britain. Dispatch No. 1. DNA, General Records Dept. of State, Dipl. and Cons. Instrs., V, 348. R.G. 59.

Aug. 16
WASHINGTON *to Timothy Pickering*

Enclosing letter from Consul Eaton; acknowledges letter enclosing request of O'Brien payment; recommendation by Pickering of Cist, position filled. MHi, Pickering MSS, XXVI, 199.

Aug. 16
WASHINGTON *to President John Adams*

Commission for marshal of Maryland made to Maj. Hopkins, President's preference for Chase noted. Isaac Williams pardon granted on consultation with heads of departments; amended patent to Wild. Has written to King to congratulate British King on escape from assassin, and to purchase jewels for Bay of Tunis. Consensus of department heads that five million dollars proper sum for settlement of British claims, awaiting instructions from President. Enclosing letter to Carlos de Yrugo. DNA, General Records Dept. of State, Report Book I, 173–77 (letterpress copy). R.G. 59; MHi, Adams Papers, John Adams Letters Rec'd, XLIX, 132. Referred to in letter John Adams to J.M., Aug. 26, 1800, agreeing to lump-sum settlement with British. DNA, General Records Dept. of State, Misc. Letters June–Dec., 1800, 125. R.G. 59; MHi, Adams Papers, John Adams Letter Book July 10, 1799—Mar. 1, 1801, 240; Adams, *J. Adams Works*, IX, 78, excerpt at 72n.

Aug. 17
WASHINGTON *to President John Adams*

Giving opinion that French changing policy, leaving only claim for compensation against them and not cause for war. Adams, *J. Adams Works*, IX, 85n.

Aug. 23
WASHINGTON *to Alexander Hamilton*

Acknowledges letter of 19th with enclosure of memorial from Governor General of Danish West Indies concerning our ships of war. Dispatches from Paris inconclusive; St. Sebastian "paragraph" may be true. DLC, Papers of Alexander Hamilton, Vol. 78; Hamilton, *Works*, VI, 460; Oster, *Marshall*, 92.

Aug. 23
WASHINGTON *to President John Adams*

Acknowledging two letters of the 11th and letter to be sent to Prince Regent of Portugal. Letter to King prepared for approval; J.M. and heads of departments agree with President explanatory clause of Article 6 of treaty preferable, lump sum for U.S. creditors next choice.

Requested letters to governors concerning Spain deferred because Col. Hawkins report indicates fulfilled; pleased letter concerning *Sandwich* approved. Enclosing letter from King concerning European wars. MHi, Adams Papers, John Adams Letters Rec'd, XLIX, 134; DNA, General Records, Dept. of State, Report Book I, 179–83. R.G. 59. (letterpress copy); Adams, *J. Adams Works*, IX, 74n. Also referred to in letter of John Adams to J.M. Aug. 30, 1800, approving instructions to King; letters to governors not necessary; will have to fight French alone; delay of delegates. DNA, General Records Dept. of State, Misc. Letters June–Dec., 1800, 126. R.G. 59. MHi, Adams Papers, John Adams Letter Book July 10, 1799—Mar. 1, 1801, 245.

Aug. 23
WASHINGTON *to Rufus King*

President prefers agreement to explanatory clause of Article 6 of treaty with Great Britain; American commissioners withdrawn from board because of unwarranted extension of British claims; instructs as alternative lump settlement; not determined if appointment of new commissioners alone agreeable. Dispatch No. 2, DNA, General Records Dept. of State, Dipl. and Cons. Instrs., V, 349–56. R.G. 59; CSmH, RK 538; Adams Papers, John Adams Letters Rec'd, XLIX, 154; ASP (For. Rel.), II, 386–87; Oster, *Marshall*, 70–77; W. R. Manning (ed.), *Diplomatic Correspondence of the United States, Canadian Relations*, (Washington, Carnegie Endow., 1940), I, 147.

Aug. 23
WASHINGTON *to Rufus King*

Letter designated "private"; stresses personal preference for explanatory clause of Article 6; unofficial reports of French treaty negotiation indicate failure. Morristown Nat'l Park.

Aug. 23 *Commissioner Georgia Boundary—*
WASHINGTON *Mississippi Territory*

Pursuant to act of Congress, Apr. 7, 1798, limits of Georgia and establishment of government Mississippi Territory, had appointed T. Pickering (Secretary of State), Oliver Wolcott (Secretary of Treasury), and Charles Lee (Attorney General) commissioners under Section 6; J.M. named in place of Pickering, adjust claims with Georgia, powers under act of May 10, 1799, until next session of Congress. Signed for President by J.M., Secretary of State. DNA, General Records Dept. of State, Misc. Temporary Commissions, 1789–1818, 83. R.G. 59. (See herein Dec. 8 and Dec. 12, 1800.)

Aug. 25
WASHINGTON *to President John Adams*

Enclosing French decrees; predicts envoys to France may return without treaty; questions whether hostilities with France should continue. Encloses dispatches from Isle de France.

Acknowledges letter of Aug. 15; will commission Lamar consul at Madeira only if American by birth not available; discusses other former applicants. MHi, Adams Papers, John Adams Letters Rec'd, XLIX, 136; DNA, General Records Dept. of State, Report Book I, 185–89. R.G. 59 (letterpress copy); excerpt in Adams, *J. Adams Works,* IX, 81 n. Referred to in letter John Adams to J.M., discussing declaration of war against France, Sept. 4, 1800. DNA, General Records Dept. of State, Misc. Letters June–Dec., 1800, 134. R.G. 59; MHi, Adams Papers, John Adams Letter Book July 10, 1799—Mar. 1, 1801, 257; Adams, *J. Adams Works,* IX, 80–81.

Aug. 25
WASHINGTON *to Rufus King*

Enclosing bill of exchange; if no appropriation, apply to general funds. Dispatch No. 3. DNA, General Records Dept. of State, Dipl. and Cons. Instrs., V, 355–56. R.G. 59.

Aug. 26
WASHINGTON *to Rufus King*

Concerning complaint of Sweden against two American letters of marque; instructions as to apology; American courts open for private loss. Dispatch No. 4, DNA, General Records Dept. of State, Dipl. and Cons. Instrs., V, 356. R.G. 59. Replied to Dec. 15, 1800, No. 94. NNHi.

Aug. 26
WASHINGTON *to William Smith*

Enclosing answer of President to Prince Regent of Portugal concerning announcement of birth of daughter. Dispatch No. 2. DNA, General Records Dept. of State, Dipl. and Cons. Instrs., V, 357. R.G. 59.

Aug. 26
WASHINGTON *to President John Adams*

Acknowledges letter of 18th; wrote to King concerning Swedish complaint. Enclosing letter from Governor of Indiana; early appointment of judges advisable; approves President's choice of William Clarke and Gov. Harrison's recommendation of Henry Vanderburgh; encloses recommendations for appointment Griffin and Claiborne. MHi, Adams Papers, John Adams Letters Rec'd, XLIX, 143; DNA, General Records Dept. of State, Report Book I, 192–93. R.G. 59 (letterpress copy).

Aug. 26
WASHINGTON *to Thomas Claxton*

Directions from secretaries of four executive departments—State, Treasury, War, and Navy—appointing Claxton agent for furnishing President's house; act of Congress, Apr. 24, 1800, $15,000 appropriated, $250 for services; oval room, second floor, drawing room of Mrs. Adams and northwest room, first floor, richly furnished; others plain and elegant, avoiding expense. Quasi-War–U.S. and France, VI, 289, from Navy Dept. Archives, General Letter Books, IV, 1800–1801.

Aug. 27
WASHINGTON *to President John Adams*

Transmitting dispatches from judge of Kentucky District (Judge Harry Innes); hopes resistence to federal court ended. Also enclosing letters from Spanish officials; recommends claim against Spain for condemnation of American vessels by French consular courts in Spain. MHi, Adams Papers, John Adams Letters Rec'd, XLIX, 144; DNA, Dept. of State, Report Book 1, 195–97. R.G. 59 (letterpress copy).

Answered in letter John Adams to J.M., Sept. 5, 1800. DNA, General Records Dept. of State, Misc. Letters June–Dec., 1800, 140. R.G. 59; MHi, Adams Papers, John Adams Letter Book July 10, 1799—Mar. 1, 1801, 254.

Aug. 27
WASHINGTON *to Henry M. Rutledge*

Concerning appointment of commissioners to negotiate with Indians; victories of Napoleon in Italian campaign. Listed in Lazare, *Book-Prices* (1926), 819; (1938), 507. Present owner unknown.

Aug. 27
WASHINGTON *to Israel Whelen*

(N.f.) Referred to in letter Israel Whelen to J.M., Sept. 3, 1800. DNA, General Records Dept. of State, Misc. Letters June–Dec., 1800, 135. R.G. 59; also in letter Israel Whelen to J.M., Oct. 16, 1800. DNA, General Records Dept. of State, Misc. Letters June–Dec., 1800, 269. R.G. 59.

Aug. 28
WASHINGTON *to Timothy Pickering*

Enclosing letter from King; dispatches from Paris concerning embassy uncertain. MHi, Pickering MSS, XXVI, 203; DLC, Beveridge Coll.

Aug. 29
WASHINGTON *Bridge Aid*

Meeting of heads of departments, Secretaries of State, Treasury, War, and Navy; $500 aid in building bridge over the Tiber; $1,000 bridge over Rock Creek. Quasi-War–U.S. and France, VI, 302–303; Navy Department Archives, General Letter Books, IV, 1800–1801.

Aug. 30
WASHINGTON *to Israel Whelen*

Acknowledges two letters of 27th; money transmitted; the ships *Hero* and *Anna Maria*. PPHi, Dreer Presidents Coll. Referred to in letter Israel Whelen to J.M., Sept. 3, 1800. DNA, General Records Dept. of State, Misc. Letters Jan.–Dec., 1800, 135. R.G. 59; also in letter Israel Whelen to J.M., Oct. 16, 1800. DNA, General Records Dept. of State, Misc. Letters Jan.–Dec., 1800, 269. R.G. 59.

Aug. 30 *to William Eaton,*
WASHINGTON *Consul of the United States to the Kingdom of Tunis*

The *Anna Maria* sailing for Tunis with cargo; demand for jewels reluctantly consented to; King directed to purchase; possible delay; Barbary Powers demands unwarranted, must not be continued; the United States unwilling to go to war; residue of stores expedited. King to be informed of affairs. Bill for $6,000 from Robinson to be paid. DNA, General Records Dept. of State, Dipl. and Cons. Instrs., V, 357. R.G. 59; TxU; Barbary Powers, I, 369–70.

Aug. 30
WASHINGTON *to President John Adams*

Acknowledges letter of 22nd; happy proceedings with Spanish approved. Enclosing letter of Stevens concerning victory of Toussaint at San Domingo; also letters of Mitchell of Charleston, S.C., and Humphries. MHi, Adams Papers, John Adams Letters Rec'd, XLIX, 146; DNA, General Records Dept. of State, Report Book I, 199 (letterpress copy). R.G. 59. Answered in letter John Adams to J.M. Sept. 9, 1800, stating will lift embargo on San Domingo if heads of departments satisfied. DNA, General Records Dept. of State, Misc. Letters Jan.–Dec., 1800, 139. R.G. 59; MHi, Adams Papers, John Adams Letter Book July 10, 1799—Mar. 1, 1801; Adams, *J. Adams Works,* IX, 82–83.

Sept. 3
WASHINGTON *to President John Adams*

Acknowledges letter of President concerning Norton claim; delicate because of provisions to British Army in Revolutionary War. Encloses Wilkins and Harrison letters of recommendation of Hollingsworth as judge of Indiana Territory. MHi, Adams Papers, John Adams Letters Rec'd, XLIX, 147; DNA, Dept. of State, Report Book I, 199. R.G. 59.

Answered in letter John Adams to J.M. Sept. 13, 1800. DNA, General Records Dept. of State, Misc. Letters Jan.–Dec., 1800, 141, R.G. 59; MHi, Adams Papers, John Adams Letter Book July 10, 1799—Mar. 1, 1801, 267; Adams, *J. Adams Works,* IX, 82–83.

Sept. 5
WASHINGTON *Money Draft*

Exchange draft for £5,875 on Paget and Bainbridge, bankers, London, payable to Oliver Wolcott; endorsed on back to J.M., and by J.M. to Rufus King. DNA, Dept. of State, Dipl. and Cons. Instrs., V, between 366 and 367. R.G. 59.

Sept. 6
WASHINGTON *to the President [John Adams]*

Received letter from Chev. de Yrugo complaining of refusal of marshal of District of New York to deliver vessel *Sandwich*, unlawfully captured by Capt. Talbot; J.M. has taken measures; discusses action if Talbot refuses to accede to order of executive; suggests applying to court to dismiss action. MHi, Adams Papers, John Adams Letters Rec'd, XLIX, 151; DNA, General Records Dept. of State, Misc. Letters Jan.–Dec., 1800, 137. R.G. 59. Answered in John Adams to J.M. Sept. 17, 1800, Same, 148; MHi, Adams Papers, John Adams Letter Book July 10, 1799—Mar. 1, 1801, 271.

Sept. 6
WASHINGTON *to John Adams*

Acknowledges letter of Aug. 26; stresses difficulty of arriving at lump sum settlement with British and preference of explanatory clause; instructions along these lines sent to King, approved by department heads. Enclosing letter from Liston, and J.M. reply; sent without President's prior approval. Preparing letter to Humphries for remonstrance to Spain concerning French consular courts. Enclosing for consideration proclamation opening trade with San Domingo; B. Dandridge applying for consulate. MHi, Adams Papers, John Adams Letters Rec'd, XLIX, 148; DNA, General Records Dept. of State, Report Book I, 201–205 (letterpress copy). R.G. 59. Referred to in two letters John Adams to J.M., both dated Sept. 17, 1800. DNA, General Records Dept. of State, Misc. Letters Jan.–Dec., 1800, 147–48. R.G. 59; MHi, Adams Papers, John Adams Letter Book July 10, 1799—Mar. 31, 1801, 269, 270.

Sept. 6 *to Robert Liston,*
WASHINGTON *Minister of Great Britain to the United States*

Replying to letter of Aug. 25, newspaper charges of British government connection with Bowles activities in Florida in inciting Indians against Spaniards cannot be prevented; hostility of people against Great Britain because of impressment and proceedings of courts of Vice Admiralty. MHi, Adams Papers, John Adams Letters Rec'd, XLIX, 150. Quoted in Beveridge, *Marshall*, II, 498–99.

Sept. 6
WASHINGTON *Presidential Proclamation*

Lifting ban on commerce between the United States and Hispaniola; signed by J.M. as Secretary of State. DNA, General Records U.S., Proclamations, R.G. 11; Quasi-War–U.S. and France, VI, 321–22, from State Dept. Archives, and *Connecticut Journal* (New Haven, Conn.), Oct. 8, 1800, DLC; *The Virginia Argus*, Oct. 7, 1800, 48, 3. (See herein Aug. 30, 1800.)

Sept. 8
WASHINGTON *to President John Adams*

Returning papers from Gov. St. Clair. Recommends appointment of Leonard if Pintard to be removed as consul at Madeira. Encloses for approval letter to Humphries for remonstrance to Spain for depredations. MHi, Adams Papers, John Adams Letters Rec'd, XLIX, 152; DNA, General Records Dept. of State, Report Book I, 207–11 (letterpress copy). R.G. 59.

Sept. 8
WASHINGTON *to David Humfries [Humphreys]*

Propounds the U.S. policy of neutrality in European war, especially toward Spain. Directs that complaint be lodged with Spain for allowing fitting out of privateers under French commissions in Spanish ports, manned by Spaniards, capturing American merchantmen; also for condemning in its courts, or allowing French consults to condemn, such captures; compensation demanded. Dispatch No. 2. DNA, General Records Dept. of State, Dipl. and Cons. Instrs., V, 358–63; Quasi-War–U.S. and France, VI, 326–31. See John Adams to J.M., Sept. 17, 1800. DNA, General Records Dept. of State, Misc. Letters Jan.–Dec., 1800, 147, R.G. 59, approving; MHi, Adams Papers, John Adams Letter Book July 10, 1799—Mar. 1, 1801, 270.

Sept. 9
WASHINGTON *to Rufus King*

Request to give good offices in appeal from condemnation of American ship *Charlotte* in Court of Vice Admiralty at Halifax. Dispatch No. 5. DNA, General Records Dept. of State, Dipl. and Cons. Instrs., V, 364. R.G. 59. Replied to Nov. 22, 1800. No. 89, NNHi.

Sept. 9
WASHINGTON *to President John Adams*

Enclosing letter to King that two million dollars is limit of lump sum chargeable to the United States in treaty settlement. MHi, Adams Papers, John Adams Letters Rec'd, XLIX, 153. Answered in John Adams to J.M., Sept. 18, 1800. DNA, General Records Dept. of State, Misc. Letters, Jan.–Dec., 1800, 145. R.G. 59; MHi, Adams Papers, John Adams Letter Book July 10, 1799—Mar. 1, 1801, 273; Adams, *J. Adams Works*, IX, 84.

Sept. 12
WASHINGTON *to President John Adams*

Apologizing for sending dispatches without cover letter. MHi, Adams

Papers, John Adams Letters Rec'd, XLIX, 155. Referred to in letter John Adams to J.M. Sept. 27, 1800 (enclosing letter of J. Cox Barnett of Bordeaux, July 27, a private letter [n.f.]); MHi, Adams Papers, John Adams Letter Book July 10, 1799—Mar. 1, 1801, 282; DNA, General Records Dept. of State, Misc. Letters, Jan.–Dec., 1800, 153. R.G. 59.

Sept. 13
WASHINGTON *to Timothy Tinsley*

Application for collectorship of Norfolk forwarded to Secretary of Treasury. Uncertain as to French negotiations. MHi, Washburn MSS, 11.1.4[25].

Sept. 13 *to Thomas Bulkely,*
WASHINGTON *Consul of the United States, Lisbon*

Request to give aid and advice to Terascon, owner of the vessel *Sea Nymph,* carried to Lisbon by British captor. DNA, General Records Dept. of State, Dipl. and Cons. Instrs., V, 364. R.G. 59; Quasi-War–U.S. and France, VI, 348.

Sept. 13 *to John Gavino,*
WASHINGTON *Consul of the United States, Gibraltar*

Request to give aid and advice to agent of Lewis A. Terascon, owner of vessel *Sea Nymph,* if British captors attempt adjudication in Gibraltar. DNA, General Records Dept. of State, Dipl. and Cons. Instrs., V, 365. Answered John Gavino to J.M., Feb. 1, 1801. DNA, General Records Dept. of State, Cons. Dispatches, Gibraltar, No. 2. R.G. 59.

Sept. 16
WASHINGTON *to David Lenox*

Instructions to request discharge of two Americans on British ships of war. DNA, General Records Dept. of State, Dipl. and Cons. Instrs., V, 365. R.G. 59.

Sept. 16 *to William Savage,*
WASHINGTON *Consul of the United States, Kingston, Jamaica*

Instructions to convey request for release of several Americans impressed by British squadron on Jamaica station. DNA, General Records Dept. of State, Dipl. and Cons. Instrs., V, 366. R.G. 59; Quasi-War–U.S. and France, VI, 355.

Sept. 16
WALNUT FARM,
WESTMORELAND COUNTY, VA. *Bushrod Washington to C. P. Wayne*

Many applications for history about to be written, waiting until ready for press. Have determined with gentleman who will assist to sell copyright; not involved in sales. Present propositions to J.M., power of attorney during absence on Southern Circuit. Turned down many offers for papers (of George Washington); would not furnish them to anyone, but do full justice. PPHi.

Sept. 17
WASHINGTON *to President John Adams*

Acknowledging letters of 4th and 5th. Suggests consideration that envoys to France may return without treaty; believes present government conciliatory and there will be no cause for war, merely compensation for past injuries. Encloses commissions for judges of Indiana Territory; one for Griffin to be returned if not approved. (Acceptance by Griffin in letter to President, Williamsburg, Oct. 18, 1800. MHi, Adams Papers, John Adams Letters Rec'd, XVI, 156.) Reminds of mentioning private business when assumed office; wishes fortnight in Richmond first of October. MHi, Adams Papers, John Adams Letters Rec'd, XLIX, 156; DNA, General Records Dept. of State, Report Book I, 213–17 (letterpress copy). R.G. 59. Reproduced in part in Adams, *J. Adams Works,* IX, 85n. J.M. went to Richmond to argue the case of *Mayo v. Bentley,* 4 Call 528 (herein 1800, Legal Practice, Court of Appeals, Va.). See Beveridge, *Marshall,* II, 494 n.2. Above letter answered in John Adams to J.M. Sept. 27, 1800. MHi, Adams Papers, John Adams Letter Book, July 10, 1799—Mar. 1, 1801, 283; DNA, General Records Dept. of State, Misc. Letters, Jan.–Dec., 1800, 152. R.G. 59; Adams, *J. Adams Works,* IX, 84–85.

Sept. 18
WASHINGTON *to Rufus King*

Remittance of bill of exchange for reimbursement of J. & F. Baring and Co.; money borrowed for expense of prize causes before Court of Admiralty and Court of Appeals, London. Dispatch No. 6. First of set of bill of exchange attached. By duplicate letters of same date, second and third set of bill of exchange sent. Duplicate and triplicate of letter in J.M. handwriting. DNA, General Records Dept. of State, Dipl. and Cons. Instrs., V, 366. R.G. 59. Replied to Dec. 10, 1800, No. 91. NNHi.

Sept. 20
WASHINGTON *to Rufus King*

Directing to renew negotiations with British as to contraband, blockades, impressment; discussion of international law on the subjects; separateness of French negotiations. DNA, General Records Dept. of State, Dipl. and Cons. Instrs., V, 367–83. R.G. 59; ASP (For. Rel.) II, 486–90; NNHi (typescript); MH, Autograph file (extract unidentified hand); ASP, IX, 23–26 (excerpt); Oster, *Marshall,* 65–69 (excerpt); Niles' Vol. II (Aug. 22, 1812), 403 (excerpt); Beveridge, *Marshall,* II, 507–14 (excerpt).

Sept. 23
WASHINGTON *to David Humphreys*

Instructions concerning claim of Gregorie and Scobie against Spain for award under treaty; right of naturalization discussed; protests payment of specie contracts with depreciated money; demand for restoration of vessels captured from British; release of Americans in Spain captured by French; protests depredations of Spanish vessels; various claims for illegal captures, documents enclosed. Dispatch No. 3. NjP, De Coppet Coll.; DNA, General Records Dept. of State, Dipl. and Cons. Instrs., V, 383–88. R.G. 59; Quasi-War–U.S. and France, VI, 331–32.

Sept. 24
WASHINGTON *to Rufus King*

Requesting efforts for release of impressed American seaman Benjamin Eastman. Dispatch No. 7. DNA, General Records Dept. of State, Dipl. and Cons. Instrs., V, 366–67. R.G. 59.

Sept. 24
WASHINGTON *to President John Adams*

Encloses letter from J. Q. Adams, minister at Berlin; received certificate of ratification of U.S. treaty with Prussia. Also encloses letter to King for approval and forwarding direct if approved. Vessel taken at Puerto Plata delivered to Spain. MHi, Adams Papers, John Adams Letters Rec'd, XLIX, 157; DNA, General Records Department of State, Report Book I, 220–21. R.G. 59 (letterpress copy).

Answered in letter John Adams to J.M. Oct. 3, 1800. DNA, General Records Dept. of State, Misc. Letters Jan.–Dec., 1800, 157. R.G. 59; MHi, Adams Papers, John Adams Letter Book July 10, 1799—Mar. 1, 1801, 218; Quasi-War–U.S. and France, VI, 426; Adams, *J. Adams Works,* IX, 86–87, reproduced in part in Same, 87n.

Sept. 25
WASHINGTON *to Israel Whelen*

Concerning shipments to Algiers (n.f.). Referred to in letters Israel Whelen to J. Wagner, Oct. 4 and 18, 1800. DNA, General Records Dept. of State, Misc. Letters Jan.–Dec., 1800, 160, 171. R.G. 59.

Sept. 26
WASHINGTON *to President John Adams*

Encloses permit for brig *Amazon* to carry passengers to France. MHi, Adams Papers, John Adams Letters Rec'd, XLIX, 158.

Sept. 29
WASHINGTON *to Israel Whelen*

(N.f.) Referred to in letter Israel Whelen to J.M., Oct 4, 1800. DNA, General Records Dept. of State, Misc. Letters Jan.–Dec., 1800. R.G. 59.

Sept. 30
WASHINGTON *Account—Secretary of State*

Account of J.M., Secretary of State, quarterly salaries, Department of State, J.M. $1,250. Total $2,750. Auditor's Office, Oct. 1, 1800. DNA, Records U.S. General Accounting Office, Misc. Treas. Accounts, 1790–1835, No. 11723. R.G. 217.

Sept.
SUPERIOR COURT, HARDY COUNTY, VA. *Law Suit*

J.M. by Charles Magill v. Johnathan Hutton. Action on bond, £99:5, payable at £49:12:6, May 6, 1799, on demand.

Oct., 1800. Judgment under rules.

May, 1801. Bail, set aside.

Sept. 9, 1801. Confessed judgment £49:12:6 and interest. Hardy County, Va. (now W. Va.) Superior Court, Record Book 1800–1803, 266–67.

Sept.
WASHINGTON *to Governor of Mississippi Territory, Natchez*

Concerning delivery of thirty-seven copies laws last session of Congress, with document. Listed in Lazare, *Book-Prices* (1931), 757. Present owner unknown.

Oct. 1
PARIS *from William Vans Murray*

Advising J.M. of signing of provisional treaty with France. In "Message from the President," etc., May 20, 1826, Diplomatic Correspondence. Annals, 19 Cong., 1 sess., 102.

Oct. 1
WASHINGTON *to President John Adams*

Acknowledges three letters of 17th, one of 18th; happy that letters to King and Humphreys approved. Agrees with suggestions for method of payment in settlement with Britain; mentions rumors concerning sailing of the *Portsmouth* (from France). MHi Adams Papers, John Adams Letters Rec'd, XLIX, 159.

Oct. 4
WASHINGTON *to Rufus King*

Enclosing bill of exchange for refund of expenses borrowed in prize cases before courts. Dispatch No. 8. DNA, General Records Dept. of State, Cons. Instrs., I, 1. Duplicate and triplicate. DNA, General Records Dept. of State, Dipl. and Cons. Instrs., V, inserted following 388.

Replied to, King to J.M., Dec. 10, 1800. No. 91. NNHi.

Oct. 4 *from Oliver Ellsworth, W. R.*
PARIS *Davis, Wm. V. Murray*

Enclosing journal of proceedings commencing Mar. 2, 1800, and convention arrived at in mission to France. DNA, Dept. of State, Dipl. Dispatches, France, Vol. 7.

Oct. 6
WASHINGTON *Appointment—Indiana Territory*

Commission to Henry Vanderburgh, until next session Congress, Judge of Indiana Territory, good behavior or existence of government, requirement to reside therein; signed for President by J.M., Secretary of State. DNA, General Records Dept. of State, Misc. Temporary Commissions, 1789–1818, Vol. B, 84. R.G. 59.

Same, to John Griffin, Virginia as third judge Indiana Territory, Same, 85.

Same to William Clark, Kentucky, Chief Justice Indiana Territory, Same, 86. Appointments authorized. Letter President Adams to J.M., Sept. 5, 1800. DNA, General Records Dept. of State, Misc. Letters Jan.–Dec., 1800, 133.

Oct. 9
WASHINGTON *Document*

Certificate of citizenship of John Johnston signed by J.M. OCHP, Jones Coll., J-K MSS, p. 32, item 43.

Oct. 11
CAMBRIDGE, MASS. *from Elbridge Gerry*

Acknowledging letters of J.M. Sept. 15 and Sept. 25 with accounts (n.f.). Refers to Gerry letter to President, July 21, 1799, for account from Pickering. Salary confirmed by President; draw bill for $1,850.48; error of Pickering in cutting in half return passage from France; also wrong guilder rate. Asks for correction, submit to President. MHi, Adams Papers, John Adams Letters Rec'd, XLII, 178. See letter President Adams to Gerry, June 13, 1800, that Adams submitting matter to J.M. MHi, Adams Papers, John Adams Letter Book July 10, 1799—Mar. 1, 1801.

Oct. 14
PHILADELPHIA *from Stephen Girard*

Concerning condemnation of brig *Sally*; appeal taken; requests letter to U.S. minister. Girard College, Stephen Girard Papers, Letter Book 7, Letter 691.

Prior to Oct. 16
WASHINGTON *to Samuel Bayard*

Concerning appointment of consul to Madeira (n.f.), Referred to in letter John M. Pintard to J.M., New York, Oct. 16, 1800. DNA, Dept. of State, Misc. Letters Jan. 8–Dec. 29, 1801, 27. R.G. 59. Also referred to in J.M. to John M. Pintard, Oct. 22, 1800, herein.

Oct. 16 *Chief Justice Oliver Ellsworth to*
HAVRE, FRANCE *President John Adams*

Resignation as Chief Justice of the Supreme Court, remaining in South France for the winter. MHi, Adams Papers, John Adams Letters Rec'd, XVI, 155.

Oct. 16, 18
WASHINGTON *to Israel Whelen*

Concerning shipment to Algiers (n.f.), Referred to in letter Israel Whelen to J.M., Oct. 30, 1800. DNA, General Records Dept. of State, Misc. Letters Jan.–Dec., 1800, 167.

Oct. 22 *to Commissioner of the*
WASHINGTON *City of Washington*

President to arrive in few days, and Mrs. Adams shortly, with servants; as many workmen as possible should be put to work; little houses in neighborhood need not be removed. Signed by J.M. and Ben Stoddard. Quasi-War–U.S. and France, VI, 492, from Navy Dept. Archives, General Letter Books, IV, 1800–1801.

Oct. 22 *to John M. Pintard,*
WASHINGTON *Consul of the United States, Madeira, Spain*

Acknowledges letter of Oct. 16, enclosing protest and account of capture of ship *Columbus* by Spanish cruisers; compensation to be demanded by the United States; personal attendance not necessary; commissioners probably will be appointed. Complaints against Pintard as consul at Madeira; proceedings suspended because of (Samuel) Bayard's letter; no application made for consulate by Leonard. J.M. wrote to Bayard concerning him; no action to be taken without hearing. DNA, Dept. of State, Misc. Letters Jan. 8–Dec. 29, 1801, 28, R.G. 59.

Answer, Pintard to J.M., Nov. 7, 1800. Same. Enclosed in letter Pintard to Aaron Burr, Mar. 1, 1801. Same, 25.

Oct. 24
WASHINGTON *to Rufus King*

Requesting aid in appeal of Girard of Philadelphia in prize case concerning ship *Sally*; citizenship of Girard. Dispatch No. 9. Girard College, Philadelphia, Stephen Girard Papers, Letters Rec'd, 1800, Letter 429; DNA, General Records Dept. of State, Dipl. and Cons. Instrs., V, following 388; Same, Cons. Instrs., I, 1 R.G. 59; John B. McMaster, *The Life and Times of Stephen Girard* (Philadelphia, J. B. Lippincott & Co., 1918), I, 385 (excerpt).

Oct. 24
WASHINGTON *to Stephen Girard*

Enclosing letter for transmittal to King; advises to include oath of citizenship and court opinion. Girard College, Stephen Girard Papers, Letters Rec'd, 1800, Letter 428. (See letter Stephen Girard to Rufus King forwarding the J.M. letter and court opinion. Girard College, Stephen Girard Papers, Letter Book 8, Letter 1.)

Oct. 25
WASHINGTON *to Gov. James Jackson of Georgia*

One hundred seventy-six copies of laws of last session of Congress shipped. Ga. Dept. of Archives and History.

Oct. 25
WASHINGTON *to Israel Whelen*

Concerning shipments to Algiers and Tunis (n.f.). Referred to in letter Israel Whelen to J.M., Dec. 2, 1800. DNA, General Records Dept. of State, Misc. Letters Jan.–Dec., 1800, 174. R.G. 59.

Oct. 28 *Ben Stoddard, Secretary of Navy, to*
WASHINGTON *Commissioner of City of Washington*

Conveying opinion of J.M. that "decent person" be placed at door of President's house to prevent interruptions to furnishing house by sight-seers. Quasi-War–U.S. and France, VI, 512, from Navy Dept. Archives, General Letter Books, IV, 1800–1801.

Oct. 30
WASHINGTON *to Richard Peters*

Thanks for book accompanying letter of 24th. Agrees strength of Jacobism partly attributable to direct tax; Federalists permitted selves to be taken in; many causes of opposition. Legislature of Pennsylvania could make "our case" not absolutely desperate. Prays future administration does as little harm as present and past. Dillon, *Marshall*, I, insert at p. 96.

Oct. [*n.d.*] *to Benjamin Hammill Phillips,*
WASHINGTON *Consul of the United States, Curaçao*

(N.f.) Referred to and answered by Phillips, Oct. 25, 1800, concerning French landings. Quasi-War–U.S. and France, VI, 500–502, from State Dept. Archives, French Spoliation. C. A. Curaçao, 1797–1801.

Nov. 4
WASHINGTON *Pardon*

Philip Desch and Abraham Schantz, Pa., insurrection; sentenced U.S. District Court eight months, $150; bad health, die if not released; signed by J.M., Secretary of State, No. 31. DNA, General Records Dept. of State, Pardon Records, I, 37. R.G. 59.

Nov. 4
WASHINGTON *to Rufus King*

Advises of claim of Col. Beriah Norton against British government for supplies furnished its army during war with the United States, under contract, part paid. Demerit of furnishing supplies diminished by source, acting as agent of inhabitants of Martha's Vineyard, neutral during war to rescue selves from British Army, from which American Army did not protect them. President pleased if paid; and in unofficial countenance, no application in public character, nation not supporting, no aid pecuniary or otherwise. Marked private. CSmH, HM 22879.

Nov. 4
WASHINGTON *Treaty with Prussia*

Proclamation of Treaty of Amity and Commerce with Prussia, signed July 11, 1799; countersigned by J.M. as Secretary of State. MHi, Adams Papers, XCVI, 226a; DNA, General Records of the U.S. Government, Treaties. R.G. 11.

[Nov.], *n.p.* *President Adams to Senate*

Draft of note submitting a treaty to Senate; will ratify understanding not to interfere with existing or prior treaty. Redrafted by J.M. stating law of nations subsequent treaty contradictory to prior considered to reserve rights granted another nation; safe to modify, if ratified without change proper to explain. MHi, Adams Papers, John Adams Letters Rec'd, XLIX, 166 e.

Nov. 5
[WASHINGTON] *to John Jay, Governor of New York*

Advising of need for request for requisition for accused forger from Canada (n.f.). Answered Jay to J.M., Nov. 15, 1800, herein.

Nov. 8
WASHINGTON *to Israel Whelen*

Concerning shipments to Algiers and Tunis (n.f.). Referred to in letter Israel Whelen to J.M. Nov. 13, 1800. DNA, General Records Dept. of State, Misc. Letters Jan.–Dec., 1800, 283. R.G. 59.

Nov. 8 *President John Adams to*
WASHINGTON *Governor of Ligurian Republic*

Advising that Frederick H. Wollaston appointed consul for U.S. port of Genoa. Countersigned J.M., Secretary of State. DNA, General Records Dept. of State, Credences, III, 112. R.G. 59.

Nov. 11
WASHINGTON *Pardon*

Pardon and remission of forfeiture, President Adams, by J.M., Secretary of State, on petition of Robert and George McCandless, Baltimore, against whom and their schooner *Milford* information in U.S. District Court, Maryland, for loading lead and gunpowder with intent to export; plea ignorance of renewal of embargo act of Congress. Pardon No. 32, DNA, General Records Dept. of State, Pardon Records, 1, 38; Petitions for Pardons and Related Briefs. R.G. 59.

Nov. 12
DEPT. OF STATE, WASHINGTON *to Edmund Randolph*

Acknowledging letter of Oct. 1, requesting (1) accounts of Thomas Pickering and any letters concerning £1,600 St. bills; (2) consular appointment of Heissel submitted to Col. Humphries; (3) bill on Longueman (?) to Gouverneur Morris; (4) copy of accounts of bankers of Holland 1794, 1795, 1796. Answer, (1) accounts removed by Pickering; (2) nothing further except letter of May 29, 1798; (3) no account, two letters being copied and sent; (4) sending banker's accounts.

In testimony *United States v. Edmund Randolph*, U.S. Circuit Court, Va. District, Ended Cases, 1804, Box Misc. Corresp. 1796–1801. V, U.S. Circuit Court Case Papers, 1804.

Nov. 13 *to Frederick H. Wollaston,*
WASHINGTON *Consul of the United States, Genoa*

Acknowledging receipt of letter of June 27; answers by predecessors apparently intercepted; encloses introductory letter to government of Genoa to act as consul. DNA, General Records Dept. of State, Cons. Instrs., I, 2. R.G. 59.

Nov. 15
PHILADELPHIA *from Stephen Girard*

Recommends Martin Bickhaus as consul to Isle of France. Girard College, Stephen Girard Papers, Letter Book 8, Letter 10.

Nov. 15
ALBANY *from John Jay, Governor of New York*

Acknowledges letter of Nov. 5, enclosing documents; Thomas Jameson alias, etc., charged with forgery in New York, fled to Canada. Returning documents with request for requisition to recover from government of Canada. NNC.

Nov. 20
WASHINGTON *to Charles Cotesworth Pinckney*

Wrote to Pinckney several days past, Maryland would have six Federalist votes; mistaken (letter n.f.); Maryland gone Anti-Federalist six to four; believed New England the same; Rhode Island doubtful; Pennsylvania Senate holding; effect of votes of South Carolina for Jefferson; North Carolina decisive. DLC, Pinckney Family Papers, Box 10; WMQ (ser. 3), Vol. XII (Oct., 1955), 643.

Nov. 20
CAMBRIDGE *from Elbridge Gerry*

Acknowledges letter of 3rd, settlement of account for expense of mission to France. Draft on General Lincoln. DLC, E. Gerry Papers, Gerry Letter Book, Ac. 1021, Loc. Regular.

Nov. 20 *to Wilhelm Anton Lendemen,*
WASHINGTON *Governor General, Danish West India Islands*

Acknowledges letter of Aug. 6. Instructions to armed cruisers of the United States require respect to flag of neutrals; Lieut. Maley of the *Experiment* dismissed. DNA, General Records Dept. of State, Cons. Instrs., I, 2. R.G. 59.

Nov. 21
WASHINGTON *to Thomas Bulkely*

Acknowledges letter of Sept. 27; a "continuation" of laws to be forwarded. No legal provision to form permanent hospital establishment abroad for American seamen; expense accumulating, should retrench. Could contribute to Royal Hospital of St. Joseph in proportion to benefits; asks details. Instructs to advise Rufus King of American vessels carried into Lisbon and illegally adjudicated at Gibralter; also Gavino. Disallows further issuance of commissions for vessels to arm abroad. DNA, General Records Dept. of State, Cons. Instrs., I, 3–4. R.G. 59.

Nov. 21
WASHINGTON *to Carlos de Yrugo*

Replying to complaint against Capt. Mallowny of the U.S. sloop of war *Ganges,* made by the captain general of Cuba and advising that matter be examined (n.f.). Referred to in letter de Yrugo to James Madison. DNA, Dept. of State, Notes from the Spanish Legation, II, note of June 4, 1801. R.G. 59.

Nov. 22
WASHINGTON *to Charles Cotesworth Pinckney*

Maryland vote divided; Federalist electors will vote for both Federalists; congratulates on sentiment for Pinckney in South Carolina; Pennsylvania Senate maintained its ground; Rhode Island vote decisive. DLC, Marshall Papers—Pinckney.

[Ante Nov. 22], Monday Morning
WASHINGTON *to President John Adams*

Note submitting draft of speech to Congress; digested by heads of departments. Not signed but designated as from Secretary of State and in J.M.'s handwriting. MHi, Adams Papers, John Adams Letters Rec'd, XLIX, 164.

[Ante Nov. 22]
WASHINGTON *to [President Adams]*

Draft for Presidential address to Senate and House of Representatives, in handwriting of J.M. MHi, Adams Papers, John Adams Letters Rec'd, XLIX, 165 a–c; Adams, *J. Adams Works,* IX, 143–46; Richardson, *Messages,* I, 305–307. Also related draft, marked "Mr. Marshall," and in J.M.'s handwriting, probably J.M.'s original draft. MHi, Adams Papers, John Adams Letters Rec'd, XLIX, 166 a–c.

J.M. was requested to prepare draft, letter President John Adams to J.M., Sept. 27 and Sept. 30, 1800. DNA, General Records Dept. of State, Misc. Letters Jan.–Dec., 1800, 152, 158. R.G. 59; Adams, *J. Adams Works,* IX, 85.

Nov. 23
ALEXANDRIA *from Charles Lee*

Enclosing letter from Steele of Mississippi Territory, whom J.M. knows well, recommending appointment of James Campbell as Attorney of the United States in that territory. Notation in J.M. handwriting. MHi, Adams Papers, John Adams Letters Rec'd, XLIX, 163.

Nov. 23 [*circa*]
RICHMOND *to Edmund Randolph*

Answers to queries of Randolph of Nov. 23 as to usages in Department of State to be offered as defense of suit against him by the United States. Secretary of State not to get quietus of moneys remitted to Europe until receipt there acknowledged, merely statement to Treasury Department and voucher. Required to settle annually; believes examination annually; was in office less than year. [Note appended.] Returning answers, prevented earlier by company. Autograph. In testimony *United States v. Edmund Randolph,* U.S. Circuit Court, Va. District, Ended Cases 1804, Box Misc. Corresp. 1796–1801. V, U.S. Circuit Court Case Papers, 1804.

Nov. 25
WASHINGTON *to Israel Whelen*

Concerning charter of vessel for Tunis (n.f.). Referred to in letter Israel Whelen to J.M., Dec. 2, 1800. DNA, General Records Dept. of State, Misc. Letters Jan.–Dec., 1800, 174. R.G. 59.

Nov. 25
WASHINGTON *to Ebenezer Stevens*

Concerning funds for cargo to Tunis (n.f.). Referred to in letter Israel Whelen to J.M., Dec. 8, 1800. DNA, General Records Dept. of State, Misc. Letters Jan.–Dec., 1800, 176. R.G. 59.

Nov. 25 *from Ben Stoddart, Secretary of Navy*

Returning papers from Sodastrom concerning schooners *Mercator,* captured by Wm. Maley, and *Charming Betsey,* recaptured from French. Quasi-War–U.S. and France, VI, 548.

Nov. 25
WASHINGTON *to Unknown*

Reproaches self; recommended Maj. Richardson as officer; impression addressee to be appointed command Second Brigade Virginia Militia. VW.

Nov. 26 *to Edward Stevens,*
WASHINGTON *Consul of the United States, San Domingo*

Has firm information that treaty concluded with France; instructs to advise Gen. Toussaint for consent to open all ports of San Domingo; encloses letter for delivery to Gen. Toussaint. DNA, General Records Dept. of State, Cons. Instrs., I, 4–5. R.G. 59.

Nov. 26 *to Citizen Toussaint Louverture,*
WASHINGTON *General in Chief of the Army of San Domingo*

Acknowledges letter of 4 Messidor and Meade communications concerning articles desires to purchase. Cannot be done through government;

private purchases permissible. DNA, General Records Dept. of State, Cons. Instrs., I, 5. R.G. 59.

Nov. 26
WASHINGTON *to Richard Soderstrom*

Acknowledges letter of 24th and 25th with letter from governor general of Danish West India Islands. Respects Danish; if cruises violation of neutral flag, a breach of instructions, Danish use their flag in manner not countenanced. Lieut. Maley dismissed. Recommends in case of *Mercator* an appeal; not determined whether United States will pay if ship was illegally confiscated. Annals, 11 Cong., H. of R., App., 2158–59; ASP (For. Rel.), III, 344; Oster, *Marshall,* 82–83.

Nov. 27 *to Unknown*

Acknowledges pamphlet written by addressee; common law as law of United States; does not disagree. Never advocated Constitution adopt it; attributed to Richmond newspaper; committee report, Mason. Sensible men both parties could agree on principle; applications differ. Discusses Isaac Williams case, privateering against British; clearly in federal courts; treaty and agreement involved; not common law crime; addressee and Ellsworth could agree. "Our" opinion English statute and common law at settlement adopted as applies to situation, not affected by Constitution. Gallatin argument on sedition law; Federalists contend court jurisdiction from Constitution and not common law. DLC, Marshall Papers, Ac. 2354; Francis Wharton, *State Trials of the United States During the Administration of Washington and Adams* (Philadelphia, Carey and Hart, 1849), 652–58; quoted in Crosskey, *Politics and Constitution,* II, 1356–57.

Nov. 28
WASHINGTON *to Governor of Lower Canada*

Request for extradition from Montreal to New York of Thomas Jameson, alias Charles Spender, alias Charles Holland, charged with forgery, pursuant to Article 27, British Treaty of Amity, etc. DNA, General Records Dept. of State, Cons. Instrs., I, 6. R.G. 59.

Nov. 28
WASHINGTON *to John Jay, Albany, N.Y.*

Acknowledges letter of 15th. Requisition for Thomas Jameson. Williams College Library.

Nov. 28 *to Robert Shore Milnes,*
WASHINGTON *Lieutenant Governor of Lower Canada*

Communicated by Liston, British minister; Thomas Jameson, alias Charles Spendor, alias Charles Holland, fugitive from justice for forgery in New York detained in prison in Montreal; request by President pursuant to treaty order to deliver to agent of Governor of New York. Manning, *United States, Canadian Relations,* I, 152–53.

Nov. 28 *to Thomas Fitzsimmons*

Concerning New York land titles; Robert Morris. Listed in Lazare, *Book-Prices* (1964), 843; (1931), 757. Present owner unknown.

Nov. 29 *Passport*

To Francis Dadier Petit de Villers, signed by J.M. PP.

Nov. *to Clerk of U.S. Supreme Court*

Note to clerk concerning case of *Blane v. Donald and Burton,* enclosing letter of Charles Young to J.M., Nov. 25, 1800, stating case dismissed last Aug. term for nonappearance; asks to certify what required and mail to Patton at Alexandria. Marked 1803.

Letter Charles Young to J.M. dated Nov. 25, 1800, Richmond. Since writing J.M. last evening through Patton saw Randolph; greatest danger to writ of error from mistake of clerk and nonappearance of counsel last August term; Tilligham's letter to Donald & Burton. Desires papers relative to being engaged as counsel in first place; engaging Lewis; reason for assuring Patton case would not come up last term. Asks to do what can to relieve; motion next Tuesday. Documents desired: certificate of clerk of pending writ, if dismissed the reason, lengthy for transcribing; from J.M. that employed, engaged Lewis, reason not come to issue last August. DNA, U.S. Supreme Court, Case Papers. Case No. 80. R.G. 267.

(See also herein 1808, U.S. Supreme Court, *Blane v. Ship Charles Carter and Donald and Burton,* 4 Cranch 328.)

Dec. 2 *to Samuel Sitgreaves,*
WASHINGTON *Agent of the United States, London*

Acknowledges letters to Sept. 29, including Sept. 23 with copy of Apr. 22. Expects by time of receipt, negotiations with Britain concluded; informal explanations of Article 6 of British treaty with new board satisfactory; return to the United States when expedient. DNA, General Records Dept. of State, Cons. Instrs., I, 6–8. R.G. 59; ASP (For. Rel.), II, 388–89; Oster, *Marshall*, 77–78.

Dec. 4
WASHINGTON *to Rufus King*

Advising Presidential preference for explanatory clause as to Article 6 of British treaty; informal agreement and new board satisfactory. Dispatch No. 9. PP, Rare Book Dept., Jay Treaty Papers, Wm. M. Elkins Coll.; DNA, General Records Dept. of State, Dipl. and Cons. Instrs., V, following 388. R.G. 59; Same, Cons. Instrs., 8–10. R.G. 59; ASP (For. Rel.), II, 389; Oster, *Marshall*, 79–80.

Dec. 5 *to W. & J. Willink, N. & J. Van Staphorst,*
WASHINGTON *and Hubbard, Bankers, Amsterdam*

Enclosing first of two sets of bills of exchange for 22,000 guilders to credit of department; good bills scarce, further remittance. DNA, General Records Dept. of State, Cons. Instrs., I, 10. R.G. 59.

Dec. 6
WASHINGTON *to Charles Cotesworth Pinckney*

Election results reviewed; South Carolina vote for Jefferson would make him President. J.M. alarmed for Federalist cause. DLC, Marshall Papers—Pinckney.

Dec. 8 *Commissioner, Georgia-*
WASHINGTON *Mississippi Boundary*

Message of President Adams nominating J.M. commissioner under Georgia boundary act. DNA, Legislative Dept., Office of Senate Financial Clerk. R.G. 46; Senate, Exec. Journal, I, 356. R.G. 46. (See herein Aug. 23 and Dec. 12, 1800.)

Dec. 9 *to Speaker of House of*
WASHINGTON *Representatives [Theodore Sedgwick]*

Transmitting report containing abstracts of returns to Secretary of State by collectors of ports, and agents in foreign countries pursuant to "Act for relief of American seamen." DNA, Legislative Div., Reports Dept. of State, 6 Cong., 2 sess. to 10 Cong., 1 sess.; also Same, Reports Dept. of State, III, 123. R.G. 59.; ASP (For. Rel.), II, 292–94.

Dec. 9
WASHINGTON *to President of the Senate [Thomas Jefferson]*

Same as above. State Dept. document. ASP (Commerce), I, 449.

Dec. 10
WASHINGTON *to Secretary of Treasury*

Returning papers with letter of Sept. 31, Arnold Henry Dohrman claim to township of land under act of Oct. 1, 1787; no law authorizing patent. Accompanying petition of Charles Tompkins on behalf of Dohrman to House of Representatives, 6 Cong. DNA, Records of the U.S. House of Representatives, File H. R., 6A–F1. R.G. 233. Replying to letter from Secretary of Treasury authorizing grant of township of land. DNA. General Records Dept. of State, Misc. Letters June–Dec., 1800, 136. (See herein, Jan. 16, 1801.)

Dec. 11 *to George C. Morton,*
WASHINGTON *Consul of the United States, Havana*

Instructions to obtain permit and freedom from arrest of John Hollins, merchant of Baltimore; property in Havana attached; wishes to enter to adjust claim concerning commission transactions. DNA, General Records Dept. of State, Cons. Instrs., I, 10–11. R.G. 59.

Dec. 12
WASHINGTON, DEPT. OF STATE *to [John Adams]*

Additional list of impressed seamen to be disposed of, same list in letter of Oct. 30 last (n.f.); strike out names duplicated. NbO; CSmH, HM 4685.

Dec. 12
WALNUT TREE FARM *from Tobias Lear*

Enclosing list of George Washington papers sent in trunk. Discusses own financial straits, bankruptcy. VW.

Dec. 12 *Commissioner,*
WASHINGTON *Georgia-Mississippi Territory*

Permanent commission as commissioner under act to establish limits of Georgia, and government Mississippi Territory. Signed, the President, by J.M., Secretary of State. DNA, General Records Dept. of State, Misc. Permanent Commissions, 1789–1802, Vol. B, 385. R.G. 59. (See herein Aug. 23 and Dec. 8, 1800.)

Dec. 12
WASHINGTON *Commissions—Judges, U.S. Attorney*

Letters patent, commissions permanent appointments to David Hopkins, marshal, Maryland District; Henry Vanderburgh, second judge, Indiana Territory; John Griffin, third judge, Same; William Clark, Chief Justice, Same; Joseph Hamilton Davies, (married to J.M.'s sister Nancy) Attorney of the United States, Kentucky District. Signed, President, by J.M., Secretary of State. DNA, General Records Dept. of State, Misc. Permanent Commissions, 1789–1802, Vol. B, 379–85. R.G. 59.

Dec. 12
WASHINGTON *Commissions—Consuls*

Commission to Henry Hammond, New York, consul for Port of Cap-Français, San Domingo. Signed, the President, by J.M., Secretary of State. DNA, General Records Dept. of State, Commissions of Consuls and Consular Agents to Foreign Countries, 1790–1829, 189. R.G. 59. Same to Bartholomew Dandridge, Virginia, consul southern part of San Domingo, excluding Petit-Goâve. Same, 190.

Dec. 13
WASHINGTON *Commission—Mississippi Territory*

Commission to John Ellis and others, Legislative Council, Territory of Mississippi, five years. Signed President, by J.M., Secretary of State. DNA, General Records Dept. of State, Misc. Permanent Commissions, 1799–1802, Vol. B, 391. R.G. 59.

Dec. 13
WASHINGTON *from W. R. Davies*

Enclosing letter from Talleyrand to Letombe with convention and instructions. DNA, Dept. of State, Dipl. Dispatches, France, VII. R.G. 59.

Dec. 17
WASHINGTON *to Collector of Customs, Providence, R.I.*

Asks for proof of citizenship of sailors impressed at Leghorn on board armed ship *Providence,* and for their liberation. Rhode Island Historical Society; Quasi-War–U.S. and France, VII, 37.

Dec. 17
WASHINGTON *to David Lenox*

Encloses documents of American citizenship of six men impressed on British ships of war; instructs attention to cases. DNA, General Records Dept. of State, Cons. Instrs., I, 11. R.G. 59; MH; Quasi-War–U.S. and France, VII, 37.

Dec. 17 *to William Savage, Agent for*
WASHINGTON *United States Seamen, Kingston, Jamaica*

Encloses documents of American citizenship of six men impressed in British ships of war at Jamaica station; immediate release and safe return to be requested of Adm. Seymour. DNA, General Records Dept. of State, Cons. Instrs., I, 12. R.G. 59.

Dec. 17
WASHINGTON *to John Gavino*

Instructions to demand release from impressment of Hercules Whitney, enclosing documents; if ship not at Gibraltar, advise other consuls or correspondents; Lenox, agent in London, advised. DNA, General Records Dept. of State, Cons. Instrs., I, 12. R.G. 59.

Dec. 18
WASHINGTON *to Charles Cotesworth Pinckney*

Burr and Jefferson votes equal; House of Representatives must choose; not intermeddling; North Carolina will decide and Burr withdraw if against him. Chagrined at Federalists' defeat. Treaty with France before Senate; unconditional ratification doubted. Ellsworth resigned from Supreme Court; Jay nominated. Returning to Richmond to practice law; wishes never again to fill political station. DLC, Pinckney Family Papers, Box 10, J. D. Shelf; WMQ (ser. 3) Vol. XII (Oct., 1955), 643–44.

Dec. 18
PHILADELPHIA *from Stephen Girard*

Recommends Martin Bickman as consul of the United States at Isle of France. Girard College, Stephen Girard Papers, Letter Book 8, Letter 37.

Dec. 19 *to Turell Tufts,*
WASHINGTON *Consul for the United States, Parimaribo*

Cautioning him to use respectful manner in addressing officers of government at Surinam; instructing to report any Americans engaged in slave trade. DNA, General Records Dept. of State, Cons. Instrs., I, 13. R.G. 59.

Dec. 19
WASHINGTON *Commission—John Jay*

Letters patent appointing John Jay, New York, Chief Justice of the U.S. Supreme Court. Signed President Adams, by J.M., Secretary of State.

DNA, General Records Dept. of State, Misc. Permanent Commissions, 1789–1802, Vol. B, 380. R.G. 59.

Dec. 22
WASHINGTON *Commissions—Marshals*

Commissions to Samuel Bradford as marshal, Massachusetts District, and Aquila Giles, same of New York District, four years. Signed, President, by J.M., Secretary of State. DNA, General Records Dept. of State, Misc. Permanent Commissions, 1799–1802, Vol. B, 387, 388. R.G. 59.

Dec. 22
WASHINGTON *to Elias Backman, Consul for the United States, Sweden*

Advising that President cannot make representation to Congress on claim for expenses denied for journey to Stockholm. DNA, General Records Dept. of State, Cons. Instrs., I, 13–14. R.G. 59.

Dec. 22
MANCHESTER, VT. *from Robert Craig*

Offer to exchange J.M.'s Buckingham land and Negroes for Richmond and Manchester land. VHi, Letter Book C, Blue Box.

Dec. 23
WASHINGTON *Commission—Northwest Territory*

Commission to Solomon Sibley, Legislative Council Territory Northwest of Ohio, residue of Henry Vanderburgh five-year term from Mar. 4, 1799. Signed, President by J.M., Secretary of State. DNA, General Records Dept. of State, Misc. Permanent Commissions, 1799–1802, Vol. B, 390. R.G. 59; MiD.

Dec. 24
WASHINGTON *to President John Adams*

Submitting application of D'Ambrugeas for passage to France, without opinion. MHi, Adams Papers, John Adams Letters Rec'd, XLIX, 168.

Dec. 25
WASHINGTON *to Ebenezer Stevens*

Advising of remittance to Whelen of $5,000 on account of cargo Stevens procuring for Tunis, enclosing list (n.f.). Referred to in letter Stevens to J.M., Dec. 8, 1800. DNA, Dept. of State, Misc. Letters Jan.–Dec., 1800, 177. R.G. 59.

Dec. 25
WASHINGTON, DEPT. OF STATE *to Rufus King*
Listed in Lazare, *Book-Prices* (1926), 819. Present owner unknown.

Dec. 26
PHILADELPHIA *from Stephen Girard*
Asks J.M. to write to Rufus King that letters sent to Girard by J.M. are being forwarded, concerning brig *Sally* appeal; enclosing letter to J.M. from Richard Peters, judge of District Court of Pennsylvania. Girard College, Letters of Stephen Girard, Letter Book 8, Letter 40.

Dec. 28
WASHINGTON *to Edward Carrington*
Desires to sell Buckingham land to raise money for Fairfax Purchase, divisible into two parts; Epperson's plantation south of Bear Branch and Snoddy's Spring Branch contains 1,600 acres; Craig proposition enclosed and referred to Carrington; Hopkins, on whom J.M. generally relies in state of distress; Copeland holds three-year note £3,800 of J.M. and brother; consider cash if purchases. Understands vote for Jefferson and Burr equal, rumor Burr two-vote majority from New York; if equal, doubtful who chosen; will take no part, no interest; choice of evils but probably in favor of Burr; will not weaken Constitution, and no undue foreign attachments. Probably compelled to be in Washington until Mar. 3. CTY, Pequot Libr.

Dec. 28
WASHINGTON *from Thomas Jefferson*
Advising list of votes for President and Vice-President in his hands; no messenger from Department of State needed. DLC, Thomas Jefferson Papers, Vol. 108, 137.

Dec. 28
WASHINGTON *to John Quincy Adams*
Asking for inquiry concerning Littlepage at request from his family. MHi, Adams Papers, John Adams Letters Rec'd, XCVII, 79. Referred to in DNA, Dept. of State, Despatches of John Quincy Adams from Berlin, No. 9, Apr. 18, 1801.

Dec. 29
PHILADELPHIA *from Stephen Girard*
Concerning recommendation for consular appointment; requests let-

ter J.M. to U.S. minister in London concerning appeal of prize case. Girard College, Stephen Girard Papers. Letter Book 8, Letter 42.

Dec. 29
WASHINGTON *to Henry Vanderburgh*

Appointment as Judge of Indiana Territory. PP.

Dec. 31
WASHINGTON *to President John Adams*

Enclosing two copies of the laws of the Mississippi Territory. MHi, Adams Papers, John Adams Letters Rec'd, XLIX, 169.

Dec.
WASHINGTON *to President John Adams*

Enclosing answer of Secretary of Senate as to names of newly elected Senators; no form of summons in files; suggests among Presidential papers. MHi, Adams Papers, John Adams Letters Rec'd, XLIX, 170.

n.d., WASHINGTON *to Jonathan Dayton*

Acknowledges letter of 5th Wagner directed to examine patents; appears Brooklyn's wheel of machine propelled by tide resembles patent of Silas Betts. OMC.

n.d. *from Timothy Pickering*

Memoranda: Aug. 2, to J.M. acknowledging his of 23rd; Aug. 2, to J.M. enclosing letter to Pinckney; Aug. 7, to J.M. enclosing letter of Capt. Richard O'Brien. MHi, Pickering Papers.

HOUSE OF REPRESENTATIVES

REFERENCES HEREIN to Annals of Congress are to *The Debates and Proceedings in the Congress of the United States* . . . . (6 Cong., Dec. 2, 1799—Mar. 3, 1801) Washington, Gales and Seaton, 1834–1856 (1851). The original documentation on which this is based is the original Journal of the House of Representatives. DNA, Legislative Branch. R.G. 46.

Jan. 3 *Slave Trade*

Voted in favor of committee report rejecting petition for Congressional laws suppressing slave trade. Annals, 6 Cong., 1 sess., 245.

Jan. 6 *Bankruptcy Bill*

On committee presenting bankruptcy bill. Same, 247.

Jan. 7 *Army Bill*

Remarks opposing resolution of Nicholas for reduction of army and to repeal acts of 1798 and 1799 augmenting the army and authorizing the appointment of certain officers. Same, 251–55.

Jan. 10 Voted for resolution of Committee of Whole disagreeing with repeal resolution. Same, 369.

Jan. 16 *Treaty with Algiers*

J.M. member committee on President's message relative to affairs with Algiers; reported balance of funds due under treaty. ASP (For. Rel.) I, 558.

Jan. 22 *Army Bill*

Remarks opposing resolution for reduction of army and repeal of army bill. Annals, Same, 395–96.

Jan. 23 *Alien and Sedition Acts*

Voted for resolution to repeal Section 1. Same, 419.

Voted against amendment to allow prosecution at common law with truth a defense. Passed. Same, 423.

Voted against resolution as amended. Same, 425.

Jan. 23 *Army Bill*

Voted against bill to suspend army enlistments. Same, 403.

Voted against amendment to eliminate supernumerary and general staff officers. Same, 404.

Jan. 29 *John Randolph, Contempt*

Supported resolution as amended in McKnight-Reynolds matter; attack on Randolph in theater not a breach of privilege of member of House. Passed. Same, 505–506.

For sustaining Speaker in ruling out of order a resolution reprimanding McKnight and Reynolds. Same, 506–507.

Jan. 30 *Bankruptcy Bill*

Voted against postponement of action on bankruptcy bill. Same, 509.

Feb. 11 Opposed amendment to exempt prior debts and transactions. Same, 520.

Feb. 12 *Army Bill Exemption*

Remarks opposing amendment to remove exemption of noncommissioned officers, musicians, and privates from imprisonment for debts over $20.00 prior to enlistment. Rejected. Same, 521–22.

Feb. 13 *Military at Elections*

Chairman of special committee for bill to restrict military personnel from voting places. Same, 522–23.

Feb. 17 *Trade with France*

Voted against new bill to continue suspension of intercourse with France. Same, 527. Bill lost.

Feb. 18 Opposed Harper substitute; favored amendment limiting exceptions to European residents. Same, 530.

Feb. 20 For suspension as passed. Same, 531.

Feb. 20 *Military at Elections*

Reported bill. Same, 527.

Feb. 21 *Bankruptcy Bill*

Voted for recommitment. Motion negatived. Same, 534.

Feb. 26 *Robbins-Nash Resolution*

Voted against discharge of Committee of Whole on resolution to censure President. Same, 557.

Feb. 27 *Thomas Nash Resolution*

Remarks opposing resolution for obtaining of record in Thomas Nash, alias Jonathan Robbins, case as an improper postponement. Same, 577; Abridgement, Debates of Congress, II, 453. Voted against. Annals, Same, 564–65, 577, 578.

Mar. 5 Opposed resolution calling on President for information. Passed. Annals, Same, 595.

Mar. 7 Speech opposing resolution censuring President for his action in the case of Thomas Nash, alias Jonathan Robbins. Same, 596–618; U.S. Supreme Court Reports, 5 Wheaton, Appendix No. 1; Oster, *Marshall*, 225–53; Moore, *American Eloquence*, II, 20–32; Abridgement, Debates of Congress, II, 457–69; *Speech of the Hon. John Marshall delivered in the House of Representatives of the United States, on the resolution of the Hon. Edward Livingston, relative to Thomas Nash, alias Jonathan Rob-*

bins. (Philadelphia, The True American, 1800); Beveridge, *Marshall*, II, 458–75.

Mar. 8 Voted for Committee of Whole disagreement to censure resolution. Annals, Same, 619.

Mar. 10 On resolution approving President's action. Passed. No vote recorded for J.M. Same, 621.

Mar. 12 *Marine Corps Bill*

Opposing in debate provision of Marine Corps Bill giving civil courts rather than courts martial jurisdiction over certain offenses; also against provision for cashiering officer failing to arrest offending member of service on shore. Same, 623–24; also DNA, Reports of Select Committees, II, 623–24. For description of debate with John Randolph of Roanoke, see Beveridge, *Marshall*, II, 447–48, quoting "Copy of a letter from a gentleman in Philadelphia, to his friend in Richmond, dated 13th March, 1800," printed in *Virginia Gazette and Petersburg Intelligencer*, Apr. 1, 1800.

Mar. 13 *Tazewell Claim*

Autograph by J.M., petition of William Tazewell, late secretary of E. Gerry, reimbursement for remaining in Paris after Gerry's departure (XYZ Affair), letters of Talleyrand, to Holland and London to advise Murray and King, captured, to Spain and Portugal. Secretary of State refused for time detained. Referred to J.M., Gordon, Pinckney. Report made to Committee of Whole House, Apr. 9, 1800 (see herein). Resolution reported and agreed; bill ordered, Apr. 16, 1800. DNA, Legislative Branch, Petitions House of Representatives; Same, Reports of Select Committees, II, 483–92. R.G. 46; Annals, Same, 625.

Mar. 13 *Military at Elections*

Drew bill, passed. Same, 626. Defeated in Senate, Apr. 14. Annals, 6 Cong. 1 sess., Senate, 151.

Mar. 19 *Presidential Borrowing*

Failed to vote on bill for President to borrow. Annals, 6 Cong. 1 sess., H. of R., 633–34.

Mar. 21 *Western Reserve Cession*

Report by J.M., member of Committee on the Connecticut Western Reserve, recommending acceptance of cession by Connecticut; bill to Committee of Whole. Annals, Same, 638; ASP (Public Lands), I, 83–88; Oster, *Marshall* 205–21.

Mar. 26 *Capt. Truxton*

Vote favoring medal to Truxton. Passed. Annals, Same, 642.

Mar. 26 *Rhode Island College Relief*

No vote. Same, 642.

Mar. 26 *U.S. Courts Bill*

Voted against postponement. Same, 644.

Mar. 27 Spoke against motion to strike from bill provision for Circuit Courts; defended new system. Same, 646.

Mar. 30 Voted against postponement; bill recommitted to committee; J.M. a member. Same, 649.

Mar. 31 *Byrd Petition*

Petition of Otway Byrd presented by J.M.; patent for lands granted to him by Virginia improperly located by surveyor on land on Paint Creek, northwest side of Ohio, ceded by Virginia to the United States. DNA, Legislative Branch, H.R. 6 A–F 5.1. R.G. 46; Annals, Same.

Apr. 2 *British Treaty*

Proposed amendment, President to determine delivery of accused on requisition, or that crime cognizable by American courts. Annals, Same, 654.

Apr. 7 *Western Reserve Bill*

Called for motion of day on bill; spoke and voted against motion to postpone. Same, 658.

Apr. 7 *Fisheries Bill*

Voted against postponement of question. Same, 659.

Apr. 8 *Western Reserve Bill*

Remarks opposing motion to amend by striking adjustment with Pennsylvania, and amendment, accepting jurisdiction only. Same, 661.

Apr. 9 *Tazewell Claim*

Report for committee to allow claim of William Tazewell. Same, 661; ASP (Claims), 239. (See Mar. 13, 1800, herein.)

Apr. 10 *Western Reserve Cession*

Voted for bill for acceptance of cession as amended. Passed. Annals, Same, 662. For bill, see Same, Appendix, 1495–96.

Apr. 14 *U.S. Courts Bill*

Voted against postponement to December. Passed. Same, 666.

Apr. 14 *Salt Tax*

No vote on salt tax continuance. Same, 667.

Apr. 15 *Disputed Election Bill*

Spoke against Senate appointment of chairman of Grand Committee to select President and Vice-President, and committee's views being final; presented substitute. Same, 670. View followed. Same, 687–710. For report on Senate bill, see DNA, Legislative Branch, Reports of Select Committees. H. of R., II, 328. R.G. 46.

Apr. 15 *Land Patents to Virginia Officers*

Spoke in support of petition of Temple Elliot and others, officers of Virginia Line, for land patents in Kentucky and Northwest Territory, prevented from locating by Virginia cession. Argued Virginia retained only enough for Continental Line. Report to disallow not agreed to. Annals, Same, 668–69, 672.

Apr. 16 Chairman committee to authorize President to grant patents to officers, where by resolution of Virginia Legislature granted, but withheld by cession. Same, 672.

Apr. 16 *Tazewell Claim*

Report of committee agreed to; J.M. on committee to bring in bill. Same, 673.

Apr. 17 *Disputed Election Bill*

Spoke against motion to strike first section; J.M.'s amendments considered. Same, 673.

Apr. 18 Spoke against postponement to December. Same, 674.

Apr. 18 *Salt Tax*

Voted against limiting to two years. Same, 675.

Apr. 18 *Tazewell Claim*

Brought in bill. Same, 675.

Apr. 18 *Land Patents to Virginia Officers*

Brought in bill. Same, 675.

Apr. 21 *Disputed Election Bill*

Supported motion for select committee, discharge of Committee of Whole on Senate bill. Passed. Same, 678.

Apr. 21 *Bill to pay Admirals of Navy*

No vote on postponement. Same, 678.

Apr. 23 *Georgia Boundary Bill—Establishment of Mississippi Territory*

Spoke against motion to strike latter part of section and separate provision for commissioners to pass on claims to Georgia lands granted and revoked by legislature. Motion passed. Same, 681–82.

Apr. 23, 24 *Copper Manufacture*

On committee for incorporating company for manufacture of sheet copper. Same, 681–82.

Apr. 24 *Mississippi Governor's Bill*

Voted for agreement with Senate amendment giving Governor of Mississippi power to prorogue Senate. Defeated. Same, 682.

Apr. 25 *Disputed Election Bill*

Made report of committee on bill. Same, 683.

Apr. 25 *Mississippi Claims Bill*

Voted for agreement with Senate amendment providing for commissioners to settle claims. Defeated. Same, 685.

Apr. 28 *Military Academy Bill*

Voted against postponement. Passed. Same, 690.

Apr. 28 *Copper Manufacture*

Bill ordered engrossed. Same, 688.

(Note: Defeat of bill involving loan of $50,000 by the government to such a company. Apr. 21, 22. Same 678–79.)

Apr. 29 *British Treaty*

Proposed amendment to 27th section of treaty. Same, 691.

Apr. 29 *Disputed Election Bill*

Spoke on voting methods. Same, 692.

May 1 Voted against striking Section 1 of Senate bill. Same, 694. Voted against amendments. Same, 694.

May 2 Voted for Senate bill. Passed. Same, 697.

May 3 *Bill Prohibiting Slave Trade*

No vote. Same, 699–700.

May 7 *Tax on Sugar*

No vote on bill for additional tax. Same, 705.

May 9 *Disputed Elections Bill*

No vote on amendment. Same, 710.

May 9–10 *Washington Mausoleum Bill*

No vote on bill for mausoleum. Same, 711–12.

Feb. 4, 1801 The Senate amended House Bill, No. 270, 6 Cong. "An act to erect a mausoleum for George Washington"; J.M., Bushrod Washington, John Eager Howard, Tobias Lear, commissioners, any three empowered to fix on plan, contract $50,000 for project, plans and model of equestrian statue; monument instead of mausoleum.

Mar. 2, 1801 House of Representatives agreed to amendments, but striking out J.M. and others as commissioners and leaving to President to select.

Mar. 3, 1801 Senate postponed on amendments, to next Congress. DNA, Legislative Branch, Senate Journal. R.G. 46.

Nov. 26, 1800 *Resignation*

Lyttleton Waller Tazewell took seat in room of J.M., resigned. Annals, 6 Cong., 2 sess., H. of R., 792.

LEGAL PRACTICE

U.S. Circuit Court, Virginia

Philip Pubkner v. Reuben Coutts.

Action on bond, 1789, £600 Va., equal to $2,000. J.M. for plaintiff.

May 28, 1799. Plea, payment. U.S. Circuit Court, Va., Order Book III, 212.

May 30, 1800. V.j. £600 Va., Value of $2,000, payable by $833.33. Same, 388.

V, U.S. Circuit Court Case Papers, 1800, containing autograph petition signed.

James Cary, endorsee of James Watson v. Jonah Watson.

Action on promissory note, $1,216.22. J.M. for plaintiff.

Record incomplete.

V, U.S. Circuit Court Case Papers, 1800, containing autograph petition signed.

Samuel Gist and McDowell, s.p. Gist, McDowell, and Thomas v. James Hill, surviving obligor of John, Mark, Thomas, Charles, and James Hill.

Action on sealed bond, 1764, £360 Va. J.M. for plaintiff.

Case continued from 1796.

Nov. 30, 1798. Cost bond for defendant. U.S. Circuit Court, Va., Order Book III, 135.

Dec. 12, 1798. Plea filed denying defendant same James Hill. Same, 189.

May 29, 1800. Attorney for plaintiff, J.M., says not instructed in promises and cannot further prosecute. Dismissed. Same, 382.

V, U.S. Circuit Court, Va., Case Papers, 1800, containing autograph petition.

George Green v. Andrew Vanbibber.

Chancery, alleging agreement, 1791, to receive merchandise for Georgia land and £200 note; when received at Williamsburg, merchandise damaged, fraud; injunction against j. on note in 1793. J.M. for defendant.

Dec., 1800. Dismissed, defendant dead.

V, U.S. Circuit Court Case Papers, 1800, containing summons endorsed executed on Apr. 25, 1794 on J.M.

Hall v. Ingram, s.p. Geo. Kipper & Ingram & Co.

Action concerning 400 acres, Halifax County, sold to defendant outstanding mortgage, 1773, £817. J.M. for defendant.

Nov. 23, 1798. Answer purchase without notice, mortgage not recorded within time limit.

May, 1800. Dismissed.

V, U.S. Circuit Court Case Papers, 1800, containing autograph answer, unsigned.

James Halton, N.Y. v. Thomas Ker.

Debt, on j. this court, £256:15:8 N.Y. value of $920. J.M. for plaintiff.

Nov. 22, 1795. Undertaking for defendant. U.S. Circuit Court, Va., Order Book II, 22.

Dec. 5, 1799. Same. Same, III, 332.

Jan. 4, 1800. V.j. above amount plus $18 and $230 damages. Same, 414.

V, U.S. Circuit Court Case Papers, 1800, containing account for mileage to Norfolk for J.M.

William Knox & Vo. v. John Darby.

Nov. 24, 1798. Action of debt; plea payment. U.S. Circuit Court, Va., Order Book III, 106.

May 29, 1799. Undertaking special bail for defendant by J.M., John Heath, John Wickham, John Minor, Thos. R. Rootes. Same, 221.

June 5, 1799. V.j. $1,589.92 and $296.77 damages. Same, 253.

May 30, 1800. Writ of *scire facias, Knox v. J.M., et al.* Quashed on rendering defendant. Same, 393.

V, U.S. Circuit Court Case Papers.

Lessee of Lambert v. Reuben Payne, et al.

Ejectment. Ouster from 140 acres, Henry County, devised by will of 1782 by George Hamer, died 1795, to Lambert, an Englishman, by subsequent will to George Gilmer; latter interest claimed not a fee. Issue also raised, but not decided, of right of alien to inherit realty.

J.M. and Edmund Randolph for defendant.

Nov. 26, 1798. Motion of Payne to be made party defendant by J.M., his attorney. Pleas, general issue. U.S. Circuit Court, Va., Order Book III, 114.

Jan. 7, 1799. Special verdict, exceptions by defendant refusal to admit evidence devise of fee intended to prior devisee; also to introduction of unprobated will. Same, 267.

May 30, 1800. Law on special verdict for defendant. Same, 391, 397.

V, U.S. Circuit Court Case Papers, containing agreement of counsel as to non-presentation of unprobated will, if probated.

Affirmed Mar. 1, 1805, in the U.S. Supreme Court. *Same v. Same,* 3 Cranch 97. J.M. did not sit in case because counsel for one of parties below. Same, 117. DNA, U.S. Supreme Court Case Papers, containing autograph signature on citation.

William Livesay v. Andrew Trouin.

Case, goods sold, £467:11:5 Md., value of $1,257.

Filed June 15, 1799. J.M. for plaintiff.

Dec., 1799. Special bail for defendant.

June 3, 1800. V.j. $1,293.54. U.S. Circuit Court, Va., Order Book III, 414.

Nov. 22, 1800. J. on bond against Vanderwall and Mosby, $2,700.74, payable by $1,350.07. Same, 422.

V, U.S. Circuit Court Case Papers, containing autograph petition, signed.

Peter Murdock and Alexander of Andrew Cochrane, s.p. Andrew Cockrane, Robert Donald & Co., Glasgow, Great Britain v. Nathaniel Pope, Va.

Debt, on bond 1771, £191:12:2 Va. Filed, Jan., 1797.

J.M. for plaintiff.

May 31, 1800. Plea of payment withdrawn, confessed j. U.S. Circuit Court, Va., Order Book III, 394.

V, U.S. Circuit Court Case Papers, containing autograph petition, signed.

Newman, Land, & Hunt, Portugal v. Joseph Mandeville, Va.

Case, on bill of exchange of defendant 1792, £210 St. value of $920.40, protested.

Filed 1797. J.M. for defendant. Bushrod Washington for plaintiff.

Answer, defendant then resident of Great Britain, declared bankrupt under its laws, 1793.

Rejoinder, no fraud.

Nov. 26–27, 1800. V.j. for defendant. U.S. Circuit Court, Va., Order Book III, 438, 439.

V, U.S. Circuit Court Case Papers, containing autograph answer.

A companion case between parties was continued Nov. 29, 1800. Same, Order Book III, 454; discontinued by plaintiff Dec. 7, 1801. Same, IV, 81.

Robert Scott and Alexander Donald. s.p. Donald Scott & Co. v. Nathaniel Pope.

Two cases on sealed bonds, 1774, £171:15:10½ Va. and £196:18:2 Va.

Filed 1797. J. M. for plaintiff.

Nov. 23, 1799. Plea payment. U.S. Circuit Court, Va., Order Book III, 275.

May 31, 1800. Confessed j. £171:15:10½ Va., value of $572.60; £196:18:2 Va., value of $656.70. Same, 393, 394.

V, U.S. Circuit Court Case Papers, containing autograph petition.

John Wilson, assignee of John Story v. Cary and Mary Pleasants, administrators of Charles Logan.

Debt. on bond £600 Pa. value of $1,600. J.M. for plaintiff.

Case continued from 1796 to 1798.

Dec. 10, 1798. Plea, payment, assets administered. U.S. Circuit Court, Va., Order Book III, 162.

Nov. 30, 1799. Abated by death of Mary. Same, 303.

May 27, 1800. Confessed j., £600 Pa., value of $1,600. Same, 366.

V, U.S. Circuit Court Case Papers, 1799.

Court of Appeals of Virginia

Philip Woodson and Graham v. Josiah Woodson et al., 2 Call 209.

Appeal from decree High Court of Chancery enforcing lease of coal mine, affirmed. J.M. for appellants in early proceedings, Call and Wickham herein.

Father of appellee leased coal mine to Graham twenty years with privilege to surrender, rentals for benefit of daughters; devised same to daughters and reversion to son Philip, appellant. Latter sold reversion to Graham, who surrendered and continued to mine. Decree issued to pay rent with interest, if surrenders thereafter to relinquish possession for remainder of term.

Held, decree right on merits, interest on rentals discretionary with Court and proper.

Fees: May, 1791, £2:8; May, 1793, £5. Account Book, 288, 362.

William Robertson v. James Campbell and Luke Wheeler, 2 Call 354.

Appeal High Court of Chancery, May 13, 1797, dismissing bill of appellant, reversed. J.M. for Campbell and Wheeler in earlier proceedings; Call for same herein.

Appellant owed Wilson on j. based on a surety bond in action on protested bill of exchange against his brother; sold Negroes, applying proceeds to debt; received advance from appellees 22,000 pounds tobacco applied to debt, at which time gave appellee bill of sale, of two Negro shoemakers, absolute in form but claimed to be for security, profits from them to be applied to interest on loan. Wilson for further substantial payments by appellant agreed to remit damages included in amount due on judgment; assigned claim to appellees who levied execution; refused to remit damages; claimed slaves sold to them conditionally and not by mortgage; injunction and accounting sought.

Held, damages remitted by agreement; applying hire and profits of slaves to interest only usurious; must apply to principal and interest; slaves transaction a mortgage, to be returned on payment; accounting ordered.

Oct. 15, 1800. Heard. Court of Appeals, Va., Order Book IV, 4.

Oct. 24, 1800. Reversed, accounting according to findings and j. thereon. Same, 17.

Fee: Mar., 1795, £2:8. Account Book, 406.

George Stephens, heirs of John Stephens v. James Cobun, 2 Call 371.

Appeal from High Court of Chancery, Mar. 14, 1798, reversing decree of County Court which ordered conveyance of land to appellant, affirmed. J.M. for appellee in earlier proceedings; Call for same herein.

Action for land by heir of John Stephens, whose widow sold to Jonathan Cobun, thence to James Cobun while appellant an infant; that John Stephens and Jonathan Cobun had agreed to a division of the 400-acre tract. Appellee claimed as purchaser from occupants alleged prior to Stephens, and a finding to this effect by j. of Board of Commissioners.

Held, j. of board conclusive under Virginia land law.

Nov. 1, 1800. Heard. Court of Appeals, Va., Order Book IV, 26.

May 8, 1800. Affirmed. Same, 32.

Fee: Sept., 1795, "Chr," £5. Account Book, 420.

William Mayo v. William Bentley, administrator of William Ronald, 4 Call 528, 534–36.

Appeal from High Court of Chancery.

Injunction against j. of appellant against appellee, County Court Powhatan reversed in part. J.M. and Daniel Call for appellee.

Decedent died Feb. 3, 1793; administrator appointed Feb. 21, Powhatan County, no published notice; Feb. 26 suit by brother of decedent on simple contract filed Henrico County; Mar. 4, confessed by administrator who had come to Henrico. Meantime, Feb. 28 suit filed by Mayo in Powhatan County on specialty; not served on administrator when confessed j. Also Carrington sued on specialty, payable Apr. 1, 1793; writ issued tenth, confessed j. May 10, 1793. Thereafter in May office j. taken by Mayo; enjoined by High Court of Chancery for mistake of clerk in failing to enter motion to set aside and plead. Held, court divided if administrator may in all instances confess j. to simple contract creditor where no notice by suit of specialty creditor; that administrator need not advertise appointment to creditors (and in only one out of ten cases does he do so; see Judge Fleming, opinion herein p. 548); that error of clerk properly relieved in equity; that administrator may prefer one of two specialty creditors' actions by confessing j. as to one and delaying the other. The decree altered the injunction as subject to payment from future assets, and placing Mayo's claim ahead of subsequent j. creditors.

Oct. 23, 24, 28, 29, 1800. Heard. Court of Appeals, Va., Order Book III, 344, 345, 349, 350.

Nov. 3. Reversed and amended. Same, IV, 27.

Note: J.M. returned to Richmond to argue this case prior to assuming chief justiceship. (See herein Sept. 17, 1800.)

LAND TRANSACTIONS
South Branch Manor, Hardy County, Virginia
(Now West Virginia)

Mar. 5 *Deed*

J.M., by Rawleigh Colston, attorney in fact, to John Fisher, thirty-two acres on Cattail Run. Consideration £9 Va. Recorded May 9, 1800. Hardy County, Va., Deed Book A, 322.

Mar. 8 *Deed*

J.M., by Rawleigh Colston, attorney in fact, to Benjamin Beene, forty-six acres in accordance with contract of sale by James Marshall. Consideration £11:16 Va. Recorded May 5, 1800. Hardy County, Va., Deed Book A, 241.

Mar. 8 *Deed*

J.M., by Rawleigh Colston, attorney in fact, to James Snodgrass, remainder interest, thirty-four acres in possession of Snodgrass of sixty acres, No. 45, leased Thomas Lord Fairfax to Lambert Hoover, Aug. 3, 1777. Consideration £7:10. Recorded May 5, 1800. Hardy County, Va., Deed Book A, 234.

Mar. 8 *Deed*

J.M., by Rawleigh Colston, attorney in fact, to Jacob Fisher, six acres. Consideration £4:13 Va. Recorded May 7, 1800. Hardy County, Va., Deed Book A, 291.

Mar. 8 *Deed*

J. M., by Rawleigh Colson, attorney in fact, to Leonard Shoab (Shobe), thirty-one acres, adjoining north back line of Manor. Consideration £8:19 Va. Recorded May 7, 1800. Hardy County, Va., Deed Book A, 297.

Mar. 8 *Deed*

J.M., by Rawleigh Colston, attorney in fact, to Robert Darling, fifty-nine acres, south side Timber Ridge. Consideration £15:19:9 Va. Recorded May 7, 1800. Hardy County, Va., Deed Book A, 298.

Mar. 8 *Deed*

J.M., by Rawleigh Colston, attorney in fact, to Robert Cunningham and Robert Porter, 104 acres. Consideration £28:12 Va. Recorded May 8, 1800. Hardy County, Va., Deed Book A, 308.

Mar. 10 *Deed*

J.M., by Rawleigh Colston, attorney in fact, to Moses Hutton, conveyance remainder interest, three tracts totaling 140 acres, leased Thomas Lord Fairfax to John Kimble, No. 44, on Aug. 3, 1773; also part on Mar. 6, 1780; No. 45 Fairfax to Lambert Hoover, Aug. 3, 1773. Consideration £24. Recorded May 6, 1800. Hardy County, Va., Deed Book A, 231.

Mar. 10 *Deed*

J.M., by Rawleigh Colston, attorney in fact, to John Hay, fifty-nine acres. Consideration £12:5 Va. Recorded May 6, 1800. Hardy County, Va., Deed Book A, 229.

Mar. 10 *Deed*

J.M., by Rawleigh Colston, attorney in fact, to James Parsons, 105 acres. Consideration £21:10 Va. Recorded May 6, 1800. Hardy County, Va., Deed Book A, 273.

Apr. 16 *Deed*

J.M., by Rawleigh Colston, attorney in fact, to John Hogbin, eighty-three acres. Consideration £20:15 Va. Recorded May 5, 1800. Hardy County, Va., Deed Book A, 275.

Apr. 16 *Deed*

J.M., by Rawleigh Colston, attorney in fact, to Alexander McKinley, seven acres. Consideration £1:19 Va. Recorded May 9, 1800. Hardy County, Va., Deed Book A, 320.

May 4 *Deed*

J.M., by Rawleigh Colston, attorney in fact, to John Renick, 6½ acres, west side South Branch of Potomac. Consideration £1:12:6 Va. Recorded Sept. 9, 1800. Hardy County, Va., Deed Book A, 350.

May 7 *Deed*

J.M., by Rawleigh Colston, attorney in fact to Joseph Obannon, conveyance of remainder interest, 17½ acres, leased Denny Martin Fairfax to Obannon, May 21, 1791. Consideration £5. Recorded Sept. 9. 1800. Hardy County, Va., Deed Book, A 345.

May 7 *Deed*

J.M., by Rawleigh Colston, attorney in fact, to Henry Kerr, conveyance of remainder interest, three tracts, 45 acres, No. 79, leased Thomas Lord Fairfax to Kerr, Aug. 3, 1773; 170 acres, No. 80, same, leased Same to Same, same date; 27 acres leased Denney Martin Fairfax to Kerr, May 21, 1791. Consideration £60. Recorded Sept. 9, 1800. Hardy County, Va., Deed Book A, 346.

July 4 *Deed*

J.M., by Rawleigh Colston, attorney in fact, to John Harness, 5¾ acres. Consideration £1:9:6 Va. Recorded Sept. 9, 1800. Hardy County, Va., Deed Book A, 348.

July 4 *Deed*

J.M., by Rawleigh Colston, attorney in fact, to George Harness, conveyance of reversionary interest, 300 acres, No. 51, leased Thomas Lord Fairfax to George Harness, Sr., Aug. 3, 1773. Consideration £63:8. Recorded Sept. 9, 1800. Hardy County, Va., Deed Book A, 351.

Sept. [entered as 1790] *Deed*

J.M., by Rawleigh Colston, attorney in fact, to Jacob Vanmeter, four tracts, 71½ acres, No. 1, leased Thomas Lord Fairfax to Henry Vanmeter, Aug. 3, 1773; 200 acres, No. 2, leased Same to Same, same date; 53 acres and 38 acres, leased, Same to Same, Mar. 6, 1780. Consideration £139:0:4. Recorded Sept. 9, 1800. Hardy County, Va., Deed Book A, 341.

Sept. [entered as 179—] *Deed*

J.M., by Rawleigh Colston, attorney in fact, to Peter Horse, conveyance of reversionary interest, fifty acres, leased Denny Martin Fairfax to

Horse, May 28, 1791. Consideration £30. Recorded Sept. 9, 1800. Hardy County, Va., Deed Book A, 353.

Nov. 19 *Deed*

J.M., by Rawleigh Colston, attorney in fact, to George Harness, Jr., and Jacob Vanmeter, Jr., ninety-two acres. Consideration £31:8:6 Va. Recorded May 5, 1801. Hardy County, Va., Deed Book A, 366.

Dec. 1 *Deed*

J.M., by Rawleigh Colston, attorney in fact, to Michael Hyer, reversionary interest, 104 acres, No. 58, leased Thomas Lord Fairfax to Leonard Hyer, Aug. 3, 1773; also 50 acres, same, leased Denny Martin Fairfax to Michael Hyer, May 21, 1791. Consideration £44. Recorded July 15, 1801. Hardy County, Va., Deed Book 5, 48.

Hampshire County, Virginia (Now West Virginia)

Jan 8. *Partition Deed*

James M. Marshall to J.M., land in Hampshire County, Va., on Potomac known as Swan Ponds; also tract called Anderson's Bottom. Consideration, relinquishment by J.M. of all his interest in certain land purchased of Denny Fairfax allotted to James, and five shillings. Recorded Sept. 7, 1802. Hardy County, Va., Deed Book A, 519.

Mar. 7 *Deed*

J.M., by Rawleigh Colston, attorney in fact, to Edward William, reversionary interest, 230 acres of 440 acres, South Branch Manor, Hampshire County, No. 5, leased Thomas Lord Fairfax to Vestry of Hampshire Parish. Consideration £10. Recorded Sept. 9, 1800. Hardy County, Va., Deed Book A, 343.

Nov. 10 *Deed*

John Foster and Jane, his wife, Alexandria, to J.M., Richmond, now Secretary of State, and James Marshall, District of Columbia, 1/6th undivided interest in 761 acres, Hampshire County, on north bank of Potomac adjoining land of William Odle, granted to Edward Smith by patent, Apr. 6, 1795; also 30 acres adjoining. Consideration. $696.66. Recorded Apr. 20, 1801. Hampshire County, Va., Deed Book 12, 308; The John Marshall House.

1801

DOCUMENTS

Jan. 1
WASHINGTON *to Alexander Hamilton*

Acknowledges letter of Dec. 26. Jefferson-Burr Presidential election contest. Objections to Jefferson's foreign and domestic policies; concurrence in Hamilton's opinion of Burr; unacquainted with Burr; taking neither side; would not continue as Secretary of State. Favors ratification of French treaty; does not approve it; ratification should include renunciation of use of American ports to fit out French privateers, most-favored-nation clause. France an encroaching nation. DLC, Papers of Alexander Hamilton, Vol. 83; Hamilton, *Works*, VI, 501–503; Oster, *Marshall*, 90–92.

Jan. 1
WASHINGTON *Commission—Secretary of Treasury*

Commission to Samuel Dexter as Secretary of Treasury; signed, President, by J.M., Secretary of State. DNA, General Records Dept. of State, Misc. Permanent Commissions, 1799–1802, Vol. B, 386. R.G. 59.

Jan. 2
WASHINGTON *Pardon*

Conrad Marks and others, U.S. District Court, Pa., misdemeanor for insurrection, now imprisoned, pardoned "for divers good causes and considerations." Signed by J.M., Secretary of State. No. 33. DNA, General Records Dept. of State, Pardon Records, I, 39. R.G. 59.

Jan. 2
WASHINGTON *to Governor of Campeathy*

Requesting that proceeds from condemnation of American vessels captured by Spanish privateer be paid to owner. DNA, General Records Dept. of State, Cons. Instrs., I, 14. R.G. 59.

Jan. 3
WASHINGTON *to Rufus King*

Request to assist in appeal of Stephen Girard from Court of Vice Admiralty in Halifax, condemnation of brig *Sally*; Curwen, his agent; Girard a citizen of the United States. Girard College, Stephen Girard Papers, Letters Rec'd. 1801, letter 8; DNA, General Records Dept. of State, Dipl. and Cons. Instrs., V, 388–89. R.G. 59.

Jan. 3 *to Robert Ritchie,*
Washington *Consul for the United States in San Domingo*

Advising appointment of Bartholomew Dandridge consul to southern part of San Domingo; addressee's function to cease in this district. DNA, General Records Dept. of State, Cons. Instrs., I, 15, R.G. 59; NjP.

Jan. 4 [erroneously dated 1800] *to Frederick Jacob Wichelhausen,*
Washington *Consul for the United States, Bremen*

Approving explanations sought in Bremen of arrest of Baltimore merchant to determine if oppressive. DNA, General Records Dept. of State, Cons. Instrs., I, 15. For reply, see F. J. Wichelhausen to J.M., Apr. 8, 1801; DNA, General Records Dept. of State, Cons. Despatches, Bremen, I. R.G. 59.

Jan. 5
Georgetown, Md. *Promissory Note*

Fifty-four days, $800, by John Stewart to J.M. Endorsed successively by J.M. and Charles Simms. Protested for nonpayment Mar. 4. DLC, Papers of Charles Simms, IV.

Jan. 5
Washington *to David Humphries (Humphreys)*

Advising that pressing of individual claims by Americans for unlawful captures and condemnations should not be allowed to obstruct general settlement with Spain by appointment of commissioners; requests support of claims of Messrs. Preble and Fisher. Dispatch No. 4. NjP, De Coppet Coll.; DNA, General Records Dept. of State, Cons. Instrs., I, 15–16. R.G. 59.

Jan. 7
Albany, N.Y. *John Jay to President John Adams*

Refusing nomination as Chief Justice of the U.S. Supreme Court because system defective, and ill health. MHi, Adams Papers, John Adams Letters Rec'd, XLV, 151.

Jan. 8
Washington *to William Cranch*

Enclosure of commission of Cranch as a commissioner of the City of Washington. MHi, Cranch MSS.

Jan. 8
WASHINGTON *to Evan Jones or William E. Hulings*

Requesting to forward to Gov. Sargent enclosed commissions to Legislative Council, Mississippi Territory. DNA, General Records Dept. of State, Cons. Instrs., I, 16–17. R.G. 59.

Jan. 9
WASHINGTON *Commission—District of Columbia*

Commission to William Cranch, Maryland, one of commissioners to survey District of territory accepted as permanent seat of government, during pleasure of President; signed President, by J.M., Secretary of State. DNA, General Records Dept. of State, Misc. Permanent Commissions, 1799–1802, Vol. B, 389. R.G. 59.

Jan. 9
WASHINGTON *Commission—Consul*

Commission to John Stuart Kern, Pennsylvania, consul for city and island Manila, Dominion of Spain; signed President, by J.M., Secretary of State. DNA, General Records Dept. of State, Commissions of Consuls and Consular Agents to Foreign Countries, 1790–1829, 191. R.G. 59.

Jan. 10
CHILLICOTHE, OHIO *from George Mathews*

Waiting for letters from New England Land Company; asks fate of Wickham's attachment and Nelson's appeal; asks J.M.'s intention to remain in office under Jefferson. DNA, General Records Dept. of State, Misc. Letters, Jan.–June, 1801, 14. R.G. 59.

Jan. 11
WASHINGTON *to William Vans Murray*

Referring to letter of J.M. to addressee of June 16, 1800, concerning unlawful capture and condemnation by French of vessel of Jeremiah Yellot at Curaçao; enclosing documentary proof for submission to Batavian Government. DNA, General Records Dept. of State, Cons. Instrs., I, 17. R.G. 59.

Jan. 12
WASHINGTON *to Job Wall*

Referring to former letter that bond as consul disapproved and draft not accepted; astonished by subsequent drafts; funds for distressed seamen exhausted; demands settlement of accounts. DNA, General Records Dept. of State, Cons. Instrs., I, 17–18. R.G. 59.

Jan. 14
WASHINGTON *Passport*

Passport to Thomas Neil, naturalized citizen, to travel abroad, signed by J.M. as Secretary of State. Listed in Kingston Galleries, Inc., Somerville, Mass., Catalogue No. 7, p. 32. Present owner unknown.

Jan. 15
WASHINGTON *from Secretary of War*

Acknowledging recommendations of J.M. for appointments in the army (n.f.). DNA, Records of the Office of the Secretary of War. R.G. 107.

Jan. 15 *to Roger Griswold, Chairman of Committee*
WASHINGTON *of Ways and Means, House of Representatives*

Justification of estimated appropriation for payments to Algiers, annuity payment, biennial present, consular present, debt to Boeris. CtY.

Jan. 16
WASHINGTON *Pardon*

John Salter and others, U.S. Circuit Court, Mass., 1799, misdemeanor against laws of the United States, six months and $200 to two months and $40. No. 34. Signed by J.M., Secretary of State. DNA General Records Dept. of State, Pardon Records, I, 40. R.G. 59.

Jan. 16
WASHINGTON *to Secretary of Treasury*

Opinion that no doubt of right of applicant to land for services under resolution of Congress, Oct. 1, 1787; but cannot make grant under executive powers; no authority. Accompanying petition of Charles Tompkins to House of Representatives, 6 Cong., on behalf of Arnold Henry Dohrman. DNA, Records of U.S. House of Representatives, File H.R., 6A–F1. R.G. 233.

(See letter J.M. to Secretary of Treasury, herein, Dec. 10, 1800. Also see bill in Congress for relief of Dohrman, Feb. 23, 1801; Annals, 6 Cong., 2 sess., H. of R., 1050.)

Jan. 18
WASHINGTON *to Rufus King*

Advises of complaints by owners of American vessels at Curaçao of seizure of two vessels by British after capture by French; claims of salvage and vessels seized; hopes no formal complaint necessary. Congress probably to pass bill reorganizing judicial system; separate Supreme Court from circuit courts. Opposition in Senate to French treaty. DNA, General Records Dept. of State, Dipl. and Cons. Instrs., V, 389–91. R.G. 59. Same, Cons. Instrs., I, 18–19. R.G. 59; Quasi-War–U.S. and France, VII, 98–99.

Jan. 18
WASHINGTON *to Timothy Pickering*

Returning personal letter. (Noted as from Rufus King, London, Apr. 22, 1800.) MHi, Pickering MSS, XXVI, 238.

Jan. 18 *James Monroe to Thomas Jefferson*

Referring to opinion of J.M. that if nine states did not concur in nominee for President of the United States, Congress may make the appointment. Hamilton, Monroe, II, 256.

Jan. 20
WASHINGTON *Nomination as Chief Justice*

Message by President John Adams transmitting nomination to Senate of J.M., Secretary of State, as Chief Justice in place of John Jay, who has declined office. DNA, Legislative Dept., Office of Senate Financial Clerk, Senate Exec. Journal, I, 371, R.G. 46.

J.M. says that he recommended Judge Paterson as successor to Chief Justice Elsworth, who had resigned; President refused, giving reason that would injure feelings of Judge Cushing; real reason suspected that Paterson opposed second mission to France. J.M. brought Jay's letter of refusal to President, who said, "I believe I must nominate you." J.M. surprised, and bowed in silence. The next day he was nominated. Marshall, *Autobiography*, 29–30.

Jan. 21 *Nomination as Chief Justice*

Newspaper report of nomination as Chief Justice of U.S. Supreme Court. *Washington Federalist* (Georgetown), Jan. 21, 1801, 3.

Jan. 22 *to John Elmslie,*
WASHINGTON *Consul for the United States, Cape Town*

Letter concerning capture received; suprised commission and instructions not received; sent directly and via London; enclosing copies and laws on captures by convoy for India. DNA, General Records Dept. of State, Cons. Instrs., I, 19–20. R.G. 59.

Jan. 22
PHILADELPHIA *Thomas B. Adams to President John Adams*

Newspaper statement that J.M. named Chief Justice of the U.S. Supreme Court contradicted. MHi, Adams Papers, XX, 198.

Jan. 23
WASHINGTON *to Unknown*

Advising number of copies of letters from George Washington to Sir John Sinclair on agricultural matters sent into the United States by Sinclair. CtHi, Hoadley Autograph Coll.

Jan. 26
WASHINGTON *to Office of Secretary of War*

Letter criticizing court-martial of Capt. Marks; recommending appointment in army. DNA, Records of the Office of the Secretary of War, Letters Rec'd., War Office. R.G. 107.

Jan. 27
WASHINGTON *Confirmation, Chief Justiceship*

Confirmation by Senate of appointment of J.M. as Chief Justice. DNA, Legislative Branch, Office of Senate Financial Clerk, Senate Exec. Journal, I, 374. R.G. 46.

J.M. states nomination was suspended (for a week) by friends of Judge Paterson and then approved unanimously. Marshall, *Autobiography*, 30.

Jan. 27
RICHMOND *Newspaper Item, Nomination*

Notice of J.M.'s nomination. *The Virginia Argus*, Jan. 27, 1801, 3. Same in *Richmond Examiner*, Feb. 6. V.

Jan. 28
WASHINGTON *to David Lenox*

Acknowledges letter of Oct. 4; proof of citizenship of various persons impressed on British ships of war enclosed. PPHi, Dreer Coll.; DNA, General Records Dept. of State, Cons. Instrs., I, 20. R.G. 59.

Jan. 28
WASHINGTON *to William Savage*

Enclosing proofs of citizenship of certain Americans impressed on British ships of war at Jamaica station; referring to earlier cases; reminder to Lord Seymour of applications to Sir Hyde Parker; requesting monthly report of seamen released. DNA, General Records Dept. of State, Cons. Instrs., I, 20–21. R.G. 59.

For reply see William Savage to J.M., Apr. 11, 1801. DNA, General Records Dept. of State, Cons. Despatches, Kingston, Jamaica, I. R.G. 59.

Jan. 28
WASHINGTON *from President John Adams*

Requesting J.M. to prepare summons to Senators for session Mar. 4, 1801. DNA, General Records Dept. of State, Misc. Letters Jan.–June, 1801, 9. R.G. 59.

Jan. 30
WASHINGTON *to Office of Secretary of War*

Concerning Indian boundary line in North Carolina; enclosure, letter to Secretary of State from Governor of North Carolina, resolution of Legislature. DNA, Records of the Office of Secretary of War, Letters Recd. War Office. R.G. 107.

Jan. 30
WASHINGTON *to Rufus King*

Advising Presidential acceptance to appointment of Sieur Blicker Olsen as Danish minister and consul general to the United States. Dispatch No. 11. DNA, General Records Dept. of State, Cons. and Dipl. Instrs., V, 391; also Same, Cons. Instrs., I, 21. R.G. 59.

Jan. 30
WASHINGTON *to John Breckenridge*

Summons to extra session of Senate. DLC, Papers of Breckenridge Family, XX.

Jan. 31
WASHINGTON *Commission—Chief Justice*

Commission to J.M. as Chief Justice during good behavior; signed by President Adams. DNA, General Records Dept. of State, Misc. Permanent Commissions, 1799–1802, Vol. B, 392. R.G. 59.

Jan. 31
WASHINGTON *from President John Adams*

Instructing to prepare letter recalling John Quincy Adams from Ministry of Prussia. DNA, General Records Dept. of State, Misc. Letters Jan.–

June, 1801, 10. R.G. 59; MHi, Adams Papers, John Adams Letter Book, July 10, 1799—Mar. 1, 1801, 319.

Jan. 31
WASHINGTON *President Adams to S. Dexter, Secretary of War*

Order directing Dexter as Secretary of State *pro hac vice* to affix seal of the United States to commission of J.M. as Chief Justice. MHi, Adams Papers, John Adams Letter Book, July 10, 1799—Mar. 1, 1801, 320; Adams, *J. Adams Works,* IX, 95–96; Beveridge, *Marshall,* II, 557–58.

Jan. 31
WASHINGTON *President John Adams to King of Prussia*

Advising of the leaving of John Quincy Adams as minister. Signed by J.M. as "Acting Secretary of State." DNA, General Records Dept. of State, Credences, I, 112. R.G. 59; MHi, Adams Papers, XCVII, 81a., also Letters Received, no number.

See letter President Adams to J.M., Jan. 31, above.

Feb. 2
WASHINGTON *Memoranda on Foreign Affairs*

Affairs with Barbary Powers, especially Tripoli, require immediate attention; J.M. wrote to O'Brien concerning commuting annuity of articles to Algiers to lump sum; $30,000 a good bargain; J.M. transferred procurement to purveyor; if remained in office would have required to be handled by Secretary of Treasury. Affairs with Spain require serious consideration of department. Urges immediate attention to claims of American merchants against British for depredations; refers to King correspondence and letter J.M. to King No. 2; difference under Article 6, fears may be concluded. Endorsed Job Wall. DNA, General Records Dept. of State, Misc. Letters Jan.–June, 1801, 12, R.G. 59; MHi, Adams Papers, Misc. Letters.

Feb. 2
WASHINGTON *to Judge Paterson*

Acknowledges letter of Jan. 26; thanks for congratulations on appointment. Regrets cannot attend Court, and cause of it; has seen only Judge Cushing. Judicial bill before Senate; same as last session; hopes will pass; separation of Judges of Supreme Court from circuit courts; later system to extend with needs of nation. NN, Paterson Papers, Bancroft Transcripts, 636, 637; NjR, Wm. Paterson Papers.

Feb. 3
WASHINGTON *to Thos. T. Garitt*

Enclosing detailed instructions and admonishing economy to Garitt, an agent for Navy Department at St. Christopher, to administer relief to captured American seamen at Guadaloupe and adjacent islands; DNA, General Records Dept. of State, Cons. Instrs., I, 22–23. R.G. 59.

Feb. 3
WASHINGTON *to John Q. Adams*

Instructing on behalf of President to return to the United States; to advise Prussian Majesty. Enclosing letter of President to King of Prussia dated Jan. 31, 1801. DNA, General Records Dept. of State, Cons. Instrs., I, 22. Same, Credences, I. R.G. 59; MHi Adams Papers, John Adams Letters Rec'd, XCVII, 80–81.

Feb. 3 *to John Breckenridge, Addressed*
WASHINGTON *as Senator-Elect for Kentucky, Lexington, Ky.*

Enclosing Presidential summons directing attendance at Senate chamber, Mar. 4, asking acknowledgment. DLC, Papers of Breckenridge Family, XX.

Feb. 3
WASHINGTON *Commission—Secretary of War*

Commission appointing Roger Griswold, Connecticut, Secretary of War; signed, President, by J.M., acting Secretary of State. DNA, General Records Dept. of State, Misc. Permanent Commissions, 1789–1802, Vol. B, 393. R.G. 59.

Feb. 3
WASHINGTON *Commission—Governor, Northwest Territory*

Commission appointing Arthur St. Clair, Pa., Governor, Northwest Territory; signed, President, by J.M. acting Secretary of State. DNA, General Records Dept. of State, Misc. Permanent Commissions, 1789–1802, Vol. B, 394. R.G. 59.

Feb. 3 *to Jonathan Trumbull, Jr.,*
WASHINGTON, DEPT. OF STATE *Governor of Connecticut*

President calling Senate Mar. 4 next; not known Connecticut appointed successor to Tracy; term expires. Enclosing summons for forwarding to new appointee. CtHi, U.S. Gov't Letters, No. 75.

Feb. 4
WASHINGTON *to Edward Thornton*

Requesting release from impressment of Presley Thornton Coke on board British ship at Halifax; enclosures (n.f.). Referred to in letter Edward Thornton to James Madison, May 12, 1801. DNA, General Records Dept. of State, Notes from British Legation, II. R.G. 59.

Feb. 4
WASHINGTON *to President John Adams*

Accepting appointment as Chief Justice of the United States, entering immediately on the duties. MHi, Adams Papers, John Adams Letters Rec'd, XXI, 216; Oster, *Marshall*, 57–58; Iles, *Little Masterpieces*, I, 97–98; Adams, *J. Adams Works*, IX, 96; Dillon, *Marshall*, I, 52–53; *Green Bag*, Vol. XIII, (Apr., 1901), 176; Beveridge, *Marshall*, II, 558.

Feb. 4
WASHINGTON *from President John Adams*

Acknowledging letter accepting appointment of Chief Justice of the U.S. Supreme Court; requesting and authorizing J.M. to continue duties as Secretary of State until "ulterior arrangements" made. DNA, General Records Dept. of State, Misc. Letters, Jan.–June, 1801, 13. R.G. 59; MHi, Adams Papers, John Adams Letter Book, July 10, 1799—Mar. 1, 1801, 321; *J. Adams Works*, IX, 96.

Feb. 4
WASHINGTON *Commission as Chief Justice*

Commission from President of the United States to J.M. dated Jan. 31, 1801, constituting J.M. Chief Justice of the United States read in open court. J.M., having taken the oath, took his seat upon the Bench. DNA, U.S. Supreme Court, Minute Book A, 114.

Feb. 7
RICHMOND *Quoit Club*

The Quoit Club, originally named the Amicable Society of Richmond, was organized Dec. 13, 1788. J.M. elected to membership Feb. 7, 1801; remained so for many years. Membership limited to twenty-five or thirty. Later became known as the Buchanan Spring Quoit Club. Edmund Berkeley, Jr., "Quoits, the Sport of Gentlemen," *Virginia Cavalcade*, Summer, 1965, 11 ff., quoting *American Turf Register and Sporting Magazine*, 1829; and Munford, *The Two Parsons*. See also *Green Bag*, Vol. VIII (Dec., 1896), 482.

Feb. 8
WASHINGTON *from Elihu Hall Ray*

Written in consequence of hint given by J.M. of suggesting to him to intimate to the President application to British government for records of Province of West Florida during their control, sent to England; their importance. CSmH, RK 242.

Feb. 10
RICHMOND *Letter of "Lucius"*

Letter I, criticizing J.M. for his alleged opinion that Congress appoint acting President in case of equal vote. V, from *Richmond Examiner.* See *Washington Federalist* (Georgetown), Feb. 10, 1801, 73.

Feb. 10
WASHINGTON *to Arthur St. Clair*

Advising of reappointment as Governor of the Northwest Territory and enclosing commission. Smith, *St. Clair,* II, 530; Oster, *Marshall,* 35. Original listed in Lazare, *Book-Prices,* (1959), 585; also in Carnegie Book Shop, Catalogue 247, 19. Present owner unknown.

Feb. 10
WASHINGTON *from President John Adams*

Instructing to file memorandum of Adams disavowing authorship of letter to Thomas Cushing, Dec., 1780; file in office of Secretary of State and publish. MHi, Adams Papers, John Adams Letter Book, July 10, 1799—Mar. 1, 1801, 326; DNA, General Records Dept. of State, Misc. Letters Jan.–June, 1801, 30. R.G. 59; V, from *Richmond Examiner.*

Feb. 11
WASHINGTON *Pardon*

Alexander Fulton, Pa., contrite and repentent for insurrection; an exile in foreign land; reformation of prisoner; pardoned of misdemeanor and treason. Signed by J.M., Secretary of State. No. 35. DNA, General Records Dept. of State, Pardon Records, I, 41. R.G. 59.

Feb. 13
RICHMOND *Letter of "Lucius"*

Letter II. Argument Congress no power to appoint Adams President in case of equal vote. V, from *Richmond Examiner.*

Feb. 17
RICHMOND *Letter of "Lucius"*

Letter III. Effect on political nature "of country if Congress power to appoint acting President in case of equal vote." V, from *Richmond Examiner.*

Feb. 18 *Treaty with France*

Countersignature as acting Secretary of State to U.S. Instrument of Ratification of Treaty with France, signed Sept. 30, 1800. DNA, General Records Dept. of State, Treaties. R.G. 11.

Feb. 18
WASHINGTON *Pardon*

Samuel Spring, U.S. Circuit Court, Mass., convicted counterfeiting bills; one hours pillory, $500, three years; punished but improverished. Pardoned of fine. No. 43. DNA, General Records Dept. of State, Pardon Records, I, 43. R.G. 59.

Feb. 19
WASHINGTON *to Robert Hays*

Enclosing commission to continue as marshal, Tennessee District. DLC, Papers of Andrew Jackson, IV, 337A.

Feb. 19
WASHINGTON *from President John Adams*

Enclosing letter of Vice-President Thomas Jefferson and resolution of Senate, requesting to arrange delivery of certificate as Vice-President to Aaron Burr. DNA, General Records Dept. of State, Misc. Letters Jan.–June, 1801, 33. R.G. 59; MHi, Adams Papers, John Adams Letter Book, July 10, 1799—Mar. 1, 1801, 327.

Feb. 19
WASHINGTON *Commission—Minister to France*

Appointment of James A. Bayard, minister plenipotentiary to Republic of France. Signed by J.M., acting Secretary of State. DNA, General Records Dept. of State, Credences, I, 113–14. R.G. 59.

Feb. 20
WASHINGTON *Commission—U.S. Attorney*

Appointment of Harrison Gray Otis as U.S. Attorney for Massachusetts District by President John Adams. Signed by J.M., acting Secretary of State. MHi, Otis MSS.

Feb. 20
WASHINGTON *Commission—Marshal*

Commission to Robert Hays, Tenn., marshal, Tennessee District, four years; signed, President, by J.M., acting Secretary of State. DNA, General Records Dept. of State, Misc. Permanent Commissions, 1789–1802, Vol. B, 395. R.G. 59; DeHi, Bayard Papers.

Feb. 20
WASHINGTON *Commissions—Circuit Judges*

Commissions: William Griffith, N.J., Judge U.S. Circuit Court, 3rd Circuit; John Lowell, Mass., Chief Judge U.S. Circuit Court, 1st Circuit; Benjamin Bourne, R.I., Judge U.S. Circuit Court, 1st Circuit; Jeramiah Smith, N.H., Same; Egbert Benson, N.Y., Chief Judge U.S. Circuit Court, 2nd Circuit; Oliver Wolcott, Conn., Judge U.S. Circuit Court, 2nd Circuit; Samuel Hitchcock, Vt., Same; Jared Ingersoll, Chief Judge U.S. Circuit Court, 3rd Circuit; Richard Bassett, Del., Judge U.S. Circuit Court, 3rd Circuit; Charles Lee, Va., Chief Judge U.S. Circuit Court, 4th Circuit; George Keith Taylor (married to J.M.'s sister Jane), Va., Judge U.S. Circuit Court, 4th Circuit. All signed, President, by J.M., acting Secretary of State. DNA, General Records Dept. of State, Misc. Permanent Commissions, 1789–1802, Vol. B, 396–401, 404–406, 411–12, 414. R.G. 59.

Feb. 20
WASHINGTON *Commissions—U.S. Attorneys*

Commissions to Frederick Frelinghuyson, U.S. Attorney, New Jersey District; John Wilkes Kitterd, Same, Eastern District Pennsylvania; Edward St. Loe Livermore, Same, New Hampshire District. Signed, President, by J.M., acting Secretary of State. DNA, General Records Dept. of State, Misc. Permanent Commissions, 1789–1802, Vol. B, 403, 407, 413. R.G. 59.

Feb. 21
WASHINGTON *to Richard Bassett*

Enclosed commission as Circuit Judge of the United States. Copy of acceptance of same date noted on document. MdHi, Bayard Coll.

Feb. 21
WASHINGTON *to Harrison Gray Otis*

Enclosure of commission as U.S. Attorney for District of Massachusetts. MHi, Otis MSS.

Feb. 21
WASHINGTON *to Rufus King*

Introducing Cooper of Virginia, NNHi.

Feb. 24
RICHMOND *Georgia Boundary Dispute*

Article signed "Scots Correspondent" criticizing J.M. receipt of eight dollars per day as commissioner of Georgia boundary dispute while Chief Justice. V, from *Richmond Examiner.*

Feb. 24
WASHINGTON *to Oliver Wolcott*

Enclosing commission to office of Judge of United States Circuit Court (Connecticut, Vermont, New York). CtHi; Gibbs, *Memoirs,* II, 495. Acknowledged by Wolcott in two letters of acceptance, Mar. 2, 1801. CtHi, Oliver Wolcott, Jr., MSS, Vol. XVI, 22 and 24.

Feb. 24
WASHINGTON *Commissions—Judges*

Commissions to Thomas Bee, S.C., Chief Judge U.S. Circuit Court, 5th Circuit; Joseph Clay, Ga., Judge, same; John Sitgreaves, N.C., Judge, Same; William McClung, (married to J.M.'s sister, Susan Tarleton) Ky., Judge U.S. Circuit Court, 6th Circuit. Signed, President, by J.M., acting Secretary of State. DNA, General Records Dept. of State, Misc. Permanent Commissions, 1789–1802, Vol. B, 418–21. R.G. 59.

Feb. 26
WASHINGTON *to Rufus King*

Since strange revolution in public opinion, future course not easily determined. Opinion as to Jefferson's domestic policy, strengthening state governments and House of Representatives; personnel of cabinet. Foreign policy uncertain; probably anti-British without war. Advice not to conclude agreement with Britain until hears from new administration. PP, Rare Book Dept.

Feb. 26
WASHINGTON *to Rufus King*

Enclosing letter of Fitzsimmons to Secretary of Navy concerning conduct of British cruisers and courts of Vice Admiralty in America; efforts of British minister sincere, but order of Cabinet in London needed to stop legalized plunder; unlawfully confiscating all American shipping to Spanish colonies, incompatible with peace; no definite instructions because of new administration, but directed to make remonstrances. Enclosing for forwarding letter of Mrs. Washington to Sir John Sinclair. DNA, General Records Dept. of State, Cons. Instrs., I, 24–25. R.G. 59.

Feb. 27
WASHINGTON *to President John Adams*

Letter enclosing abstract of cases of depredations by British on commerce of the United States commencing the beginning of 1800 in accordance with order of House of Representatives of Feb. 24. Order not set date; many cases no complaint to Governor; letters from consul, President Chamber of Commerce, Philadelphia; conversations indicate no British order authorizing depredations; letter of Fitzsimmons. DNA, Legislative Division, Messages from President, 6 Cong., House of Representatives, also in Same, Reports of State Dept. to House of Representatives, III, 133. R.G. 267; ASP (For. Rel.), II, 345–46; ASP, IV, 312–15; Oster, *Marshall,* 69–70 (letter only).

Feb. 27 *to Speaker of House of*
WASHINGTON *Representatives (Theodore Sedgwick)*

Correcting omission of case of British capture in report to President. DNA, Legislative Division, Messages from President, 6 Cong., House of Representatives; also in Same, Reports of State Dept. of House of Representatives, III, 133. R.G. 267; ASP (For. Rel.), II, 345; ASP, IV, 312–13; Oster, *Marshall,* 70.

[Feb.], *n.p.* *from Humphrey Marshall*

Recommending William McClung for appointment as U.S. Circuit Court Judge, Kentucky. (Appointed by President John Adams, Feb. 24, 1800.) MHi, Adams Papers, John Adams Letters Rec'd, II, 215.

Mar. 2
WASHINGTON *from Thomas Jefferson*

Concerning countersigning letters as Secretary of State; need for commission after Mar. 4. Requests clerk to draw up appointment document. J.M. to administer Presidential oath. DLC, Thomas Jefferson Papers, Vol. 110, 18821.

Mar. 2
WASHINGTON *to Thomas Jefferson*

Acknowledging letter of same date. Necessity for request to act as

Secretary of State; letters signed. Acceptance to administer Presidential oath; form of oath. DLC, Thomas Jefferson Papers, Vol. 110, 18825; Oster, *Marshall*, 182–83.

Mar. 2
WASHINGTON *to Col. William Davies*

Introducing Dr. John Bullus. Listed in Lazare, *Book-Prices*, (1945), 632. Present owner unknown.

Mar. 3
WASHINGTON *Statement of Account—Salary, Secretary of State*

Account of J.M. as Secretary of State to Auditor of Treasury, salary as Secretary of State, Jan. 1–Feb. 3, 1800, thirty-four days at $5,000 per annum, $472.22. Errors excepted, Feb. 28, 1801. Registered, above date. DNA, Records U.S. General Accounting Office, Misc. Treasury Accounts, 1790–1835, No. 12116. R.G. 217.

Mar. 3
WASHINGTON *Commission—Judges*

Commissions to Philip Barton Key, Md., Chief Judge U.S. Circuit Court, 4th Circuit; Charles Magill (who acted as attorney in fact for J.M. in Hardy County land transactions), Va., Judge, Same; William Tilghman, Chief Judge U.S. Circuit Court, 3rd Circuit; William H. Hill, N.C., District Judge, North Carolina District; Jacob Read, S.C., Same, South Carolina District; Elizah Paine, Vt., Same, Vermont District; Thomas Gibbon, Ga., Same, Georgia District. Signed, President, by J.M., acting as Secretary of State. DNA, General Records Dept. of State, Misc. Permanent Commissions, 1789–1802, Vol. B, 415–17, 422–24. R.G. 59.

Mar. 4
WASHINGTON *from Thomas Jefferson*

Request to act as Secretary of State until successor appointed. DLC, Thomas Jefferson Papers, Vol. 110, 18835; DNA, General Records Dept. of State, Misc. Letters June–Dec. 1801, 30. R.G. 59.

Mar. 4 [erroneously dated 1781]
WASHINGTON *to Thomas Jefferson*

Acceptance of request to act as Secretary of State until successor appointed. DLC, Thomas Jefferson Papers, Vol. 110, 18847; Oster, *Marshall*, 182.

Mar. 4
WASHINGTON *to Charles Cotesworth Pinckney*

Acknowledges letter of Feb. 11; thanks for friendly expression on appointment. J.M. impressed with importance of judiciary; will endeavor not to disappoint friends. Judge Bay left for Mississippi Territory; gave letters of introduction to Governor and secretary. New political years and new order begins; Adams left at four o'clock, Jefferson inaugurated at twelve. Hopes for public prosperity and happiness under Democrats; latter divided between speculative theorists and absolute terrorists; Jefferson not classed with latter but if aligns with them, calamity for country.

Continued at four o'clock: J.M. administered oath; inauguration speech well judged and conciliatory. Charleston Libr. Society, Charleston, S.C.; AHR, Vol. LIII (Apr., 1948), 519–20.

Mar. 13
RICHMOND *Appointments—Relatives*

J.M. accused of "taking particular care of his family" in judicial appointments; signed "From a Scots Correspondent." V, from *Richmond Examiner.*

Mar. 16
WASHINGTON *Patent Entry*

Patent to William Stillman for veneering plough in cabinet-making; signed by J.M., Secretary of State. DNA, U.S. Patent Office, Restored Patents, I, 1790–1803, 433–35, R.G. 241.

Mar. 18
RICHMOND *to James M. Marshall*

Answering letter of Mar. 12; chagrined at development of principle which may be imputed to himself in failure to deliver commission as Justice to Cranch; did not examine commission; if words omitted by clerk, correct copy in office of Secretary of State will cure. Did not send out commissions because "apprehended" nondelivery of signed and sealed commission does not affect office for a fixed term, such as that of Justice, unlike indefinite term, as of marshal, which President can revoke. Would have sent out signed and sealed commission but for extreme hurry and absence of Wagner as secretary to President. Passed Pennock notes to Brown and Benton for bills; sent to Murdock with instructions; advises bring in deed to Winchester for transmission to Norfolk. Mortified at circumstances in appointment of Chief Judge of the District; negligence arising from belief

Johnston would accept; thought Cranch sent an express. Asks for date of meeting at Winchester. Instructs to pay Steward six dollars, money from Maj. Taylor. DLC, Beveridge Coll.

Mar. 31
WASHINGTON *to———*

Concerning depositions on publication in Kentucky of certificates for soldiers Illinois regiment. VW.

Apr. 4
WASHINGTON *Statement of Account—Chief Justice*

Account of J.M., salary as Chief Justice, Feb. 4–Mar. 31, 1801, at $4,000 per annum, $622.22. Registered above date. Controller's Office, Apr. 2, 1801. DNA, Records U.S. General Accounting Office, Misc. Treasury Accounts, 1790–1835, No. 12206. R.G. 217.

Note: The salary of the Chief Justice was $4,000 per annum; that of Associate Justice, $3,500, paid in quarterly installments. See for example, Same, Nos. 12698; 13015; 13296; 13607; 17884; 21748; 21993. In 1816, Congress refused to increase the salaries. Annals, 14 Cong. 1 sess. H. of R., 194, 231–33.

Apr. 25
RICHMOND *Appointment of Clerk—William Marshall*

William Marshall, J.M.'s brother, was appointed Clerk of Court by the newly constituted U.S. Circuit Court, Judges Philip Barton Key and George Keith Taylor sitting. V, U.S. Circuit Court Va., Order Book IV, 1.

Apr. Court *Law Suit*

J.M. v. John Cooke and Joseph Chilton, debt, replevin for goods taken by distress for rent and restored. Judgment for plaintiff £100 payable by £50. County Court, Fauquier, Minute Book 1800–1801, 773.

Aug. 12 *to U.S. Attorney*

Order to Treasury for balance of salary. Listed in Lazare, *Book-Prices* (1941), 47. Present owner unknown.

Oct. 10
WASHINGTON *to William Cushing*

Concerning importance of U.S. Supreme Court. MHi.

Nov. 14
WASHINGTON *Auditor's Office Account*

Adjustment of account of William Tazewell, secretary to Elbridge Gerry, envoy to France, showing $600 chargeable to J.M., late Secretary of State, for sum received from Gerry and accounted for to him by J.M. DNA, Treasury Dept., Auditor's Office, 12853. R.G. 39.

Dec. 7–12 *Unconstitutionality of Court Repeal Act.*

A series of five articles signed "A Friend of the Constitution" attacking proposed abolition of federal Circuit Courts in repeal of Judiciary Act of 1801 as unconstitutional: independence of judiciary from legislative control; office during good behavior; abolishing office illicit attempt to remove incumbent; rulings of Court of Appeals Virginia holding act of 1787 unconstitutional; judges of Court of Appeals required to sit in new Circuit Courts; same as to act of 1792, conferring injunction power on District Court; need for independence of judges, protection of rights of person, republican government, freedom from party domination or power, political preferences, protection of minority. *Washington Federalist* (Georgetown), Dec. 7, 8, 9, 10, 11, 12.

These were probably written by J.M. and probably represent his position at that time; the same signature used in later articles (see herein June 28, 1819); his alleged close association with this publication. (See Beveridge, *Marshall*, II, 532n, 541, 547n.)

Dec. 8
RICHMOND *Law Suit*

J.M. v. Jacob Smith. Action of debt on note of hand; petitioner came by attorney; default j. £20 and interest. County Court, Henrico, Order Book X, 179. (See herein Feb. 1, 1802.)

Dec. 11
WASHINGTON *Bushrod Washington to C. P. Wayne*

Answer to Wayne's letter of Dec. 10. Proposal for publication and sale of copyright of *Life of Washington* in United States; $100,000 minimum amount for American copyright. PPHi, Dreer MSS.

COMMISSIONER OF SINKING FUND

J.M., AS CHIEF JUSTICE, became and acted as a Commissioner of the Sinking Fund to retire the public debt of the United States. Other members were the President of the Senate, the Secretary of State, the Secretary of the

Treasury, and the Attorney General. Acts of Congress, 1 Cong., 2 sess., act of Aug. 12, 1790, Annals, II, 2370; Same, 3 Cong., 2 sess., act of Mar. 3, 1795, Annals, IV, 1519–26.

Annual Reports of Commissioners of Sinking Fund to Senate

Dec. 17, 1801 Report signed by J.M. with Abraham Baldwin, President of Senate pro tem; James Madison, Secretary of State; Albert Gallatin, Secretary of Treasury; Levi Lincoln, Attorney General. DNA, Register's Office, Reports of the Commissioners of the Sinking Fund. Legislative Branch. R.G. 63; ASP (Finance), I, 699.

June 7, 1802 J.M. did not attend meeting. ASP Same, II, 9.

Feb. 5, 1803 Report of 1803 not signed by J.M. Same, 23.

Feb. 6, 1804 Report of 1804 not signed by J.M. Same, 84.

Feb. 8, 1805 Report signed by J.M. with A. Burr, President of Senate; Albert Gallatin, Secretary of Treasury. Same, 120.

Feb. 5, 1806 Report signed by J.M. with George Clinton, President of Senate; James Madison, Secretary of State; Albert Gallatin, Secretary of Treasury; John Breckenridge, Attorney General. Same, 172.

Feb. 5, 1807 Report signed by J.M. with same except C. A. Rodney, Attorney General, in place of Breckenridge. Same, 227.

Feb. 5, 1808 Same. Same, 269.

Feb. 4, 1809 Report not signed by J.M. Same, 322.

Mar. 18, 1809 J.M. not attend meeting. Same, 370.

(June 23, 1809 Powers of Commissioners. Letter Gallatin, Treasury Dept. to House of Representatives, June 20, 1809. Same, 369–70.)

Feb. 4, 1811 Report not signed by J.M. Same, 472.

Feb. 5, 1812 Same. Same, 528.

Feb. 8, 1813 (Dated Feb. 6.) Report signed by J.M. with William H. Crawford, President of Senate pro tem; James Monroe, Secretary of State; Albert Gallatin, Secretary of Treasury. Same, 603.

Feb. 7, 1814 (Dated Feb. 5.) Report not signed by J.M. Same, 821.

Feb. 6, 1815 Same. Same, 897.

Feb. 7, 1816 Report signed with John Galliard, President of Senate pro tem; James Monroe, Secretary of State; A. Dallas, Secretary of Treasury. ASP (Finance), III, 73.

Feb. 7, 1817 Report signed with John Galliard, President of Senate pro tem; William H. Crawford, Secretary of State; Richard Rush, Attorney General. Same, 169.

Feb. 10, 1818 Report signed with John Galliard, President of Senate pro tem; John Q. Adams, Secretary of State; William H. Crawford, Secretary of Treasury; William Wirt, Attorney General. Same, 242.

Feb. 5, 1819 Report not signed by J.M. Same, 401.

Feb. 5, 1820 Same. Same, 473.

Feb. 7, 1821 Same. Same, 665.

Feb. 6, 1823 Report signed with Daniel D. Tompkins, Vice-President; John Q. Adams, Secretary of State; William H. Crawford, Secretary of Treasury. Same, IV, 227.

Feb. 6, 1824 Same. Same, 462.

Feb. 5, 1825 Report not signed by J.M. Same, V, 227.

Feb. 8, 1826 (Dated Feb. 6) Report signed with John C. Calhoun, Vice-President; Richard Rush, Secretary of Treasury; William Wirt, Attorney General. Same, 299.

Feb. 7, 1827 Report signed with Nathaniel Macon, President of Senate pro tem; Henry Clay, Secretary of State; Richard Rush, Secretary of Treasury; William Wirt, Attorney General. Same, 607.

Feb. 6, 1828 (Dated Feb. 4) Report signed with John C. Calhoun, Vice-President; others than Macon the same. Same, 857. DNA, Register's Office, Reports Commissioners of Sinking Fund, Legislative Branch. R.G. 63.

U.S. SUPREME COURT

February term, Feb. 2–Feb. 10.

Feb. 2, 3. Cushing only, adjourned for insufficient number.

Feb. 4. J.M.'s commission presented. J.M., Cushing, Chase, and Washington attended balance of term. U.S. Supreme Court, Minute Book A, 114–17.

August term, Aug. 3–12.

Aug. 3. Paterson, Moore, Washington, adjourned insufficient number.

Aug. 12. Above with J.M. and Chase. Same, 117–20.

December term, Dec. 7–31.

Dec. 7. Cushing only, adjourned.

Dec. 8, 9. J.M., Cushing, Paterson, Chase, Washington; adjourned, no case ready.

Dec. 10–31. Same members, except Chase absent Dec. 10. Same, 121–26.

Accommodations for Court

Jan. 20
Washington

from Commissioners of City of Washington to President of Senate and Speaker of House

Concerning making of accommodations for Court. DNA, U.S. Supreme Court, Office of Clerk; *Documentary History of the Construction and Development of the United States Capital Building and Grounds* (1904), 58 Cong., 2 sess., *H.R. Report No. 646.*

Jan. 21
Washington

Resolution—Courtroom

Vice-President communicated to Senate letter from Commissioners of City of Washington requesting room in Capital temporary accommodations of Supreme Court of the United States. Resolution of consent. 6 Cong., 2 sess., Senate, Annals, 734.

Jan. 23
Washington

Resolution—Courtroom

Resolution of House of Representatives, suitable apartments in part of Capitol completed for Courts of the United States, also District of Columbia; on completion of Capitol permanent quarters. Annals, 6 Cong., 2 sess., H. of R., 959.

Opinions

Silas Talbot v. Hans Frederick Seeman, 1 Cranch 1, 26–45, also 4 Dallas 34.

Error to U.S. Circuit Court, New York, decreeing restoration of ship without salvage, reversing U.S. District Court, New York, which decreed restoration on payment of one-half salvage; reversed, decreeing restoration on payment of one-sixth salvage.

Libel filed in 1799 by officers and crew of U.S. ship of war *Constitution* for recapture of ship *Amelia* of Hamburgh, armed and with cargo from Bengal, captured by French cruiser, manned by French and proceeding to French port for adjudication.

Held, that recapture was lawful under general principles of law and under the circumstances, acts of Congress of 1798 and 1799, although not applying to neutrals, and that of 1800 covering neutrals passed subsequent to capture, considered pertinent; that meritorious service performed; condemnation by French extremely probable under edict of Jan. 18, 1798; that amount of salvage determinable by court, act of Congress of 1799 fixing salvage at one-half of value for recapture of ships of nations in amity with the United States construed to apply to only co-belligerents; partial hostility with France recognized; public laws of foreign nation subject to judicial notice without proof as fact.

George Wilson v. and adv. Richard Mason, devisee of George Mason, 1 Cranch 45, 87–103.

Error to U.S. Court, District of Kentucky, upon cross caveats for same land.

J. for Mason, reversed.

Mason in 1780 under Virginia act of 1779 made two entries of Kentucky land—one for 8,400 acres on Panther Creek commencing "four miles above the west fork," another for 8,300 acres beginning at the upper corner of the former. Later in 1780 he made another entry for the 8,400 "four miles above the forks of Panther Creek where it mouths into Green River" and surveyed the two tracts accordingly. The West Fork of Panther Creek was 12½ miles above the mouth of the Creek entering Green River. In 1783, Wilson, knowing of the error, entered and surveyed a large tract including the 8,300-acre survey.

Held, Mason's second entry of 8,400 acres was a removal, that of 8,300 acres was not removed and title thereof entirely on survey; legislation construed to require entry as basis of title, must be certain in order to give notice; actual notice of survey without proper entry does not bar subsequent entry and survey by another; also that compact between Virginia and Kentucky preserving land titles could not adopt Virginia law making state District Court decisions on caveats final so as to exclude federal court jurisdiction.

Note: Counsel for plaintiff in error Alexander Hamilton Daviess was first western lawyer to plead before the Court; subsequently married J.M.'s sister; was part owner of the Wilson claim.

United States v. Schooner Peggy, 1 Cranch 103, 108–10.

Error to U.S. Circuit Court, Connecticut, reversing U.S. District Court. Prize case, decree of condemnation, reversed. French armed vessel bound from San Domingo to France with dispatches; decree of condemnation of Circuit Court, Sept. 23, 1800; writ of error to Supreme Court, Oct. 2, 1800.

Held, not "definitely condemned" and therefore restored under convention with France, Sept. 30, 1800. Treaty declared supreme law of the land (109). Intimated power of Court to consider a law of Congress unconstitutional. "If the law be constitutional . . . I know of no court which can contest its obligation." (110)

Jacob Resler v. James Shehee, 1 Cranch 111, 117. *Per curiam,* attributed to J.M.

Error to U.S. Circuit Court, District of Columbia, Alexandria. Action for malicious prosecution; j. for defendant in error, plaintiff below, affirmed.

Action originally brought in Court of Hustings, Town of Alexandria, by Shehee, alleging Resler procured warrant for his arrest by mayor of Alexandria alleging received one box of tallow valued at two dollars stolen by Negro slave from person unknown, knowing it to be stolen, acquitted. In action for malicious prosecution thereafter filed office judgment entered for want of plea, and writ of inquiry awarded; cause transferred to U.S. Circuit Court under act of Congress; defendant failed to plead for two terms of latter court; on third term sought to file special plea of justification, merely stating above facts; plea refused; bill of exception taken; plea of general issue; v.j. for plaintiff $1,000. Held, Virginia practice applicable, liberal in allowing pleas to office j. at next term, but at subsequent term mere discretion, and here facts of plea admissible under general issue.

Note: Case of *Downman v. Downman's Executors,* 1 Washington 26, cited to show Virginia practice. J.M. was counsel for one of the parties in this case. (See herein 1791, Legal Practice, Court of Appeals, Va.)

Turner v. Fendall, 1 Cranch 116, 129–37.

Error to Circuit Court, District of Columbia, Alexandria. J. against plaintiff in error, affirmed. Judgment creditor issued writ of *fieri facias,* and sheriff obtained money from sale of property seized; before paying into court, he levied execution on another *fieri facias* against the money in his hands, based on a judgment had against judgment creditor.

Held, sheriff liable for failure to turn money in to court.

LEGAL PRACTICE

U.S. Circuit Court, Virginia

Hunter Banks and Co., Va. v. William Hill Sergeant, Va., and William Constable, New York.

Chancery, accounting for commercial transaction. J.M. for defendant Constable in earlier proceedings. (Sergeant an alleged factor for Constable.)

Nov. 22, 1791. Defendant Constable filed petition for removal of cause from High Court of Chancery under act of Congress. U.S. Circuit Court, Va., Order Book I, 49.

May 29, 1794. Commissioners appointed. Same, 379.

Dec. 5, 1794. Commissioners of court substituted. Same, 444.

Nov. 2, 1797. Continued. Same, III, 2.

June 4, 1800. Report of commissioners set aside. Same, 417.

May 9, 1801. Findings of fact and decree for complainant against Constable, 33,325 lbs. tobacco, or specie at twenty shillings Va. per 100 lbs. Same, IV, 74.

Same, Record Book Index, Civil Apl., Nov. T, 1801.

V, U.S. Circuit Court Case Papers, containing autograph.

Fee: July 10, 1789, £6. Account Book, 204.

Court of Appeals of Virginia

William Starke Jett, executor of Richard Bernard, who was executor of William Bernard v. William Bernard, son and devisee of William Bernard, 3 Call 10.

Appeal from decree High Court of Chancery, Sept. 28, 1798, in which appellee plaintiff and appellant and Thornton and Anne Bernard, infants, defendants, affirmed. J.M. for appellant in earlier proceedings; Call for same herein.

Legacy to wife 40,000 weight crops of tobacco and tobacco debts; to son Richard, 20,000 weight of same. Commissioner reported deficiency of estate to pay both, wife first entitled, charged to defendant for misconduct as executor. Court of Chancery held no misconduct, legacies abate proportionately, affirmed.

Apr. 16, 1801. Heard. Court of Appeals, Va., Order Book IV, 49.

Apr. 23, 1801. Affirmed. Same, 64.

Fee: Sept., 1792, £7. Account Book, 336.

Bullock v. Goodall and Clough, 3 Call 39.

Appeal from High Court of Chancery, May 12, 1798, enjoining j.

County Court of Hanover, May, 1795, fining appellee, sheriff of the county. £264:8:9 for not returning execution, affirmed. J.M. was counsel for Bullock in earlier proceedings; Call for him herein.

Execution issued in 1792 by appellant on j. £497:1:11¾ against his father's estate; levied by appellant through his deputy; property sold at auction to appellee for £264:8:9; evidence that estate had no further property; execution was not returned by sheriff. In 1795 appellee moved and obtained fine against appellant for failure to make return, £264:8:9. Injunction issued by High Court of Chancery against j. on grounds return held at request of appellee until settlement made between him and deputy.

Held, injunction affirmed; evidence indicates withheld at request of appellee; no advantage to sheriff or loss to appellee; fine was excessive and violated Bill of Rights.

Nov. 1, 1800. Abated, death of appellant, *scire facias* executrix. Court of Appeals, Va., Order Book IV, 27.

Apr. 13, 1801. Set aside. Same, 43.

May 1, 1801. Reawarded. Same, 94.

Oct. 12, 1801. Heard. Same, 99.

Oct. 14, 1801. Affirmed. Same, 100.

Fee: July, 1795, £5. Account Book, 418.

James Innes, Attorney General, and John Pendleton, Auditor of Public Accounts (Commonwealth of Virginia) v. Caron de Beaumarchais, 3 Call 107.

Appeal from decree of High Court of Chancery, Sept. 26, 1796, and order of Oct. 5, 1796, reversed in part and affirmed as to residue by equally divided Court. J.M. counsel for Beaumarchais in early proceedings.

In 1778, Beaumarchais' vessel arrived at York Town with military stores which sold to Virginia; contract between M. Chevallie the supercargo, and Armstead, State Agent, payment on basis of six shillings "Virginia currency" for each livre of cost of goods in France, payment in part by 1,500 hogheads of tobacco to be credited at £4 per hundred, balance in Virginia treasury warrants bearing 6 per cent.

Claim was made for payment on basis of contract as for specie and not paper money; deposition that at time of sale Chevallie turned down offer of merchants to purchase at four shillings, six pence specie per livre, payable in tobacco at twenty shillings per hundred for each livre.

In 1785 claim referred by Governor to Solicitor, who fixed the amount in pounds and reduced to specie on basis of five paper dollars to one specie, as specified in act of 1791; and Auditor refused settlement on any others basis. Petitions to legislature 1792–93 refused. Part payment was made and credited at nominal amounts from time to time.

The Court of Chancery held no proof of contract on basis of six shillings and decreed on same basis as offer of merchants—four shillings, six pence per livre in specie, £125,595:2:1¼.

On appeal to Court of Appeals, held court jurisdiction; contract for paper money not specie; by two judges, adjustment for rate of depreciation under Section 5 of act of 1781 by court on four-to-one basis; by two, that five-to-one basis apply; by all that basis of tobacco credit be twenty shillings per hundred, not sixteen, and that interest stop in 1785. Initial decree of court that no scale set by it because of division amended on rehearing to affirm up to amount based on four-to-one scale (£11,732:15:2) the minimum amount all agree due.

Oct. 15, 1801. Innes dead, successor Philip Naiborne; Pendleton resigned, successor P. Samuel Sheppard; Beaumarchais dead, representatives André Toussant de la Rue and Eugenie de Beaumarchais, his wife. Court of Appeals, Va., Order Book III, 100.

Oct. 16–20, 1801. Heard. Same, 101, 102.

Nov. 2, 1801. Decree. Same, 115.

May 7, 1803. Reheard on decree. Same, 267.

May 10, 1803. Decree amended. Same, 274.

Fees: July, 1792, "Chevallie," £35; Mar., 1793, £15. Account Book, 332, 406.

(See herein 1789, Legal Practice, *Beaumarchais v. Smith.*)

See also report of House of Delegates of Virginia on petition of M. Chevallie. Journal of House of Delegates 1792, 146, 147, 157; Same 1802–1803, 18; Petition to Governor, Oct. 1793. H. R. McIlwaine (ed.), *Official Letters of the Governors of Virginia* (Richmond, Virginia State Library, 1926), I, 286–87.

See also *The Auditor v. Chevallie,* 5 Call 107 (1804), declaring above decision was on a four-to-one basis and affirming ruling of Court of Chancery on that basis by a divided court.

Alexander Spotswood v. Edmund Pendleton, John Campbell, Bernard Moore, Benjamin Pendleton, and Henry Fields the younger, with William Pannell, John Wharton, Ezekiah Brown, and Charles Porter; also Same v. Edmund Pendleton, and above through Fields, with William Moreton, Robert Pollard, William Underwood, and William Chisham, 4 Call 514.

Appeals from High Court of Chancery, Sept. 21, 1796, dismissing bills of appellant, affirmed. J.M. for Pendleton, Pannell, and others in earlier proceedings. Call and Randolph for same herein. Bills alleged appellant heir of lands in Orange, Culpeper, and Spotsylvania Counties entailed from father who died in 1768; six appellees named executors; Moore alone qualified and became his guardian; latter had two acts of Assembly 1764 passed authorizing sale of land with consent of others named to pay debts; fraudulently obtained and approved by King in Council; bills of exchange of testator sufficient to pay debts; sale improperly made through agents; misapplication of proceeds; purchasers named defendants liable because of knowledge of transaction and misapplication. In defense pleaded estate encumbered with debt, bills of exchange worthless; sales mostly to tenants at estimated prices; no counter bids; variance of lots sold from leases arose from subsequent surveys; purchaser innocent; proceeds applied. Chancery Court dismissed on grounds sales within statute; action for title improperly brought in equity.

Held, by various judges, fraud in obtaining statute not proved; beneficial to estate; statute conclusive; sales by agents supervised by trustees proper; variance in quantity on surveys not material; purchasers not responsible for application of funds. One judge, that court had jurisdiction; two judges, not necessary to decide because bill dismissed.

Oct. 28, 1799. Continued. Court of Appeals, Va., Order Book III, 349.

Nov. 6–7, 1800. Heard. Same, Order Book IV, 31, 32.

May 9, 1801. Affirmed. Same, 90.

Fees: Mar., 1794, £50; also Oct.–Nov., 1793, "Pannell," £2:8. Account Book, 382, 374.

Samuel Young v. Sir Peyton Skipwith and Same v. Same and Sherwood, Daniel and John Hicks, executors of Amos Hicks.

Appeal from decrees of High Court of Chancery, May 27, 1795. J.M. for appellant.

Oct. 26, 1796. Continued. Court of Appeals, Va., Order Book III, 140.

Oct. 27. Heard. Same, 141.

Nov. 5. First case appeal dismissed as not final decree. Second case continued for rehearing. Same, 146.

Oct. 12, 1798. Apr. 11, 1799, Oct. 14, 1799. Continued. Same, 246, 279, 334.

Apr. 28, 1801. Appellant dead, revived, affirmed. Same, IV, 77.

Fee: Dec., 1791, £7. Account Book, 308. (This fee was undoubtedly for early stages of the proceedings. It is not known how far J.M. proceeded.)

LAND TRANSACTIONS
Fauquier County, Virginia

Sept. 11 *Land Contract*

Agreement of James M. Marshall to sell part of Manor of Leeds land lying between Cobler and Rattlesnake Mts.; several occupants; to J.M., Rawleigh Colston, John Ambler; sale price twenty shillings per acre; latter authorize J.M. to resell on joint account. In final division of Manor of Leeds rated at this price; possession now, rents for proprietors until purchase price paid thereon. NIC.

Sept. 28 *Land Contract*

J.M., Rawleigh Colston, and James M. Marshall to sell to William Clarkston, 422 acres of Manor of Leeds on which John Pope Williams resides; at forty shillings per acre, one-fourth cash, balance in three payments. Signed by J.M. for self and as attorney in fact for Colston. Recorded May 26, 1806. Fauquier County, Va., Deed Book 16, 394.

Henrico County, Virginia

Apr. 4 *Deed*

Thomas Franklin, wife and children of Thomas Franklin, deceased, and others to J.M., twenty acres in Henrico County next to land of Abraham Cowley; £20. Recorded May 1, 1809. Henrico County, Va. Deed Book 8, 401.

South Branch Manor, Hardy County, Virginia (Now West Virginia)

Feb. 7 *Deed*

J.M., by Rawleigh Colston, attorney in fact, to William Rennicks, conveyance of reversionary interest, five tracts: 128 acres, No. 23, leased Thomas Lord Fairfax to Jonathan Heath, Aug. 3, 1773; 284 acres, No. 4, leased Same to Rennicks, same date; 108 acres, leased Same to Same, Mar. 9, 1779; 148 acres and 51 acres, leased Same to Same, May 21, 1791. Consideration £246. Recorded Sept. 7, 1801. Hardy County, Va., Deed Book A, 389.

Mar. 8 *Deed*

J.M., by Rawleigh Colston, attorney in fact, to Thomas McClung, 7½ acres. Consideration [unreadable]. Recorded May 8, 1801. Hardy County, Va., Deed Book A, 368.

Mar. 12 *Deed*

J.M., by Rawleigh Colston, attorney in fact, to Jesse Welton, thirty-four acres. Consideration £11 Virginia. Recorded Mar. 15, 1801. Hardy County, Va., Deed Book 5, 43.

May 1 *Deed*

J.M., by Rawleigh Colston, attorney in fact, to Patrick Lynch, conveyance of reversionary interest, 205 acres, No. 15, leased Thomas Lord Fairfax to Lynch, Aug. 3, 1773. Consideration £75. Recorded Sept. 5, 1801. Hardy County, Va., Deed Book A, 387.

June 1 *Deed*

J.M., by Rawleigh Colston, attorney in fact, to Adam, Felix, Mary, and Hannah Sea, heirs of George Sea, reversionary interest, 216 acres leased Thomas Lord Fairfax to Michael Sea, Aug. 3, 1773. Consideration £200. Recorded Sept. 8, 1801. Hardy County, Va., Deed Book A, 394.

June 1 *Deed*

J.M., by Rawleigh Colston, attorney in fact, to James Cunningham, reversionary interest five tracts: 28 acres, No. 36, leased Thomas Lord Fairfax to Samuel Hornbeck; 71 acres, No. 25, leased Same to Same; 45 acres, No. 37, leased Fairfax to William Ashby; 137 acres, No. 24, leased Fairfax to Simon Hornbeck; 44 acres, No. 26, leased Fairfax to Daniel Hornbeck, all leases executed Aug. 3, 1773. Consideration £76. Recorded Sept. 9, 1801. Hardy County, Va., Deed Book A, 413.

June 6 *Power of Attorney*

J.M. empowering Charles Magill, Winchester, attorney to execute deeds, releases, conveying reversion of interest in South Branch Manor to purchasers. Recorded, Superior Court, Sept. 8, 1801. Hardy County, Va., Deed Book A, 407.

June 8 *Deed*

J.M., by Rawleigh Colston, attorney in fact, to William Cunningham, Jr., reversionary interest, 235 acres, No. 33, leased Thomas Lord Fairfax to Isaac Hornbeck, Aug. 3, 1773; 222 acres on drains of South Branch of Potomac, leased Same to Same, June 8, 1777; 140 acres, leased Same to

Leonard Harness, Aug. 3, 1773. Consideration £600. Recorded Sept. 8, 1801. Hardy County, Va., Deed Book A, 399.

June 8 *Deed*

J.M., by Rawleigh Colston, attorney in fact, to William Cunningham, reversionary interest four tracts: 110 acres, No. 58, leased Thomas Lord Fairfax to Israel Ward, Aug. 3, 1773; 148 acres, 149 acres, and 123 acres, above leased Denny Martin Fairfax to Cunningham, Nov. 20, 1790. Recorded Sept. 8, 1801. Consideration £800. Hardy County, Va., Deed Book A, 403.

June 13 *Lease*

J.M., by Charles Magill, attorney in fact, to Lawrence Shook, for natural lives of lessee, Samuel Shook, and Isaac Welton, forty-six acres South Branch Manor, yearly rent twenty-five shillings Virginia per hundred acres. Recorded Sept. 9, 1801. Hardy County, Va., Deed Book A, 433.

June 13 *Lease*

J.M., by Charles Magill, attorney in fact, to Lawrence Shook, 140 acres, No. 83, same leased to Henry Francisco, Sr., Aug. 3, 1773, for lives of Henry Miller, Daniel Miller, and Welton Miller, yearly rent twenty-five shillings Virginia per hundred acres. Recorded Sept. 9, 1801. Hardy County, Va., Deed Book A, 435.

Aug. 15 *Deed*

J.M., by Charles Magill, attorney in fact, to William Rennick, Jr., reversionary interest in two tracts: 242 acres, No. 32 leased Thomas Lord Fairfax to George Rennick, Aug. 3, 1773; 254 acres, leased same to Felix Seymour, same date, such part in possession of grantee. Consideration £63:4. Recorded Sept. 9, 1801. Hardy County, Va., Deed Book A, 417.

Aug. 15 *Deed*

J.M., by Charles Magill, attorney in fact, to James Machir, reversionary interest in four tracts: 252 acres, No. 11, leased Thomas Lord Fairfax to Thomas McCarty, Aug. 3, 1773; 81 acres, leased Fairfax to William Welton, same date; 5 acres and 16 acres leased Denny Martin Fairfax to James Machir, July 15, 1789. Consideration £200. Recorded Sept. 9, 1801. Hardy County, Va., Deed Book A, 419.

Sept. 5 *Deed*

J.M., by Charles Magill, attorney in fact, to Henry Pringle, reversionary interest, 46½ acres and 34 less 1½ acres. Consideration $100. Recorded Oct. 14, 1801. Hardy County Va., Deed Book 5, 60.

Sept. 8 *Deed*

J.M., by Rawleigh Colston, attorney in fact, to William Cunningham, reversionary interest, three tracts: 291 acres, No. 34, leased Thomas Lord Fairfax to Joseph Petty; 261 acres, No. 38, leased same to Herbert Brink; 558 acres, No. 36, leased same to John Westfall, all on Aug. 3, 1773. Consideration $500. Recorded Sept. 8, 1801. Hardy County, Va., Deed Book A, 396.

Sept. 8 *Deed*

J.M., by Rawleigh Colston, attorney in fact, to William Cunningham, reversionary interest, four tracts: 68 acres, No. 57; 242 acres, No. 42; 133 acres, No. 53, all leased Thomas Lord Fairfax to Cunningham, Aug. 3, 1773; also 12 acres, No. 35, leased Fairfax to John Singleton, same date. Consideration $700. Hardy County, Va., Recorded Sept. 8, 1801. Deed Book A, 401.

Sept. 8 *Deed*

J.M., by Rawleigh Colston, attorney in fact, to Andrew Burns, fifty-eight acres. Consideration £13 Virginia. Recorded Sept. 8, 1801. Hardy County, Va., Deed Book A, 406.

Sept. 9 *Deed*

J.M., by Charles Magill, attorney in fact, to Richard Seymour, reversionary interest, three tracts: 42 acres, No. 74, leased Thomas Lord Fairfax to John Westfall, Aug. 3, 1773; 136 acres, No. 75, leased Fairfax to Abraham Clark, Sr., Aug. 3, 1773; 58 acres, leased Denny Martin Fairfax to Richard Seymour, May 28, 1791. Consideration £59. Recorded Sept. 9, 1801. Hardy County, Va., Deed Book A, 412.

Sept. 9 *Deed*

J.M., by Charles Magill, attorney in fact, to James Cunningham, reversionary interest, ninety-eight acres, No. 22, leased Thomas Lord Fairfax to Daniel Hornbeck, Aug. 8, 1773; also ninety-eight acres, leased Denny Martin Fairfax to James Cunningham, Nov. 27, 1790. Consideration £24. Recorded Sept. 9, 1801. Hardy County, Va., Deed Book A, 415.

Sept. 9 *Deed*

J.M., by Charles Magill, attorney in fact, to Jacob Fisher, reversionary interest, ninety-five acres, No. 35, leased Thomas Lord Fairfax to John Singleton, Aug. 3, 1773. Consideration £20. Recorded Sept. 9, 1801. Hardy County, Va., Deed Book A, 422.

Sept. 9 *Deed*

J.M., by Charles Magill, attorney in fact, to Adam Fisher, forty acres. Consideration £9 Virginia. Recorded Sept. 9, 1801, Hardy County, Va., Deed Book A, 426.

Sept. 9 *Deed*

J.M., by Charles Magill, attorney in fact, to Thomas Jones, ——— acres. Consideration £3:13 Virginia. Recorded Sept. 9, 1801. Hardy County, Va., Deed Book A, 427.

Sept. 9 [1800] *Deed*

J.M., by Charles Magill, attorney in fact, to Job Welton, 34 acres at Sink Hole Ridge; 19¼ acres on east bank of Lunies Creek. Consideration £13:6:3 Virginia. Recorded Sept. 9, 1801. Hardy County, Va., Deed Book A, 429.

Sept. 9 *Deed*

J.M., by Charles Magill, attorney in fact, to Adam and John Fisher, two tracts: sixteen acres adjoining own lot on Parsons Run, also thirty-four acres. Consideration £18:16. Recorded Sept. 9, 1801. Hardy County, Va., Deed Book A, 430.

Sept. 10 *Deed*

J.M., by Charles Magill, attorney in fact, to Peter Higgins, reversionary interest in four tracts: 33 acres, No. 18, leased Thomas Lord Fairfax to Conrad Moore; 35 acres, No. 20, leased Same to Peter Sternburger; 212 acres, No. 21, leased Same to Samuel Beall; 72 acres, No. 19, leased Same to Jacob Yocum; all leases executed Aug. 3, 1773. Consideration £98. Recorded Sept. 10, 1801. Hardy County, Va., Deed Book A, 437.

Sept. 10 *Deed*

J.M., by Charles Magill, attorney in fact, to William D. Lucas, reversionary 117¾ acres and 35 poles of 242 acre tract, No. 32, leased Thomas Lord Fairfax to George Rennick, Aug. 3, 1773. Consideration £30:11:8. Recorded Sept. 10, 1801. Hardy County, Va., Deed Book A, 439.

Sept. 10 *Deed*

J.M., by Charles Magill, attorney in fact, to Joseph Inskeep, reversionary interest, three tracts: 295 acres, No. 38, leased Thomas Lord Fairfax to Joseph Inskeep; 133 acres, No. 13, leased same to Christopher Cocke; 92 acres, an island on west side of South Branch of Potomac, opposite mouth of Hutten's Run; all leases executed Aug. 3, 1773. Consideration £110. Recorded May 7, 1803. Hardy County, Va., Deed Book B, 85.

Sept. 10 *Deed*

J.M., by Charles Magill, attorney in fact, to Job Welton, reversionary interest, fifty-five acres, No. 82, leased Thomas Lord Fairfax to Ephraim Richardson. Consideration £33. Recorded Oct. 14, 1801. Hardy County, Va., Deed Book 5, 58.

Sept. 10 *Deed*

J.M., by Charles Magill, attorney in fact, to Job Welton, reversionary interest, 5¾ acres. Consideration £0:31 Va. Recorded, Oct. 14, 1801. Hardy County, Va., Deed Book 5, 59.

Sept. 10 *Deed*

J.M., by Charles Magill, attorney in fact, to John Harness, Sr., fifty acres. Consideration £18:4 Va. Recorded Jan. 14, 1802. Hardy County, Va., Deed Book 5, 93.

Sept. 30 *Deed*

J.M., by Charles Magill, to Henry Pringle, twenty-three acres. Consideration £6:15 Va. Recorded Oct. 14, 1801. Hardy County, Va., Deed Book 5, 60.

1802

DOCUMENTS

Jan. 2
LONDON *from Rufus King*

(Nearly six months after J.M. left office of Secretary of State) King received last official letter of J.M., and private one. Difficulties in executing Articles 6 and 7 of Treaty of 1794 settled; explains terms. NNHi.

Jan. 22
WALNUT FARM *Bushrod Washington to C. P. Wayne*

Concerning negotiation for sale price of American rights to *Life of Washington*. PPHi.

Feb. 1
RICHMOND *Law Suit*

J.M. v. Jacob Smith and Elisha Pace. Motion on bond and property tendered for discharge of Smith's body taken on execution. (See Dec. 8, 1801, herein.) Default j. $54.58, payable by $27.29. County Court, Henrico, Va., Order Book X, 199.

Feb. 2
[WASHINGTON] *Account to Auditor—Whalen*

Statement of account of Israel Whalen to U.S. Auditor's Office; amounts advanced by J.M. while Secretary of State to various persons employed for brigatine *Sophie.* Barbary Powers, II, 64.

Mar. 26 *John Rutledge, Jr., to James A. Bayard*

Repeal of Judiciary Act wounded Federalist party; public sentiment opposed. Conversed with J.M., who stated firmness of Supreme Court may be depended upon. DeHi, Bayard Papers.

Mar. 27 *Life of Washington*

Announcing forthcoming biography of George Washington, described as authentic, accurate, and elegant performance; suggests defer subscriptions to daily proposals for works on life of Washington. *Washington Federalist* (Georgetown), Vol. II (Mar. 27, 1802), 279.

Apr. 2
WALNUT FARM *Bushrod Washington to C. P. Wayne*

Concerning contract on *Life of Washington,* will consult with J.M. PPHi.

Apr. 5
RICHMOND *to Oliver Wolcott, Jr.*

Thanks for copy of last judicial bill sent; great solicitude; uncertain what destiny decreed us (the Supreme Court). Contains defect; assumes will be corrected, as not party or political question; mode of carrying causes Circuit to Supreme Court; repealed bill attended to it. Terms of 5th Circuit inconvenient to bar; presumes will request change. Regrets June term put down; immediate operation of bill will be insisted on. Considers bill repealing internal revenue and every other measure favored by those repealing the judicial system to pass. Expects statehood in Northwest Territory if vote considered necessary by those in office; surprised considers three votes necessary. Jury tax unreasonable; discourage resort to federal courts. CtHi, Oliver Wolcott, Jr., MSS, Vol. 48, 30.

Apr. 6
RICHMOND *to William Paterson*

Acknowledging letter of Mar. 29; forwarding enclosed letter to Judge Washington; not seen publication requested. Will promote interests of Princeton College; regrets its misfortunes. Bill to Senate concerning courts less burdensome than expected; has constitutional scruples concerning Circuit Court duties of Supreme Court justices, but considers matter decided. Regrets loss of June term; had hoped for consultation of judges. NN, Papers of Wm. Paterson, Bancroft Transcripts, 639–41; NjR, Wm. Paterson Papers.

Apr. 19
ALEXANDRIA *to Justice William Cushing*

Expects passage by Congress of law abolishing June term of Supreme Court and requiring sitting on Circuit Court bench; J.M. believes unconstitutional; presumes Court holds contrary opinion; if so, will conform; asks Cushing's opinion. MHi, R. T. Paine, V 4.

Apr. 19
ALEXANDRIA *to Justice William Paterson*

Apparently no session of Supreme Court June next, and shall be directed to ride circuits. Desires sentiments of judges concerning duty to sit in Circuit Court under act; respects authors of original act and those acting under it, but questions whether change after appointments distinguishes. Points to seriousness of refusal to act and reaction of public. Enclosed letter to Judge Cushing. NN, Papers of Wm. Paterson, Bancroft Transcripts, 643–47; NjR, Wm. Paterson Papers.

Apr. 19
ALEXANDRIA *to Justice Samuel Chase*

Letter similar to those of Justices Cushing and Paterson (see above) sent to Chase (n.f.). See answer of Chase to J.M., dated Apr. 24, 1802, herein.

Apr. 22
WASHINGTON *Statement of Account—Mediterranean Powers*

Account of J.M. as Secretary of State, expenditures in fulfilling engagements of the United States with Mediterranean powers, Aug. 20, 1800—Mar. 3, 1801, $59,813.90. Registered, above date. Accounting Office, Oct. 22, ———. Comptroller's Office, Nov. 26, 1808. DNA, Records U.S. General Accounting Office, Misc. Treas. Accounts, 1790–1835, No. 12888. R.G. 217.

Apr. 22
WASHINGTON *Statement of Account—Seamen*

Account of J.M. as Secretary of State, for relief and protection of seamen, 1800—Mar. 3, 1801, $15,000. Registered, above date. Comptroller's Office, Nov. 28, 1808. DNA, Records U.S. General Accounting Office, Misc. Treas. Accounts, 1790–1835, Nos. 12889–90. R.G. 217.

Apr. 22
WASHINGTON *Statement of Account—Mines*

Account of J.M. as Secretary of State, exploring copper mines Lake Superior, Nov. 24, 1800—Mar. 3, 1801, Richard F. Cooper, $1,500; Dec. 4, 1800, bill on J.M. by W. Hooper, agent, to Wm. Cooper, $500; Nov. 25, 1800, receipt by Cooper $1,000 draft by J.M.; Dec. 24, 1800, same, $500; Sept. 14, 1800, draft on J.M. by Cooper to Nicholas Low, $1,000. DNA, Records U.S. General Accounting Office, Misc. Treas. Accounts, 1790–1835, No. 12,891. R.G. 217.

Apr. 22
WASHINGTON *Statement of Accounts—Spain*

Account of J.M., Secretary of State, expenditures carrying out Treaty of Friendship United States and Spain, June 21, 1800—Mar. 3, 1801, $11,840. Registered date above. Comptroller's Office, Nov. 21, 1808. DNA, Records U.S. General Accounting Office, Misc. Treas. Accounts, 1790–1835, No. 12892. R.G. 217.

Apr. 22
WASHINGTON *Statement of Accounts—Prize Claims*

Account of J.M., Secretary of State, prosecution of claims prize causes, claims of American citizens to captured property, Sept. 20, 1800—Mar. 3, 1801, $43,399.99. Registered, above date. Errors excepted, Mar. 3, 1801. Accounting Office, Oct. 22, 1801. Comptroller's Office, Nov. 27, 1808. DNA, Records U.S. General Accounting Office, Misc. Treas. Accounts, 1790–1835. No. 12893. R.G. 217.

Apr. 24
BALTIMORE *from Justice Samuel Chase*

Acknowledges letter of Apr. 19; has seen act repealing Judiciary Act of 1801 and reviving former system; also act setting up circuits and assigning Justices. Suggests conference of Justices at Washington July or August; lay result before President. Desires to yield to opinion of other justices, but conscience must be satisfied; his need of office to support family. His opinion repealing act unconstitutional in abolishing appointments, commissions, and salaries of Circuit Court judges. Duty of Congress to establish inferior courts; power over them; when established, hold office during good behavior, removable only by impeachment. Uniform opinion until lately Supreme Court power to declare act of Congress void; no judicial remedy for circuit judges. Objects to Supreme Court justices holding Circuit Court because supporting unconstitutional law; deprivation of office of circuit judges unconstitutional; for Supreme Court to exercise original jurisdiction beyond enumerated cases violates constitutional procedure for appointment. Sitting of justices in Circuit Court under prior act distinguished, never questioned, but now would injure rights of other judges. NN, Papers of Wm. Paterson, Bancroft Transcripts, 633–97; NNHi.

May 3
RICHMOND *to Justice William Paterson*

Quoting letter from Judge Bushrod Washington, refusing access by Judge Benson to George Washington papers, similarly had refused Alexander Hamilton; not allow use for party purposes. Judge Washington considers question of sitting as circuit judges settled, J.M. gratified if majority so hold. Judge Chase is opposed, desires meeting in Washington. J.M. writing to Judge Moore (n.f.). Paterson requested to write to Judge Cushing. NN, Papers of Wm. Paterson, Bancroft Transcripts, 651–57; NjR, Wm. Paterson Papers.

May 5
RICHMOND *to Rufus King*

Thanks for letter of Jan. 12, received few weeks before. Commends on accomplishment of difficult negotiations; accomplished what deemed impractical; treaty with great European nation acceptable to all. Present administration claim extricated from twenty-four million dollar debt in which former administration involved it; friends of "ancient state of things" also claim credit; depends on accident, if Adams or one of his political opinion had been elected, treaty would have had other reception; payment of lump sum called by critics national degradation and abandonment of national interest; a free-will offering to Britain of those seeking war with France rather than giving small loan to France for gratitude due. Surprised Britain agreed after advantage of fifth commissioner; credit to American negotiators but also respect to English minister. Hopes national tribunals will continue prudence in exposition of treaty of peace. No change in public opinion as to question of Union, disposition to coalesce with present majority gone; minority recovering strength and firmness. Political tempers will long exist after those now tossed at rest. NNHi; King, *Life*, IV, 116–18; Oster, *Marshall*, 84–85. See Warren, *Supreme Court*, I, 565n.

May 5
PRINCETON, N.J. *Honorary Degree*

Trustees of the college of New Jersey (Princeton) voted to confer the degree of LL.D. on J.M. Princeton University Archives, Manuscript Minutes, III, 81. (See herein Oct. 29, 1802.)

June 3 *Justice William Cushing to*
SCITUATE, MASS. *Justice William Paterson*

Answered Paterson's letter of 6th (May); also letter to Chief Justice; immediately thereafter received Paterson's concerning circuit judges with extract of letter from J.M. and opinions of Judges Chase and Washington. Result is concurrence of three in favor of old practice and inclination of J.M. that such might be opinion of majority, prevailing opinion. No need to meet at Washington in August, as suggested by Chase; he will be left to exercise "singular jurisdiction." NNHi. (See herein June 11, 18, 1802.)

June 11
NEW BRUNSWICK *from Justice William Paterson*

Quotes from letter from Judge Cushing, May 29, in answer to his of the 6th enclosing J.M. letter concerning need of commission for justices to act as circuit judges, originally doubtful, now abide by practice. Paterson will advise when second letter to Cushing, May 25, answered. NN, Papers of Wm. Paterson, Bancroft Transcripts, 767; NNHi.

June 14 *George Washington Memorial*

Terms of subscription to George Washington Monument or Mausoleum; J.M., Bushrod Washington, Benjamin Stoddard to select design; subscriptions not more than one eagle, $10.00; surplus amounts used for

National University proposed by Washington. *Washington Federalist* (Georgetown) June 4, 1802, 328. Copied from *Boston Sentinel.*

June 18
New Brunswick *from Justice William Paterson*

Received letter from Judge Cushing, June 3, in answer to his of May 25; refers to views in former letter; if majority favor old practice (approval of Supreme Court Justices sitting in Circuit Court because old practice), no need for August meeting. NNHi; NN, Papers of Wm. Paterson (typescript).

June 30
Washington *Account—Secretary of State*

Statement of account as Secretary of State, general account current with U.S., $187,212.53. Registered, above date. Accounting Office, Nov. 28, 1801. Comptroller's Office, Dec. 10, 1808. DNA, Records U.S. General Accounting Office, Misc. Treas. Accounts, 1790–1835, No. 12907. R.G. 217.

Aug. 20
Washington *to Polly Marshall*

Visit with Mrs. Washington; pleased with Jacquelin. VW; Mason, *Polly,* 143 (dated 1800).

to Maj. Thomas Massie,
Aug. 31, *n.p.* *Addressed to Frederick, Care of Col. Meade*

Proposes trade of some of his Buckingham tract for addressee"s Faquier land. Will be in Winchester Saturday, then to the Allegheny, on return in Martinsburg until late September. Instructions endorsed for bearer to obtain answer. VHi.

Sept. 17
Philadelphia *from C. P. Wayne*

Circular for subscriptions to publication of J.M.'s history of the late Gen. George Washington. MHi, Adams Papers, Letters Rec'd, XXI, 330a.

Sept. 22, *n.p.* *Contract*—Life of Washington

Contract between Bushrod Washington of Mount Vernon, Virginia, and Caleb P. Wayne of Philadelphia for publication by latter of the "Life of the late Gen. George Washington," which is now preparing under the inspection of B. Washington; five volumes intended; manuscript of three volumes to be delivered within approximately two years; Wayne to have copyright in the United States, North and South America, West Indies; European rights reserved. Royalty one dollar per volume, payment commence on publication of first three volumes. Price per volume not to exceed three dollars. Wayne to promote sale, not assign without consent. PPHi.

Sept. 24 — Life of Washington

Subscription notice by C. P. Wayne of *Life of Washington*, under supervision of Bushrod Washington. (J.M. not named as author). *Washington Federalist* (Georgetown) Oct. 25, 26, 1802, 384, 385.

Oct. 29 — *Honorary Decree—Princeton*

Item describing annual commencement exercises, Princeton; degrees of Doctor of Law conferred on J.M. and Elaphalet Pearson, professor of Oriental Language and Belles-Lettres, Oxford. *Washington Federalist* (Georgetown) Oct. 29, 1802, 388. (See herein May 5, 1802.)

Nov. 19
MOUNT VERNON — *Bushrod Washington to C. P. Wayne*

Enclosing certificate of purchase by Wayne of American copyright to *Life of Washington*, corroborating accepted proposal. Not intended as a party work, despite what Democrats say. PPHi.

Nov. 21
RICHMOND — *to Charles Cotesworth Pinckney*

Writing *Life of Washington*; asks details of attack on Savannah in 1779, Gen. Lincoln's siege of Charleston. Disgusted with political world and disheartened generally. Rumor that an eminent personage fatigued almost beyond bearing with a great democratic and religious writer. Congressional election contest in Virginia. DLC, Pinckney Family Papers, Box 11; WMQ (ser. 3), Vol. 12 (Oct. 1955), 644–46.

U.S. SUPREME COURT

UNDER THE JUDICIARY ACT of 1789 (Sept. 24, 1789, 1 Stat. 73) the Court held two annual sessions, one commencing the first Monday in February, the second commencing the first Monday in August.

The Judiciary Act of 1801 (Feb. 13, 1801, 6 Cong., 2 sess. ch. 4; 2 Stat. 89) provided for sessions commencing first Monday in June and December. The Amendatory Act of 1802 (Apr. 29, 1802, 7 Cong., 1 sess., ch. 31; 2 Stat. 156) restored the former sessions; the August session, however, was abolished as a business session, except for motions and continuances. (See Annals, 7 Cong., 1 sess. H. of R., 1236.) As a result there was no business session of the Court between Dec. 19, 1801, the termination of the Dec., 1801, term, and Feb. 8, 1803, the commencement of the February term. The August session, 1802, was attended by Justice Chase Aug. 1, and all cases on the docket were continued.

In the course of debate on the repeal bill, J.M. and his landholdings were brought into discussion. Nichols proposed an amendment to the bill setting the minimum jurisdictional amount at $500, avowedly to prevent the Marshalls from bringing actions for quitrents in federal courts. He stated that the estate of Lord Fairfax, with quitrents due, was confiscated by Virginia; nevertheless, his heirs sold their rights, which assignees contend are unimpaired and which they might wish to gain advantage of in federal instead of state courts. The $500 was intended to be beyond amount of any single claim. The Journal contains the following insertion: "It is understood that the present assignees of the claims of Lord Fairfax, are James M. Marshall, General Lee, and a third individual, and that they maintain their claims under the British Treaty." The amendment lost thirty-seven to thirty-seven, by vote of Chairman. The limit was set at $400. Annals. 6 Cong. 1 sess. H. of R., 897.

By act of May 4, 1826, the session of the first Monday in February was moved to the second Monday in January. (4 Stat. 160). The change was effective in 1827 and applied in 1828.

U.S. CIRCUIT COURT, 5TH CIRCUIT VIRGINIA AND NORTH CAROLINA

Editor's Note:

The Judiciary Act of Sept. 24, 1789 (1 Stat. 73), divided the country into thirteen districts along state lines with two districts in Virginia and Massachusetts. North Carolina and Rhode Island were not provided for until after they joined the Union in Nov., 1789, and 1790, respectively.

The country was divided into three circuits—the Northern, Middle, and Southern—each having a Circuit Court composed of two Supreme Court justices and a District Judge of the Circuit. Virginia was placed in the Middle Circuit. The requirement of two justices was not strictly adhered to; for example, the first term of the North Carolina Circuit Court, Nov. 8, 1791, was attended by Justice James Iredell and District Judge John Sitgreaves; the Nov., 1790, term of the Virginia Circuit Court, by Justice John Blair and District Judge Cyrus Griffin; the May, 1792, term, by Justice James Wilson and the District Judge; the Nov., 1792, term, by

Justice William Cushing and the District Judge. Under the act of Mar. 2, 1793 (1 Stat. 333), only one Justice was required to attend sessions.

During the period of J.M.'s extensive practice before the Virginia Court, the following justices sat on the bench of that court: James Wilson, John Blair, James Iredell, Thomas Johnson, William Cushing, and William Paterson.

The Judiciary Act of 1801 (Feb. 13, 1801, 6 Cong., 2 sess., 2 Stat. 89) set up six circuits attended by separately appointed circuit judges and eliminated "circuit riding" by the Supreme Court justices, whose numbers were reduced from six to five. The eastern and western districts of Virginia and the District of Maryland constituted the 4th Circuit. North Carolina, South Carolina, and Georgia constituted the 5th Circuit. During the period of its existence, the 4th Circuit was manned by Philip Barton Key of Maryland, Chief Judge, and George Keith Taylor and Charles Magill, both of Virginia; the 5th Circuit, by Joseph Clay, Jr., of Georgia (Chief Judge), Dominick A. Hall, and Henry Potter of North Carolina, the latter being superseded in 1802 by Edward Harris of North Carolina. Potter in turn became District Judge of North Carolina and thereafter sat with J.M. for many years in Circuit Court. All of the judges of the 4th and Potter of the 5th Circuit were appointed by President Adams, J.M. assisting therein as Secretary of State.

This system was abolished by the act of Mar. 8, 1802 (2 Stat. 132), and the act of Apr. 29, 1802 (2 Stat. 156), as amended by the act of Mar. 3, 1803 (2 Stat. 244), and reverted largely to the system under the Judiciary Act of 1789. The country was divided into six circuits, the District of Virginia and that of North Carolina constituting the 5th Circuit. The court was constituted as before of one Justice of the Supreme Court and the District Judge of the district, the law allowing court to be held by one or both of these, and establishing two annual sessions.

The first term of the Virginia Court under the act of 1802 commenced Nov. 2, 1802, and was attended by J.M. The district judges successively attending with him were Cyrus Griffin, Saint George Tucker, George Hay, and Philip P. Barbour. The court throughout its life had a comparatively heavy docket and extended sessions, attended regularly by J.M. and with varying attendance of the District Judge of the time.

Sessions of the North Carolina Circuit Court held at Raleigh were short, reflecting a light calendar. During the first years to 1807, sessions were from five to six days each; commencing with the latter date, they did not exceed three days, and on one occasion, lasted only one day. J.M. was regular in attendance, missing only four terms: June, 1806; May,

1807; Nov., 1814; and, necessarily, May, 1835. Length of sessions and J.M.'s attendance at both courts are noted herein yearly where information is available.

U.S. Circuit Court, Virginia

November term, Nov. 22–Dec. 10.

J.M. attended alone.

V, U.S. Circuit Court, Order Book IV, 182–272.

Opinions

Manuscript drafts of opinions of J.M. delivered in U.S. Circuit Court, Virginia and North Carolina, in J.M.'s handwriting showing corrections and deletions, from November term, 1803, to May term, 1831. Am. Philos. Soc. Libr.

Note: The manuscript of *Wallis v. Thornton,* 2 Brockenbrough 422 (May term, 1831) and of *Hopkirk v. M'Conico,* 1 Brockenbrough 220, May term, 1812, contain summaries of the pleadings. The first manuscript sheets of opinions are missing in *Gaines v. Spann,* 2 Brockenbrough 81 (May term, 1823) and *United States v. Maurice,* 2 Brockenbrough 96 (May term, 1823). The opinions in *Livingston v. Jefferson,* 1 Brockenbrough 190, November term, 1811, appear in two drafts, the first incomplete. The case of *Wormeley v. Wormeley,* 1 Brockenbrough 330 (November term, 1817) has a draft of the decree, the opinion noted by J.M. is missing. All appear with additional opinions to 1833 in Brockenbrough.

John Murdock & Co. v. John Shelton's Executors.

Debt on bond. J.M. for plaintiff.

Dec., 1796. Filed.

Oct., 1797. Court order.

Nov., 1797. Court order confessed.

May 27, 1799. *Scire facias,* death of defendant. U.S. Circuit Court, Va., Order Book III, 372.

Nov. 22, 1800. Same. Same, 438.

Apr., 1802. Continued.

Nov. 22, 1802. Abated by death of defendant. Same, IV, 184.

This is the first case J.M. sat on in Circuit Court (under act of 1802).

V, U.S. Circuit Court Case Papers, 1802, wherein J.M. is designated as counsel for plaintiff in early proceedings.

John Murdock & Co. v. Nathaniel Pope

Debt, on bond £737:1:6½, value of $2,123.59. J.M. for plaintiff.

1796, 1797, 1798. Attachments.

1799, 1800. Continued.

Dec. 19, 1800. Plea, payment.

Apr. 30, 1802. V.j. above amount, payable by $985.51. U.S. Circuit Court, Va., Order Book IV, 156. Circuit Judges Key and Taylor sat on case, acting under Judiciary Act of 1801.

V, U.S. Circuit Court Case Papers, 1802, wherein J.M. is designated as counsel for plaintiff in early proceedings.

John Tabb's Administrators v. Samuel Gist, 1 Brockenbrough 33, 44–61; 6 Call 279.

Bill for an injunction sought by administrators of John Tabb, deceased, to set aside judgments obtained by Gist, a London merchant, against Tabb, an American tabocco merchant, as surviving partner of Richard Booker and Co. and related partnerships formed by that company and for resettlement of accounts. Claim made that Tabb mentally deranged, failed to set up defense that not member of several of the partnerships and instead set up trust for payment; that Gist indebted to Tabb on private account for excess commissions on shipments of tobacco which should be set off. J.M. in providing for accounting by commissioners and further proof stated administrators might present defense of nonmembership in partnerships, that a member of partnership not held as partner in further partnerships created unless consented or acquiesced in their joint operation, that by withdrawal from a partnership not released from partnerships formed by it previously, that further proof be had on disputed agreement as to commission and status of partnership; private claims may be set off against partnership liabilities; interest be calculated on accounts due; special commercial agreements for commissions were terminated by the Revolutionary War; and that both parties submit all letters and letter books.

U.S. Circuit Court, North Carolina

December term, Dec. 30–Jan. 5, 1803.

J.M. and District Judge Henry Potter sat throughout.

DNA, U.S. Circuit Court, N.C., Minute Book, as dated.

LEGAL PRACTICE
(Of Earlier Date)

The following are cases in which J.M. had been engaged prior to going on the Bench.

Court of Appeals of Virginia

Anthony Thornton, trustee of Joseph Robinson v. Gawin Corbin, 3 Call 191.

Motion to set aside order of court dismissing appeal by Thornton from decree High Court of Chancery, May 17, 1789, for redocketing, rule discharged. Call for Thornton.

J. M. had been retained as counsel before appointment as Chief Justice; did not mark himself on docket or advise who would finish; appeal dismissed Apr., 1801, for want of prosecution. Roote had sought counsel for Thornton. Affidavit of J.M. that employed, and would have appeared if present; no fee, but attributed that to being so frequently from home; did not think would be heard so soon; thought he had been marked.

Held, insufficient, Thornton should have applied for new counsel himself after Marshall appointment.

(The Court subsequently reversed itself and heard the case on its merits.)

May 5, 1801. Appeal dismissed, failure defendent to appear. Court of Appeals, Va., Order Book IV, 87.

Nov. 18, 1801. Motion to show cause why not set aside decree. Same, 130.

Apr. 12, 1802. Continued. Same, 134.

Apr. 14, 1802. Heard. Same, 141.

Apr. 17, 1802. Rule discharged. Same, 154.

May 12, 1802. Orders of May 5, 1801, and Apr. 17, 1802, set aside; appeal put on docket; certified to Superior Court of Chancery, Richmond. Same, 197.

Nov. 5, 6, 1802. Heard, continued. Same, 223.

Apr. 26, 27, 1803. Heard. Same, 255.

May 5, 1803. Decree of High Court of Chancery affirmed. Same, 265.

Zachariah Johnson v. John Brown, 3 Call 227.

Appeal from decree High Court of Chancery, May 18, 1799, dismissing bill of appellant for conveyance of land from appellee who held under later entry but senior survey and grant, affirmed.

The Court stated Johnson, a recent assignee of the entry, was purchaser of a state claim; no caveat filed; delayed surveying for forty years; survey failed to follow his entry. J.M. was probably counsel for Johnson in early stages, Randolph herein. Court of Appeals, Va., Order Book IV, 109, 157, 204, 207.

Fees: Apr., 1792, £4:10; Aug., 1793, "Chr," £1. Account Book, 322. 368.

For other fees for matter between same parties, see Mar. 31, 1786, £2:8; Oct. 4, 1788, £2:8. Account Book, 66, 168.

William Allen v. Carter Bassett Harrison et al., 3 Call 251.

Appeal from High Court of Chancery, decrees of Mar. 15, 1800, and Sept. 7, 1794, ruling after-acquired land passed to heirs and not residuary devisee, affirmed. J.M. represented Harrison in early proceedings. Call herein.

Testator devised "James City County land" to son John, who predeceased him; residue to John and son William James. City land in question was purchased by John after making his will which left entire estate to his father, the testator. Heirs claimed land as against William who claimed under residue clause.

Held, after-acquired land not pass by will, following English rule, and not affected by Virginia Act of 1785 where not expressly so stated; will of testator inconsistent with such intent. Court of Appeals, Va., Order Book IV, 202, 203, 209.

Fee: Mar., 1794, £6. Account Book, 382.

David Ross v. Elizabeth and Richard Overton, 3 Call 268.

Appeal from District Court, Richmond, Sept. 12, 1800, j. for appellee on award on arbitration bond for rent and improvements, £6,000 payable by £3,530, affirmed. J.M. was counsel for Overton in early proceedings. Call, Nicholas, and Randolph represented Overton herein.

Lease in 1783 by Overton to Ross of land, mill, and fishing adjoining City of Richmond; lessee made improvements under terms of lease; gristmill destroyed by ice.

Award and judgment for rents and value of mill. Insertion of date of bond left blank in submission held not a variance; liability of lessee for destroyed improvements affirmed; English law noted. Court of Appeals, Va., Order Book IV, 208, 209, 224.

Fees: Oct. 22, 1789, £2:10; June, 1792, £4:16; Mar., 1793, "Overton," £2:8. Account Book, 220, 330, 352.

Mary and William Yerby, infant children of George Yerby v. George Yerby, administrator of George Yerby, and devisees, 3 Call 289.

Appeal from High Court of Chancery, May 17, 1800, dismissing bill by appellants against appellees, affirmed. J.M. involved as counsel in earlier proceedings; Warden for appellant, Wickham for appellee herein.

Children of second marriage claimed revocation of prior will giving all to children of first marriage; evidence intended to amend will, also that declared intention to leave devise or bequest to second marriage children.

Held, implied revocation of will by marriage and children here rebutted by existing children at date of will, and expressed intent not to revoke. Court of Appeals, Va., Order Book IV, 243, 249.

Fee: Mar., 1795, £5:12:6. Account Book, 406.

LAND TRANSACTIONS

Fauquier County, Virginia

Mar. 30 *Mortgage*

John Cooke, Fauquier County to J.M., Jr., Richmond, ninety acres of leased land resided on by mortgagor with slaves, animals, and household furniture; to secure payment of £51:5:10 Va. and 1,063 lbs. tobacco, Dec. 25 next, with interest from Apr. 7, 1792. Payment receipted Nov. 27, 1819, by Jno. Scott, agent for J.M. Recorded Sept. 27, 1802. Fauquier County, Va., Deed Book 15, 227.

Hardy County, Virginia (Now West Virginia)

Mar. 5 *Deed*

J.M., by Charles Magill, attorney in fact, to Morgan and Andrew Burns, forty-two acres, surveyed by John Foley, May 29, 180——. Consideration £12 Va. Recorded May 5, 1802. Hardy County, Va., Deed Book A, 449.

Mar. 12 *Deed*

J.M., by Charles Magill, attorney in fact, to Rudolph Shobe, sixteen acres. Consideration £4 Va. Recorded Apr. 14, 1802. Hardy County, Va., Deed Book 5, 112.

May 5 *Deed*

J.M., by Charles Magill, attorney in fact, to Valentine Powers, reversionary interest, forty-two acres, No. 84, leased Thomas Lord Fairfax to grantee, Aug. 3, 1773. Consideration £20:10:3. Recorded May 5, 1802. Hardy County, Va., Deed Book A, 448.

May 5 *Deed*

J.M., by Charles Magill, attorney in fact, to Frederick Sellers, reversionary interest, ninety-five acres, leased by Denny Martin Fairfax, Dec. 4, 1790. Consideration £24. Recorded May 6, 1802. Hardy County, Va., Deed Book A, 470.

May 5 *Deed*

J.M., by Charles Magill, attorney in fact, to Job Welton, reversionary interest ——— acres, No. 45, leased Thomas Lord Fairfax to Jonathan and Alexander Simpson, Aug. 3, 1773. Consideration £15. Recorded May 7, 1803. Hardy County, Va., Deed Book B, 94.

May 6 *Deed*

J.M., by Charles Magill, attorney in fact, to John Welton, forty-five acres. Consideration £11. Recorded May 6, 1802. Hardy County, Va., Deed Book A, 463.

May 6 *Deed*

J.M., by Charles Magill, attorney in fact, to Andrew Byrns, *et al.*, twenty-five acres, surveyed by John Foley, Oct. 27, 1801. Consideration £6:11:3 Va. Recorded May 7, 1802. Hardy County, Va., Deed Book A, 498.

Aug. 12 *Deed*

J.M., to Charles Magill, attorney in fact, to Job Welton, five acres. Consideration $4.25 current money of the United States. Recorded Sept. 7, 1802. Hardy County, Va., Deed Book A, 513.

Sept. 7 *Deed*

J.M., by Charles Magill, attorney in fact, to Conrad Carr, seventeen acres. Consideration £4:5 Va. Recorded Sept. 7, 1802. Hardy County, Va., Deed Book A, 511.

Sept. 7 *Deed*

J.M., by Charles Magill, attorney in fact, to Conrad Carr, forty-nine acres. Consideration £12:5 Va. Recorded Sept. 7, 1802. Hardy County, Va., Deed Book A, 514.

Sept. 7 *Deed*

Rawleigh Colston, by Charles Magill, his attorney, and Elizabeth, his wife; J.M., by Charles Magill, his attorney, and Mary Willis, his wife; James M. Marshall and Hetty, his wife; James Machir, and Rebecca, his wife, to Isaac and Jacob Vanmeter, 1,550 acres. Resurvey, tracts granted by Thomas Lord Fairfax to Thomas Bryan Martin, Apr. 7, 1748, surveyed by James Greene, commencing at Manor line branch of Boston's Run, 4/5 to Vanmeters, 1/5 to James Machir and Vanmeters.

Consideration £3,000. Recorded Sept. 7, 1802. Hardy County, Va., Deed Book A, 520.

Acknowledgment of signatures of Elizabeth Colston, Mary Willis Marshall, and Hetty Marshall before justices of Berkeley County, Va., Court, Sept. 8, 1802, Sept. 24, 1802. Hardy County, Va., Deed Book B, 105–107.

Sept. 8 *Deed*

J.M., by Charles Magill, attorney in fact, to Philip Yoakam, reversionary interest, 265 acres, No. 47, leased Thomas Lord Fairfax to Yoakam, Aug. 3, 1773. Consideration £90. Recorded Sept. 8, 1802. Hardy County, Va., Deed Book A, 524.

Sept. 8 *Deed*

J.M., by Charles Magill, attorney in fact, to Edward Williams, twenty acres. Consideration £5:11:6 Va. Recorded Jan. 12, 1803. Hardy County, Va., Deed Book 5, 174.

Dec. 13 *Deed*

J.M. and Mary Willis, his wife; James M. Marshall and Hetty, his wife, to Abel Seymour, Hardy County, reciting conveyance of South Branch Manor by Denny Fairfax to J.M., that J.M. with authority of persons interested sold considerable part to tenants holding for life, unsold part property of J.M. and James M. Marshall; that James for self and J.M. contracted to sell to Seymour remaining leased lands, approximately 9,371 acres; unleased land approximately 1,629 acres; and rents arrears £1,112; consideration £2,284 Va.; excepting land contracted to be sold prior to Oct. 1 previous. If deficiency in amount of land or rents seller make good for rents and for land at £13 per hundred acres plus 25 per cent. Rents and proceeds of sales since September last to Seymour.

Consideration payable one-fourth Mar. 1, 1804, and one-fourth in succeeding years. Granting clause of deed covering remaining title of J.M. and James M. Marshall, five shillings. Acknowledged by J.M., above date,

Court of Hustings, Richmond; recorded Apr. 13, 1803, Hardy County, Va., Deed Book 5, 187.

James M. and Hetty Marshall did not sign the above.

1803

DOCUMENTS

Jan. 2
RALEIGH *to Polly Marshall*

Journey not disagreeable; lost $15.00 from waistcoat pocket; Peter discovered failed to bring breeches; no tailor available; returning in four or five days. The John Marshall House; DLC, Marshall Papers, Acc. 2535; WMQ (ser. 2), Vol. III (Apr., 1923), 82–83; Beveridge, *Marshall,* III, 101–102; MHi; Mason, *Polly,* 152–53.

Jan. 14
RICHMOND *to Samuel Hunt*

Acknowledges letter of Dec. 26; was fellow passenger on voyage from Bordeaux. Intends being in Washington in February; felicitations on "event;" General Morris mentioned. MH, Autograph file.

Jan. 28
RICHMOND *Law Suit—Buckingham County Land*

Bill in equity, High Court of Chancery, injunction against John Pendleton selling land held by deed of trust to secure mortgage. J.M. acquired Buckingham County land from Charles Minor Thurston, 1790, part encumbered by mortgage Thurston's grantor to Caron de Beaumarchais, now dead, John A. Chevallie, agent; last payment on purchase 1796. Bill asks order Thurston settle differences caused by Webb being credited by Beaumarchais on debt for house in Washington at time Thurston bought from Webb; title bad and credit removed. Injunction granted. MB, Chamberlain MSS.

Feb. 7, *n.p.* *to James M. Marshall*

Has considered bill, copy of which sent to James by Fitzsimmons; amendments proposed "by our counsel." Agrees "our claim" should be introduced in present suit as proposed, expeditiously. Discretion allowed counsel to adopt ideas, hints J.M. gave. Discusses whether Gouverneur Morris not necessary party; hopes not, but believes so. Whole interest of

Morris in New York property is equity of redemption in 1,500,000 acres; other land undisposed of when deed under which "we" claim executed subject to judgment transferred to Gouverneur Morris before "our lands" contribute. Suggests claim be made in bill; Holland Company should have satisfied judgment equity of redemption in lands to which they have legal title; injunction lies against sale of land conveyed to others to secure debt where held property in own hands sufficient to satisfy. Mason deposition must be taken. CtY, Hay MSS.

Feb. 17
PHILADELPHIA *C. P. Wayne to Bushrod Washington*

Postmasters obtaining subscriptions to *Life of Washington*; allusion to "unfaithful collectors." PPHi, Dreer MSS; DLC, Beveridge Coll. (J.M. erroneously described as addressee.)

Mar. 2
WASHINGTON *to Jonathan Trumbull, Jr.*

On return from long trip into country last fall found Trumbull treatise on report of investigating committee of last session of Congress, valuable work. Always considered report for content and manner most disreputable acts of present administration. CtHi, Jonathan Trumbull, Jr., U.S. Gov't Letters, 75.

Mar. 16
RICHMOND *to Robert Harper, Baltimore*

Concerning case of Robbs and Wood. Listed in Lazare, *Book-Prices*, (1936), 673. Present owner unknown.

Mar. 18
RICHMOND *to George Simpson, Cashier*

Arrangement for drawing salary as Chief Justice through the Bank of the United States. PPHi, Etting Jurists Coll.; DLC, Beveridge Coll.

Mar. 20
PHILADELPHIA *from C. P. Wayne*

Requesting copy of second volume of *Life of Washington* manuscript. PPHi.

Apr. 27
GEORGETOWN Life of Washington

Statement signed by C. P. Wayne denying that Phillips of London purchased manuscript copy of *Life of Washington* to publish; also denying that manuscript destroyed in fire. *Washington Federalist,* Apr. 27, 1803.

July
KENTUCKY *Tax List*

Entry with Auditor for listing taxes of nonresidents, Kentucky; listed as second-rate land by H. Marshall, agent for J.M., 1,000 acres on Clay Lick Creek, 1,000 acres on Lost Creek, a branch of the Ohio. KyHi.

Aug. 12
MOUNT VERNON *Bushrod Washington to C. P. Wayne*

Letter from J.M. concerning time of completing first two volumes of *Life of Washington* (n.f.); visit by Wayne with J.M. proposed. PPHi, Dreer MSS.

Aug. 13
FRIGATE *Constitution* *from Tobias Lear*

Indignant at report circulating that he suppressed part of diary of Washington; traced via Rev. William Kirkland, through another from J.M.; Jefferson gave favor to Kirkland. Hurt sale of *Life of Washington.* Leaving copy through Gen. Lincoln of letter to J.M., Dec. 12, 1800; inventory of papers and letters delivered to J.M. at Washington. Leaving country for some years. DLC, Papers of James Madison, XXVI, 11.

Aug. 15
RICHMOND *to Oliver Wolcott*

Refers to letter from Wolcott Aug. 4; expenses of Col. William Davies in claim of Virginia for expenditures during Revolutionary War. Gratified by Wolcott's transfer to New York. CtHi, Oliver Wolcott Papers, Vol. 53.

Sept. 8
SUPERIOR COURT, HARDY COUNTY, VA. *Law Suit*

J.M. by William Naylor, his attorney, v. Ann Simpkins. Ejectment, ninety-seven acres, part of Swan Pond tract, Hampshire County, lease executed May 10, 1801. Sept. 9, judgment for plaintiff. Superior Court Common Law Book, Hardy County, Va. (now W. Va.) 1803–1807, 35–38. May 7, 1802, service and conditional order on defendant; Sept. 7, 1802, conditional order set aside, defense filed; May, 1803, continued, Sept. 8, 1803, v.j. for plaintiff. Superior Court, Hardy County, Va. (now W. Va.),

Common Law Book, 1797–1803, 414, 454, 484. Same, Record Book 1797–1800, 456–58.

Oct. 7, *n.p.* *to Cashier of Bank of the United States*

Order by J.M. to pay quarter salary to Macmurdo and Fisher. TKL.

Oct. 23
PHILADELPHIA *C. P. Wayne to Bushrod Washington*

Concerning meeting, J.M. to receive copy of *Life of Washington*; effect of delay. PPHi, Dreer MSS.

Nov. 9
PHILADELPHIA *C. P. Wayne to Bushrod Washington*

Delay in receiving copy for *Life of Washington*; dissatisfaction of subscribers. PPHi, Dreer MSS.

Nov. 21
RICHMOND *to Benjamin Lincoln*

Letter from Lear, rumor in Boston suppressed part of Washington diary, attributed to J.M. by Rev. Kirkland. Relates facts: regular diary commenced 1781; June 1, 1791, to Sept., 1794, missing; less than 150 pages; put in pack; Bushrod Washington does not have. Lear transmitted trunk to J.M. in Washington; receipt signed without examining; thanks for copy. Trunk brought to Richmond. Bushrod Washington sent other trunks through Lear; latter in Richmond 1802, examined trunks; took journals; informed lost. J.M. thought incredible, not made public, but mentioned to person from whom Kirkland received; never accused Lear. Copy of letter to Kirkland. MHi, Benjamin Lincoln Papers.

Dec. 16
PHILADELPHIA *C. P. Wayne to Bushrod Washington*

Meeting with Marshall (J.M.'s son); manuscript of first volume of *Life of Washington*; excessive length; J.M.'s name on title page; problem of composition. PPHi, Dreer MSS.

Dec. 23
RICHMOND *to C. P. Wayne*

Title page of *Life of Washington*; objection to name as author in filing copyright; length of Vol. I; schedule for completion and printing of Vol. II and III; contract with Morgan; personal supervision of copying; court duties. Son at Princeton. PPHi, Dreer MSS; DLC, Beveridge Coll.

Dec. 29
RICHMOND *Richmond Academy*

Act of Virginia Legislature establishing The Richmond Academy, J.M. trustee. V, Virginia Acts, Dec., 1803, 28–29, Chap. XXII; Hening, Stat., XVI, 34.

U.S. SUPREME COURT

FEBRUARY TERM. Feb. 7–Mar. 2.

Feb. 7. Paterson alone; adjourned.

Feb. 8–11. J.M., Paterson, Chase, Washington; adjourned, business not prepared.

Feb. 12. Moore added.

Feb. 14. Moore absent.

Feb. 15. Chase absent; adjourned insufficient number.

Feb. 17. Chase back.

Feb. 18–28. Moore back

Mar. 1, 2. Chase absent.

U.S. Supreme Court, Minute Book A, 128–36.

Aug. 1. Chase; all cases continued. Same, 136–37.

Feb. *Rules of Court*

Damages where writ of error to delay, 10 per cent of judgment; 6 per cent per annum where real controversy.

Rule concerning date for delivery of cause to clerk, filing record; procedure by plaintiff where failure to file; assignment of errors. U.S. Supreme Court Clerk's Records. R.G. 267. Autograph. Published in 1 Cranch, flyleaf. Rules and Orders XVI–XVIII.

Joseph Fenwick v. John Stricker and Henry Payson, administrators of George Sears, use of Judah Hays, 1 Cranch 259.

Holding administrator having letters of administration in Maryland may not sue in District of Columbia after separation from Maryland without letters of latter. No opinion of Court. Case notes of J.M. in record file. DNA, U.S. Supreme Court, Case Papers, Case No. 122. R.G. 267.

OPINIONS

William Marbury, Dennis Ramsay, Robert Townsend Hooe, and William Harper v. James Madison, Secretary of State, 1 Cranch 137, 153–181.

Original case. Mandamus to deliver commissions as justices of peace, District of Columbia. Nominations made by President Adams, approved by Senate; commissions signed and sealed, not delivered by Mar. 4, 1801; refused by Madison; also certificate of nomination and approval refused by Secretary of Senate. Rules discharged.

Held, applicant has right to commission, appointment complete, right to office vested and beyond discretion of executive; right enforcible by judicial action; mandamus proper remedy to obtain delivery of commission; Section 2, Article III of the Constitution is exclusive as to original jurisdiction of the Supreme Court and is violated by provision of Judicial Act giving general jurisdiction in original mandamus proceedings; the Supreme Court has power to declare an act of Congress in violation of the Constitution void, as in this case.

Dec. 18, 1801. Motion for rule on James Madison, Secretary of State, to show cause why mandamus not issue, continued.

Aug. 2, 1802. Continued.

Feb. 10, 1803, Witnesses examined.

Feb. 12, 1803. Same.

Feb. 24, 1803. Rule dismissed, court no jurisdiction to issue mandamus in this case.

DNA, U.S. Supreme Court, Case Papers, Original Cases. R.G. 267; DNA, U.S. Supreme Court, Minute Book A, 124, 127, 130, 134. R.G. 267; DNA, U.S. Supreme Court, Docket Book A, 112. R.G. 267.

Opinion announced. *Washington Federalist* (Georgetown) Feb. 25, 1803, 436; published in full, Same, Mar. 14, 16, 1803, 443, 444. Dillon, *Decisions*, 1–41; Cotton, I, 1–43; Marshall, *Writings*, 1–28.

Bailey & Clark v. Robert Young & Co., 1 Cranch 181, 190–94.

Error to Circuit Court, District of Columbia, Alexandria.

Action on case, goods sold and delivered, j. for defendant in error, plaintiff below, affirmed.

Sale of 400 bushels of salt, $283.

Held, seller may recover in action despite endorsement of promissory note by buyer as conditional payment; need not proceed against maker of note first. DNA, U.S. Supreme Court, Case Papers, Case No. 110. R.G. 267.

Wilson v. Lenox & Maitland, 1 Cranch 194, 207–211.

Error to Circuit Court, District of Columbia, Alexandria.

Action of debt against endorser, j. for defendant in error, plaintiff below, reversed.

Bill of exchange £300, made in Alexandria on London drawee payable to Wilson, protested for nonpayment.

Held, Virginia law applicable requires declaration to state costs of protest. DNA, U.S. Supreme Court, Case Papers, Case No. 113, R.G. 267.

R. T. Hooe & Co. v. William Groverman, 1 Cranch 214, 219–39.

Error to Circuit Court, District of Columbia.

Action of covenant on charter party by owner of vessel for demurrage at English port, j. for defendant in error, plaintiff below, reversed.

Charter party provided hirer of entire vessel liable for demurrage caused by his default; owner supplied mariners. Vessel detained at Falmouth, England, as provided; detained for three months on suspicion of being French.

Held, hirer not liable for actions of captain or for demurrage.

Citation signed by J.M. DNA, U.S. Supreme Court, Case Papers, Case No. 114. R.G. 267.

Gabriel Wood v. William Owings and Job Smith, assignees of William Robb, bankrupt, 1 Cranch 239, 250–52.

Error to 4th Circuit Court, Baltimore.

Action in case money had and received, j. for defendants in error, plaintiff below, reversed.

Action by assignees in bankruptcy, July 12, 1800, against creditor receiving payment from trustees under deed of trust of land for creditors; deed executed and delivered May 30, 1800, acknowledged June 14.

Held, deed effective May 30; not an act of bankruptcy or in fraud of creditors under Federal Bankruptcy Act effective June 2, 1800. DNA, U.S. Supreme Court, Case Papers, Case No. 99. R.G. 267.

United States v. Simms, 1 Cranch 252, 256–59.

Error to Circuit Court, District of Columbia, Alexandria.

Indictment for suffering faro game at Alexandria, District of Columbia, contrary to Virginia law, by the United States, dismissed; affirmed. Held, acts of Congress of 1801 assuming government of District of Columbia, declaring Maryland and Virginia law in effect and providing for collection of fines, penalties, and forfeitures in name of the United States require collection thereof by same action as heretofore by the state and not directly by the United States. DNA, U.S. Supreme Court, Case Papers, Case No. 111. R.G. 267.

Thompson v. Jameson, 1 Cranch 282, 290.

Error to Circuit Court, District of Columbia, Alexandria.

Action of debt, j. for defendant in error, plaintiff below, based on decree of court of equity, reversed.

Attachment in state chancery court in nature of foreign attachment by Jameson against Hadfield; decree £860:12:1 with interest from certain day to date of decree, declaring Jameson became surety in open court; declaration was for principal only.

Held, fatal variance. J.M., in addition, stated action of debt not lie because not declared Thompson undertook to pay for Hadfield. DNA, U.S. Supreme Court, Case Papers, Case No. 127. R.G. 267.

Mandeville & Jameson v. Joseph Riddle & Co., 1 Cranch 290, 297–99.

Error to Circuit Court, District of Columbia, Alexandria.

Action in case, money had and received, J. for defendant in error, plaintiff below, reversed.

Action on promissory note executed at Alexandria by Gray, endorsed to Mandeville, by him to McClenachan out of state.

Held, Virginia law applicable; under statute endorsee may sue immediate endorser (not determined if for face value or consideration paid), may not sue remote endorser. (An exhaustive discussion of law, Note A, Appendix of 1 Cranch. No indication that J.M. wrote this.) DNA, U.S. Supreme Court, Case Papers, Case No. 129. R.G. 267.

Hugh Stuart v. John Laird, on behalf of Laird and Robertson, Glasgow, Great Britain, 1 Cranch 299.

Error to U.S. Circuit Court, Virginia. J. for defendant in error, plaintiff below, affirmed. Opinion by Justice Paterson. J.M. "having tried case below, declined giving an opinion" (p. 308).

Action of covenant by British creditor, j. for plaintiff Dec. 17, 1801, before what was then 4th Circuit, eastern district of Virginia. Court held by circuit judges under Judiciary Act of 1801; levy of execution returned breach of forthcoming bond for delivery of slaves executed on.

Dec. 2, 1802. Motion for execution against bondsmen to Circuit Court, now the 5th Circuit under Judiciary Acts of Mar. 8 and Apr. 29, 1802, which returned to Judiciary Act of 1789, Chief Justice of Supreme Court presiding, and abolished court under 1801 act. Defense, act of Mar., 1802, unconstitutional; abolishes court and deprives judge of office despite good behavior; that of April, because Supreme Court limited to appellate jurisdiction and judge given original.

Held, Congress power to transfer cause from one court to another; practice and acquiescence in Supreme Court Justices sitting on circuit "ought not now be disturbed."

Autograph notation that writ of error issue, and signature on writ of error and citation. DNA, U.S. Supreme Court, Case Papers, Case No. 141. R.G. 267.

For consultation with justices on issue of this case, see (herein) letters to William Paterson, Apr. 6, 19, May 3, 1802; to William Cushing, Apr. 19, 1802; from Samuel Chase, Apr. 24, 1802; from Paterson, June 11, 18, 1802; Cushing to Paterson, June 3, 1802.

Dec. 17, 1801. Before U.S. Circuit Court, 4th Circuit, Philip Barton Key, Chief Judge, Judges George Keith Taylor and Charles Magill. Action of covenant, v.j. $1,734.54. U.S. Circuit Court, Va., Order Book IV, 122.

Nov. 23, 1802. Before U.S. Circuit Court, 5th Circuit, J.M. sitting. *Laird v. Hugh Stuart and Charles Z. Carter*, in debt, motion on a forfeited forthcoming bond. Continued. Same, 190.

Nov. 29, 30, Dec. 1, 1802. Continued. Same, 224, 234, 241.

Dec. 2, 1802. Special plea by defendant, demurrer. Same, 247.

Dec. 3, 1802. J. for plaintiff on demurrer, j. $3,581.22 the penalty of bond, payable by $1,640.71. Same, 249.

Thomas Hamilton v. James Russell, 1 Cranch 309, 314–18.

Error to Circuit Court, District of Columbia, Alexandria.

J. for defendant in error, defendant below, affirmed.

Action of trespass, levy by Russell on personal property of Robert Hamilton claimed by Thomas under recorded bill of sale; property remained in possession of Robert.

Held, bill of sale fraudulent against creditors where possession allowed in sellers hands. DNA, U.S. Supreme Court, Case Papers, Case No. 132. R.G. 267.

Hepburn & Dundas v. Colin, 1 Cranch 321, 329–32.

Error to Circuit Court, District of Columbia. J. for defendant in error, defendant below, affirmed.

Action of debt on agreement to arbitrate accounts and creditor accept rights of debtor in defaulted sale of 6,000 acres Ohio land on basis of $21,112 on award. Debtor suing for excess of this amount over award, tendered deed of assignment on condition release first be given. Held, condition beyond terms of agreement tender could be refused. DNA, U.S. Supreme Court, Case Papers, Case No. 130. R.G. 267.

Charles Abercrombie v. Dupuis, 1 Cranch 343.

Error to Circuit Court, Georgia. J. for defendant in error, plaintiff below, reversed.

Petition alleged plaintiff resident of Kentucky, defendant of Georgia.

Held, no jurisdiction, must allege citizens of different states, following *Brigham v. Cabot,* 3 Dallas 382. J.M. stated did not know his opinion if a new question. DNA, U.S. Supreme Court, Case Papers, Case No. 134. R.G. 267.

Joseph Hodgson v. Samuel Dexter, 1 Cranch 345, 363–65.

Writ of error to U.S. Circuit Court, District of Columbia, Washington. J. for defendant in error, defendant below, affirmed.

Action of covenant on lease. Dexter, Secretary of War, under order of President, May 15, 1800, to move executive offices Philadelphia to Washington, leased house on Pennsylvania Avenue, eight months, $400, as quarters for War Department, the lease executed to him and successors. Building burned Nov. 8, 1800; action for failure to reconstruct against Dexter personally.

Held, face of agreement shows intended as public contrac; Dexter not personally liable. DNA, U.S. Supreme Court, Case Papers, Case No. 137. R.G. 267.

Lloyd v. Alexander, 1 Cranch 365, 366.

Writ of error to U.S. Circuit Court, District of Columbia, Alexandria.

Writ quashed for failure to be accompanied by citation on defendant. DNA, U.S. Supreme Court, Case Papers, Case No. 125; R.G. 267.

U.S. CIRCUIT COURT, VIRGINIA

May term. May 23–June 7.

May 23. J.M. alone.

May 24–June 3. J.M. and District Judge Cyrus Griffin.

June 4–7. J.M. alone.

U.S. Circuit Court, Va., Order Book IV, 273–332.

June 4 Bill of review granted in *Thomas Blaine v. The Ship Charles Carter, Donald & Burton and Robert Burton,* j. of U.S. Circuit Court, Dec. 9, 1799, dismissing libel by Blaine, upon bottomry bonds claiming against executor's creditors, after allowing ship to make several voyages without asserting lien. Affirmed in U.S. Supreme Court, *Same v. Same,* 4 Cranch 328, (Mar. 8, 1808) opinion by Justice Chase. J.M. gave no opinion "having decided case in Circuit Court" (note 1, p. 331). DNA, U.S. Supreme Court, Docket Book A, 189. R.G. 267. U.S. Circuit Court, Va., Order Book IV, 255, 325.

November term. Nov. 22–Dec. 13.

Nov. 22–24. J.M. alone.

Nov. 25–Dec. 3. J.M. and District Judge Cyrus Griffin.

Dec. 5–13. J.M. alone.

U.S. Circuit Court, Va., Order Book IV, 333–420.

Dec. 1, 1803 J.M. absented self from hearing of *James Markham Marshall v. Peter Baker,* action on case, plaintiff not appearing, nonsuited. U.S. Circuit Court, Va., Order Book IV, 372.

William Wilson v. Peter Light.

Nov. 29, 1794. Case; plea general issue; depositions. J.M. for defendant. U.S. Circuit Court, Va., Order Book I, 421.

May 23, 1796. Continued. Same, II, 113.

May 26, 1797. Abated by death of plaintiff. Same, 219.

The same case was revived or a related case was later filed, 1798. Action for $10,000 money advanced.

June 5, 1799. Depositions. U.S. Circuit Court, Va., Order Book II, 257.

May 29, 1800. Continued. Same, 382.

Dec. 1, 1803. *Nancy Wilson, executrix, and Andrew Bagg and James Bryson, executors of William Wilson v. Peter Light* was tried with J.M. as judge. V.j. for defendant. Same, IV, 373.

Same, Record Book, Index, Civil, Nov. T, 1803.

V, U.S. Circuit Court, Va., Case Papers, containing notation on affidavit, "Jno. Marshall, Esq."

Fees: Nov., 1792, £2:10; Nov., 1794, £7 (with an additional case). Account Book, 342, 400.

George Cabell v. Frederick Avery and Hezekiah L. Wright.

Autograph notation allowing injunction against j. of court in favor of Avery and against Cabell.

V, U.S. Circuit Court Case Papers (filed with 1805 papers).

Dec. 5, 1803. Dissolved. U.S. Circuit Court, Va., Order Book IV, 390.

Opinions

Thomas Blane v. William Drummond, 1 Brockenbrough 62, 64–71.

Action of debt on a bond brought in name of Blane, the obligee; defense that Blane a British subject took bankruptcy under English law whereby all rights vested in assignees who have exclusive right to sue; reply that British consul of Norfolk authorized by assignees to bring action in Blane's name.

On demurrer, held under Virginia law bonds assignable only by act of party, not be operation of foreign law; that right to personal property and equitable rights governed by English bankruptcy law, right of action governed by law of forum, no extraterritorial operation intended as to right of action. Demurrer overruled, j. for plaintiff.

Owen v. Adams, surviving partner of Hunt and Adams, 1 Brockenbrough 72, 72–76.

Action by London merchant on an account commencing 1784. Copy of account from books submitted, kept by clerk since dead; sworn as conforming to original entries but no evidence as to handwriting of original. Collateral evidence of account submitted in letter of defendant admitting a balance due in general terms.

Held, following *Blackstone's Commentaries* that books of accounts not of selves admissible evidence; used to refresh memory of entry maker; if latter dead, handwriting proved, then admissible. Also necessary to prove books original books of entry.

J. reversed and commission for depositions in Great Britain.

U.S. CIRCUIT COURT, NORTH CAROLINA

June term. June 15–21.

December term. Dec. 29–June 3, 1804.

J.M. and District Judge Potter sat throughout.

DNA, U.S. Circuit Court, N.C., Minute Book, as dated.

Opinions

Gibson et al. v. Williams, 2 Haywood 281. Brunner's Coll. Cas. 19.

Scire facias to subject defendant heir to payment of j. debt recovered against executor of ancestor. Plea, nothing by devise; as to land descended, mortgaged and paid to creditors, also payments to value of land. Later, sold equity of redemption, question value above debts paid for ancestor.

Held, *per curiam,* by payment of debts entitled to land descended to amount such payments worth; as to part of land charged not value at time of descent to heir but value time sold; heir not liable for interest on balance.

June 16, 1803. V.j., value of real estate subject to claim $707.33⅓. DNA, U.S. Circuit Court, N.C., Minute Book, above date.

Teasdale v. Jordan, administrator of Branton, 2 Haywood 281, Brunner's Coll. Cas. 19.

Administrator permitted to amend answer by adding plea, where judgments taken against him to amount of assets in hands since answered. Opinion by J.M., Potter assenting.

Dec. 31, 1803. V.j. for plaintiff $2,201.68; that defendant fully administered. DNA, U.S. Circuit Court, N.C., Minute Book, above date.

Hardy Sanders v. John Hamilton, 2 Haywood 226, 282, Brunner's Coll. Cas. 20.

Hamilton sold slave to Sanders, latter sued by third person, Hamilton agreed to make good damages. Recovery had against Sanders, who sued Hamilton.

Held, damages value of slave at time of recovery, not present time; record of recovery evidence of eviction and amount of damages.

Dec. 31, 1802. V.j. $2,000. DNA, U.S. Circuit Court, N.C., Minute Book, above date.

June 4, 1803. New trial granted. Same.

Jan. 1, 1805. V.j. $1805.44. Same.

Wilkings v. Murphey, administrator, 2 Haywood 282, Brunner's Coll. Cas. 21.

Action on obligation of intestate, plea statute of limitations, replication that intestate assumed within three years. Evidence that administrator assumed within three years, testator dead ten years.

Held, doubtful if admission of administrator can take debt out of statute of limitations; plea should have been that administrator not testator, admitted; error to admit evidence. Reversed with leave to add count.

Murray and Monford v. Jonathan and Daniel Marsh, 2 Haywood 290, Brunner's Coll. Cas. 22.

Action by endorsee on note.

Held, endorser to plaintiff may be witness for him where endorsed before bankruptcy; record of proceedings of bankruptcy not require certificate of presiding judge, as required under federal statute in case of state judgments; attestation of clerk of District Court sufficient; if objection to witness and proof thereon, counterproof may not be made by witness; must be outside testimony; deposition not showing parties in caption or body defective; where plaintiff pressed for trial and nonsuited for unavailability of evidence, may not allege surprise to set aside nonsuit. Order. DNA, U.S. Circuit Court, N.C., Minute Book, Jan. 2, 1803.

Hamilton v. Jones et al., 2 Haywood 291, Brunner's Coll. Cas. 24.

Scire facias issued against heirs and devisees of deceased to subject land descended to judgment against executor. Latter had pleaded assets fully administered, and finding in his favor. Before *scire facias* known to him, Arrington purchased from one of the defendant heirs who refused to plead personal assets in hands of executor to satisfy judgment.

Held, Arrington permitted to make plea.

Dec. 31, 1803. New trial granted. DNA, U.S. Circuit Court, N.C., Minute Book, above date.

June 18, 1804. V. j., assets in hands of executor sufficient to satisfy. Same.

Hamilton v. Sims, 2 Haywood 291, Brunner's Coll. Cas. 24.

Action against heir to subject assets received to bond obligation of ancestor.

Plea, "nothing by descent or devise." Advised by Court if found against him would be judgment "*de bonis propriis*" against heir for whole debt regardless of finding of value of assets received; plea withdrawn and land devolved in remainder set forth in new plea. Per curiam.

June 18, 1804. Juror withdrawn in case. DNA, U.S. Circuit Court, N.C., Minute Book, above date.

Jan. 3, 1805. Confessed j., $350. Same.

Jones and wife v. Walker et al., 2 Haywood 291, Brunner's Coll. Cas. 25.

Held *per curiam,* appeal in admiralty case takes matter out of inferior court, but latter holding goods may sell to preserve them; that where uncertainty as to order of sale, court record kept on slips of paper, proof allowed of order; purchaser of property not affected by later decree in appellate court as to rights between libelant and claimant.

Robert Ogden, Jr., administrator of Samuel Cornell v. Richard Blackledge, executor of Robert Salter. Not reported.

Action against executor of estate on bond, 1775; filed 1790. Plea, North Carolina act of 1715 limiting action to seven years from death; reply, act repealed by act of 1789 repealing other laws within purview of act, despite act of 1799 declaring act of 1715 in force. Demurrer.

On division of opinion, Justice Potter and J.M., question submitted to U.S. Supreme Court on certificate of division, the first case under the act authorizing such practice. DNA, U.S. Circuit Court, N.C., Minute Book, Jan. 5, 1803.

The Supreme Court declared the act of 1715 repealed, and that statute of limitations suspended as to British subjects until Treaty of Peace of 1794. *Same v. Same,* 2 Cranch 272 (1804). J.M. did not sit in cause "having formed a decided opinion on the principal question while his interest was concerned." Same, note 2.

Mar. 6, 1804. Certificate of opinion. DNA, U.S. Supreme Court, Docket Book A, 155. Case No. 140. R.G. 267.

June 18, 1804. In Circuit Court, verdict and j. for plaintiff $250, defendant fully administered, act of 1789 no bar, plea of act of 1715 and Treaty of 1783 overruled. DNA, U.S. Circuit Court, N.C., above date.

June 17, 1805. Finding, no payments; that sufficient real estate descended to heirs to satisfy j. Same.

For earlier ruling of Circuit Court holding 1715 act repealed and revival act of 1799 unconstitutional, see *Robert Ogden v. D. Witherspoon.* DNA, U.S. Circuit Court, N.C., June 4, 1800.

LEGAL PRACTICE
(Of Earlier Date)

U.S. Circuit Court, Virginia

William Wilson v. Peter Light.

(See herein 1803, U.S. Circuit Court, Va.)

Court of Appeals of Virginia

Edmund Cowles et al. v. William Browne, executor of John Cooper, Thomas Cowles, and William Walker, 4 Call 477.

Appeal from High Court of Chancery, decree of May 12, 1800, dismissing bill of legatees under power of appointment, alleging unequal and improper exercise thereof, affirmed. J.M. was counsel for legatees in earlier proceedings; Call their counsel herein.

Will of wife holding slaves as separate property, Thomas Cowles trustee, left them to husband for life, requesting at decease to give "in such manner and proportion as he shall think proper" to various nephews, children of two brothers. During his lifetime arranged conveyance by Brown to one legatee of land of lesser value than four slaves received (legatee admittedly still having recourse against Brown); sold some slaves along with own and gave a legatee one of bonds for purchase price; gave another legatee four slaves and later exchanged for eight and money. In his will he made unequal distribution, stating some legatees would free slave, to which objected.

Held, no showing of fraud, nor requirement for equal distribution, disapproving of English practice.

Fee: June, 1795. £5. Account Book, 416.

LAND TRANSACTIONS

Fauquier County, Virginia

Nov. 12 *Land Agreement*

Agreement, J.M., Richmond, by Charles Marshall, his agent, with Joseph Chilton, permitting building of merchant mill and race on land formerly leased by J.M. to Thomas Smith, twenty acres, Fauquier County, consent of Smith, option to take at end of lease at appraisal. On above date assigned Chilton to Robert Hereford; agreed to by J.M. with promise to give new lease. Recorded Apr. 27, 1804. Fauquier County, Va., Deed Book 15, 586–87.

Hardy County, Virginia
(Now West Virginia)

Mar. 11 *Deed*

J.M., by Charles Magill, attorney in fact, to William Cunningham, reversionary interest, three tracts: 133 acres, No. 33, east side South Branch of Potomac, leased Thomas Lord Fairfax to Casper Bogart, Aug. 3, 1773; 154 acres, No. 54, west side South Branch of Potomac, leased same to Michael Harness, same date; 53 acres, leased Denny Martin Fairfax to Harness, May 28, 1791. Consideration £74. Recorded May 9, 1803. Hardy County, Va., Deed Book B, 97.

Mar. 11 *Deed*

J.M., by Charles Magill, attorney in fact, to William Cunningham, eleven acres. Consideration £2:15. Recorded May 9, 1803. Hardy County, Va., Deed Book B, 100.

Mar. 11 *Deed*

J.M., by Charles Magill, attorney in fact, to Joseph Inskeep, sixty acres and seventy acres. Consideration £34 Va. Recorded May 9, 1803. Hardy County, Va., Deed Book B, 107.

Mar. 17 *Deed*

J.M., by Charles Magill, attorney in fact, to Peter Higgins, reversionary interest, two tracts: 368 acres, leased Denny Martin Fairfax to John Higgins, Nov. 19, 1791; 480 acres, leased same to same, June 10, 1790. Consideration £212. Recorded May 7, 1804. Hardy County, Va., Deed Book B, 285.

May 9 *Deed*

J.M., by Charles Magill, attorney in fact, to Joseph Obannon, reversionary interest, 137 acres, No. 37, leased Thomas Lord Fairfax to Henry Marsh, Aug. 3, 1773. Consideration £34. Recorded May 9, 1803. Hardy County, Va., Deed Book B, 103.

May 9 *Deed*

J.M., by Charles Magill, attorney in fact, to Moses Welton, reversionary interest, 105 acres, No. 65, leased Thomas Lord Fairfax to Jonathan Simpson, Aug. 3, 1773. Consideration £26:5. Recorded May 9, 1803. Hardy County, Va., Deed Book B, 110.

May 9 *Deed*

J.M., by Charles Magill, attorney in fact, to Strother McNeill, reversionary interest, 130 acres, No. 16, leased Thomas Lord Fairfax to Andrew Young, Aug. 3, 1773; also tract on east side South Branch of Potomac, leased Denny Martin Fairfax to John Pancake, Dec. 4, 1790. Consideration £49:10. Recorded May 10, 1803. Hardy County, Va., Deed Book B, 128.

Aug. 12 *Deed*

J.M., by Charles Magill, atorney in fact, to Alexander Simpson, reversionary interest, ninety-seven acres, No. 65, leased Thomas Lord Fairfax to same, Aug. 3, 1773. Consideration £10. Recorded Sept. 7, 1803. Hardy County, Va., Deed Book B, 215.

Randolph County, Virginia
(Now West Virginia)

Sept. 8 *to W. R. Bernard*

J.M. agreeing to sell his land on Randolph's Creek, subject to agreement with tenants. Listed in Lazare *Book-Prices* (1937), 596. Present owner unknown.

1804

DOCUMENTS

Jan. 9
Alexandria *Promissory Note*

To Charles Simms, $800, fifty-seven days. DLC, Papers of Charles Simms; V, 35216.

Jan. 10
RICHMOND *to C. P. Wayne*

Acknowledging letter of Jan. 2. Omission of certain footnotes approved; objection to use of name as author of *Life of Washington*; will abide by decision on point by Bushrod Washington and Wayne; if used, judicial title to be omitted. Corrections in punctuation, paragraphs, and spelling authorized. Second volume, contents, copy after February term of Supreme Court. PPHi, Dreer MSS; DLC, Beveridge Coll.

Jan. 10
RICHMOND *to C. P. Wayne*

Sheets of second volume of *Life of Washington* received. Leaving for North Carolina. Copy of third volume to Bushrod Washington. PPHi, Dreer MSS; DLC, Beveridge Coll.

Jan. 10
RICHMOND *to Bushrod Washington*

Urging omission of name as author of *Life of Washington*; if used, judicial title not annexed (n.f.). Referred to in J.M. to C. P. Wayne, same date (herein).

Jan. 22
RICHMOND *to C. P. Wayne*

Letter of Jan. 10 received. Method of citing references in *Life of Washington*; omission of notes, authorized to shorten; need for plates and cuts, Gordon's *History* a source. PPHi, Dreer MSS; DLC, Beveridge Coll.

Jan. 23
RICHMOND *to Samuel Chase*

Letter of Jan. 13 acknowledged. J.M. consulting brother William and Wickham concerning rejection of Taylor testimony in Callender case (James T. Callender, publisher of an anti-Federalist newspaper, convicted in Richmond May, 1800, for violation of the Alien and Sedition Act in federal Circuit Court, Justice Chase presiding. See Wharton, *State Trials*, 688–718); coming to Washington in February; bringing list of jurors, writ in Callender arrest. Opinion that no ground for impeachment; doctrine of attaint, writ of error available; reversal of judicial action by legislature suggested as preferable to removal of judge. Has not written to Moore; setting out for Washington; Nelson dead. PPHi, Etting Jurists Coll.; DLC, Beveridge Coll.; Beveridge, *Marshall*, III, following 176.

(Edward S. Corwin comments that this letter is misdated and should be Jan. 23, 1805. See MVHR, Vol. VI [Mar., 1920], 381.)

(For testimony of J.M. as to above in Chase impeachment trial, see herein Mar. 2, 1804.)

Jan. 24
BOSTON *Academy of Arts and Sciences*

J.M. elected Fellow of the Academy of Arts and Sciences. *Book of Nominations of the Academy, 1802–1818.*

Feb. 2
RICHMOND *to James M. Marshall*

Received letter from Morris concerning testimony at Indian Queen; written lawyers to press issue. Inquires of payment to addressee of $500 by Hopkins Mar., 1802. Bill for state bank pending, objections. Burr to be dropped by Democrats. Outlines basis of loan by Morris of 250,000 guilders, based on security of U.S. bonds and stock of Pennsylvania Land Company. DLC, Beveridge Coll. (incomplete, mutilated).

Feb. 7
WASHINGTON *to C. P. Wayne*

Transmitting assignment of copyright to *Life of Washington.* Title to introduction; spelling, capitals, etc., contents, dates, arrangement of material; time for copy of second volume; copiers; correction of copy. B. Washington and remittance of Morgan money. PPHi, Dreer MSS; Beveridge Coll.

Mar. 2
WASHINGTON *Chase Impeachment Trial*

Deposition by J.M. sworn before John Randolph, chairman of committee of inquiry into conduct of Samuel Chase and Richard Peters; when first heard of Jonathan Snowden statement to chairman regarding conversation between Judges Chase and Washington in his presence concerning trial of James Thomson Callender, has no recollection; since has indistinct recollection, asserts not serious, would have different opinion of both if such motives of judicial conduct had been attributed to one and acknowledged by other without reproach. *The Virginia Argus,* Apr. 14, 1804, 1.

Mar. 25
RICHMOND *to Bushrod Washington*

Difficulty with copyists; awaiting stage to send to Philadelphia. On return to Philadelphia from Jersey, asks attentive reading and correcting; Morgan. Changes in conclusion of first volume and start of second. PPHi, Dreer MSS.

Mar. 27
RICHMOND *to C. P. Wayne*

Two copies of second volume of *Life of Washington* by stage to B. Washington, Philadelphia, by Davidson; copyists incorrect; Hardy's Tavern. Change in text by Washington. PPHi, Dreer MSS.

Mar. 28
RICHMOND *to Bushrod Washington*

Copy sent to Philadelphia by Davidson. Reading, correction in text; maps, alterations, Gordon's *History*, maps of Long Island, New Jersey, Philadelphia, Allentown, Princeton; third volume, ready in May. PPHi, Dreer MSS; DLC, Beveridge Coll.

Apr. 1
RICHMOND *to James M. Marshall*

Acknowledges letter of Mar. 15 concerning Leymon payment and settling accounts with Colston. Going to North Carolina early in June. Opinion in Winchester case indicates compromise did not settle question of title. Judge Tucker; Clarksons not filed bill; fears it and Beverly case. *(Beverly v. Martin,* see herein 1807, U.S. Circuit Court, Va.) Verdict in Staunton case involving purchase of $60,000 note for Alexander; conveyance of stock; appeal if verdict against Morris includes J.M. and James. Virginia bank law giving discretion to legislature disapproved by J.M., not trust a dollar to it. News of England. Received articles of impeachment against Judge Chase; alarming to friends of pure and independent judiciary, if such exist. DLC, Beveridge Coll.

Apr. 29
RICHMOND *to Bushrod Washington*

Errors in spelling (in *Life of Washington)*; son assist correcting; paging and length of volumes; number of subscriptions. PPHi, Dreer MSS; DLC, Beveridge Coll.

Apr.
RICHMOND *to Bushrod Washington*

Letter acknowledged with notes of alterations in *Life of Washington,* correction of repetition of Braddock's defeat; problems of length and division of volumes. Short's corrections; requests severe correcting; copyists; expurging criticism of author of the "Farmer's" letters; corrections as to Washington and Braddock expedition. PPHi, Dreer MSS; DLC, Beveridge Coll.

May 6
RICHMOND *to Benjamin Lincoln*

Acknowledges letter of Apr. 25; denies implied Lear secreted journal of Gen. Washington, also that gave receipt for papers in a trunk. MHi, Norcross MSS.

May 17
RICHMOND *to C. P. Wayne*

Correction in quotation from Burke; corrections in spelling; time for third volume (*Life of Washington*). PPHi, Dreer MSS; DLC, Beveridge Coll.

May 27 *from John Page, Governor of Virginia,*
RICHMOND *to J.M. as Chief Justice*

Requesting order for safe custody of Thomas Logwood. V, Exec. Letter Books 1803–1807, 85.

May 30
RICHMOND *Confinement of Prisoner*

Order of Council of State of Virginia establishing guard at prison, confinement of Thomas Logwood; requesting general government to take charge; conversation of Governor with J.M., doubts power of court. V, Exec. Papers, Box 1804, May–July, File May.

May 30
RICHMOND *from Gov. Page*

Requesting opinion in writing of doubts as to power of court to direct guards in Logwood confinement. V, Exec. Letter Books 1803–1807, 84.

May 31
RICHMOND *to Gov. Page*

No power to order guard for security of Logwood, convicted of felony in federal court, rescue threatened; suggests applying to the Executive of the United States. CVSP, IX, 399.

June 1
RICHMOND *to C. P. Wayne*

Official business delayed corrections in sheet of first volume (*Life of Washington*); proof sheets of second volume. Leaving on 12th. Errors of printing in printed work; congratulations on printing. PPHi, Dreer MSS; DLC, Beveridge Coll.

June 6
RICHMOND *to C. P. Wayne*

Acknowledging letter of May 27. Maps to appear separately; pleased with first volume (*Life of Washington*). PPHi, Dreer MSS, DLC, Beveridge Coll.

Editions of *The Life of George Washington*:

Philadelphia, C. P. Wayne, 1804–1807. 5 vols. Atlas.

Same, 1805–1807.

Second edition, revised and corrected by author. Philadelphia, J. Crissy, 1832. 2 vols.

Atlas to above. Philadelphia, J. Crissy, 1832.

Second edition and Atlas. Same, 1833.

Same, 1839. 2 vols.

Same, Philadelphia, J. Crissy and Thomas Cowperthwait & Co., 1840. 2 vols.

Same, Philadelphia, E. C. Markley & Son, 1848, 2 vols.

Same, Philadelphia, Crissy and Markley, and Thomas Cowperthwait & Co., 1850. 2 vols.

Same, Fredericksburg, Va., The Citizens' Guild of Washington's Boyhood Home, 1926. 5 vols.

Same, New York, Wise, 1925. 5 vols.

Same, New York, Walton Book Co., 1930. 2 vols.

John Marshall, *History of the Colonies planted by the English on the Continent of North America, from their settlement, to the commencement of that War which terminated in their independence*. Philadelphia, A. Small, 1824. (First volume of above).

The Life of Washington, written for the use of schools, Philadelphia, James Crissy, 1838. Numerous imprints and reprints thereof.

London, R. Phillips, 1804–1807. 5 vols. (British).

Paris, Dentu, 1807. 5 vols. and Atlas (French).

Translation of original Vols. II–V by J. Werninck. Haarlem, A. Loosjes, 1805–1809. 10 vols. and Atlas (Dutch).

Hamburg, Campe, 1805–1806. 4 vols. (German).

List of subscribers to *The Life of Washington*, first edition, 1804. ScU, South Caroliniana Libr.

n.d., n.p. *Notes by J.M.*

Three fragments, notes and instructions to copyist to copy certain letters and documents (from George Washington papers for use in writing *Life of Washington*) period May, 1757, Col. Stanwix; earlier period, Sir John St. Clair, Gov. Fauquier, Gen. Forbes, Lord Fairfax, Gouverneur Morris, letter to Gov. Dinwiddie, Sept. 8, 1756, mentioned. DLC, John Marshall Papers.

n.d., n.p. *Notes by J.M.*

Autograph notes for corrections and insertions, insertion of letters, refers to Col. Washington's activities against French and Indians. Listed in Argosy Book Stores, Inc., Catalogue 450, 19. Present owner unknown. (Probably same as above.)

n.d., n.p. *Notes by J.M.*

Notes on U.S. history, on back of invitation by John Breckenridge to J.M. and Thomas Marshall for dinner, four o'clock, Thursday. DLC, John Marshall Papers, Var. Accessions.

Text of Vol. V, by copyist. PPHi.

Four pages of text, autographic. MdHi, Kennedy MSS.

Four pages of text, autographic, on French relations, Congress. MH, Houghton Libr.

Autograph notes taken on Washington Letter Books, period 1792–93. Three pages. DLC, Beveridge Coll.

Notes on English and French colonies in America, in French. VW.

June 10
RICHMOND *to C. P. Wayne*

Setting out for North Carolina, taking sheets of second volume (*Life of Washington*) which received; returning about 25th, hoping further sheets. Delivered third volume to Washington, two copies to be delivered to Wayne in Philadelphia. PPHi, Dreer MSS; DLC, Beveridge Coll.

June 27
RICHMOND *to C. P. Wayne*

Returned from North Carolina; sent printed sheets, second volume

(*Life of Washington*); punctuation errors, additions concerning combination against Washington; unwilling allusion made to author of papers. PPHi, Dreer MSS; DLC, Beveridge Coll.

June 27
RICHMOND *to C. P. Wayne*

Enclosure of letters of George Washington to Patrick Henry dated Mar. 27 and 28, 1778, concerning anonymous letter (written by Benjamin Rush) forwarded by Henry, and involving the Gates and Conway faction, for inclusion in note in third volume of *Life of Washington*. PPHi, Dreer MSS.

July 4
PHILADELPHIA *C. P. Wayne to Bushrod Washington*

Suggestions for making changes in text concerning Conway cabal against Washington requested by J.M.; Wayne instructions not to open box or see text; suggests Charles Chauncey open and reseal. Difficulties with Weems; requests for change of contract; 5,000 subscribers; $2,000 sent. PPHi, Dreer MSS.

July 5–8
RICHMOND *to C. P. Wayne*

Returning sheets with corrections; inspection of proof sheets; misapprehension as to correcting errata. Omission of notes third chapter. Objects to second edition while fourth volume pending; too hurried. Third volume being forwarded by Bushrod Washington; limited printing requested. Leaving on 20th; spending rest of summer in mountains for health, taking first volume.

July 8. Wishes to take first and second volumes to mountains for correction. PPHi, Dreer MSS; DLC, Beveridge Coll.

July 20
RICHMOND *to C. P. Wayne*

Letter acknowledged with sheets of second volume; notes second edition of first volume postponed. Will read first volume for corrections and forward. Leaving for upper country, to Front Royal, Frederick County, Va. Errors in manuscript not composition. Takes *Gazette of the United States*; acknowledges favorable comment of *Political and Commercial Register* and an unnamed paper. Reluctance in agreeing to be named as author mentioned; requests unfavorable comments to be forwarded to assist in correction. PPHi, Dreer MSS; DLC, Beveridge Coll.

July 20
PHILADELPHIA *from C. P. Wayne*

Concerning insertion of material on Conway cabal and filling blanks. PPHi, Dreer MSS.

Aug. 4
RICHMOND Life of Washington

Favorable review of first volume, reprinted from *Philadelphia Register. The Virginia Argus,* Aug. 4, 3; also Sept. 1, 1804, 3.

Aug. 10
FRONT ROYAL, VIRGINIA *to C. P. Wayne*

Acquainted with Maj. Jackson. Use of word "enemy" in *Life of Washington* to be eliminated; mystified by errors in first volume; hopes printing limited. Leaving for the Allegheny, returning last of month. Several rereadings necessary. James Marshall's Russian leather-bound copy; copy of second edition by son to Whig Society in Princeton. PPHi, Dreer MSS; DLC, Beveridge Coll.

Aug. [between 10 and 20] *to C. P. Wayne*

Answered by Wayne to J.M. Aug. 20, 1804, following (n.f.).

Aug. 20
PHILADELPHIA *from C. P. Wayne*

Letter with insertion acknowledged; filling in blanks in copy of third volume; use of word "enemy". Magazine of Philadelphia and newspaper of New York with adverse criticism forwarded. Warns against disclosing revised edition. Whig Society and James Marshall books delivered. Advises no hurry in revision; present prospects no republication. Four volume desired by September. Printing 7,200 or 7,300 including 1,000 for sale; first volume printed in London in May. Costs increased by excessive length of volumes; maps costly. Requests few lines for proposal of second edition at later date. PPHi, Dreer MSS; DLC, Beveridge Coll.

(J.M. worked on the revision for a second edition for many years. See Bushrod Washington to C. P. Wayne, Nov. 26, 1816 [herein]. Arrangements were made for its publication in 1821. See J.M. to Bushrod Washington, Dec. 27, 1821 [herein]. The second edition appeared in 1832. See J.M. to Cary and Lea, May 5, 1832 [herein.])

Sept. 3
FRONT ROYAL, VIRGINIA *to C. P. Wayne*

Acknowledges letter of Oct. 20, returned from the Allegheny. Errors in plan of *Life of Washington*, introductory volume omitted; regrets carelessness of work, pressure of constant application; want of interest in first volume; drop republication of first volume. Shortening of third volume; fourth volume delayed, copiers quit, returning to Richmond in October, ready in February. Need for closer examination; postponement of second edition. PPHi, Dreer MSS; DLC, Beveridge Coll.

Sept. 5
PHILADELPHIA *from Benjamin Rush*

Addressed to Front Royal, Virginia, letter of few days prior sent to Washington. Requests erasure from George Washington letter to P. Henry of Apr. 27, 1778, reflecting on him; heard of intended use in Vol. III of *Life of Washington*. Rush acknowledges authorship of anonymous letter to Henry, Jan. 12, 1778. PPL.

Sept. 8
FRONT ROYAL *to C. P. Wayne*

Letter of Aug. 22 received. Content with diminution of third volume by Wayne; desires both copies of tenth chapter from Judge Washington; length of work; examination of second volume, discusses third and fourth. Not discuss republishing, first edition should be in hands of public; wishes number of copies had not exceeded subscribers. PPHi, Dreer MSS; DLC, John Marshall Papers.

Oct. 4
RICHMOND *to Noah Webster*

Acknowledging leter of Aug. 21; just returned from tour in mountain country for health of family. Agrees to give attention to suggested corrections in J.M.'s *Life of Washington*. Procuring Webster's book concerning introduction of representation in Massachusetts. Pierpont Morgan Libr., N.Y.; Emily Ellsworth Ford Skeel, *Notes on the Life of Noah Webster* (New York Priv. Print., 1912), I, 542–43.

Oct. 4
RICHMOND *to C. P. Wayne*

Acknowledges letter of Sept. 16 with sheets of second volume miscarried. Just returned to Richmond. Sending daily corrected sheets of first and second volumes; anxious for second edition; regrets alteration of type made necessary. Obliged to Webster for correction of fact. Omission of part of Washington letter requested by Dr. Rush approved. Lost copiers; seeking new ones. PPHi, Dreer MSS; DLC, Beveridge Coll.

Oct. 10
RICHMOND *Life of Washington*

Favorable review of second volume, just appearing. *The Virginia Argus*, Oct. 10, 2.

Oct. 30
RICHMOND *to C. P. Wayne*

Acknowledging letter of Oct. 9, printed sheets of Vol. III, *Life of Washington*, corrections of Vol. I; use of information in anonymous letter (Benjamin Rush, the author) concerning battle of Trenton and date of battle of Long Island. PPHi, Dreer MSS; DLC, Beveridge Coll.

Nov. 2
RICHMOND *to Gen. John Eager Howard*

Inquires concerning battles of Cowpens, Guilford, Hobkirk's Hill, Camden; General Greene's information incomplete. PPHi, Dreer American Prose, VI.

J.M. wrote a letter to William Washington, South Carolina, containing the same inquiries. See William Washington to J. E. Howard, June 3, 1805. ICHi.

Dec. 21
RICHMOND *to C. P. Wayne*

Acknowledges letter of Dec. 3; not clear about reprinting of corrected copy; volumes lost at sea; second edition should be corrected from printed copy. J.M. not satisfied with published volumes, too hurried; wishes to read and correct at leisure. PPHi, Dreer MSS; DLC, Beveridge Coll.

Dec. 25
MOUNT VERNON *Bushrod Washington to C. P. Wayne*

J.M.'s need for prompt remittance of money. PPHi, Dreer MSS.

Dec. 30
MOUNT VERNON *Bushrod Washington to C. P. Wayne*

Concerning his time to prepare second edition of *Life of Washington*. PPHi, Dreer MSS.

U.S. SUPREME COURT

FEBRUARY TERM, Feb. 6–Mar. 6.

Feb. 6. J.M. alone, adjourned.

Feb. 7–Mar. 6. J.M., Cushing, Chase, Washington. U.S. Supreme Court, Minute Book A, 138–51.

August term. Chase, all cases continued. Same, 152.

Justice Alfred Moore terminated service Jan. 26, 1804.

Justice Paterson was seriously injured in a coach accident Oct., 1803, and was unable to attend. See letter Paterson to J.M., June 31, 1803. NjR.

George Capron v. Henrianus Van Noorden, 2 Cranch 126.

Writ of error to U.S. Circuit Court, North Carolina, reversed.

Trespass in the case. Declaration stated defendant Van Noorden, "late of Pitt County"; did not state plaintiff an alien, citizen of any state, or place of residence. V.j. for defendant, error brought by plaintiff for lack of jurisdiction of court.

Held, court no jurisdiction, record not show diversity; plaintiff may take advantage of error in his favor even though chose court.

Jan., 1804. Record filed.

Mar. 5, 1804. Order reversing.

DNA, U.S. Supreme Court, Docket Book A, 177; Minute Book A, 150. Case No. 168. R.G. 267.

Rebecca G. McIlvaine v. Daniel Coxe's Lessee, 2 Cranch 280; on reargument, 4 Cranch 209. (1808).

Error to U.S. Circuit Court, New Jersey. J. for defendant in error, plaintiff below, affirmed. Opinion by Justice Cushing.

Coxe, a citizen of New Jersey, adhered to British cause during Revolution and sought to become British subject; in 1802 was bequeathed New Jersey land. State law denied right of expatriation; jury hearing as basis of confiscation for breach of allegiance, which was done in 1789.

Held, not an alien under New Jersey law, status not affected by Treaty of Peace, could inherit.

J.M. did not sit, "having formed a decided opinion on the principal question, while his interest was concerned." Note to 2 Cranch 280. The Court did not pass on the question of whether or not an alien could inherit, an issue debated in the case and of interest to J.M. as involving the right of Denny Fairfax to inherit under the will of Thomas Lord Fairfax.

St. George Tucker et al., Judges of General Court for benefit of Rebecca Backhouse, administrator of John Backhouse, v. John Baylor. Not reported.

Writ of error to j., U.S. Circuit Court, Virginia, on forthcoming bond executed by John Baylor and Thomas R. Rootes to judges on behalf of Rebecca Backhouse arising from writ of *fiere facias* in said court against goods and chattels of Lucy Armstead; slaves seized by deputy marshal.

May 24, 1803. J. by Circuit Court $3,478 against Baylor, payable by $1,739.

Writ of error to U.S. Supreme Court endorsed by J.M., "Let a writ of error issue."

Notice to Tucker *et al.* of writ signed by J.M.

Order for record endorsed by J.M.

Feb. 24, 1804. Affirmed by consent of counsel of both parties.

DNA, U.S. Supreme Court, Docket Book A, 164. Cases Nos. 150, 151; Minute Book A, 145.

DNA, U.S. Supreme Court, Case Papers. Case No. 150. R.G. 267.

St. George Tucker et al., Judges of General Court for benefit of Murdocks Donald and Co., v. John Baylor. Not reported.

Writ of error to j., U.S. Circuit Court, Virginia, on forthcoming bond executed by John Baylor and Thomas R. Rootes to Judges on behalf of Murdocks Donald and Co. arising from writ of *fiere facias* in said Court against goods and chattels of Lucy Armstead.

May 24, 1803. J. by Circuit Court $3,018.06, payable by $1,509.03. Writ of error to U.S. Supreme Court endorsed by J.M., "Let a writ of error issue."

Notice to Tucker *et al.* of writ signed by J.M.

Order for record endorsed by J.M.

Feb. 24, 1804. Affirmed by consent of counsel of both parties.

DNA, U.S. Supreme Court, Docket Book A, 164. Cases Nos. 150, 151; Minute Book A, 145.

DNA, U.S. Supreme Court, Case Papers. Case No. 151. R.G. 267.

Thomas Young v. John Walker and Anthony B. Forman, executors of Henry Forman, et al.

Writ of error to U.S. Circuit Court, North Carolina, affirmed.

Jan. 3, 1804. Admiralty, appeal from District Court of Pamplico District, reversed; error to U.S. Supreme Court. DNA, U.S. Circuit Court, N.C., Minute Book, as dated.

Supreme Court proceedings:

Mar. 2, 1804. Record filed.

Feb. 6, 1808. Affirmed.

DNA, U.S. Supreme Court, Docket Book A, 185; Minute Book B, 83. Case No. 178. R.G. 267.

Opinions

Abraham Faw v. Philip Marsteller, 2 Cranch 10, 22–33.

Appeal from Circuit Court, District of Columbia, Alexandria, sitting as Court of Chancery. Decree for appellee, petitioner below, reversed and amended.

Action for rental due on perpetual ground rent, £26 per annum, on one-half–acre lot in Alexandria, executed 1779. The Virginia act of Nov., 1781, abolished paper money, set a scale of depreciation for basing contracts and debts incurred since 1777, with an escape clause in case of injustices (Section 5).

Held, Section 5 applicable, but decree for payment during existence of paper money adjusted by scale and thereafter in species at amount specified, erroneous; basis should be actual annual value at date of contract in specie or equivalent as determined by jury. Note: depreciation reached proportions of 500 to 1. Autograph decree. DNA, U.S. Supreme Court, Case Papers. Case No. 152. R.G. 267.

Later proceedings, Same, Case No. 233.

J.M. advised counsel rule requiring statement of points of case in writing enforced even though one point involved. 2 Cranch 11, note 1.

Edward Pennington v. Tench Coxe, 2 Cranch 33, 51–64.

Error to U.S. Circuit Court, Pennsylvania. J. for defendant in error, plaintiff below, reversed.

Case in which Court knowingly passed on a feigned issue based on wager between Pennington, a sugar refiner of New York, and Coxe, a citizen of Pennsylvania, involving the construction of a federal revenue act. Ruled that the act of 1802 repealing internal taxes, as applied to the act of 1794 laying duties on snuff and refined sugar, excluded the payment of tax on sugar refined before, but shipped after the enactment of the repealing act. The Court disregarded the feigned nature of the cause, stating instead that it had "great difficulty," that this was a question "on which the most correct minds may form opposite opinions," and that "after the most attentive examination of the laws, and the argument of counsel, a judgment has at length been formed." DNA, U.S. Supreme Court, Case Papers. Case No. 146. R.G. 267.

Alexander Murray v. Schooner Charming Betsy, 2 Cranch 64, 116.

Appeal from U.S. Circuit Court, Pennsylvania, reversing in part U.S. District Court of Pennsylvania.

Libel under Nonintercourse Law of 1800. Decree of District Court ordering restoration of vessel and proceeds of cargo and damages, reversed by Circuit Court as to damages only. Supreme Court reversed latter, allowing damages but disapproving of method of assessment.

American-owned ship, lightly armed, and cargo sailed from Baltimore to Danish St. Bartholomew and St. Thomas; cargo sold at former, ship at latter to Shattuck, born American but long resident of St. Thomas, took oath of allegiance to Denmark. Sailing to Guadaloupe (French) with new cargo captured by French privateer, and thereafter by U.S. frigate *Constellation*; cargo sold; ship libeled in Philadelphia.

Held, Nonintercourse Law not applicable, Shattuck not a resident of the United States or a citizen under its protection, having made self subject of foreign power; question of expatriation generally left open; that no salvage allowable, no imminent danger of being condemned as prize and not threat to American commerce; that no probable cause to excuse captor from actual damage; determination of damages by assessors rather than jury and without stating basis error.

Capt. Murray was reimbursed for damages assessed by act of Congress, Jan. 31, 1805. Autograph decree. DNA, U.S. Supreme Court, Case Papers. Case No. 115. R.G. 267.

Head & Amory v. The Providence Insurance Co., 2 Cranch 127, 163–69.

Error to U.S. Circuit Court, Rhode Island.

Action in case on two insurance policies by plaintiff in error, j. on one policy only, reversed.

One policy on cargo from Malaga to Veracruz to Spain, other on Spanish brig Cuba to Spain. Vessel laying at Cuba; correspondence between insured of Boston and agent of insurance company at Providence, the former seeking cancellation at 25 per cent premium, on condition of Cuban approval, of cargo policy only; the company seeking cancellation of both without condition. Finally, company assented by letter to cancellation of cargo policy; in meantime, insured received word of capture and condemnation by British. Circuit Court charged jury correspondence created contract for cancellation.

Held, questionable if correspondence a contract and not mere negotiation; if intended as former, articles of incorporation require signature by president or officer, corporation cannot effect by parol; evidence of custom of merchants cannot vary legal requirement. Autograph decree. DNA, U.S. Supreme Court, Case Papers. Case No. 142. R.G. 267.

Note: This decision was to plague corporate law for many years.

Little et al. v. Barreme et al., 2 Cranch 170, 176–79.

Appeal from U.S. Circuit Court, Massachusetts, reversing U.S. District Court as to damages.

Decree releasing vessel and assessing damages against captor, affirmed.

Libel of Danish vessel and cargo captured by U.S. frigates, vessel sailing from French port to St. Thomas (Danish). Nonintercourse Act of 1799 permitted Presidential instructions to public vessels to capture ships sailing to French port; capture made under instructions covering vessels sailing from or to French port.

Held, instructions of President illegal, not excuse captain from damages for illegal seizure. J.M. stated was inclined to opposite view on latter point, but convinced by his brethren and "receded from this first opinion."

Dunlop & Co. v. Ball, 2 Cranch 180, 184–85.

Error to U.S. Circuit Court, District of Columbia, Alexandria. J. for defendant in error, defendant below, reversed.

Action on bond executed 1773 in Virginia where defendant resided; plea presumption of payment by lapse of more than twenty years. Trial court ruled barred, excluding from twenty-year period only war period 1775 to 1783.

Held, error, actual disability of British creditors to recover in Virginia courts extended to 1793; presumption of payment rebutted.

John Barker Church, Jun. v. Hubbart, 2 Cranch 187, 232–39.

Error to U.S. Circuit Court, Massachusetts. J. for defendant in error, defendant below, reversed.

Action on insurance policies on American ships trading from New York to one or two Portuguese ports in Brazil, excepting seizure or risk of illegal trade with Portuguese. Vessel cleared from Rio de Janeiro seized as approached Parma within four or five leagues of land as attempting illegal trade.

Held, seizure within exception which was interpreted to include attempt to trade; error in proof of Portuguese law, certificate of consul or Secretary of Foreign Affairs insufficient; must be by properly authenticated copy.

Also held, objection to charge of trial court in bill of exceptions proper, even if no ruling sought below. Autograph decree. DNA, U.S. Supreme Court, Case Papers. Case No. 166. R.G. 267. Copy opinion. MB.

Note: Comments on belligerent seizures of neutrals on high seas; profitableness of unlawful trade with Portuguese colonies.

William Mason v. Ship Blaireau, 2 Cranch 240, 263–71.

Appeal from U.S. Circuit Court, Maryland, affirming as amended decree of U.S. District Court, reversed in part, decree amended.

Libel for salvage by crew and owners of ship and cargo of British merchant ship against French ship rescued after fired on and left sinking by Spanish; brought 3,000 miles to Baltimore. Lower court allowed salvors three-fifths of proceeds (which was $62,000), of which $4,800 to owners of rescuing ship, balance to crew and officers, except Capt. Mason, who embezzled part of proceeds.

Held, salvage reduced to one-third of proceeds, one-third of which to owners of rescuing vessel and cargo, balance to crew and officers, including sailor on rescued ship, and excluding captain; that Court has jurisdiction where all parties aliens, at least when all parties assent. Autograph decree. DNA, U.S. Supreme Court, Case Papers. Case No. 175. R.G. 267.

Samuel Adams, qui tam v. Daniel Wood, 2 Cranch 336, 340–42.

Certified on division, U.S. Circuit Court, Massachusetts.

Action of debt for penalty under act of 1794 prohibiting carrying of slaves from the United States to foreign country.

Held, act of 1790 requiring no person be prosecuted, tried, or punished for fine or penalty except within two years of date incurred applied to penalties under later passed acts, and to actions of debt for penalty.

Autograph decree. DNA, U.S. Supreme Court, Case Papers. Case No. 144.

Note: Argument slave traders taking circuitous route to Africa, more than two-year sailing time to return.

Reilly v. Lamar, Beall, and Smith, 2 Cranch 344, 356–57.

Appeal from Circuit Court, District of Columbia.

Denial of injunction to appellant to stay levy of execution on j., affirmed.

Beall, a resident of Washington, had j. against Reilly, who claims sold Georgia land to Smith, who agreed to pay Beall, also discharge under insolvency law of 1700 by assignment dated May 23, 1801.

Held, payment through Smith not established; inhabitants of District of Columbia ceased to be citizens of Maryland at date of separation; court of Maryland no power to discharge. Held, also where appeal allowed in court below, need be no citation.

Note: Did not decide if separation first Monday in Dec., 1800, when Congress provided for removal of government to Washington, or Feb. 27, 1801, when provided for government of District.

The United States v. James G. Fisher et al., assignees of Peter Blight, bankrupt, 2 Cranch 358, 385–405.

Error to U.S. Circuit Court, Pennsylvania. J. for defendant in error, defendant below, on agreed case, reversed.

The United States asserted priority in bankruptcy proceedings over general creditors on claim as endorsee of bill of exchange.

Held, clause of act of 1797 giving it priority where "any revenue officer, or other person becomes indebted to the United States" is applicable, not restricted to claims against revenue agents despite prior provisions of act so limited; act constitutional as incidental to Congressional power to pay debts, and despite interference with state revenue powers.

Note: Statement "necessary and proper clause" does not mean indispensible; Congress choice of means; state sovereignty subordinate to federal supremacy as to delegated powers; Court not unmindful of its "solumn duty" to declare a law unconstitutional.

Also see oral statement of J.M. stating his personal view not a devastavit in administration of estate, and notice required. p. 390, n. 1.

Dillon, *Decisions,* 42–47 (in part); Cotton, I, 44–63; Marshall, *Writings,* 29–30 (excerpt).

Telfair et al., executors of Rae and Sommerville v. Stead's Executors, 2 Cranch 407, 418.

Writ of error to decree of Circuit Court, Georgia, for defendants in error, affirmed.

Bill by British creditor brought in 1792 for debt of partnership subjecting land and other properties bought by partnership assets in hands of deceased partner and others to payment of debt; heir of debtor not joined.

Held, "received word" that under Georgia law heir of debtor need not be joined in action.

Graves and Barnewall v. Boston Marine Insurance Co., 2 Cranch 419, 438–44.

Appeal from U.S. Circuit Court, Massachusetts. Decree dismissing bill of appellants, affirmed.

Insurance policy in name of one joint owner of vessel "as property may appear"; bill brought to include interest of other joint owner and to correct mistake.

Held, policy covers only interest of named; evidence of knowledge of insurer insufficient even though named owner intended to cover both.

Hepburn and Dundas v. Thomason Ellzey, 2 Cranch 445, 452–53.

Certified on division from U.S. Circuit Court, Virginia.

Held, under Judiciary Act citizen of District of Columbia cannot bring action in federal court against citizen of Virginia on grounds of diversity, the District not being a "state." Admitted situation "extraordinary" but "a subject for legislative not for judicial consideration." Dillon, *Decisions*, 48–50; Cotton, I, 64–67; Marshall, *Writings*, 31–32.

Note: Argument of E. J. Lee that disability of citizens of District to vote for national offices not singular; seven-eights of free white inhabitants of Virginia in same position, one-half female, one-half under age, not over one-half of remainder freeholders. Pp. 451–52.

U.S. CIRCUIT COURT, VIRGINIA

May term. May 22–June 8.

May 22–June 1. J.M. and District Judge Cyrus Griffin.

June 2–8. J.M. alone.

U.S. Circuit Court, Va., Order Book IV, 421–498.

November term. Nov. 22–Dec. 13.

Nov. 22–27. J.M. and District Judge Cyrus Griffin.

Nov. 28–Dec. 13. J.M. alone.

U.S. Circuit Court, Va., Order Book V, 1–71.

U.S. CIRCUIT COURT, NORTH CAROLINA

June term. June 15–21.

J.M. and Judge Henry Potter sat throughout, excepting the 21st, Potter only.

December term. Dec. 29–Jan. 5, 1805.

Dec. 29. Judge Potter only.

Dec. 31–Jan. 5. J.M. and Judge Potter.

DNA, U.S. Circuit Court, N.C., Minute Book, as dated.

OPINIONS

McAlister et al. v. Berry et al., 2 Haywood 290.

Action by heir to set aside conveyance of real estate inherited to executor, represented to him debts owing by testator large, fall on estate of heir whereas fund provided for payment.

Held, misrepresentation even though party imposed on of sound understanding and had time to detect; division of property ordered, executor credited with personal payments of debts chargeable against it and improvements made.

Decree. DNA, U.S. Circuit Court, N.C., Minute Book, July 3, 1804; June 18, 1805. Order adjusting charges and accounts. Same, June 20, 1805; Jan. 1, 1806; June 24, 1806.

LEGAL PRACTICE

(Of Earlier Date)

COURT OF APPEALS OF VIRGINIA

Barnett & Co. v. Smith & Co., 5 Call 98.

J.M. acted as counsel for Barnett & Co. in previous proceedings in this cause. Original action on note £500 by Smith & Co. against Barnett & Co., as acceptor, j. for plaintiff. Bill of review here sought on grounds of new evidence of forgery and credits due; that is, new testimony as to payment by witnesses not formerly available; dismissed on grounds not proved, affirmed. Counsel for Barnett claimed that bill, once received and former decree not pleaded, opened whole evidence, and answer of Smith admitted credits not allowed.

The court was divided in reasoning, Judge Tucker dissenting that allowance of bill opened entire record; three judges denied this point. Judges Roane and Lyons noted that greater flexibility allowed in American than was English practice. Four of the five judges agreed that the bill was properly denied on its merits.

Fee: Oct., 1790, "Barnett & Co. v. Smith, Young and Hyde," £5. Account Book, 262.

Staples v. Webster, 5 Call 261.

Appeal from High Court of Chancery decree dismissing bill to require release of land, affirmed. J.M. was counsel for Webster in earlier stages; Call and Wickham herein.

Staples was agent of Webster in making survey of lands under entry. Between expiration of act of 1791 setting one year for returning survey on entry and act of 1792 extending the period, he made entry of part of same land claiming Webster's rights had lapsed for failure to return survey. Webster thereafter did so under the later act and received a patent.

Held, Staples' actions could gain no equitable rights, that the filing of a caveat was required to contest the patent.

Fee: July, 1795, £6:18. Account Book, 418.

LAND TRANSACTIONS

n.d. [*circa* 1804] *n.p.* *Land Contract*

To Joseph Thompson, adjoining that previously sold; money due on first sale Sept., 1804, on this one Sept., 1805, ten shillings per acre. Witness, Charles Lee. VU, McGregor Library, No. 1106.

Fauquier County, Virginia

July 13 *Deed*

J.M. and Mary Willis, his wife, Richmond, to James Morgan, Faquier County, 3½ acres and house, part of Oak Hill tract, Fauquier County, on main Road; $200. Recorded Nov. 27, 1815. Fauquier County, Va., Deed Book 20, 90–91.

Sept. 28 *Deed*

J.M. and Mary Willis to Robert Hensford, Fauquier County, the Mill Lott, being part of Oak Hill, survey of Charles Kemper, also from mouth of Hensford's Mill Tailrace north eighteen poles, being twenty acres along the race and pond; excepting rents of present lease; $500 Virginia current. Recorded July 27, 1807. Endorsed Sept. 3, 18 ——, examined and delivered to Thos. Phillips, owner. Fauquier County, Va., Deed Book 16, 781.

Sept. 28 *Lease*

Agreement J.M. with William Ash, Fauquier County, to execute new lease of land part of Oak Hill in place of old lease dated July 25, 1793, held by Ash as assignee. Fauquier County, Va., Deed Book 15, 687.

Hampshire County, Virginia
(Now West Virginia)

Aug. 21 *Deed*

James Clarke, Hampshire County, Va., to J.M., tract on Potomac River (Hampshire County) known as Anderson's Bottom, occupied by Clarke under lease from Denny Fairfax. Consideration £500. Recorded Sept. 4, 1804. Hardy County, Va., Deed Book B, 387.

1805

DOCUMENTS

Jan. 15
MOUNT VERNON *Bushrod Washington to C. P. Wayne*

Acknowledges letter; $1,000 credit sent to J.M., also next $1,000; requests $2,100 for self. Note concerning Col. McClean. PPHi, Dreer MSS.

Jan. 19
RICHMOND *to George Logan*

Acknowledges letter of Jan. 5 on return from North Carolina. Error as to writer of petition to King (his belief that the Address of Congress to the King of 1774 written by Richard Henry Lee; see Charles J. Stillé, *The Life and Times of John Dickinson, 1732–1808* (Philadelphia, J. B. Lippincott & Co., 1891), 147n.; WMQ (ser. 3), Vol. XXII (Apr., 1965), 195, chagrined; Dickinson mentioned. PPHi, Logan Coll., V, 59.

Jan. 28
RICHMOND *to George Logan*

Acknowledges letter of Jan. 17 and extract from Dickinson. Omission of authorship of petition to King by Dickinson not from improper motive, will be corrected. PPHi, Logan Coll., V, 60.

Jan. *to William Washington*

Inquiring concerning military actions at Cowpen, Guilford, and Hobkirk's Hill (n.f.). Referred to in Washington to J. E. Howard. June 13, 1805. ICHi, Washington Coll.

Feb. 16
WASHINGTON *Justice Chase Impeachment*

Testimony of J.M. concerning his request to have Col. Harvie discharged from jury service, and Judge Chase's conduct of the trial of Callender. Annals, 8 Cong., 2 sess., 262–67; Everett S. Brown (ed.), *William Plumer's memorandum of proceedings in the United States Senate, 1803–1807* (New York, Macmillan, 1923), 291; Charles Evans (reporter), *Report of Trial before the High Court of Impeachment, composed of the Senate of the United States . . . for High Crimes and Misdemeanors* (Baltimore, Priv. Pr. for Samuel Butler and Geo. Keatinge, 1805), 71. See Beveridge, *Marshall*, III, 192–96.

Feb. 19
WASHINGTON *to C. P. Wayne*

Acknowledges letter of Feb. 15. Sheets of third volume forwarded; addition concerning Capt. McClean; various corrections; reduction of Vol. IV; shipment of books to Charleston. PPHi, Dreer MSS; DLC, Beveridge Coll.

Feb. 27
WASHINGTON *to C. P. Wayne*

Vol. IV sent by Hopkinson; roughness in text caused by shortening; copyist's errors in capital letters, punctuations, spelling to be watched for. Use of maps; third volume corrected to be forwarded; wishes to correct proof sheets fourth volume; correction in authorship of petition to the King. PPHi, Dreer MSS; DLC, Beveridge Coll.

Mar. 1
WASHINGTON *from Thomas Jefferson*

Requesting J.M. to administer Presidential oath. DLC, Papers of Thomas Jefferson, Vol. 147.

Mar. 16
RICHMOND *to C. P. Wayne*

Correction in fourth volume of word "quarter"; substitution of word. Commencing fifth volume; will take year. Received $150 from Weems. PPHi, Dreer MSS.

Apr. 28
RICHMOND *to Thomas Fitzsimmons*

Concerning litigation over Genessee land, Robert Morris, 50,000 acres;; claim of Gouverneur Morris. Listed in Lazare, *Book-Prices* (1927), 751; (1934), 630. Present owner unknown.

June 27
RICHMOND *to C. P. Wayne*

Acknowledges sheets of second volume on returning from North Carolina; punctuation and alteration. Insertion of additional material concerning combination against George Washington; Gen. Mifflin; preservation of papers. PPHi, Dreer MSS; DLC, Beveridge Coll.

June 29
RICHMOND *to C. P. Wayne*

Acknowledges letter of June 13; just returned from North Carolina.

Binding of books for Adams; Frenau papers not arrived, advise Hopkins; time for return of the *Aurora* desired, extended to six months from October. J.M. leaving for mountains for health until October; work suspended; letters forwarded from Richmond. Regrets introductory volume; difficulty in holding civil administration to one volume. Chest of books from Mount Vernon miscarried. PPHi, Dreer MSS.

Sept. 8
FRONT ROYAL *to C. P. Wayne*

Acknowledges letter of Aug. 22. Shortening third volume; errors; regrets cannot revise proof sheets. Striking certain adverbs; discusses republication; sheets of second volume miscarried. PPHi, Dreer MSS; DLC, Beveridge Coll.

Sept. 16
PHILADELPHIA *Bushrod Washington to C. P. Wayne*

Has had many applications for printing of planned history (Papers of George Washington). Will consider proposal. J.M. power of attorney to act while Washington on Southern Circuit. PPHi, Dreer MSS.

Sept. 27
RICHMOND *to Polly Marshall*

Reached Richmond day before; nothing amiss with family. Morgan delivered $50.00 to Polly at the Oaks to pay brother Charles for his son John's expense. Vexed at bad management of plantation. The John Marshall House, Richmond, Va.; Mason, *Polly*, 165.

Oct. 5
RICHMOND *to C. P. Wayne*

J.M. suffered "bilious intermittent" and fever; wrote B. Washington; fever in Philadelphia. Needs *Frenau's Gazette*. Hopkins of Richmond; also *Aurora*; papers sent, returned in absence; official duties November to March. Inquiry concerning military, *Gazette of the United States*, *Gazette of Virginia*. Delay of research; will complete volume in Spring; inaccurate, revised copies second edition, number of revised copies. Morgan and Washington, everything left to latter. PPHi, Dreer MSS; DLC, Beveridge Coll.

Oct. 7 *Deposition*

William McCleery v. Henry Lee.
Debt.

Continued, commission to take deposition of J.M. and Thomas Wilson. District Court, Fredericksburg, Law Orders E, 1804–1806, 213.

Oct. 14.
MASON COUNTY, KY. *Estate of Thomas Marshall*

Inventory of estate of Thomas Marshall (colonel) father of J.M., Mason County, Ky., Will Records, Book B, 437.

Oct. [or Sept.]
RICHMOND *to Bushrod Washington*

Asking to communicate with C. P. Wayne (n.f.). Referred to in J.M. to Wayne, Oct. 5, 1805, herein.

U.S. SUPREME COURT

FEBRUARY TERM. Feb. 4–Mar. 6.

Feb. 4. Cushing and Paterson, adjourned.

Feb. 5. J.M., Cushing, Paterson, Chase, Washington.

Feb. 6. William Johnson commission (Mar. 26, 1804), in place of Alfred Moore.

Feb. 6–Mar. 2. Above and Johnson.

Mar. 2–6. Johnson and Chase absent.

U.S. Supreme Court, Minute Book A, 153–66.

August, first Monday. Chase, all cases continued. Same, 167–69.

Richard S. Hackley v. Stephen Winchester, 2 Cranch 342.

Writ of error to U.S. Circuit Court, Virginia, affirmed.

Action on running account by member of mercantile firm for moneys advanced on bills of exchange for goods, account originally with plaintiff assigned to firm with debtor's knowledge and consent. Account included credits by plaintiff for sale of debtor's goods sold by plaintiff as factor and charges against such credits for insolvency of buyers. Defendant sought to prove losses of latter due to fault of plaintiff, evidence refused.

Held, plaintiff can bring action for benefit of assignee, debtor can offset claims against assignee; cannot offset claim for misconduct as factor, debts not guaranteed.

May 29–31, 1804. V.j. for plaintiff $4,155.17. U.S. Circuit Court, Va., Order Book IV, 444, 448, 455.

Mar. 4, 1805. On error to U.S. Supreme Court, affirmed *per curiam.* DNA, U.S. Supreme Court, Docket Book A, 191.

May 22, 1805. J. and mandate of Supreme Court filed, execution ordered. U.S. Circuit Court, Va., Order Book V, 74.

Autograph signature and interlineations on bill of exceptions. VHi; DNA, U.S. Supreme Court, Case Papers, Case No. 185. R.G. 267. Also signatures on petition for writ of error and citation. Case Papers, same.

Opinions

Harrison Huidekoper's Lessee v. James Douglas, 3 Cranch 1, 65–73, also 4 Dallas 392.

Certified division of opinion from U.S. Circuit Court, Pennsylvania.

Ejectment to try title of the Holland Company to large tracts of land in Pennsylvania, north and west of Ohio and Alleghany Rivers and Conewango Creek purchased from state under act of Assembly of Apr. 3, 1792.

Held, purchaser excused from condition to cultivate part in two years, build habitation and occupy for five years where persisted in efforts during two years but prevented by force of arms of enemies of the United States (Indians); title vests.

Autograph opinion. DNA, U.S. Supreme Court, Case Papers. Case No. 208. R.G. 267.

The United States v. Robert T. Hooe & Co., 3 Cranch 73, 88–92.

Error to U.S. Circuit Court, District of Columbia. J. for defendant in error, defendant below, affirmed.

Collector of revenue of the United States indebted to government and unable to pay all his debts conveyed land in trust to Hooe, then surety on his bond, as security, and also as security for endorsement of Hooe on money borrowed by collector from bank.

Held, no constructive fraud; no statutory lien by government under statute where no suit brought or act of insolvency or bankruptcy. Refused to rule costs could not be assessed against government.

Francis Peyton v. Richard Brooke, 3 Cranch 92, 96.

Error to U.S. Circuit Court, District of Columbia, Alexandria.

Execution on j. included costs of execution, returned *non est*; *alias ca. sa.* issued and forthcoming bond executed adding costs of second execution. On motion for execution on bond, held, addition of costs of *alias ca. sa.* proper under Virginia law.

Notice given members of bar that both parties must furnish Court statement of case, otherwise continued or dismissed.

J.M. entered into considerable colloquy with counsel.

William Hodgson v. Marks Butts, 3 Cranch 140, 155–58.

Error to U.S. Circuit Court, District of Columbia, Alexandria.

J. for defendant in error, defendant below, affirmed.

Action by mortgagee of freight of schooner to recover from captain money received as freight and applied to indebtedness of owner to himself and employees. Mortgage had two witnesses.

Held, ambiguous Virginia recording statute requiring three witnesses interpreted to apply to personalty, in keeping with "best judicial opinions of that state," especially in absence of special statute applying to mortgaging of personalty.

United States v. Benjamin More, 3 Cranch 159, 170–73.

Error to U.S. Circuit Court, District of Columbia, Washington.

Writ dismissed for lack of jurisdiction.

More was a justice of peace of the District of Columbia appointed under the act of Feb. 27, 1801, which provided for compensation of the justices by fees assessed in individual cases. The fee system was repealed by the act of May 3, 1802. More was indicted for receiving fees subsequent to the repeal, and brought before the Circuit Court of the District of Columbia which allowed a demurrer to the indictment on grounds that the 1802 act violated Article 3 of the Constitution by diminishing the compensation of judges during their term in office. Judges Cranch, a Federalist, and James M. Marshall supported this view. Chief Justice Kilty dissented on grounds that Article 3 applied only to judicial power of the United States generally and not to that of a particular territory.

Marshall avoided this explosive political question without comment, dismissing the writ of error pressed by the government on the grounds of lack of jurisdiction of the Supreme Court, that the statute in question did not apply to appeal or writ of error in criminal cases from the Circuit Court of the District of Columbia, not having been expressly given.

Abram Faw v. Daniel Roberdeau's Executor, 3 Cranch 174, 177–78.

Error to U.S. Circuit Court, District of Columbia, Alexandria. J. for defendant in error, defendant below, reversed.

Action by resident of Maryland for building materials lent and sold to testator 1786 in Virginia; claimant passed through Alexandria in 1786 but did not become resident until 1795; testator died 1794.

Virginia statute barred actions against executors and administrators based on claims more than five years before death, excepting persons out of state, action to be brought within three years after disability removed.

Held, temporary entrance into state removes disability and starts running of statute, provided debtor in state which not alleged.

Ray v. Law, 3 Cranch 179, 180.

Appeal from U.S. Circuit Court, District of Columbia.

Appeal from decree of lower court confirming order to sell mortgaged real estate denied by lower court on ground not final; petition to Supreme Court for record.

Held, order final and appealable, sundry papers filed not sufficient, assumed lower court would transmit record.

Nathan Levy v. John Gadsby, 3 Cranch 180, 186.

Error to Circuit Court, District of Columbia, Alexandria. J. for defendant in error, defendant below, affirmed.

Action against Gadsby on note made by former partner of Levy and his debtor to Gadsby and endorsed to Levy; written agreement between Levy and maker that considerably smaller amount than face of note be credited to debt. Plea, usury and general issue.

Held, writing admissible to show usury under general issue even though previously denied under special plea; issue if written agreement usurious for court, not jury; endorser may plead usury.

The Marine Insurance Co. of Alexandria v. William Wilson, 3 Cranch 186.

Error to U.S. Circuit Court, District of Columbia, Alexandria. J. for defendant in error, plaintiff below, affirmed.

Action against insurance company on policy covering vessel, Oct. 24, 1802, providing that void if unsound on survey; defense claimed unsound, survey made Nov. 26, 1802, after voyage commenced.

Held, survey not referring to date of sailing insufficient to prove unsound then.

J.M. declined giving opinion, remote degree interested by ownership of stock of company. Justices Washington, Paterson, and Cushing gave seriatim opinions.

Richard S. Hallet and Jacob Bowne v. Ebenezer Jenks et al., 3 Cranch 210, 218–19.

Error to High Court for the Trial of Impeachments and Correction of Errors of New York. J. for defendant in error, plaintiff below, affirmed.

Action on insurance policy on American vessel, en route from Newport to Havana in distress entered French port for repairs; forced by authorities to sell cargo and load with local goods. Sailed for St. Thomas; captured by British.

Held, not a violation of policy as a trading with France contrary to act of Congress of 1798.

Stephen Cooke v. William Graham's Administrator, 3 Cranch 229, 235.

Error to U.S. Circuit Court, Alexandria. J. for defendant in error, plaintiff below, reversed.

Declaration on bond stated as of Oct. 3, 1799, on oyer appeared dated Jan. 3, 1799. Bad rejoinder demurred to by plaintiff below.

Held, demurrer applied to first error, fatal variance.

William Milligan, administrator of Milligan v. John Milledge and wife, 3 Cranch 220, 232–35.

Error to U.S. Circuit Court, Georgia. Dismissal of bill of plaintiff in error, reversed.

Action to trace assets of deceased debtor in hands of legatees and devisees and subject to payment of debt. Plea in bar filed denying have assets, naming persons in South Carolina who have, asking dismissal.

Held, error to dismiss, mere denial of facts not plea in bar; failure to join persons out of state not grounds for dismissal.

William Wilson v. John Codman's Executors, 3 Cranch 193, 204–10.

Error to U.S. Circuit Court, District of Columbia, Alexandria. J. on demurrer for defendant in error, plaintiff below, affirmed.

Action by assignee of promissory note against maker alleging assignment for value received; in replication stated assigned in trust to satisfy existing debt.

Held, allegation immaterial, no departure. Also held, defendant not entitled to continuance where executor appears to prosecute case of deceased, but may demand papers of appointment; payments made by maker to payee, who was also agent of endorser not attributable to note where the two had a running account and shown on their own account.

U.S. CIRCUIT COURT, VIRGINIA

May term. May 22–June 11.

May 22–29. J.M. and District Judge Cyrus Griffin.

May 30. J.M. alone.

May 31–June 7. Both.

U.S. Circuit Court, Va., Order Book V, 72–160.

November term. Nov. 23–Dec. 16.

J.M. and Judge Griffin throughout.

U.S. Circuit Court, Va., Order Book V, 161–264.

Opinions

Cunningham Corbet et al., assignees of Minzies, v. Edward Johnson's Heirs et al., 1 Brockenbrough 77, 79–85.

Bill in equity for payment of bonds executed by deceased against his heirs and devisees and executor of his co-executor. Heirs claimed recourse should first be had to personal estate by joining executor of other co-executor of Johnson who owed the estate, and going against his executor's bond.

Held, at law creditor could elect to go against land in hands of heir or personal representative, but in equity latter must be included and personal assets first exhausted. He need not go further, however, than the legal representative in following personal assets. Sale of real estate in hands of heirs and devisees decreed.

Robert Dunbar v. Miller, Hart and Co., 1 Brockenbrough 85, 90–96.

Motion to dissolve an injunction obtained by Dunbar, a Falmouth, Virginia, merchant, against defendants, London merchants, restraining execution of judgment on a note. Latter executed in settlement of extensive and complicated dealings, with proviso for deduction of proceeds of shipment of tobacco by Dunbar completed but not yet accounted for. Shipment made with understanding not fully expressed if war in France would be directed to other market after arrival at Cork, sent to France despite war and poor price received by compromise, Dunbar claiming violation of orders, claimed invoice rather than actual price received.

Held, acquiescence in transshipment to France by proviso in note with knowledge; settlement not completely adjusted and opened for correction of errors in sales on half commissions, difference of exchange, erroneous interest; otherwise injunction dissolved.

Waddington v. Henry Banks et al., 1 Brockenbrough 97, 98–102.

Application to direct trustee to sell land held in trust to satisfy claim, so ordered.

Henry Banks, surviving partner of Hunter, Banks and Co. sold lot to Fulwar Skipwith, no conveyance by deed; latter sold to F. Graves with bond for good title joined in by Banks; Groves sold and assigned bond to Stockdell, who mortgaged and pledged the bond to Young and then conveyed to James Brown to secure debt to Alexander Donald; on foreclosure deeded to Donald, who conveyed in trust to Daniel Call to sell and pay proceeds to Waddington. Banks having bought up the pledged bond from Young claimed merger of legal and equitable title and amounts paid to Young and that due from Young to Stockdell.

Held, Banks held title as trustee, had not proved fairness of transaction, had notice of equity of purchasers; ordered to execute deed to trustee Call for sale of property by commissioners and payment of Waddington.

U.S. CIRCUIT COURT, NORTH CAROLINA

June term. June 15–21.
June 15. Judge Henry Potter only.
June 17–20. J.M. and Judge Potter.
June 21. Judge Potter only.

December term. Dec. 31–Jan. 4, 1805.
Dec. 31–Jan. 2. J.M. and Judge Potter.
Jan. 3–4. Judge Potter only.
DNA, U.S. Circuit Court, N.C., Minute Book, as dated.

Opinions

Buchannon Dunlop & Co. v. John West, Marshal, 2 Haywood 346, Brunner's Coll. Cas. 27.

Held, *per curiam,* sheriff or marshal seizing property on execution and neglecting to sell liable in damages for what property would have produced on sale.

June 17, 1805. V.j. for plaintiff, $2,975. DNA, U.S. Circuit Court, N.C., Minute Book, as dated.

Teasdale v. Branton's Administrator, 2 Haywood 377; Brunner's Coll. Cas. 28.

Verdict had against administrator who had plead assets fully administered; execution returned no goods. *Scire facias* asking judgment against administrator's own property. Pleas: no judgment of record, no devastavit found. Record showed verdict but no judgment entered in original suit. Demurrer to plea.

Held *per curiam,* loose practice in the state (North Carolina) must presume judgment on verdict; practice of state to allow *scire facias* on suggestion of devastavit and not follow English practice of prior inquiry and finding.

Demurrer allowed, finding that there is such a record. DNA, U.S. Circuit Court, N.C., Minute Book, Jan. 4, 1806.

Anonymous, 2 Haywood 378; Brunner's Coll. Cas. 29.

Held *per curiam,* party bringing *scire facias* against bail not entitled to interest on the judgment levied on.

Grubb's Administrator v. Clayton's Executor, 2 Haywood 378; Brunner's Coll. Cas. 30.

Former suit brought in state court, statute of limitations of 1715 pleaded and, on call made, determined by Court of Conference to be in effect; thereafter reply filed and later entire bill dismissed by plaintiff. Action brought in federal court; pleas, former dismissal as bar, and 1789 three-year statute of limitation. Plaintiff had administrator in England but not in the United States during three years prior to suit.

Held, *per curiam* not a dismissal on merits; not barred by terms of statute where out of state unless after three years of administrator appointment.

United States v. Holtsclaw, 2 Haywood 379. Brunner's Coll. Cas. 31.

Indictment for counterfeiting.

Held *per curiam,* person well acquainted with bank paper can give competent evidence if bank paper genuine or forged, need not have seen president and cashier writer or correspond with him to testify as to handwriting.

Bail set. DNA, U.S. Circuit Court, N.C., Minute Book, June 19, 1805.

Or verdict of guilty, fined $10.00 and three years. Same, Jan. 1, 1806.

COURT OF APPEALS OF VIRGINIA

James M. Marshall brought a number of cases to enforce his right to lease payments and his title to lots in the town of Winchester.

James M. Marshall v. Daniel Conrad, 5 Call 364.

Error to Frederick County, Va., Superior Court. Ejectment, j. for defendant in error, defendant below, reversed.

On agreed case, defendant holding under lease from Thomas Lord Fairfax, rent reserved unpaid for eighteen years, five shillings per lot annually, payment refused, entry.

J. for defendant reversed. Judge Roane dissenting.

Held, Lord Fairfax had fee in Northern Neck by original grant; rent reserved not quitrents abolished as to aliens by Virginia acts of Oct., 1777, and May, 1779; devise Lord Fairfax to Denny Fairfax approved; alien can take by devise; no office of escheat prior to Treaty of 1794 with Great Britain and act of 1784; lease constituted appropriation, compromise of Oct. 10, 1796, ended all dispute. Judge Roane contended rents were quit-rents and not affected by compromise, not appropriated by Fairfax.

Agreed case of twenty-four items included principal documents on which Marshall title to Manor of Leeds based. Superior Court, Frederick, Order Book 1797–1800, 472, 511–15, Oct. 9, 1799; Same, Land Record Book 1799–1809, 1–35.

Judgment of lower court, Same, Order Book 1800–1802, 30–34. Apr. 29, 1800.

Related case; *James M. Marshall v. Henry Bush*, Same, Order Book 1797–1800, 472.

LAND TRANSACTIONS

Fauquier County, Virginia

Sept. 21 *Deed*

J.M. and Mary Willis to John H. Clarke, reversion to part of lot now in possession of Clarke under lease from Thomas Smith, part of Oak Hill, 1,804⅛ acres (Fauquier County); consideration £70:14:4. Recorded Sept. 5, 1832. Faquier County, Va., Deed Book 33, 86–87. Above acknowledged and ordered recorded. Superior Court, Fauquier County, Va., Order Book 1832–1833, 142.

Mason County, Kentucky

Sept. 10 *Deed*

J. M. to Robert Johnson, assignee of Simon Kenton's right as locator, one-third interest in 1,934 acres, Mason County, Ky., on the waters of the Ohio. Executed by Thomas Marshall, attorney in fact of J.M. Mason County, Ky., Deed Book H, 417. (See herein June 14, 1799, for patent to J.M.) This land adjoins the 50¼-acre tract of J.M. (see June 14, 1799) and a survey of 5,413 acres for J.M., Jr., assigned to Thomas Marshall. Both tracts were on an entry of 10,659½ acres by J.M., Jr., Jan. 11, 1783. (See herein latter date.)

City of Washington

Feb. 28 *Deed*

By Thomas Munroe, superintendent, City of Washington, to J.M., John Hopkins, James Marshall as tenants in common, lots 1, 2, 7, 8, 9, 12,

13 in square 219 of City of Washington, District of Columbia Deed Records, Liber V/12, Folio 47.

1806

DOCUMENTS

Feb. 4
QUINCY *from John Adams*

Acknowledges receipt three volumes *Life of Washington*; praises condition, ornamental, more enduring than mausoleum would have been. Hopes for healthy, long life, less rancorous enemies than himself. MHi, John Adams Letter Book, "Public and Private," Mar. 23, 1801—Nov. 1812, 80.

Feb. 13
WASHINGTON *to James M. Marshall*

Acknowledges letter of Feb. 1 with enclosure of Tucker letter; annoyed by latter. Difficulty of prosecuting claim for rents against people of Winchester, Shenandoah lands belong to James; statute of limitations; pressed by business of court; suit in chancery possible; back rents due Denny Fairfax; Court of Appeals unfavorable. Payment by Ambler (mentions letter concerning Ambler [n.f.]); Edmonds payment; J.M. seeking to raise money. Mortgage for residue, suggests Murdock of England; asks concerning conveyance of residue of land. Powers of attorney necessary; meeting in Richmond end of May with addressee and Colston. MoSW. Olin Libr., Bixby Coll.; DLC, John Marshall Papers, Ac. 2738.

Mar. 30
RICHMOND *to Jonathan Williams*

Answering letter enclosing constitution of Society for the Improvement of Military Science in the United States and advising of honorary membership; excuses for delay, North Carolina Circuit Court duties in January, Supreme Court February, forgot; accepts membership and lauds purpose; sorry cannot contribute to remnant of military skill in country. NNHi.

Apr. 1
TRENTON *Bushrod Washington to Caleb P. Wayne*

Speaks of letter from J.M. to Wayne which left (in Philadelphia); to send the fourth volume of *Life of Washington* to Dawes (n.f.).

Requests payment on book account; J.M. required to pay out about $3,000 in May and dependent on it. (Leeds Manor purchase.) Washington needs $40 or $50 immediately and $500 for purchase of horses. Will send last volume on return home. PPHi.

Apr. 5
HAPPY CREEK *James M. Marshall to John Ambler*

Letter from J.M. enclosing letter from Ambler, Feb. 21 (n.f.). Payment on contract needed to satisfy Fairfax. Ambler has 4,000 acres interest in Manor; William Marshall will accept offer to sell share. VU, Coles Coll., No. 4640.

Apr. 21
RICHMOND *to [Oliver Wolcott]*

Inquiring as to George Washington's approval of Jay Treaty; rumor he was influenced by the Fauchet letter; orders of British Cabinet. Comments Democrats discovering Republic's government may have secrets. CtHi, Oliver Wolcott, Jr., MSS, Vol. 48. Answered, Wolcott to J.M., New York, June 9, 1806. Same.

May 7 *Law Suit*

J.M. v. Edmund Lacy and Samuel Coleman, dismissed by agreement of parties. County Court, Henrico, Quarterly Court, Order Book XII, 420.

May 31 *Power of Attorney*

J.M. and James M. Marshall executed power of attorney to William Murdock in execution of conveyance by Philip Martin of residue of Fairfax purchase (n.f.). See Deed, Oct. 18, 1806, herein.

June 27
RICHMOND *to Caleb Wayne*

Concerning *Life of Washington*; acknowledges receipt of payments. Listed in Lazare, *Book-Prices* (1945), 591; (1965), 953. Present owner unknown.

June 28
RICHMOND *to Oliver Wolcott*

Acknowledging letter corroborating view that Fauchet letter did not influence George Washington to approve Jay Treaty. Work completed; prepared for charges and abuse. CtHi, Oliver Wolcott, Jr., MSS, Vol. 48.

July 6
RICHMOND *to John Adams*

Apologizes for use without permission of Adams' letters to George Washington concerning command of army to be formed in 1798; late perusal of letters allowed no time. Thanks for friendly expressions in letter Feb. 4 last. Recognizes intolerant spirit toward Adams. Expects odium on self for writing *Life of Washington*. Undertook with false hope would be anonymous. Attempted to detail turbulent events without unnecessarily wounding dominant party, but no concealment of truth. Mrs. Marshall's compliments to Mrs. Adams. MHi, Adams Papers, Letters Rec'd. June 5, 1805–Dec., 1806, XXII, 49.

July 14
BLADENSBURG, VA. *Bushrod Washington to Caleb P. Wayne*

Forwarding last volume *Life of Washington* by stage. Deliver one copy to Morgan; deposit $1,000 in Bank of the United States, one-half to J.M. and one-half to Washington. PPHi.

July 17
QUINCY *from John Adams*

Acknowledges letter of sixth; will consult letter book for four letters to George Washington. Relates political conditions and pressure on him to elevate Washington to army; was opposed to it; believed purpose of advocates to favor Hamilton. MHi, John Adams Letter Book, "Public and Private," Mar. 23, 1801—Nov., 1812, 90; Beveridge, *Marshall*, III, 257–58 (excerpt).

Oct. 29, *n.p.* *to Cashier, Bank of the United States, Philadelphia*

Order to pay Murdo and Fisher, $1,000. NIC.

Nov. 9
RICHMOND *to Jonathan Williams*

Apologizes for neglect in answering letter; indisposition and tour to mountains for summer and large part of autumn. Encloses note for five dollars, amount required from each member (of the Society for the Improvement of Military Knowledge in the United States). If additional requisitions, advise. Wishes the institution (West Point) well. NNHi.

Dec. 24
RICHMOND *to Cashier, Bank of the United States, Philadelphia*

Order to pay James Brown $1,000 of J.M.'s quarterly salary. DLC, Beveridge Coll.

n.d., n.p. *Deposition of J.M.*

Deposition of J.M. concerning action of *Rawleigh Colston, administrator of Thomas Webb v. Morris and Braxton,* District Court, Richmond, before Lem Bent, commissioner; was counsel for Colston in action, favorable judgment, much time to exceptions by Morris counsel; appeal decided on. Benjamin Harrison, Jr., objected to by Colston as security on appeal bond; disinclined to make objection because of friendship with Harrison; Colston made in person; appeal dropped. J.M. counsel for Harrison in all suits in court; does not believe Harrison could have paid j. against Morris and Braxton; at time Morris credit high; would have relied on it; J.M. was consulted frequently by Colston concerning collection of j. In evidence *Francis Webb et al. v. Rawleigh Colston,* Superior Court of Chancery, Winchester, Frederick County, Va., Record Book 1784–1820, 1, 86.

CAMBRIDGE, MASS. *Honorary Degree*

J.M. received an LL.D. degree from Harvard University. *Quinquennial Catalog of the Officers and Graduates of Harvard University, 1636–1910* (Cambridge. Mass., Harv. Univ. Press, 1910), #672.

U.S. SUPREME COURT

FEBRUARY TERM. Feb. 3–Mar. 5.

Feb. 3–7. J.M., Paterson, Washington. Court adjourned, insufficient number.

Feb. 8. Johnson appeared, but Court adjourned because no counsel ready.

Feb. 9. John Breckenridge sworn in as Attorney General.

Feb. 19. Cushing appeared; attendance of all above for rest of session, except for absence of Chase from Mar. 1, Washington for two days, and J.M. the last day.

No August term.

DNA, U.S. Supreme Court, Minute Book B, 1–29.

February Term *Rules of Court*

Autograph document containing Rules of Court that causes delivered to clerk sixth day of term for trial in term, others may be continued; proceedings where writ of error a supersedeas to judgment of federal court and record not filed in six days; proceedings in causes not docketed at August term and failure of plaintiff in error to assign error, or of defendant to plead to issue. Designated Rule XIX. DNA, U.S. Supreme Court, Orders Concerning Rules of Court 1792–1848. R.G. 267. Printed in 1 Peters vii.

The Marine Insurance Co. of Alexandria v. John and James H. Tucker, 3 Cranch 357.

Error to U.S. Circuit Court, District of Columbia, affirmed.

Action on policy of insurance on vessel for voyage from Jamaica to Alexandria; ship sailed from Jamaica intending to go to Baltimore, thence to Alexandria; captured before reached point of division.

Held, an intended, not actual, deviation.

This cause was argued Feb. 20, 21, 1806, j. rendered Mar. 4, 1806. J.M. although present declined to give an opinion in the case, or as stated in the report "did not sit"; probably for interest. DNA, U.S. Supreme Court, Minute Book B, 9, 23. See also 3 Cranch 384.

Opinions

Hannay v. Eve, 3 Cranch 242, 247–49.

Error to U.S. Circuit Court, Georgia. Decree dismissing bill on demurrer, affirmed.

Resolution of Congress of 1781 provided that British vessels brought by crew to American ports deemed their prize. British vessel in distress en route from Jamaica to New York with supplies for British troops brought in, libeled and distributed to captain and crew. Action by owners against captain on alleged agreement between captain and crew to give them a share.

Held, agreement in fraud of resolution, not enforcible in American court.

Note: Minority of Court believed morally owners entitled to recover, and, war being over, should be allowed.

Montalet v. Murray, 3 Cranch 249.

A ruling on practice that where plaintiff in error fails to appear, the defendant may dismiss the writ of error, or may open the record and pray for affirmance. Costs go of course.

Announced as a Rule of Court, 3 Peters, frontispiece.

Sarah and Abigail Silsby v. Thomas Young and Enoch Silsby, 3 Cranch 250, 261–66.

Error to U.S. Circuit Court, Georgia. Dismissal of bill for accounting of plaintiff in error, reversed.

Testator provided trust of proceeds of estate, £1,500 to nephew when twenty-one, interest on £1,000 to each of two sisters, surplus to nephew, provided if proceeds not sufficient for annuities deficiency taken from nephew's bequest; became insufficient by subsequent bankruptcy of executor.

Held, deficiency taken from nephew's share though occurring subsequent to date of decease; no loss of annuity by interference in placing trust funds, or laches, in checking executor.

Strawbridge et al. v. Curtiss et al., 3 Cranch 267, 267–68.

Appeal from U.S. Circuit Court, Massachusetts. Dismissal of bill of appellant affirmed.

Ruling that the federal courts have no jurisdiction under the diversity of citizenship provision of a cause where several joint parties complainant were citizens of Massachusetts where suit was brought, and several parties defendant were similarly citizens of Massachusetts, excepting one who was a citizen of Vermont and was served in that state. The Court reserved opinion on the question where several parties represented distinct interests and diversity existed between certain ones.

Gordon v. Caldcleugh et al., 3 Cranch 268, 269–70.

Error to court of equity of State of South Carolina. Writ of error dismissed.

Bill in equity in state court by resident of South Carolina against several British subjects and two South Carolinians; motion to remove to U.S. Circuit Court under Section 12 of Judiciary Act allowed on grounds South Carolina defendants mere stockholders.

Held, Court no jurisdiction to review state court under Section 25 of Judiciary Act, because privilege under federal statute granted and not denied.

Note: Writ omitted to allege state court highest court in equity of state.

M'Ferran v. Taylor and Massie, 3 Cranch 270, 280–82.

Error to District Court, Kentucky. Decree of specific performance of contract to purchase land by plaintiff in error, plaintiff below, reversed and amended as to damages.

M'Ferran contracted to purchase of Taylor Kentucky land, 200 acres in consideration of two horses valued at £40, to which was later added 300 acres adjoining in consideration of one horse valued at £48. M'Ferran was to choose the 500 acres either from a 1,000-acre tract described as on

Hingston's Fork of Licking, or from 5,000 acres Taylor had for location. In fact, the 1,000 acres was on Slade Creek, another branch of the Licking, and less valuable. Taylor's other land was on a military warrant for 6,000 acres, 1,000 of which was on Paint Creek (Ohio), claimed not included in the choice, and his interest in which he sold. M'Ferran sought delivery of 500 acres out of this tract. The District Court held this tract excluded, gave M'Ferran opportunity to choose from the other tracts; if he failed to do so, Taylor to make the choice and convey.

J.M. in giving the opinion of the Court would have affirmed, leaving M'Ferran to action at law for damages rather than directing court of equity to grant damages for an unimportant deviation in description. He stated, however, he was "perfectly content" with the opinion which he was "directed to deliver," which was that the 1,000 acres on Paint Creek was not included in the choice, but an issue be drawn as to damages for inability to deliver land on Hingston's.

Wilson v. Speed, 3 Cranch 283, 290–93.

Error to District Court, Kentucky. Dismissal of caveat by plaintiff in error, reversed.

Wilson obtained certificate for settlement rights to 400 acres in Kentucky for raising crop and building cabin in 1776, and right of pre-emption to 1,000 acres adjoining; caveat against Speed who sought to survey part of each under treasury warrant entry. Wilson sought to introduce as witness his assignee of the 1,000 acres to prove that the assignment was for his own benefit and that reassignment was in fact by Wilson himself to persons for whose benefit bringing action.

Held, witness not incompetent for interest, but facts if proved would not warrant action by Wilson; error to dismiss and not decide on merits of caveat as to 400 acres.

Buddicum v. Kirk, 3 Cranch 293, 297–98.

Error to U.S. Circuit Court, District of Columbia. J. for defendant in error, defendant below, affirmed.

Action on bond against heir of obligor; plea, payment by delivery of wheat and assignment of debts. Notice of deposition by defendant to attorney at law for certain date and on adjournment from day to day; actually taken with intervening days.

Held, deposition taken under Virginia law; notice should be on attorney in fact, but may be waived; not taken according to notice, but waived by examination and failure to object; former guardian competent to testify for former ward where latter of age at date of trial; evidence of assignment of debts and accounts without proof of their collection by assignee is some evidence of payment.

Douglass & Mandeville v. M'Allister, 3 Cranch 298, 300–309.

Error to U.S. Circuit Court, District of Columbia. J. for defendant in error, plaintiff below, affirmed.

Assumpsit for nondelivery of flour by agent under contract to receive flour and give principal at his option flour or money. Defendant below asked for instruction to jury setting damages at time option, which Court, being divided, did not do.

Held, Court should give opinion on point relevant to issue, but failure to charge no reversible error because verdict was based on value at date contended for.

Simms and Wise v. Slacum, 3 Cranch 300, 306–309.

Error to U.S. Circuit Court, District of Columbia. J. for defendant in error, plaintiff below, reversed.

Action by sergeant of court against surety on prison bounds bond.

Held, error to refuse to charge jury where release by certificate from insolvency court obtained by prisoner fraudulently without participation of surety or magistrates, surety not liable.

Dissenting opinion by Justice Paterson.

Theophilus Harris v. Johnston, 3 Cranch 311, 317–19.

Error to U.S. Circuit Court, District of Columbia, Alexandria. J. for defendant in error, plaintiff below, reversed.

Action for goods sold and delivered. Harris bought of Johnston rum and sugar, gave as conditional payment a note endorsed to him and by him, both in blank; a receipt indicated seller was Dunlap and Johnston. Johnston endorsed the note to Dunlap.

Held, if sugar solely owned by Johnston and rum by Dunlap and sale of latter made by authority of Dunlap, Johnston may maintain suit for both in own name; recovery may not be had on original sale where note accepted as conditional payment passed on.

Dixon's Executors v. Ramsay's Executors, 3 Cranch 319, 323–24.

Error to U.S. District Court, District of Columbia. J. for defendant in error, defendant below, affirmed.

Held, an executor cannot maintain suit in District of Columbia under letters testementary of a foreign country; right to sue governed by law of forum.

Scott v. Negro London, 3 Cranch 324, 329–31.

Error to U.S. Circuit Court, District of Columbia, Alexandria. J. for defendant in error, plaintiff below, reversed.

Assault and battery to try freedom. Nonresident owner had slave brought into state by another who did not make statutory oath; owner moved into state himself within year and took required oath that moving into state not intended as evasion, no intent to sell, slaves not imported from Africa or West Indies since Nov. 1, 1778.

Held, satisfied Virginia act of 1792 freeing slave brought into state and kept one year unless owner removes into state and gives oath within sixty days.

Wise v. Withers, 3 Cranch 331, 335–37.

Error to U.S. Circuit Court, District of Columbia. J. for defendant in error, defendant below, reversed.

Trespass against collector of militia fines for distraint of property of justice of peace of District of Columbia, fined by court-martial for failure to serve in militia.

Held, justice of peace a judicial and executive officer not subject to militia duty; court-martial no jurisdiction; officer acting thereunder liable.

The United States v. Grundy and Thornburgh, 3 Cranch 337, 349–56.

Error to U.S. Circuit Court, Maryland. J. for defendant in error, defendant below, affirmed.

Action for money had and received against assignee in bankruptcy of vessel for money received from sale of ship, claim based on false registry of ownership by bankrupt in failing to disclose part ownership by alien, contrary to act of 1792, resulting in forfeiture.

Held, government had option to proceed against owner or vessel, but not against assignee who sold vessel before seizure.

Manella, Pujals & Co. v. James Barry, 3 Cranch 415, 439–48.

Error to U.S. Circuit Court, Maryland. J. for defendant in error, defendant below, affirmed.

Plaintiff of Spain transmitted through confidential agent large order for tobacco indicating to be made in six to eight shipments in name of American seller, and subject to instructions of agent. Two shipments made in neutral vessels captured by French and British, a third sent in name of Italian on instruction of agent (the United States being in near war with France) also captured by British.

Held, seller not liable, no specific instructions to ship in American vessels, and agent full power to control shipments.

Ex parte Burford, 3 Cranch 448, 449.

Habeas corpus to U.S. Circuit Court, District of Columbia, Washington, granted.

Despite its lack of appellate jurisdiction in criminal cases, the Court held that under the Judiciary Act of 1789, it had power to grant original writs of habeas corpus. Marshall remarked that the act and the Constitution were obscure, but the Court, "favoring liberty," was willing to grant the writ and, in addition, felt bound to do so by earlier decision in *The United States v. Hamilton,* 3 Dallas 17. Prisoner was committed to county jail in the District of Columbia under warrant stating that on testimony of creditable persons, the justices of peace were given to understand that the defendant, a shopkeeper, was not of good name and fame, an evildoer and disturber of the peace, and should be confined pending filing a $4,000 bond for life. On habeas corpus to the Circuit Court, that Court remanded the prisoner to jail, reducing recognizance for good behavior to $1,000 for one year.

Held, that the original warrant of commitment was illegal for want of stating a good cause certain, supported by oath; that the Circuit Court had not proceeded *de novo,* but acted only on the original proceedings. In granting the habeas corpus, the Court warned the justices that if they acted anew in the matter, they must take care that their proceedings be regular.

William Maley v. Jared Shattuck, 3 Cranch 458, 487–92.

Appeal from U.S. Circuit Court, Pennsylvania, reversing decree U.S. District Court dismissing libel, and granting damages.

This case closely parallels that of the *Charming Betsy* (herein 1804, U.S. Supreme Court) in countenancing what was undoubtedly a frequent evasion of the Nonintercourse Act prohibiting trade by Americans with the French.

American vessel trading with St. Thomas, a Dutch port, in 1799 was there sold to Shattuck, a native-born American since removed to St. Thomas and taking allegiance to the Dutch. From there it proceeded in trading to San Domingo, former French territory held by Toussaint, where it was seized by American public man-of-war, the *Experiment,* directed with an American officer on board to proceed to Cape Francois for determination. En route seized by British vessel of war and adjudged a prize at Jamaica.

Libel was brought by Shattuck against Maley, the captain of the *Experiment,* in District Court; dismissed. The Circuit Court, Justice Washington sitting, reversed the ruling, allowing over $33,000 damages.

Held, Jamaica Court of Admiralty was not conclusive as to ownership, that Shattuck had acquired commercial rights of domicile in St. Thomas; that there was insufficient suspicion of American or French ownership to warrant seizure; that seizure by the British did not excuse the captor from obtaining an adjudication of ownership; and that Shattuck recover, with certain adjustments of items of damage.

Lawrason v. Mason, 3 Cranch 492, 495–96.

Error to U.S. Circuit Court, District of Columbia. J. for defendant in error, plaintiff below, affirmed.

Assumpsit on open letter of defendant to buyer of corn that would become security for purchase.

Held, action lies against writer, buyer bankrupt, "bound by every principle of moral rectitude and good faith," and assumpsit "at least as proper as any other."

Sands v. Thomas Knox, administrator of Raupzat Heyleger, 3 Cranch 499, 503.

Error to Court for the Trial of Impeachments and the Correction of Errors, New York. J. for defendant in error, plaintiff below, affirmed.

Trespass by administrator of Danish subject against collector of customs, port of New York, for illegal seizure of vessel in alleged violation of Non-intercourse Act of 1798. American vessel sailed from the United States to Danish port of St. Croix under bond for voyage; vessel sold there to testator, taken for trading purposes to French San Domingo and thence to the United States.

Court refused argument; act not apply to vessels owned by foreigners residing outside the United States, following *Charming Betsy* case (herein 1804, U.S. Supreme Court).

U.S. CIRCUIT COURT, VIRGINIA

May term. May 22–June 17.

May 22–June 6. J.M. and District Judge Cyrus Griffin.

June 7–17. J.M. alone.

U.S. Circuit Court, Va., Order Book V, 265–369.

November term. Nov. 22–Dec. 19.

Nov. 22. J.M. alone.

Nov. 24–Dec. 2. J.M. and Judge Griffin.

Dec. 3. J.M. alone.

Dec. 4–9. Both, Judge Griffin absenting self part of Dec. 9 for case in which he was plaintiff.

Dec. 10–19. J.M. alone.

U.S. Circuit Court, Va., Order Book VI, 1–124.

June 6 Mandate of U.S. Supreme Court affirming U.S. Circuit Court, Virginia, in *William Randolph, executor of Peyton Randolph v. John Tyndale Ware, executor of William Jones,* 3 Cranch 503, dismissing bill in equity claiming credit against judgment based on goods shipped, lost, claimed buyer's duty to insure, promised to insure, which failed to do. J.M. did not sit in Supreme Court, having decided the case below. U.S. Circuit Court, Va., Order Book V, 328. For earlier proceedings see Same, Order Book IV, 69, 125, 491; Order Book V, 143.

The United States v. William Heth, Collector for District of Petersburg, 3 Cranch 399.

Case certified from U.S. Circuit Court, Virginia, on division of opinion, ruling collector not limited to 2½ per cent as provided in act of May, 1800, on bonds for duties on goods imported where moneys collected after passage of act of June, 1800, allowing 3 per cent. Opinions by Justices Washington and Paterson. U.S. Circuit Court, Va., Order Book V, 43 (Dec. 4, 1804, order certifying). J.M., being one of judges opposed below, did not sit at hearing of cause, 3 Cranch 414.

The United States v. John Johnson.

Indictment for misdemeanor, theft from mail.

May 23, 1806. Indictment of grand jury returned. Plea, not guilty; verdict, guilty. J. taken under consideration.

U.S. Circuit Court, Va., Order Book V, 269, 270.

No record of entry of j.

Autograph case notes of J.M. concerning jurisdiction of court, sufficiency of indictment, embezzlement required, route covered.

V, U.S. Circuit Court Va., Case Papers.

James M. Marshall v. Major General Phillip Martin, Leeds Castle, Great Britain, Philip Bush, Sr., Isaac Little, Henry Baker, and Joseph Gamble.

Two bills in chancery, one dated Oct. 28, 1803, one June 14, 1805. Both dismissed by plaintiff in 1806.

No order book entries. Indexed as "Chy. 1805."

V, U.S. Circuit Court, Va., Case Papers.

Philip Martin v. Hugh Murphy.

Ejectment, leasehold 317 acres Hardy County, Va., filed Jan. 1, 1803, title of cause *John Goodtitle v. Hugh Badtitle.*

Nov. 30, 1805. Affidavit that Hugh Murphy in possession, served copy declaration, not appear; order if not appear next court not make self and those claiming under defendants; plead general issue; confess lease, entry and ouster; enter common rule to insist on title only at trial, j. to be entered for defendant with award to United States of writ of *habere facias possessionem.* U.S. Circuit Court, Va., Order Book V, 201.

J.M. and Cyrus Griffin sitting.

May 23, 1806. Dismissed, plaintiff not prosecuting. Same, 269. Same judges sitting.

Declaration and notice dated Sept. 16, 1805, in J.M.'s handwriting.

V, U.S. Circuit Court, Va., Case Papers.

Opinions

William Short v. Skipwith, 1 Brockenbrough 103, 105–18.

Claim of principal against agent in accounting for losses by breach of trust allowed.

Short, then in Paris, in 1787 and 1788, instructed Skipwith, as agent, to withdraw military certificates from hands of previous agent Benjamin Harrison, Jr., invest interest in Virginia certificates; failed to do so; in 1789 turned assets over to James Brown, excepting a part of interest money, who invested interest in certificates.

Held, although executed tardily, Skipwith not liable for increase in value of Virginia certificates between 1787 and 1789; liable for money retained with simple interest, plus loss from failure to invest in certificates in 1789; on loan made by agent to third person to buy certificates which he failed to collect or transfer, liable for certificates and interest; no commission allowed on collection of loan which agent borrowed by previous agreement with principal.

Autograph opinion. V, U.S. Circuit Court, Va., Case Papers.

U.S. CIRCUIT COURT, NORTH CAROLINA

June term. June 20–25.

Judge Henry Potter alone.

December term. Dec. 29–Jan. 2, 1807.
J.M. and Judge Henry Potter.
DNA, U.S. Circuit Court, N.C., Minute Book, as dated.

Opinions

Thomas Mutter's Executors v. John Hamilton, 2 Haywood 346, Brunner's Coll. Cas. 27.

Held, *per curiam,* injunction not allowed to stay trial or judgment when cause ready for trial, even though bill contains facts enough to warrant granting.

June 18, 1805. V. j. for Mutter's executors on written obligation, $1,462.75. DNA, U.S. Circuit Court, N.C., Minute Book, as dated.

June 20, 1805. Injunction allowed on making bond double amount, also commissions to mayor of Petersburg and magistrate of County of Granville to take answers, pleas, and demurrers of defendants. Same.

Jan. 1, 1806. Injunction dissolved on hearing. Same.

——— *v. Lewis' Executors,* 2 Haywood 346, Brunner's Coll. Cas. 27.

Lewis died 1780; demurrer to plea of seven-year statute of limitations, act of North Carolina, 1715, disallowed.

Held, *per curiam,* Act of Limitations suspended during war as to British adherents unable to sue; revived at end of war, but if not seven years prior to repeal by act of 1789, not a bar.

Lessee of George William Coventry, also known as William Earl of Coventry v. Josiah Collins. Not reported.

Ejectment and trespass, j. for defendant; error to Supreme Court dismissed.

June 20, 1804. Plea not guilty, jury impaneled, demurrer to evidence tendered and joined. Jury discharged.

Jan. 5, 1805. Motion by defendant to discharge demurrer to evidence; plaintiff opposed.

June 18, 1805. Discharge of demurrer order by Potter only, J.M. "utterly refusing any opinion thereon"; jury again impaneled; exception by plaintiff.

Jan. 3, 1806. V.j. for defendant, error to Supreme Court.
DNA, U.S. Circuit Court, N.C., as dated.

Supreme Court proceedings:
Feb. 4, 1807. Record filed.
Feb. 4, 1807—Aug., 1816. Continuances.

Feb. 4, 1817. Plaintiff in error called, writ of error dismissed for non-appearance.

DNA, U.S. Supreme Court, Docket Book A, 292. Case No. 288. R.G. 267.

Thomas Hart v. Peter Mallett's Executors. Not reported.

Action of debt.

June 24, 1806. Plaintiff allowed after verdict to amend declaration to insert citizenship of defendant, North Carolina; v.j. $1,973.94 debt and $2,654 damages. Forty days allowed defendants to issue writ of error to U.S. Supreme Court.

No record of such proceedings.

DNA, U.S. Circuit Court, N.C., Minute Book, as dated.

LAND TRANSACTIONS

Fairfax Purchase, Various Counties of Virginia

Oct. 18
London, England *Deed*

Philip Martin, Leeds Castle, Great Britain, brother and heir at law of Denny Martin Fairfax, to Rawleigh Colston, Frederick County, J.M., and James M. Marshall, both of Richmond, as tenants in common the Manor of Leeds, Fauquier, Loudon, Frederick, and Shenandoah counties, Virginia; 119,927 acres surveyed by John Warner, Nov. 15, 1736 (V, Northern Neck Grants, 1736–1742, E, 28); 26,534 acres surveyed Nov. 15, 1736 (Same, 38); 13,928 acres surveyed Mar. 10, 1748 (Same, 524); subject to grants, leases, and promises prior to May 17, 1793; grantees agree to pay three annuities to grantor's sisters each £100 charged by codicil of Lord Fairfax' will; £14,000 receipted. Executed in London, J.M., by his attorney William Murdock, who acted under power of attorney dated May 31, 1806, executed by J.M. and James M. Marshall. V, *Marshall's Lessee v. E. Foley*, Circuit Superior Court of Fauquier County, Virginia, Land Causes 1833–1850, III, 8, at 40–44. (See herein Aug. 30, 1797, note; also Tyler's, Vol. XXXIV [Jan. 1926], 57.)

The original of this deed was thought to be in the hands of James M. Marshall, lost by his executor, later found with Gen. James Williams, Shenandoah County, Va., attorney for Rawleigh Colston, and entered in evidence before examiner in *United States v. M. F. Morris et al.*, 174 U.S. 196 (which see herein 1899).

Hardy County, Virginia
(Now West Virginia)

Apr. 10 *Deed*

Hugh Murphy, Hardy County, to J.M., Richmond, 249 acres in Hardy County on Abraham Creek in the Alegania [*sic*] Mountain, received under will of father. Consideration $100. Recorded May 12, 1806. Hardy County, Va., Deed Book C, 196.

May 10 *Deed*

J.M., by Charles Magill, attorney in fact, to Adam Fisher, reversionary interest, 117 acres being ⅓ of 350 acres, No. 39, South Branch Manor, leased Thomas Lord Fairfax to Adam Fisher, Aug. 3, 1773. Consideration £29:5. Recorded May 13, 1806. Hardy County, Va., Deed Book C, 202.

May 13 *Deed*

J.M., by Charles Magill, attorney in fact, to Jacob Fisher, reversionary interest, 117 acres, being ⅓ of 350 acres, No. 39, South Branch Manor, leased Thomas Lord Fairfax to Adam Fisher, Aug. 3, 1773. Consideration £29:5. Recorded May 13, 1806. Hardy County, Va., Deed Book C, 203.

May 13 *Deed*

J.M., by Charles Magill, attorney in fact, to William Cunningham, reversionary interest 124½ acres, 21 poles, being ⅓ of 350 acres, No. 39, South Branch Manor, leased Thomas Lord Fairfax to Adam Fisher, Aug. 3, 1773. Consideration £31. Recorded May 13, 1803. Hardy County, Va., Deed Book C, 205.

Hampshire County, Virginia
(Now West Virginia)

Jan. 1 *Lease*

J.M., to Daniel Collins, tract on North Branch of Potomac, part of Anderson's Bottom, now in tenure of James Clarke and John Ohara, except thirty acres conveyed to Ohara, ninety-nine acres in tenure of Ohara; term of lease fourteen years from Mar. 1, 1807; yearly rental $300. Recorded May 5, 1806. Hardy County, Va., Deed Book C, 150.

Mason County, Kentucky

Nov. 8 *Tax List*

List of land for taxes by H. Marshall, agent, 1,000 acres on North

Fork of Licking, Mason County, Ky., for James M. Marshall, surveyed in name of J.M., patented by Thomas Marshall, KyHi.

CITY OF RICHMOND, VIRGINIA

Dec. 24 *Deed*

J.M. and Mary Willis, his wife, to Daniel Call, attorney at law, two one-half-acre lots, Richmond, Nos. 781, 782, Plan of Richmond, to grantor from Francis Lightfoot, holding under will of Arthur Lee and recorded in General Court; consideration $3,000. Recorded Feb. 9, 1807. Richmond City Hustings and Chancery Court, Deed Book 4, 572–74.

1807

DOCUMENTS

Jan. 6
RICHMOND *Hallerian Academy*

Act of Virginia Legislature incorporating Hallerian Academy; J.M. a trustee. Virginia Acts, Dec., 1806, Chap. LXXXIII, 33; Hening, Stat., XVI, 335.

Feb. 3
WASHINGTON *to William Wirt*

Giving opinion concerning case of Lee and Coulson (n.f.). Referred to in letter William Wirt to J.M., Feb. 12, 1807 (herein).

Feb. 12
RICHMOND *from William Wirt*

Acknowledging letter of Feb. 3, agrees with his opinion as to case of Lee and Coulson. Murdock deposition enclosed; executors of Ann Gideon renounced execution and probate of her will in England, does not know significance. Sample attorney; asks J.M. to furnish deeds of conveyance for tender; advises to obtain complete powers; chancery term at Williamsburg. MdHi, Wm. Wirt Letter Book, 88–89.

Mar. 30
RICHMOND *to David Daggett, of New Haven, Conn.*

Answering letter of Mar. 21; opinion of Supreme Court in various publications correct; Judge Livingston on bench when habeas corpus issued; his death. CtY, Rare Book Room.

June 29
RICHMOND *to Justice William Cushing*

Aaron Burr trial, difficulties; should consult with justices. Asks opinion on constructive treason, use of evidence of one party of conspiracy, situs of overt act, extent two witnesses needed. English law discussed. Same letter to Judge Washington (n.f.). Resumé of questions asked, probably in handwriting of Cushing. MHi, R. T. Paine, Vol. 4. Quoted by Horace Gray in Dillon, *Marshall* I, 72; also Beveridge, *Marshall,* III, 481.

Sept. 5 *to Richard Peters*

Congratulations on publishing his admiralty decisions. PPHi, Peters MSS.

Sept. 27 *from B. Henry Latrobe,*
WASHINGTON *Surveyor of the Public Buildings, United States*

Suggesting superior accommodations for Supreme Court might be obtained in alteration of north wing of Capitol. Asks permission to propose to President. DLC. Latrobe MSS.

Nov. 23
RICHMOND *to Richard Peters*

Acknowledging letter of Aug. 10, reports of admiralty decisions; need for reports of Supreme Court. Burr case most unpleasant; left for mountains, to North Carolina circuit, to Richmond; criticism for following the law. PPHi, Peters Coll. Vol. 10, 122. Excerpt in Beveridge, *Marshall,* III, 529–30.

Dec. 24
RICHMOND *Trust Deed—Masonic Lodge*

Grantland to J.M. and Joseph Darmstadt and others, trustees for "Masonick" Society for City of Richmond, tenement in Richmond where Collin Dowdell resides, rented at fifty shillings per month, to collect rents commencing Jan. 16, 1808, until writ of elegit, District Court of Richmond, satisfied. Recorded Jan. 11, 1808. Richmond City Hustings and Chancery Court, Deed Book 5, 155.

Dec. 30 *to Cashier, Bank of the United States, Philadelphia*

Order to pay James Brown on order $1,000 from quarterly salary due Jan. 1. NN, Montague Coll.

U.S. SUPREME COURT

FEBRUARY TERM. Feb. 2–28; J.M. attended throughout.

Feb. 2. J.M., Cushing, Johnson present; Henry Brockholst Livingston presented commission and took seat in Court; Humphrey Marshall, Henry Clay admitted to practice.

Feb. 3. Washington appeared, but Cushing and Chase noted ill; the former was out the balance of the term; the latter appeared Feb. 4 and sat throughout except for three days. Livingston was absent from Feb. 17 to end of term.

August term, first Monday; Chase, all cases continued.

DNA, U.S. Supreme Court, Minute Book B, 31–59.

Justice William Paterson died Sept. 9, 1806.

Humphrey Marshall and wife v. James Currie, 4 Cranch 172.

Error to U.S. District Court, Kentucky. J. for defendant in error, defendant below, reversed. Opinion by Justice Johnson.

The case involved the validity of entry made by Thomas Marshall, J.M.'s father, claimed by Humphrey, J.M.'s brother-in-law and cousin, and his wife, J.M.'s sister. Action against older patentee claiming under prior entry. The entry based on marked trees was held sufficiently definite because of courses and distances making it only location.

It appears that J.M. sat at the argument of the cause. U.S. Supreme Court, Minute Book B, 44 (Feb. 27, 1807).

OPINIONS

Jennings v. Carson, 4 Cranch 2, 20–29.

Appeal from U.S. Circuit Court, Pennsylvania, reversing U.S. District Court. Admiralty, refusal to decree restitution of prize, affirmed.

In 1778, the American privateer *Addition,* owned in part by Carson, captured the sloop *George,* owned by Jennings, a Dutch inhabitant of St. Eustatius, en route to Egg Harbor and allegedly carrying supplies to the British. The sloop was condemned as a lawful prize in the New Jersey state court; but on appeal to the Continental Court of Appeals created by act of Congress during the war, the decree was reversed and restitution ordered. Pending the appeal, the ship was sold under order of the state court and the proceeds held by the marshal.

The present action commenced in U.S. District Court, District of Pennsylvania, was to enforce the decree of restitution against the legal representatives of Jennings, since deceased. The decree of this court allowing relief was reversed by the Circuit Court, which reversal in turn was affirmed by the Supreme Court on grounds that, although the District Court had jurisdiction over decrees of the old Continental Court of Appeals, the relief of restitution could not be had against the captor because the vessel and its proceeds were in the hands of the original court.

It further ruled that that court had power to sell the ship as a perishable, even pending appeal; and further that no claim for damages could be had against the captor, who had probable cause to make the capture. Marshall alluded to the carelessness with which the papers of the Continental Court of Appeals were kept.

Rhinelander v. The Insurance Company of Pennsylvania, 4 Cranch 29, 41–46.

Case certified from U.S. Circuit Court, Pennsylvania, on division of opinion.

The owners of the American ship the *Manhattan* brought action on a policy of $12,500 on freight valued therein at $50,000. The ship was under charter to third persons and, on its return voyage from Batavia in 1805, was captured by a British armed vessel, manned and libeled at Bermuda as a prize of war. The ship and cargo were both acquitted, but appeal was taken and still pending as to the cargo. The insured owner, meanwhile, and shortly after the capture, by letter offered abandonment to the insurance company. After the decree of acquittal, he gave security for the cargo, which was brough to New York. The Insurance Company refused to give countersecurity to relieve him from his obligation. Prior to arrival of the cargo in New York, the insured sued for recovery under the policy as a total loss.

J.M., speaking for a unanimous Court, ruled that the taking of a neutral vessel by a belligerent as a prize constitutes a total loss and warrants abandonment by the insured to the underwriters while ship is still in possession of the captors. Speaking for a majority of the Court, he ruled that the rights of the parties are fixed at time of offer of abandonment and are not affected by subsequent events.

Of particular interest is J.M.'s statement of the importance of the question to the commercial interests of the country and the need to settle the question clearly. Contradicting the frequent claim that he ignored precedent are his many references to English cases and texts, and his statement that these cases received the attention of the Court. He stated that in the absence of direct authorities, he acted on general principles, analogy, and reasonable construction of the contract.

Montalet v. Murray, 4 Cranch 46, 47.

Error to U.S. Circuit Court, Georgia. Action on promissory note, j. for defendant in error, plaintiff below, reversed.

Action brought by a citizen of New York, claiming as assignee of note made by defendant, a French citizen, payable to one whose residence and citizenship did not appear in the declaration.

Held, federal court had no jurisdiction over cases between aliens; did not appear on record diversity of citizenship, and court had no jurisdiction.

(See herein, 1806, U.S. Supreme Court, same case, 3 Cranch 249.)

The United States v. Willings and Francis, 4 Cranch 48, 55–59.

Error to U.S. Circuit Court, Pennsylvania, reversing U.S. District Court. Debt, on customs bond, reversal of j. against defendant in error, affirmed.

During the period in question, 1802, American-owned vessels importing goods from abroad were given the privilege of duties some 10 per cent less than those imposed on goods imported in foreign bottoms. Under the act of Dec. 31, 1792, registration of American vessels was required, and, in case of sale to another American, reregistration. Upon entry from a foreign port, the owner was required to give oath as to ownership and transfers of ownership, and to give oath that no foreigner had any part of ownership.

In the present case, the ship *Missouri* sailed from Philadelphia for Canton (China) registered in the name of Willings and Francis. While the ship was at sea, in Feb., 1801, a part was sold to other Americans, orally and without bill of sale and without change of registry. On the day of return to port and before report of entry was made, the part ownership was orally resold to Willings and Francis, who made oath reciting the above facts. Bond was required by the collector of customs based on foreign rather than domestic duties amounting to a difference of $702.05.

Held, the registration act be liberally construed; that no new registration required in case of transfer while at sea to protect the shipment from alien duties.

Oneale v. Long, 4 Cranch 60, 61.

Error to U.S. Circuit Court, District of Columbia, Washington.

Action on debt on surety bond against one of several sureties; j. for defendant in error, plaintiff below, reversed.

Bond was filed in appeal from judgments of justice of peace and signed by Oneale and another, rejected by justice of peace; without Oneale's knowledge, a third surety added and bond accepted.

Held, by unanimous Court, not liable; some justices, for reason bond void by interlineation; others, that vacated by original rejection.

Smith and others v. Edward Carrington and others, 4 Cranch 62, 69–73.

Error to U.S. Circuit Court, Rhode Island. Assumpsit by plaintiff in error on an agency account, j. for defendant in error, reversed.

Agents in Hamburgh had placed insurance on Carrington's ship for voyage from the United States to Hamburgh, on the ship and cargo from Hamburgh to Havana, and on intended return to Hamburgh. Instead of so returning, the ship came directly to the United States. The issue of the case was whether the agent had received due notice of the change of destination prior to paying the premium to the underwriter, an amount of some $13,000, which admittedly under Hamburgh law he could not demand returned to him. The evidence of defendant included a copy of a letter of defendant who was then in Canton, China, to the Philadelphia correspondents with no proof that it was a true copy. The issue was left to a jury under directions of the court which were excepted to, and verdict and judgment given to plaintiff on items of the account, excluding the premiums advanced.

Held, error to receive unauthenticated letter as evidence, verdict based thereon reversed; also exceptions may be taken to misdirection of jury; party may demand ruling of court on point of law, but not direction to jury on both law and fact.

Ex parte Bollman and Ex parte Swartwout, 4 Cranch 75, 93–101, 123, 124, 125–36.

Motion for habeas corpus to marshal of District of Columbia to bring up bodies of Erick Bollman and Samuel Swartwout committed by U.S. Circuit Court, District of Columbia, for treason, and for a certiorari to bring up the record. Granted.

Preliminary question as to jurisdiction of court to issue habeas corpus from commitment.

Held, that court had jurisdiction under Sec. 14, Judiciary Act; that constitutional under appellate jurisdiction. Justice Johnson dissented, supported by one other Justice not present (Chase or Cushing). On merits, affidavit of Gen. Wilkinson; held, that affidavit before one magistrate usable by another in making commitment; certificate of office of magistrate approved; division of opinion if paraphrase of contents of letter of Burr admissible; letter shows no reference to enterprise against the United States, Mexico only; bearer of letter acquainted with contents.

Wilkinson affidavit as to statements of Swartwout: division of Court if "revolutionizing" referred to U.S. territory; Burr levying men did not constitute an assembly, necessary to treasonable act; seizures at New Orleans, mere threat of robbery.

Statute on misdemeanor of levying war against friendly power imprecise, place indefinite.

Court (four justices: J.M., Chase, Washington, and Johnson) unanimous that crime not committed in District of Columbia, cannot be tried there.

The reporter referred to J.M.'s opinion in Burr treason trial, 4 Cranch, Appendix B, to clarify passages in opinion, probably referring to statements as to assemblage of men and situs of crime.

Dillon, *Decisions*, 51–81; Cotton, I, 68–95; Marshall, *Writings*, 33–52.

Ex parte James Alexander, 4 Cranch 75, note 1.

Habeas corpus to military officer to bring up Alexander, a New Orleans attorney, seized by orders of Gen. Wilkinson and transported to Washington.

Discussion by Justices Chase and Johnson if court power to issue habeas corpus, if mere auxiliary writ, if judge in chamber may issue it. J.M., that matter taken up without reference to precedents next day. Meantime prisoner discharged by Circuit Court.

French's Executrix v. The Bank of Columbia, 4 Cranch 141, 153–64.

Error to U.S. Circuit Court, District of Columbia, Washington. Assumpsit on promissory note, j. for defendant in error, defendant below, reversed.

Held, laches of payee of promissory note in failing to demand payment of maker and to give notice of nonpayment to accommodation endorser bars remedy against such endorser; direction to jury to contrary; error.

The United States v. Zebulon Cantril, 4 Cranch 167–68.

Certified on division of opinion from the U.S. Circuit Court, Georgia.

Held, that the act of Congress of June 27, 1798, will not support an indictment for knowingly uttering a counterfeit bill of the Bank of the United States because the law itself was repugnant in referring to the counterfeit bill as being issued by the bank and signed by officers. In the session of 1806–1807 the law was amended to correct the defect.

Sthreshley and Obannon v. The United States, 4 Cranch 169, 171.

Error to U.S. District Court, Kentucky. Debt on official bond, j. for the United States, reversed.

Action by the United States on bond of collector of revenue for duties on distilled spirits due and uncollected during office, appointment revoked, $2,285.83.

Held, in absence of neglect of duty, collector liable to turn over only revenue actually collected.

Note: Humphrey Marshall represented the plaintiff in error.

Wood v. Lide, 4 Cranch 180, 181.

Error to U.S. Circuit Court, Georgia.

Held, a writ of error served before its return date by filing a copy for the adverse party in the office of the clerk of courts may be returned at a later date, even into a subsequent term of court; appearance of defendant waives objection to irregularity.

U.S. CIRCUIT COURT, VIRGINIA

May term. May 22–June 30 (Burr Trial).
May 22–29. J.M. and District Judge Cyrus Griffin.
May 30–June 1. J.M. alone.
June 2–29. J.M. alone.
U.S. Circuit Court, Va., Order Book VI, 124–216.

Special session: Burr Trial. Aug. 3–20.
Aug. 3–5. J.M. alone.
Aug. 7, 10, 11, 13. Both.
Aug. 15. J.M. alone.
Aug. 17–31. Both.
Sept. 1–Oct. 20. J.M. alone.
U.S. Circuit Court, Va., Order Book VI, 216–48.

November term. Nov. 23–Dec. 19.
Nov. 23–24. J.M. alone.
Nov. 25–Dec. 12. Both.
Dec. 14–19. J.M. alone.
U.S. Circuit Court, Va., Order Book VI, 248–344.

George Ashton et al., executors of Thos. Muter et al. v. Ann Byrd, administratrix of Aliway Byrd, executor of Robt. Munford et al.

Dec. 14, 1807. Autograph decree, on exceptions to report of commissioners, report altered, reserved for final decision, questioned rents and profits, judgments, improvements.

V, U.S. Circuit Court, Va., Case Papers, 1824.

Entered in U.S. Circuit Court, Va., Order Book VI, 244–46.

Further proceedings in Same, Order Book XI, 451, 486; Order Book XII, 146.

Robert Beverley et al. v. Philip Martin.

Writ of right, involving surveys of 4,055 acres and 3,045 acres, North Branch of Rappahanock, called Hedgman, near Buck Run; James M. Marshall for Martin.

June 9, 1804. Survey ordered by surveyor of Fauquier County, U.S. Circuit Court, Va., Order Book IV, 497.

Dec. 17, 1806. Rule suspended. Same, VI, 112.

June 5, 1807. Order to dismiss if not surveyed and tried next term.

Same, 173. J.M. excused himself from case on this date but not at earlier dates.

V, U.S. Circuit Court, Va., Case Papers.

James Hopkirk, surviving partner of Alexander Spiers, John Bowman & Co. v. Henry Bell, executor of David Bell, 3 Cranch 454.

Mandate of U.S. Supreme Court (Mar. 4, 1807) on certificate of division of opinion U.S. Circuit Court, Virginia, ruling that Virginia limitation of actions is rendered inoperative by Treaty of Peace with Great Britain as to debts contracted before treaty and not barred at date of treaty; agent for collection is not a factor within meaning of proviso against exemption of persons beyond the seas. J. for plaintiff. U.S. Circuit Court, Va., Order Book VI, 272.

J. order of Supreme Court. DNA, U.S. Supreme Court, Minute Book B, 52. R.G. 267.

Ridley and Pringle v. David Ross & Co. and Wm. Hay.

Chancery. Action against agent for value of tobacco collected and not accounted for; j. for complainant.

The receipt of tobacco by agent in 1781 when destruction by enemy imminent held reprehensible and suspicious, especially where appropriated to personal use.

Held, liable for value at time collected and not at present date. J. for $891.24.

Autograph decree, also autograph document for submission by parties to arbitration of accounts with notations.

V, U.S. Circuit Court, Va., Case Papers.

Opinions

James Calloway, surviving partner of Trents and Calloway v. M. and J. Dobson, administrators of John Dobson, deceased, surviving partner of Dobson, Daltera, and Walker, 1 Brockenbrough 119.

Motion to amend answer of defendant in injunction proceedings against judgment obtained by defendant, English merchant, against plaintiff for balances due from trading transactions alleging fraud. Answer failed to include a shipment to defendant of tobacco included in obtaining judgment, and issue on it made up for jury.

Held, in equity amendment not permitted to include transaction in answer after opinion of court and testimony, danger of abuse.

The Aaron Burr Trial

Apr. 1 Opinion on termination of preliminary hearing holding Aaron Burr to trial for misdemeanor, not treason, and setting bail; on question of probable cause.

As to waging war against foreign friendly power: Deposition of Eaton introductory to that of Wilkinson; Burr letter to Wilkinson proved by Wilkinson's interpretation of cipher, already decided admissible by Supreme Court, J.M. favors; cipher indicates parties arranged key; military enterprise described and intended against the United States or foreign power; shows means provided; sufficient to show probable cause.

As to treason: Eaton's affidavit shows mere intent to commit, attack New Orleans and revolutionize. Wilkinson's alone held by Supreme Court to refer to expedition against Mexico; with Swartwout testimony, enough to show expedition to revolutionize in the United States; but although Swartwout testimony shows suspicion troops actually assembled for purpose, failure of government to offer affirmative proof diminishes suspicion; no probable cause shown. Bail, $10,000. *United States v. Burr,* 25 Fed. Cas. 2, 12–15, Case No. 14692n. Robertson, *Burr,* I, 11–18; Coombs, *Burr,* 4–11; *The Examination of Col. Aaron Burr before the Chief Justice of the United States, etc.* (Richmond, Grantland, 1807), 30–36; Beveridge, *Marshall,* III, 375–79 (quoted in part).

Remarks of J.M. in setting bail. *Examination of Burr, supra,* 38. For affidavits and depositions, see 4 Cranch 455–68, App., note A, Documents accompanying the President's message of Jan. 22, 1807; *Message from the President of the United States, transmitting a copy of the proceedings and of the evidence exhibited on the arraignment of Aaron Burr, and others before the Circuit Court of the United States, held in Virginia, in the year 1807* (Washington, Way, 1807).

Original papers of the cause, V, U.S. Circuit Court Case Papers, 1807.

Apr. 2 Autograph undertaking for appearance by Nicholas Perkins; also signed by J.M. V, U.S. Circuit Court Case Papers, 1807.

May 22 Ruling marshal may summon only twenty-four grand jurors; two substituted by marshal removed. *United States v. Burr,* 25 Fed. Cas. 55, 56, Case No. 14693.

Admonition if opinion formed to withdraw. Same, 57.

Proper question to jurors if opinion, if expressed. Same, 58.

Ruling opinion not only formed, but must be expressed to excuse. Same, 59.

May 22 Charge to grand jury. *United States v. Burr,* 25 Fed. Cas. 55, 59, Case No. 14693; Coombs, *Burr* 20.

May 26 Opinion by J.M. on motion for commitment on charge of treason that Court had power to commit; circumstances jury impaneled not affect; regrets hearing may stir publications unfavorable to justice. *United States v. Burr,* 25 Fed. Cas. 25–27. Robertson, *Burr,* I, 79–81; Coombs, *Burr,* 23–26; Beveridge, *Marshall,* III, 421–22 (quoted in part).

May 27 Ruling that government may produce evidence chronologically, but overt act must be proved; thereafter ruled overt act must be proved first. *United States v. Burr,* 25 Fed. Cas. 55, 60, 61, Case No. 14693.

May 27 Ruling that Wilkinson affidavit not proof of overt act, not admissible at this time, so decided by Supreme Court, that Court divided on competency of attacked letter. *United States v. Burr,* 25 Fed. Cas. 55, 60. Case No. 14693; Robertson, *Burr,* I, 94–96; Coombs, *Burr,* 28–29.

May 28 Ruling that affidavit of Jacob Dumbaugh presented by prosecution not admissible, not state place of taking; certificate of Governor not state that person taking oath the same as one of same name certified as a magistrate. *United States v. Burr,* 25 Fed. Cas. 27–30, Case No. 14692c; Robertson, *Burr,* I, 97–101; Coombs, *Burr,* 30–34.

May 28 J.M. asked to be relieved of ruling as to necessity for bail on examination for treason in addition to bail for misdemeanor; Burr consented to $10,000 additional bail. Robertson, *Burr,* I, 103–105; Coombs, *Burr,* 35–36.

May 28 Bail of $10,000 for appearance next day to hear charges, entire amount by Burr, $2,500 each by Luther Martin, Thomas Taylor, John G. Gamble, and William Langbourne. V, U.S. Circuit Court, Va., Order Book VI, 133; Robertson, Burr, I, 106; *United States v. Burr,* 25 Fed. Cas. 55, 62. Case No. 14693.

June 9 Burr's motion for *subpoena duces tecum* of letter from Gen. Wilkinson to President, Oct. 21, 1806, and orders to army and navy; J.M. discussion and request for argument on authority to issue writ. *United States v. Burr,* 25 Fed. Cas. 30, 31. Case No. 14692d; Robertson, *Burr,* I, 113–18.

June 9 Supplemental charges to jury withheld for argument. *United States v. Burr,* 25 Fed. Cas. 55, 63. Case No. 14693.

June 9 Discussion as to status of Dr. Bollman pardon. *United States v. Burr,* 25 Fed. Cas. 55, 63–64. Case No. 14693.

June 10 Reprimand to counsel to confine argument to power to issue subpoena to President. Robertson, *Burr,* I, 147–48.

June 10 Opinion that under Constitution, Eighth Amendment, and by reference to act of Congress in capital cases, accused has right to process of court before indictment; that unlike the British monarch, the President is subject to general subpoena (as admitted) and likewise *subpoena duces tecum,* no disrespect to office; the Wilkinson letter material for cross-examination, does not appear to endanger public safety, a question cognizable on the return; original must be provided. As to military order, material to defense, but subpoena should be directed to Secretary of department. *United States v. Burr,* 25 Fed. Cas. 30, 32–38, Case No. 14692d; Robertson, *Burr,* I, 173–88; Coombs, *Burr,* 41–53; Beveridge, *Marshall,* III, 443–47 (quoted in part).

Order. U.S. Circuit Court, Va., Order Book VI, 220.

Remarks of J.M. justifying his words that government wishes conviction. Robertson, *Burr,* I, 189.

June 15 Instructions to grand jury to inspect only papers of witness part of narrative and of person indicted. *United States v. Burr,* 25 Fed. Cas. 55, 64–65. Case No. 14693.

June 18 Opinion of J.M. on plea of self-incrimination to questions concerning letter in cipher and German, alleged to have been composed by Burr, addressed to Henry Wilburn, alias Erick Bollman, to be used in connection with testimony of latter before grand jury. Witness claiming privilege; Willie, reputed secretary to Burr. Questions asked if presently understood contents.

J.M. announced Court to judge if any answer will furnish evidence against witness or may disclose fact essential link in chain of testimony sufficient to convict of crime; if so, witness giving oath sole judge, subject to purging.

Held, must answer, present knowledge not justify inference or proof knew before trial; possible misprision of treason if knew at time of copying.

After answer of "no", allowed to answer that Burr wrote ciphered part and he copies it. *United States v. Burr*, 25 Fed. Cas. 38–41. Case No. 14692e; Robertson, *Burr*, I, 242–245; *Burr*, 67–70.

June 24 Indictment of Burr for treason and misdemeanor returned by grand jury. *United States v. Burr*, 25 Fed. Cas. 55, 70. Case No. 14693; Robertson, *Burr*, I, 305–306.

June 24 Ruling that bail required of Burr. *United States v. Burr*, 25 Fed. Cas. 55, 70. Case No. 14693; Robertson, *Burr*, I, 308.

June 25 On motion of Burr, confined in jail of Henrico as debtor, habeas corpus issued to marshal to bring forthwith to court. U.S. Circuit Court, Va., Order Book VI, 201; Robertson, *Burr*, I, 312.

June 26 Affidavit of counsel, Edmund Randolph, John Wickham, Benjamin Botts unable to confer; no separate room, deprives of assistance of counsel. U.S. Circuit Court, Va., Order Book VI, 202.

Order to marshal to remove Burr to front room, house of Luther Martin, shuttered, padlocked, guard. Same, 203; Robertson, *Burr*, I, 350–54.

June 25 Instructions to grand jury that might call Burr as witness. *United States v. Burr*, 25 Fed. Cas. 55, 71. Case No. 14693; Robertson, *Burr*, I, 327–28.

June 26 Habeas corpus awarded. Plea, in court, not guilty to treason charge. Trial in County of Wood where alleged committed great inconvenience, venire facias to marshal of this district to bring forty-eight qualified men, twelve from Wood County, as venire Aug. 3. U.S. Circuit Court, Va., Order Book VI, 203. Robertson, *Burr*, I, 354–57.

June 26 Benjamin Latrobe, appearance bond as witness against Burr. U.S. Circuit Court, Va., Order Book VI, 204.

June 27 Ruling on Burr motion for attachment of Wilkinson for contempt in obstructing justice, that witnesses be heard. *United States v. Burr,* 25 Fed. Cas. 41, 48–49. Case No. 14692f. Robertson, *Burr,* I, 257–67.

June 27 Ruling by J.M. on motion to attach Gen. Wilkinson for contempt for obstructing justice in connection with questioning and transporting of James Knox to Washington.

Held, payment of money to witness not made for purpose of corrupting witness; forcible transportation made under order of civil court; Wilkinson not responsible for court action or status of deputies. Robertson, *Burr,* I, 354–57; Coombs, *Burr,* 90–93.

June 27 Instructions to marshal that witnesses against Burr entitled to pay for attendance during period to return of venire process, distance of travel and return great. U.S. Circuit Court, Va., Order Book VI, 204.

June 29 Instructions to marshal witnesses on behalf of Burr paid same attendance as those of the United States. Same, 210.

June 30 Order on motion of the United States and pursuant to letter from Governor of Virginia and action of Council of State offering apartment in jail; marshal to admit visitors; Burr transferred there until Aug. 2. Same, 215; *United States v. Burr,* 25 Fed. Cas. 55, 74. Case No. 14693. Robertson, *Burr,* I, 357–59.

Aug. 3 Aaron Burr brought to bar. U.S. Circuit Court, Va., Order Book VI, 216.

Aug. 5 Instructions to counsel as to order of trying case. *United States v. Burr,* 25 Fed. Cas. 55, 75. Case No. 14693.

Aug. 5 Appearance bonds for four witnesses for government. U.S. Circuit Court, Va., Order Book VI, 217.

Aug. 7 Same for three more such witnesses. Same.

Aug. 10 Same, eight more such witnesses. Same, 218.

Burr acknowledges list of 131 jurors and venire, defects waived. Same.

Four jurors accepted by Burr. Same.

Aug. 10–11, 15 Ruling that person on venire who expressed opinion, based on rumors, that Burr had treasonable design was disqualified. *United States v. Burr,* 25 Fed. Cas. 55, 77–87. Case No. 14693; Robertson, *Burr,* I, 369–703; Coombs, *Burr,* 107–108.

Aug. 11 Opinion of J.M. as to disqualification of jurors for entertaining judgment as to guilt; disqualified if believe guilty of entire crime or essential point; if made up mind of treasonable designs anterior to indictment, not ground for challenge; but where opinion relates to designs up to time of indictment, ground for challenge. *United States v. Burr,* 25 Fed. Cas. 49, 50–52. Case No. 14692g. Robertson, *Burr,* I, 414–20; Coombs, *Burr,* 128–33.

Venire exhausted by challenges, order for forty-eight more. U.S. Circuit Court, Va., Order Book VI, 219.

Aug. 13 Appearance bond, one juror of the United States. Same.

Aug. 15 On motion of Burr *subpoena duces tecum,* Attorney General to bring forthwith into court letter Gen. Wilkinson to President, Oct. 21, 1806, mentioned in message to Congress. Same, 220.

Appearance bond for eleven witnesses of the United States. Same.

Aug. 17 Burr acknowledged list of four more witnesses, waived defects. Same, 221.

Aug. 17 Selection of jury completed. Same.

Aug. 18 Opinion as to order of evidence in Eaton testimony that the Court will not require evidence as to overt act charged in indictment to precede that of intention; corroborative or confirming evidence as to other plans in Washington or elsewhere must follow that corroborated, shows merely general evil intention. *United States v. Burr,* 25 Fed. Cas. 52, 53–54. Case No. 14692n. Robertson, *Burr,* I, 469–72; Coombs, *Burr,* 147–50.

Aug. 20 Appearance bond, one witness for Burr, one against. U.S. Circuit Court, Va., Order Book VI, 222, 223.

Aug. 24 Same, one against Burr. Same, 224.

Aug. 31 Opinion on motion to exclude further evidence, and exclude collateral evidence. Motion granted, case submitted to jury. *Charge to jury*: Under Constitution, treason consists of "levying war"; should be construed according to English construction of statute of 25th of Edward III, from which borrowed; "spurious doctrine" that in treason by levying war, guilt of principal attached to accessory may be accepted, although English cases are indecisive how indictment should read; under U.S. Constitution, those performing a part in prosecution of war may be indicted for levying, but not persons who merely counsel and advise, or who perform no part although engaged in the conspiracy; whether principal and accessory doctrine can apply in such case must be determined by the Supreme Court.

J.M. upholds doctrine announced in Supreme Court in *U.S. v. Bollman and Swartwout* (herein 1807, U.S. Supreme Court) that person engaged in conspiracy need not be present at assemblage if performs a part.

The overt act must be an open assemblage in force for purpose and capable of making war against government, in keeping with English and American authorities and not altered by *Swartwout* case. Indictment under common law and Constitution must state place and overt act and proof be of charge as laid; although accused need not be present at place overt act laid, disavows existence of doctrine of constructive presence in treason cases. Even if procurement of assemblage treasonable, both assemblage and procurement overt acts and under Constitution require direct proof actually or constructively present at assemblage, or of its procurement. Even under doctrine of procurer as accessory, necessary that conviction of principal precede; but not applicable under Constitution. Here indictment for levying war on Blennerhassett's Island and proceeding down river to seize New Orleans; assemblage proved, but not presence of accused as alleged, all other testimony irrelevant. Declares no choice in decision. *United States v. Burr,* 25 Fed. Cas. 55, 159–80. Case No. 14693; 4 Cranch, 469–508; Robertson, *Burr,* II, 401–43; Coombs, *Burr,* 307–54; Beveridge, *Marshall,* III, 504–13 (quoted in part).

Dillon, *Decisions,* 82–165; Cotton, I, 96–181; Marshall *Writings,* 53–111.

Sept. 1 Verdict of jury, not guilty. Jury discharged. (J.M. sitting alone.) U.S. Circuit Court, Va., Order Book VI, 226; *United States v. Burr,* 25 Fed. Cas. 55, 180–81. Case No. 14693; Robertson, *Burr,* II, 446.

Sept. 3 Opinion and ruling that Burr discharged of treason, held under indictment for misdemeanor. $5,000 bond required; that Burr being in court, order of Court supplied place of capias. *United States v. Burr,* 25 Fed. Cas. 187, 188–89. Case No. 14694; Robertson, *Burr,* II, 481–503; Coombs, *Burr,* 370. U.S. Circuit Court, Va., Order Book VI, 228.

Sept. 4 Opinion of J.M. concerning submission by President of letter from Gen. Wilkinson, Nov. 12, 1806, power of Court to withhold part considered contrary to public interest and proper respect for President's opinion; that President and not District Attorney decide and send with restrictions; Court could adopt methods to prevent publication of part. *United States v. Burr,* 25 Fed. Cas. 187, 190–92. Case No. 14693; Robertson, *Burr,* II, 533–37; Coombs, *Burr* 373. U.S. Circuit Court, Va., Order Book VI, 229.

Sept. 5 Order that persons serving subpoenas against Burr receive compensation. U.S. Circuit Court, Va., Order Book VI, 230.

Appearance bond, $5,000 for Burr. Same.

Sept. 7 Plea of not guilty by Burr. Same. 231.

Order witness for Burr be paid attendance. Same, 232.

Sept. 9 Jury selected. Same, 233.

Sept. 9 Opinion of J.M. rejecting evidence in trial for misdemeanor of beginning, setting on foot, or providing means of military expedition against Spain, committed at Blennerhassett's Island, Wood County, Virginia; that declarations of third persons not part of transaction, not in presence of accused, excluded; acts of accomplices not proving object and character of expedition excluded; acts of accused in another district cause for prosecution not admissible unless prove charge laid; testimony that expedition military and directed against Spain admissible. *United States v. Burr,* 25 Fed. Cas. 187, 193–99. Case No. 14694; Coombs, *Burr,* 374–75.

Sept. 15 Verdict, not guilty. U.S. Circuit Court, Va., Order Book VI, 236.

Oct. 17 Autograph entry that Burr appeared before him under oath to affidavit to summons of listed persons as witnesses. V, U.S. Circuit Court, Case Papers.

Oct. 20 Opinion of J.M. on motion to commit Burr and Blennerhassett, levying war on island at mouth of Cumberland River, Kentucky, overt acts at Bayou Pierre, Mississippi Territory, and Mississippi River.

Held, no power to commit for trial in Territory but evidence allowed to explain Cumberland meeting; plea of autrefois acquit because of importance, sitting as examining magistrate; that meeting of Cumberland not an act of levying war, weight of evidence object of expedition against Mexico, no acts of hostility or resistance to government; as to misdemeanor charge, not at war with Spain despite crossing of Sabine by Spanish forces; question if dependent on war, otherwise for settlement on Wachita, for jury. Burr and Blennerhassett committed for waging war against Spain while at peace (autograph item, commencement of ruling "The Attorney of the United States . . . charge Aaron Burr . . . with treason . . . and in the Mississippi River between the places above named . . . ." [one page]. V, U.S. Circuit Court Case Papers); Israel Smith and others dismissed; no district for trial named; on motion of government, committed to Ohio. *United States v. Burr*, 25 Fed. Cas. 201, 202–207. Case No. 14694a; Coombs, *Burr*, 379–90. See Beveridge, *Marshall*, III, 527.

Writ of habeas corpus to bring Burr from jail Henrico County where confined as debtor. Committed to marshal; kept until transported to Ohio on charge of military enterprise against Mexico, province of Spain. U.S. Circuit Court., Va., Order Book VI, 245.

Note: Indictments were returned against Burr and Harman Blennerhassett in U.S. District Court of Ohio, and record of case, depositions, etc., filed there, but the case was never seriously pressed and was finally dismissed in 1819.

U.S. CIRCUIT COURT, NORTH CAROLINA

May term. May 12–14.
Judge Henry Potter alone.

November term. Nov. 12–16.
J.M. and Judge Potter.
DNA, U.S. Circuit Court, N.C., Minute Book, as dated.

LAND TRANSACTIONS
Hardy County, Virginia
(Now West Virginia)

May 1 *Deed*

J.M., by Charles Magill, attorney in fact, to Jacob, Leonard, Peter, and Daniel Hoofman, six tracts, South Branch Manor, Hardy County: 140 acres, No. 85, and 22 acres, No. 86, leased Thomas Lord Fairfax to Christopher Hoofman; 6 acres, leased Same to Same, Mar. 9, 1779; 19 acres, 26 acres, and 17 acres, leased Denny Martin Fairfax to Same, May 21, 1791. Consideration £67:2. Recorded May 9, 1807. Hardy County, Va., Deed Book C, 330.

Randolph County, Virginia
(Now West Virginia)

Nov. 3 *Deed*

Joseph Harness and Rebekah, his wife, Ross County, Ohio, to James Marshall, Frederick County, and J.M., Richmond, one-half interest, 28,702 acres, Randolph County, Va. (now W. Va.), on Black Fork Cheat, survey dated June 28, 1794, conveyed to grantor by George Harness, Sept. 6, 1806. Consideration £1,392:12 Virginia. Recorded Nov. 7, 1807, Hardy County, Va., Deed Book C, 375.

Richmond City, Virginia

Aug. 13 *Deed*

J.M. to Thomas Marshall, Richmond, two one-half-acre lots, Plan of Richmond, Nos. 791, 792, being northwesternmost lots of square in which J.M. resides; five shillings. No witnesses; acknowledged Jan. 21, 1808. Richmond City Hustings and Chancery Court, Deed Book 5, 160.

1808

DOCUMENTS

Feb. 9
Washington *to James Taylor, of Richmond, Va.*

Acquainted with Gen. John Blackwell and his war record; lieutenant in Minute Battalion of Culpeper; met at Culpeper Courthouse, Aug., 1775; marched to Williamsburg, Great Bridge, and Norfolk; lieutenant 3rd Virginia Regiment 1777; appointed captain; prisoner at Charleston. KyHi.

Feb. 23
Washington *Joseph Story—Practice*

Joseph Story admitted to practice before U.S. Supreme Court. DNA, U.S. Supreme Court, Minute Book 1790–1828, Vol. B, 71. R.G. 267.

May 20
RICHMOND *to James M. Marshall*

Acknowledges letter. Col. Thurston's deed; suit with Stevens; Fitzhugh's note in hands of Williams for suit at Staunton; suit with Harrison, administrator. Brother William conversation with young Harrison concerning settlement. Nephew Tom in brother William's office. VU, McGregor Libr., Marshall Family Papers, No. 2988.

June [*n.d.*], *n.p.* *Executor's Deed—William Heth*

J.M., et al., executors of Col. William Heth and Widow Heth, to Daniel Lee, land in Frederick County, Va. VU, McGregor Libr., Marshall Family Papers, No. 1106.

Sept. 21
RICHMOND *to Charles Cotesworth Pinckney*

Acknowledges receipt of letter on 20th, forwarding enclosed letter to Gen. Lee. Federalists expect South Carolina to support Pinckney; otherwise, Federalists will miscarry; New York meeting of Federalists. Perilous times; Democratic party hostile to Constitution; internal changes give serious alarm. External danger, lose independence to France. J.M. withdrawn from politics, in profession and agriculture; does not read newspapers. Three of four Federalists in next Congress; Presidential election and general ticket lost. Wife at Frederick with brother; J.M. going there. (Cover endorsed "Hand by Gen'l Washington) DLC, Pinckney Family Papers, Box 11; WMQ (ser. 3), Vol. XII (Oct., 1955), 646–48.

Sept. 28
RICHMOND *to Cashier, Bank of the United States, Philadelphia*

Order to pay quarterly salary, Oct. 1 to James Brown. PP, Rare Book Dept.

Oct. 19
RICHMOND *to Charles Cotesworth Pinckney*

Federalists of Virginia support Monroe in Presidential election, over Madison, prefer his foreign policy; group are oppressed minority. Criticizes Democrats, subservient to France, antagonistic to Great Britain, loss of self-government. DLC, Pinckney Family Papers, Box 11; WMQ (ser. 3) Vol. XII (Oct., 1955), 648–49.

Nov. 7 *to [Peter Minor] Secretary,*
RICHMOND *Albemarle Agricultural Society*

Acknowledging plan of James Barbour, use funds of society as prizes for production of wheat and corn and recovery of fields; address of President. Signed by J.M. and others as Committee of Correspondence of State Agricultural Society. (J.M. was president of first State Agricultural Society in Virginia.) Printed from autograph original in *The Southern Planter,* Vol. XLIV, (June, 1883), 236a–265. Nat'l Agric. Libr., U.S. Dept. of Agriculture.

Nov. 21
RICHMOND *to James M. Marshall*

Acknowledges letter of Oct. 30; arrived before set out for North Carolina. Court decision in James M. Marshall case criticized; recommends dismiss and refile after privy commission examination of sister to deed. Fairfax survey of part of Swan Pond land lost, no grant; tenants withholding rent; if found, suit in federal court for title under treaty; state court will not support compromise. Proportion of debt of estate of M—— as between Colston and J.M. and James; believes proportion between self and James M. is five-ninths and four-ninths respectively. Elections in South Carolina unfavorable to Federalists. Embargo supported in North Carolina; also war with England. Just returned from North Carolina. VHi.

Dec. 19
RICHMOND *to Timothy Pickering*

Acknowledges copies of speeches in Senate on embargo; opposed to embargo; fears will result in war on England, protector of civilized world from tyrant. MHi, Pickering MSS, XXVIII, 412; Beveridge, *Marshall,* IV, 14–15 (excerpt); Henry C. Lodge, *Life and Letters of George Cabot* (Boston, Little, Brown, 1877), 489.

U.S. SUPREME COURT

FEBRUARY TERM. Feb. 1–Mar. 16.

J.M., Cushing, Chase, Washington, Johnson, and Livingston attended the opening session.

Feb. 8. Thomas Todd presented commission and took his seat.

Except for short intermittent absences the full Court sat throughout, J.M. attended every day.

No August session.

DNA, U.S. Supreme Court, Minute Book B, 62–97.

Thomas Blaine v. The Ship Charles Carter, and Donald & Burton et al., 4 Cranch 328.

Error from U.S. Circuit Court, Virginia. Dismissal of libel by holder of bottomry bond for repairs, etc., as against prior execution by creditor, affirmed.

Notations and signatures of J.M. on order for record, citation, petition for writ of error. DNA, U.S. Supreme Court, Case Papers. Case No. 183. R.G. 267.

Mar. 8, 1808. Opinion by Justice Chase, affirming on grounds that holder of bottomry bond lost right of performance by delay in enforcement and by allowing ship to make several voyages without asserting his lien. Notation, J.M. "having decided case" in Circuit Court gave no opinion (note 1, p. 331).

Libel by Blaine in U.S. District Court, Virginia, on two bottomry bonds on ship owned by McCawley, one executed in London by the ship master for cost of repairs, for prior bottomry bond, wages, etc., in 1796, the other executed by owner in Virginia the same year for advances made for repairs and to discharge executions against the ship. Donald & Burton claimed under execution on judgment against McCawley on which writs of *fieri facias* issued from U.S. Circuit Court before warrant of arrest in libel. Decree issued Feb. 12, 1798, in favor of Blane, on entire first bond and part of second for repairs.

V. U.S. District Court, Order Book IV, 25–33. Reversed, Dec. 6, 1799, on appeal. U.S. Circuit Court, Va., Order Book III, 336.

Appeal was taken to the U.S. Supreme Court, which on Feb. 8, 1800, dismissed the proceedings for want of statement of facts; review from Circuit Court by writ of error not appeal. Reported, 4 Dallas 22. Also DNA, U.S. Supreme Court, Minute Book A, 107. Same, Docket Book A. Case No. 76. Error proceedings were now instituted in the Supreme Court, the record returned and filed Aug. 2, 1800. The writ was quashed for nonappearance of counsel Aug. 14, 1800. DNA, U.S. Supreme Court, Minute Book A, 110. During this period J.M. was employed as counsel for Blane and engaged Lewis to handle the case, being assured that the case would not be taken up in the August session. See letter Charles Young to J.M., Nov. 25, 1800, and J.M.'s note to clerk of courts herein. Charles Lee now entered the case, made motion to withdraw the record, Aug., 1801. Matter was continued Dec. 2, 1801, nonappearance of defendant in error; again Aug. 3, 1802; on Aug., 1803, entry "Off by order of plaintiff." DNA, U.S. Supreme Court, Case Papers. Case No. 80; Same, U.S. Supreme Court, Docket Book A, 92.

The Supreme Court Case Papers of Case No. 80 contain an order to certify the record dated June 1, 1801, endorsed by J.M., filed Aug. 3, 1801, with autograph notation "Let a citation and writ of error issue upon the petitioner complying with the terms prescribed by law." There is also an opinion marked 1803, referring to Justice Moore, which affirms the Circuit Court and is identical to Justice Chase's opinion of 1808.

It contains also the letter of Charles Young to J.M., Nov. 25, 1800, indicating Randolph consulted as counsel for plaintiff in error asking for certificate as to employment of J.M. as counsel, his engaging Lewis, assurances could not come up next court; also asking for certificate of clerk if writ of error pending or dismissed, reasons, if record can be copied.

Note of J.M. to Clerk of Court dated 1803 encloses above letter; asks he certify what asked, send answer to Robert Patton, Alexandria. Meantime a bill for revival and filing of record in U.S. Supreme Court was filed Dec. 6, 1802, in U.S. Circuit Court, Virginia, and allowed June 4, 1803. U.S. Circuit Court, Va., Order Book IV, 225, 335. The record of the instant proceeding was filed August term, 1804, and the case repeatedly continued to date of argument, Feb. 22, 1808. DNA, U.S. Supreme Court, Docket Book A, 189. R.G. 267.

Opinions

Fitzsimmons v. The Newport Insurance Co., 4 Cranch 185, 197–202.

Error to Circuit Court Rhode Island. Action on insurance policy on vessel, denial of recovery for breach of warranty, reversed.

The *Big John* was insured with warranty as American property, Charleston, South Carolina to Cádiz, Spain. On departure, it was not known that Cádiz was under blockade by the British. The *Big John* was stopped there by the blockading squadron and detained for eleven days with a prize master on board. Captain on questioning stated his intention to continue to Cádiz if released. Vessel was taken to Gibraltar and condemned on this ground.

Held, mere intention to break a blockade as stated in the adjudication and shown by extrinsic evidence was neither under the law of nations nor the treaty between the United States and Great Britain a breach of blockade so as to violate the warranty.

Marshall v. The Delaware Insurance Co., 4 Cranch 202, 205–208.

Error to Circuit Court, Pennsylvania. Action on insurance policy of vessel, cargo, and freight as total loss denied. Affirmed.

Insured vessel, a neutral, was captured by a belligerent and libeled as a prize of war. Sentence on July 9, 1806, was in favor of the vessel and on the afternoon of 19th, restitution made. The owner in New York heard of the capture on the 17th and on the morning of the 19th his agent by his order abandoned to the insured.

Held, the right to abandon for total loss depends not on information but actual fact and the decree for restitution on the 9th terminated the technical loss even though the actual restitution was later than the offer to abandon.

The United States v. The Brig Union, The Sloop Sally and Cargo, and The Sloop Deborah and Cargo, 4 Cranch 216, 217–18.

Appeal from judgments of U.S. Circuit Court, Delaware, affirming dismissal by District Court, in three separate libels against three vessels for alleged breach of revenue laws denied for lack of proof of jurisdictional amount of $2,000 for each involved.

The United States had one witness testify in open court as to value. An appraisment made in the court below was introduced showing each vessel worth less than $2,000.

Held, the latter was the best evidence and appeal dismissed. Motion thereafter by the United States to obtain affidavits of value was denied.

Pawling and others v. The United States, 4 Cranch 219, 221–24.

Error to District Court, Kentucky. Debt action on official bond against sureties. J. for appellee, reversed.

Bond to cover collector of revenue signed by Pawling, Todd, Adair, and Kennedy as sureties. Defense that their signatures conditional on obtaining two others as co-sureties, that collector held it merely in escrow and that delivery of bond to supervisor of revenue was not authorized. Bond on its face was absolute.

Held, the sustaining of a demurrer to the defense evidence was error.

Daniel Grant v. John and Jeremiah Naylor, 4 Cranch 224, 234–36.

Error to U.S. Circuit Court, Maryland. Action of assumpsit on guaranty of commercial account. J. for appellee, reversed.

Appellant signed letter guaranteeing commercial transactions of John Hackett and his son Alexander, erroneously addressed to John and Joseph Naylor and Co., instead of John and Jeremiah Naylor and Co. The latter received the guaranty and delivered goods of £2,168 Sterling to Hackett and Grant, who became insolvent.

Held, error and in derogation of the statute of frauds to allow parol evidence by Naylors that they were intended as recipient of the guaranty.

The decision was by a divided Court.

Rose v. Himely, 4 Cranch 241, 268–93.

Appeal from U.S. Circuit Court, South Carolina, which in libel action reversed District Court restitution of part of cargo of American schooner *Sarah* to appellant, reversed.

The *Sarah*, after trading with the rebels at San Domingo in 1804 and while returning to the United States with a cargo belonging in part to appellant, was seized by a French privateer more than ten leagues from San Domingo shores, taken to Baracoa, Cuba, and cargo sold without condemnation to one Cott, master of the American vessel *Example*, and taken to Charleston, South Carolina. Here Rose, the supercargo of the *Sarah*, brought libel and was awarded restitution.

Meantime, condemnation was had in San Domingo courts, commenced after the South Carolina proceedings, and based on an *arrêt* issued after seizure of vessels within two leagues of the coast of San Domingo. This decree was submitted in the appeal to Circuit Court which reversed the restitution order.

The Supreme Court justices were widely divided on the issues. J.M., supported by Washington, held that the San Domingo court decree was a nullity issued without jurisdiction, interpreting the *arrêt* as a municipal regulation allowing seizure only within two leagues, but in any case illegal on the high seas; and decree made without possession of the vessel.

Livingston, Cushing, and Chase refused to pass on the first point but concurred in the second. Johnson dissented, interpreted the *arrêt* as permitting seizure on high seas, which he upheld as a right of a belligerent; further, the possession of the French captor gave the right to adjudicate.

(For further proceedings in this case, see herein, *Himely v. Rose*, 5 Cranch 313 (1809). Principle overruled in *Hudson and Smith v. Guestier*, 6 Cranch 281.)

Copy opinion. DNA, U.S. Supreme Court, Case Papers. Case Nos. 248–50. R.G. 267.

Hudson and others v. Guestier; and *LaFont v. Bigelow*, 4 Cranch 293, 293–97.

Error to U.S. Circuit Court, Maryland. J. for appellees in their action of trover for cargo against purchasers at condemnation sale, reversed.

These cases were argued in connection with *Ross v. Himely*, 4 Cranch 241 (herein). Here the brig *Sea Flower* was captured within territorial waters of San Domingo, then in a state of insurgency, by a French privateer for violation of French municipal law prohibiting intercourse with the port, and carried to a Spanish port, Baracoa, Cuba. While there, the vessel and cargo of coffee and logwood were condemned in the court of the French island of Guadaloupe, and purchased by appellee.

The Court was widely divided. J.M. and Washington for appellee on grounds that the seizure was in territorial waters and therefore seizure for violation of a municipal regulation was legal, and that possession in a neutral court was sufficient to give the French court jurisdiction, and the purchaser right to the cargo.

Justices Chase and Livingston dissented on the latter point. Justice Johnson concurred, considering the first point immaterial. Justice Todd later expressed concurrence with Justice Johnson.

(For further proceedings see *Same v. Same*, 6 Cranch 281, herein 1810, U.S. Supreme Court.)

Alexander v. Harris, bailiff of W. Crammond, 4 Cranch 299, 301–305.

Error to Circuit Court District of Columbia, Alexandria. Action of replevin by tenant for premises seized in distress for rent. J. for lessor for double rent, affirmed.

The defendant-appellee set up as a defense for the distress a lease of three years on which $111.67 was in arrears and unpaid. The plea or reply by the tenant was that the rent claimed was not in arrears and unpaid at time of distress. At the trial the alleged lease for three years was supported by testimony of a lease for one year and continued possession for two years by consent. The Court below instructed the jury that if no new agreement had been made for the two years, the allegation of a three-year lease was supportable.

Held, the charge was erroneous but the plea of the tenant of no rent arrears admitted the demise as alleged.

Chappedelaine, residuary legatee, and Closrivierre, administrator de bonis non of Chappedelaine v. Decheneaux, executor of Dumoussay, 4 Cranch 306, 308, 309–16.

Error to Circuit Court, Georgia. Bill in equity to set aside agreed account stated between partners or to correct and to ascertain subsequent accounts. Lower Court's adoption of auditor's report as corrected affirmed with alteration of interest item.

The two testators together with Boisfeillet, Du Bignon, and Grand Closmesle jointly purchased the islands of Sapelo, Blackbeard, Jekyll, and half of St. Catharines off Georgia, Dumoussay keeping the accounts. In 1792, the latter and Chappedelaine signed an agreed account between them alleged to be fraudulent showing an account due Dumoussay. The lower court appointed auditors who found patent errors in the agreed account and large amounts due from Dumoussay in subsequent accounts.

Held, the suit between trustees of aliens is within the jurisdiction of federal courts, and that although an account stated will generally bar a suit for accounting, it may be reopened where shown to be erroneous.

The Mayor and Commonalty of Alexandria for use of John G. Ladd v. Thomas Patten and sureties, 4 Cranch 317, 320–21.

Error to Circuit Court, District of Columbia, Alexandria. Action of debt on official bond as vendure master. J. for appellee, reversed. Patten was sued for money in his hands from vendue sale of goods for Ladd. He also owed Ladd for goods privately sold to him and made payments which he claimed should be applied to and satisfy his official sale. The lower court instructed the jury that if Patten at time of payment did not direct how the account was to be applied, the creditor might apply it as he pleased, but that he must act immediately or application by law is to the vendue account.

Held, error to charge that the election of the creditor was lost if not exercised immediately.

Jacob Mountz and John Mountz and Henry Knowles, his sureties, v. Hodgson and Thompson, 4 Cranch 324, 327–28.

Error to Circuit Court, District of Columbia, County of Washington. Writ directed against refusal of Circuit Court to quash execution. Writ of error quashed for lack of jurisdiction.

J. was had by defendants in error against Jacob Mountz and George Reintzel. Maryland law allowed stay of execution for six months if defendant confessed judgment before two justices of peace, and thereafter permitted execution without proceeding by *scire facias.* Mountz acting alone so confessed judgment before John Ott, a justice of peace, and Daniel Reintzel, mayor of Georgetown. After six months, peremptory execution was taken which appellants sought to quash on grounds that judgment was not confessed before two justices and not be codefendant Reintzel.

Error was brought from refusal to quash. A majority of the Court quashed the writ of error, some of the judges on grounds that error will not lie to such a ruling, and others that the writ should be to the judgment of the justices of peace and not the Circuit Court.

The United States v. Gurney and others, 4 Cranch 333, 341–46.

Question certified from U.S. Circuit Court, Pennsylvania. Action on a bond to pay money at Amsterdam.

The agreement between the United States and Gurney, merchants of Philadelphia, was that in consideration of $205,000 advanced, Gurney was to repay to Willink and Van Staphorst, bankers to the United States, at Amsterdam 500,000 guilders in three installments, the second one of which was to be on Mar. 1, 1803. This installment was paid on May 16, the others at the named dates, the last on June 11, 1803. The agreement called for demand by the United States at Philadelphia in case of default, in which case 20 per cent damages was to be added. On June 14, 1803, Albert Gallatin, Secretary of the Treasury, demanded payment of the second installment plus 20 per cent penalty and interest.

Held, acceptance of the second installment late waived the penalty but not interest from date due to date of payment.

Peisch and others v. Ware; and *The United States v. The Cargo of The Ship Favourite*, 4 Cranch 347, 358–66.

Appeal from U.S. Circuit Court, Delaware, affirming U.S. District Court, salvage and forfeiture of wreck, affirmed.

Vessel broke anchor in Delaware Bay and drifted asea without mast or anchor after abandonment by crew; towed to a shoal and cargo salvaged by Thomas Rodney and Ware, hiring forty-eight hands and six boats for sixteen days and twelve nights, Owners Peisch and others refused to pay one-half of $14,000 valuation, erroneously thinking law required submission; submitted to arbitrators, who awarded that amount. Meantime, the wine, brandy, and cordials were libeled by the United States for violation of revenue laws as unmarked and duties not paid.

Held, not liable for forfeiture because revenue law requirements applied only to regular importations. As to salvage, four justices approved one-half, two because of binding award, two because proper amount; three dissented as excessive, but acquiesced in decree. Autograph opinion. DNA, U.S. Supreme Court, Case Papers. Case No. 268. R.G. 267.

Shearman v. Irvine's Lessee, 4 Cranch 367, 369.

Error to U.S. Circuit Court, Georgia. Ejectment, j. for defendant in error, affirmed.

Alexander Baillie received grants from Georgia for land in Camden County in 1766. Irvine claimed title as his heir and held possession until Sept. 10, 1804, the date of alleged ouster by Shearman. The latter claimed error for refusal to nonsuit claiming the Georgia act of 1767 required entry within seven years after acquiring title.

Held, such a construction of the statute was "inadmissible," that there was no requirement of actual entry where title and possession was undisturbed and not contested at time of acquisition.

Alexander v. The Baltimore Insurance Co., 4 Cranch 370, 373–82.

Error to Circuit Court, Maryland. J. for appellee in action for total loss against it as underwriters of insurance on vessel, affirmed. The ship *John and Henry* was insured for voyage from Charleston to Port Republican or other port in Bite of Leogane. On Oct. 2, 1803, she was captured by a French privateer and taken to Mole St. Nicholas, where the French commandant appropriated the cargo, agreeing to pay for it in coffee. On Oct. 29 she sailed for Cape Francois, a port off her route, to receive the payment, and was captured and condemned by a British squadron blockading the port. Abandonment and claim of total loss was made by the insured on the basis of the seizure of the cargo at the Mole.

Held, coverage was on the ship alone, that loss of the voyage by the cargo was not loss as to the ship; also that diversion of Cape Francois was abandonment of the voyage. J.M. went to unusual length in examining English authorities claimed to the contrary.

Mathews v. Zane, 4 Cranch 382.

Error to the Supreme Court for Muskingum and State of Ohio under 25th section of Judiciary Act, affirmed.

The question raised was if the U.S. Supreme Court had appellate jurisdiction over a judgment of a state court in case involving claim of one citizen of Ohio over another such citizen, both claiming title to the same land under act of Congress of 1800.

The Court "hesitated," but on "consultation together and deliberation," the majority decided that Article III of the Constitution extended the construction of the Judiciary Act and allowed such jurisdiction, intending that construction of the laws of the United States and rights and titles thereunder be construed uniformly.

Young v. The Bank of Alexandria, 4 Cranch 384, 396–98.

Error to Circuit Court, District of Columbia, Alexandria. Rule by defendant in error to show cause why a writ of error to the Supreme Court from judgment in its favor in Circuit Court should not be quashed, denied.

The bank was organized under a Virginia law of 1792 which allowed it to bring summary action in court against its debtors and denying them right of review. A Virginia act of Jan., 1801, continued its charter. The act of Congress of Feb., 1801, establishing a Circuit Court in the District of Columbia provided for review of its judgments in cases involving over $100, with a saving clause preserving rights theretofore granted.

Held, Virginia had a right to legislate concerning the District of Columbia despite its cession of 1789–1790 until Congress acted, but that the saving clause in the federal act did not apply, Virginia having no power to legislate concerning federal courts.

Spiers v. Rebecca Willison, 4 Cranch 398, 400.

Error to District Court, Kentucky. Detinue for slaves, j. for defendant in error, reversed.

Defendant in error, plaintiff below, was allowed to offer parol evidence that while Kentucky was part of Virginia, her grandmother gave her slaves by a deed which was lost. The Court refused plaintiff in error requested charge that under Virginia law a gift of slaves must be by writing recorded.

Held, error, that parol evidence may explain the possession but not the required deed in writing.

Ramsey v. Lee, 4 Cranch 401, 402–403.

Error to Circuit Court, District of Columbia, Alexandria. Detinue for slave, j. for defendant in error, affirmed.

Mrs. Gordon in 1784 made an oral gift of a slave to Ramsey. The latter's mother in 1790 claiming as legatee of Mrs. Gordon deeded the slave to Wilson, who conveyed to Lee in 1804. Ramsey and his mother continued to live with the Wilsons until 1805, then took the slave. The court below charged the jury that a verbal gift of slave coupled with possession was void.

Held, a proper charge.

Stead's Executors v. Elizabeth and Caroline Course, widow and daughter of Daniel Course, 4 Cranch 403, 412–14.

Error to Circuit Court, Georgia. Dismissal of bill in equity to subject land to payment of debt, affirmed.

Appellant brought action against Elizabeth and Caroline Course, daughters of Daniel Course, to subject 450 acres of land in Chatham County, Georgia, purchased by Daniel at tax sale claimed to be without authority and fraudulent. The purpose was to set aside the sale and subject the land to payment of judgment held against Rae and Somerville, Robert Rae, deceased, having held the land from John Rae, the original grantee. On the question of collusion it appeared that Daniel Course was a son-in-law of Robert Rae's widow, who in turn married Samuel Hammon, who had authorized the sale. The defendant below answered, setting up the purchase, claiming it lawful and without fraud. Issue was made on the sufficiency of the plea.

Held, the plea was insufficient in not alleging and proof not made of conformity to Georgia law which allowed tax sale of land only if other assets are exhausted and then only so much as needed to satisfy the tax. Autograph decree. DNA, U.S. Supreme Court, Case Papers. Case No. 217. R.G. 267.

Higginson v. Mein, 4 Cranch 415, 418–20.

Appeal from U.S. Circuit Court, Georgia. Dismissal of appellants bill to foreclose mortgage, reversed.

Alexander Wylly, a resident of Georgia, in 1769 executed a bond and mortgage on land in Georgia to Greenwood and Higginson of London. In 1784 his estate was confiscated for adherence to the British and the mortgage property sold to James Houston. In 1796 it was sold with notice upon execution of judgment against James Mossman, executor of Houston. Action in 1802 against purchaser's agent for the debt and foreclosure was dismissed.

Held, the lien of the mortgage and the debt thereof due a British subject was not confiscated by Georgia, merely sequestered, and if confiscated, was restored by the treaty with Britain; the statute of limitations did not bar the claim because mortgagor's possession was not adverse, and a savings clause preserved the rights of persons beyond sea. As to presumption that debt paid due to lapse of time, the Court made this an issue on remand.

Justice Livingston dissented without opinion, probably on grounds that the lien of the mortgage had been confiscated.

Pollard and Pickett v. Dwight et al., 4 Cranch 421, 428–33.

Error to U.S. Circuit Court, Connecticut. Action of covenant upon warranty of title of deed. J. for defendant in error, reversed.

Suit commenced by foreign attachment in County Court of Hartford, Connecticut, against Pollard and Pickett of Virginia claiming that they had no title to Virginia land in Wythe County sold by them. They removed the case to federal Circuit Court, on which District Judge Pierpont Edwards sat alone since the death of Justice William Paterson, Sept., 1806. Dwight was permitted to give oral testimony that the survey of 1794 on which patent to the land of 1795 was fraudulent, and that there were claims against part of the land.

Held, that Pollard and Pickett by appearing waived objection to nonservice of process; that Circuit Court can be held by one judge regardless of vacancy of Supreme Court Justice; that it was error to allow parol testimony to show deed voidable or to show title in others.

The United States v. The Schooner Betsy and Charlotte and Her Cargo, 4 Cranch 443, 452.

Appeal from Circuit Court, District of Columbia reversing District Court forfeiture of vessel and cargo for violation of act prohibiting commercial intercourse between United States and San Domingo, reversed.

The vessel sailed from Alexandria, entered Cape Francois, returned to Alexandria, where seized. Claimant denied voluntarily entered Cape Francois, vessel having cleared from Alexandria to St. Jago de Cuba entered in distress.

Held, place of seizure determines jurisdiction of court; her seizure in port navigable from sea by vessel of ten tons and cause falls within District Court jurisdiction in admiralty, not at law; trial by jury dispensed with. Cases of *The United States v. La Vengeance,* 3 Dallas 297, and *The United States v. Schooner Sally, of Norfolk,* 2 Cranch 406 followed, the absence of specific enforcement provisions in Embargo Act not distinguishing. Justices Chase and Livingston dissented; Justice Todd no opinion, absent at argument.

U.S. CIRCUIT COURT, VIRGINIA

May term. May 23–June 17.
May 23–June 13. J.M. and District Judge Cyrus Griffin.
June 13–17. J.M. alone.
U.S. Circuit Court, Va., Order Book VIII, 1–110.

November term. Nov. 22–Dec. 15.
Nov. 22–27. J.M. alone.
Nov. 28. Both.
Nov. 29–Dec. 7. J.M. alone.
Dec. 8–10. Both.
Dec. 12–15. J.M. alone.
U.S. Circuit Court, Va., Order Book VIII, 110–222.

Philip Martin v. Jacob Weekly and James M. Marshall et al. Not reported.

Chancery bill alleging survey by Fairfax of Manor of Leeds, 1747–1748, Gooney Run added to Leeds but unappropriated, surveyed after death but survey lost. Feb., 1793, Denny Martin sold Manor of Leeds and other Virginia lands to James M. Marshall. Commonwealth claimed escheated, inquest of office traverse filed District Court of Dumfries, j. for Commonwealth appealed to Court of Appeals, pending and repeatedly argued, reversed and quashed after compromise J.M. and Commonwealth. Earlier *Denny Fairfax v. David Hunter* in U.S. Circuit Court claiming under treaty of peace, writ of error to U.S. Supreme Court dismissed. Weekly purchased from Virginia Land Office. Philip Martin inherited, willing to convey, but James Marshall would not accept while adversary proceedings.

Answer of James M. Marshall willing to accept.

June, 1808. Case dismissed.

Autograph bill by J.M., also answer of James M. Marshall.

V, U.S. Circuit Court, Va., Case Papers.

Opinions

M'Call, Smilie and Co. v. Harrison et al., 1 Brockenbrough 126, 127–30.

Plaintiff, an English firm which prior to Revolutionary War had business house in Virginia in 1770, received bond from debtor and as security a deed of trust to trustees of land. By mistake the name of John McCall and Co. used in deed.

Held, purchaser of land pay plaintiff.

Murdock, Donald and Co. v. Shackelford's Heirs, 1 Brockenbrough 131, 132–35.

Action to subject real estate in hands of heirs to payment of judgment, denied. Deceased received land under father's will for life, to his children at his death subject to estate to wife; if died without heirs of body to his brother.

Held, an executory devise in tail after estate for life, remainder in fee to children; the life estate not chargeable for debts after death.

J. Murdock and Co. v. William Hunter's Representatives, 1 Brockenbrough 135, 139–46.

Bill in chancery by plaintiff, English merchants against devisee of Hunter to subject Virginia land to payment of bond executed by Hunter in 1774 attested by witness now dead whose handwriting was proved as only proof of execution of bond. The answer stated Hunter died with large personal estate, lapse of thirty years in pressing claim, recourse lost. Administrators of estate dead.

Held, proof of execution of bond by proof of handwriting of dead attesting witness sufficient in absence of opposing circumstances; J.M. followed judicial decisions in England pronounced after the Revolutionary War, stating decisions before the war have authority of appellate decisions, those after accepted as opinions of distinguished men especially if not change established rule. Also, in absence of allegation that legatees had personal property, need not be joined to satisfy claim ahead of real property. Case continued for further proof of execution, and proof of assignment of bond to plaintiff.

U.S. CIRCUIT COURT, NORTH CAROLINA

May term. May 12–13.
J.M. and Judge Henry Potter.

November term. Nov. 12–14.
Nov. 12 (Sat.) Potter alone.
Nov. 14. Both.
DNA, U.S. Circuit Court, N.C., Minute Book, as dated.

Henry Rose et al. v. Lewis and R. Groenig. Not reported.

Appeal to U.S. Supreme Court from decree of U.S. Circuit Court, N.C. condemning vessel to captor, reversed.

Ship *Sarah* seized by captor outside territorial waters claimed by French government of San Domingo, taken to foreign port, condemned by Court of San Domingo for violation of French law prohibiting trade and authorizing seizure within two leagues. Held, a marine trespass, not authorizing seizure or condemnation, restored to owner less insurance and expenses of bringing vessel to the United States.

Feb. 18, 1806. Record filed.
Mar. 2, 1808. Reversed.
DNA, U.S. Supreme Court, Docket Book A, 254; Minute Book B, 87. Case No. 250. R.G. 267.

LAND TRANSACTIONS

District Court, Frederick County, Virginia

By ruling of General Court, June 13, 1808, in case adjourned from District Court of Winchester, *John Miller v. James M. Marshall and I.S. Woodstock*, I Va. Cas. 158, writ of prohibition issued against James M. Marshall and justice of peace for Frederick County from proceeding before justice of peace against a landowner for recovery of rent reserved on fee.

Fairfax Estate, Various Counties, Virginia

Oct. 5 *Partition Deed*

Deed of partition Rawleigh Colston and Elizabeth, his wife, Berkeley County, to J.M., Richmond, and James M. Marshall, Frederick County, reciting conveyance from Philip Martin to grantees in common of Manor of Leeds and agreement of grantees to partition, conveyance to Colston by deed of same date of his share in severalty, 26,535 acres between Ashby's Gap and Snicker's Gap, releasing residue of Manor of Leeds. Recorded General Court, Richmond, June 12, 1811. Entered as evidence in *Marshall's Lessee v. Weaver,* Circuit Court of Fauquier County, Va., Land Causes, II, 700, at III, 2–3f.

See (herein), Aug. 30, 1797, note; also *United States v. M. F. Morris, et al.,* 174 U.S. 196, wherein original deed entered in evidence (herein 1899).

Oct. 5 *Partition Deed*

J.M. and James M. Marshall and wives to Rawleigh Colston; division of lands in Loudon, Fauquier, Frederick, and Shenandoah counties, Manor of Leeds and Goony Manor, received in severalty from Philip Martin; in consideration of release to Colston of 26,535 acres and 13,466 acres Colston releases interest in balance. Recorded in General Court, Richmond, June 12, 1811, in Frederick County, Aug. 2, 1814. Frederick County Records, Deed Book 36, 302; VU, McGregor Libr., Marshall Family Papers, No. 1106. See *United States v. M. F. Morris et al.,* wherein certified copy entered in evidence (herein, 1899).

Greene County, Ohio

Apr. 12 *Deed*

2,000 acres in Virginia military district (Ohio) to Thomas Underwood; in execution of original contract between J.M. and James Harrison Gordon and John Bryce; land to J.M. by grant from the United States, patented Feb. 20, 1796. Greene County, Ohio, Deed Book 1A, 509.

Hampshire County, Virginia
(Now West Virginia)

Mar. 12 *Deed*

Benjamin Wiley, Alleghany County, Maryland to J.M., ninety-six acres on North Branch of Potomac, Hampshire County, granted to Alphens Guston, June 10, 1788, beginning at three chestnut oaks at top of mountain. Consideration $200 mint money of the United States. Recorded Apr. 10, 1808. Hampshire County, Va., Deed Book 15, 460.

Hardy County, Virginia (Now West Virginia)

June 8 *Deed*

J.M., by Charles Magill, attorney in fact, to George Harness, Sr., 156 acres, South Branch Manor. Consideration £39. Recorded Sept. 7, 1808. Hardy County, Va., Deed Book C, 429.

Mason County, Kentucky

Sept. 10 *Deed*

J.M., by Thomas Marshall, attorney in fact, to Robert Johnson, Scott County, Ky., assignee of the rights of Simon Kenton to one-third interest as locator, one-third undivided interest in 1,934 acres on the Ohio River in Kentucky. Mason County, Ky., Deed Book H, 417.